EARTHEN VESSELS AND TRANSCENDENT POWER

The *American Society of Missiology Series,* in collaboration with Orbis Books, seeks to publish scholarly works of high merit and wide interest on numerous aspects of missiology — the study of mission. Able presentations on new and creative approaches to the practice and understanding of mission will receive close attention.

Previously published in
The American Society of Missiology Series

American Society of Missiology Series, No. 25

EARTHEN VESSELS
AND
TRANSCENDENT
POWER

American Presbyterians in China, 1837–1952

G. Thompson Brown

ORBIS BOOKS

Maryknoll, New York 10545

The author is grateful to and acknowledges permission from publishers and several archives for the photographs that follow page 160. In particular, he thanks the Presbyterian Department of History, Montreat, North Carolina, for permission to reproduce photos 5, 13–14, and 20–23; to the Frank Brown collection in the same archives at Montreat for photos 24 and 25; to the Department of History, Presbyterian Church, U.S.A., Philadelphia, for photos 2, 7; to the same archives in Philadelphia for the historic photos (15 and 16) taken by Rev. Charles A. Killie at the time of the Boxer Rebellion.

Photo 1 is taken from Walter Lowrie, *Memories of the Rev. Walter M. Lowrie: Missionary to China* (New York: Carter and Bros., 1849). Photo 3 is taken from Helen Coan Nevius, *The Life of John Livingston Nevius* (New York: Fleming H. Revell, 1895). Photo 4 is taken from Daniel W. Fisher, *Calvin Wilson Mateer: Forty-Five Years a Missionary in Shantung, China* (Philadelphia: Westminster Press, 1911). Photo 6 is taken from Nettie DuBose Junkin, *For the Glory of God: Memoirs of Dr. and Mrs. H. C. DuBose of Soochow, China* (Lewisburg, Va., privately printed by the family, n.d.). Photos 8 and 18 are taken from Arthur Judson Brown, *The Lien-Chou Martyrdom* (New York: Pamphlet of Board of Foreign Missions, c. 1906). Photo 9 is owned by First Presbyterian Church, Wilmington, North Carolina, and is found also in Lawrence D. Kessler, *The Jianqyin Mission Station: An American Missionary Community in China, 1895–1951* (Chapel Hill: University of North Carolina Press, 1996). Photo 10 is taken from B. A. Garside, *One Increasing Purpose: The Life of Henry Winters Luce* (New York: Revell, 1948). Photo 11 is taken from Yu-Ming Shaw, *An American Missionary in China: John Leighton Stuart and Chinese-American Relations* (Cambridge: Cambridge University Press, 1992). Photo 12 was taken from the Randolph-Macon Woman's College Alumni Bulletin, Fall 1992. Photo 17 is undated and was taken from a missionary photo album in the author's possession. Photo 19 is from the *Records of the Centenary Missionary Conference* (Shanghai: Centenary Conference Committee, 1907).

The Catholic Foreign Mission Society of America (Maryknoll) recruits and trains people for overseas missionary service. Through Orbis Books, Maryknoll aims to foster the international dialogue that is essential to mission. The books published, however, reflect the opinions of their authors and are not meant to represent the official position of the Society.

Copyright © 1997 by G. Thompson Brown

Published by Orbis Books, Maryknoll, New York, U.S.A.

Manufactured in the United States of America

Library of Congress Cataloging-in-Publication Data

Brown, G. Thompson (George Thompson), 1921-
    Earthen vessels & transcendent power : American Presbyterians in
China, 1837-1952 / G. Thompson Brown.
      p. cm. – (American Society of Missiology series ; no. 25)
    Includes bibliographical references and index.
    ISBN 1-57075-150-1 (cloth)
    1. Presbyterian Church – Missions – China – History. 2. Missions,
American – China – History. 3. China – Church history – 19th century.
4. China – Church history – 20th century. I. Title. II. Series.
BV3415.2.B76 1997
266′.5151 – dc21
                                                                          97-38238
                                                                                            CIP

Dedicated to the memory of
Frank A. and Charlotte Thompson Brown,
my parents,
who served a collective seventy-two years
in the Chinese Empire,
Nationalist China, and
the People's Republic of China

Contents

Part 1
THE NINETEENTH CENTURY
Dynasty, Foreign Devils and the Kingdom of God

Part 2
THE TWENTIETH CENTURY
War Lords, Nationalism and the Emerging Church

Preface to the Series

The purpose of the American Society of Missiology (ASM) Series is to publish —
without regard for disciplinary, national, or denominational boundaries —
scholarly works of high quality and wide interest on missiological themes from
the entire spectrum of scholarly pursuits relevant to Christian mission, which is
always the focus of books in the Series.

By "mission" is meant the effort to effect passage over the boundary between
faith in Jesus Christ and its absence. In this understanding of mission, the basic
functions of Christian proclamation, dialogue, witness, service, worship, liberation, and nurture are of special concern. And in that context questions arise,
including, How does the transition from one cultural context to another influence the shape and interaction between these dynamic functions, especially in
regard to the cultural and religious plurality that comprise the global context
of Christian mission?

The promotion of scholarly dialogue among missiologists and scholars in
other fields of inquiry may involve the publication of views that some missiologists cannot accept, and with which members of the Editorial Committee do
not agree. Manuscripts published in the Series reflect the opinions of their authors and are not understood to represent the position of the American Society
of Missiology or of the Editorial Committee. Selection is guided by such criteria
as intrinsic worth, readability, and accessibility to a range of interested persons
and not merely to experts or specialists.

The ASM Series Editorial Committee
James A. Scherer, Chair
Mary Motte, FMM
Charles Taber

List of Maps

Abbreviations

ABCFM	American Board of Commissioners for Foreign Missions
AH	*Assembly Herald*
AP	*American Presbyterians: Journal of Presbyterian History*
APMP	American Presbyterian Mission Press
AR	*Annual Reports, Board of Foreign Missions, Presbyterian Church in the U.S.A.*
AR(PCUS)	*Annual Reports, Executive Committee of Foreign Missions, Presbyterian Church in the U.S.*
BFM	Board of Foreign Missions, Presbyterian Church in the U.S.A.
BMB	*Bi-Monthly Bulletin*, PCUS China Missions
BSF	Board Staff File (Incoming and outgoing correspondence with missionaries), Department of History, Philadelphia
CC	PCUSA China Council Minutes
CHA	*The Church at Home and Abroad*
CIM	China Inland Mission
CMS	Church Missionary Society
CR	*The Chinese Recorder*
ECFM	Executive Committee of Foreign Missions, PCUS
FM	*The Foreign Missionary*
HFR	*Home and Foreign Record of the Presbyterian Church, U.S.A.*
IBMR	*International Bulletin of Missionary Research*
KMT	Kuomintang
LMS	London Missionary Society
MC	*The Missionary Chronicle*
MCD	Missionary Correspondence Department (PCUS) letters
MR	*Presbyterian Monthly Records*

MS	*Missionary Survey*
NPM	Northern Presbyterian China Mission
PCUS	Presbyterian Church in the U.S. (South)
PCUSA	Presbyterian Church in the U.S.A. (North)
PDH(Phil)	Presbyterian Department of History, Philadelphia
PDH(Mont)	Presbyterian Department of History, Montreat
PRC	People's Republic of China
PS	*Presbyterian Survey*
RAB	Religious Affairs Bureau, PRC
RCA	Reformed Church in America
SPM	Southern Presbyterian China Mission
TM	*The Missionary*
WWW	*Woman's Work for Woman*

Note on the Spelling of Chinese Words

A word must be said about the complex problem of spelling Chinese names and places. The traditional way of rendering the Chinese characters into English is known as the Wade-Giles system. This was used throughout the missionary period. However, missionary usage was not standardized and often the same city or person's name is spelled in different ways. A new system, known as *Pinyin,* has been adopted by the Chinese government and is used in all current documents, newspapers, maps, etc. In this work *Pinyin* is used throughout, following the practice of current Western historians. Exceptions have been made in the case of certain names and places that have been firmly fixed in the English language, such as Chiang Kai-shek, Sun Yat-sen, Canton, Peking, Hong Kong, Yangtze River. In the case of treaties (Treaty of Nanking, Treaty of Tientsin) the old spelling has not been changed. The first time a word is used, the old Wade-Giles spelling is put in parentheses. In direct quotes of missionary documents the old spelling has not been changed. The Chinese custom in regard to personal names is to put the surname or family name first. This practice has been followed except in the case of Chinese who have preferred to follow the Western order and the old spelling.

List of Pinyin and Wade-Giles Equivalents

Pinyin versions of the following places names are given first. The Wade-Giles version of the same place is given in parentheses.

Beijing (Peking)
Baoding (Paoting)
Changde (Changteh)
Chengdu (Chengtu)
Chenzhou (Chenchow)
Chongqing (Chungking)
Dai (Tai) (people)
Dao Guang (Tao-kuang)
Dengzhou (Tengchow)
Fujian (Fukien) Province
Fuzhou (Foochow)
Guangdong (Kwangtung) Province
Guangxi (Kwangsi) Province
Guangzhou (Canton)
Haikou (Hoi-How)
Hankou (Hankow)
Hangzhou (Hangchow)
Hebei (Chili) Province
Hengyang (Hengchow)
Huaian (Hwaianfu)
Huaiyin (Tsing-Kiang-Pu)
Huayuan (Hwai Yuan)
Huizhou (Kochow)
Jiaxing (Kashing)
Jiaji (Kachek)
Jiangyin (Kiangyin)
Jiangsu (Kiangsu) Province
Jiangxi (Kiangsi)
Jiaozhou (Kiaochow)
Jinan (Tsinan)
Jining (Tsining or Chiningchow)
Jiulongjiang (Kiulungkiang)
Kunming (Yunnanfu)
Ledong (Nodoa)

Lianyungang (Haichow)
Lianzhou (Lien Chow)
Linyi (Ichow)
Nanjing (Nanking)
Nanxuzhou (Nanhsuchow)
Ningbo (Ningpo)
Qiantang River (Chientang River)
Qingdao (Tsingtao)
Qiongzhou (Kiungchow)
Qujiang (Sheklung)
Rehe (Jehol)
Shandong (Shantung) Province
Shantou (Swatow)
Shenyang (Mukden)
Shouzhou (Showchow)
Shunde (Shunteh)
Sinchang (Tunghiang)
Suqian (Suchien)
Suzhou (Soochow)
Tianjin (Tientsin)
Taizhou (Taichow)
Tengxian (Tenghsien)
Weixian (Weihsien)
Xiamen (Amoy)
Xian (Sian)
Xiangtan (Siangtan)
Xuzhou (Suchow)
Yancheng (Yencheng)
Yangjiang (Yeungkong)
Yantai (Chefoo)
Yixian (Yihsien)
Yuanjiang (Yuankiang)
Zhejiang (Chekiang) Province
Zhenjiang (Chinkiang)

Foreword

Earthen Vessels and Transcendent Power by G. Thompson Brown is an exciting contribution to the history of Christianity and Christian mission. It tells the important story of American Presbyterian missionary involvement in China in the nineteenth and twentieth centuries and gives us fresh clues to the dynamism of the Christian Church in China today.

In this book, Brown weaves together the story of American Presbyterian missionaries and their Chinese Christian colleagues with the dynamic of the fast-changing history of China from the mid-nineteenth to the mid-twentieth centuries. He tells of the life experience and the ministry of Presbyterians in mission — their triumphs and their failures — and how the Holy Spirit used these "earthen vessels" to plant the seeds of the gospel. Most importantly, he connects that story to the life of the Chinese people and the changing dynamics of Chinese society.

Few are better prepared to tell this story. G. Thompson ("Tommy") Brown, born in China of Presbyterian missionary parents, had a distinguished career as a missionary in Korea, as a professor in seminaries in Korea and the United States, and as director of the International Mission Program of the Presbyterian Church (U.S.A.). Following that latter assignment, Brown served as China Consultant for the Presbyterian Church during the 1980s as the church in China gained new strength in dynamism and its witness. He has a deep love for the people and the churches of China and a profound respect for those who are faithful in the mission of Jesus Christ. Both of these themes come through clearly in this work.

We live in a time in which many are gaining appreciation for the fact that we only truly understand our present when we are connected to our roots. This book reminds the American church that its principal calling is to be a "missionary society" through the example of faithful American Presbyterian missionaries. It also provides a fresh understanding of the church in China by taking a new look at those who planted the gospel in that great nation.

China, probably as much as anywhere in the world, has helped us to realize that the seeds of the gospel, when planted in faithfulness, bear great fruit. The vitality of the Christian church in China today is cause for us to reassess an earlier pessimism (so alive in the West in the 1960s and 1970s) concerning the missionary movement in that nation.

As Brown points out clearly, many mistakes and moral and theological failures were made in that effort. However, this mission also represented great faithfulness on the part of many who responded to God's call to go into all the world and share the gospel. In God's good time, God used the work of these earthen vessels to bring forth a dynamic and alive church in China, which we know today.

Once I picked up *Earthen Vessels and Transcendent Power,* I found it very hard to put down. This is an exciting book that tells an exciting story of the work of the Holy Spirit in the lives of American and Chinese Christians. I have confidence that you will find it just as difficult to put this book down once you begin to read this exciting story.

CLIFTON KIRKPATRICK, Stated Clerk,
Presbyterian Church (U.S.A.)

Acknowledgments

It would be impossible to list all those who have helped in the writing of this history. But I wish to acknowledge a few whose contributions were indispensable. Years ago, James Bear, my mentor at Union Theological Seminary in Virginia, provided the stimulus for the writing of mission history. His monumental five-volume unpublished manuscript, *The Mission Work of the Presbyterian Church of the United States in China* was the basic source material for the Southern mission. Clifton Kirkpatrick, Bob Abrams, Gwen Crawley, and Insik Kim of the Worldwide Ministries Division gave encouragement along the way and the Division provided a subvention for the book's publication. The National Endowment for the Humanities gave a travel grant to visit archival centers in the United States. Frederick Heuser, Michelle Francis and their respective archivists at the Presbyterian Departments of History in Philadelphia and Montreat contributed their time in locating and retrieving mission records and photographs. The Henry Luce Foundation provided a research grant for travel to China and opportunities for interviewing Chinese historians and church leaders. Columbia Theological Seminary was my "home base" and extended numerous opportunities for the gathering of material through its China program. President Douglas Oldenburg's enthusiastic support of the China Missionary Reunion in 1994 added encouragement and furnished an occasion for the exchange of information and experiences with the China missionary community. Grateful thanks is extended to my missionary colleagues and Chinese Christian leaders for responding to questionnaires and interviews. James Scherer and his editorial committee for the American Society of Missiology Book Series read the manuscript and offered valuable advice. And, most important, thanks is extended to Bill Burrows, editor of Orbis Books, and Catherine Costello for their technical assistance, ecumenical vision and willingness to boldly act in faith in the publication of a Presbyterian mission history! And finally, there is my wife, Mardia, and our children, who provided support, wise counsel, and understanding of the life of the missionary family in Asia.

G. Thompson Brown
Decatur, Georgia
July 1997

xxiii

Introduction

The Rebirth of the Church in China

A visitor to China in the year 1997 initially would hardly be aware of the presence of Christianity. Few church buildings, steeples or crosses can be seen. The media contain scant religious news. Announcements of church services do not appear in daily papers. One looks in vain for Christian hospitals or academies. Evangelists do not appear on television screens. Crusades in public places are unknown.

But, as time passes, an astute observer gradually becomes aware of a vital, contagious Christian presence. Down alleyways and behind walls Christian churches are filled to capacity for Sunday services. Christian acquaintances, if asked, tell of meeting regularly in private homes for worship, Bible reading, and prayer. A briefing by the staff of the China Christian Council at their office on Yuen Ming Yuen Road in Shanghai reveals that a quiet revival has been sweeping across the land since the first churches were reopened in 1979. This has been in spite of a tightening up of restrictions on the Christian community since the Tiananmen Square massacre of 1989. Forty-five new pastors were ordained on 5 January 1992 at the meeting of the Fifth National Christian Conference.[1] In a mass baptismal service held in Hangzhou on 5 July 1992, 308 candidates were received into the Christian church with 206 choosing baptism by sprinkling and 102 baptism by immersion. Many of these were young people.[2] More than 11 million Bibles have been printed and distributed since 1980 and the Bible is now the second most widely published book in the country after the *Selected Works of Mao Zedong*.[3] Jiangsu Provincial Christian Council leaders report that there are now fifteen hundred churches and "meeting points" in the province, 95 percent of which are newly built.[4] The latest statistics of Protestant Christianity are all the more amazing since twenty years ago China watchers said that the church was all but dead:

Organized churches with buildings	12,000
Home meeting places	25,000
Seminary trained pastors	2,700
Seminaries	17
Seminarians	1,000
Bibles printed since 1992	13 million[5]

1

How many Christians are there in China today? Nobody knows for sure but the latest estimate given by the China Christian Council runs from 9.1 to 13.7 million for Protestants.[6] Other estimates are considerably higher. Figures for Roman Catholics run as high as 10 million.[7] Old churches are being reopened or new ones built at the rate of ten a week. And this has been going on for the past ten years! This period of rapid, sustained church growth is probably unprecedented in modern church history.

How did all this happen? To understand the present in China one must always look to the past. The history of the Protestant church in China is buried in the early days of the nineteenth century. So to grasp the meaning of what is happening today, we must probe deeply and search for roots.

An analogy from archeology may be helpful. A present thriving community may be built on top of layers of accumulated history. The community may or may not be aware of the cultural heritage of which it is a part. The debris of more recent layers may hide what lies below. Each layer contains clues that must be sorted out and analyzed so that the present can be better understood.

Beneath the present flourishing Christian community in China lie thirty years of suppression and abuse that culminated in the Great Proletarian Cultural Revolution (1967–1977) when all churches in the land were closed. Digging deeper, earlier layers can be identified with labels such as "Great Leap Forward" (1957–1958), "The Anti-Rightist Campaign" (1957), "The Hundred Flowers" (1956) and "The Accusation Meetings" (1951). During these years relationships with worldwide Christianity were broken and the church became isolated. Christian hospitals, universities and medical schools were nationalized. Presbyteries, synods, general assemblies and ecumenical councils were dissolved. Continuity with the past and with the world church was broken. In short, the institutional memory of the church was erased.

Penetrating beneath this thirty-year period into the missionary era that precedes it is difficult and painful. It is difficult because many of the leaders of this period, both Chinese and missionary, are no longer with us. Written records, minutes and reports were for the most part destroyed during the Cultural Revolution. It is painful, because in trying to recreate this period one touches the raw nerve of Chinese patriotism on the one hand, and on the other threatens deeply held missionary convictions.

How should the impact of the missionary movement be interpreted today? For years the official interpretation of the state was quite simple. The missionary cause was inexorably linked with the imperialism of the Western powers. Western religion and Western colonialism were but two sides of the same coin. Both were identified with the Opium Wars and the Unequal Treaties. For example, exhibits in the Guangdong Historical Museum in Canton portrayed missionary hospitals and schools as forerunners of Western economic, political and cultural imperialism. In the Nanjing Museum an exhibit portrays the opening of a school in 1898 by the Rev. J. Y. McGinnis, a Presbyterian missionary in Jiangyin (Kiangyin), and gives it a sinister interpretation. The school's purpose was obviously to subvert the citizens of Jiangyin. In the end, the missionaries made few converts and failed miserably to achieve any lasting results. So read the official interpretation.

Here the Chinese Communist Party is exercising an ancient imperial prerogative: Each dynasty has the license to rewrite the history of the previous dynasty. The history of the past shapes the present and is dangerous, if left uncontrolled, because it can motivate rebels, counter-revolutionaries and reformers. History is too emotionally charged to be left alone. It must be hermetically sealed off from the present so that only one orthodox view of the past is permitted.

Charges that the missionary movement was closely linked to Western colonialism in China cannot be dismissed easily and must be carefully examined. The ambiguous role assigned the China missionary by Western historians must likewise be scrutinized. Paul A. Cohen, in the *Cambridge History of China*, has written that the missionaries came, not like the traders to extract profits or the diplomats to obtain concessions, but to serve the Chinese people. He then asks a provocative question:

> Why, then, of all those who ventured to China in the last century, was it the missionary who inspired the greatest fear and hatred? If there is any one answer to this question, it is that the missionary was deeply — and unavoidably — committed to the proposition that the true interest of the Chinese people could be served only by means of a fundamental reordering of Chinese culture.[8]

Cohen's answer may be as good as any but it raises other questions. If they inspired fear and hatred on the part of some, they also inspired intense loyalty on the part of others. If they demanded changes in the traditional Chinese culture, they were strangely like the Chinese Communists who outdid the missionaries in advocating the destruction of the old traditions.

The prejudices and, at times, fanaticism of the missionary cannot be denied. But neither the Communists' nor the Western secular explanation can account for the strength and vitality of the present-day Christian movement. The Communist Party is now expressing alarm at defections to Christianity taking place within its ranks. *Wei Shi,* a Communist Party magazine of Jiangsu Province, is very much on the defensive as it reports that some cadre members are abandoning communism in favor of Christianity. Eight senior cadre in Funing County had become devout believers.[9]

The role of the missionary in China needs reevaluation. Much of what was written between 1950 and the mid 1970s was colored by the assumption that the missionary enterprise ended in "debacle" and that Christianity in China has ceased to exist as an organized religion.[10] History has now proved that neither of these assumptions is true.

What really was the contribution that the missionaries made? What were their weaknesses and failures along with their triumphs? Such an evaluation would be of benefit not only to an understanding of the Chinese church but to the modernization of the Chinese nation to which the missionary movement made a profound contribution.

There are signs that a more positive view of the missionary era is emerging in China. Scholars are more open and less doctrinaire in their treatment of religion and missions.[11] Scholarly journals are eager to pursue the various aspects of the missionary involvement in the early modernization of the nation. An international conference on issues relating to the missionary enterprise in the Qing dynasty is being proposed.[12] Cracks are appearing in what was once the official "hard line" as links with the past are beginning to surface in greater detail.

A news story in the Beijing press links the prestigious *Chinese Medical Journal* with its missionary beginnings one hundred years ago:

> More than 7,000 doctors, nurses and administrators gathered in Beijing's Science Hall yesterday to celebrate the 100th anniversary of the *Chinese Medical Journal*, China's oldest medical publication. The journal, a monthly magazine in English, was launched by the China Medical Missionary Association in Shanghai in March 1887 under the name of the *China Medical Missionary Journal*.[13]

On the occasion of the centennial celebration of the founding of the oldest hospital in Beijing, the administrator paid tribute to the spirit of the founders. Now known as "Hospital Number 6," it was formerly the Presbyterian Douw Hospital. The hospital staff, facilities and the scope of its medical practice have grown enormously, but the administrator warned of a deterioration of the hospital's fine old traditions of medical service:

> In the past, when we had a patient needing a blood transfusion, a call in the corridor would produce a long line of nurses willingly offering their blood. Such spectacles no longer appear.... Physically, we are growing up healthily, but spiritually we are losing.... We miss our old traditions, and will try to bring them back fully.[14]

The Drum Tower Hospital in Nanjing (Nanking) celebrated its centennial in May 1993 and invited representatives from the Disciples, Methodist and Presbyterian mission boards to take part in the festivities. A portrait of the founder, Dr. William E. Macklin of the Disciples of Christ Mission, standing with Dr. Sun Yat-sen was prominently displayed in the reception hall. A news story in the Nanjing secular press praised the sacrificial work of the founder and noted the contribution the missionary staff of the hospital had made to the welfare of the city.[15]

Graduates of Christian colleges, nonexistent since they were merged with state schools in the early 1950s, have organized alumni associations in order to keep alive the identity of their schools. *The New York Times* carried the story of a meeting of the Hangzhou Christian College alumni:

> On the wooded Dragon Hills of Hangzhou, the Chinese lakeside city, about 400 college faculty members, alumni and local journalists gathered

recently to celebrate the 140th anniversary of one of the oldest Christian colleges in China.[16]

Hangzhou alumni have launched a campaign to restore their old college and reestablish relationships with its founder, the Presbyterian Church in the United States of America (PCUSA).

Correspondence from Christian friends in Suzhou (Soochow) has asked for information about the first missionaries who came to their city. The letter was written on behalf of the Chinese People's Political Consultative Conference, "which is coming to recognize the good work done by our missionaries and wants to list them in the city history."[17] The stele in the church yard mentioned a Rev. "Du" and gave his name in Chinese characters. The letter asked: (1) what was his full English name? (Rev. Hampden Coit DuBose of the Presbyterian Church, U.S.); (2) was he the first missionary to come to our city? (he was the first to stay any length of time); (3) what else was known about his life and work? (he arrived in Suzhou in 1872 and served there until his death in 1910; he led a crusade against the infamous opium trade).

A letter from a schoolteacher and boyhood friend of the author in Xuzhou (Suchowfu) asked for information on the beginnings of the Presbyterian mission in that city. City authorities are constantly asking for such information and little is remembered because the old records were destroyed. They wanted names and dates of those who had served in the city.[18]

Chinese Christians are searching for their roots. Bits and pieces of information are being dug out of the past like broken shards from an archeological dig. More information lies buried in the archives of mission boards in the United States. To this must be added memoirs and biographies, church journals and the State Department consular records. For a composite picture, all these must be sorted out, pieced together and analyzed.

This is not to say that the "Three-Self" (Self-governing, Self-supporting, Self-propagating) postdenominational church in China today is the same as the church of the missionaries. It most certainly is not. There are profound differences, but the differences cannot be understood until a comparison is made with the former era. There is radical discontinuity with the past. But there is continuity as well. The 1911 Union Version of the Bible is still the most popular translation. Two-thirds of the hymns in the new hymnbook published by the China Christian Council came from the missionary era. To the despair of those who would introduce new forms of worship, most congregations still follow the rituals and liturgies they remember from the mists of years gone by.

The history of American Presbyterian missions forms a good case study for the broader Protestant movement of which it was a part. At least seventeen hundred American Presbyterian missionaries served in China between the years 1841 and 1952. They served in twelve provinces and over fifty cities of the Empire/Republic — from Peking in the north to the tropical island of Hainan in the south. Over two hundred of them died and were buried in China. For the most part they lived out their lives in peace and harmony with their Chinese neighbors but eighteen died what might be considered martyr's deaths.

And they are a part of America's religious and secular story, too. Presbyterian missionaries went to China, came home and were never the same again. The foreignness of China rubbed off on them. Chinese ministers and educators came to Protestant seminaries and it would be difficult to say who taught whom the most. For better or worse Chinese presbyteries were members of the Synod of New York for twenty-two years. For another thirty-six years one or more Chinese synods were subject to the PCUSA General Assembly. Six China missionaries were elected to the position of moderator of the Presbyterian General Assembly.[19] Women found their calling as church professionals in China before the same opportunities were open to them in the churches back home. Before the term "human rights" had been coined, Presbyterian missionaries in China were learning what its practice meant. It was in China that American Presbyterians — North and South — learned to work together again after the terrible War Between the States had torn them apart. Time and again the missionary movement, of which China was so important a part, contributed a sense of meaning and direction, vigor and vitality to the church at home.

For Presbyterians China was the first "foreign field" begun by their assembly. It was also the largest. For over one hundred years "China Missions" was the single largest item in the benevolent budget of the General Assembly. Year after year members of Presbyterian churches responded with sacrificial giving to causes in China that they would never see.

Presbyterian China missionaries played a leading role in molding relationships between the two countries. Whether this role was a proper one can be debated but there is no question that they were political and social activists, taking sides on all the issues of the day — from the Opium Wars to the recognition of Red China. In the words of Professor John Fairbank:

> In China's nineteenth-century relations with the West, Protestant missionaries are still the least studied but most significant actors in the scene.... Protestant missionaries were aggressive individualists in thought and attitude, often in conflict with the established order in China.... Only the missionaries sought direct contact with the common people in the two civilizations. They were the principal if not the sole link between village China and small-town America.[20]

Presbyterian missionaries served as U.S. consuls (Divie McCartee); influenced the wording of treaties (W. A. P. Martin); supported and opposed the Taiping rebellion (Martin and McCartee); campaigned against the opium trade (Hampden DuBose); instigated clubs to reform the ruling dynasty (Gilbert Reid); organized anti-footbinding leagues (Mary and Charlotte Thompson); denounced the treatment of Chinese laborers in the United States (the Canton Mission); opposed the sale of scrap iron to Japan (Frank A. Brown); and served as advisors for diplomatic missions (Frank W. Price). At the end it was a former Presbyterian missionary (John Leighton Stuart) who served as the last American ambassador to nationalist China on the mainland. Another Presbyterian missionary (Pearl S. Buck) perhaps more than any other literary figure influenced how a generation of Americans would think about the Chinese people.

This is the story of and about American Presbyterians. But they were a part of a missionary community made up of thousands from other churches who left their homes to serve in China. And so it is their story too. As the years rolled by the differences that had separated their churches at home became less important. The various strands of Protestant Christianity began to run together, resulting in the formation of the united Church of Christ in China. It was not a perfect union but nevertheless a giant step forward and, perhaps, the forerunner of the present day postdenominational expression of the Christian community.

A mission history can only trace the course of human events connected with a divine enterprise. The missionary at times was a hindrance to, and sometimes a vehicle for, furthering that enterprise. For the church can only be established by God's own mighty acts on soil that to us may be foreign — but no soil is foreign to the Spirit of God. For "we have this treasure in earthen vessels to show that the transcendent power belongs to God and not to us" (2 Cor. 4:7).

Part 1

The Nineteenth Century

Dynasty, Foreign Devils and the Kingdom of God

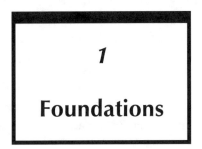

1

Foundations

The missionary enterprise of American Presbyterians in China began in a theological dispute. Presbyterians do not do anything precipitously. The issue must first be debated from every side. The issue was not whether Christians had an obligation to take the saving gospel of Jesus Christ to the "heathen." At least in principle there was general agreement on this. As early as 1744 David Brainerd, ordained by the Presbytery of New York and supported by a missionary society in Scotland, had engaged in missionary activities among the Indians along the Delaware River. Presbyterian missionaries, supported by independent societies, had gone to Syria and Lebanon in 1823.

The debate was over the nature and mission of the Church of Jesus Christ. Should a church through its own denominational board appoint and support missions to the Indian nations and distant lands or was this best left to independent societies? It was not an easy decision. Some felt that missions could best be carried out by individual Christians who could organize their own societies. This was the way the modern missionary movement had begun in England when William Carey had been sent to India by the Baptist Missionary Society in 1793. This was the way it had started in America. The American Board of Commissioners for Foreign Missions (ABCFM) had been organized by members of Congregational churches in New England as an independent society and it had become the agency of choice for Presbyterians. Presbyterians were members of the board and there was no particular complaint with the way the ABCFM was working.

The Church *Is* a Missionary Society

But others saw the situation quite differently. For them it was a question of the mission of the church of Jesus Christ. If it was not to engage in mission to the regions beyond, then what was it? If the church wished to be true to its New Testament mandate, how could it ignore its missionary obligation? Mission was not an elective that individual church members could choose or not as they saw fit. Rather, it belonged to the very nature of what it meant to be a member of Christ's church and was too important a matter to be left to independent societies. And so there was a growing conviction that the Presbyterian Church

11

needed its own mission agency to carry out the mandate Christ had given to his church. This "conceptual change" in mission strategy was well expressed at that time by John Holt Rice of Union Seminary in Virginia:

> The Presbyterian Church *is* a missionary society, the object of which is to aid in the conversion of the world, and every member of the Church is a member for life of said society, and bound, in maintenance of his Christian character, to do all in his power for the accomplishment of the object.[1]

The issue was complicated by the "Old School"/"New School" division within the General Assembly. A number of issues involved in the dispute have been long since forgotten. But in the area of missions an issue of considerable importance was at stake. The New School supported a continuation of the voluntary principle: "Missions is a matter for individual Presbyterians to decide about and carry out simply in voluntary association with other like-minded Christians." The Old School advocated the organic principal: "Missions is a function of the church as a collective, disciplined body and therefore to be carried out through its constituted judicatories."[2] It is an issue that is still with us today.

In 1812, 1828 and 1831 overtures were presented to the General Assembly asking the Assembly to establish its own board, which would have responsibility for sending the gospel of Christ to the regions beyond. Each time the General Assembly declined to act, referring Presbyterians who wished to engage in such activities to the ABCFM. Old School advocates in Pennsylvania decided that they could wait no longer and asked the Synod of Pittsburgh to establish its own foreign mission agency. In 1831 the Synod constituted the Western Foreign Missionary Society which was accountable to and supported by the Synod.

Between the years 1832 and 1837 the Western Foreign Mission Society sent twenty-one missionaries to the Indian nations and thirty-nine missionaries to Liberia and India. They intended their society to be a stopgap until they could persuade the General Assembly to take over the work.

Finally in 1835 they met with success when the General Assembly voted to appoint a committee that would confer with the Synod of Pittsburgh on the transfer of the work of the Western Foreign Missionary Society to the Assembly.

But the next year, after long and acrimonious debate, the General Assembly under New School pressure reversed its previous action by a vote of 110 to 106 and declined to proceed with the action approved the previous year. The Synod of Pittsburgh felt betrayed but did not give up. A campaign was begun to get the Assembly to proceed with the original plan. Momentum for a denominational board began to build. To gain broader support, the name was changed to "Presbyterian Foreign Missionary Society" and the headquarters was moved to New York.

The strategy was successful. The General Assembly of 1837, meeting in Philadelphia and dominated by Old School advocates, approved the overture from the Synod of Pittsburgh by adopting the following resolution by a vote of 108 to 29:

> Resolved, that the General Assembly will superintend and conduct, by its own proper authority, the work of Foreign Missions of the Presbyterian Church, by a Board appointed for the purpose and directly amenable to said Assembly.[3]

Having made the decision, the Assembly went about it in a big way. The Board of Foreign Missions of the Presbyterian Church in the United States of America (BFM) was constituted with a membership of eighty members — forty ministers and forty elders. Its first meeting was held 31 October 1837 in Baltimore. The Synod of Pittsburgh transferred its thirty-seven missionaries (11 ministers, 5 teachers, 1 printer, 20 women) and assets of $5,784 to the new General Assembly board. One of the first actions of the Board was to appoint the Honorable Walter Lowrie Corresponding Secretary. Lowrie then held the position of Secretary of the U.S. Senate, and had previously served as senator from Pennsylvania. At this or the next meeting of the Executive Committee the decision was made to start work in China.

The China Decision

Why China? In making the decision to open work in China, the new Board gave the following reasons:

Size. China's enormous population. One-fourth of the human race was at stake.

Ignorance of the true God. The almost complete ignorance of the true religion called for action on the part of Christians everywhere. Yet comparatively little had been done.

One written language. The board was impressed by the "remarkable fact" that the people in this vast country were united in a common written language and could be reached through the publication and distribution of the Bible, which had only recently been translated. Evangelization through the printed word would play a major role in the new mission.

China is "open and waiting for the Gospel." Foreign residence was forbidden within the empire except at one point (Macau) because the government was apprehensive of European politics but the educated people of China were anxious to receive books of Western learning. Millions of Chinese lived in the "Eastern Archipelago" (Malaysia) and were accessible to missionary labors. Here was the place to begin.[4]

The opinion that China was "open and waiting for the gospel" was hardly a realistic appraisal of the religious situation at the time. China was not waiting to receive a new religion. It was perfectly satisfied with the ones it had. And yet, unknown to the members of the Board, events just over the horizon would dramatically change the whole situation.

To begin the China mission it was decided that two ordained men, a printer and a physician were needed. Rev. John A. Mitchell and Rev. and Mrs. Robert W. Orr were appointed. A physician and a printer could not be found. Instructions given by the Board to its first China missionaries were to proceed to the Eastern Archipelago, visit various points and then decide on the best location. What was desired was a place that was healthy, where people and property would be protected and where there was a goodly number of Chinese. They were to engage in preaching, establish schools and operate a printing press. Missionaries should "submit to the laws of the place."[5]

In its first report to the home church, the Board singled out the opium trade as the principal obstacle to the spread of the gospel in China:

> The contraband trade of *opium,* is at this time the greatest barrier of the Gospel into China. . . . What a spectacle is presented here! The government of a nation not possessing the Bible, and unblessed by the light of the Gospel, laboring to protect their people from a moral pestilence, which is carrying dismay and poverty and wretchedness through the land . . . and the merchants of the other governments, nominally Christian, employing ships and capital and bribes to force that very evil upon them.[6]

Prophetic words indeed! The long shadow of the opium trade would continue to plague the missionary efforts in China for the next one hundred years.

The Missionary Enterprise in the United States

The China venture of the Presbyterian Church can best be understood in the context of events taking place in the American scene in the early decades of the nineteenth century. The youthful American Republic was in a mood of optimistic, confident expansion. The frontier was moving steadily westward. The Louisiana Purchase (1803) had doubled the land mass of the United States. In the War of 1812 the United States had challenged Great Britain over the issue of freedom of American ships on the high seas. The Monroe Doctrine (1823) had declared that henceforth the Western hemisphere would be free from European intrigue and domination. By the 1830s clipper ships from New England were challenging the British monopoly in the enormously profitable China trade and were bringing back tales of a strange and exotic people. In 1844 James K. Polk was elected president on a policy of "Manifest Destiny," the annexation of Texas, and the expansion of the United States from the Atlantic to the Pacific. The young republic was eager to assume a leadership role in world affairs.

Slavery was one of the few clouds on the horizon. In 1808 Congress had declared an end to the African slave trade but the Missouri Compromise (1820) had left the issue of slavery within the United States unresolved. In 1821 the abolitionist movement founded the American Colonization Society in Liberia for the resettlement of African slaves.

On the religious scene, the "Second Great Awakening" was sweeping the country. Camp meetings and revival services were leading lay and clergy alike to a new sense of responsibility for personal witness. The Presbyterian and Congregational churches had entered into the Plan of Union (1801) in which both denominations cooperated in the organization of new congregations as the frontier moved westward. The sending out of William Carey (1793) and Robert Morrison (1807) by missionary societies in Great Britain challenged Protestants in America to do the same. In 1806 a band of students meeting at Williams College took refuge during a rain storm under a haystack, held a prayer meeting and offered themselves for foreign mission service. This led to the formation of the ABCFM in 1812.

Motivation for mission was as varied as the volunteers who were sent. Charles W. Forman cites a number of reasons: altruistic service, the plight of the "heathen," the sense of obligation, the value of the human soul or simply the call of Christ. "There was a minimum of theory and a maximum of practice."[7] Valentine Rabe characterizes the movement as a "mixture of youthful enthusiasm, and ecclesiastical conservatism, traditionalism, and free innovation."[8]

Some have seen in the nineteenth-century missionary enterprise an extension of American expansionism — a spiritualized "manifest destiny" to conquer the world. The religious and cultural imperialism of the missionary and the exploitation of commercial interest were but two sides of the same coin. But Arthur Schlesinger, Jr., cautions against pushing the analogy too far:

> If from time to time the missionary effort facilitated the capitalist effort, the missionaries themselves remained a force independent of, and often at odds with, both the white trader and even more the white settler.[9]

Missionaries undoubtedly identified the American values of liberty, individuality and industry too closely with the Christian gospel. Their strident use of military metaphors was unfortunate and contributed to the easy identification of their mission with nationalistic endeavors. But missionaries were more often than not at loggerheads with the entrepreneurs and diplomats who saw them as troublemakers. The missionary movement will never be understood if it is viewed simply as an appendage to a political, social or economic endeavor. It had its own distinct ethos, purpose and goals.

The Middle Kingdom in 1837

On the eve of the arrival of the first Presbyterian missionaries, China's world view was one of splendid isolation. Both in area and in population China was the largest country in the world. Outer Mongolia, Turkestan, Tibet and Taiwan were all part of China's vast domain.

China knew herself as "Zhong-guo" or "The Middle Kingdom." It was the center of the universe and Chinese civilization was the standard against which all other cultures were judged.

Outside their domain there were either the vassal states or the barbarians. Other distant countries on the periphery did not concern them. China was completely self-sufficient and had no needs — cultural, economic or religious — that could not be satisfied from within her own boundaries. Diplomacy consisted of receiving tribute from inferior peoples dependent upon China's goodwill. In 1793 the Emperor Qianlong (Ch'ien-lung) rebuffed the diplomatic mission of Lord Macartney to Peking with these words to the British sovereign:

> You, O King, from afar have yearned after the blessings of our civilization, and in your eagerness to come into touch with our converting influence have sent an Embassy across the sea. . . . Yesterday your Ambassador petitioned my Ministers to memorialize me regarding your trade with China, but . . . Our Celestial Empire possesses all things in prolific abundance and lacks no product within its own borders.[10]

The Chinese misreading of Western culture was matched by the Western ignorance of China. The ethnocentrism of the East was matched by the arrogance of the West:

> Each felt that the other belonged to a lower order of civilization. It would be difficult, indeed, to image a more violent non-meeting of minds.[11]

Early Protestant missionaries were totally unprepared to deal with Chinese culture. China's civilization extended in an unbroken line back to the days of the mythical rulers — Yao, Shun and Yu (circa 2200 B.C.). Could Christianity relate to such an ancient, monolithic and sophisticated civilization without some accommodation? The historian Kenneth Scott Latourette raised the question over sixty years ago and it is still relevant today:

> In the only countries where Christianity has triumphed over a high civilization, as in the older Mediterranean world and the Nearer East, it has done so by conforming in part to older cultures. Whether it can win to its fold a highly cultured people like the Chinese without again making a similar adaptation remains an unanswered question.[12]

The Qing or Manchu dynasty was ruling China when the Protestant missionaries entered the country. Their homeland was in the steppes north of the Great Wall and they were considered foreigners by native Chinese. They had come to power in 1644 when their "banner" armies had penetrated the Great Wall of China and had overthrown the Ming dynasty, which had been weakened by peasant revolts and corrupt eunuchs. The cycle had followed the inevitable pattern of dynastic decline.

In the year 1837 Dao Guang (Tao-kuang), the sixth emperor of the Qing, was on the dragon throne. The dynasty ruled through a dual system of Manchu and

Chinese officials. Manchus were exempt from forced labor, paid lower taxes and had other privileges. Anti Manchu sentiments were pervasive throughout the empire.

Jean Chesneaux characterizes the period as "a conjunction of crises," citing the following pressures that threatened the empire:

Rampant population increase. For a hundred years the population had been growing without any comparable increase in arable land. This demographic pressure lowered the standard of living, led to famines and resulted in peasant migrations.

The rise of secret societies. In China the classic form of protest against the established order was the secret society. The White Lotus Society in the north and the Triad in the south defied the authorities and terrorized the countryside.

Deterioration in government services. In spite of the population increases there was a decline in public services. Dikes and canals fell into disrepair. District officials and tax collectors became more corrupt.[13]

The Three Religions of China

The classical understanding of religion in China is expressed in the saying "Ju, Shih, Tao, San Chiao" — "Confucianism, Buddhism, Taoism — the Three Teachings."[14] To be linked in this way meant that they were not mutually exclusive. "The shrines of each are open to all and availed of by all."[15]

Confucianism

Confucius (551–479 B.C.) was primarily concerned with the problem of bringing social order out of chaos during a time of political and social turbulence. How do human beings live in relationship to one another? The answer lay in following the way of the ancients. Of supreme importance were the "five relationships" — between king and subject, father and son, husband and wife, older brother and younger brother, friend and friend. In a well-ordered Confucian society everyone knew one's assigned role and what duties it entailed.

The teachings of Confucius created a society that was unalterably conservative. Emphasis on a male-dominated society meant that the abuse of women was institutionalized. Footbinding, child marriages, concubinage and the infanticide of girl babies are a few examples.

But one must also recognize the positive role Confucius played in molding Chinese society. For Confucius, good government was primarily a matter of moral example.

> In a day when might was right, he argued that the ruler's virtue and the contentment of the people, rather than power, should be the true measures of political success.... Confucius was China's first great moralist, the founder of a great ethical tradition in a civilization which above all others came to concentrate on ethical values.[16]

The influence of Confucius on family and education has been enormous. The solidarity of the Chinese family endured even the ravages of the Cultural Revolution. Education was the key to advancement as access to high office was through a national examination system.

Confucius was only peripherally concerned with humanity's relationship to the Divine. In a famous response to questions about spirits and the future life he replied:

> While still unable to do your duty to the living, how can you do your duty to the dead...not yet understanding life, how can you understand death?[17]

Buddhism

It was in this neglected realm of the spirit world that Buddhism complemented the teachings of the great sage. Unlike the humanism of Confucius, Buddhism was concerned with the philosophical questions of life and death and suffering. The historic Buddha, known in China as Sakyamuni, had lived and taught in northern India around 500 B.C. The essence of his teachings is contained in the Four Noble Truths. All life is suffering. Suffering is caused by desire. To put an end to suffering one must cease to desire. Elimination of desire is through the Eight Fold Path.

Buddhism was introduced into China in the first century A.D. It adapted well to Chinese culture but in the process experienced the same fate as other ideologies that have tried to transform the Chinese. Buddhism itself underwent a change. From the original Theravada came the Chinese version of Mahayana:

> In place of the godless religion of the historic Buddha, the Mahayanists have myriads of godlike Buddhas in eons of time.... the emphasis in Mahayana Buddhism shifted from enlightenment through "one's own strength" to salvation through "the strength of another...." Mahayana thus provided compassionate, comforting gods for every human need.[18]

In times of strong prosperous dynasties, Confucianism was predominant. In times of disintegration, disorder and suffering, Buddhism came into its own. Buddhism has had a strong attraction for women and peasants at the bottom rungs of the social order. Buddhism softened the harsh rigidities of the Confucian system with its emphasis on kindness and mercy.

Taoism

The third member of China's religious triad had its origin in the teaching of the sage Laotzu. The term itself comes from the Chinese "Tao" — which has been variously translated into English as "the Way," "the Power" or the "Logos" of the fourth gospel. Its enigmatic character is seen in the opening lines of the Taoist classic *The Tao Te Ching* (The Way and the Power):

The Tao which can be defined is not the eternal Tao; the name by which it can be named is not its eternal name. When nameless, it is the origin of the universe; when it has a name, it is the mother of all things.[19]

As Confucius emphasized man in relationship to society, Laotzu emphasized man in communion with nature. Withdrawal, nonconformity and freedom of individual expression have been Taoist themes. Poets and painters were often Taoist. Taoism represented the protest of the individual against the stifling conformity of Confucian orthodoxy. It was said that when a man held office he was a Confucian; when he was out of office he became a Taoist. In succeeding years Taoism degenerated into superstition and magic. It is "the most difficult of all religions in China to describe because it is the most amorphous."[20]

By the time the Protestant missionaries had arrived a rigid, ultraconservative Confucianism was the state orthodoxy. For several hundred years Buddhism had been in decline. Taoism was scorned by scholars as superstition unworthy of their attention.

Sensitive missionary observers would detect points of contact between Christianity and "The Three Teachings." They could agree with many of the ethical principles taught by Confucius. The Buddhist emphasis on mercy and compassion would strike a resonant chord in Christian ears. The Taoist awe and humility before the mysteries of the universe did not seem far from the kingdom of God.

And yet there were fundamental differences that the early missionaries felt could not be compromised: the Confucian ancestral sacrifices, the Buddhist images and idols, the Taoist incantations and magic. Could the Christianity the missionaries brought be adapted to Eastern thought-forms without losing its own soul? And yet without some adaptation how could its gospel become relevant? There would be no easy answers.

China's Relationship with the West

Dynastic decline could not have come at a worse time. For much of her long history, the civilization of China had surpassed that of Europe. Fairbank has pointed out that

China under the T'ang and Sung and right down to Marco Polo's day was a far greater civilization in both size and accomplishment than its contemporary, medieval Europe.... Consider how the main flow of influence over the long course of history had been from China to Europe, not the other way: first, the silk trade...paper...printing...porcelain... cast-iron, canal lock-gates, the wheelbarrow, the stern-post rudder...the compass...gunpowder, and all the rest.[21]

All this was forgotten by Western diplomats and missionaries who experienced China at the low point of its long history.

Portuguese navigators were the first to reach China over the sea route around the Cape of Good Hope, and through the Straits of Malacca. By 1514 they had reached the southern coast of China and established a trading post at Macau on a small peninsula south of Canton. For the next three hundred years Macau was the place where European merchants met Chinese mandarins for trade.

The British arrived on the scene in 1699 and obtained permission to establish a trading compound, called a "factory," on the Pearl River just outside Canton. In the beginning, Westerners wanted things Chinese more than the Chinese wanted things Western. Tea, silk and porcelain china were much in demand in Europe. They were exchanged for manufactured goods from England, silver dollars from Spain and cotton from India.

On the Chinese side the monopoly was held by a guild of merchants called the "Cohong." On the foreign side it was held by the British East India Company. As long as the foreigners could be kept in their place they were welcomed, for there were enormous profits to be made on both sides. Fraternizing and social mingling were prohibited. Foreign traders could not bring their wives to live with them in the Canton factories, nor could they ride in sedan chairs or enter the walled city of Canton. Each year at the end of the trading season they returned to Macau.

In the early years of the nineteenth century, there was an enormous expansion of trade through the "Canton System" and in 1834 the monopoly of the British East India Company ended. China was on the threshold of a new chapter in East-West relations.

Early Christian Missions to China

When did Christianity first come to China? The event is chiseled into the stone of the remarkable Nestorian Monument of Xian (Sian), erected in 781 but not unearthed for nearly a thousand years. The monument tells of the arrival of the monk Alopen at the capital city of the Tang dynasty in the year 635. The missionary, who had crossed the deserts and high mountains of Central Asia via the Silk Road, was received with honor by the emperor. Nestorian communities were established in the trading centers of the empire and for some decades the new religion enjoyed considerable success. But Nestorian Christianity never ceased to be a foreign religion. After several hundred years it disappeared from China's soil. Dr. Samuel H. Moffett suggests there were religious, theological, missiological and political reasons for its decline. Of the four, the political was probably decisive: "the fall of an imperial house on which the church had too long relied for its patronage and protection."[22]

A second attempt to introduce Christianity into China was made in the thirteenth century. Marco Polo's account of his travels and the fabulous civilization he found in China aroused intense interest among the people of Europe. In 1294 a Franciscan monk, John of Montecorvino, arrived in Cambaluc (later Peking) bearing a letter from Pope Nicholas III to the emperor Kublai Khan. He had taken three years to make the trip and in the meantime Kublai had died. But the missionary was welcomed by the court of the Yuan (Mongol) dynasty. Again there was initial success but during the later part of the fourteenth century the Franciscan mission began to decline. Again the church was not able to overcome its foreignness. The church at home, suffering from the ravages of the Black Plague, was not able to sustain the advance across the vast distance. The Franciscans were identified with the Mongols (a foreign dynasty) and when the Mings (a native dynasty) came to power, the Christian presence in China again came to an end.

Two hundred years were to pass before another attempt would be made. This time it would be the Jesuits' turn. Success was achieved when a brilliant young priest by the name of Matteo Ricci secured a residence at the capital city of Peking in 1601. Ricci was a scholar and a scientist. A breakthrough was made when Ricci and his companions exchanged the saffron garb of the Buddhist priests for the long robes of the Confucian scholars. Another triumph came when the Jesuits were asked to undertake the reform of the Chinese calendar. Ricci had a prodigious memory and his feats of reciting long lists of Chinese characters won the respect of the scholars.[23] By his patience, scholarly ways and respect for Chinese customs he won the confidence of the rulers.

Roman Catholicism prospered in China during the seventeenth century. Other Roman Catholic orders entered China with the Spanish and French traders. A native Chinese was consecrated bishop in 1685. Not until the twentieth century would there be another. By the end of the century there were about seventy-five foreign priests in China. Half of these were Jesuits. Christians probably numbered about three hundred thousand.[24] As evidence of the favor that Christianity enjoyed at the Manchu court is this astonishing testimony to the death of Jesus Christ attributed by Bishop K. H. Ting to the Emperor Kangxi (1661–1722):

> With his task done on the cross,
> His blood forms itself into a streamlet.
> Grace flows from West Heaven in long patience:
>> Tried in four courts,
>> Long walks at midnight,
> Thrice denied by friend before the cock crew twice,
> Six-footer hanging at the same height as two thieves.
> It is a suffering that moves the whole world and all ranks.
> Hearing his seven words makes all souls cry.[25]

But Christianity fell on hard times during the eighteenth century. One reason was undoubtedly the "Rites Controversy." Ricci and the Jesuits had made every attempt to adapt Christianity to Chinese customs. They used classical Chinese names for God that had pagan connotations. They were tolerant of Confucian ceremonies honoring the ancestors. The Dominicans and Franciscans felt the Jesuits had gone too far. The issue was complicated by jealousy between the orders. The Jesuits had been there first and were the court favorites. As the dispute grew in intensity, appeals were made to Rome. Rome vacillated, siding first with one group and then the other. Finally in 1742 Pope Innocent XIII issued a decree that was a final rejection of the Jesuit position. There could be no accommodation of Catholic dogma and practice with Chinese culture.[26]

The aftermath of the controversy was a divided and weakened Christian mission. Chinese emperors had been alienated. Intermittent persecutions took place. Increasingly Christianity was viewed as a hostile and alien force. In 1811 an imperial edict prohibiting the practice of Christianity throughout the realm was issued. Missionary priests were expelled but some stayed and were hidden by their parishioners. The last Jesuit astronomer at the court in Peking died in 1838 and was not replaced. Latourette estimates that the number of Catholic Christians had declined by a third to not more than 220,000.[27]

The issue of the foreign nature of Christianity, which was faced by the Nestorians, the Franciscans and the Jesuits, would surface again and again in the succeeding years.

The Coming of the Protestants

Robert Morrison and his wife, Mary, Scottish Presbyterians under the appointment of the London Missionary Society, arrived in Canton in 1807. They had been refused passage by the British East India Company and had been given a free ride on an American ship. Morrison immediately began the study of the Chinese language, and being of a scholarly disposition, he made rapid progress. His residence in Canton was precarious until it was legalized by his appointment as translator by the same East India Company that had once refused him passage. Morrison spent his time translating the Bible and preparing a Chinese-English dictionary. In his journal entry for 16 July 1814 he records an historic occasion — the baptism of his first convert, Tsae A-Ko, "at a spring of water issuing from the foot of a lofty hill by the seaside, away from human observation."[28]

In a letter to his missionary society written on 25 November 1819, another historic occasion is recorded:

> FATHERS AND BRETHREN, By the mercy of God, an entire version of the books of the Old and New Testaments, into the Chinese language, was this day brought to a conclusion.[29]

In 1813 William Milne and his wife arrived in Macau but were expelled almost immediately by the Portuguese. They moved to Malacca, where there was greater freedom for Protestants under Dutch rule. Here Milne, with backing from Morrison, established the Anglo-Chinese College, which had the dual purpose of acquainting Europeans with the Chinese culture and giving Chinese a Western education within the context of the Christian faith.

Milne's major contribution was in the publication of Christian literature. His pamphlet entitled *The Two Friends* became the best known treatise for the Christian faith and passed through seventeen editions and the printing of several hundred thousand copies. Its success was attributed to its literary style and the way it captured the Chinese spirit by presenting Christianity in the form of a rational dialogue between two cultured Chinese gentlemen.[30]

These were difficult days for the small Protestant missionary community. Milne's wife died of dysentery. Mary Morrison died in childbirth in 1821. Milne died the next year. All were under forty.

New volunteers began to arrive. The first American, the Rev. Elijah Bridgman, under appointment by the ABCFM, came in 1830. His most significant contribution was, again, through the printed page. He edited *The Chinese Repository,* which served to introduce Western and Chinese civilization to each other. Bridgman's widely read publications presented Western geography, history, science and government from a Christian perspective.[31]

The first medical missionary, Peter Parker, arrived in 1834. Both Bridgman and Parker were given free passage by D. W. C. Olyphant, an American shipper in the Canton trade.[32] Parker opened the Canton Ophthalmic Hospital and his operations on cataracts and tumors dramatically demonstrated the superiority of Western medicine. His fame spread far and wide and his patients included leading Chinese merchants and Cantonese officials.[33]

We are now on the eve of the arrival of the Presbyterians. A score of Protestant missionaries had established a base of operations in Canton and Macau. The enterprise was scarcely thirty years old. The first pioneers had passed from the scene. Morrison died in 1834 and was buried beside his wife, Mary, in the Protestant cemetery in Macau. The Bible had been translated and was in print. The Christian message was being disseminated through the printed page. Several schools had been established and a hospital founded. Christian converts numbered not more than a hundred — most of whom were in the employ of foreigners. Imperial edicts still prohibited the dissemination of the Christian faith or the residence of Christian missionaries.

These first missionaries brought with them all the prejudices of their countrymen. There is no record that they were given any preparation for a cross-cultural mission. Indeed, there is no way that such preparation could have been given. Definitions for "racism," "ethnocentricity" and "acculturation" do not appear in the 1831 edition of Noah Webster's *American Dictionary.* Webster's sole definition of "culture" is "the act of tilling and preparing the earth for crops."[34] Missiology, cultural anthropology and cross-cultural studies had yet to be invented. Indeed, these missionaries and those that followed would lay the foundations for these disciplines. Coming to China as teachers, they would become learners and find that they along with those whom they wished to teach would be changed by the message they brought.

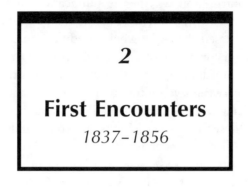

2

First Encounters
1837–1856

Singapore

On 6 December 1837, Rev. John A. Mitchell, Rev. Robert W. Orr and Mrs. Eliza Carter Orr set sail from New York to Singapore.[1] Their voyage around the Cape of Good Hope on a sailing vessel took 115 days, which was considered a good passage for that season of the year. Singapore, a British trading post that had been established in 1819 by Sir Stamford Raffles on the southern tip of the Malay Peninsula, was the logical place to begin until China itself was open for foreign residence. It had overtaken Malacca, the site of the Anglo-Chinese College started earlier by Morrison and Milne, as the most important transportation and commercial center between India and the China coast. Chinese comprised a large percentage of the population.

Property was purchased for residences and a school and the missionaries began the study of the Cantonese dialect. In 1839 Orr baptized his first convert, Tan Kwang, his Chinese language teacher from Siam.

But tragedy soon struck. Mitchell was stricken with a fever and died on 2 October 1838 less than six months after he had arrived. Soon thereafter the Orrs buried an infant daughter. Later Mr. Orr's health began to fail. In 1841 it became necessary for the family to return to the United States.

New recruits were on the way. Rev. and Mrs. Thomas L. McBryde arrived in 1840 and Dr. and Mrs. J. C. Hepburn the next year. A small school was begun. But McBryde found it difficult to live in the intense heat and his health began to break.

Another recruit, the Rev. Walter M. Lowrie, son of the Board secretary, sailed from New York in January 1842 at a time of great uncertainty as to what was happening in China. War had broken out between Great Britain and China over opium and related issues. What effect would this have on Christian missions? His instructions from the Executive Committee were to proceed to Macau, survey the situation there and then proceed to Singapore, where the small missionary band would make decisions about the future of the enterprise. When

Lowrie arrived in Macau he was surprised to find the McBrydes already there, as they had made the move to a cooler climate because of health.

The situation in China had changed significantly from the time Lowrie had left New York. England and China were about to sign a peace treaty that would open China to foreign residence. Lowrie was in a quandary. Was the sea trip back to Singapore, where only the Hepburns remained, necessary? Finally, he decided to follow his instructions and booked passage on the *Sea Queen.*[2]

It was not a happy voyage. The captain swore incessantly, the steward was filthy and the food was often uneatable. Because of adverse monsoon winds they made little progress. Running short of supplies, they changed course for Manila, which they reached in sixty-five days, still no nearer to Singapore.

Lowrie tried again, booking passage on the *Harmony*, but this time it was even worse. They were caught in a gale, driven far off their course toward a reef known as the "North Danger." Men were sent aloft but could see nothing. Suddenly, the ship struck the rocks with tremendous force. The pumps were unable to keep the water out and the ship was abandoned. They pushed off from the sinking ship in the lifeboats as darkness was falling. The nearest land was Luzon, some four hundred miles away.

On the fourth day as they were approaching land a storm broke out that threatened to capsize the small boats. At 2 A.M. the wind and seas abated and Lowrie wrote, "We began to hope that our lives might be spared." As morning dawned, they could see the waves breaking on the rocks but were able to beach the boat in a small cove. "With one consent, we gathered together under the trees and offered up our thanksgiving and praise to God." Spanish officials arranged for their return to Manila, where Lowrie was offered free passage back to Macau.

McBryde and Lowrie advised the Board to give up the Singapore venture and concentrate all their efforts on China. Hepburn sold the property and closed down activities only recently begun. They buried an infant child in Singapore and in June 1843 moved to Macau.

Six years had passed since the Board had made its China decision. Eight missionaries had been appointed. Of these one had died, two had returned home because of health and the health of two others was precarious. The work in Singapore had been abandoned. But the Opium War and the resulting treaties were to bring a new era for East-West relationships.

The First Opium War and the Treaty of Nanking

An understanding of the Opium War and the Unequal Treaties is essential for an understanding of the China mission, for these events cast a long shadow over the Christian movement for the next one hundred years. Problems began with the rapid expansion of trade through the port of Canton, which outgrew the merchant guild system. Exports from China, principally tea and silk, were in great demand in the West. Indian cotton was needed in China for its infant textile industry and the trade was mutually beneficial. All went well until China's domestically grown cotton began to take care of its needs. What could be used for import into China to pay for the tea and silk being exported to the West? British merchants came up with an ideal product — readily available in India, easily transportable, in great demand in China and enormously profitable: opium!

There had long been a market for opium in China. Periodically the government took steps to outlaw the use and import of opium but with little success. Bribes, the self-interest of officials and the enormous profits involved made its control all but impossible. As the trade increased, opium addiction became a serious social problem. In 1839 imperial statutes were adopted that outlawed the traffic and levied heavy punishments both for traders and users of opium.

The Manchu Court appointed an incorruptible Confucian, Lin Zexu, as the Imperial Commissioner at Canton to enforce the new prohibitions. He immediately came into conflict with both British and Chinese traders. In two months he made 1,600 arrests and confiscated 11,000 pounds of opium. He demanded that the foreign traders surrender their stock. When they refused, he confined the 350 foreign traders to their Canton factories for six weeks. The traders finally capitulated and turned over 20,000 chests of opium. These Lin burned in a great public ceremony, scattering the ashes over the harbor.[3]

Dissatisfaction among the British with the Canton system had been smoldering for some time. There were complaints over the treatment of British subjects who had been convicted and punished according to Chinese law, which appeared capricious and cruel to Europeans. Manchu officials continued to regard British diplomats as tribute bearers from a vassal state. They had rebuffed repeated attempts on the part of British to establish diplomatic relationships with the central government in Peking. Now the forceful detention of British subjects and the confiscation of British cargo offered an excuse to settle the issue by force of arms.[4]

The war, which consisted primarily of naval engagements, was fought intermittently around Canton and along the coast. Strangely, trade at Canton continued during the hostilities with the American merchants handling British interests. But the conflict was hopelessly one-sided. Chinese forces were no match for the British gunboats and shore parties. The reforming Commissioner at Canton was recalled in disgrace and the Manchu court sued for peace.

The first of the infamous Unequal Treaties was signed at Nanjing in 1842. The significant terms of the treaty were: (1) The merchant guild system at Canton was abolished in exchange for free trade regulated by tariffs, which averaged between 4 and 10 percent; (2) Hong Kong, then a barren island, was ceded to Great Britain; (3) five "treaty ports" — Canton, Xiamen (Amoy), Fuzhou (Foochow), Ningbo (Ningpo) and Shanghai were open to British residence and trade; (4) an indemnity of 21 million Mexican silver dollars was paid to Britain to cover the confiscated opium and the cost of the war; (5) British subjects were granted extraterritoriality when residing in the treaty ports, which meant that they were subject to British rather than Chinese law; (6) within the treaty ports British subjects could buy land and open schools; (7) British warships could anchor in treaty ports and travel in Chinese waters.[5] Although not involved in the conflict, the United States and France were given similar concessions in treaties signed in 1843 and 1844 under the "most-favored-nation clause."

Missionaries were not mentioned in the treaties. The only reference to religion was in the French and American treaties, which granted permission to foreigners to build hospitals, schools and, surprisingly, "places of worship." How did the phrase get into the treaty? Some historians have contended that it was at the insistence of Elijah Bridgman and Peter Parker, who served as interpreters for the American delegation and were looking out for missionary interests.[6] However, Peter Parker remembers it differently. In his memoirs he wrote that it was a member of the Chinese delegation who proposed the addition:

> On coming to the seventeenth article of the treaty, which provided for leasing of ground, building places of business and residences, cemeteries, and hospitals, at the treaty ports, Pwan-Sze Shing, whose father and mother had been my patients . . . knowing the gratification it would afford me, suggested the additional and most important provisions, "Urh Le pae T'ang," (and Temples of Worship).[7]

As citizens of the nations that had made the treaties missionaries gained two important privileges: (1) the right to reside and propagate their religion in the treaty ports and (2) legal protection of their own country's laws. Travel into the interior was not mentioned.

There was no reference to opium in the treaties but trade in the commodity was tacitly condoned and expanded all along the coast. And along with the increase in the trade, there was a corresponding increase in opium addiction and social problems.

It was under these ominous circumstances that the Presbyterians made their first move into China.

Xiamen

After the closing of the mission in Singapore, a decision had to be made as to where to begin in China. The Board left the matter with the small band of missionaries on the scene, who decided on Xiamen, one of the five treaty ports opened by the Treaty of Nanking. Xiamen was four hundred miles north of Canton, was said to have a more healthy climate and was further removed from the adverse influence of the foreign traders. Also, Xiamen was on an island just off the mainland and would provide some security in case there was trouble.

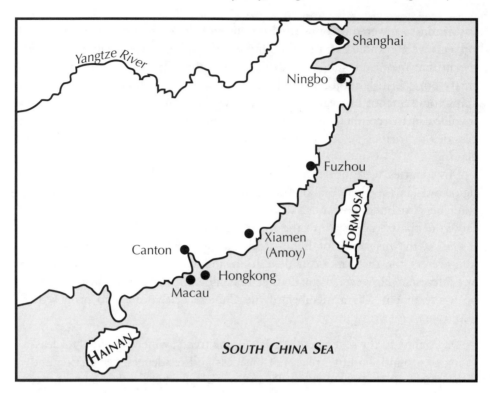

South China Coast 1850

The McBrydes spent the summer of 1842 at Kulangsu, a small island commanding the entrance to the harbor, which had been seized by British forces. The English officers received them kindly, and offered the use of their facilities. McBryde wrote of his poor health and slow progress in the study of the language.[8]

Lowrie made a visit to Kulangsu in September 1843 and one event during his stay created an international incident. At that time there was considerable uncertainty as to how far beyond the limits of a treaty port the missionaries might travel. Lowrie and David Abeel, the forerunner of the Reformed Church in America (RCA), who had a working knowledge of the local dialect, decided to "test the waters." They engaged a boat and proceeded up the river some forty miles to the city of Zhangzhou. When they landed they were met by a large crowd of men and boys who followed them through the streets with stares of wonder and bewilderment, as they were the first foreigners these people had seen. The Chinese were good-natured and polite but extremely curious. One man carefully examined Lowrie's clothes and tried to investigate how his pantaloons were put on. Lowrie and Abeel secured a room at a local inn and while they were preparing their supper of rice and eggs, Mandarin officials appeared and after some discussion announced that the treaty that had just been signed allowed foreigners permission to trade only in the five ports and that they would have to leave immediately. Abeel replied that they were Americans who only desired to cultivate friendly relations and that though the treaty allowed foreigners to trade at the five ports, it did not prohibit them from travel elsewhere. When the Mandarins heard that they were Americans, their attitude changed, for they had heard good reports of Americans. A compromise was worked out and the foreigners were taken to the dock, where they spent the night on board a river boat that was technically not in the city proper. The next day they toured the city in sedan chairs provided by the officials and left on the evening tide. The trip made a deep impression on Lowrie, who wrote in his memoirs his first impressions of China: (1) the crowded cities, (2) the openness of the people, (3) the widespread use of opium and (4) the necessity for humility, self-denial and patience in keeping with the words of the Lord — "to the poor the Gospel is preached."

The trip came to the attention of Sir Henry Pottinger, the senior British official in Hong Kong. He was incensed, fearing that the treaty he had carefully put together might be jeopardized. Pottinger issued a statement denouncing the visit of foreigners from another country who had forced their way into a Chinese city, defied the local authorities and passed themselves off as British citizens. Lowrie was just as incensed that his actions and integrity had been misrepresented. He replied in an open letter setting the British official straight: They had made it clear to the Chinese that they were Americans, they had not forced their way into the city but had quietly reasoned with the Mandarins and in the end had departed when told to do so. No complaints had been raised by the Chinese officials, and Sir Henry had no authority over citizens of another country.[9]

Sometime in 1843 Mr. McBryde's health broke down completely and it was necessary for the family to return home. But the next year eleven new missionaries arrived in Canton, bringing new life to the endeavor. Six arrived on the sailing ship *Cohota* and after they had disembarked, Dr. Hepburn, the senior member of the group, presided at what might be called the first meeting of the China mission. After a season of prayer for divine guidance it was decided that three stations would be opened and the following assignments were made: *Xiamen:* Dr. and Mrs. James C. Hepburn, M.D., Rev. John Lloyd, Rev. Hugh A. Brown; *Ningbo:* Rev. Walter M. Lowrie, Dr. Divie B. McCartee, M.D., Rev. and Mrs. Richard Q. Way, Rev. and Mrs. Augustus W. Loomis, Rev. and Mrs. Michael S. Culbertson; *Canton:* Rev. Andrew P. Happer, M.D., Mr. and Mrs. Richard Cole (printer).

The Hepburns arrived in Xiamen a few months after the departure of the McBrydes and were joined by John Lloyd and Hugh Brown. But health problems disrupted the well-laid plans. Dr. Hepburn came down with malaria and he and Mrs. Hepburn left for home in 1845.[10] Brown contracted an eye disease, for months could neither read nor write and he returned home in 1848. Lloyd died of typhus fever the same year. With no missionaries on the horizon, the work that had been begun was turned over to the RCA Mission, which was making Xiamen the center of its China endeavor.

Ningbo

Ningbo was destined to be the first Presbyterian mission station that stood the test of time. It would become a model for much of the work that would follow. Pioneer Presbyterian missionaries in Shanghai, Shandong (Shantung) and Peking all had their start in Ningbo. Rev. Elias Inslee, forerunner of the Southern Presbyterian Mission, spent his formative years there.

Ningbo was chosen as the "chief station" of the mission for three reasons: (1) Ningbo was north of Canton and the climate was healthier, (2) the dialect was closer to *Mandarin*, which was spoken throughout the northern provinces, and (3) the people were not yet "corrupted as at Canton, by foreign influence."[11]

Dr. Divie Bethune McCartee was the first to arrive. The date was 21 June 1844. He traveled up from Hong Kong on the *Eagle,* an American "opium schooner," as these were the only ships sailing the China coast. The British consul, Mr. Thom, offered hospitality until he could rent a house.

Ningbo was described by an early missionary as an ancient city whose walls, thirty feet high and six miles in circumference, were built in the year 1333. The population was about 250,000. The streets were narrow and the houses and shops crowded together. "All the customs, habits, and occupations of the people [were] the same as they have been for many centuries."[12] As with many Chinese port cities, Ningbo lay some miles up river as a protection against pirates that infested the coast. The harbor was always crowded with small craft. Ocean schooners anchored down river. Pontoon bridges, which were opened to permit junks to pass, connected the branches of the city.

When McCartee arrived one other missionary was residing in the city — Miss Mary Ann Aldersey, an English lady of independent means who had opened a school for girls.[13]

McCartee had difficulty sleeping due to the intense heat and the strange sounds at night: the junk men getting up anchor, the booming of the Buddhist monastery bell, the cry of the night herons and the clamor of the patrols along the city wall. As the hot months wore on, he moved to Chusan, an island off the coast, which was cooler. Here he was joined by Rev. and Mrs. Richard Way, who had been transferred to the China mission from Siam. On Chusan a dispensary was started and Christian witness begun:

> Every morning their Chinese teacher reads a suitable tract, or a portion of the sacred Scriptures at the Dispensary, and these are distributed as far as practicable in the city.[14]

In the fall, McCartee and the Ways returned to Ningbo and soon afterward McCartee secured rooms in the Yiu-sheng-kwan Taoist monastery. The reason for the move was twofold:

> I came here because I found that I could do little either in the way of practice, or of acquiring the language, while living among the Europeans

and Americans; and, although it required some little resolution to break away from society as it were, and live entirely in the midst of natives, yet I have been amply repaid for it in the success I have met with both in increasing my knowledge of the language and medical practice.[15]

He had Morrison's dictionary and translation of the Bible. But the Ningbo dialect was very different. In Canton he had obtained a list of useful phrases in the Chinese characters. When shown these, a local scholar could tell him the Ningbo equivalent. By a process of trial and error a simple dictionary of the Ningbo dialect was prepared. Thus he became proficient in the use of medical terms and the colloquial language of the people.

His relationship with the Taoist monks was a pleasant one. They were happy to receive the $6 a month rent for the two rooms which McCartee used as a residence and dispensary. The stream of patients probably enhanced the reputation of the monastery. They took no offense at the Christian tracts McCartee displayed, and from the younger monks McCartee learned a good deal of the Ningbo dialect, customs and legends.

The number of patients grew rapidly. McCartee wrote that in four months he had seen five thousand patients and performed ninety operations. In order to get to know his patients better, McCartee began the practice of home visitation. In this way he gained a number of friends among the more respectable class of inhabitants. At each home he was expected to sit awhile, smoke a pipe and drink a cup of tea with the master of the house. Through these contacts he had an opportunity of "proclaiming from house to house the glad tidings that there is a 'balm in Gilead,' and a physician there who can heal the worst maladies and minister comfort and healing to the wounded spirit."[16]

Walter Lowrie arrived in April 1845 and took up residence in the monastery with McCartee. Rev. and Mrs. Michael Culbertson and Rev. and Mrs. Augustus Loomis arrived the same month after a stormy voyage of thirty-eight days from Hong Kong.[17]

Soon thereafter the Ningbo Mission was formerly organized with eight members. According to the rules of the Board only ordained ministers were considered "missionaries." Dr. McCartee and the ladies counted as "assistant missionaries." But the rules were irrelevant: Dr. McCartee, from the standpoint of both seniority and ability, exercised the dominant leadership role.[18] From the first, an annual day of prayer and fasting was observed. This practice continued for many years.

How were these first missionaries received by the local populace? While there was no enthusiastic welcome, they were treated with courtesy and respect. This was all the more surprising when one remembers that Ningbo had been bombarded by the British during the Opium War. Lowrie wrote in 1845:

The people are as civil and obliging as could reasonably be expected, considering the severe and uncalled for treatment they received during the war, and the thoughtless course of some English officers, in destroying the public buildings for firewood. We are better treated here, by far, than a Chinaman would be in New York or London; though it does occasionally ruffle one's temper to hear himself called a pah-kwei, or *white devil*, with some other such choice epithets.[19]

On 18 May 1845 a memorable event occurred with the organization of the Presbyterian Church of Ningbo. It was probably the first Protestant church on China's soil.[20] However, none of the first members were natives of Ningbo. The members consisted of the missionaries, Miss Aldersey, two of her girls, and the "bearer" of the infant son of the Ways who had accompanied them from Siam. Services were first held in English as only McCartee had sufficient knowledge to preach in Chinese.

In July the Coles arrived, bringing with them the printing press. Printing of the Chinese characters with metallic divisible type was still in the experimental stage and had to be tested by trial and error. Four thousand different characters had to be arranged according to their different radicals and frequency of usage. Nevertheless, in its first two years of operation, 635,000 pages were published — mostly Scripture portions.[21]

But Lowrie expressed disappointment that the translations of the Scriptures were almost unintelligible to the average Chinese reader:

> I am losing faith in the doctrine, "The Bible without note or comment" at least as far as the Chinese are concerned.... The most intelligent of them fall into frequent and gross mistakes as to its meaning.... Some people say the Bible is an Oriental book, and the Chinese are an Oriental people, therefore, they can easily understand it.... The Chinese are as much beyond "the East" on one side as America is on the other; and therefore the remark is very unfounded.[22]

To meet this need Lowrie plunged into the study of the Chinese classics and the preparation of biblical texts with notes. He began a dictionary of the "Four Books" of Confucius and confessed to a real veneration for the sage. He wrote tracts on the Sabbath, the Shorter Catechism and a commentary of Luke.

In December 1846 Lowrie made his first attempt at public preaching. On Sundays a notice would be put up outside the door of his house saying there would be preaching in the afternoon. At the appointed time the door would be opened and Lowrie's language teacher would invite people in. Lowrie would begin the service and in a few minutes an audience of fifty to one hundred people would have gathered. By the time he had finished, new people would have come in so he would start over again.

A boys' boarding school was begun in 1845 by Mr. Way. Applicants were carefully screened and twenty-three of the most promising were received. Strangely, boarding schools preceded day schools because the early missionaries felt they needed to have control over the students in order to instill both a degree of Western education and the elements of Christianity. Students were apprenticed to the mission by their parents for a specified term of years and were provided free room and board. The course of study included the Chinese classics, geography, Western history, arithmetic and the Bible.

The first native of Ningbo to be baptized was one of the boys in the school, Yuing Ko-Kuing. He was given careful instruction for eight months and admitted to the church in 1846. But to the great disappointment of the missionaries, he was later suspended from the church because of his participation in the "idolatrous rites" of the ancestral tablets. Forty-three years later McCartee had the joy of witnessing his reception into the church again.[23]

The years 1846–1847 were critical for the Ningbo missionaries. They suffered from discouragement, dissension, sickness and suspicion from the local populace. The summer of 1846 was one of intense heat and drought. "The heavens over us were as brass, and the earth as powder and dust beneath our feet."[24] Some were near death and Dr. McCartee gave thanks for their deliverance:

> While on every mission station in China, death has entered and taken away some, and sickness has driven others from their field of labor, we desire fervently to thank our Heavenly Father that still, "*We* are all still here."[25]

The drought caused the crops to fail and a severe earthquake was taken by the people as an evil omen. Rumors of poisonings and the activities of demonic spirits abounded. It was blamed on the presence of the foreigners, who had upset the balance of nature.

In 1846 the station was cheered by the arrival of Rev. John W. Quarterman. But in this same year Mr. and Mrs. Cole were "separated from the mission by the unanimous recommendation of the brethren."[26]

In 1847 the mission suffered the tragic loss of one of its most promising members. Lowrie had been invited to join the interdenominational Bible revision committee then meeting in Shanghai. It was a tribute to his scholarship and the growing importance of the American Presbyterian Mission. During the course of the meetings a messenger from Ningbo arrived asking him to return home because of an emergency. He left Shanghai on 16 August 1847 for the trip to Ningbo crossing Hangzhou Bay on a small vessel. His faithful servant told the Ningbo missionaries what happened. Suddenly, a pirate ship was seen bearing down upon their small craft. Discharging their firearms, the pirates boarded the ship with swords and spears plundering everything in sight. Concerned that the foreigner would testify against them they decided to throw him overboard. He was pushed over the rail, and as they did this Lowrie threw up on the deck a copy of the book he had been reading — Bagster's edition of the Bible in Hebrew, Greek and English.[27] Lowrie floated around in the water for some time and then sank out of sight.[28]

Beginning the next year, the fortunes of the mission took a turn for the better. Three missionary couples arrived in 1849 and another two couples the next year. As the numbers increased, property was needed for residences but the first plot purchased was used as a cemetery. Mr. Moses Coulter, who arrived to take over the printing press, was stricken with dysentery in 1852 and was buried there. The constant bouts of malaria, dysentery and tropic fevers took the lives of others and made more adequate housing essential.[29] In 1848 the mission leased for one hundred years a piece of land on the north bank of the river on which were built a dispensary and foreign-style residences.

The first church building was dedicated in 1851 or 1852. Rev. Michael Culbertson, who had had some architectural training at the Military Academy at West Point, designed the building with Doric columns and a flight of stone steps in front. It was known as the "Yiaesu Kyiao Kong-we Dong" (Meeting Hall of the Church of Jesus). Large numbers of curious citizens were attracted by the ringing of the first church bell.

In the beginning public church services were noisy and disorderly. They were interrupted by frequent comings and goings and continuing conversations among those who had come to watch. The Chinese did not mean to be rude but had no custom of communal worship. "Private meetings" were held with small groups who wished to inquire more seriously into the nature of Christianity.

This public preaching to "promiscuous audiences" did not bear much visible fruit. Most of the early converts came from the schools or by employment. Why then the large building and the chapel preaching? The early missionaries felt they

> needed to witness in a visible way to the religion of Christ before the people at large...so a church building was called for...a house of God, where may be witnessed the solemn yet simple worship...to the deity.[30]

For the first few years, converts averaged about one a year. An increase is first noted in 1852 when four were received. The next year ten were baptized. Of these one was Lu Sin-sang, later ordained as an elder "and head of a noble line of Christians."[31]

Initially, missionaries were confined by the Treaty of Nanking to the city proper. But as time went on, missionaries pushed their interpretation of the treaty to the limit and in 1848 began systematic itineration in neighboring towns.

As the work expanded the need for native workers soon became apparent. In 1854 a "helpers training class" was formed and taught by Messrs. Rankin and Martin.[32] The class began with three young men, Lu Kyiae-dzing, Dzing Shih-nyiao and Kying Ling-yu. They were taught Bible, theology, composition and speaking. All completed the course and served for many years in the employment of the mission. Ordinations would come later.

The accomplishments of the first ten years are given in the *Annual Report* for 1855:

Since the establishment of the Mission in June 1844, thirteen male and eleven female missionaries have been connected with it. Of this number, two have been removed by death, and three have returned to the United States; one family had its connections with the Mission dissolved, and two other families have been removed to another station; the rest are still in the field.... Twenty-four adults have been received into the church by baptism...twelve males and twelve females; of these two have been cut off from the communion of the church, two have been removed by death, and twenty remain.... The boarding schools for boys and girls are in a flourishing condition; two printing presses are in constant use; three substantial houses of worship have been erected...and an immense amount of relief has been rendered to the sick by the medical missionary.[33]

Canton

One might have thought that the missionaries in Canton would have met with greater acceptance due to the longer association of the city with the foreigners. But the reverse was true due to the British occupation of the city and its bombardment during the first Opium War. Although "opened" as a treaty port in 1842, the walled city was closed to missionaries because of strong anti-foreign sentiments whipped up by local gentry. Under these trying circumstances the Presbyterians tried to gain access to the city.

At the meeting of the mission in 1844, the Rev. Andrew P. Happer, with degrees in both theology and medicine, was assigned to this task. Several attempts to move into the city failed because of intense opposition. But a school for boys was begun in Macau. In 1846 Happer was joined by the Rev. and Mrs. William Speer and Rev. John B. French. Mrs. Cornelia Speer died and was buried in Macau in 1847.[34] In 1847 Happer and French made the move to Canton with some thirty of their boarding school students. The two single men did not remain single long. Happer married Elizabeth Ball, the eldest daughter of Rev. Dyer Ball of the ABCFM, and in 1851 French married her younger sister, Mary.[35]

The mission was first located on "Old-Clothes Street" in the native city. After twice being driven out of these quarters they secured temporary housing in the Danish compound. Here the missionaries and school boys were all crowded into the same house. Finally, a fine piece of property was leased about a mile from the foreign factories on the river front. But they were left homeless again when a typhoon blew the roof off. By 1850 repairs had been made and the property sufficiently expanded to include space for a day school, chapel and residence.[36] Robert E. Speer has described the early days of the Canton mission:

They were shut up at first in their own houses, and could only visit the neighboring streets by stealth. It was two years before Mr. French could

rent a chapel "in a long dark alley," and three before Dr. Happer secured
another "near a public street." In this chapel the Mission began that daily
preaching to the heathen which has never ceased to this day, save during the Arrow War [Second Opium War] when the dwelling houses of the
missionaries were destroyed, the schools broken up, and evangelistic work
was suspended.[37]

In 1854 two new couples, who would long be remembered in Canton, arrived: Dr. John G. and Mrs. Abby Kerr, and Rev. Charles F. and Mrs. Mary
Preston. Dr. Kerr immediately took over the work of the dispensary from the
overworked Happer, who had been running the school, prescribing medicines
on weekdays and preaching twice on Sundays.

Preston became a master at preaching in the colloquial dialect. For twenty-
two years, with the exception of one furlough in America and evacuation during
the Arrow War, he preached daily at one of the city chapels. Dr. Speer described
the impact he had on listeners in these words:

> He was perhaps the best speaker of Chinese in Southern China, and
> though not an impassioned speaker in English, he took fire when he be-
> gan to preach in Chinese. . . . Men from the country would come again and
> again, filled with wonder, to hear the marvelous speech of the winsome,
> cordial, gentleman, who knew their hearts and could speak to them so
> that they understood the Word of Life.[38]

But the results of the preaching of which Dr. Speer wrote came later. In the
early years there were few conversions. The *Annual Report* of 1855 told of only
one known conversion during the first seven years.

Peter Parker's Canton Ophthalmic Hospital, supported by the foreign community and the China Medical Society, achieved great success and Parker
became a celebrity. In 1846 he was appointed Chargé d'Affaires of the U.S.
diplomatic mission. Parker was deeply offended when his mission board, the
ABCFM, terminated its relationship with him on the grounds that his government employment was incompatible with that of a missionary.[39] His service at
the hospital was no longer possible and the China Medical Society transferred
its management to Dr. Kerr, who remained a missionary of the Presbyterian
Board. Its services were broadened to include all branches of medicine. Dr. Kerr
reported that during 1856 he treated nearly twenty thousand patients, the principal diseases being "of the eye and of the skin, ulcers, rheumatism, dyspepsia,
dropsy, and afflictions of the lungs."[40]

In 1856 the work at Canton was disrupted by the Second Opium War (Arrow
War). There was much destruction of mission property, and all activity ceased
for the next two years as missionaries took refuge in Macau or returned to
America.

Shanghai

In the meantime, the focus of Christian missions was rapidly moving to the north. Shanghai, opened as a treaty port in 1842, was destined to become the great transportation hub for the Yangtze valley. It would be the center of missionary activity and ecumenical cooperation for the next one hundred years.

In 1842 Shanghai was little more than an unimpressive town with no historical or cultural significance on the mud flats of the Huangpu River some seventeen miles from where it flowed into the Yangtze. But the British had recognized its strategic location because of its safe anchorage, which was free from typhoons, its commanding presence at the mouth of the mighty Yangtze and the growing importance of the trans-Pacific trade.

During the First Opium War a British flotilla shelled the Wusong forts at the mouth of the Yangtze and then sailed up the Huangpu to hoist the British flag over Shanghai. The *Illustrated London News* described the capture of the city:

> The battleship *Nemesis*...set fire to the city of Shanghai which was occupied by our troops, its public buildings burned, its rich granaries, the property of the government, given up to the people. An incessant cannonade was kept up for two hours ere the enemy showed any symptom of submission.[41]

In opening the treaty port for trade, the British staked out their concession on a square mile of open fields along the banks of the Huangpu outside the walls of the Chinese city. The French did the same.[42] A projected American settlement never materialized as American interests merged with the British to become the International Settlement. The concessions became for all practical purposes self-governing enclaves with their own electrical system, water mains, sewage and police protection. Consular courts settled disputes and disciplined offenders. During times of revolution the security of the zone attracted Chinese business interests. Lowrie describes the sight in 1847:

> A forest of masts of junks filled the river...the foreign residences form quite a town, and when all are finished will be a settlement quite unequalled in China. Some of them are very expensive, and everything indicates an expectation of this place becoming, at no distant day, the head-quarters of influence in China.[43]

In 1850 the American Presbyterians made the decision to begin work in Shanghai because of its growing importance. The Board instructed Rev. and Mrs. J. K. Wight to leave Ningbo and open the new station. They were accompanied by Rev. and Mrs. Michael Culbertson as Mr. Culbertson had been appointed the Presbyterian delegate on the Bible translation committee to take the place of Walter Lowrie. Property was purchased near the South Gate of the Chinese city. Here, residences, a chapel and a school were built. A shop was also rented near the center of the International Settlement and fitted up with tables and benches for use as a chapel.[44]

Mission work in Shanghai was slow. One factor was the health of the early missionaries. In 1852 the Rev. and Mrs. John Byers arrived but Mr. Byers developed a cough and it became apparent that he could not live in the Shanghai climate. They departed on the same ship on which they had arrived but John Byers died at sea a few days before the ship reached New York.

When Walter Lowrie was murdered by the pirates, his younger brother, Reuben, was preparing for college. The event made an indelible impression on the young man of eighteen. After graduation from Princeton Seminary he volunteered for China service and arrived in Shanghai in 1854 with his wife, Amelia.

Lowrie's gifts, like that of his brother, were in the literary field. During the brief years he labored in Shanghai, he worked on a dictionary of the colloquial dialect, a commentary of the Gospel of Matthew and a number of tracts that were used in Christian day schools. He died in Shanghai in April 1860 of an intestinal disease. The day before his death Mrs. Lowrie gave birth to a son who one day would return with his mother to serve in the land where his father and uncle had lived and died.

Bible Translation

It soon became apparent that a new version of the Bible was needed. Morrison and Milne had completed the translation of the Old and New Testaments in 1819 but this had been done in the foreign enclaves of Macau and Malacca. Its accuracy and readability were largely untested in China proper. As missionaries began to preach, many inaccuracies appeared. It was of utmost importance that the new translation should be a united effort in which all Protestants cooperated, for if conflicting versions were circulated, Chinese would come to the conclusion that missionaries were preaching different religions. In 1843 a meeting of British and American mission representatives was held in Hong Kong to plan for a new Union Version of the classical language (Wen Li) that would command the respect of Chinese scholars. Four delegates were chosen for their seniority and knowledge of Chinese: Walter Henry Medhurst and John Stronach of the London Missionary Society (LMS), Bishop William J. Boone of the Protestant Episcopal Church and Elijah C. Bridgman of the ABCFM. To this august group young Walter Lowrie was elected.

One critical issue dominated the early discussions. It was the "term question" — what was the best Chinese word to use in translating the Christian Deity? The Catholics had used the term "Tien Chu" (Lord of Heaven). In their first translation Morrison and Milne had used "Shen" — a generic term that could be used for all kinds of deities from the high gods of heaven to the spirits of the ancestors. More recently, Medhurst, one of the most experienced Chinese linguistic scholars, had begun to use the term "Shang Ti" (Supreme Ruler), which had the advantage of being a more personal term. Its disadvantage: it was the name of a well-known Chinese idol. For example, the Taoist abbot at the monastery in Ningbo where McCartee was staying came across the term "Shang Ti" in some of McCartee's literature and exclaimed in great surprise that the doctor was a disciple of the same god to whom the monastery offered sacrifices!

When the delegates met in Shanghai they very quickly lined up on the two sides of the issue. The British members, Medhurst and Stronach, strongly favored Shang Ti while the Americans, Boone and Bridgman, preferred Shen. Lowrie had studied the matter thoroughly and took the side of his American colleagues but as the junior member of the committee was reluctant to speak.

So the case stood when the delegation began their deliberations on Matthew 1:23. Bridgman proposed that they use Shen. Boone seconded the motion. All knew that Lowrie would have supported the motion and it would have passed by a vote of three to two. But the motion was never put, and the debate went on for the next three weeks. It was at this point in the discussions that Lowrie was called to return to Ningbo and met his death at the hand of pirates.

The issue was never resolved. Rev. Michael Culbertson joined the committee in August 1850. By that time the committee had divided into two factions. The LMS members continued their work on a Shang Ti version, which was published by the British and Foreign Bible Society in 1852 or 1853 and became known as the Delegates Bible. Culbertson joined the translators working on a Shen version, who were principally Americans and financed by the American Bible Society. In May 1862 Culbertson reported the completion of the task on which he had labored for eleven years:

> I have been permitted to bring to its close the great work on which I have been engaged for so many years — the translation of the Bible. On the 17th of March, 1851, our Committee consisting of five members began their work. On the 27th of March, 1862, I brought it to a close, having been left single handed by the lamented death of my only remaining colleague, Dr. Bridgman, in November last. The other members of the Committee,...were obliged by ill health to withdraw before we had finished....I feel deeply grateful to my Heavenly Father that I have been permitted at last to see the end of this task.[45]

To this day, Christians in China are still divided on the term question. In the Catholic version of Scripture God is Tien Chu. For Protestants two versions of the Bible are in common use. For some God is Shen; for others, Shang-Ti.

The significance of these years between the Opium Wars lay not in the number of converts but in the foundations that were laid for the future. The first encounters had taken place. Of the forty-nine Presbyterian missionaries appointed, scarcely one-half remained. But this number had now weathered the critical beginning years. The Chinese language, if not mastered, had become for most a workable tool. Missionary residence had been established in three of the cities of the empire. Working relationships were in place in a few schools and dispensaries. Precious few conversions had occurred but the seeds of the Christian faith had been planted.

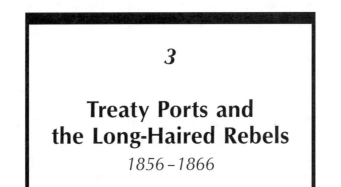

3

Treaty Ports and the Long-Haired Rebels

1856–1866

At the midpoint of the nineteenth century the Christian movement in China was in a precarious state. From the beginning its fortunes had been tragically linked with the Opium War and the Unequal Treaties. A missionary presence had been established on the periphery of the Middle Kingdom. Conversions to Christianity had been painfully slow. The great inland cities and the provinces of the interior were as yet beyond reach. The decade between the Arrow War (Second Opium War) and the end of the Taiping Rebellion (1856–1866) was a critical time both for China and for the missionary enterprise. Would the Qing dynasty survive? Could the Christian movement penetrate to the heart of the Empire?

It was a decade of continuing internal and external crises for the Qing dynasty.[1] The defeat by Britain had discredited the central government and weakened its control over the provinces. There was a marked increase in the rise of secret societies, which fomented revolt. Piracy increased along the China coast as trade shifted from inland waterways to the South China Sea. The decline in inland traffic brought unemployment to boatmen, porters and coolies. The food supply was not sufficient to keep up with the population increase, resulting in frequent "famine years." Maintenance of canals and dikes deteriorated. In 1852 the Yellow River broke loose from its banks and shifted its course to the north of the Shandong peninsula with disastrous results for millions of peasants whose lands were flooded.

In 1850 the old Daoguang Emperor died and was succeeded by the anti-foreign Xianfeng (1851–1861). China had signed the Treaty of Nanking under duress and officials dragged their feet in its implementation. Anti-foreign outbursts in Canton made treaty enforcement there all but impossible. British attempts to establish direct diplomatic ties with the court in Peking were rebuffed.

The trade in opium increased significantly. In 1842 Westerners sold 33,000 chests of opium to China. By 1853 the amount had risen to 52,000 chests. But foreign trade as a whole did not increase as had been expected. The trade in

41

opium meant less money to import other commodities. Trade through Canton dropped dramatically as treaty ports to the north were opened.

The Rev. Michael Culbertson, writing from Shanghai in 1856, reviewed the progress of Protestant missions in these words:

> It is now nearly half a century since the first Protestant missionary entered China. During this period 190 missionaries have been sent out, under the patronage of 21 different societies. Of these, 101 are still laboring in this field, including a few who are temporarily absent from their posts. Through the labors of these missionaries, there are now in China something more than 600 persons connected with churches of the various evangelical denominations.... The number of church members may seem to be small... but it is quite large enough to refute the objections so often raised on the ground of a want of success.[2]

The Arrow War (Second Opium War)

A minor incident in 1856 provoked a new war. Canton authorities, professing to be searching for pirates, seized a Chinese-owned craft, the *Arrow* of Hong Kong registry flying the British flag. The crew, all of whom were Chinese, were detained. On this flimsy excuse, Britain went to war.[3] This time France also declared war, using the pretext that a French priest had been murdered in Guangxi.[4] Again the war was one-sided. Canton was briefly occupied. The Dagu forts guarding the sea approach to Peking were stormed. China, facing rebellion from the Taipings, was incapable of continuing the war and sued for peace.

The resulting Treaty of Tientsin was signed by China, Britain and France in 1858. Similar treaties were signed with Russia and the United States although they had not taken part in the conflict. The treaty contained fifty-six articles, the most important being the following:

- The treaty powers were granted diplomatic recognition and residence at the court in Peking.

- Eleven more treaty ports were opened.[5]

- The Kowloon peninsula was ceded to Great Britain.[6]

- Citizens of the treaty powers were given the right to travel in the interior.

- France and Great Britain each received eight million taels (ounce) of silver as war indemnities.

- The opium trade was legalized.

- Religious toleration clauses, which differed somewhat in wording, were included in each of the various treaties.

The American treaty read as follows:

The principles of the Christian religion, as professed by the Protestant and Roman Catholic churches, are recognized as teaching men to do good, and to do to others as they would have others do to them. Hereafter those who quietly profess and teach these doctrines shall not be harassed or persecuted on account of their faith. Any person, whether citizen of the United States or Chinese convert, who, according to these tenets, shall peaceably teach and practice the principles of Christianity shall in no case be interfered with or molested.[7]

But hostilities did not end with the signing of the treaty drafts, which needed ratification by the various governments. When the British and French ministers arrived in Tianjin (Tientsin) the next year to exchange ratification documents, they were denied passage to Peking. The issue was probably more of "face" than substance as the Americans and Russians ratified their treaties in Tianjin without difficulty. But the British and French insisted on traveling to the capital city for the ratification. They tried to force their way up the river with a small naval detachment, and were repulsed with heavy casualties. The next year the British and French returned with a combined force of over seventeen thousand troops, defeated the larger imperial forces and entered Peking in October 1860. The emperor and his court fled beyond the Great Wall to the province of Rehe (Jehol). When a British negotiator was seized while under a flag of truce and twenty of his men executed, Lord Elgin, the British plenipotentiary, ordered the destruction of the emperor's summer palace (Yuan Ming Yuan) with its priceless art treasures.[8] The conventions agreed to earlier were quickly signed by Prince Kung, the emperor's brother.

The military activities of the war did not appreciably affect the Presbyterian missionaries in Ningbo and Shanghai. They were far from the scene of battle. America was neutral and the local populace was not all that much concerned about the matter, which they viewed as a quarrel with the Manchu dynasty.

In Canton it was another matter. Here the Presbyterian Mission was in the middle of the battle zone as British gunboats shelled the city. The *Annual Report* for 1857 told the story:

The most serious event in the history of these missions is the suspension of all missionary labor at Canton, in consequence of the outbreak between the British and the Chinese of that city.... The destruction of both the dwelling houses occupied by the mission families, with much valuable property...the loss of manuscripts and books not easily replaced; the breaking up of the schools; and the closing of the hospital, dispensary and chapels, are among the immediate and sad results of this disturbance.[9]

Missionaries withdrew to Macau and the work in Canton was not resumed until two years later.

The irresponsible actions of foreign traders and mercenaries after the war ended did more damage to missionary relationships than the war itself. The

French attempted to imprison coolies and ship them abroad as if they were slaves.[10] Portuguese sailors, no better than pirates, harassed the port of Ningbo and offshore islands.[11] Missionaries were lumped with other foreigners and suffered abuse as "yang gweiza" (foreign devils).

Missionaries and the Colonial System

The treaties signed between 1842 and 1860 created a colonial system that regulated relationships between China and the Western powers for the next eighty years. From the standpoint of many Chinese patriots today (Christians, non-Christians, Marxists and others), the missionary movement was compromised by its association with this system and the treaties that were forced upon the Chinese people. For an understanding of the Chinese church today, it is essential that we confront the issues this raises. In 1979 Bishop K. H. Ting (Ding Guangxun), President of the China Christian Council, wrote:

> The recognition of the historical relatedness of the missionary movement to western economic, political and military penetration into China is all-important to any understanding of what Chinese Christians have strived to do and be, and to any consideration as regards future relations with Chinese Christians.[12]

A starting point might be the observation that from the beginning the colonial masters and the missionaries viewed each other with considerable hostility. To the colonial powers missionaries were nuisances and troublemakers. On the other hand, early missionaries displayed no great love for the traders, whose morals often contradicted everything the missionary represented. Latourette referred to the missionary and the diplomatic/business communities as "two reciprocally suspicious camps":

> Between the missionary and his fellow countrymen in business and government service a great gulf was usually fixed. Some on both sides succeeded in crossing it, but as a rule the foreign merchants and consuls were severely critical of the missionary and his work, while the missionary looked with thorough disapproval upon the life led by the average non-missionary foreigner.[13]

Both Carey and Morrison were denied passage on the ships of the East India Company. In 1793 one of the directors of the East India Company is said to have proposed the following resolution:

> The sending out of missionaries into our Eastern possessions is the maddest, most extravagant, most costly, most indefensible project which has ever been suggested by a moon-struck fanatic. It strikes against all reason and sound policy; it brings the peace and safety of our possessions into peril.[14]

But as time went on, it would seem that a "marriage of convenience" took place between the missionary and the colonial system. Each found that the other was needed. The same East India Company that had refused Morrison passage later employed him as an interpreter. Morrison found it impossible to live and work in Macau without some kind of official status, which only the East India Company could grant. The treaties opened up the right of residence within China and the right to propagate the new religion. Missionaries knew the language and the customs of the people and could not be ignored. They had an influential constituency back home and they wrote letters. A symbiotic relationship developed between the two sides with each receiving benefits from the arrangement. But it was an uneasy alliance that neither side completely accepted.

The missionaries did protest the worst aspect of the colonial system, which was the legalization of the opium trade. The Board of Foreign Missions (BFM) made this clear in their statement of 1837. In mission conferences held in 1877 and 1890 resolutions were adopted urging the British government to suppress the traffic. Christians in England and the United States took the lead in condemning it. William Gladstone and the Earl of Shaftesbury led the attack in the British Parliament, and in 1843 the House of Commons adopted the following resolution:

> That it is the opinion of this House that the continuance of the trade in opium, and the monopoly of its growth in the territories of British India, are destructive of all relations of amity between England and China, injurious to the manufacturing interest of the country . . . and utterly inconsistent with the honor and duties of a Christian kingdom.[15]

However, the resolution did not have the force of law and the trade continued. Not until 1906 was the trade finally brought to an end due to the efforts of the Anti-Opium League and China missionaries. In the words of the eminent historian John King Fairbank, this was "surely one of the longest-continued international crimes of modern times."[16]

Missionaries served as interpreters for the Western powers during the treaty negotiations and to this extent were linked to the trade they denounced. In some cases they probably influenced the writing of the treaties in favor of the religious toleration clauses and the rights of missionaries. Samuel Wells Williams, a former missionary of the ABCFM, and Presbyterian W. A. P. Martin accompanied the American delegation to Tianjin as interpreters and helped to negotiate the treaty that ended the Second Opium War. Ralph Covell, in his biography of Martin, carefully documents the involvement of the Presbyterian missionary. Martin saw no conflict between serving on the American diplomatic delegation and his missionary calling on the grounds that he might "promote the missionary cause in the treaty renewal and have some weight in securing the desired provisions for liberty of conscience."[17] He and Williams probably took no part in major policy decisions but there can be little doubt that their influence was felt in the wording of the religious toleration clause. It must be remembered, however, that treaties with Britain, France and Russia had already been signed and each of these contained religious toleration clauses.[18]

Martin was ambivalent on the military action of the British. Christian conscience got in the way of the practical advantages of a decisive British victory! On the one hand Martin wrote: "In the dispensation of Providence it seems to be necessary that these conceited Asiatics should be humbled by the Sword, before they are exalted by the Gospel."[19] On the other hand, Martin was most critical of the British renewal of the war:

> The war was rekindled, and the Chinese were accused of bringing it about by treachery. But were they wrong in barring the way to a city that was not opened by treaty?...Not only were they [the British] aggressors in firing the first shot, they were clearly wrong in the whole issue....It is a thousand pities that the occasion for unchaining England's thunder should be in one instance to exact payment for the destruction of a prohibited drug, in another to procure satisfaction [for an insult]...in a third a mere quibble of words.[20]

The worst aspect of the toleration clauses was to grant to Chinese converts the protection of foreign laws. In Latourette's judgment:

> This provision in part removed Chinese Christians from the jurisdiction of Chinese officials, for any alleged persecuting could be referred by the missionaries to a consul or minister for presentation to the imperial authorities. It led to abuse, because not infrequently Chinese professed conversion to obtain the assistance of the missionary and the Consul in lawsuits.[21]

The religious toleration clauses accented the foreign nature of the new religion. It is little wonder that in the succeeding years loyal Chinese have condemned Christianity with the phrase "win a convert: lose a citizen."

French Roman Catholics were probably the chief offenders in seeking legal protection from their consuls for their converts.[22] But some Protestants also abused their privileges under the treaties. Thus, the whole Christian community was implicated.

At times American missionaries served as consuls in the treaty ports where they resided. The British appointed consuls from their professional foreign service, but in the early years the United States resorted to part-time, unpaid consuls because they lacked funds and trained personnel.

In Ningbo, McCartee served on a number of occasions as the American consul. Whenever a ship, other than the British, entered the port he would proceed with the necessary processing. He was not paid a salary but received "commissions." On one occasion he acted as judge when American beachcombers and deserters were apprehended by Chinese authorities for criminal acts. He sentenced an offender to thirteen months' imprisonment for breaking into a Chinese money changer's shop.

McCartee saw no conflict of interest between serving as U.S. consul and being a missionary. Apparently, neither did the Chinese Christian community. Rev. Woh Cong-Eng, first pastor of the church in Ningbo, attributed the long years of cordial relationships the mission and church had with the officials to McCartee's consular activities:

> The American government wished Dr. McCartee to act as consul for Ningpo. He long declined, saying he had no time for any but his religious duties; but finally consented to take the office temporarily. All his dealings with officials were most friendly and he never lost an opportunity to explain the Gospel to them in his interviews. It was probably in a good measure due to this perfect understanding that the officials of Ningpo have always been willing to protect the Christians in their jurisdiction.[23]

But among the missionary community there were deep-rooted differences of opinion as to the propriety of this practice. Elias B. Inslee, who arrived in Ningbo in 1857, is sharply critical of a colleague for accepting the consular post:

> Mr. Way has accepted the Consulate again. It would doubtless have been more to his own credit and that of the mission had he let it alone, for it involves a necessary connection with opium merchants and seamen that in my opinion ought not to exist.... The U.S. Marshall here for Mr. Way was, and I believe is, the proprietor or keeper of a most notorious bawdy house called the Ningpo Hotel.[24]

Undoubtedly the missionaries used the special privileges that the colonial system provided them for all they were worth. They pushed their own interpretation of the treaty provisions to the limit. They too closely identified the cause of missions with that of Western civilization. But one must remember that the missionary was a child of the times.

Citizens of China 150 years ago were much less likely to be offended by the connection between the state and religion than we are today. After all, this is how their system operated. And there is no doubt that many Chinese wished to open the doors of their country to the Westerners and their new ideas. The wars were with a foreign dynasty and many native Chinese shed few tears when the Manchu regime was humbled. In the end the Chinese people would judge the newcomers not so much by their involvement with foreign governments but in their personal relationships. The new religion would be proved true or false by the way in which its witnesses lived, what they taught and how they died.

Missionary Methods

The end of hostilities and the signing of the peace treaties brought a surge in missionary appointments. During the nine years from 1857 to 1866 the BFM sent to China thirty-six new missionaries (counting husbands and wives). However, during this same period there were twenty-six losses due to death, sickness or resignation. Taking into account the opening of new work in Shandong (Shantung) Province in 1860, the number of missionaries working in the south remained about the same. With the new appointments, the Presbyterians became one of the three largest Protestant missionary bodies then at work in China.[25]

Missionary methods were by trial and error for no one had yet worked out a sure-fire strategy for the conversion of the Chinese Empire. The only certainty was that the Gospel of Jesus Christ was "the power of God unto salvation" (Rom. 1:16). But cultural differences were enormous. And what was "gospel" and what was "culture" was not all that easy to distinguish.

But a pattern of mission strategy was emerging. For the Presbyterians this involved the following features:

Wide Itineration

Missionaries were fascinated by the China that lay beyond the walls of the treaty ports. What was the "real" China — the China unspoiled by association with a Western mercantile culture of gunboats and merchants, opium smugglers and profiteers every bit as pagan as the Chinese "idolaters"? Itineration beyond the treaty ports had begun earlier but it was not legitimized until the Treaty of Tientsin. In many cases these missionary travelers found a more receptive audience in the country than in the cities where they resided.

Henry Rankin of Ningbo told of a month's trip he took in 1855 with R. H. Cobbold of the Church Missionary Society (CMS) in which they visited fourteen walled cities, most of which had never before been visited by foreigners, and were well received:

> Wherever we went we preached in temples, or other such places as were suitable, and widely distributed tracts and portions of the Scriptures. We were greatly prospered every step of our journey, and have been permitted to return with, I hope, grateful hearts for God's protection, and for the abundant blessings which we daily enjoyed.[26]

In 1859 Rev. and Mrs. Samuel Gayley of Shanghai made an extended trip to Suzhou and then followed the Grand Canal as far as the "Precious Girdle Bridge." Gayley cautioned others to "proceed with great prudence" so that these opportunities would not be spoiled by a too aggressive advance.[27]

City Chapels

Daily preaching was held in five city chapels in Ningbo and three in Shanghai. Those who came were for the most part nonbelievers who would drop in out of curiosity or genuine interest in the new faith. Chapel services were well attended but few individuals made decisions for Christ. These should not be confused with the more formal church services held on Sunday for baptized Christians, catechumens and their families.

It is hard to evaluate the effectiveness of the chapel preaching as there were few tangible results. Most of the conversions still came from the schools, personal relationships or missionary employment. Nevertheless, through the chapel preaching a much wider circle of city people was becoming introduced in some measure to the Christian faith.

The Printing and Distribution of Christian Literature

A high priority for the Presbyterians was the mission press. Mr. William Gamble, an experienced printer, arrived in 1858 to take over this work, bringing with him a new font of Chinese metallic type and a electrotyping machine. In 1860 the press was moved to Shanghai, where new buildings were constructed and a new cylinder press installed. Gamble instituted techniques that revolutionized the printing industry in China.[28]

In 1859 the production of the press reached over 7 million pages.[29] The press was largely self-supporting as printing jobs were paid for by the various mission agencies. Year after year, the printing of the scriptures, in various forms and colloquial dialects, continued to be the largest production item. Other items included religious books, tracts, magazines, calendars, dictionaries, and medical and educational textbooks. During these years the Presbyterian Press became the most widely known and respected printing establishment in China.

Schools – Day or Boarding?

The emphasis on the boys' and girls' boarding schools continued. The course of study for the boys' school in Ningbo is thus described:

> Our object is to give the pupils, first, a thorough knowledge of Gospel truth, by which they may secure their own salvation; and second, to make them familiar with their own literature, by which they may be more influential for good among their countrymen.[30]

In the girls' school the mornings were devoted to study and the afternoons to work projects such as sewing. One vexing problem for the girls was the betrothal of pupils to "heathen" boys while they were still in school.

In Shanghai the Rev. John Farnham developed an exceptionally fine education program. A new school building was built at the South Gate compound and in 1862 radical changes were made in educational methods. Instead of rote memory Farnham emphasized reason and logic. Even more revolutionary was the merger of the boys' and girls' schools. The girls cooked for the boys as well as themselves. The system worked quite well.

There was considerable discussion as to the relative merits of day or boarding schools. *The Annual Report* for 1857 spoke of the advantages of the day schools:

> It is probable that the educational labors of the missionaries in China, will eventually be devoted mainly, as in India, to day schools. These are much

less monopolizing than boarding schools in their demands on missionary time and strength.... They offer the prospect of bringing a large number of scholars under Christian influence.[31]

Yet most of the church members in the early years came from the boarding schools. This had both advantages and disadvantages. It provided a trained leadership for the church, but it also meant that most of the Christians were in the employ of the mission. The question of foreign dependence would plague the mission for many years. Becoming a Christian was linked with the monetary advantage of working for a foreign institution. The mission tried to prepare graduates for secular employment by teaching various trades, but this had limited success. Of the eight graduates of the boys' boarding school in Ningbo in 1857, four began work in tailor shops, two were employed by the press and two became teachers in mission schools.[32]

"Native Assistants"

As the years went by, more and more of the administration and teaching was taken over by Chinese who had themselves been trained in the schools. They became mission employees and were called "native assistants" or "helpers." In 1859 Elder Zia Ying-tong took over the management of the boys' school under the supervision of Rev. J. L. Nevius. This set the pattern for the future. In the report for 1861 fourteen assistants are listed as serving in the Ningbo field: five were catechists, seven school teachers and two colporteurs (Bible salesmen).[33] The growth of the church from this time on can be attributed to the faithful, sacrificial labor of these early Chinese leaders, who often suffered persecution and abuse from family and clan.

Breakthrough at San Poh

In 1857 the long-awaited and prayed for breakthrough occurred. But it happened in a most unusual place and in a way that the missionaries could not have foreseen. A "grass-roots" awakening broke out in San Poh ("North of the Hills"), a region some twenty-five miles north of Ningbo. The people of the area were notorious for their turbulent and lawless character but also noted for their energy, courage and independence. It was a great surprise to all that such a place would be among the first to witness the triumphs of the Gospel.

Elder Zia Ying-tong began the work in the area and met with an unexpected response from the people:

Here he met with so much encouragement that he was released from his engagements in Ningpo, to spend his time exclusively in efforts for the good of this people.... The interest was at one time so great that it was with difficulty that three persons could attend to the crowds that came to hear the strange doctrine of the Cross. Some were influenced by mere curiosity, some by a wish to oppose the new religion, and some, we hope, by a real desire to know and obey the truth.[34]

Nevius first visited the area in May 1857, was amazed at the size of the gathering and baptized the first seven converts. He wrote that the significance of the event was not just the large numbers but the way it had happened. He noted two features:

First, the work was carried on "entirely by natives." It was the native preacher Zia and other Chinese assistants who had the impact on the village. In fact, the missionaries avoided visiting the place "for fear of drawing the minds of the people from the Gospel to us, and also to avoid exciting the prejudices and opposition of the higher classes by our presence."[35]

Second, the new converts received no financial benefit from becoming Christians. Nevius contrasted the new San Poh Christians with those of Ningbo:

> It is a most interesting and encouraging fact connected with the work in San-Poh, that none of the converts, except the reformed opium smoker, whose services we are desirous to obtain, received any pecuniary aid from us. In Ningpo, almost every convert is supported by funds of the Church. …We are now happy to be able to point to a little company of believers, who, in a worldly point of view, are only losers by being connected with us, and can only be regarded as actuated by a love for Christ and his gospel.[36]

The San Poh revival had a profound effect on Nevius and the "Nevius Plan" for missionary work, which he later developed more fully in Shandong and which had such an impact on the beginnings of the Presbyterian work in Korea.

The revival movement at San Poh, which continued over the next five years, had a marked effect on the overall rate of church growth in the Ningbo area. In 1859 thirty-four new members were received, the largest number for any one year up to that time.[37] In 1862 the church at the village of Yu Yiao in the San Poh region was organized as a separate congregation. Note the statistics for that year:

Ningbo City Church

Additions	18
Deaths	2
Suspensions & dismissals	11
Total membership	80

Yu Yiao

Additions	30
Deaths	2
Suspensions & dismissals	2
Total membership	61

The 1864 statistics report four organized churches with a total membership of 177. Churches in outlying areas grew faster than the central church in Ningbo. In ten years the rate of growth had exploded.[38] In this same year another milestone was passed:

> The members of the church at Yu Yiao held a meeting and elected one man to the office of ruling elder, and two deacons. These are … the *first members* of the church being *elected to any office* who have *no dependence whatever* for support on the foreign members of the mission, i.e., they are tradesmen, and not teachers or native assistants.[39]

The Presbyterian church in Shanghai had a later start than the church in Ningbo. The first congregation was organized in 1860 at the South Gate compound and was composed of the missionary families and the first convert, a young man named Ve Nae-kwae who was Reuben Lowrie's language teacher. His conversion is recounted by Mr. Farnham:

> He one day entered Mr. Lowrie's study and found the latter in tears. Touched by his employer's evident grief, he asked what was the matter, whether the home mail had brought sad news. He answered in substance: "No; but every mail brings letters from father hoping for the conversion of the Chinese, and I can only write back every time, there are none yet who believe. … Nae-kwae was moved by this, and in course of time gave himself unreservedly to Christ, the first fruit of Mr. Lowrie's ministry to the Chinese.[40]

Four Christian employees of the press were added the next year but these were not Shanghai men. No new members were reported in 1862. Shanghai was "by far the most discouraging mission station" wrote Mrs. Nevius in 1864.[41] Sickness and death among the missionaries and the turmoil of the Taiping Rebellion undoubtedly contributed to the slow growth. The proximity to the great Western commercial metropolis with all its corruption and vice certainly had a negative effect. Yet some progress was made. Rev. John S. Roberts wrote soon after his arrival in 1862:

> We now have, I may say, almost nightly preaching in four places with encouraging audiences. Our schools are all doing well. Our little church, numbering twelve members, has its weekly prayer meeting, and a portion of them, Bible classes three times in the week.[42]

Presbyteries

A Presbyterian church without a presbytery would be an anomaly, but how and when and by whom should they be established in a land that knew not Calvin and Knox?[43] Should a presbytery in China be linked with the "mother church" in the United States? Or should the missionaries wait until the Christian community decided what form of church government was best for their land and culture? Should ordained missionaries be voting members of the Chinese presbytery? These were some of the knotty ecclesiastical problems missionaries and the home church faced.

In the year 1848 the General Assembly of the PCUSA instructed its China missionaries to organize presbyteries in each city where they lived and worked. Ordained missionaries were told to transfer their membership from their home presbyteries to the ones being organized in China. The China presbyteries were to become members of the Synod of New York until such time as a Synod of China could be formed.

At the time, the action of the General Assembly seemed reasonable. But it was probably precipitous. There were then no Chinese elders or pastors and as yet no organized congregations. Placing the Chinese presbyteries under the authority of the Synod of New York accented the foreign nature of the church. Later, the organic linkage with the church in America made it more difficult to unite with Chinese churches formed by Presbyterian missions from other lands.

Whatever the case, the Canton missionaries were quick to follow the instructions of the General Assembly and in December 1848 the Presbytery of Canton was organized by Reverends Andrew Happer, John French and William Speer. With the resignation of Speer in 1849, a quorum was no longer present; the presbytery was suspended and no meetings were held for ten years. Years later Rev. Henry Noyes, stated clerk of the presbytery, adds this comment:

> It was fourteen years after the organization of the Presbytery before it had a church under its care, and thirty-five years before it licensed a native minister.[44]

The Presbytery of Ningbo was formed in 1849. All the members were missionaries. A second meeting of the presbytery held in 1849 or 1850 sent an overture to the General Assembly of the PCUSA asking advice on the subject of the marriage of professed Chinese Christians with non-Christians. The U.S. Assembly wisely declined to take action and referred it back to the Presbytery of Ningbo.[45] Candidates for the ministry were received and assigned to individual missionaries for training. In 1853 the presbytery voted to translate into the Ningbo dialect portions of the Presbyterian Form of Government and the Shorter Catechism.[46]

In 1857 three native assistants were ordained as elders and received into the presbytery: Zia Ying-tong, Zi Kyin-san and Lu Kao-dzing. All served mission and church with distinction. Elders Zi and Lu were teachers in the schools. Zia was largely responsible for the revival in San Poh.

A memorable day for the presbytery came in 1864 when six young men had completed the requirements for ordination. But some missionaries were not ready to take this most important step arguing that further instruction was needed. Once ordained, the Chinese ministers would have the same status and voting privileges as the missionaries. In a letter to the home board, Rev. Samuel Dodd told of the sharp disagreement and the debate "to ordain or not to ordain." He argued convincingly that they should proceed with the ordination of the "six young men who had been native assistants and candidates for the ministry from four to ten years." Nevius carried the day with his exhortation: "Get Presbyterianism on its legs and it will run alone."[47]

The first to be ordained was Zia Ying-tong, who was installed as co-pastor with Mr. Dodd of the San Poh church. Kying Ling-yu was ordained as pastor of a second church in the San Poh field but died after only two years of service.

The minutes of the October 1867 meeting of Ningbo Presbytery indicate another milestone. The presbytery met with two missionaries, four Chinese ministers and six Chinese elders. Rev. Zia was elected moderator and for the first time, the Chinese members exceeded the number of missionaries.[48]

Shandong Mission

In May 1861 Rev. and Mrs. Samuel Gayley and Rev. and Mrs. J. A. Danforth moved from Shanghai to the newly opened treaty port of Dengzhou (Tengchow) on the tip end of the Shandong promontory.[49] Shandong, where Confucius had lived and taught, was the heartland of China's ancient civilization. In the mid-nineteenth century it was desperately poor, and far removed from the Western commercial penetration. Both the Gayley and Danforth families had suffered from the heat and humidity in Shanghai and it was thought the five-hundred-mile move north would be good for them.

A new station in the north was good mission strategy. But paradoxically, the Shandong venture proved to be the most costly endeavor yet in terms of missionary lives. In time, however, Shandong would become the largest and in some ways the most successful mission of the Presbyterian Church in China.

At the time, Rev. and Mrs. J. B. Hartwell of the Southern Baptist Mission were the only other foreigners in Dengzhou and they gave the Presbyterians a warm welcome and entertained them in their home until they could find a suitable place to stay. Rev. and Mrs. John L. Nevius arrived in Dengzhou the next month. Because of Mrs. Nevius's health, the Board had transferred them to the Japan mission but Nevius could not forget his China call and had asked to return to China and the Shandong assignment. Less than five months after arriving at Dengzhou, Mrs. Danforth died, the cause of death unknown. Mr. Danforth's health was shattered in body and mind and a man was employed to take him home on the long voyage around the Cape of Good Hope.

During the autumn of 1861 the province of Shandong was ravaged by bandits probably associated with the Taiping rebels. Villages were burned, people killed and livestock driven away. Dengzhou was besieged by the rebels but was saved by its high city walls. During the "Bandit Year" Rev. J. Landrum Holmes and Rev. T. M. Parker of the American Episcopal Mission were murdered by one of the marauding bands on the road between Dengzhou and Yantai (Chefoo). In these troubled times, missionaries engaged in relief work, providing food, medicine and clothing. The cordial relationship with the people dates from this event.

In July 1862, Rev. and Mrs. Charles Mills sailed from Shanghai to Yantai to join the Shandong Mission. This was the "cholera year" and during that summer more than one thousand persons died every day in Shanghai of the dread disease. These included two of the Mills children and Michael Culbertson, who died a few months after completing his work on the translation of the Bible. Samuel Gayley met them in Yantai to escort them to Dengzhou. Yantai was in the throes of the epidemic and three members of the missionary community had died there in the space of several days. Gayley made arrangements for the necessary animals and carts but stayed behind to help bury the dead, catching up with the Mills party at an inn along the way. The next day the third Mills child died. On the way, Gayley was stricken and died shortly after reaching home.

Dr. and Mrs. McCartee of Ningbo had been assigned to Yantai to begin medical work and entered the harbor at the height of the cholera epidemic. He was the only foreign doctor present but had no drugs. He immediately began taking care of those that were afflicted in every way he could. His presence and practice undoubtedly saved the lives of a number from the missionary community. The loss of life in and around Yantai was about one-third of the population.[50]

During the winter of 1864 two missionary couples, Rev. and Mrs. Calvin Mateer and Rev. and Mrs. Hunter Corbett, left New York on the sailing vessel *Saint Paul*. The long voyage took 165 days around the Cape of Good Hope. The ship was ruled by a tyrannical captain whose treatment of passengers and crew brought the ship almost to the point of mutiny. Sunday services were prohibited. Due to lack of proper food, scurvy broke out. On reaching Shanghai the passengers proceeded to press criminal charges against the captain with the American consul. After profuse apologies from the captain the case was dropped.

But the ordeal of the missionaries was not over. They took the steamer *Swatow* for Yantai, which is the first record we have of steam transportation along the China coast. But the ship ran aground on a reef as they neared their destination. Fearing the ship would break up during the night, passengers and crew were brought ashore. They wandered for five hours in the snow and ice, and at the point of exhaustion found lodging in a peasant farmhouse where they enjoyed the warmth of the "kang" (a raised, heated platform) and breakfasted on rice and sweet potatoes. When it was light, they saw in the distance their ship still afloat on the reef. The men returned to the ship and were able to remove most of their belongings. After three days they were rescued by a British gunboat that was anchored in Yantai harbor. Although they nearly did not make it, these two shipwrecked couples would give to China 155 combined years of service! Together with the name of Nevius, Corbett and Mateer would become the legendary triumvirate that planted the Christian church in Shandong.[51]

With all the troubles encountered it was a wonder that anything was accomplished. But the acts of mercy and compassion shown during the bandit and cholera years broke down some of the suspicion. Itineration into the country began almost immediately. Before his death Gayley preached to a crowd attending an annual festival in the nearby city of Laichowfu. A man named Ning Tsung heard the message. His heart was touched and he become the first convert leading his family and neighbors into the new faith. It was in his village that the first church was organized. In the *Annual Report* for 1862 this notation appears:

> By the blessing of God our time of sowing has also been one of reaping. Six persons have been received into the church by baptism.[52]

Rental or purchase of property was most difficult. During the early years all the missionaries resided in the Kwan Yin (Goddess of Mercy) Temple, which was rented to them by an opium-smoking priest who needed the money. Mateer told of the removal of a two-hundred-pound image of the goddess to make more room for the living. No one wanted it and for years it lay in his attic.

Although Dengzhou was originally designated as the treaty port, the city of Yantai had much the better harbor and became the center of commerce and trade. Presbyterian work began there when the McCartees arrived during the cholera epidemic. But McCartee was never able to obtain a suitable place for his medical work and at the request of Ningbo station returned south.

The Corbetts moved to Yantai in 1865, occupying first an abandoned "haunted" house and later a house that was free of demons but was flooded every time the nearby stream overflowed.

On one of Corbett's first itinerary trips, he spent the Sabbath at the inland city of Laiyang. A scholarly man named Wang Tsei followed Corbett back to the inn to inquire more fully about what he had heard and spent the night there in the study of Mark. Corbett continued with the story:

> Three weeks later he came to my home, saying that he could neither sleep nor eat until he found hope in Jesus. He spent the summer with me in earnest study, and in the autumn of 1865 he and two others were baptized.... Mr. Wang became an eloquent preacher, whose labors God greatly blessed in the saving of souls.... When he first returned to his home after his conversion his kind and gentle manner, so different from the stern and overbearing ways of former years, filled his wife and son with fear that what the people were saying of the foreigners' power of witchcraft might be true, and that this changed man had become a victim. After a few days Mrs. Wang had an experience of her own. She argued that if the Christian religion had power to make her husband gentle and kind it must be true.[53]

The Taiping Rebellion

In 1851 a peasant uprising in Guangxi Province broke out that became known in history as the Taiping Rebellion.[54] For fifteen years the rebellion ravished China from one end to the other and came perilously close to overthrowing the Qing Dynasty. The loss of life incurred during the revolution is incalculable but some estimates run as high as 50 million. Since the origins of the rebellion were linked to Protestant Christianity, it had a profound effect upon the Christian movement. The Taipings are also significant because historians of the People's Republic of China look on the movement's leader, Hong Xiuquan, as a forerunner of the Communist Revolution.[55]

Hong Xiuquan was born in 1814 into a poor but self-reliant Hakka family in Guangxi.[56] He is one of the strangest personalities in Chinese history! Hong showed some promise as a scholar and passed the preliminary Confucian examinations for court appointment. But later attempts to pass the provincial examination resulted in repeated failures, which left him embittered and neurotic. On a trip to Canton in 1833 or 1834 he was handed a tract which was known in English as "Good Words to Admonish the Age," written by Liang Fa, an early Protestant convert.[57] It included passages of scripture and offered a blueprint for the redemption of the Chinese people through Christian monotheism, its tone of moral seriousness and filial piety following the tradition of Confucius. But, according to Liang Fa, morality was not enough as human nature could only be changed by faith in Christ and the transformation of the Holy Spirit.

Hong put the small booklet away for future reference. With the subsequent failure to pass the Confucian examinations, Hong had a nervous collapse and was confined to his bed for forty days. He later declared that during his illness he had been carried to heaven and brought before a venerable old man who said he was the creator of mankind. The old man complained that the human race had forgotten him and was worshiping demons. He rebuked Confucius for neglecting the true doctrine. In another vision he met a middle-aged man called the "Elder Brother."[58]

On rereading the booklet he had received in Canton, Hong became convinced that the old man of the vision was the Christian God and that the Elder Brother was Jesus Christ. He also became convinced that he was the younger brother of Jesus Christ and had been commissioned to destroy the idols and bring the Chinese people to a worship of the true God. He and his cousin, Hong Rengan, baptized each other and began to teach their new doctrine.

Hong's efforts to break up idols and Confucian tablets made it necessary for him to leave his native village. He made his headquarters in "Thistle Mountain" in the rugged area of eastern Guangxi and began to gather a number of discontented and marginalized elements of society to his cause. He organized the group under the name of the "Pai Shang Ti Hui" (Society of God Worshipers), using, significantly, the Protestant term for God. On hearing that there was a foreigner preaching a doctrine similar to his in Canton, Hong traveled to the city in 1847 with his cousin to learn more about the Christian faith. There he met an independent Baptist missionary named Isaachar Roberts and spent several months studying the new doctrine. But Roberts apparently had some misgivings and declined to give him baptism. Hong's money ran out and he returned to Thistle Mountain.

By 1850 the Society of God Worshipers began to take on political and military dimensions. Preaching gave way to rebellion. The social disorders in Guangxi added momentum. Landless peasants, unemployed coolies, charcoal burners, disbanded soldiers and deserters joined the movement. A stern moral code was enforced. All private property was turned over to the organization. Tools and farm instruments were made into arms. Gunpowder was manufactured in charcoal ovens. Soldiers who died in battle were told they would go straight to heaven.

In 1851 the movement broke out of its native province and began the march toward national conquest. One fortified city after another fell. Hong announced the establishment of the "Kingdom of Heavenly Peace" (Taiping Tianguo). To emphasize the universal nature of the kingdom, four of his lieutenants were named "wangs" (kings) of the four points of the compass. Hong reserved for himself the title "Heavenly King." To the Manchu authorities they were known as the "Long Haired Bandits." As they advanced through Central China to the Yangtze valley they were supported by spontaneous uprisings of peasants. Harsh officials and landlords were put to death. Taxes were forgiven. Land registers and loan contracts were burned.

The strategic tri-city area of Wuhan on the Yangtze fell in January 1853. Here, in what later military strategists believe was a tactical error, the revolutionaries turned east along the lower Yangtze instead of continuing the drive northward toward the capital. Nanjing fell in March. Surviving Manchu soldiers and officials were put to death. The city, renamed "Tianjing" (Celestial Capital), became their headquarters for the next eleven years.

Later in 1853 the march to Peking was renewed but the initiative had been lost and the advance faltered some seventy miles south of the capital. The Taipings did not receive the support of the peasants in the north as they had in the south. Winter was hard on the southerners who were ill equipped for the bitter cold. The remnants of the northern armies were annihilated and the threat to the Qing dynasty passed.

But for another decade the Taiping rule encompassed large portions of central China. In its early days it followed the utopian tradition of peasant communism. Men and women had equal rights. Footbinding and the wearing of queues were abolished. Idols and Confucian tablets were destroyed. Opium, gambling, prostitution and adultery were forbidden and violations severely punished. It is little wonder that both missionaries and the Chinese Communist Party had such a fascination with the Taipings!

But this early period of an integrated communal society did not last. As the leaders became entrenched, they demanded the privileges and trappings of power and luxury. Two of the original "kings" died in battle. Hong, jealous of the power of his subordinates, had two of the remaining kings assassinated.

The Taipings received a new lease on life in 1859 with the arrival of Hong Rengan, the nephew, who had first accompanied the Heavenly King on his memorable visit to Isaachar Roberts. Hong at one time had been in the employ of the London Missionary Society and had a better understanding of the Christian faith than the others. He belatedly joined the Taiping cause perhaps thinking he could swing the movement toward traditional Christianity and accommodation with the West. He was given the title "Shield King" and made prime minister. With more competent leadership, Taiping armies were again victorious as they pushed south into the lower Yangtze delta.

Hong attempted to win the favor of the Western powers by making promises of trade and commerce. Missionaries were invited to Nanjing to take part in religious instruction. But the promised reforms never materialized. The Heavenly King became more irrational in his behavior, and withdrew to the inner rooms of his palace quarters, which he shared with his concubines. The Western powers became alarmed when the advances of the Taipings threatened Shanghai. With the ratification of the Treaty of Tianjin, it became all the more important to support the Empire from which new treaty rights had been wrung. British and French business interests mobilized a small force of Western mercenaries, which was placed under the command of an American adventurer, Frederick Townsend Ward. Ward and the "Ever Victorious Army," as his force was soon named, successfully defended Shanghai and when Ward died in battle, Major General Charles George Gordon of the British army took command.[59] Taiping troops were repulsed and were never again a threat in the lower Yangtze valley. Hong's rapprochement with the West had failed and in 1861 he was deposed.

A combination of Manchu and provincial troops finally gained the upper hand. In 1864 Nanjing was recaptured. The Heavenly King, either died from sickness or committed suicide before the city walls were breached. A terrible massacre followed as tens of thousands of Taiping soldiers were put to death.

The Taipings and Christian Missions

The perplexing relationship between the rebellion and Christian missions has been much debated. To what degree can the Taipings be called "Christian"? Was the Christian mission responsible in any way for the uprising?

At first glance it would appear that the Taipings took from Christian books a substantial amount of theology. They printed a "Taiping Bible" that contained much of the Old Testament and the complete New Testament. They emphasized the concept of a creator God, the Ten Commandments, opposition to idol worship, the rite of baptism, observance of the Sabbath, heaven and hell. Jesus was acknowledged in some undefined sense as a savior.

But much of Christian doctrine was repudiated. The Incarnation, the Atonement, and the deity of Christ were rejected. Little was said about the teachings of Jesus. The cross as a Christian symbol was unknown.

To Christian dogma much was added. Note the following confused Taiping exposition of the Trinity by Hong Xiuquan:

There is only one Supreme God. Christ is the First Son of God....The Eastern King is a beloved Son of God, and, together with the Great Elder Brother and Myself, was born of the same Mother. The Father knows that there are some mistakes in the records of the New Testament....He also knows that the people on earth mistakenly think that Christ is God. ...Moreover, I Myself ascended to the High Heaven, saw the Heavenly Father, the Heavenly Mother, the Great Elder Brother and the Heavenly sister-in-law many times.[60]

Latourette's evaluation is to the point:

The Taiping movement was a Chinese sect, displaying some interesting results of contact with Christianity, but drawing most of its beliefs and characteristics from its Chinese environment and the erratic genius of its leaders.[61]

Eugene Powers Boardman, in his extensive study of the Taiping documents, concluded: "The Taiping religion still was not Christianity."[62]

But was it reformable? With patience and further exposition of the scriptures could it have become a vehicle for the conversion of the Chinese Empire?

Missionaries were not of the same mind. W. A. P. Martin believed that the rebellion could be used for the evangelization of China. He made several attempts to reach the "Celestial Capital" against the advice of his colleagues and the American High Commissioner. Martin left Shanghai by river boat "in a thunderstorm in order to elude the vigilance of the High Commissioner." After some close encounters with imperial forces and river pirates he gave up the attempt and years later admitted the venture had been "foolhardy."[63]

Dr. McCartee, who had opposed Martin's venture, agreed to serve as interpreter for an American flotilla seeking assurances from the Taipings that American interests would be protected. The U.S.S. *Saginaw,* a side-wheeled steamer, picked up McCartee in Ningbo, joined the *Dacotah* and *Harford* in Shanghai and proceeded up the Yangtze. Admiral Stribling asked McCartee to translate a document he wished to present to the Taipings asking them to protect U.S. citizens engaged in trade. McCartee suggested adding "and citizens engaged in preaching, teaching, or healing the sick, and all in their employ." The phrase was added.

The squadron anchored near a Taiping fort a few miles below Nanjing. Here McCartee took one of the small boats, the coxswain and five men and landed. He walked up to the walls of the fort alone. The rebels opened the gate and McCartee entered the rebel camp. He asked that arrangements be made for an audience with the Heavenly King. He and American officials would be back the next morning. The next morning, a guide, horses and mandarin chairs were waiting and the officials were taken to the Heavenly City where a council of state was waiting and tea and betel nuts were offered. Admiral Stribling presented his document and McCartee explained it. Some slight changes were made and they were asked to stay for lunch at which the "young prince" asked a blessing. Later the Taipings were invited to see the ships and their big guns.[64]

In Shanghai John Farnham and Charles Mills were caught in the cross-fire between imperial forces supported by a company of British soldiers and the long-haired rebels. Farnham described the encounter:

> They were a horrid-looking set of fellows, resembling South Sea islanders, with long black hair hanging over their foreheads and down their necks.... They were armed with a great variety of weapons... rifles... double-barrelled fowling-pieces... swords... long knives.... Their leader was mounted upon a fine horse — a well-dressed, good-looking young man.... "Whither away?" he exclaimed, as we sprang into the street to make our escape. Knowing that the rebels worshipped God and destroyed all idols we replied, "We worship God, and wish to go to a place of safety." "I, too, worship God," he replied. "Remain where you are; you are safe. My followers will not meddle with any foreigner."[65]

The Rev. Isaachar Roberts had the best opportunity to evaluate the movement because of his previous association with its leaders. At the invitation of his former pupils he arrived in Nanjing in October 1860 and lived there for about a year. He became completely disillusioned with both the conduct of the rebels and their perversion of the Christian faith. Roberts believed that the Heavenly King had become insane.[66]

In the end the Taiping Rebellion failed because of dissension among the leaders, their failure to win the support of the peasants in the north and the neurotic character of their founder. Foreign intervention may have hastened the downfall but it did not alter the inevitable result.

The cause of Christian missions was grievously damaged by its early association with Taiping ideology. Timothy Richards, one of the most discerning missionaries of the time, believed that Christianity continued to suffer from the Taiping legacy of ill-will for the next fifty years.[67]

Chapter 4

To the Heart of the Empire
1867–1893

During the terrible times of the Taiping Rebellion the Empire appeared at the point of collapse. It had been humiliated by the Unequal Treaties, paralyzed by internal inertia and corruption and weakened by the onslaught of the Taipings. Had the Qing dynasty lost the "mandate of heaven"?

The Restoration

But the Manchus showed remarkable powers of recuperation. The dynasty staged an amazing recovery, which resulted in twenty-five years of relative peace. It is a period known by Chinese historians as the Restoration.[1]

Restoration was made possible by a number of factors. New leadership emerged and assumed positions of power and authority. The anti-foreign Xian-feng Emperor died "in exile" when, in 1861, French and British troops occupied Peking and the court fled north of the Great Wall. Cixi, concubine of the dead king, raced back to the capital to take possession of the imperial seals. Her five-year-old son, Tongzhi, was declared the heir apparent and ascended to the dragon throne. Cixi became the Empress Dowager and the dominant force in Chinese politics for the next forty years.

A shift in the balance of power from Peking to the provinces and from Manchu to Chinese leadership brought about a renewal of loyalty to the throne. It was not the Manchu "banner armies" but provincial armies loyal to provincial commanders that defeated the Taipings. Two of the ablest men of the period were Zeng Guofan (1811–1872) and Li Hongzhang (1823–1901). Zeng had raised and led the Hunan army, which was largely responsible for the defeat of the Taipings. Li, general of the Anhui army and later governor-general of various provinces, became the architect of Chinese statecraft for the next four decades. Both were Chinese whose power bases came from the central provinces.

The Western powers, having wrung concessions from the Manchus, now found that it was in their own self-interest that the dynasty survive. Their role switched from one of hostility to one of support. Nothing would be gained if

China were dismembered or the authority of the central government further weakened.

Foreign affairs were handled through a newly created office, the *Zongli Yamen,* tacitly recognizing the fact that other nations were equal powers and not barbaric tribes to be dealt with by minor officials on the fringes of the Empire. In 1868 the first Chinese diplomatic mission, led by Anson Burlingame, an American diplomat in the employ of the court, was sent abroad.

A few first steps were taken toward modernization. In 1872 the Chinese Educational Mission brought 120 long-gowned young Chinese boys to Hartford, Connecticut, to receive a Western education while continuing their classical Chinese studies. But, alas, they became Americanized — hiding their queues, adopting Western dress, developing athletic skills and undignified ways. One of the first to return married an American girl and was converted to Christianity. The project was quickly abandoned.

Longer-lasting results were obtained in the modernization of the Imperial Maritime Customs Service. Robert Hart, an extraordinarily unobtrusive and efficient Irishman, was employed to direct the collection of tariffs and supervise the other duties of the customs service, which included the improvement of harbors, dredging of river channels and even a postal service. Hart administered the service in the interests of the government with efficiency and integrity from 1863 to 1908, bringing in a regular source of revenue equal to nearly one-fourth of the total government income. Fluent in Chinese and sensitive to cultural differences, he became one of the most influential men in the government.

And so by fits and starts China moved toward modernization. Arsenals, a few textile mills and an iron smelting plant were built. Some naval ships were purchased from Krupp in Germany. The propriety of building railroads was heatedly debated. A private company built a narrow-gauge railroad from Shanghai to Wusong at the mouth of the Yangtze. But then the government, under pressure from the Confucian conservatives, reconsidered the enterprise, purchased the line and had it destroyed.

The term "Restoration" aptly describes the aim of the dynastic leaders. Their goal was to "restore," not to make new. Intensely Confucian in philosophy, they sought to use Western technology as a *means* to achieve traditional Chinese *values.* Reform was not what the dynasty had in mind. But reform was what was needed. Modernization came too little and too late. The result was the disastrous defeat in the Sino-Japanese War of 1894–1895, which brought this period to a close.

Anti-foreign Movements

The end of the Taiping Rebellion ushered in a period of increased anti-foreign agitation, which is illustrated by the celebrated Tianjin incident of 1870 when a Roman Catholic cathedral and orphanage were destroyed and the French consul, twenty priests and nuns and an undisclosed number of Chinese converts were killed.

The reasons for the anti-foreign outbursts throughout the Empire are not difficult to uncover. Resentment because of the humiliation of the opium wars and Unequal Treaties was often in the background. The Christian movement was identified by Confucian conservatives as synonymous with the disastrous Taiping Rebellion. The number of missionaries was rapidly increasing and as they aggressively penetrated into the interior they created more opportunities for friction.

A key issue in many of the disputes was the purchase of land in the interior. American and Chinese understanding of land ownership was quite different. Missionaries felt that once the property had been purchased, often at prices substantially higher than the going rate, they should be able to build on the property or do with it as they wished. But in Chinese society individual property rights were never absolute. The clan had the right to disapprove the sale. The *feng sui* (wind-water) influences of the place could be disturbed by the height of the building. And if all the proprieties were not observed, anti-missionary demonstrations could result.

A key role was played by the gentry — the class of scholars, landowners and local functionaries that exercised enormous influence in Chinese society. The gentry had been decimated by the Taipings and were now anxious to recover their elitist position. The presence of the foreign teachers usurped their role as the custodians of traditional learning.

The missionaries believed that the common people heard them gladly and were grateful for the educational, medical and humanitarian services they brought. But the gentry poisoned the minds of the peasants against them. During these decades tracts and pamphlets containing slanderous attacks against the missionaries have been traced to gentry authors.

Not all of the anti-foreign "incidents" were anti-Christian. Some were the result of bandits and lawless elements in the society that victimized foreigners and wealthy Chinese alike. Some incidents were caused by secret societies whose motive was to discredit the ruling dynasty by fomenting disorder. The massacre of nine Protestant missionaries of the CMS and their children in Kucheng, Fujian (Fukien), in 1895 by a society of "Vegetarians" may be a case in point.

Government officials, for the most part, sought to uphold the treaty provisions that protected foreign rights and recognized the humanitarian benefits the missionaries brought. Note the following proclamation issued by the Prefect of Nanjing around the year 1895:

> Be it known that foreigners here renting or otherwise setting up halls do so to save and to help the poor.... Shameless villains who... invent reports and create disturbances... will first be thoroughly examined, then strictly dealt with.[2]

Paul A. Cohen investigated thirty-four major incidents that involved missionary loss of life, personal injury or property damage during the decade

1860–1870. Of the number, twenty-seven cases involved Roman Catholics, three cases involved Catholics and Protestants and three cases involved Protestants. Reasons cited by Cohen for the animosity to the Catholics include the following: the abuse of treaty rights, the excessively large indemnities claimed for property loss, the support of unscrupulous converts in court cases and the arrogance of French officials in relating to Chinese magistrates.[3]

But the Protestant missionaries cannot avoid taking some of the blame. They pushed to the limit their "rights" under the treaties and when trouble erupted they often expected the American consul to come to their rescue.

The position of the Presbyterian Board was that Americans did not lose their rights as citizens just because they were missionaries. While the treaties provided for the redress of grievances, the Board expected missionaries "to exercise moderation and prudence" and that "appeals to the secular arm should always and everywhere be as few as possible."[4]

But moderation and prudence did not always characterize the missionaries' demands. Irwin T. Hyatt cited examples where they pestered the American consul to intervene for near frivolous reasons, such as the repair of tombstones.[5]

Hyatt cited a more serious case involving Calvin Mateer's intervention in the case of a Chinese convert. The incident illustrates the dilemma facing the missionary when a "brother in Christ" suffered persecution and even torture for the sake of the gospel. To intervene or not? A peasant farmer, Miao Hua-yu, heard Mateer preach, experienced a dramatic conversion, became an ardent evangelist and a favorite of Mateer. Later he ran afoul of the authorities, and was arrested for "preaching strange words which caused men to wonder" and for "introducing foreigners into the city." Given a chance to recant, Miao refused and suffered two hundred blows from the bamboo rod. Miao still refused to recant, and by "singing hymns, praying on his knees, and disrespectful talking" he so enraged the officials that five hundred additional blows were administered. When Mateer heard what had happened he rushed to his aid. When he saw him at the point of collapse, with a chain around his neck and his body disfigured, he was overwhelmed with grief for his friend who had suffered such extreme persecution for the sake of the gospel. He appealed to Samuel Holmes, the Yantai consul. Holmes pressured the magistrate and within a week Miao was released. But later developments showed that the issue was not as clear-cut as Mateer had thought. Miao proved to be a disappointment. Acquaintances characterized him as a "reckless boaster and deceiver." His preaching bordered on inciting the villagers to rebellion. He used his close relationship with the foreigners to enhance his standing in the community. The officials had been at least partly right in their assessment of Miao's character. Mateer learned from the experience to make no further appeal to the consul. In 1872 he wrote he was convinced that "bad results come from our efforts to assist [Chinese] Christians." In 1873 Mateer was "stoned and roughed up worse than on any occasion since he had begun itinerating. He sought no redress."[6]

The attitude of the Chinese toward the foreigners is seen in a new light when compared with the behavior of Americans toward Chinese who were then immigrating to the United States. Chinese immigration received legal sanction in the Burlingame Treaty of 1863. But as immigration increased it aroused intense opposition from labor unions, which claimed the Chinese were taking jobs away from them. Also, Chinese immigrants did not conform to the American ideal of the "melting pot." The Chinese did not "melt." The Burlingame Treaty was violated repeatedly by municipal and state courts, which discriminated against Chinese and ignored acts of brutality against them. In 1876 a notorious incident took place in Rock Spring, Wyoming, when riots occurred between white laborers and some four hundred Chinese immigrants who had come to work on the Union Pacific railroad. Armed railroad workers crossed the tracks and invaded "China town," shooting, looting and burning as they went. The carnage resulted in twenty-eight charred and mutilated bodies of Chinese laborers. None of those implicated in the attack were brought to trial.[7] In 1892 the U.S. Congress adopted the Geary Act, which, in clear violation of the treaties signed with China, ended Chinese immigration.[8] With such complete disregard for the rights of Chinese living in the United States, there is little wonder that riots against foreigners living in China took place.

The State of the Mission at Home

While there was relative peace in China, the terrible conflict between the states had begun back home. When the "Old School" General Assembly met in Philadelphia in May 1861, most of the southern states had withdrawn from the Union. When the Assembly adopted the Gardiner Springs Resolution pledging allegiance to the Union, commissioners from the southern presbyteries felt they had no alternative but to withdraw.[9]

The effects of the Civil War and the resulting withdrawal of the southern constituency had a marked effect on the missionary enterprise of PCUSA. The departure of the southern churches resulted in the loss of $30,000 annually, which was about 20 percent of the total contributions. The expense of transmitting funds to China during wartime went up 40 percent.[10]

A number of missionaries from the southern states had served under the New York Board, but only a few were in China at the time of the division.[11] The Board lost the services of an able and experienced secretary, the Rev. John Leighton Wilson. Mr. Wilson resigned at the outbreak of the war and returned to his native South Carolina. Apparently the parting was amicable and Lowrie expressed great regret at his leaving. But even in the midst of this tragic and bitter war, all missionary ties were not broken. In 1862 Lowrie acknowledged receipt of $2,000 from "the southern church" for the support of missionaries from the southern states under the New York Board.[12]

The Board quickly rebounded from the damage done to the cause during the war. Missionary appointments to China continued without abatement. In 1863 Lowrie wrote that "business in the North was never more prosperous."[13]

In 1870 the reunion of the Old and New School Assemblies brought an enlarged constituency to new mission opportunities. The old debate as to whether missions should be conducted through the Assembly's agency or through independent societies was now beside the point. A number of New School missionaries under the ABCFM were transferred to the Presbyterian Board.

In the late 1870s the Board began to experience financial difficulties in supporting its expanding mission force. Help came with the establishment of women missionary societies. John C. B. Webster has underlined the importance of this development:

> In 1870, immediately after the reunion of the Old and New Schools, two regional Presbyterian societies were formed in Philadelphia and New York.... These Women's boards were autonomous but worked in close conjunction with the Board of Foreign Missions in recruiting and supporting single women missionaries, specifically for work among women and children rather than for "general missionary work" which was the Board's domain.[14]

In 1871, total contributions from "Women's Boards" came to $7,327. In this year the magazine *Woman's Work for Woman* was started and in five years contributions had risen to $114,000.[15]

The establishment of Women's Boards signaled the rising importance of women for the missionary enterprise. The revised *Missionary Manual* of 1889 states that women with full-time mission assignments were entitled to vote on all issues.[16] Slowly, what had begun as an all-male preserve was changing.

Rapid Expansion of China Missions

Protestant missions in China were now at the "takeoff" point. With the ratification of the Tianjin treaty and the defeat of the Taipings, most of the provinces were now "open" for foreign residence. The transcontinental railroad crossing of North America in 1869 and the advent of regular steamship service across the Pacific between 1870 and 1880 made transportation quicker and cheaper. The Student Volunteer Movement was in full swing and China constituted a "particularly appealing mission field to college and university students."[17]

In 1864 there were 189 Protestant missionaries in all of China. By 1889 this number had increased to 1,296 (589 men, 391 wives, 316 single women). In 1869 the number of baptized Protestant church members was estimated at around 5,700. By 1893 the number had increased nearly tenfold to 55,000 with a Christian constituency of well over 100,000.[18]

During the three decades between 1867 and 1897 the Presbyterian Board sent 257 missionaries to China. But for every ten new appointments there were four losses. Attrition can be attributed to the following reasons: resignation, 70; death, 28; death of spouse, 5; transfer to other missions, 13, for a total of 116.[19]

Of those appointed between 1837 and 1895, seventy-seven, or 22 percent of the total, lasted less than five years. But if the missionary made it through the first five years the probability was that long years of service in China would result. One hundred and eight (31 percent) served more than thirty years.[20]

What kind of missionaries were appointed during this thirty-year period? Although there are ambiguities and overlaps, the following breakdown is approximately correct:

Ordained clergy (all men)		80
Evangelists	69	
Educators	11	
Medical doctors		39
Men	24	
Women	15	
Women's work & education		
(all single women)		60
Printing/literature (all men)		6
Wives		72
Total		257

Note the large number of medical doctors. In the preceding thirty-year period only three doctors (Hepburn, McCartee and Kerr) had been appointed and only one of these (Kerr) had been able to develop a substantial medical practice.

Note also the large number of women (seventy-five) who were appointed as professional missionaries in medical and educational work. The single woman missionary soon became indispensable because she alone had access to the women's quarters in the homes of China. And it was here that the missionary movement was to have its greatest success. The foreign mission field became the first vocational opportunity the church offered to professional women.

Professional women were all single when appointed. But life in China must have had its romantic opportunities for many did not remain single long. Of the seventy-five single women appointed during these years, twenty-five married soon after arriving in China. After marriage most divided their time between their professional assignments and children in the home.

Kathleen Lodwick's characterization of Presbyterian women missionaries in Hainan would be true for those in other places:

> As a group the women were very well-educated — nearly all had some post-high school education. Generally, they came from upper-middle class families who had been able to afford education for their daughters. Most, but not all, came from Presbyterian families.[21]

There is no evidence that missionary appointees were given any special orientation prior to their arrival in the field. Ordained missionaries took the same course of study as seminarians preparing for service in the United States. The training for medical doctors was no different from that for licensed medical personnel at home. When they arrived in China, language study was considered essential but formal language instruction in a school came later. A new missionary was provided the services of a full-time Chinese language teacher. In 1886 the Board deplored the fact that some missionaries were not getting the language and insisted on language examinations for all new missionaries.[22] But from the number of works they published, some were gaining a mastery of the language.[23]

Policies and Practices

Formal mission statements as to the purpose of the China mission are hard to find. This was before the time when church agencies had became obsessed with goals and priorities! For the China missionary, the purpose of the mission was self-evident: *It was to claim the Chinese Empire for Jesus Christ.*

There was general agreement as to what should be done. Now that the provinces were open, the mission should push forward into the interior as rapidly and aggressively as possible. Here the peasants were more open to the gospel than in the coastal cities. China would never be won if the missionaries stayed in the treaty ports. The heart of the Empire must be claimed for Christ. Missionary residences should be built in central locations. Here worshiping congregations should be brought into being. A period of careful instruction as a catechumen should precede baptism. Schools should be established for both boys and girls so that the Christian constituency could read the Bible. Classes should be formed for the training of mission "helpers." These would become the nucleus of a native clergy.

Medical work was necessary in order to break down hostility. Hospitals should be started in each central location. Medicine was thus viewed as auxiliary to the main thrust of evangelism. However as the number of medical professionals increased, this began to change. Medical practice, reflecting the compassion of Jesus Christ, began to assume an importance of its own.

The classic mission "station" thus consisted of a church, hospital or clinic, one or more schools and missionary residences. From these centers, missionary evangelists itinerated into the surrounding countryside establishing "substations" where Christian communities would be formed under the leadership of Chinese associates. Insofar as possible, "comity" agreements were worked out with other Protestant mission bodies so as to avoid unnecessary duplication and competition.[24] Chinese religious practices and cultural traditions that were alien to the gospel should be abolished. These included ancestor worship, concubinage and footbinding. The printing and distribution of Christian literature was essential because of the Chinese veneration of the written word.

The 1889 edition of the *Missionary Manual* looked forward to "the speedy establishment of a self-supporting and self-propagating church."[25] The omission of the first element of the triad — self-government — may be significant.

Was success in "self-support" possible if self-government was ignored? "Self-support" remained during these years an elusive target. It was the goal to which all gave lip service but it was assumed that its achievement lay in the distant future. In the meantime there was no alternative to the building of churches and the employment of church workers with American money. A lone, dissenting opinion was registered by the Rev. John L. Nevius.

During these years the relationship between the Board in New York and the missionaries in the field began to change. In earlier times strong-willed individuals operated on their own. The early years were characterized by Latourette as "biographical rather than institutional."[26] Mission organization was weak; the leadership of the national church almost nonexistent; the Board was too far removed in time and distance to provide guidance or restraints. But in 1875 a White Star steamer carrying mail crossed the Pacific in sixteen days. Relationships with the home Board would never be the same! New York was now near enough to make intervention inevitable. And the large number of new missionaries made a greater degree of administrative control necessary.

Thus the New York Board began to assume a more activist role. Decisions made on the field were overruled.[27] The Board defended its right to terminate relationships with missionaries if there was sufficient cause.[28] The China mission was prodded to move more rapidly toward ordaining native pastors.[29] The missionary body was urged to exercise greater control over missionary assignments and to act collectively in making requests for appropriations.[30] In 1892 a young Princeton graduate named Robert E. Speer became the Corresponding Secretary for the China field. He would give brilliant, forceful leadership to the mission program at home and abroad for the next forty years.

What had been a loose confederation of individuals was moving in the direction of centralized authority. But the changes were made not without resistance and frustration on the part of missionaries — sometimes with the Board and sometimes with each other. Nevius protested the Board's right to unilaterally amend the *Missionary Manual* and took his case to the General Assembly.[31]

At times the Board expressed exasperation with the quarrels of its China missionaries.[32] In Ningbo, McCartee and Martin disagreed on nearly every conceivable issue. Martin favored the early baptism of converts. McCartee would delay baptism until there was true "sorrow for sin." Martin favored the use of "Shen" for the deity; McCartee favored "Shang Ti." Martin wanted to give native assistants greater responsibilities. McCartee felt that this violated Presbyterian order. Here were two brilliant, strong-willed individuals constantly at odds, and each appealing to the Board to do something about the other. McCartee puts his finger on the problem:

> We are composed of very heterogeneous materials. Some were brought up as Congregationalists. . . . Some of us were brought up among the strictest kind of old school and anti-new measure Presbyterians. Some . . . think sessions are out of place on the mission field. Some ladies prefer not to be

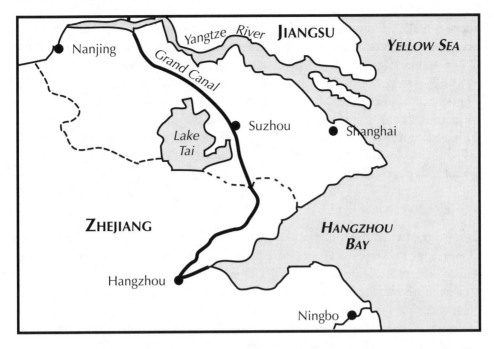

Central China and Yangtze River Delta 1880

connected with the Presbyterian church on the field but have "all things in common with those of other missions."[33]

In Canton there was a sharp rivalry between John G. Kerr and Andrew Happer. Here again were two extremely able missionaries, each of whom made lasting contributions to the Christian movement but who simply could not get along.[34]

With the rapid increase in missionary personnel and the growing institutionalism of the work, a better way of relating missionaries to each other and to the Board was needed. But with the expansion of mission stations all the way from Canton to Peking, administration on the field could not be handled by one central body. Consequently, in 1868 the Board adopted a plan for three separate China Missions: (1) the Central China Mission, (2) the North China Mission, and (3) the South China Mission. In 1889 Shandong became a separate mission. In 1893 Hainan Mission was added. Each mission had responsibility for its own personnel assignments and budget requests.

The Central China Mission

A closer look at the progress of each of these China missions as they penetrated further inland to the great cities of the empire is now in order.

Mission work in Shanghai and Ningbo continued much along the same lines as in the preceding period. Ningbo lost some of its importance as trade began moving through the port of Shanghai. As the oldest center of Presbyterian work it made good progress in the development of a native clergy. In 1893 there were ten organized churches in the Ningbo area with nine ordained pastors and 760 communicant members. In Shanghai three centers of Presbyterian work developed. At the South Gate there was a self-supporting church, Lowrie High School for Boys and the Mary Farnham Girls' School. In the International Settlement a second church was started near the site of the Presbyterian Press. In Hongkew a third church was begun. But evangelistic work in the great metropolis was slow. In 1895 the three Shanghai churches had a combined communicant membership of 210.[35]

Hangzhou (Hangchow)

Hangzhou, with a population of one million and the capital of Zhenjiang (Chekiang) Province, was considered a prime site for the next station. It was one of the most beautiful cities of China — to quote the well-known saying: "Heaven above, Suzhou and Hangzhou beneath." It had been the capital of China during the Southern Sung Dynasty (1135–1270 A.D.) and renowned as a center of the silk and tea industry. Situated at the southern terminal of the Grand Canal, it lay about half way between Ningbo and Shanghai.

Rev. John Nevius first visited the city in 1858 in company with the American Consul and Mr. Russell of the Church Missionary Society.[36] At West Lake they met a party of Mandarin officials who were quite startled at the sudden encounter and asked them to leave. In 1859 Nevius returned and secured accommodations at the Six Harmony Pagoda. He was well received and returned to Ningbo to bring his wife back to the city. Mrs. Nevius described her new residence in a Taoist temple as charmingly located on a high hill just a few minutes walk from the center of the city.

Later in 1859 the attitude of the officials changed when the British and French fleets attacked the Daku forts. The city magistrates asked the American consul to recall the missionaries who returned to Ningbo.

Hangzhou was intermittently occupied by both Taiping and imperial forces with widespread destruction. Messrs. David Green and Samuel Dodd visited the city in 1864 and found it in ruins. Over half the houses had been burned. In 1865 the Green family moved to Hangzhou and rented a house on "Leather Market Street."[37] This same year the Hangzhou church was organized with thirteen members.

The opening of work in Hangzhou was greatly facilitated by Chinese evangelists from Ningbo who had been itinerating in this area and had established groups of believers. Van Evera pays high tribute to Rev. Tsang Nyin Kw'e, who accompanied Green, served as preacher for the street chapels and later was the first pastor:

> He shared the responsibility for the work and again and again came to the
> support of the church in difficult situations.... His patient labor during

the long years of his pastorate was the chief factor in the growth of this congregation.[38]

In 1867 the Ningbo Boys' Academy was transferred to Hangzhou. The move of the school was hotly contested by the Ningbo missionaries.[39] The BFM intended to make Hangzhou the principal station of the province and to phase out some of the work in Ningbo. But because of strenuous objection, both stations were kept at full strength. The Academy prospered in its new location as more and more of its students came from Christian homes.

Hangzhou statistics for the year 1893 are as follows: churches and preaching points, 5; ordained Chinese pastors, 2; unordained preachers, 3; Bible women, 2; communicant members, 124; boys' boarding school pupils, 50.[40]

Suzhou (Soochow)

This city of gardens and canals with a population of half a million was the location for the next mission station. It too had been devastated during the Taiping Rebellion. Albert Rawlinson described the beginnings of Presbyterian work in these words:

> Mr. Charles Schmidt, a European, was in the employ of the Chinese government during the Taiping rebellion. After its close he engaged in business, but was unsuccessful. In a conversation with Rev. David D. Green, when he said he had been unfortunate in business because of the hard times, Mr. Green asked if he did not think God had something to do with it. The words brought him silently to acknowledge God, and prepared the way for his conversion. He had married a Chinese wife, and both became members of the Presbyterian church in Shanghai. Supported in part by his own means, he undertook evangelistic work in Suchow in 1868.[41]

Rev. and Mrs. George Fitch moved to the city in October 1872, the same week that Rev. and Mrs. Hampden DuBose of the Southern Presbyterian Mission arrived.[42] Others followed but for years the work was carried on by Chinese evangelists as ill health depleted the number of missionaries. Progress was slow. But China missionaries were eternal optimists and the future was always bright. The 1887 report read:

> The people are attentive and civil, but thus far there is little to encourage in outward results. We preach on in hope.... As yet there is little to show for all the years of work here, but there is a splendid opportunity for labor.[43]

In 1891 an outbreak of anti-foreign violence threatened the missionaries in the lower Yangtze valley. It began with rumors that two Chinese Roman Catholic women at Wuhu had been using magic to corrupt little children. Mobs destroyed the Roman Catholic mission in that city and the riots spread to other cities along the Yangtze River. Missionary women and children were evacuated from Suzhou at the insistence of the U.S. consul. Rev. David Lyon remained in the city and appealed to the local magistrate for protection when the chapel was broken into and his life was threatened by ruffians who followed his sedan chair down the street shouting "Kill the foreign devil!" The magistrate came in person and quelled the violence. Arrests were made and troublemakers were beaten.[44]

Statistics for 1893 are as follows: churches and preaching points, 7; ordained Chinese pastors, 0; unordained preachers, 3; Bible women, 2; communicant members, 35; pupils in boys' boarding school, 30.[45]

Nanjing (Nanking)

This strategically important city on the Yangtze River some two hundred miles north of Shanghai had been the capital of the early Ming dynasty. Here the *lingua franca* was the Mandarin dialect, spoken throughout the northern provinces. Nanjing was destined to become a strategic center for Protestant union activities which would include a hospital, a university and a theological seminary. Its importance is underlined by the fact that today it is the headquarters of the China Christian Council, the Nanjing Seminary and the Amity Foundation.

The Protestant missionary presence began with the arrival of the Rev. George Duncan of the CIM in 1867 not long after the city of the Taipings had been re-taken by the imperial armies. Duncan was unable to rent a room but a Buddhist priest permitted him to sleep in an upper chamber of the Drum Tower from sunset to sunrise. During the day the room had to be vacated so Duncan frequented the public places and tea rooms and preached the Christian message.[46]

The Revs. Albert Whiting and Charles Leaman of the Presbyterian Mission arrived in the summer of 1875 and rented a house near the South Gate of the city.[47] They were ordered to leave when a mob gathered to protest their presence. But Whiting had a copy of the imperial order from Peking directing governors and officials to provide protection to the foreigners stating that their right of residence was permitted by treaty. On seeing the imperial order, the officials changed their attitude abruptly. Protection was provided and right of residence established. Later their families joined them. Mrs. Whiting was probably the first lady in foreign dress to appear in Nanjing.

In 1878 Whiting obtained permission of the mission to travel north to aid in the distribution of famine relief. He arrived in Taiyuan, capital of Shanxi Province, and shortly afterward contracted "famine fever" and died. Mrs. Whiting returned to her parents' home in Turkey and for several years the work in Nanjing was suspended. Mrs. Whiting subsequently returned to Nanking and resumed her work there among Chinese women. In 1883 she married Rev. Robert Abbey, who had joined the station.

Here, as in Suzhou, progress was slow. One of the bright spots was the continuity provided by Elder Hu,

> who is as good, if not better, than a foreigner. He has been at his post, from morning till night (eating his rice at the chapel).... In the spring he was interrupted for a few days, on account of the chapel having been

looted by a mob; but before we had arranged about it with the officials he was back at his post.[48]

One bitter disappointment was the failure to establish an organized church with its own ordained pastor after fifteen years of hard work. Nanjing was Mandarin-speaking territory and trained pastors in Ningbo or Shanghai were of little help. One successful project was the Nanking Girls' Boarding School, which attracted students from four provinces. Upon graduation they became teachers, Bible women or wives of Christian workers.

Statistics for the year 1893 are as follows: churches and preaching points, 7; ordained Chinese pastors, 0; unordained preachers, 5; Bible women, 2; communicant members, 64; pupils in boarding schools, 49.[49]

The North China Mission

Peking

The Presbyterian presence in Peking was first established by a most unconventional missionary in a most unconventional manner. W. A. P. Martin had accompanied the American delegation that negotiated the signing of the Treaty of Tientsin in 1858 and had an itch to carry the gospel to the capital city. The Board discouraged the idea, citing the need to act with caution since Peking was not a treaty port.[50] But Martin would not take no for an answer. In June 1863 he wrote to the Board Secretary reiterating his request, noting that Peking "now swarms with Jesuits who are straining every nerve to preoccupy it to the exclusion of Protestants."[51] Without waiting for an answer he moved first to Tianjin and then with the help of diplomats S. Wells Williams and Anson Burlingame, he obtained temporary quarters in a temple three miles outside the West Gate of the Imperial City. No funds were available as the Board had not authorized the move so Martin secured a loan from Williams to purchase property and make repairs. As happened more than once in dealing with its missionaries, the Board recognized the *fait accompli*, as the *Annual Report* for 1864 lists the new station:

> Peking; the capital of the country; occupied as a mission station in 1863: mission laborers — Rev. William A. P. Martin, D.D. and his wife; two native Christian assistants.[52]

Martin began his ministry in a "low-profile" manner. There were quiet home meetings and personal conversations. Daily preaching began at a chapel. Although there were large crowds, they came mainly out of curiosity. One person was baptized the first year, and six in each of the next two years, equally divided between Chinese and Manchus, aged from mid-teens to old men. Most came from the peasant class but among them was one young officer whose yellow belt indicated his imperial status.

Soon after he arrived Martin began a school for boys, which he named "Truth Hall Academy." By the second year there were twenty students. Mrs. Martin taught some classes and their own two boys, and visited among the Chinese women. Martin repeatedly appealed to the Board for another missionary to help in the work, which he felt was of such strategic importance. But for the first five years the Martins were alone. Martin felt keenly the lack of Board support, but he made influential friends. Sir Robert Hart made an annual contribution of fifteen hundred taels to the work of the academy from customs revenue.

Martin became known as a scholar and writer. He published a series of lectures, known in English as *Evidences of Christianity,* which became a best-seller. It went through thirty Chinese editions and was translated into Japanese and Korean.[53] The reason for its appeal was its use of Chinese thought forms to explain Christian theological concepts.

Martin's translation of Henry Wheaton's *Elements of International Law,* which was the standard text of the day, brought him to the attention of the imperial court and led to an invitation to teach in the school just established by the government for the training of young men to serve as interpreters in the fledgling Chinese foreign service. Martin accepted the offer, which eventually led to full-time employment with the government, resignation from the Presbyterian Mission and a brilliant career as president of the institution that was the precursor of the Imperial University of Peking.

"Few Americans have been so widely and deeply involved in Chinese life as W. A. P. Martin." So wrote Martin's biographer, Ralph Covell, who cited as evidence for his claim: Martin's sixty-six years residence in China, his high government position, his efforts to modernize state education, his friendship with high-ranking officials, his published works and his role in interpreting Chinese culture to the West.[54]

The reunion with the New School General Assembly in 1870 brought into the mission ABCFM missionaries Rev. Joseph L. Whiting and Rev. Daniel C. McCoy and their wives, who were already stationed in Peking. In 1874 the location of the mission shifted from the southern to the northern portion of the city where a new chapel was opened.

The 1893 *Annual Report* gave these statistics: number of churches, 3; ordained Chinese pastors, 3; other Christian workers, 4; Bible women, 2; boarding school pupils, 72; communicant members, 311.[55]

These were small humble beginnings. Yet the record told of how the gospel began its penetration into the Forbidden City:

A Chinese woman having in some way gained some little knowledge of the truth, made several calls upon the ladies of the mission with a view of learning more about the Christian faith. It appeared she was one of the women in waiting on the wife of the Sixth Prince (Prince Kung). Her visits to the mission finally came to the knowledge of the Prince, but he raised no objection, and her study of the truth continued. By degrees she began to interest other female members of the court, and at last accounts a voluntary Bible-class of over thirty was studying on each Sabbath in the imperial court of China.[56]

The An Ting and Douw Hospitals

In 1881 Dr. B. C. Atterbury arrived and began a medical practice that became the first major Western medical center in the capital city, pioneering in the fields of medical education, nursing and care of women.[57] In 1883 Atterbury purchased at his own expense a small building, and with some repairs, converted it into a hospital. He described this small beginning in a letter to the church back home:

> It is in many respects well adapted to its purpose; and though small, accommodating about twenty in-patients, it will, I trust, aid much in our work in this city. Fitted up somewhat as such institutions are at home, and warmed with a large American stove, the two wards look quite pleasant and cheerful.[58]

The first year two thousand patients were treated at the hospital and the dispensary that was started in the northern part of the city. Most of the patients paid something for their food and medicine. Along with the medical work, there was preaching of the gospel and distribution of Christian tracts.

In 1887 a building program was completed at the cost of $11,000 using the Chinese "pavilion plan" of having a number of small structures rather than a single big one. Three pavilions, accommodating ten patients each were named after the benefactors that provided the funds: "Bakewell," "Dodge" and "Douw." There were also accommodations for an operating room, a chapel, a doctor's residence and an "opium refuge." Funds for the Douw pavilion, for which the women's hospital was named, were given by Miss D. M. Douw of Albany, New York. The men's hospital was named "An Ting" (Tranquility) after the gate in the northern sector of the city wall near which the hospital was located. In 1888, Dr. Mariam E. Sinclair arrived, and with Miss Janet McKillican, R.N., took over the women's work.

Cases treated included all the ills to which human frailty is subject: malaria, attempted suicides, insanity, opium addiction (50 percent success rating reported), "animal possession" (hedgehog, weasel, fox, snake and rat) and "demon possession." A strong catharsis often was enough to drive the invading spirit away. The hospital treated beggar children from the streets as well as Manchus and eunuchs from the emperor's palace. Dr. Sinclair was often invited to visit well-to-do women and official families in their homes. Hospital staff accompanied missionary evangelists on their country trips. In 1886 a class was begun for the training of Christian young men in the practice of Western medicine. Lectures made use of the medical textbooks translated by Dr. Kerr of Canton. Four medical students (two Manchus and two Chinese) were graduated in 1888.

The 1893 *Annual Report* gave the following statistics for the combined hospitals and dispensary: out-patients, 29,930; in-patients, 247; surgical operations, 889.[59]

The Shandong Mission

During the thirty-year period between 1865 and 1895 the Shandong Mission grew to become the largest and, in many ways, the most successful work of the PCUSA in China. By the year 1895, 63 missionaries, nearly 40 percent of the total, were on the role of the Shandong Mission. They were deployed in 6 stations with 36 organized churches, well over 300 "preaching points," 7 ordained Chinese pastors, 199 "teachers and helpers" and 3,797 baptized members.[60] There were more converts in Shandong than in all the other missions combined.

What lay behind this success? A number of answers were suggested by Shandong missionaries.[61]

The superior character of the people: Shandong was the "home of the sages" (Confucius, Mencius) and their moral influence for good continued to permeate the province.

The good judgment of the early pioneers: Shandong had the good fortune to have "a remarkable trio of missionary families" (Nevius, Corbett and Mateer) who gave long uninterrupted years to the development of the work. All died and were buried in Shandong.[62]

Extensive itineration: In the words of the 1893 report:

> "The great work of the Shantung Mission is that of itineration, a work really of bishops and not unlike that of the early apostles who extended their influence over the widely scattered cities."[63]

The mission sought aggressively to push into the interior, starting new stations at strategic points. From these stations the missionary evangelists radiated out to smaller market towns and villages by donkey, ox cart or *shenza,* a strange hammock contraption suspended between two mules.

The use of trained native evangelists: The Shandong mission developed a plan by which lay evangelists were given instruction in theological classes held in the various centers. These unpaid lay workers took over the work in the villages under the direction of a missionary or native pastor.[64]

The Dengzhou Boys' School

Certainly, one of the reasons for the success in Shantung was the remarkable development of the boys' school in Dengzhou under the leadership of Calvin and Julia Mateer. Calvin always said that the school was Julia's idea. It began as a modest project inspired by Julia when she realized that she and her husband would be childless. Why not begin a small school for young Chinese boys? What they began would become "the first missionary institution to achieve true collegiate standing" in China.[65]

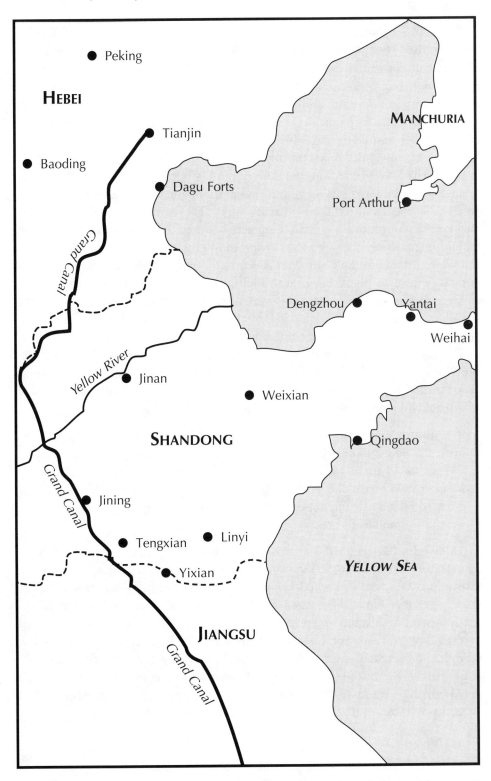

North China and Shandong 1890–1905

The school opened at the Kuan-yin Tang (Temple to the Goddess of Mercy) in September 1864 with six boys recruited from poor, illiterate families. The parents had consented to their enrollment because instruction would be given in the Confucian classics and food, clothing and books were free. At first the results were disappointing and it was Julia who kept the school alive. But after eight dismal years a change occurred. Calvin Mateer's biographer, Irvin T. Hyatt, Jr., writes that a key factor was Calvin's own sense of mission. The school would be his and Julia's passion for the rest of their years.[66]

Standards were raised in the selection of students. The curriculum was revised according to a threefold formula that combined "Chinese Classics, Western Science, and Religious Instruction."[67] The writing of essays in the vernacular was introduced. Calvin designed his own laboratory apparatus and taught the science courses. The strong emphasis on science was necessary, Calvin said, because the Confucian educational tradition led the student "like a donkey, with eyes hooded and head tied fast to the center of the mill." Mathematics and science in large doses was needed to lift the donkey's hood and stimulate the mind to think for itself.[68] Religious instruction depended above all else on the direct personal contact between teachers and students.

The enrollment grew from twenty-two in 1874 to thirty-four in 1876. The superior quality of the educational program began to receive attention from all over North China as more students were added. Calvin and Julia worked well as a team. Julia gave most of her time to the younger boys:

> If a student's clothing were dirty, she had it cleaned; if the clothing was torn, she had it mended. If the place was very dirty, she would supervise a clean up. If there was sickness she would supply medicines. When the weather was muggy she would caution [the students] to avoid drafts.... In every coming and going, in every look of distress or joy, there was nothing she did not notice and rectify.[69]

In 1898 Julia Mateer died and was buried in Dengzhou. In a ceremony commemorating her sixtieth birthday held several years earlier, graduates of the institution she loved presented her with an inscription in gilt letters with the title "Character Nourishing Aged Mother." Calvin died in 1908 at the age of seventy-two. At his funeral service, these remarkable statistics of the school graduates were read: total receiving diplomas, 205; teachers in government schools, 38; teachers in church schools, 68; pastors, 17; evangelists, 16; literary work, 10; business, 12; railroad, post office, customs, 7; others, 15; deceased, 22. Graduates were scattered among thirteen denominations and sixteen provinces, and served in a hundred schools.[70]

Jinan (Tsinan)

Having established mission centers on the coast, the Shandong Mission had as its goal during these years the thrust into the interior. In 1871 Rev. Jasper S. McIlvaine reached Jinan by traveling south from Peking over tortuous roads by donkey and ox cart. The city was then the capital of the province with a population of two hundred thousand. McIlvaine took up residence in quarters he rented in an inn inside the East Gate of the city. He began regular preaching, which was probably the first time the gospel had been proclaimed in the city. McIlvaine suffered a nervous breakdown, due in part to intense loneliness, and returned to the United States to regain his health. He came back in 1874 and persuaded the Shandong Mission to open a permanent station at Jinan. Rev. and Mrs. J. Fisher Crossett and Rev. and Mrs. John Murray joined the station in the next two years. Difficulty was encountered in renting property due to opposition from the gentry and for some years the street chapel consisted of a "twenty-five by six foot matting-covered passageway between the missionary home and the main street."[71]

A small group of Christians from the countryside began to gather for regular worship services. To provide a place for them to meet, McIlvaine was finally able to purchase a site for a chapel on the main market street with $5,000 from his father's estate. But before the property could be secured Jasper McIlvaine died of acute pneumonia. He was described by colleagues as "a man of unusual gifts, scholarly attainment and consecration."[72]

The purchase of the land brought years of trouble for the station. Negotiations had been badly handled. The property's conspicuous location on the city's thoroughfare was bitterly opposed by the city gentry. A mob attacked the chapel, reduced the property to shambles and dragged the Rev. Gilbert Reid, the only missionary there at the time, through the streets leaving him in a semi-conscious state. He was rescued by a friendly constable. After protracted negotiations, the dispute was settled through the intervention of Chester Holcomb, Secretary of the Legation in Peking in 1885. The property on the main street was exchanged for a smaller site in a less prominent part of the city and a sum of money paid the mission to compensate for the difference in the property value.[73]

In 1882 the Presbytery of Shandong convened in Jinan and organized a church of 24 members with two elders and one deacon. The congregation experienced steady growth and in 1895 reported a communicant membership of 165.

The Rev. Stephen A. Hunter, M.D., and his wife arrived in 1879 to begin medical work. In 1892 the city authorities gave permission for the building of the McIlvaine Memorial Hospital, constructed with funds received as a part of the land swap arranged earlier. In 1893 nearly six thousand patients, plus opium addicts, were treated in the new building.[74]

Weixian (Weihsien)

The long itineration trips of Corbett and Nevius from Yantai into the interior of the province began to produce good results. But it was difficult to reach the area because of the impassable roads. In 1883 the Shandong Mission decided to open a new station at the important city of Weixian, about equidistant between Yantai and Jinan. Two evangelistic couples, Rev. and Mrs. Robert Mateer and Rev. and Mrs. J. H. Laughlin, were commissioned to begin the work. John Laughlin described the first years at the station in this report:

> During the first two years of our residence in Wei Hien our services were held in a rented room in a neighboring village. It was a wretched place, small, smoke-begrimed, hot in summer, cold in winter, and inconveniently located.... The Sabbath congregations have from the first been encouraging. The resident Christians with the 15 or 20 boys of Mrs. Mateer's class of "inquirers," and the curious spectators make up a fair congregation.[75]

The station experienced a tragic loss in the death of the two young missionary wives: Annie Laughlin in 1884 and Sadie Mateer in 1886. A chapel, intended as a memorial to Mrs. Laughlin, was built with funds received from friends in Philadelphia.

Much of the work was in itinerating throughout the region. In 1887 Mateer told of visiting two hundred villages, being well received and finding a ready audience in nearly every place, most of which had never heard of the Christian religion. Miss Fannie Wight described her work with country women in an article, "The Luxuries of Itinerating":

> I am now in a smoky-walled, damp, dark, smelling inn, where the glimmer of a candle gives us a sickly light. Mrs. Laughlin [Jennie Anderson, second wife of John H.] is rocking her baby on a *kang* opposite me: she is singing "There is a happy land."...My *kang* is behind me, and I have sat there all day...women and children around me; interesting and delightful it has been to me to tell them of Heaven and of Christ....The next trip was taken in a two-wheeled cart, without springs. Deep were the ruts and great was the bouncing....Some of the women were quite advanced, and two of them learned to read the twelfth chapter of Romans....It was a delight to teach them.[76]

Weixian showed rapid progress from the first. The 1894 statistics are most impressive: 2,362 communicant members, 13 organized churches, 4 ordained Chinese pastors, 130 outstations where regular services were held, 939 pupils enrolled in 27 city and country schools, 17,356 patients treated in the Mateer Memorial Hospital by Dr. W. R. Faries and Dr. Mary Brown.[77]

Linyi (Ichow)

In 1890 a third station was opened in the interior at the large city of Linyi, 150 miles southwest of Yantai. Rev. and Mrs. W. P. Chalfant and three new missionary couples were assigned to open the work.[78] A small "wheelbarrow inn" on the outskirts of the city was secured from Mr. Djang, a wealthy new convert. Because of Mr. Djang's standing in the community and his steadfast support of the missionaries, the station began without the opposition received in other places. This peaceful relationship was broken by a strange incident that occurred in 1893. Rev. Charles Killie was attacked by two Chinese who threatened to kill him if one hundred ounces of silver were not paid by the next morning. Killie managed to get away but the incident provoked a riot founded on stories circulated by the two men that the foreigners had stolen lost children. The mission premises were attacked and searched, and several employees dragged off to the *yamen* and beaten. When the extortion attempt came to light the authorities acted with vigor to apprehend the villains and punish them in accordance with Chinese law. To the horror of the missionaries, who had appealed for mercy, each was given one thousand blows and required to go to the mission premises and perform the humiliating "kow-tow" ceremony of knocking their heads on the ground. At the suggestion of intermediaries the missionaries gave the two men, who were in a desperate condition, enough food to last awhile. The official issued a proclamation attesting to the treaty obligations to respect the residence of the foreigners. The declaration was framed in glass and hung at the gate of the mission compound.

For the missionaries the significance of the event was that it was settled with dispatch by Chinese authorities without any appeal to the American consul. Missionary comment compared the "reckless disregard of treaty obligations" on the part of American authorities regarding Chinese laborers in the United States with "this edict issued in an interior district of Shantung" that served as "a conspicuous testimony for the political and diplomatic honor of the Chinese government."[79]

Church services began in a small carpenter shop. Itineration by missionaries, lay evangelists and Bible women in the surrounding villages brought in a large harvest. By the year 1898, 280 communicants had been baptized.

Medical work began soon after the station was opened by Dr. Charles Johnson for the men and Dr. Anna Larson for the women. They worked out of a small dispensary and visited patients in their homes. In 1893, over four thousand men and women were treated. Anna Larson died on Christmas Day, 1897. Her death made a deep impression on the citizens of Linyi and the gentry of the city sent immense wreaths of artificial flowers to lay on her casket.

Jining (Tsining or Chiningchow)

The first attempts to enter the city on the southern border of Shandong failed when Dr. Stephen Hunter and Rev. William Lane were driven out of the city by a mob in 1892.[80] Later that year provincial authorities gave permission for the purchase of land and a second attempt was made. This time they were successful. Spacious buildings on a conveniently located plot of land were purchased from a rich man who had lost his wealth in the Taiping Rebellion. Rev. and Mrs. J. H. Laughlin were transferred from Weixian to begin the work.[81] They were soon joined by Dr. and Mrs. Isaac L. Van Schoick, Rev. and Mrs. William Lane and Mr. Lane's mother, Mary Lane, who wrote of their journey and entrance into the city:

Noah's dove was not more rejoiced to find a resting place for the sole of her foot, than were the weary missionaries who arrive at Chiningchow, 19 October 1892. A journey of 500 miles and twenty days on the road, first on Chinese junk, then in ox-carts, lastly by *shenza*. . . . predisposes one to appreciate home comforts. We removed the bells from our mules, and under cover of darkness entered the gate of the city and silently wended our way along the street, no one the wiser, until we arrived at the mission compound.[82]

They were spared the hostile crowds but the people of the city, never having seen foreigners before, thronged into the compound and for days watched the strangers unload their belongings and set up housekeeping. Mrs. Lane remarked that having a mother-in-law in the party was a distinct advantage:

Old women hobble about to get a glimpse of me, remarking of Mrs. Wm. Lane, "Oh, she is all right, she has her mother-in-law with her." . . . At last, a refuge has been found for that much-reviled class. In far off China, they will find appreciation and a work to do. Come on, mothers-in-law![83]

Learning from earlier disasters the missionaries made a distinct effort to court the officials. They were invited to a magic lantern show. The chief official responded by inviting one of the ladies to show the slides to the women of his household. The gate of the compound was opened and by degrees small groups of women and children entered to observe the swing set up in the playground. A Sunday School became a focal point for contact with the Chinese mothers.

The medical work was carried on by Drs. Van Schoick, Henrietta Donaldson and Mary Hill. After five years of sacrificial service, Dr. Van Schoick returned with his wife to America with a fatal illness caused by exposure to some disease.

Itineration throughout the area brought results. Laughlin and Lane began classes for inquirers and these formed the nucleus of the future church. In the first year thirteen were baptized. It would be the first-fruits of a great harvest. Lane wrote of the prospects before them:

This field to the west of the canal and within Shantung consists of about 15 counties, and probably has a population of 5,000,000. To be Christ's apostle to this vast region and its multitude, is certainly calculated to rouse any latent powers there is in one. With such a work life is tremendously worth living![84]

The Nevius Methods

In 1880, the Rev. John L. Nevius began work at a new country field some three hundred miles inland from Yantai. Remembering the breakthrough that had been achieved at San Poh years before, he began the development of a new plan for starting country churches. He wrote to the home board: "I am trying to make the work independent and self-supporting from the first."[85] It was a revolutionary idea. The traditional method had been to build a church with mission funds and then send in a salaried Chinese "helper" to be the pastor who worked under close missionary supervision. In time it was hoped that the subsidies could be reduced and the churches would become self-supporting. But this had not happened. Once the subsidies were begun it became very difficult to wean the church off foreign aid.

Nevius's plan was different. The Christians would be asked to provide their own place of worship — generally a large room in a private home. Worship was led by a seasoned Christian who lived in the village. These leaders would be given training in Bible classes held in a central place. Leaders who attended the Bible classes would be provided food and lodging while in training but no other financial aid. Nevius visited his churches twice a year. He employed several helpers who operated somewhat as "circuit riders" but were not pastors of local churches.

Nevius wrote that his principles were the results of years of experience and bitter failures. Christianity should disturb the cultural patterns of its adherents as little as possible. To take a new believer out of his calling, whether he was a farmer or a shopkeeper, and pay him to do the work of witnessing to Christ often did more harm than good. The use of foreign funds made it appear that Christianity was a foreign religion under the control of foreign agents.

As the years went by, Nevius felt that his plan was working. The number of meeting places increased to over sixty. One thousand adults were baptized in the first seven years the plan was in operation. In 1885 Dr. Nevius published several articles in the *Chinese Recorder* outlining his methods. Presbyterian missionaries newly arrived in Korea saw the articles and were much impressed. At the invitation of the Korea missionaries, Dr. and Mrs. Nevius visited Seoul in June 1890 and shared with the new missionaries his methodology. The "Nevius Methods" became the guiding principles for both the northern and southern Presbyterian Mission in Korea for the next fifty years.

But in China Nevius was only partly successful. Calvin Mateer was adamantly opposed to his plan. Some of his methodology was incorporated in the procedures of the Shandong Mission. But the key element that called for the use of unpaid Christians rather than salaried agents was too radical a change.

As Nevius grew older he could not keep up with the strenuous country itineration. He hoped that younger missionaries would carry this on but this did not happen. So the Nevius "experiment" came to an end after ten years. Three years after the historic visit to Korea, he died at his home in Yantai and was buried in the missionary cemetery overlooking the Yellow Sea. He was sixty-four years old.[86]

The South China Mission

The growth of the church in Guangdong Province was slower than in the regions further north. The humiliation the people of Canton had experienced during the opium wars was not quickly forgotten. The war with France over Indochina in 1884 was another affront to China's dignity and selfhood.

The treatment of Chinese in America has been mentioned. Most of these immigrants came from the Canton delta, and this created enormous problems for the South China Mission:

> It is impossible to appreciate the difficulties of the work in the Canton Province, and to make due allowance for any elements of discouragement in the results, without taking into consideration the influence of the Chinese Exclusion Bill passed by the United States Congress, and the bitterness of feeling which it has created in all official circles.[87]

In 1886 the Canton Mission asked the General Assembly of the PCUSA to protest the passage of the exclusion bills which violated treaty obligations. The statement warned that the honor of Christianity was at stake and grave consequences to the China mission would result if the church at home was silent.[88] In 1893 Dr. Speer and a delegation representing seven mission boards went to Washington to advocate the repeal of the "obnoxious" laws against Chinese. But all this had little effect. It was ironic that in those areas of China that had a long acquaintance with the Christian West, Christian missions would have the hardest time. Where we were least known, in the interior of Shantung, the gospel message had the best chance to be heard.

Canton

Denied access to the interior by circumstances beyond their control, the Canton missionaries concentrated on the great city at the mouth of the Pearl River. Membership growth was slow but progress was made. Six churches were organized and by 1895 these had a combined membership of 746.[89] The first pastors were all missionaries although they undoubtedly had unordained Chinese assistants.

It was not until 1884 (twenty-two years after the first church was organized) that Canton Presbytery ordained its first three ministers, who were installed as pastors and added to the roll of Presbytery. But the *Annual Reports* for 1893–1895 again list missionaries in charge of all city churches. One wonders what happened. Would membership growth have been faster if transfers to native clergy had taken place sooner?

The educational work was more successful. The Canton Mission developed an extensive network of day schools, boarding schools and training schools for Christian workers. The 1893 *Annual Report* lists 40 such schools with a total enrollment of 1,485 students under Christian instruction. The Boys' School, with an enrollment of 100 in 1893, provided Christian education for the sons of native Christians. The advanced department provided training for mission workers in the chapels and schools.

The Canton Girls' Seminary was under the care of Misses Electa Butler, Harriette Lewis and six native teachers. One hundred and ninety were enrolled in

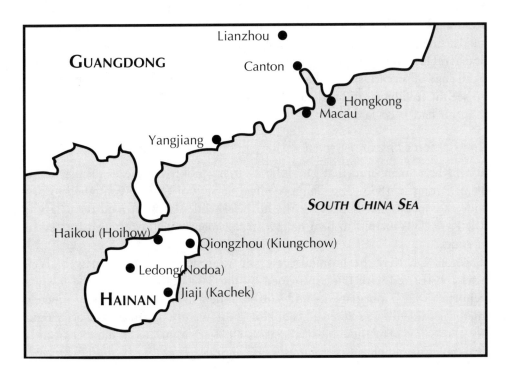

South China and Hainan 1900

1894. The school concentrated on training teachers and Bible women but also received any "respectable woman who desires to learn Bible truth" and many of these were non-Christians. The Bible, Shorter Catechism, church history and music made up the curriculum. Activities included a missionary society (for support of Bible women in the country) and the Dorcas Society (sewing projects for the poor and needy).[90] The following two institutions played significant roles in the development of the Christian mission in South China:

A Christian College for Canton

In 1884 the Canton Mission presented to the BFM a proposal for the establishment of a Christian college at Canton with a carefully worded rationale. Such an institution would service an area as large as France and embracing a population of 30 to 40 million. There was a growing demand for a knowledge of English and Western science. The college would provide an educated ministry and qualified teachers for the church. Presbyterians were in the best position to undertake such a project — the Southern Methodists were starting a college in Shanghai and the Northern Methodists one in Fuzhou.[91]

The BFM gave conditional approval to the proposal and Dr. Happer, in the United States at the time, began the solicitation of funds. Within two years he had raised $100,000. In 1886 a board of trustees was organized and Happer was elected president. He returned to Canton the next year and began the implementation of the plan by beginning a school in rented quarters for the teaching of English and science. But in the next two years little progress was made. Happer became discouraged and his declining health delayed the plans further. He resigned as president, returned to the United States and died in 1894 at the age of seventy-six. He had served in China forty-five years. He did not live to see the fulfillment of his dream but the foundations for a Christian college in Canton had been laid.[92]

The Canton Christian Hospital

It will be remembered that Dr. John G. Kerr took over the medical work of Peter Parker in 1855. The China Medical Society of Canton continued to provide the operational budget for the hospital while the BFM paid the salary of Dr. Kerr. This proved to be a happy arrangement which continued for several decades.

Under Dr. Kerr the hospital grew and prospered. In 1867 a new building was constructed with funds provided by the Society. In that year the hospital reported 18,477 out-patients and 400 in-patients. In 1880 a class of nineteen medical students was received. Four of these were women, a rare occurrence for those days. For these medical classes Dr. Kerr translated a number of medical texts including a six-volume work entitled *The Theory and Practice of Medicine*.

Dr. Mary Niles arrived in 1883 and took over the female wards. Her activities are described in the 1890 *Annual Report*:

> She has performed 683 surgical operations and 164 patients have been visited in their homes, 275 calls having been made. She has thus reached many firesides of the poor, and also of the wealthy and influential [including the wife of the Provincial Governor], always carrying the Gospel message.[93]

In 1885 Dr. John Swan joined the Canton Mission and for the next fifteen years these three made up the professional staff with Chinese assistants who were trained in the medical classes.

In 1889 the hospital reported the following statistics:

	Males	Females	Totals
Out-patients	13,758	3,415	17,173
In-patients	945	379	1,324
Operations	1,543	616	2,159
Total patients treated			40,300[94]

The hospital was more than a place for the healing of bodies. Mrs. Kerr began a school that taught patients a profitable vocation that they could use when discharged. The Christian witness is described in the report for 1892:

The patients are gathered into classes on Sunday mornings, and religious instruction is given by the physicians and members of the church. ...Christian books are kept in the wards for those who can read.... Mr. Wang, the blind colporteur, has gone daily from ward to ward instructing the patients.[95]

In the beginning the hospital admitted all who came free of charge. Later, patients were required to pay a small fee.

Lianzhou (Lien Chow)

As noted above, the Canton Mission had been slow in starting new stations in the interior. Prodding came from the BFM to push more aggressively into the countryside: The Canton Mission should "radiate more widely from the center in which they had been placed for more than forty years."[96] In 1883 Rev. J. C. Thomson, M.D., and Rev. Wellington White succeeded in renting property at Lianzhou, two hundred miles up the West River. The strategic importance of the city is described in this report:

Three rivers meet at or near Lien Chow which drain fertile and populous valleys. Within a radius of thirty miles there must be nearly one thousand villages, containing a population of several hundred thousand people. To the west it is only two days journey into the borders of Kwangsi [Guangxi] province.... To the north it is only one day's journey into the great province of Hunan with its nineteen millions of people and not a single resident missionary.[97]

Violent anti-foreign outbursts occurred in 1885, forcing the missionaries to close the dispensary and withdraw, but the church continued under the leadership of its loyal pastor. Two years later the situation improved and the missionaries returned.

Miss Johnson started a school and Dr. Machle opened a dispensary. Dr. Eleanor Chesnut took over the medical work for women. The next year 6,720 patients were treated. Evangelistic work was begun among the Ius and Hakka tribes in the nearby mountains and a second church was started. In 1894 the two churches reported a membership of 110.

This incident in a chapel started across the border in Hunan illustrates both the opposition and the faithfulness:

Our religious service was invaded one Sabbath morning by a mob of twenty men, led by the son of the official of the town. Our native helper was seized and beaten, and taken off to be imprisoned. He effected his escape, however, while on his way to prison. The Christians re-assembled, and a native brother reopened the service. They were again attacked, and their leader beaten and taken to prison, where he received two hundred blows with the bamboo, but was immovable in his loyalty to the Christian faith, and flatly refused to worship the idols into whose presence he was

brought. A subsequent appeal to the authorities secured promise of protection, whereupon seven persons requested baptism, and, after examination,
five of them were received.[98]

A good beginning had been made but the welfare and safety of the believers
and missionaries remained precarious.

Yangjiang (Yeung Kong)

In 1886 the Rev. J. C. Thomson, M.D. opened, a clinic at Yangjiang, a city
250 miles southwest of Canton near the coast. Placards were posted against
the missionaries and some opposition was shown but no violence encountered.
The medical aid that Dr. Thomson was able to give during a cholera epidemic
led to a more friendly reception on the part of the gentry. Five converts were
baptized in 1889, which was the beginning of the church in this area. A reading
room was opened where those passing by could drop in, look over the Christian
literature and enjoy a cup of tea. In 1890 the number of out-patients treated
was 16,548.[99]

In 1893 the Thomsons were joined by two brothers, Rev. Andrew Beattie
and David Beattie, M.D., their two wives and two Chinese pastors. The enlarged missionary team engaged in evangelistic work, day schools and visitation
among the women.

The next year a deadly plague swept through the province leaving tens of
thousands dead. The disaster was blamed on the presence of foreigners and
riots broke out. A violent mob broke into the Beattie residences and wrecked
the two homes. The two families with their children took refuge in the *Yamen*,
where they were protected. The station was closed but not for long.[100]

Hainan Island Mission

The account of how work began on the island of Hainan is one of the most
unusual stories in the annals of China missions. In 1869 a sea captain from
Denmark described as a red-bearded giant of a man came to China and entered
the employ of the Canton Customs Service. As captain of a steam launch his
task was to do battle against the increasing number of pirates and smugglers.
It was a task made more difficult by the periodic encounters with the typhoons
that laced the South China Sea.

His name was Carl C. Jeremiassen, and while in the employ of the Customs
Service he "came in contact with a vital Christianity" that transformed his life.
Desiring to change his career from being "a seeker of criminals for punishment
to a seeker of souls for salvation," he began work on Formosa as an independent missionary.[101] Before long he decided that he needed some medical training
if he was to succeed in his new calling. He made the acquaintance of Dr. Kerr
and served an apprenticeship in the Canton hospital. Then, singlehandedly, he

began work on Hainan, the tropical island separated from the extreme tip of southern China by a scant twelve-mile channel.

Hainan Island is volcanic in origin and approximately 150 miles long and 115 miles wide. In the first century A.D., the island was conquered by the Chinese, who pushed the Tai and Laos aboriginal tribes back into the mountains. Later the Hakkas, with their distinctive culture and language, migrated from the mainland. The population of the island in the mid-nineteenth century was between 1 and 1.5 million people. No Protestant mission work had been started there prior to the arrival of Jeremiassen.

Ledong (Nodoa)

In 1881 the pirate chaser turned missionary settled in Haikou (Hoihow) and began long, extensive treks into the interior dispensing medicine and gospel truths. He traveled with a faithful servant who was dumb and a colporteur provided by the British and Foreign Bible Society. In the course of three years a small group of converts had been gathered at the inland town of Ledong. As Jeremiassen was not an ordained minister, he appealed to the Presbyterian Mission in Canton to send someone to instruct and baptize the new converts. Rev. H. V. Noyes came to Ledong in 1884, examined twenty-five inquirers and baptized nine of them, who formed the nucleus of the church. Jeremiassen appealed to the Presbyterian Mission to continue the good work that had been begun. In 1885 Dr. Henry M. McCandliss and the Rev. and Mrs. Frank P. Gilman were appointed by the BFM to serve on the island. In this same year Jeremiassen became a member of the Presbyterian Mission. In 1888 Dr. McCandliss married Olivia Kerr, the daughter of Dr. Kerr, and Jeremiassen married Jeanne Sutter from Switzerland. These three couples formed the pioneer band of missionaries on the island.

During the "Hakka Rebellion" in 1886–1887, General Fang was dispatched by the Viceroy of Guangdong to put down the insurrection. Several thousand of his men were stationed at Ledong. During the hot summer months an epidemic of malaria broke out and many of the troops died. Jeremiassen began to treat the sick men with quinine. All under his care recovered and the grateful general asked how he could repay his benefactor. Jeremiassen proposed that a plot of land and a suitable building be given where the sick could be cared for. General Fang responded enthusiastically — land was given and a thatched-roof building raised. This became the site for the mission compound with its dispensary, manse and chapel.

Haikou

The McCandliss and Gilman families moved to the treaty port of Haikou but had difficulty buying property. For several years they used the ancestral hall of the Tang family until a plot of land on the waterfront was purchased.

Work on the island proceeded along the lines followed on the mainland but there were some differences. Note the multicultured Christian congregation that formed the church in Ledong:

> Sunday congregations vary from thirty to seventy.... Regular Sunday evening services are held in the street of the market. These are curious meetings... Singing and a large, well-illuminated picture of some Bible subject draw the crowd. Hakka, Mandarin, Limko, Hainanese or Cantonese are used, according to the crowd that gathers.... There are twenty-two professed Christians at Nodoa.[102]

Because of the different tribal languages a Mission Press was established at Ledong where scriptures and tracts were printed in the Hainanese Romanized colloquial dialect.

Mr. and Mrs. Jeremiassen became something of a legend on the island as they traveled on long trips into the mountains. Their annual report for 1894 tells of one such trip:

> The first four months of the year were for the most part spent among the aboriginal tribes.... We stayed among the Tahan hills for about a fortnight, having daily services and healing the sick.... From there a good half day's journey brought us to Fanja which is built up in the valley just under the head of the Five-finger mountain range. We made Fanja our headquarters for a fortnight while we made daily visits to the numerous villages hidden away among the mountain glens where we found the people very much interested in what we had to tell them about God and his wonderful dealings with men.[103]

Jeremiassen was an individualist and worked best independently. In 1898 he ended his relationship with the Presbyterian Mission in order to have greater freedom to work in his own way. In 1901 he suffered an attack of influenza. Mrs. Jeremiassen was finally able to persuade him to board a ship in order to seek medical care in Haikou but it was too late. He died at sea at the age of fifty-four.

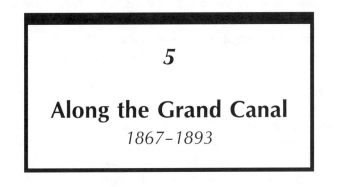

5

Along the Grand Canal
1867–1893

The Missionary Calling of the Southern Church

It is now necessary to return to the year 1861 and pick up the story of the initiation of a China mission by the Presbyterians in the South.[1] How would brothers who had so recently been engaged in a terrible armed conflict relate to each other? Would problems emerge between two competing American Presbyterian missions in China? Or would the southerners bring to China additional resources for witness and service?

The new mission enterprise would also be significant for American Presbyterians. Here would be opportunities for cooperation in a land where the old animosities could be forgotten. The first faltering steps toward participation in joint mission could be taken. The healing process could begin. Especially for the South, the China mission would provide a chance to end the isolation the war and slavery had brought and challenge the church to look beyond the tragic situation at home and to reach out to the world.

When the first General Assembly of the southern church met in Augusta, Georgia, in early December 1861 it took two actions that would have a lasting effect on its overseas mission program. First, it elected John Leighton Wilson the Secretary for Foreign Missions. It was an inspired decision. Wilson had served for nineteen years as a missionary of the ABCFM in Western Africa and eight years as a secretary of the Presbyterian Board in New York. When hostilities became imminent he resigned this position and returned to his native state of South Carolina. When urged to stay by colleagues in the North, he wrote: "My mind is made up. I will go and suffer with my people."[2]

The second action of the Assembly was the adoption of an extraordinary statement expressing its resolve to undertake a mission to the world in spite of the wartime conditions at home:

Finally, the General Assembly desires distinctly and deliberately to inscribe on our church's banner as she now first unfurls it to the world, in immediate connection with the Headship of her Lord, His last command: "Go ye into all the world and preach the gospel to every creature," regarding this as the great end of her organization, and obedience to it as the indispensable condition of her Lord's promised presence."[3]

What motivated this ringing call to foreign missions? Such a concern may seem strange in view of the Assembly's stance in defense of slavery. Was the concern for evangelism abroad a cover-up for attitudes at home? Prior to 1861 Presbyterians in the South had shown only limited interest in world missions.

The statement came from the "heart and mind of John Leighton Wilson."[4] And Wilson's opposition to slavery was well known. He was viewed with suspicion by some of his contemporaries in the South because he had served under the Boston-based ABCFM and with the BFM in New York, both of which had well-known abolitionist sympathies. During his years of service in Africa he had seen the ravages of the slave trade and had supported efforts to end the infamous traffic.[5] He and his wife had inherited slaves but early in his missionary career had freed them all.[6]

The theology and structure of the missionary enterprise in the South were understandably similar to that of the New York Board. But in one respect a change was attempted. The term "executive committee" was deliberately chosen, rather than "board," due to the influence of Rev. James Henley Thornwell whose views dominated the Assembly. Thornwell's point was that the boards had become too large and too independent of the Assembly. The BFM numbered over one hundred members. The executive committee was to be a "mere instrumentality" of the Assembly and not an agency with independent authority.[7] However, as the years progressed, the difference between board and executive committee would be increasingly difficult to discern.

Several of Wilson's policies, as noted by his biographer, were ahead of his times and had an impact on mission strategy in China. Wilson believed that the native church should be independent of European or American control. He also supported the union of Presbyterian bodies working in the same area.[8]

During the war years the Executive Committee limited its work to the Indian nations in Oklahoma that had signed treaties with the Confederacy. Dr. Wilson served as secretary for both the Foreign and Domestic mission committees. The Committee had its offices in Columbia, which was near Wilson's home.[9]

In 1866, one year after the surrender at Appomattox, the Executive Committee received a letter from Elias B. Inslee offering his services for a China mission. The times were anything but ripe for a major new commitment. On the home front there was

an empty treasury...dismantled churches and manses...men of wealth and substance suddenly reduced to poverty...little visible means of supporting a home ministry...the carpet-bag system, under which the country groaned for years.[10]

Nevertheless, the Committee published Inslee's letter in the church paper and an appeal was made for $500 for the new cause. A new era in the foreign mission enterprise was about to begin.

The Founder

What kind of man was Elias B. Inslee? In the records he appears as a shadowy, enigmatic figure about which not much is known.[11] One thing is certain: He was not the typical "Southern Presbyterian." He was born of Scottish ancestors in New Jersey in 1822 and moved to Alabama as a young man, where he acquired a trade as carpenter and builder. Believing he was called to the ministry, he went to Scotland and entered the theological seminary of the Free Church. He married a Scottish highland lass, Euphemia Ross, returned to the United States, was ordained by the Presbytery of Mississippi and soon thereafter was appointed a missionary to China by the BFM. The Inslees arrived in Shanghai on Christmas Day, 1856, and were assigned to Ningbo.

Inslee's missionary service in China was spirited and stormy. He and his family lived simply in a Chinese house, identified with the people and began to speak the Ningbo dialect fluently. An infant son died of smallpox. He and his wife started a school. But country itineration was the activity in which he excelled. He told of one three-month trip:

> We distributed 2,200 books in 22 cities...some of which were not before visited by missionaries or other foreigners....The people generally were open and ready to receive us....The proper way to travel in China is to walk....We must go among the people if we would teach.[12]

For reasons unknown, Inslee felt alienated from his fellow missionaries and wanted to work independently. He declined to join the Ningbo Presbytery and resented mission rules that required an accounting of funds contributed by friends in America. In 1861 the Board terminated his relationship and Inslee returned to the United States. Inslee felt he had been fired because of his southern sympathies. Dr. Bear has examined the records carefully and concluded that this was almost certainly not the case. Inslee, an able and dedicated missionary in many respects, was recalled because of personality clashes with fellow missionaries and his desire to operate independently.[13]

For the next few years, little is known of Inslee's whereabouts. In 1864 he returned to China as an independent missionary supported by friends in Canada. Defrauded by the shipping company of his passage money, he ran out of funds and for a time he was employed by the London Missionary Society. He wrote of baptizing sixteen converts and starting a girls' school. Euphemia died in 1866 at the age of twenty-six, "faithful to the last." She left him with "four motherless children," making his return home necessary. It was under these circumstances that he wrote to the Executive Committee offering his services as one who was "as desolate as the desolated South."[14]

Inslee's difficulties in China must have been known to the Executive Committee as Wilson was probably still with the New York Board when Inslee was dismissed. But references were favorable and Inslee made a good impression when he met with the Committee. He was appointed a missionary to China and $400 appropriated as an outfit allowance. A supplemental $200 was approved "for a lady in case one went with him." The lady in question was Eugenia Young, who said yes to Inslee and the China venture with the wedding taking place in the First Presbyterian Church of New Orleans. The Inslees sailed from New York in June 1867 for "Aspinwall" (Colon) where they took a "queer little train and crossed the Isthmus of Panama." A second steamer took them to San Francisco, and from hence to Nagasaki and Shanghai.[15]

Hangzhou

Inslee chose Hangzhou as the place to begin. When the Inslee family arrived, missionaries of the Church Missionary Society, American Baptists and Northern Presbyterians were at work in the city. Inslee's relationship with the Northern Presbyterians was cordial but he made it clear he intended to start a new work under new auspices. The sign posted over the property read "American Southern Church."

Inslee had visited the city with John L. Nevius and was familiar with the local scene. He found he could get along with the Ningbo dialect and rented property for a residence, a street chapel and a girls' school. Years later Mrs. Inslee described their home life in Hangzhou:

> We had neither doors nor windows, so we had to protect ourselves from the November wind by hanging up sheets. Nevertheless, we were very happy, and Mr. Inslee worked night and day to put in partitions, windows and doors....As a protection against a vandal horde of rats...Mr. Inslee made me a safe for food of bamboo split in halves, which was quite fine in its resemblance to a pipe organ....Occasional little tea parties among themselves, and games of wiley bright and hide the switch in the little court, with mamma as their leader, were about all [the children's] pleasures.[16]

The work began along the lines previously established by the Northern Presbyterians in Ningbo. Mr. Inslee started a girls' boarding school early in 1868 with Mrs. Inslee teaching music and arithmetic. Inslee described the school program and some of its problems relating to footbinding and marriage:

> We try to get them between the ages of seven and twelve. We shall remove the bandages from their feet as soon as practicable. They cannot study with their feet in such terrible pain....The feet, though crippled, can be restored even when fifteen years old....Articles are drawn up that they are not to be forced into marriage relations by parents even after graduat-

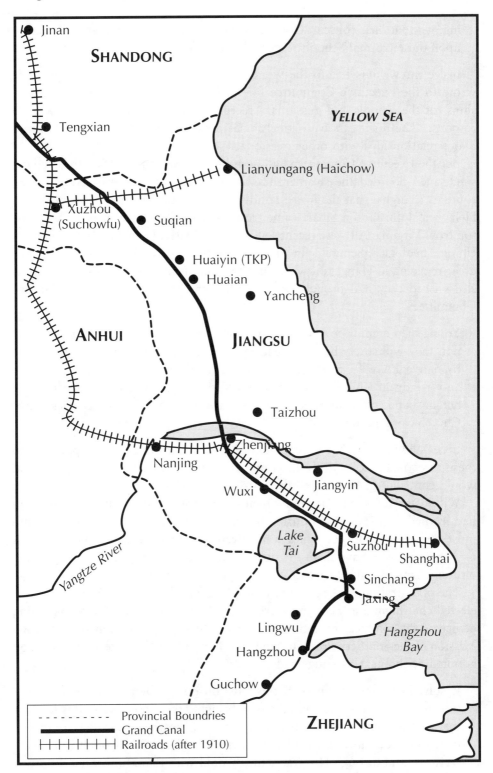

Southern Presbyterian Missions 1867–1937

ing, without their consent. Our future success in China will mainly depend upon these Normal Schools, especially those for girls.[17]

Inslee threw himself into the work with high ambitions for the future. He wrote to the Executive Committee for medicines, a self-inking press, scholarships for the schools and missionary recruits. For seven months there was no response. The first years were lonely ones for the Inslee family as little is said about relationships with other missionaries.

But the Executive Committee had been busy. In September 1868 three young single men boarded the steamer *Alaska* in New York and traveled the same route to Shanghai that the Inslee family had taken the previous year. Benjamin Helm and John Linton Stuart came from Kentucky, and Matthew Hale Houston from Virginia. All were recent seminary graduates: Helm and Houston from Union Theological Seminary in Virginia and Stuart from Princeton. There was great rejoicing in Hangzhou when these appointments were announced but Inslee wished they had brought wives with them. His advice to the Executive Committee:

> Young men coming to China should by all means be married. If they are not, they will surely be unsettled, unsatisfied, and always held in distrust by natives. A wife, to the Chinese mind, is always a sign of good faith, and a lady in China with a missionary spirit can be quite as useful as her husband, often more so.... Ladies are the cheapest missionaries the Church can send out.[18]

Inslee's advice may have been sound, but he was wrong in its application to these three men. Collectively they, and the wives they would bring to China, would contribute 146 years to the mission enterprise.

Within several weeks the young men were settled in their quarters. Houston had learned to prepare food during his years in the Confederate Army and did most of the cooking. Few rules were given for language study and each was on his own. Inslee gave them the questionable advice to avoid the study of the written characters and concentrate on speaking the vernacular.

The organization of the mission took place on 5 December 1868. Inslee was elected chairman, and Houston secretary. A letter from Dr. Wilson containing advice on the conduct of meetings was read. The society was named the "China Mission of the Southern Presbyterian Church in the United States." A resolution adopted at the next meeting read:

> Resolved that the members of this Mission do hereby record their gratitude to God for His great goodness in bringing them together in this land, that they may make known his salvation to the heathen. They declare that their only hope in this work is the grace by which God worketh in His servants; and through His grace, they would with thankful hearts, devote themselves and all that is theirs to do the work to which the Lord has called them.[19]

Under the tutelage of Inslee the three young missionaries plunged into the work with great enthusiasm. Inslee preached daily in the chapel but with scant results. He baptized one family in 1869 but later had serious doubts as to their motives and other applications were deferred. He also began the dispensing of medicines, which contributed to their general favorable reception by the people. The girls' school progressed with Mrs. Inslee giving it much of her time. A boys' school was begun with Houston in charge. An acre of land was purchased on the side of a hill with a commanding view of the Qiantang (Chientang) River and West Lake.

Low Ebb

But more was attempted than could be carried out. Language misunderstandings confused everything. There was never enough money and transmitting what there was from South Carolina was unpredictable. Health breakdowns followed due to climate and living conditions. To complicate things further, Inslee insisted they open a new mission station.

In July 1869 Inslee accompanied Helm and Stuart 150 miles up the Qiantang River to Guchow, the proposed location for the new work. But no one would rent them property. The best they could get was the second floor of a small building, which was reached by means of a ladder. On the first floor was a restaurant and an opium den. After weeks in the nearly unbearable heat of summer, more comfortable quarters were found. Helm's health broke down and he moved back to Hangzhou to help with the school, leaving Stuart alone. Stuart wrote of his intense loneliness. There were no visible results from his preaching. The letter concluded:

> I begin to feel very much downcast with reference to preaching under such circumstances, but last Sunday my neighbors came in and behaved with great propriety. I trust the Lord to give me strength to stand firm, and preach his word with all boldness, relying on his almighty power and grace. But I am more and more convinced of the wisdom and goodness of our Lord when he gave us his example of sending forth his disciples "two by two."[20]

In spite of heroic efforts, Guchow was finally abandoned because of the lack of response, the miserable living conditions, insufficient missionary personnel and problems of health. The destiny of the mission would lie on Hangzhou's other waterway that led to the north — the Grand Canal.

These years were a struggle for the survival of the mission. There were delays in sending funds from Columbia. Controversy broke out in the church papers at home over the nonsupport of the China missionaries and Dr. Wilson was blamed.[21] The situation improved when an arrangement was worked out with Olyphant and Co. for the transmission of funds. Thomas and Eliza Converse arrived in 1868 but lasted only a year because of a health breakdown. Anti-foreignism was on the rise and the *Annual Report* for the year 1870 told the sad story:

> This mission…has been sorely afflicted during the year. First, in the re-duction of their working force, second, in repeated attacks of sickness… and third, in the unsettled conditions of the country — threatening at times the interruption of all missionary work.[22]

Early in 1870 Inslee's health began to fail. The diagnosis was "dropsy" and a change to a cooler climate was prescribed. But a summer in Yantai brought no improvement. Mrs. Inslee, pregnant at the time, described the trip from Hangzhou to Shanghai with her sick husband to catch the steamer home:

> My last babies, twins, were born on a Chinese boat. We expected to make the trip in two and one-half days, but a storm kept us five days on the way. The bamboo roof leaked so badly that the only dry place on my bed was under my back. I was carried on a litter from the boat through the streets of Shanghai in broad day light.[23]

Inslee never recovered and died in Amite County, Mississippi in April 1871 at the age of forty-eight. His last words: "I leave my wife and children to God and to the Church." The Executive Committee and the church responded by raising the sum of $6,500 for their support.[24]

Inslee is characterized by his colleagues as a man of "rough and rugged char-acter," which is illustrated in an incident that took place while he was traveling on a small coastal ship:

> A pirate ship bore down upon them. Everyone was alarmed. Other mis-sionaries went down below deck to pray but Mr. Inslee had an old cannon rolled out, and he himself fired it with such an effective blast that the pirates turned and fled. The owners of the ship, Olyphant and Co, afterwards gave him a free pass on any of their ships anywhere at any time.[25]

His years with the Southern Presbyterian China Mission (SPM) were few but his contribution was substantial: the fortuitous selection of Hangzhou as the starting point, identification with the life-styles of the people and emphasis on both evangelism and education. Most important was his training of three young men on whom, humanly speaking, the future of the enterprise would depend.

Recovery and Advance

From low ebb in 1871 the tide began to turn. At last some new reinforcements arrived. Although financial problems were ever present, the home church began to recover from the destitution of the Civil War. Missionary health improved with more permanent housing. Fluency in the language made communication more effective. And most important, some results began to appear.

During the three years between 1871 and 1874, nine new missionaries arrived. In 1871, Miss Evelyn Withrow, engaged to be married to Matthew Houston, made the trans-Pacific crossing with a company of Northern Presbyterians. Houston met her in Japan where the wedding took place. In 1872 Rev. Hampden C. DuBose and his bride, Pauline McAlpine, arrived with Mrs. Anna Randolph. In 1873 Rev. John Davis, Mr. George Painter and Miss Anna Safford were appointed. In 1874 Stuart, who had gone home in 1873 for health reasons, returned with his bride, Mary Horton.

Mary Horton and Linton Stuart's courtship is worth recounting. Mary was a southern belle from Mobile, Alabama. At the age of twenty-two she was engaged to be married to a lieutenant of the Confederate navy. But these plans were shattered when her fiancé was killed in the battle of Mobile Bay. Mary was brokenhearted and lost interest in life and for a while her family was in despair about her health. Then, quite suddenly, she announced to her parents that she was volunteering for service in the newly begun mission to China. Family and friends were shocked and tried to talk her out of the wild idea. But Mary was adamant and wrote to the Executive Secretary, Leighton Wilson, who responded that they were not appointing single women to China because life there was too harsh and dangerous. However, he added, it just so happened that John Linton Stuart, a single missionary to China, was on furlough and would be at the meeting of the General Assembly to be held in Columbus, Georgia. He would like for her to meet him.

Mary attended the Assembly and was introduced to Linton by the board secretary. When the Assembly was over Linton followed Mary back to Mobile, where he was invited to preach at Mary's church. A whirlwind courtship followed and before the family realized it, Mary and he had made their decisions on love matters and missionary matters. The wedding took place at the Government Street Presbyterian Church and within a few months the newly-weds were on a slow boat to China.[26]

As reinforcements arrived, construction began on schools, residences and a chapel. But a setback came when the authorities wanted back the fine plot of land that had been purchased on the hillside overlooking the river. The ubiquitous *feng sui* had been disturbed by the foreigners' presence. A plot of land in the northern part of the city and funds to rebuild were offered in return. The swap was in the best interests of friendly relations but it meant starting over again. There was another drawback. The land was poorly drained and steamy hot in summer. Missionaries began to experience malaria chills and fever, the cause of which was then unknown. They tried everything. The planting of sunflowers was thought to be of help. More important was curtailing the use of manure, better drainage and the practice of taking refuge in the nearby hills during the heat of summer.

The work developed along the lines that had been initiated by the Northern Presbyterians.

Language and literature. Nothing much could be accomplished until a certain proficiency in language was gained. In the words of an early missionary, this was a herculean task:

> Learning Chinese is Work for Men with Bodies of Brass, Lungs of Steel, Heads of Oak, Hands of Spring Steel, Eye of Eagles, Lives of Methuselah![27]

As language skills increased, the preparation of Christian literature became possible. Miss Safford completed a child's catechism called "Peep of Day." Helm translated "Jesus Loves Me," which became the most popular hymn for Chinese children ever written. Painter worked on a biblical geography.

The Chinese guest room. Christian witness began in the missionary home. Dr. P. Frank Price has described the importance of receiving guests in conformity with Chinese etiquette:

> One of the first requisites of each missionary home was...a Chinese guest room. This was adorned with appropriate scrolls on the walls and had the proper arrangement of furniture, which consists of a large table and two chairs at the end opposite the door.... The guest on entering must take the "lowest seat," which is the chair nearest to him on his left, and when the host enters the guest must show great reluctance in going forward...until the host by insistent perseverance persuades him to take the first seat of honor at the left of the table facing the door.... With patience must the host or hostess answer over and over the same questions, "How far is it to America?" "How old are you?..." And being a missionary he must watch for an opening in which to state intelligently the object of his coming to China.[28]

Work among women. All the ladies of the station engaged in the visitation of women. Almost always they were politely received. During one year Mrs. Du-Bose visited over one hundred homes — in many of which a number of women had gathered to meet their newly arrived foreign neighbors. By the year 1884 Hangzhou Station had in its employ five "Bible women" who accompanied the missionary ladies on their visits.[29]

Street chapel preaching. Street chapels were open several hours during the day. Passersby would come in out of idle curiosity. On the walls would be suitable inscriptions such as the Ten Commandments, the Beatitudes or John 3:16. Tracts would be given out. Informal preaching by the missionary or co-worker would take place as people gathered.

Religious pilgrimages. A unique feature of the work in Hangzhou was the use of religious pilgrimages as preaching opportunities. Tens of thousands of pilgrims would come each year on festive occasions to visit the famous Buddhist and Taoist temples near West Lake. Missionary evangelists would visit the shrine areas, engage in open-air preaching, and distribute their literature. This practice did not seem to be offensive to the practitioners of the other religions, and in fact, the presence of the foreigners may have added to the festive occasion.

Boarding schools. Mrs. Randolph's school for girls proved to be a success from the very beginning, and quickly became known as one of the best girls' schools in China.[30] The report for the year 1879 gave a description of the program:

> The number of pupils is 29. A written contract is made with the parents of every girl received into the school; 1st, she is to remain a given number of years to complete her education. 2d, that she is not to be subject to the cruel practice of foot-binding. 3rd, that she is not to be betrothed to a heathen husband.... A number of girls have been made the subject of divine grace, and several of the graduates have been married to Christian husbands.[31]

The success of the school was attributed in no small measure to Mrs. Randolph's "right hand woman," Mrs. Ah-tse, who had graduated from Miss Aldersey's school in Ningbo years before.

The boys' school, under Mr. Painter, had rough going. The report for 1875 told of seven students who were asked not to return, one who ran away and another who was taken home by parents. The next year conditions of the school improved with four uniting with the church and several graduates employed as lay preachers. But Painter's health broke down and in 1880 he asked to be relieved of school work. Stuart took over.

Day schools. The development of day schools came after that of the boarding schools. Because they required less financial support and needed simpler buildings and not as much missionary supervision, they could be started quite easily and multiplied quite rapidly. Houston wrote in 1875:

> A new feature of great interest has been added to our work. I mean the neighborhood schools. We now have six of these in the city [Hangzhou] with 250 students.[32]

Most of the work was carried on by Chinese teachers. Half the time was given to the study of the Bible and Christian books and half to the study of the Confucian classics.

Organization of the church. The church in Hangzhou had its beginning in March 1869 when a man and his wife were received by baptism, another man by transfer and the first communion service was held. But there was not much growth until 1877. Seven were received in that year, eight in 1878, and thirteen in 1879. Steady growth continued until the church had a membership of forty-six by the year 1883. The church was under Houston's care but the conduct of the services were largely in the hands of "native assistants." Converts came from the schools and from families who had some direct relationship with the missionaries.

Suzhou

With the closing of the work in Guchow and the arrival of new missionaries, the mission began searching for another place to begin work. Stuart and DuBose made several visits to Huzhou (Huchow), on the southern end of Tai Hu (Great Lake). On one trip they lived a while on a houseboat and on another at a nearby Buddhist temple. But efforts to rent property failed.

In 1872 Stewart and DuBose visited Suzhou and became very much impressed with the possibilities there. The city, located on the Grand Canal a hundred miles north of Hangzhou, was noted for the beauty of its gardens and at the time had a population of three hundred thousand inhabitants. It had suffered great destruction during the Taiping Rebellion. Mr. Muirhead, veteran missionary of the LMS, was preaching daily in a crowded chapel. Rev. and Mrs. George F. Fitch of the Northern Presbyterian China Mission (NPM) arrived at about the same time as the Southern Presbyterians. The authorities were friendly and a house was rented that was large enough to serve as residence and chapel. Hampden and Pauline DuBose moved to Suzhou in the fall of 1872 and became the founders of the new station. In his memoirs DuBose told of the curiosity of the people and a conversation about the new arrivals:

> "Have you seen them?"
> "How do they look?"
> "They have white faces."
> "The man has a long black beard and says he is only twenty-six years old. In our country only old men grow beards. . . . "
> "What about the lady?"
> "She has a soft voice and smiles and is as pretty as the 'Goddess of Mercy.' "[33]

DuBose began to preach daily at his street chapel about a year after he had arrived and wrote of the experience:

> It is a joy to me to again speak of God . . . nearly the same thing every day. But as we have almost an entirely different congregation each time, one sermon is a far more valuable piece of property than in the course of a pastorate at home. . . . Yet though I preach thus hand-cuffed, I do rejoice. . . . The door is opened, those passing along the street stop and look in. Being invited to enter they come in and sit down, or perhaps they stand and read some of the mottoes that hang on the wall.[34]

Soon John Davis and Miss Safford joined the station. Each lived in a different part of the city. Here again health problems plagued the missionary community as Suzhou was crisscrossed with canals and malaria was rampant. Julius Augustine DuBose, aged thirteen months, died in October 1874.

This same year an anti-foreign mob paraded through the streets of the city breaking up the services in the chapel and forcing its way into the missionary quarters. DuBose's forehead was cut by a flying stone and some personal goods were stolen. When the police arrived the mob melted away. In 1876 the "paper men terror," as it was called, spread throughout the province. Malicious rumors, possibly started by the White Lotus Society, charged that Roman Catholic priests were sorcerers who made paper men that bewitched innocent Chinese, causing boils to break out.

As at Hangzhou, day schools were initiated with some success. But a boys' boarding school that opened in 1876 had hard going. The mission debated the issue as to whether the two boys' boarding schools (in Hangzhou and Suzhou) were worth the considerable cost to keep them open. Also, schools for boys were being run by other missions: the Northern Presbyterians in Hangzhou and the Southern Methodists in Suzhou. In 1883 the mission voted to close both schools, but was badly divided on the issue and laid the matter before the Executive Committee. The Committee upheld the majority and the schools were closed. It was a bitter disappointment for Rev. and Mrs. DuBose.

In 1874 the church was organized and the first four converts baptized. DuBose told of the dilemma they faced when one of the converts, a barber by trade who had heard the gospel in the street chapel, wished to become a Christian but could not close his shop on the sabbath:

> We decided that it was a case in which the Master would have mercy and not sacrifice. His wife, a heathen woman, advised him to join the church, because, she said, he was a better man since he had been a Christian.[35]

One "cheering feature" of the small congregation was its independence:

> Its members are all men of business, who heard the gospel in the street chapel, believed, and were received into the fellowship, and none look to the foreigners for temporal assistance.[36]

In 1876 Suzhou station bought a houseboat, the *Star of Salvation,* to travel the many canals throughout the region. It would be the forerunner of many a mission boat that would carry evangelists, medicines and Christian literature into remote regions that were otherwise inaccessible. The pleasing feature of the boat consisted not of its speed but the comfort it provided its occupants one hundred miles from home.

Miss Safford, the pioneer in women's work, meticulously recorded her activities for five years in the 1877 *Annual Report:* 1,200 visits made, 8,000 persons reached, 143 pupils taught, 25 villages visited, 1,712 books and papers distributed, and 5 books printed in the Suzhou dialect. Although the visible results were not all that great, she believed much had been accomplished in removing prejudices and suspicions, and creating a climate for friendly relationships.[37]

But the church grew more slowly in Suzhou than in Hangzhou. DuBose wrote in 1879:

> The Yang Yoh-Hong chapel has now been open seven years; about 4,000 sermons preached in it with net results of four converts. The Methodist put "fruit" as proof of one's ministry. I suppose they would forbid us to preach. Calvinism has long patience.[38]

The Expanding Mission

The fifteen-year period from 1884 to 1899 is characterized by Bear as a time of growth and expansion:

> In 1883 missionaries were working in two stations [Hangzhou and Suzhou]. In 1897 the Mission had occupied twelve stations [two were later given up]. . . . In 1883 there were fifteen missionaries on the China roll. In 1899 the ten stations were occupied by 71 missionaries. . . . The Executive Committee had sent out to the China field 64 new missionaries. . . . There were losses in these years but there was a net gain of 56 in personnel.[39]

In twelve years church membership increased fourfold from 58 to 271.

In the United States the times were good and there was a growing enthusiasm for missions in the South. The China Mission budget increased from $16,354 in 1883 to $41,931 in 1899.[40] The exchange rate was favorable and costs were low.

Changes took place in the Executive Committee. In 1884 J. Leighton Wilson resigned because of poor health and Dr. Houston, who had retired from China after his wife's death, was elected his successor. Nine years later Houston resigned in order to return to China as a missionary. In 1894 the Assembly elected Rev. S. H. Chester as the Secretary, and he served until 1926.

Some small gains were made in the rights of women missionaries. Previously, the ladies were required to have their work reports read at the annual meeting by one of the men. But beginning in 1884 each made her own report. In 1885 the following rule was adopted:

> No action shall be taken by the Mission in any matter directly affecting the work of an unmarried lady missionary until the lady has first been informed of the action proposed and has had the opportunity to submit her views on the subject to the mission.[41]

During these years the expansion of the mission took place in two directions. First, the work in the large cities of Hangzhou and Suzhou was strengthened and new stations were begun in the area south of the Yangtze. As this work developed, the mission was drawn into closer cooperation with the Northern Presbyterians. A second direction was pioneer work north of the river. Here the Southern Presbyterians would blaze a new trail.

South of the Yangtze

Zhenjiang (Chinkiang)

In 1882 the mission appointed a committee to choose a location for a third station. The committee visited five cities and chose Zhenjiang for a number of reasons: (1) its location was on the south bank of the Yangtze where the Grand Canal crossed the great river; (2) it was a treaty port at the center of a densely populated area; (3) there were no other Presbyterian missionaries in the city. DuBose, one member of the committee, described the city in these words:

> Chen-kiang [Zhenjiang] is the first open port on the Yang-tse. The original native city [is] surrounded by its fine wall of clean, new-looking brick.... The foreign settlement, with its large houses, lies about a mile distant.... There are thirty or forty foreigners; only one lady. Steamboats stop daily, going up and down.[42]

The city had been captured by the British during the First Opium War after a fierce battle in which scaling ladders were used to mount the city walls. Out of a Manchu garrison of four thousand, only five hundred survived, many committing suicide rather than be taken prisoner. The city again suffered terribly during the Taiping Rebellion. Due to these events the prediction was that work would be slow and difficult for the "missionaries of the place have been identified with war, opium, and rebellion."[43]

Woodbridge arrived in 1883, but left soon afterward to meet his fiancée, Miss Jeanie Woodrow, in Yokohama where they were married. They returned to Zhenjiang and set up housekeeping in a rented house on the waterfront. In 1884 they were joined by Rev. and Mrs. Henry M. Woods. Because of the health problems encountered in Hangzhou and Suzhou, the Executive Committee strongly recommended they settle on higher ground. Remarkably, they were able to purchase land on a hilltop west of the city because the graves, which cover most of the hillsides in China, had already been removed when the site was cleared for a fort during the Taiping Rebellion. It was said the property was haunted, but the missionaries said they would rather face the ghosts of the hills than the microbes of the Hangzhou swamp and the Suzhou canals.

The report for 1885 told of the beginning of the work:

> At... Chinkiang, the brethren have each opened a chapel, and preaching services are held daily. The two chapels lie on either side of the Grand Canal, and a great number of the floating population is reached. Some work has also been commenced by Mrs. Woods and Mrs. Woodbridge. The people are generally polite and attentive.[44]

One wonders why "each of the brethren" opened his own chapel. Was it because of differences? This could have been the case as the annual meeting of the mission in 1887 took three days to settle a dispute between them.[45] Woods, at his request, was assigned to the new station that was being opened north of the Yangtze where he would begin a long and distinguished career. Woods's place at Zhenjiang was taken by James E. Bear, Sr.

In the early years the preaching in the chapels produced very few visible results. After ten years only five communicant members were reported. Animosity against the foreigner, and especially the British, was strong due to the fighting during the Opium War. In 1889 a riot broke out when a Sikh policeman employed by the British struck a Chinese beggar in the British concession. The English consulate and the Southern Baptist mission were burned to the ground. The American Consulate was plundered. The Presbyterian property, being some distance from the city, escaped unharmed. Woodbridge wrote that the wonder was there were not more outbreaks considering all the Chinese had suffered at the hands of the "Christian nations":

> I write this to the credit of the Chinese. Had such an uprising occurred in England or America, with all its attending circumstances, not a Chinaman would have escaped.[46]

After ten years of discouraging growth, a change is noted. In the year 1898 four chapels, three native evangelists, one day school and twenty-five communicant members were reported.[47]

Sinchang/Jiaxing (Kashing)

For some time the city of Jiaxing, with a population of about 150,000 and located about halfway between Hangzhou and Shanghai on the Grand Canal, had been viewed as a desirable site for a mission station. In 1880 Rev. Samuel Dodd of the NPM had made an attempt to enter the city but had been driven out. In 1891 the Southern Presbyterians tried but again the attempt was rebuffed. But an agent for the mission, Elder Hu, was able to rent a six-room house in the small town of Sinchang some nine miles northwest of Jiaxing. Hu, a man of integrity and long years of service, moved in and began a Christian witness. In February 1892 he was joined by Rev. P. Frank Price, one of the most able and distinguished missionaries of the southern church. In April Mr. Price married Miss Esther Wilson of Hangzhou and brought his young bride of twenty-six back with him to the new station. They were soon joined by Miss Annie R. Houston, M.D. In a letter home, Mrs. Price described the pattern of daily work. In the morning, study and visitation were the order of the day. In the afternoon

> we open the doors at two o'clock, and Mr. Price receives the men in one room, Miss Houston her patients in another, and I, the women in another. The men come in great numbers, and Mr. Price with the help of his native assistant, talks with them, answers their numerous questions, and explains the Gospel to them. Miss Houston had generally from ten to twenty patients with every kind of disease.... I have from forty to fifty [women] at a time talking to them. From four to five o'clock we have a short service in the chapel, and all are invited in.[48]

In 1893 Annie Houston married Rev. Brown Craig Patterson and joined him in mission work north of the river. Her place was taken by Wade Hampton Venable, M.D., and his wife, Eliza Talbot, whom he had met on the long voyage across the Pacific. They were married the day after their ship docked in Shanghai.

Dr. Price records "two notable days" of prayer and fasting by missionaries and the Christian community that deeply affected the life and work of the station: prayer for cooperation and brotherly love, prayer for rumors to cease, prayer for more workers, prayer for adequate funds.[49]

Prayers were answered in a remarkable way. A "high day" in July was the organization of the Sinchang church with five members; false rumors circulated by the literati ceased at least for a while; several new church workers arrived; two thousand cases were treated in the dispensary by Dr. Venable and Mrs. Price; and Rev. and Mrs. Waddy H. Hudson joined the station in 1894. By the year 1899 a second preaching point had been opened, an industrial school opened and the membership of the Sinchang church had grown to fifty-eight.

In 1895 attempts to enter the city of Jiaxing were finally successful when Venable rented quarters which were described by Dr. Chester who visited the city as a "three roomed mud hovel"

> where Dr. Venable and Mr. Hudson spent one whole winter without kindling a fire, except under the dirt oven in which they cooked their meals. The air was so damp that on cold nights the icicles would gather on their beards which they let grow for protection.[50]

Early the next year their families joined them when property large enough for several residences and a small hospital was purchased inside the North Gate. In the *Annual Report* for 1897 Venable reported 7,264 patient visits, 8 major operations, 556 minor operations and 26 cases of attempted suicide by taking overdoses of opium.[51] Hudson told of the evangelistic work:

> On Sundays we had first a Sabbath School, then a preaching service for Christians and inquirers only.... At night the natives hold a service conducted entirely by themselves.... One young man has asked for baptism. ... We are told that Kia-hing [Jiaxing] is a veritable stronghold of idolatry. ... There seemed to be a peculiar fear of the Gospel.[52]

The possibility of mob violence was always near. Once a child's skull was found at the front door. No doubt it had been placed there by those circulating rumors that the foreigners were stealing children, but it was discovered and disposed of.

Since Sinchang was originally started as a stepping-stone to Jiaxing and the two locations were only nine miles apart, Sinchang station was eventually closed. The church there had been well established and continued to grow after the missionaries left.

Jiangyin (Kiangyin)

Attempts were made in 1892 to gain an entrance to Wuxi at the northern end of Lake Tai and astride the Grand Canal. But property could not be purchased and the people were unresponsive. After five years of effort, the station was closed. But from Wuxi access was gained to the walled city of Jiangyin ("Rivershade") located on the southern bank of the Yangtze twenty five miles to the east.[53] Here at the point where the mighty river narrows to a width of a mile, the twelve-inch guns of the Jiangyin fort could deny all ships passage up the river.

The scene is described by an early missionary:

> Spread out before us is a scene of wondrous charm: on the north flows the Yangtze River, bearing upon her waters a great variety of river craft, from the small "sampan" of the fisherman to the...stately steamers that pass to and fro, all through the day or night. To the south lies the city, with its wall of brick and stone thirty feet high.... All round about the city are beautiful farming lands, intensively cultivated and presenting the appearance of an elaborate garden.[54]

The ancient pagoda inside the West Gate had preserved amicable relations with the spirits of the air and water but had failed to protect the city from the onslaughts of the Taipings, who destroyed large sections of the city.

In 1895 a new era began for the ancient city when two foreigners, Reverends Robert Haden and Lacy Little, established residence in the city. With a little medical training, Haden began to diagnose patients and to dispense quinine and other remedies. Little began to explore the mysteries of the Chinese language and the Chinese personality. On the other hand the Chinese found the presence of two single American males in their midst equally mystifying. The explanation that they had come to be of benefit to the people of the city was beyond comprehension. A simpler explanation: they were there as representatives of the American government to spy out the land.

A Chinese house was leased for ten years from a landlord who was an opium addict and in dire need of money. One-half the lease money was paid in advance. A difference of opinion surfaced when it was announced that the windows and doors had not been included in the lease price. An amicable settlement was reached but in the negotiations the Chinese doctor representing the landlord "lost face" and vowed to get even. His revenge came in a strange and unexpected manner. He removed the body of a child from a neighboring graveyard and buried it in the back yard of the mission residence at night. Days later the doctor charged that the foreigners were using the bodies of children for their malevolent practices and had buried such a child in their yard. The unsuspecting missionaries invited the mayor and an inspection party to search the premises in order to prove their innocence. Following the guidance of the doctor the body of the child was dug up and exhibited and a riot ensued. The property was ransacked and as their personal belongings were being looted, the two missionaries sprinted the distance to the Jiangyin forts, taking refuge in the quarters of the German gunnery instructor.

But providentially, the plot was uncovered, the doctor was sent to prison and the Chinese authorities paid for the property damage. Buildings were rebuilt and the work of the station returned to normal except that weddings took place, which altered the state of the single men. Lacy Little married Pauline DuBose of Suzhou and Robert Haden, Eugenie Hilbold of Zhenjiang.[55]

When the station at Wuxi was closed, Dr. and Mrs. George Worth and Rev. J. Y. McGinnis moved to Jiangyin. Lacy Little and George Worth had been close friends in college and were delighted to be together again. The arrival of the Worths initiated a love affair between Jiangyin Station and the First Presbyterian Church of Wilmington, North Carolina (Dr. Worth's home church), that would continue for the next thirty years.

Dr. Worth took over the dispensary and the number of patients multiplied rapidly. A reaction to the false charges related to the riot produced a surge of good will on the part of the magistrates and the people. Many applied for church membership but the missionaries were apprehensive that they came from unworthy motives:

> We have constantly refused to assist them by securing official aid for their protection in lawsuits, as we wish them to clearly understand that the Kingdom of Jesus is not of this world.... We might have baptized them by the hundred had it seemed wise to do so.[56]

North Jiangsu

In crossing the Yangtze into northern Jiangsu, the mission moved out of the Yangtze delta into a new region. Here the great north China plains began and the Mandarin dialect was universally spoken. Here the staple crops were wheat and barley rather than rice. The area was subject to periodic droughts and floods and often poverty-stricken. It had been neglected by government officials and was often infested with bandits and secret societies. Northern Jiangsu had more in common with Shandong to the north than Jiangsu, south of the river.

Absalom Sydenstricker was the architect of the plan to push north. For some months after his arrival in 1880 he and Mrs. Sydenstricker had lived in Shandong for health reasons, and had became familiar with the pattern of work in which Nevius and other Northern Presbyterians were engaged. Returning south he asked to be assigned the task of starting work north of the river. His dream was to link up Presbyterian work in the cities of the Yangtze River valley with the work of Presbyterians in Shandong. No other Protestant missions were at work in most of the area. The plan had the hearty endorsement of both missions.[57]

Access to the area was furnished by the Grand Canal, as roads were nonexistent. This engineering masterpiece was begun in the sixth century A.D. when a network of local canals was connected, linking the Yangtze with the Yellow River. By the thirteenth century these had been expanded into a grand trunk line extending eleven hundred miles from Hangzhou in the south to Tianjin in the north. During its glory days the canal was the primary route over which tribute grain was brought from the Yangtze delta to the capital city. A fleet of six thousand junks, a horde of boatmen and an army of bureaucrats were employed to operate the system and keep the grain moving north. During the late Qing dynasty the upkeep on the dikes was neglected, allowing the canal to deteriorate. But until the coming of the railroad in 1911 it was the only transportation system available, and even today the canal is used by river barges, which haul an incredible volume of freight.[58]

Missionary travel was most often by houseboat. A boat could be rented for the trip and accommodations prepared to one's liking. At times the boat would be towed by steam launch. More often sail, oars and the tow path were used to propel the boat forward. Speed was no consideration. The boat would tie up along the bank for the night. Travel of the Mark Grier family for the 150-mile distance between Zhenjiang and Huaiyin during the winter of 1897 is described in a letter:

> The boat was a large one and very comfortable as boats go. Our first care was to hang up curtains, stop up the windows where glass was lacking, paste up the cracks with paper, and so try to keep out the cold wind. With these precautions and an oil stove, and plenty of fur and cotton wadding, we did not suffer from cold. After an hour or so, we stopped in the middle of the river [Yangtze] — wind too high to cross.... We cross the river by night...then at Yangchow, encountered such a blockade of boats that it was impossible to proceed. Huge boats going to Peking with the yearly tribute of lumber...blocked the canal so we simply waited.... One boat ran aground.... The men got out and pushed and pulled.... After this delay we went on steadily, though slowly and reached Tsing-Kiang-Pu [Huaiyin] nine days after leaving Chinkiang.[59]

Huaiyin (Tsing-Kiang-Pu [TKP])

Early in 1887 the Sydenstricker family made the move up the canal and settled at Huaiyin (TKP) where a house was rented.[60] Mr. Sydenstricker's associate in the country work was an elder trained by Dr. Nevius in Shandong. Mrs. Sydenstricker had a Bible woman to help in the women's work. In order not to be conspicuous the Sydenstrickers dressed in Chinese clothes. The neighbors treated them with kindness.[61]

They were joined in the fall by the Henry Woods family who had been transferred from Zhenjiang. Rev. Henry McKee Woods was the first of three remarkable brothers to serve in China — all assigned to Huaiyin (TKP). In 1888 Dr. Edgar Woods arrived with his China-born wife, Frances Smith, the daughter of Bishop and Mrs. Dreslen Smith of Shanghai. Edgar is considered the pioneer medical missionary of the SPM.[62] The third brother, James Baker Woods, M.D., arrived in 1894. Total years of service in China of the three brothers was 106 years![63]

Henry Woods began preaching on the street and in tea houses. Sydenstricker itinerated far and wide into north Jiangsu. They were soon joined by Rev. and Mrs. James Graham and Miss Ellen Emerson. A boys' and a girls' school were begun. The "Jesus Hall Love and Mercy Hospital" was opened on rented land inside the East Gate in 1891. A special proclamation by the city magistrate provided official sanction for the new venture. In the year 1893 six thousand persons were treated. Medical work undoubtedly contributed to the reception of the gospel as progress here was a little faster than it had been further south.[64] In 1894 the *Annual Report* gave these statistics: nineteen communicants added by examination; seven infants baptized; twenty-five total number of communicants; seven thousand books and tracts distributed; six thousand persons received medical assistance.[65]

But there were bitter losses. Henry and Josephine Woods lost a six-year-old son, Edgar. Georgia, daughter of Rev. James R. and Mrs. Sophie Peck Graham died at the age of three. The Sydenstrickers lost four children during "the vicissitudes of their pioneer missionary life."[66]

Suqian (Suchien)

The next major stop on the Grand Canal as it wound its way through the north China plain was Suqian, a city of seventy-five thousand about sixty miles north of Huaiyin (TKP). The veteran Sydenstrickers and two newcomers, B. C. Patterson and Mark Grier, were assigned the task of opening the station. The four became five when Patterson married Dr. Annie Houston of Jiaxing and brought to the team the added skills of a medical doctor.

Negotiations to purchase property began in the fall of 1893 and took about a year to be consummated. A house was purchased and property for a chapel was rented. But the further north the foreigners moved the more isolated they became and the more they were viewed with curiosity and suspicion. When the newcomers arrived in the fall of 1894 some of the gentry posted vile placards against the foreigners and were able to have the property contracts cancelled. So rental negotiations began again. After some difficulty a Chinese inn was rented. The newcomers remained behind closed doors and when they ventured into the streets, they wore Chinese clothes. In order to remove suspicion, the gate was opened every afternoon for any and all to come and see the newcomers. Mrs. Patterson was the first white woman to come to Suqian and created quite a sensation. People came by the droves, out of curiosity to be sure, but some stayed to buy books and hear the new teaching. A dispensary was opened with Mrs. Patterson treating the women and Mr. Grier, who had had some medical training in the United States, treating the men. As the medicine woman's skills became known the number of patients increased dramatically. There were 4,207 patient visits the first year.

Changes took place in the membership of the station. Sydenstricker was reassigned to Zhenjiang, having worn himself and his family out in the pace he had set in pioneer itineration. Mark Grier married Nettie Donaldson of the NPM in Shandong, bringing another medical doctor to the station. William F. Junkin arrived in 1897. He would be the bulwark of the station for the next forty years.[67]

These were famine years in North Jiangsu. A letter in *The Missionary* described the dreadful scene:

> For three years the crops have been a failure.... You would pass along the road and see the willow and elm trees barked for a distance of four or five feet. Further on the children would be up in the trees gathering their dinner — the young leaves of the mulberry and willow... further along a whole family was lying down on the floor, unable to raise their heads; all down with famine fever. Another house, typhus. Another, confluent smallpox.[68]

Patterson and Junkin spent much of their time distributing relief goods. Lacy Little from Jiangyin arrived to help and described how the aid was administered:

> [We would] go into the country on wheelbarrows accompanied by a soldier apiece (to keep the beggars from thronging us)... giving tickets to those families that were most destitute.... By this method Messrs. Patterson and Junkin and the writer were enabled to give relief to nearly 1,600 families.[69]

In the wake of the famine would come the bandits. Junkin describes one encounter with the "tue fei" (dirt robbers) who

> relieved me of all the belongings I had with me, even to the outer garments on my back! It was not funny to be robbed, but I had to laugh afterwards at the thought of the sight I presented as I sat in the "high seat" of the Yamen of the town... rather scant of dress, telling my troubles to the official across the table in his silk robes.[70]

The *North China Herald* of Shanghai paid a fine tribute to Mrs. Patterson for her work during these trying circumstances:

> One of the most heroic women in China is Mrs. B. C. Patterson, M.D. of the Southern Presbyterian Mission, Suchien, North Kiangsu. Eighty miles from any other foreign lady, herself and baby exposed to famine fever while her husband was away helping the starving thousands, she had in nine months had 8,000 patients and expects to remain at her post during the heated term, ministering to the sick and suffering.[71]

But for all their good works, few converts were won. Members were gained one year — lost the next. In fact in one year (1897) for reasons unknown all the members were suspended from membership and a new beginning was made.

Breakthrough at Lingwu

The long-awaited and prayed for breakthrough occurred in a place and in a way that no one could have predicted. In 1895 two mission-employed evangelists in Lingwu, forty miles north of Hangzhou, were withdrawn because of lack of funds. This forced the company of believers to be on their own. What began as a loss became an opportunity as "there developed a life and strength among the members higher than had ever been known before."[72] Matthew Houston moved to the town and lived alone in the Chinese community. He proposed that the church select a council of three members with whom he would consult on all matters. Houston taught a Bible class in which all who could read took turns reading their verses and expounding their meaning. Houston raised questions and offered further exposition if necessary. The morning worship service was entirely in the hands of the council, which selected one of their number to lead it. In the afternoon separate services were held for Christians and non-Christians with a member of the council leading the non-Christians and Houston speaking to the Christians. During the first year, ten new believers were baptized.

The next year even more startling results were achieved. Twenty new members were received and contributions tripled. The church selected three of its number to serve as evangelists to visit nearby villages. They were paid the wage of a common laborer from the contributions of the members. The church had to be enlarged. No mission funds were used.

Dr. Houston described his experience at Lingwu as the most striking evidence of God's power that he had ever witnessed.[73] But, alas, Presbyterian polity had not been followed! The church council, composed of men who were neither elders nor deacons, had administered the Sacrament of the Lord's Supper. There had not been enough time to follow the cumbersome ecclesiastical process. More serious, unmarried women had been allowed to preach.

Houston became convinced that his theological views had changed and his ordination vows required him to report these changes to his presbytery (Louisville). Colleagues in Hangzhou could not talk him out of it. For Houston it was a matter of conscience. The mission, with great reluctance, appointed a committee to hear his case.

The most substantive issue concerned the status of women in the church. Houston persisted in his views that the scripture prohibited married women from serving as "preachers" but not single women or widows. This view had been vindicated at Lingwu. Having heard Dr. Houston out, the mission was really not anxious to pursue the matter further and wished it could be dropped. There was deep affection for Dr. Houston and everyone recognized the remarkable results that had been achieved in Lingwu. But neither did the mission wish to go on record as condoning action contrary to the standards of their church. In the end they granted him permission to return to the United States and present his views to his presbytery.

Louisville Presbytery was just as reluctant as the mission committee to try

Dr. Houston for heresy and tried to dismiss the case by warning him of "dangerous tendencies." But Houston was not content to let the matter lie. The case dragged on, the patience of the presbytery began to wear thin and in the end it acted to "divest the Rev. M. H. Houston of the office of the ministry, and order his name stricken from the roll."[74]

It was a tragic ending to an illustrious career. But the incident shows that cross-cultural mission is dangerous and that not all casualties are from disease. Changes demanded in a missionary encounter are not always one way. Sometimes they affect not only the convert but the one who came to do the converting. Dr. Samuel Chester paid this high compliment to Matthew Hale Houston's integrity of character:

> For the sake of bearing a witness to what he believed to be the truth, he gave up all church honors and emoluments and retired to live on a meager income of such occasional evangelistic work as he was physically able to do, until his death at Augusta, Georgia on January 18, 1905. His character was of the stuff of which martyrs are made.[75]

Linton Stuart took over the work at Lingwu after Houston left. He continued the same plan that Houston had inaugurated but brought it back in line with Presbyterian procedures. The congregation continued its growth and closed the year 1899 with seventy-six communicant members — nearly double the number of any other congregation in the Southern Presbyterian field with the exception of the city church in Hangzhou. Equally important, the church was well on the way to achieving self-government, self-support and self-propagation.

What were the learnings of the Lingwu experience? In some ways they paralleled the Nevius experience in San Poh forty years earlier, emphasizing the importance of (1) decision making by the community of believers; (2) reliance on local leadership and resources; (3) the realization that polity that had worked well in Geneva or Edinburgh was not necessarily the best for the Chinese culture.[76]

After twenty-five years, what had been accomplished? Fairly accurate statistics are available for the year 1895:

Mission stations	9
Organized churches	4
Chapels	22
Schools	20
Students	335
Dispensaries	9
Persons treated during year	31,102
Ordained Chinese pastors	1
Unordained preachers	9
Bible women	9
Members added during year	73
Total communicant members	301[77]

These were the days of small beginnings. Nevertheless, a foundation had been laid for substantial growth in later years.

Perhaps the China mission had made a deeper impact on the church at home. After the isolation of the Civil War and the Reconstruction Era, Presbyterians in the South were rejoining brothers and sisters in the North and in other lands in world mission. This story is told in the next chapter.

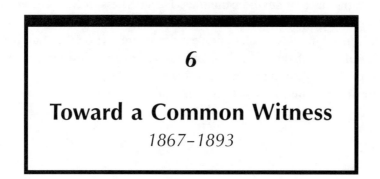

6

Toward a Common Witness
1867–1893

In 1889 there were at least forty-one Protestant missionary societies at work in China.[1] One must ask the question as to the degree of cooperation between them. Of particular interest is the relationship between the Northern and Southern Presbyterians.

Presbyterians North and South

In the early years one could read the minutes of one mission and hardly be aware of the existence of the other although both were at work in some of the same cities. But soon this began to change. From the first, personal relationships were cordial. Marriages inevitably drew the two bodies closer together and in each case the wife followed her husband into the other mission.[2] Assistants employed by the Southern Presbyterians received their training in the northern mission. When funds from home were slow in arriving, the southerners got advances from their northern cousins, although this was embarrassing.

The first reference to any cooperative endeavor came in 1885 when Bishop G. E. Moule of the Church Missionary Society invited all the Protestant missionaries and native workers in Hangzhou to take part in a series of outdoor evangelistic preaching services. All participated.

As time went on the relations between Presbyterians north and south grew closer. Undoubtedly the personal relationship between the board secretaries, Walter Lowrie and Leighton Wilson, had much to do with this:

> Their friendship was very deep and warm. Twenty years after Dr. Wilson came South, Dr. Lowrie visited him in Baltimore to confer with him about mission work in Africa and to urge that our church establish a mission on the Congo.[3]

Fraternal delegates were exchanged between the two missions. Sydenstricker patterned his work in North Jiangsu after that of Nevius in Shandong. In Hangzhou the boys' school of the NPM and the girls' school of the SPM each received children sent by the other mission without expense. In 1898 Messrs.

Joshua Garritt (NPM) and George Hudson (SPM) conducted a joint class for training eight young men for the ministry.[4] There were no significant theological differences between the two missions. In 1893 the PCUSA Board and the PCUS Executive Committee urged their missionaries in central China to engage in closer cooperation.[5] Plans for cooperation in a college and a seminary were initiated. But it was years before general resolutions could be translated into specific plans for action.

Some differences in practice did develop. The Northern Presbyterians were spread much wider over China and developed a national perspective. The Southern Presbyterians, concentrated in a smaller geographic area, were more regional in their outlook. The New York Board tended to exercise more authority over the field body. The Executive Committee for the most part left field policy to the mission. A larger proportion of the northern mission's resources was committed to the educational work.

Differences did develop between the missions that were south of the Yangtze and those in North Jiangsu and Shandong. Southern Presbyterians south of the river became closely aligned with their Northern Presbyterian colleagues in the cities of the Yangtze delta while the Southern Presbyterians in North Jiangsu became more closely linked with the Northern Presbyterians in Shandong. Here the linguistic, cultural and economic differences of the two regions played a part. As a result of these differences the Southern Presbyterians divided their work in 1900 into two missions — Mid China and North Jiangsu.

A United Presbyterian Church for All China?

Closer cooperation inevitably raised the question of the establishment of one Chinese Presbyterian church for the whole country. There was widespread commitment to this ideal but the goal of how it could be achieved was an enigma that would take years to solve. Different patterns had been followed by the various missions in starting their churches. Each related to their home boards in different ways. Difficulties of travel and differences in dialects further complicated the problem.

By the year 1890 there were eight different Presbyterian missions serving within the Chinese Empire. These are listed below with the date of their arrival and the area of work:

1. *Reformed Church of America* (1842). Xiamen.

2. *Presbyterian Church in the U.S.A — North* (1844). Five missions along the China Coast and Yangtze Valley.

3. *Presbyterian Church of England* (1847). Shantou (Swatow), Xiamen, Hakka minorities and Taiwan.

4. *Presbyterian Church in the U.S. — South* (1867). Jiangsu and Zhejiang provinces.

5. *Irish Presbyterian Church* (1869). Manchuria.

6. *Canadian Presbyterian Church* (1872). Taiwan, Henan.

7. *United Free Church of Scotland* (1878). Manchuria.

8. *Church of Scotland* (1878). Yichang (Ichang), Hubei.[6]

Of the eight missions the PCUSA was by far the largest and the only mission whose work extended over a large area of the Empire. With the annexation of Taiwan into the Japanese Empire in 1895, English and Canadian missions on the island joined in the establishment of the Presbyterian Church of Formosa which was independent of the China mainland. The Irish Presbyterians and the United Free Church of Scotland formed a united church in Manchuria when this area came under Japanese dominance.

Three divergent patterns were followed in the organization of the churches in China proper. At an early date the PCUSA had established presbyteries that were placed under the Synod of New York. In 1870 the General Assembly instructed the presbyteries of Canton, Ningbo, Shanghai, Shandong, Fuzhou, Japan and Siam to meet and form the Synod of China, still under the PCUSA Assembly. China missionaries questioned the advisability of such a union, citing linguistic problems and travel costs. The New York Board agreed to bear the travel expenses. The organizational meeting of the synod was held in Shanghai on 20 October 1870. All presbyteries were represented except Fuzhou, Japan and Siam which never sent delegates.[7] The third meeting of the Synod held in 1874 reported these statistics: 27 missionary ministers, 13 Chinese ministers, 22 churches, 67 "preaching places," 569 adult male baptized members, 525 adult female baptized members, 223 adults baptized during the year, 133 infants baptized during the year.[8]

In 1898, at the request of the China presbyteries, the PCUSA General Assembly divided the Synod of China into the Synod of North China and the Synod of Central and Southern China.[9] The division reflected the linguistic differences and difficulties of travel. Representatives of the presbyteries of Peking, Jinan, and Shandong met in 1898 in the Presbyterian Church of Yantai to form the Synod of North China. Seventeen ministers (fourteen missionaries, three Chinese) and seventeen elders (all Chinese) were enrolled. The Synod of Central and Southern China was convened in the Lowrie Memorial Presbyterian Church in Shanghai, the same year. Representatives came from the presbyteries of Canton, Hangzhou, Ningbo and Shanghai. The synod membership consisted of twenty-seven ministers (eleven missionaries, sixteen Chinese) and eight elders (all Chinese) from the four presbyteries of Canton, Hangzhou, Ningbo and Shanghai. Minutes of the two synods were kept in both English and Chinese. The conduct of the meetings closely followed American procedures. But two actions of the northern synod related specifically to the China context: a meeting of the "Anti-Footbinding Society" and a resolution urging Christians not to "appear hastily in the Courts as participants in lawsuits."[10] There was little mention of finances. Presumably, this was handled by the mission organization.

The Southern Presbyterians, who came on the scene thirty years later, at first followed the same plan that had been initiated by the northern church. In 1873, at the suggestion of Dr. Wilson, the mission petitioned the General Assembly to establish the presbytery of Hangzhou, which would be placed under one of the synods of the church in America. This proposal was approved by the Assembly.

But in the meantime, Dr. Houston wrote to the home board that missionaries were having second thoughts about the advisability of such an action. Two objections were raised. The first was blatantly racist. They did not want to be members of "a mixed presbytery," composed of two races (Chinese and Caucasian). As time went on, Chinese members would dominate the organization and missionaries would find themselves outnumbered, outvoted and subject to the discipline of "immature" Christians of another race. The second reason had more merit:

> Another reason why it is unadvisable for foreigners and natives to be joined in one presbytery, is that it tends to prevent the union of the native Christians.... There are four branches of the Presbyterian Church now operating in China — the English, Scotch, and Northern, besides our own. Where foreigners are united with the natives in a presbytery, the presbytery ... attaches to the foreign Assembly.... If this state of things exists, how can the native Presbyterians come together in an organized capacity?[11]

Since the mission had not yet ordained any Chinese ministers, Houston proposed to delay the organization of a China presbytery until Chinese ministers and elders could take part.

The Assembly of 1876 rescinded its previous action on the grounds that it had no power to establish a presbytery on foreign soil. A far-reaching policy was established: There would be no appendages of the Southern Presbyterian Church in foreign lands:

> We ought not to seek to propagate our own distinctive Presbyterian body in various parts of the world, but rather to disseminate simply the principles and doctrines that we hold.... No heathen land can be thoroughly evangelized except through the agency of its own people. The foreign missionary, with the blessing of God, may set the ball in motion, and for a time shape its course. But it is for men raised upon the soil to continue and extend the work.[12]

It was not until 1885 that three men elected by the Hangzhou church were ordained to the position of ruling elder: Wu Sin-'O, Yu Foh-Tsang and Sang Kien Dang. All were in the employ of the mission. All served faithfully and well. Another ten years elapsed before the first pastor was ordained. Dzen An Lin was ordained and installed as the pastor of the Hangzhou church in 1895. He was fully supported by the Hangzhou congregation. Pastor Dzen was trained in a theological class of the NPM and his wife had been trained in the Hangzhou Girls' School. He was described as an "able preacher, and, in manner and bearing, a polished Chinese gentleman, though coming up from the humbler walks of life."[13]

In the absence of a presbytery, annual conferences of workers were held. George Hudson described the fourth such conference, held in 1899:

> In spite of the six dialects used, nearly all the speakers were well understood.... Three... theological students were examined by the Mission's committee.... The chairman was Mr. Dzen of Hangchow, the first native to hold this distinction. In presiding he was tactful and courteous. In addition to a very excellent paper, "The Present Condition of the Church in China," he frequently gave a clearcut synopsis of the several discussions as they closed.... Mr. Sen of Sinchang commanded the respect of all by his penetrating grasp of essentials. Mr. Liu of Soochow aroused a lively debate over the changes necessary in marriage and funeral customs.... Of the foreigners, Dr. Davis seemed to be the most impressive, Mr. Stuart was always solid, Dr. DuBose eloquent and aggressive; Mr. Woodbridge showed literary culture.[14]

From the vantage point of the present day, it would appear that both PCUSA and PCUS patterns for establishing a Chinese church were flawed. The PCUSA had established functioning ecclesiastical bodies in which both missionaries and Chinese pastors and elders participated. This was no mean achievement. But the policy of placing Chinese synods under the jurisdiction of the American General Assembly accented the foreign nature of the enterprise.[15] Furthermore, such an arrangement made it more difficult to establish a united church with other mission boards.

On the other hand, the PCUS action against establishing "mixed presbyteries" had racist overtones. The ringing affirmation of 1876 not to start Southern Presbyterian churches on foreign soil was in the right direction but the policy delayed the transfer of authority to Chinese pastors and elders.

A third plan was developed by missionaries of the Reformed Church in America (RCA) and the English Presbyterian Church in Shantou (Swatow) and Xiamen. This proved to be the best model and pointed the way to the future.

The theological basis for this model can be found in the writings of John Campbell Gibson, of the English Presbyterian Mission. Gibson believed that the Presbyterian system, with its emphasis on the authority and dignity of the elder, was peculiarly suited to the social structure of the Chinese people. "The Chinese," he wrote, "have really been Presbyterians before they became Christians."[16] Thus the introduction of the Presbyterian order in China did not need the validation of the church in the West, but arose simply because of its practical suitability to the local scene. Missionaries should cooperate with native ministers and elders in organizing a presbytery that should be "self-governing, self-supporting and self-propagating."[17]

So when the first church organization was formed it made no sense to link it with either of the churches abroad. In 1862 the Xiamen "Tai-hoe" (Presbytery or "Classis" as it was known by the RCA) was organized, which consisted of the missionaries of the two overseas churches, two Chinese pastors and six elders. This became the first church of the Reformed faith and Presbyterian order in China that was independent of the parent churches in England or America.

The union was immediately accepted by the Presbyterian Church of England but strongly opposed by the General Synod of the RCA, which instructed its missionaries to withdraw from the union and form a classis that would be under the jurisdiction of the home church. A strenuous debate on the issue continued for the next several years and came to a head when five senior RCA missionaries in Xiamen submitted letters of resignation in protest of the General Synod's action. Their conviction was that

[it was] not only unnecessary but wrong to establish two different churches of like faith and order, to the distraction of the Chinese brethren, the waste of missionary energy and the needless division of the body of Christ.[18]

In 1864 the RCA board gave in, removed its opposition and allowed its missionaries to join the union presbytery.[19]

In the "Amoy Plan," as it came to be called, the structures of the two missions were kept distinct. Missionaries retained their relationship to their home church but sat as "provisional" voting members of the Tai-hoe and were eligible to hold office. In case of misconduct the Tai-hoe had the power to withdraw its recognition of the missionary, including his right to vote and hold office. Each mission was responsible for administering funds originating from Britain or America, while the Tai-hoe administered funds contributed by Chinese Christians. Only pastors of self-supporting churches were eligible for ordination and were then called by vote of the congregation. The Amoy Plan was the forerunner of a truly "Three-Self" (Self-governing, Self-supporting, Self-propagating) church but it would be years before it could be applied to a national church in China.

Despite many differences, the movement for forming a united church holding the reform faith and Presbyterian order continued to build. The PCUSA Synod of China, meeting in Shandong in 1874, sponsored a conference to explore ways of establishing a united Chinese Presbyterian church. Representatives came from all Presbyterian missions plus the ABCFM and the English Baptists. The conference proposed the establishment of a Presbyterian Confederation that would encourage cooperation and consultation. Benjamin Helm, who attended the meeting, wrote of the strong sense of unity and commitment to a united church:

It may seem to some in the States that such a step was ill-advised, if not improper, on the part of the Mission, seeing that the Churches from which we come do not so much as hold fraternal correspondence. But the case is quite different out here; those questions which have separated [us]...have no place in China....We are not here to establish a Southern or a Northern, but a *Chinese* Presbyterian Church.[20]

A Plan of Union was unanimously adopted by representatives of the five Presbyterian missions (Northern and Southern Presbyterian, United Church of Scotland, Canadian and Irish Presbyterian) at the General Conference of Protestant Missionaries held in Shanghai in 1890. It would have linked existing presbyteries in one Synod for all China, which would meet every five years. But for reasons not entirely clear, the plan floundered and nothing came of it.[21] As is often the case, the translation of general resolutions into specific actions was no easy matter. Inertia, the pressure of other priorities, distances and the reluctance to exchange the known for the unknown prevailed. Organic union of the Presbyterians would have to wait until the twentieth century.

But the movement toward union did result in some concrete cooperative projects. One such venture was the establishment in 1901 of a weekly Christian newspaper under sponsorship of the Presbyterian and Reformed missions. The Rev. S. I. Woodbridge of the SPM was elected editor. The newspaper was named the *Chinese Christian Intelligencer* ("Tung Wen Pao") with editorial offices in Shanghai. By 1907 the paper had thirty-five hundred subscribers and reached most of the provinces of China.[22]

The Missionary Conference of 1890

One manifestation of the essential unity of Protestant missions was the remarkable General Conference of Protestant Missionaries held at Shanghai, 7–20 May 1890.[23] Invitations were extended to all Protestant missionaries then serving in China. To the surprise of the planning committee, 445 missionaries, about one-third of the total number in China, attended the conference. They represented 36 different mission boards and societies. Almost an equal number were men and women. The largest number were from the China Inland Mission (84). Next was the Northern Presbyterians (49). There was one serious deficiency: Only two members of the conference were Chinese — Rev. and Mrs. Y. K. Yen of the American Protestant Episcopal Church. All the addresses and minutes were done in English and only a brief account of the meeting was made in Chinese. In spite of shortcomings it was a great ecumenical gathering held twenty years before the Edinburgh Missionary Conference of 1910.

The format of the conference called for addresses to be given on timely subjects as assigned by the conference committee. A sampling of the topics addressed reveal the issues and concerns of the Protestant community of that day:

- "Relation of Christianity to Universal Progress"
- "Service of Song in China"
- "The Place of the Chinese Classics in Christian Schools"
- "Evils of the Use of Opium"
- "How far should Christians be required to abandon Native Customs?"
- "Orphanages, Asylums for the Blind, Deaf and Dumb"
- "Scientific Terminology . . . Means of Securing Uniformity"
- "Church Discipline"

Conference speakers represented the great diversity of the missionary movement. Hudson Taylor of the conservative China Inland Mission gave the opening sermon. Timothy Richards, the brilliant Welsh missionary, who was deeply involved in reform and relief efforts, spoke on "Relations of China Missions to the Chinese Government." Yet in spite of different points of view, the characteristic feature of the conference was the spirit of harmony.

One presentation that touched off a sharp exchange was the paper presented by W. A. P. Martin entitled "The Worship of Ancestors — A Plea for Toleration." Martin recognized the fact that the most serious obstacle to the conversion of the Chinese was the ancestral rites. His thesis:

> Let us then, instead of proposing to abolish the system, ask ourselves the
> further question, whether it is not capable of being modified in such a way
> as to bring it into harmony with the requirement of the Christian Faith?[24]

There was immediate disagreement. A resolution introduced by Martin's colleague, C. W. Mateer, and seconded by Hudson Taylor, calling for the conference to record its sharp dissent from Martin's conclusions was overwhelmingly adopted.

The conference members asked some hard questions of themselves, their methods and their attitudes. Y. K. Yen deplored the way some missionaries maligned the Chinese character, and pled for greater sympathy, patience and understanding.[25] John L. Nevius spoke of the failures of the past. Public preaching did not make an impression on the Chinese listeners as they had no tradition of formal, public discourses. Conversation, teaching and healing the sick were better forms of presenting the gospel. The use of unpaid Chinese volunteers was superior to the use of "resident paid agents."[26]

Women's work was highlighted. Mrs. J. L. Stuart read the paper of Miss Safford (who was ill) entitled "A General View of Women's Work." Miss Harriet Noyes presented the paper "Girls' Schools" and Miss Mary Niles, M.D., spoke on "Medical Mission Work in China by Lady Physicians." The women gave thanks for the great increase in the number of "lady-workers" and the advancement of the work among the women and girls. They took a strong stand against footbinding and the marriage of Christian girls to heathen men.

The ladies, rather pointedly, addressed one appeal to the men of the conference: Wives "should have every encouragement and assistance from their husbands, to enable them to engage in direct mission work."[27] Another appeal was addressed to the Christian women of all Protestant countries, calling for sending more women missionaries so that the wives, mothers and daughters of China might achieve their "full development into lively members of the great household of faith."[28]

One lasting contribution was the appointment of permanent committees for the revision of Bible translation and the preparation of textbooks for Christian schools. Another contribution was the statistical data compiled by Rev. J. W. Davis of Suzhou, a summary of which appears below:

	Total Protestant	*Presbyterian*
Missionaries	1,296	259
Ordained Chinese pastors	211	41
Unordained helpers	1,266	315
Female workers	180	26
Total communicant members	37,287	12,347
Organized churches	522	95
Fully self-supporting churches	94	42
Hospitals	61	18
Patients treated in 1889	348,439	99,138
Pupils in schools	16,836	3,497[29]

Compared with the China masses, it was but a very small beginning. But in comparison with the past, the growth was considerable. The number of Christians had more than doubled in the space of ten years.

The conference issued two appeals. One was a memorial directed to the Emperor of China expressing thanks for protection, answering false charges and "showing that everywhere we inculcate loyalty, peace and charity, and that in all our work we seek nothing but the best interest of China and the Chinese." A second appeal was addressed to "all Protestant Churches of Christian Lands" asking that they send to China "one thousand men within five years from this time."[30] Latourette noted that in the next five years, 481 men and 672 women were recruited and sent to China.[31] The appeal had not gone unanswered.

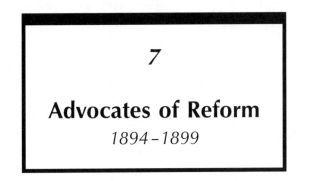

7

Advocates of Reform

1894–1899

During the last decade of the nineteenth century, the Qing dynasty faced new crises that laid bare the impotence of the Empire, the incapacity for reform and the inevitability of revolution. During the "Self-strengthening Movement" following the Taiping Rebellion the Manchu rulers had eased the strains within the empire by a sharing of authority with Chinese provincial governors. A pragmatic working relationship with the Western powers had been worked out. For a short time a reform movement showed signs of promise but it was blocked by reactionary forces. The dynastic cycle was spiraling downward and could not be reversed.

The missionary outlook during this period vacillated from optimism to despair. On all sides were signs of change. Railroads were being built. Telegraph and postal services were established. Steam launches plied the waterways. The clamor for Western education was increasing. Missionaries became involved in the drive for modernization. During this period the *Annual Reports* contain enthusiastic references to a new openness and reform:

The great gates, closed for centuries, are slowing swinging open.[1]

By slow degree the suspicions of the people are removed.[2]

One of the encouraging features of the year is the increase of friendliness from the upper classes.[3]

Never before was there manifested so decided a change from the old conservative and obstructionist policy to . . . an increasing welcome of Western civilization.[4]

But along with these optimistic references, there were ominous reports of "mob violence against foreigners," hostility on the part of Chinese soldiers, attacks on street chapels by "lewd fellows of the baser sort," and the distribution of anti-foreign literature.[5] In some districts there were official proclamations supporting the good work missionaries were doing and the right to preach their "doctrine."[6] But in Shandong proclamations denouncing Christianity were widely posted.[7]

Some developments were positive. Other trends were threatening. Conditions seemed to be building up to some kind of climax and the signs seemed to say that it could go either way.

The Sino-Japanese War (1894–1895)

The first Sino-Japanese War signaled the beginning of the six turbulent years that lay ahead. The war began over a conflict of interests in Korea, traditionally a vassal state of China but where Japan was flexing its newly developed military muscles. In 1894 the Tonghak Rebellion broke out in the southern provinces, threatening the rule of the reigning dynasty.[8] The Korean court appealed to China for assistance. This China was only too happy to give as it strengthened its claims of suzerainty. Troops were dispatched and the revolution was put down. But Japanese troops had also entered Korea ostensibly at the request of the pro-Japanese faction of the court. A face-off resulted between the two armies and each side refused to budge. China sent reinforcements via a British chartered steamer but the Japanese learned of the vessel's sailing and sank it, drowning 950 Chinese soldiers. On 1 August 1894 both countries declared war.

It was a most uneven contest. A Chinese army was defeated near Pyongyang. A naval engagement resulted in the decisive defeat of the Chinese fleet, which was hopelessly outclassed by the more modern Japanese ships. Japanese landing forces captured Port Arthur in Manchuria and Weihaiwei in Shandong.

China sued for peace. Terms forced on China by the treaty of Shimonoseki in 1895 were humiliating: (1) China gave up all claims to Korea, which was pronounced "independent" but soon became a "protectorate" of Japan. (2) Taiwan and the Liaodong Peninsula in Manchuria were ceded to Japan. (3) A huge indemnity was paid to cover Japan's cost of the war. Terms would have been worse except for the attempted assassination of the Chinese negotiator, the redoubtable Li Hongzhang, by a Japanese fanatic. Li was only superficially wounded, but Japan lost "face" in the event and was anxious to settle the matter as quickly as possible. Later, due to pressure from the Western powers, Japan returned the Liaodong Peninsula to China.

China had long considered the island people of Japan to be their inferiors and the humiliation suffered at their hands had repercussions across the Empire. Attempts to create a modern fighting force had been inept. Funds appropriated for the modernization of the navy had been diverted by the Empress Dowager and her favorite eunuch to the construction of a marble boat at the Summer Palace.

The war revealed more than military ineptitude. It laid bare the failure of the Qing establishment to make common cause with China's millions.

> The war pitted Japan, which had become a modern state in which nationalism bound the government and people together in a common purpose, against China, where government and people by and large formed separate entities.[9]

The "Scramble for Concessions" and "Missionary Rights"

China's weakness made it vulnerable to a new round of encroachment by the foreign powers. It appeared to be a ripe melon waiting to be carved up into spheres of influence.

The Russians demanded rights to build a railroad across Manchuria. The Germans used the murder of two Catholic priests in Shandong as a pretext for seizing Jiaozhou (Kiaochow) Bay. The French consolidated their protectorate over Indo-China and demanded concessions in Guangdong and Guangxi. The British negotiated a lease for ninety-nine years on the New Territories, extending Hong Kong's foothold on the Kowloon peninsula.

The United States had not sought special spheres of influence in China and became alarmed at what was happening. In 1899 Secretary of State John Hay issued a series of communications known as the "Open Door Notes," which insisted that the rights of all nations to trade freely with China should not be restricted in any so-called sphere of influence. "The territorial and administrative integrity of China" should be respected. Although not free from self-interest, the "Open Door" policy did advocate the independence of China as a matter of political justice and self-determination and it undoubtedly acted as a brake on further encroachments.[10]

With the more active involvement of the Open Door policy, the United States moved toward a stronger commitment to support the rights of American missionaries. The French and English had aggressively supported the rights of their subjects while the policy of the United States had been one of "studied ambiguity."[11] But now the United States reassessed its policy.

> By the end of the decade Washington had dramatically broadened its definition of missionary rights and demonstrated its willingness to defend the exercise of those rights, even in the face of undiminished Chinese opposition.[12]

A study of the files of the U.S. Consulate at Yantai for the 1890–1900 decade shows the strong sympathetic support given Presbyterian missionaries in Shandong by Consul John Fowler. Most cases were settled amicably with the cooperation of Chinese officials but the consul did not hesitate to make demands when he felt that treaty obligations had been violated.[13]

But consular intervention should not be overemphasized. Consul Fowler made a report to Washington of the serious anti-foreign cases throughout the Empire in which American authorities had become involved during the years 1883–1895. Fifty-five cases are listed, of which twenty-eight involved missionaries.[14] This is a small number when spread over the whole Empire during a twelve-year period. Except for a few times of intense opposition, such as the Boxer year, missionaries lived out their terms of service in peace and harmony with their Chinese neighbors.

The support given American Protestants fell far short of that demanded by the French. In 1899 an imperial edict, urged by the French minister, stated that Roman Catholic bishops were to have direct access to viceroys and governors and were to be considered of the same rank. Lesser clergy were to rank with provincial officials. The State Department asked its minister in Peking, the Honorable E. H. Conger, to obtain the same privileges for Americans. The ambassador spoke at the annual meeting of the Southern Presbyterians in 1899 and asked if they wanted the same treatment. The mission's reply was a categorical no.

> *Resolved,* that the members of the Southern Presbyterian Mission ask nothing more than the rights of private citizens of the United States.... Right relations between Church and State forbid missionaries to claim "equal rank with viceroys and governors."[15]

When the ambassador found that most Protestant missionaries took the same position, he did not pursue the matter further.

Missionaries and the Reform Movement

The debacle of the war with Japan and the encroachment of the Western powers brought new impetus to the demands for reform that were sweeping the Empire. Professor Hao Chang cites a number of factors that propelled the country toward transformation, among which was "the intellectual activity of Christian missionaries in the 1890s."[16] Missionaries were not only evangelists of a new faith but the "cultural brokers" of Western secular ideas. This they accomplished, writes Dr. Chang, through three institutions: schools, private associations and newspapers. Each of these can be illustrated in the mission programs of the day.

Schools

By 1900 approximately forty thousand students attended Christian institutions. This was but a fraction of the student population but Jessie G. Lutz has pointed out that the contribution made to the reform movement by the schools far exceeded the size of the student body.[17] Mission schools emphasized such subjects as modern science, mathematics, world history and English. This prepared graduates for employment by commercial trading companies and the new government bureaus such as the railroads, telegraph service, and maritime customs. Christian schools received students "on the margins of Chinese society" as they charged little tuition and so provided "an avenue of mobility for families with modest income." Christian schools emphasized education for women who with few exceptions were excluded from the traditional academies. Mission schools "played a role in bringing medical education to China and in establishing a formal certification required for doctors." Textbooks prepared for mission schools were important in developing a vocabulary for the physical and social sciences.

The most prestigious school in the land to be identified with the reform movement was the Tung-wen Kuan (School for Interpreters) in Peking, of which W. A. P. Martin was president. By the year 1896 a number of graduates of the institution were serving as interpreters and consuls in China's infant foreign service. Martin, who was granted the rank of Mandarin of the Second Class in 1898, became one of the most influential advisors to reform-minded Chinese officials.

Associations

Missionaries were great organizers and were instrumental in the formation of numerous societies that aimed to promote special causes or address one or more social problems. The following examples are among those that were most successful:

Both the *YMCA and YWCA* had their early beginnings in Presbyterian schools. One of the first YMCAs was organized on the campus of the Hangzhou Christian College in the late 1880s.[18] The first YWCA was established by Miss Esther Wilson (Mrs. P. Frank Price) in 1890 at the Hangzhou Girls' School.[19] The "Y" became organized on a national scale in 1896 with the visit of John R. Mott and the holding of a national convention. From the schools the movement spread to the port cities where it had a far-reaching influence among those in business and the professions.

Anti-footbinding leagues were another example of missionary organizations that sought to bring about social change. For centuries the practice of footbinding had deformed the feet of little girls, whose limbs would be wrapped tightly with bandages while still quite young. After the bandages had been in place for a number of years, they could not be removed without intense pain. The women would then be fated to hobble around on their bound feet for the rest of their lives. The origins of the practice are unknown but are related to the erotic interest of the men in the delicate "lotus feet" of their women.

Annual reports and missionary letters cite in strongest terms their opposition to this age old practice. This letter from a young single missionary to her mother in Atlanta, Georgia, could be repeated in missionary literature again and again:

> Thursday we organized an Anti-Foot-Binding Society and there were quite a large number of women who promised to unbind their feet — I hope it will do some good. Charlotte was elected Vice-President — one of the Chinese women is President.[20]

When the Southern Presbyterians opened their school for girls in Hangzhou, one of the requirements for admission was that the bandages must be removed from the feet of the little girls age seven to twelve. In 1896 the Presbyterian Girls' School in Nanjing was finally successful in "setting the last pair of bound feet free" from among its twenty-eight girls.[21]

In order to be successful, the movement had to reach the men as mothers feared they would be unable to arrange good marriages for their daughters if they had large, unbound feet. In 1878 after considerable debate, the Presbyterian Synod took official action against footbinding and from that date reports of the Anti-Footbinding League became regular features of the meetings.[22]

One of the most successful missionary enterprises was the *Anti-Opium League*. The terrible effects of the drug are well documented in the literature of the day. Jonathan Spence's "well informed guess" is that there were 40 million opium users of whom 15 million were addicts.[23] During these years over five thousand tons of opium were imported annually from India.

In 1896 Dr. Hampden DuBose of Suzhou organized the Anti-Opium League, which was supported by missionaries of all denominations, other Westerners and Christian and non-Christian Chinese. For years DuBose carried on an extensive correspondence with officials of the British government, Chinese viceroys and the International Commission against Opium in the Hague. In 1902 when on furlough he met with President Theodore Roosevelt and interviewed officials of the State Department. As a result of these visits, U.S. consuls in China were instructed to prepare annual reports on the ravages of the opium trade.

Success came in 1906. The British Parliament unanimously adopted the following resolution: "The Indo-Chinese opium trade is morally indefensible, and the Government is requested to bring it to a speedy close."[24] In this same year DuBose made the acquaintance of the newly appointed governor of Jiangsu, who was sympathetic to the anti-opium cause. Governor Chen introduced DuBose to the viceroy of Central China, Tuan Fang. In the resulting interview the viceroy suggested that DuBose draw up an anti-opium "memorial" (petition) to the Throne and have it signed by all the missionaries in China. DuBose secured 1,333 signatures and bound these with his memorial with a yellow silk cover which was dispatched to the viceroy who forwarded it to the emperor. On 20 September 1906, the imperial edict against opium was issued and dispatched to all parts of the realm. Remarkably, it was a near verbatim copy of the memorial written by DuBose. In the annual report of the League for the year 1906, Dr. DuBose wrote of the rapid progress that had been made:

> Opium dens were closed by the thousands, all opium smokers were registered, mass meetings were held in the interest of the campaign, and great bonfires were built in public places for the burning of opium and opium pipes.[25]

Reform clubs were formed in various cities of the Empire among government officials who believed that radical changes were needed in the affairs of government. In this, the Welsh missionary Rev. Timothy Richards took the lead. His leadership of the movement is acknowledged by Professor Hao Chang:

> Under his vigorous and imaginative leadership the society not only greatly expanded its activities but adopted a new approach, aiming its efforts primarily at persuading the Chinese elite of the value of Western culture.[26]

Gilbert Reid of Shandong became closely associated with the movement and resigned from the Presbyterian Mission in 1895 to organize a ministry entitled Mission among the Higher Classes:

> Gilbert Reid, a missionary to the upper classes among the Chinese, has been instrumental in the formation of a reform club in Peking. The library and reading room of the club will be supplied with books and papers on science and politics, while the plan includes also courses of lectures and a daily paper.[27]

Newspapers and the Press

Southern Methodist missionary Rev. Young J. Allen founded the *Church News* (Chiao-hui hsin-pao) in 1868, which had a profound influence upon the educated elite of the day. This became a channel for spreading Christian news and beliefs as well as serving as a forum for social and political discussion. "It achieved a degree of influence on the Chinese elite that was unprecedented since the beginnings of large-scale missionary activities in China."[28] The Presbyterian Press served as printers for much of the new reform literature. In 1898 it printed 45 million pages![29]

Did missionaries identify the Kingdom of God too closely with that of Western civilization? Some, like W. A. P. Martin, felt that radical social changes were needed. Only after the pattern of Western civilization was accepted would the Chinese be receptive to Christianity. Others, like Hampden DuBose, who also worked tirelessly for social change, were conscious of the danger of equating Christianity with Western progress:

> Are railroads a means of grace? Have they a sanctifying influence? What have men-of-war to do with the coming of the Prince of Peace?.... There is no necessary connection between civilization and salvation. If God chooses to bless these outward movements, well and good, but let the church rely solely on the "foolishness of preaching," and the power of the Holy Ghost.[30]

New Stations

As the reform movement picked up steam, the penetration of missionaries into the interior also accelerated. Railroads opened up the hinterland and alleviated the suffering during famine years as grain from areas of plenty could be rushed to areas of scarcity. But railroads were not an unmixed blessing. They were built with the loans and expertise of the West. They symbolized the exploitative power of the foreigner. They deprived the canal boat operators and the coolies of their livelihood. To the superstitious Chinese peasant, the iron rails that cut across the plains, vaulted the rivers and bored through the mountain ranges destroyed the harmony of nature. They showed no respect for the ancestral rice lands and desecrated the graves of the ancients. Even the name given

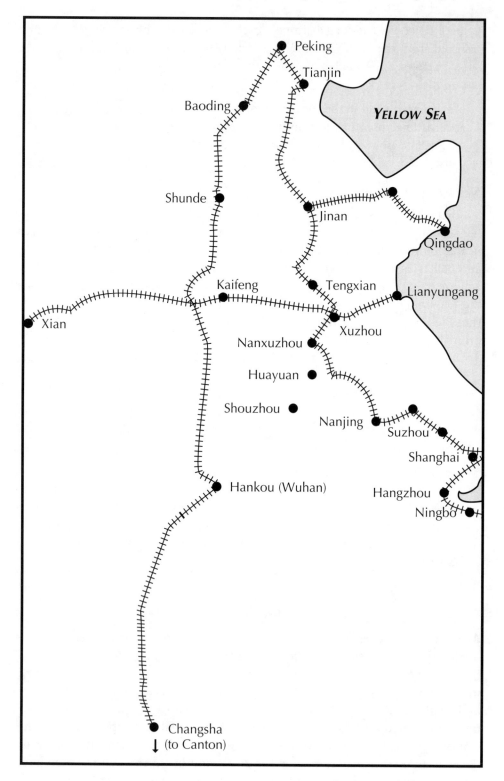

North, Central China and Railroads 1900–1915

to the locomotive that belched forth smoke and ashes — *hwa cha* (fire cart) — personified its sinister origin. Could not these chariots of fire be responsible for all the misfortunes that had overtaken China? Missionaries and the railroads were of the same stuff and would be tarred with the same brush. The three new Presbyterian mission stations started during these years were associated with the coming of the railroads.

Baoding (Paoting), 1893

For years the New York board had urged the North China Mission to expand its work beyond Peking into the countryside. An opportunity to do this arose when the contract was let for the building of the Peking-Hankou Railroad. The railroad would pass through Baoding, an important walled city and capital of Hebei (Chili) Province some 110 miles southwest of Peking.[31]

A cathedral in the city gave evidence of the strong Roman Catholic presence for over a hundred years. Both the American Board (ABCFM) and the CIM had worked there which is why the Presbyterians had avoided the city. But with its growing importance, another mission in the city would be welcomed. In 1893 land was purchased outside the North Gate of the city with the help of the ABCFM. Veteran missionaries Rev. and Mrs. J. L. Whiting were the first to arrive.

The work proceeded in the conventional manner with daily preaching by Rev. James Lowrie at the city chapel, the treatment of patients at the dispensary opened by Dr. George Taylor and the visitation of the women by Mrs. Amelia Lowrie.[32] Graduates from Dengzhou College provided indispensable assistance. Some of the gentry requested that a school for boys be opened that would teach the new "Western learning." The school was begun but those who had asked for it lost interest when they found out that Christian doctrine was "a part of the package." A school for girls was more successful. Soon the dispensary was recording one thousand patients a month. Adult baptisms were between five and ten a year and by 1900 membership numbered approximately one hundred.

The reception given to the newcomers was mixed. The officials showed appreciation for the work of the dispensary, but others were ready to resort to physical violence. The following incident was reported in the *New York Sun* of 11 March 1894:

> Some soldiers who were here in Paotingfu, on the way to the seat of war [the Sino-Japanese conflict], entered the street chapel of the Presbyterians while the Rev. J. Walter Lowrie was preaching, knocked over the benches, tried to get his watch and spectacles, and seemed ready to make an attack upon his person. An outcry out of doors led the soldiers to run out into the street, and Mr. Lowrie closed the chapel. The mob raged outside . . . until sunset, but could not get in.[33]

In 1898 a mob assaulted the Roman Catholic cathedral over the interference of foreign priests in local lawsuits. On this occasion the Presbyterians were spared. But two years later the ax would fall on all.

Qingdao (Tsingtao), 1898

The seizure of Jiaozhou Bay by the Germans in 1897 and the construction of modern port facilities at Qingdao had an immediate effect on the Presbyterian work in Shandong. The projected rail line inland to the provincial capital of Jinan decreased the importance of Dengzhou and Yantai and increased the importance of Weixian, which would be on the new line.

Even before the Germans arrived, the Presbyterians had eyed Qingdao for a mission station. Frank Chalfant described the magnificent harbor as able to hold "the navies of the world."[34] A later generation of missionaries would discover that Qingdao was an ideal summer resort with the finest beaches in the Orient.

The Shandong Mission assigned the task of opening the new station to Rev. and Mrs. Paul D. Bergen. In 1898 they rented a small thatched-roof house outside the city but Mr. Bergen came down with typhus fever and the German authorities served notice that the house must be torn down for sanitary reasons. Rents were high and as the Board had no funds, the Bergens bought land and erected a house at their own expense. Rev. and Mrs. L. J. Davies arrived the next year. Later the German government gave the Presbyterians a hilltop site with views of sea and mountains.

When the Bergens arrived construction was well under way:

> The Germans are developing a modern city at Tsingtau. They are grading streets, digging sewers, demolishing the dirty and overcrowded Chinese quarters, erecting fine buildings, constructing wharves and warehouses, improving the harbor...opening coal mines, running steamers between Tsingtau and Shanghai, and constructing a railroad and telegraph lines into the interior.... Tsingtau is rapidly becoming one of the chief cities of Shantung.[35]

Among the throngs of Chinese coming to the city seeking work were Christians from Presbyterian congregations in the interior. Bergen found 150 Christians among the newcomers and a number of these were graduates of Dengzhou College, who were much in demand by the city administrators. Sunday worship services were begun and almost from the beginning the church became self-supporting. Bergen wrote of the Christian community:

> I must say that, on the whole, we have no reason to be ashamed of our Christians. They have kept together pretty well, and seem to appreciate better than ever before that they are one in Christ. Some are growing rapidly rich and some have to labor as coolies, and this, as elsewhere occasionally produces jealousies among the little flock.[36]

Two German Protestant missions were at work when the Bergens arrived — the Berlin Mission and the Weimar Mission. Presbyterian "native evangelists" assisted the German missions and pupils from Presbyterian families attended the German mission schools. Regular church services were held in the German chapel until they could build their own church. A division of territory was worked out with the Presbyterians continuing in the area in which they had previously worked from Weixian and the Germans beginning work in unevangelized territory. Medical work was unnecessary because of the availability of medical care at the new German mission hospital. The only restriction imposed by the German authorities was that German rather than English should be taught in the mission schools. Public offices and businesses were closed on Sunday — which made church attendance easier.

A budget crisis at home made it difficult to make grants for the new work. This was "a blessing in disguise" necessitating "a resort to the Korean method of self-support from the outset."[37] As the congregation grew, they purchased a lot in the heart of the city on which they built a brick and stone sanctuary. In 1901 the Presbytery of Shandong organized the congregation with a hundred members to which the Rev. Ting Li Mei, a graduate of Dengzhou College, was called. From the first Ting's salary was provided by the congregation.

The German occupation provided better transportation and economic benefits. But the harshness of German troops in seizing territory for mines and the railroad added to the hostility against all foreigners across the province.

Xuzhou, 1897

The third station opened during this period was also linked to the railroads. Xuzhou was a large walled city with a population of about two hundred thousand at the extreme northwestern corner of Jiangsu Province. Formerly on the Yellow River, it had been left high and dry when the river changed its course in the 1850s. It was destined to become a major railroad junction on the Tianjin-Pukou Railway linking the capital in the north with Nanjing and Shanghai in the south. Crossing this major trunk line at Xuzhou was the Lung-Hai Railroad running from Lianyungang (Haichow) on the Yellow Sea westward to Xian. As a major railroad junction it would be the site of many decisive battles fought during China's civil wars and the war with Japan.

But all that was in the future. In 1895 Xuzhou was isolated and difficult to reach. One missionary family recorded twenty-six days of travel to reach the city from Shanghai via steam launch on the Yangtze, house boat along the Grand Canal and then overland by cart.[38] Xuzhou had resisted all attempts by both Roman Catholic and Protestant missionaries to secure a toehold within the city walls.

Rev. Absalom Sydenstricker first visited the area at the request of Rev. Alfred Jones of the English Baptist Mission who had baptized five Christians in the city but was unable to care for them because of the long distance to be traveled from his base in Shandong. It was partly with Xuzhou in mind that Sydenstricker had opened the station at Suqian, seventy miles away on the Grand Canal. When the Sydenstrickers were reassigned to Zhenjiang because of health, Hugh White and Mark Grier were given the task of opening work in Xuzhou. Both were newlyweds. Rev. Mark Grier had married Miss Nettie Donaldson, M.D., of the Northern Presbyterian Mission in Jining and the Rev. Hugh White had married Augusta Graves of Hangzhou.

White visited the city with Sydenstricker in 1895 but they were attacked by a mob and sought refugee in the *Yamen* (Office of the magistrate.)[39] The next year White and Grier tried again. They stayed twenty days in an inn, but were then forced to leave.

A third attempt in December 1896 is described by White:

> On arrival, the refusal of several inns to receive us did not look very encouraging, and after spending the night in a house [outside the city walls] not quite so well furnished as the White House or Vanderbilt's palace, that landlord also began to squirm. But the Lord's time had come.[40]

They were about to be ousted, but two of the city officials came with the shocking good news that the newly appointed *Taotai* (chief magistrate) was concerned about their lodging and would help them find a location in the city. Because of intervention by foreign diplomats in Peking he had been instructed to help both Catholic and Protestant missionaries get peaceably settled.

The Catholics had secured land and had begun to build. Grier and White purchased property inside the West Gate consisting of four old Chinese houses. But the property could not be left vacant for long. Mark would remain while Hugh returned to Suqian to get his wife. The Griers would move in the spring after the birth of their first baby. White returned to Suqian with the good news of the property purchase. Mark would be returning shortly "in time for Christmas dinner." Christmas came but no Mark. A fine goose dinner was waiting. Nettie was broken hearted. The hours of the evening passed slowly. Then about two o'clock in the morning he staggered in

> faint and half dead from cold — his clothes frozen to his body! His cart, in crossing a frozen river, had fallen in; and he had gotten soaked in the icy water. Also he had been robbed, his suitcase containing all his money and valuables, and even his glasses, had been stolen from the rear of the cart. But he was *home again.... It was Christmas after all!*[41]

The two foreign women did not venture outside the small compound for the first six months. To do so would mean being cursed and pelted with mud and stones. Signs had been posted on the street saying that the two women were actually men and were masquerading as women in order to trap unsuspecting children. Something had to be done to break down the hostility and suspicion. One day Mark announced that he and Nettie would dress their newly arrived daughter, Isabel, in her new Chinese clothes and all three of them would venture out together on the street. Perhaps the baby would help break down suspicion.

Immediately a large crowd gathered to see the small "foreign devil." She was not all that different from a Chinese baby! The crowd laughed and Isabel laughed back. They were human beings after all. Then one man said "let me hold it" and to Nettie's astonishment Mark passed the small precious package into the arms of the Chinese gentleman. Others wanted to hold the baby and Nettie watched with apprehension as her baby made the rounds throughout the throng. The ice was broken.

The next day a Mrs. Lee came to call. After the customary greetings she asked, "Where did you get that baby you showed us yesterday?" "It's my baby," replied Nettie. "It couldn't be yours, for the notices say you are a man pretending to be a woman." "But it *is* my baby" replied Nettie. Mrs. Lee came back with a challenge: "Well, if you are its mother, then nurse it!" Mrs. Grier proceeded to nurse the child. Seeing was believing.

Mrs. Lee was the first to come to Dr. Grier's clinic and the first woman to be baptized in the Xuzhou field. The laughter of a little child had brought her.

The old houses in the compound were repaired. Women began to come to the clinic in droves as the magic of the foreign medicine woman began to circulate around the city. Mark Grier, who had had some medical training before leaving America, saw men patients. On serious cases, his wife took over. In 1904 Dr. A. A. McFadyen arrived. He would give thirty-five years of service to the Xuzhou men's hospital. In 1905 10,000 treatments were given and 325 in-patients accommodated in the two hospitals.[42]

Building more substantial facilities began in 1900 with the arrival of a shipment of Oregon pine, thirty-six days in transit from Shanghai by barge during which time Mark Grier camped on top of the lumber. In 1902 the Julia Farrior Stanford Boys' School opened and soon reached its capacity of twenty-five scholars. The Girls' School was opened in 1911 under Mary and Charlotte Thompson and in the first year enrolled sixty-two students.[43]

The Christian community began with the five members baptized by Mr. Jones and grew rapidly. A church building with a capacity of 350 was erected in 1905. Soon it was inadequate. The organization of the church dates from 1906 with 2 elders, 2 deacons, 104 communicant members. The report that year states:

> The church was organized on Presbyterian lines, is not under the jurisdiction of the Presbyterian Church in the U.S., but is one of the units which it is hoped will ultimately form the Presbyterian Church of China.[44]

These were famine years in north Jiangsu and at times the entire energy of the station was spent in distributing relief. Following in the wake of famine was disease. Missionary strength was depleted because of sickness and forced evacuations. Death took its toll on missionaries and their small children.[45]

"The 100 Days"

A reform movement led by a Cantonese Confucian scholar, Kang Youwei, came close to breaking the grip of the traditional orthodoxy and achieved power briefly during what has become known as the "100 Days" of 1898.

Kang began with a radical reinterpretation of Confucius that enlisted the ancient sage on the side of the reformers! The traditional texts that emphasized the conservative nature of the classics were forgeries. The original manuscripts supported the doctrine of institutional reform. "In Kang's view, Confucius was above all, a great innovator."[46] Thus Kang skillfully disarmed the conservatives, provided legitimation for reform, and sanctioned a radical attack on the imperial orthodoxy.

After the catastrophic defeat by Japan, Kang secured the signatures of thirteen hundred scholars who were taking the civil service examination in Peking and petitioned the throne to initiate institutional reforms. It is doubtful that the emperor ever saw the message. But with Russian advances in Manchuria and the German seizure of Qingdao the clamor for reform could no longer be stifled. Kang again appealed to the throne and this time there was a positive response.

The new initiative came at an opportune time. In 1895 the Empress Dowager, who had dominated Chinese politics for years, cancelled elaborate plans for her sixtieth birthday party because of the defeat by Japan and retired to the Summer Palace. The young Emperor, Guangxu, turned twenty-four and assumed the prerogatives of the throne. Under the influence of a reform-minded tutor he became enchanted with the publications of Chinese reformers and the literature of the West. On one occasion he ordered 160 books published by the Presbyterian Press and the Bible Society.[47]

On 11 June 1898 the Emperor, closely advised by Kang, issued the first of a series of reform decrees initiating the 100 Days of reform. There is evidence that missionaries influenced the initiation of the program.[48] There followed a steady stream of decrees aimed at the modernization of the Chinese state. They ranged across the whole gamut of national life. The civil service examinations were revised to include a knowledge of Western learning. Subsidies to Manchus were abolished. The Imperial University of Peking was established and W. A. P. Martin was appointed dean of the faculty.

At first it seemed that the Empress Dowager supported the reforms. But her silence was due more to misgivings about the rampant anti-Manchu sentiments sweeping the country. The wily "Old Buddha" was merely biding her time. As the summer wore on the reform edicts became more radical. Neither Kang nor the Emperor had had any experience in the art of governing. Some proposals were utopian and could scarcely have been implemented by the most ardent administrator. They challenged the vested interests of everyone in authority — Manchu princes, the Grand Council, Chinese literati, military commanders, and the eunuchs.

On 21 September the Empress Dowager, ostensibly at the request of the

Grand Council, reasserted her authority as regent in a coup d'etat. Troops under the command of a loyal confidant were secretly brought to the capital. The Emperor was seized by guards and eunuchs loyal to the Dowager and confined to the "Ocean Terrace," a small island in the interior of the palace grounds. Kang Youwei escaped with the aid of British consular officials. Six reformers were executed. Others found refuge in Japan. The 100 Days of reform had come to an end.[49]

The reform movement ended in failure but many of its proposals would be reintroduced in the early years of the twentieth century by the same "Old Buddha" who had first so bitterly opposed them. But in the meantime the Manchu court, in a backlash against the reformers, turned to support a fanatical cult that plunged the Empire and the Christian movement into the deepest crisis yet to be faced.

Presbyterian Missions at the End of the Nineteenth Century

Before proceeding to the momentous events of 1900, let us pause and consider the status of the Presbyterian work. Sixty years had passed since their arrival on the mainland. Since time in the Orient is measured in sixty-year cycles, it is appropriate now to review the record.

The expansion of the work force is impressive. In 1899 the Northern Presbyterians numbered 196 missionaries organized in 6 missions and 19 stations. An educational network had been established consisting of 23 academies and 244 elementary day schools in which over 3,000 scholars were enrolled. Three fledgling institutions of college level had been begun. Sixteen hospitals and thirteen dispensaries were in operation, treating over 150,000 patients a year. The Presbyterian Press, the most prestigious publishing house in the country, was turning out four million pages of Christian literature each month.[50]

The Southern Presbyterians had likewise experienced rapid growth since their arrival in 1867. In 1899 they numbered seventy-one missionaries, fifty of whom had been appointed within the last ten years. Ten stations had been started. Medical work had been begun in four locations. Two high schools and sixteen elementary schools were in operation. Cooperation with the Northern Presbyterians was in progress.[51]

The PCUSA and PCUS senior mission executives visited China in the year 1897 and their comments on the issues of the day help put the program in perspective.[52] Dr. Speer stated his opinions forcefully and convincingly. He respected the decisions made on the field but on occasion disagreed sharply. Chester's report is more descriptive and he appears more willing to leave decisions with the missions. There is no record that the two met while in China although they were there at approximately the same time.

There was little basic difference in policies. For both evangelism was central. The overriding purpose was to establish a Chinese church. Fearing that missionaries would be sidetracked by peripheral demands on their time and money, Dr. Speer again and again called them back to the central purpose:

> We need to work with more common absorption of purpose toward the great central aim, planting in China in a native Church the forces of the spirit of Christ, full of grace and truth and charity.[53]

Dr. Speer cited the many strengths of the Presbyterian missions and took pride in what had been accomplished. He applauded the high standards that were required for baptism and the character of native workers. He rejoiced in the confidence and friendliness that existed between missionaries and Chinese workers. He applauded the fine spirit of cooperation of the various missions and cited as an example the relationship with the Southern Presbyterians in Hangzhou.[54]

On other issues Speer was quite critical. The mission had moved too fast in creating a complex church structure. At Ningbo they had "organized a church before they had a convert and . . . a presbytery before they had a church."[55] The foreign structure was one that emphasized "proper procedure" but lacked "energetic aggressiveness." Chinese would want to make modifications and should be encouraged to do so. To quote Dr. Speer again:

> The preservation of the greatest simplicity of organization will contribute to the efficiency of the native Church and the native workers. It is a misfortune to build up the organization . . . more rapidly than the life within will bear.[56]

Speer neglected to say that the impetus for organizing the first presbyteries had come from New York.

Speer saw the lack of self-support as the key problem. In 1899 there were only ten fully self-supporting Presbyterian churches. In the Ningbo field churches organized forty years ago were still receiving as much subsidy as they had at the beginning.[57]

There were understandable reasons for this: poverty of the people, lack of a benevolence tradition, the necessity for a well trained clergy and unclear lines of authority between church and mission.[58] Yet a more vigorous appeal for self-support should be initiated. He cited with approval the Nevius Plan and the Shandong policy whereby

> the people provide the place of worship, though it be but a humble home, and supervising them by an itinerant evangelist, to whose support they shall be induced to contribute as soon and as liberally as possible.[59]

Speer was distressed that many of the younger missionaries "seem to have given up chapel preaching." Instead they had moved toward "an unjustifiable development of educational work." Schools were needed but their "one aim is to raise up Christian leaders" rather than provide education for the general public. There was danger that students would be "trained out of touch with their people and emerge unfitted for leadership."[60]

Speer had words of praise for the medical work but wished that there was more "medical itineration" and "evangelistic utilization."[61] He had some provocative words of caution about the extensive works of charity:

> This enormous philanthropic representation of Christianity has prevented our making one definite and unmistakable impression — that we are preaching Jesus.... The people of China [regard] Christianity as a great charity and not as an authoritative message from God to His children.[62]

One can understand a board secretary's reluctance to endorse each and every work of charity. But the missionary, face to face with the agony and pain of those who suffered, could not but make appeals to the church at home, even though at times these were unauthorized. Contrary to the policies of the Board, they secured support for the deaf, the dumb, the blind and the insane. But for these acts of charity, the Christian movement was remembered long after the memory of other institutions had faded.

Dr. Chester's observations paralleled those of Dr. Speer. He reiterated the primacy of preaching.[63] He was glad to report that the Southern Presbyterians were among the "most strenuous supporters" of the policy of self-support. He believed that the mission should own as little property as possible since it often became a source of trouble. But ownership of residences was preferable to renting because of the health factor. The medical work needed to be upgraded. Only those with the best training should be sent out and these should be provided with full and necessary equipment.[64]

On one issue he was highly critical of mission policy:

> If I should offer any criticism of our past policy...it would be that there has all along been too much scattering of forces. Stations have been opened faster than we have been able to man them for effective work, with the result that new missionaries have often been pushed into places of responsibility before they were prepared.[65]

Mission policy of the Southern Presbyterians differed from that of the northerners in two respects. First, the southerners were slower to ordain Chinese pastors. They felt that ordination should be delayed until full support was provided by the congregation. Second, there was less emphasis on educational institutions. The Executive Committee warned against starting schools before the Christian constituency was able to share in their cost.[66]

The Gospel and Chinese Culture

But the basic problem facing the missionary lay not in the administration of the program but in the Chinese culture, which seemed all too often impervious to the gospel of Jesus Christ. How could Americans present the gospel to Chinese people whose culture and civilization was so different from their own? By the end of the nineteenth century a mainstream "Presbyterian" viewpoint was beginning to crystalize.

Both Speer and Chester spoke with great respect for Chinese civilization. Dr. Chester wrote:

> The mission of the church in China is not to civilize the Chinese. They had a civilization which is very different from ours, but which is very old and elaborate, and which...suits them in some respects better than our civilization ever will....The church's business in China is to...establish the kingdom of God; and God's instrument for that purpose...is the preaching of the gospel.[67]

Speer commented that a few missionaries "fiercely denounce" the Chinese religions without any qualification. A few at the other extreme "are content with kindly enlightening intercourse without much preaching of the gospel." The majority, including most Presbyterians, are in-between. They "speak respectfully of the Chinese religions" but present "uncompromisingly the full orbed light of Christ."[68] Speer cites this conversation between a Presbyterian missionary and one from another mission:

> "Well, Mr. J., have you got any patent way of preaching the Gospel? You seem to be having more success than we are." "Well, no," I replied, "but we try not to irritate needlessly, and we ground our teaching as far as we can on the reason and sense of man." "O, bosh!" he said. "I know that nonsense. The world is damned. Believe and be saved, is my preaching."[69]

One of the greatest obstacles to Christian discipleship was ancestor worship. Here were strong differences of opinion. A few Protestants and most Roman Catholics were willing to make some accommodation to the Confucian ceremonies. The great majority of Presbyterians were utterly opposed to it. Dr. Speer concurred with this view but argued that Christians should be "urged to keep their tombs in such good repair...as to disprove the charge of irreverence and unfilial conduct."[70]

Polygamy was likewise a major obstacle to church membership. There was general agreement that polygamy contracted subsequent to baptism could not be tolerated. But what about husbands who had taken second wives prior to conversion? Speer wrote that he was absolutely opposed to their being received into the church.[71] But some missionaries believed that in some circumstances the husband could be baptized and received into the church without requiring that the second wife be put away. A case in point was the baptism of a man with two wives in Xuzhou by Rev. Mark Grier. Dr. Samuel Laws of Maryland heard about it and protested the action vigorously. He sent an indictment to Grier's Presbytery of South Carolina, and attacked Dr. Chester for permitting this to happen. Chester supported his missionaries as did the Executive Committee and the PCUS General Assembly of 1906.[72]

The issue of whether the Chinese classics should be taught in mission schools was another point of disagreement. The opposition was strongest among the younger generation of students who had lost all respect for the old ways. They argued that the classics were full of superstition, their rote memorization was useless and the archaic language could no longer be understood.

Dr. Hayes of Dengzhou College advocated a more cautious approach. The classics formed the foundation for Chinese literature. The Greek and Latin classics, even more pagan than the books of Confucius, had long been used in the Christian schools of the West. Rather than eliminate the classics, their rote memory could be minimized and they could be taught in an intelligent and rational way.[73]

Ten Years of Church Growth

In spite of seemingly insurmountable obstacles, there was real progress. Viewed in terms of the hundreds of millions within the Chinese Empire it was small indeed but compared with past years the advance was substantial. Note selected statistics taken from the missions of the Northern Presbyterian Church for the ten-year period 1889–1899:

	1889			1899		
	Members	*Churches*	*Pastors*	*Members*	*Churches*	*Pastors*
Canton	509	8	3	2,266	20	3
Hainan	—	—	—	57	2	—
Central	943	15	15	1,625	20	19
Shandong	2,260	16	1	5,429	41	14
Peking	140	2	1	380	3	2
Totals	3,852	41	20	9,757	86	38

Note: "Members" represents baptized adults in good standing who had undergone a period of instruction. "Churches" represents organized congregations who had elected elders and were led in most cases by an ordained Chinese pastor. These congregations would be at least partially self-supporting. "Pastors" were ordained Chinese clergy. Statistics come from the *Annual Reports* for the two years.

The report shows that real, solid progress was made. Growth of communicant members was about 250 percent. The Christian constituency (including children, inquirers, students in mission schools) would be four to five times this number. The number of organized churches and ordained pastors had doubled. There would be many other places of regular worship led by lay workers.

But the rate of growth was quite uneven. Some missions had experienced very slow growth. The Canton Mission, after years of slow growth, had exploded — showing a fourfold increase in members. The years of steady preaching by missionaries in the street chapels was finally having its effect. Some of this growth was the result of Chinese who had been converted to Christianity in the United States and had returned to the Canton area. Ningbo had a large number of pastors because of its long history but many of these were still being subsidized.

In Shandong the progress was most significant in all categories. Note the dramatic increase in the number of ordained ministers and in self-support. Three reasons were given for the Shandong advance: (1) the emphasis initially given to self-support by Nevius and others; (2) the fact that Shandong churches were in rural areas where there was greater receptivity; (3) the aggressive mission policy of wide itineration.[74]

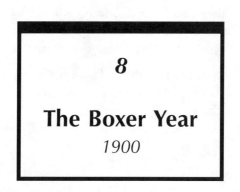

8

The Boxer Year

1900

How to explain it — the Terror that swept over North China in the summer of 1900? What were the causes of the bizarre uprising of the *Yihetuan,* usually translated into English as "The Righteous and Harmonious Fists," more popularly known as the "Boxers"? Comparisons are hard to come by: The Indian Sepoy Mutiny of 1857? The massacre of Chinese railroad workers by citizens of Rock Springs, Wyoming, in 1885? The Chinese Cultural Revolution of the 1960s? Or "ethnic cleansing" in Bosnia in 1993? The list of possible causes of the uprising goes on and on: the "scramble for concessions," the railroads, the German seizures in Shandong, the Yellow River floods, the failed Reform Movement, the enigmatic personality of the Empress Dowager — and, of course, the missionaries. Nearly one hundred years later the assignment of fault is probably impossible and unnecessary. Better, one should simply tell the story and note its effect on the missionary enterprise.

It is necessary to devote a chapter to this one year for reasons that at first may not be self-evident. The year was a turning point in China's search for a national identity. The life-and-death crises of the times laid bare the character of missionaries and Chinese Christians. The dramatic nature of the events focused the spotlight of world opinion on the China Christian mission. The outcome of the chaotic events tested the mettle of the mission board and church at home in their resolve to "win China for Christ." How serious were they about an endeavor that was far more demanding and complex than first envisioned? And when all the fury had been spent, the uprising would set the stage for a new beginning.

The Righteous and Harmonious Fists

For years the Righteous and Harmonious Fists had been known as one of the innumerable secret societies of China that had fomented rebellion against the established order.[1] In the spring of 1899 reports began to surface that the society had reemerged under the banner "Support the Qing and Exterminate the Foreigners." They claimed that all the ills of the nation could be attributed to the foreigners, whom they called the *Ta Mao-tzu* (great hairy men) who had to be exterminated or expelled from the country. Only then would China return to its former glory. A popular jingle expressed the sentiment:

> When at last all the Foreign Devils
> Are expelled to the very last man,
> The Great Qing, united, together,
> Will bring peace to this our land.[2]

The movement began to gain the support of a number of disparate groups that felt that they had suffered from the foreigner's presence: the literati, Manchu princes, coolies and boatmen thrown out of work by the railroads, peasants whose fields had been destroyed by floods and roving bandits who had nothing to lose. Armed bands were recruited from among the peasants and loosely organized into units of from twenty-five to fifty young men under a leader who had complete command authority. They engaged in elaborate drills of slow motion calisthenics from which they gained the name "boxers." They boasted that these exercises would confer magical charms that would protect them from the firearms of the aliens. Shandong was their heartland, which meant an inevitable confrontation with the Presbyterians.

The first reference to the Boxer disturbances appears in a letter written in the spring of 1899 by Charles Killie of Linyi to the Presbyterian Board. Christian families were being "plundered, beaten, tortured, and killed" and they feared that worse was yet to come.[3] Reports from the Shandong Mission indicate the movement was gaining ground:

> Rebellion added to the horror of the year. Mobs formed in various parts
> of the province. The "Boxers" and the "Great Sword Society" became
> ominously familiar names.[4]

The troubles escalated when the Shandong governor, Yuxian, came out openly in support of the Boxer cause. Boxer bands were subsidized, given official sanction and encouraged in their attacks on railroads, foreigners and Chinese Christians. Foreign diplomats in Peking put pressure on the court to have Yuxian removed. He was transferred to the governorship of Shanxi and Yuan Shikai was appointed governor of Shandong in December 1899. Yuan, a strong administrator with army backing, was able to blunt the Boxer menace within the province, but for the next eight months the situation was out of control.

In March 1900 John Fowler, the U.S. Consul at Yantai, reported a number of ominous signs in his dispatches to Washington. Anti-foreign propaganda was appearing throughout the province and it was believed that the agitation was supported by the officials. In January 1900 a Boxer band beheaded an Anglican missionary some fifty miles southwest of the provincial capital. He warned: "We are on the eve of the most serious trouble," and urged Washington to take strong action.[5]

The action now shifts to Peking. Yuxian, the expelled governor of Shandong, had powerful friends at the court and succeeded in persuading the Empress Dowager to support the Boxer movement. At first this was done surreptitiously but in April, against the advice of most of her advisors and the governors of all the southern provinces, the Dowager issued edicts that sanctioned the movement. The Dowager's reasons have been debated. Did she believe in their miraculous powers? Did she think the foreigners were attempting a coup that would force her abdication in favor of the reform-minded emperor? Or did she think she could control the movement and use it to solidify her hold on the throne? Whatever the case, the Boxers now became more radical in their resolve to exterminate the foreign menace and began the destruction of railroads, telegraph lines and mission stations.

A Rescue Operation

In June Consul Fowler warned all American citizens in the province to flee to places of safety. But there was no way for some to get out. Fowler chartered the Japanese ship *Kwanko Maru* and asked the Rev. George Cornwell, Presbyterian missionary in Yantai, to take charge of the rescue operation.[6] Cornwell sailed with the ship to an inlet on the north coast of Shandong, some two hundred miles west of Yantai. There the steamer waited at the rendezvous point. During the next five days small groups of refugees began to arrive from the interior — a French Roman Catholic bishop, English Baptists and their children from Chingchowfu, Canadian Presbyterians from Henan, a party of Presbyterian women and children from Weixian, another large group from Jinan, a French consul and his party of twenty Chinese soldiers assigned as guards. In all eighty foreigners and Chinese were evacuated. In his report to Consul Fowler, Cornwell told of the harrowing experience of finding food and shelter while they waited, difficulties encountered in trans-shipping the refugees from junks and lighters to the steamer, contrary tides, high seas and reports that roving bands of Boxers were approaching.[7]

Fowler believed that by now most foreigners had been evacuated from Shandong but there was bad news from Weixian. And there was no news at all from the Americans at Baoding. What was happening in Peking was a mystery. Messages to the capital were accepted by the Chinese Telegraph Office but only in plain English. Confidential messages using the consular codes were refused. Had hostilities begun?

Destruction and Escape at Weixian

At the Presbyterian compound in Weixian all was normal until the evacuation message was received from Consul Fowler. Most of the station members then proceeded to the rendezvous point where they were evacuated by Cornwell's steamer. But Miss Emma Boughton and Miss Charlotte Hawes were itinerating in country villages at the time and could not be reached. Rev. Frank Chal-fant volunteered to remain in the station until the single ladies returned and then accompany them to Qingdao. On Sunday 24 June the usual church ser-vices were held. On Monday preparations for leaving were interrupted when an angry mob attempted to climb over the compound wall. Chalfant sent a message to the local magistrate requesting protection. As the situation was get-ting worse, he got his revolver, which he intended to use to frighten the mob away. Chalfant's stirring eye-witness account in his report to Consul Fowler is a thriller:

> I found the windows of the dispensary being smashed by a howling mob of at least one hundred.... I warned them off, fired several shots over their heads. They greeted me with a shower of bricks and stones and yelled: "The Big Knife Society fears not guns!... " I knew that these expressions referred to their superstitious beliefs that they are invulnerable. At once I decided to disabuse their minds of this false idea and seeing they were on the wall and about to enter the compound I ran forward amid a hail of missiles and fired into the crowd.... I took my position at the north-west corner so as to command two sides of the place and warned the mob not to come near. Just then I noticed a man lying dead about the spot where I had fired last. I must have killed him for there were no other shots fired except mine.... I reminded the mob that they had now evidence that they could be killed like any other man. This seemed to make them a lit-tle undecided and kept them at bay for nearly an hour.... [Then] I heard one voice say: "The Yamen [officials] will not protect them!" They then made an onslaught from two sides and after a few more shots I had to retreat barely escaping injury from the large missiles hurled with intent to kill.... Reaching my house by a side entrance, the ladies and I barricaded doors and windows and took refuge upstairs. Soon (8:00 P.M.) the chapel was seen on fire. I noticed there were no rioters in my front yard and so I ordered our party to escape. We went down, passed through my front window, found a ladder on the porch — a most fortunate thing.... At that time the chapel and two residences were burning and they were igniting the house next to mine. One of these men saw us and cried: "the devils are escaping, kill!"... It was now after sunset and growing dark.... No one pursued us, though many were climbing over the wall to loot the buildings. The nearest and only retreat was Fangtze, the German mining shaft 30 li [10 miles] south.... Keeping clear of villages and roads we went through the fields reaching Fangtze at midnight where we were cordially received and provided with food. Four loyal Chinese — two of them ser-vants, escorted us to this place. Next morning the "Chi huin Tsen" [district magistrate] called and expressed sorrow(?) for the occurrence of the night before. He asked me to deal leniently with him and brought me a present of tea.[8]

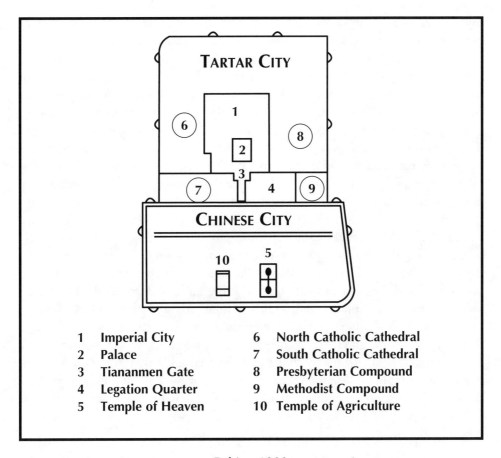

1   **Imperial City**   6   **North Catholic Cathedral**
2   **Palace**   7   **South Catholic Cathedral**
3   **Tiananmen Gate**   8   **Presbyterian Compound**
4   **Legation Quarter**   9   **Methodist Compound**
5   **Temple of Heaven**   10   **Temple of Agriculture**

Peking 1900

A few days later a party of Chinese soldiers escorted the missionaries and German engineers to safety in Qingdao.

"Siege Days" in Peking

In the meantime the Boxers had begun swarming into Peking at the invitation of the Empress Dowager. Engaging in their mystical incantations, they took over public buildings and began the looting of foreign property. On 10 June an international force of two thousand men left Tianjin for Peking but was attacked by the Boxers and forced to turn back. On 20 June Boxers murdered the German ambassador while he was on his way to the Foreign Office for an interview. Supporters of the Boxer cause presented the Dowager with a dispatch reportedly having been sent by the international force, couched in insolent language, demanding her immediate abdication. The dispatch was a forgery but the Dowager believed it was authentic and went into a rage. News that the international force had stormed the Dagu forts at Tianjin added provocation. On 21 June the Dowager issued a declaration of war against the foreign powers and dispatched an order throughout the Empire ordering all foreigners to be exterminated. On this day the siege of the legations began.[9]

Normal activities continued in the schools and hospital at the Presbyterian mission station until May.[10] In spite of the evidence that the government was supporting the Boxers, most people felt that bloodshed would not be permitted in the capital city. But as the storm clouds intensified, the schools were closed and the pupils sent home. News filtered in of the looting of foreign residences. The local magistrate announced that he could no longer provide protection. A missionary council met and decided that all would gather in the Methodist Mission compound and that they would ask for the protection of the American and British legations. The American Legation assigned twenty marines for this purpose and the British furnished ten rifles which ten missionaries quickly learned to use. A food supply was gathered for an anticipated siege.

On the night of 13 June the Boxers, protected by imperial soldiers, went on a rampage destroying every mission building and church except the Methodist compound and the Roman Catholic "Pei Tang" (North Cathedral). The streets were strewn with the mutilated bodies of hundreds of Chinese Christians. An attack was made on the Methodist compound but it was repulsed.

Inexplicably, for days the attackers waited while gathering strength for a second attack. But during the lull the embattled Christian community at the Methodist compound decided to make a break for the Legation Quarters where most of the foreign community had gathered. Eyewitnesses describe how the dangerous journey proceeded:

> At eleven o'clock in the forenoon, the long procession passed through the mission gate into Filial Piety Lane.... First in the ranks marched the twenty marines, followed by the missionary women and children.... Then came the one hundred and twenty-six school girls marching in simple, quiet dignity as if they were on their way to a religious service or school exercise. Hundreds of Chinese women and little children followed by a large company of men and boys were next in order. The handful of missionary men, armed with rifles or revolvers, closed the line of march. It was a brave, sad caravan proceeding on its way from danger into danger.[11]

Remarkably, they were not molested during the march.

The Legation Quarters were defended by 450 legation guards, 475 civilians (mostly missionaries and the diplomatic staff of eleven countries) and 2,500 Chinese Christians. Walls and sandbags provided a formidable barricade. Shops within the confines of the legation area provided canned goods and grain. Horses and mules belonging to the military establishment furnished meat. Good wells provided water.

For seven stifling weeks of summer the defenders held out. They were subject to intermittent attacks and a continuing fuselage of shrapnel. The Legation walls could surely have been overrun had the attackers acted decisively. But the Boxers were uncoordinated and advanced to the attack dancing and reciting magic incantations. Jung Lu, the army commander, despised the Boxers and refused to permit the heavy artillery to be used. At times even the Empress Dowager seemed to waver in her resolve. In one of the most bizarre incidents of the siege, on 16 July the hostilities were halted to permit the Dowager to send watermelon, wine, vegetables, ice and a conciliatory message to those besieged. Then the bombardment began again.

On 4 August an international force of nineteen thousand Japanese, Russian, British, American and French troops left Tianjin. They entered Peking on 14 August, and lifted the siege. As the foreign troops entered the city, the Empress Dowager left in great haste with a small party on what was euphemistically called "the Dowager's Tour of the Western Provinces."

The PCUSA *Annual Report* for 1901 summarizes the participation of the Christian community in the legation defence:

> Though among the most frequently exposed to fire, the missionaries lost not a man. All important committees had missionaries as chairmen and among their most active members. The American Minister testified at the close of the siege, expressing the sentiment of the diplomatic corps, that, had not the missionaries and native Christians been present, no one could have survived the summer.[12]

The Martyrs of Baoding

But most of Hebei province was still under the control of the Boxers. For months no word had been received from the ABCFM, Presbyterian or CIM missionaries at Baoding, 110 miles southwest of the capital. It was rumored that all foreigners in the city had been killed. Not until October were the foreign forces ready to dispatch a relief column to subdue the countryside, find out what had happened at Baoding and rescue any survivors.

Rev. J. Walter Lowrie, a member of Baoding station, had been absent when the Boxers took the city. Distraught with anxiety over the fate of his missionary and Chinese colleagues, he volunteered his services as interpreter for the staff of General Campbell, commander of the British contingent of the relief column. After they arrived in Baoding, Lowrie's message to the Board at home reported the heart-wrenching news: "We have arrived at our destination and, alas, all that we have heard is true. All are in the heavenly home."[13]

The "all" included Dr. George Y. Taylor, M.D., Rev. Frank E. Simcox, Mrs. May Gilson Simcox, three Simcox children, Dr. Cortland Van R. Hodge, M.D., Mrs. Elsie Sinclair Hodge of the Presbyterian mission and seven missionaries and children of the ABCFM and the CIM missions.

How they died is not entirely clear as there were no missionary survivors, but from Lowrie's investigation and the report of the Board secretary, Dr. Arthur J. Brown, which he made when he visited the city a year later, bits and pieces emerge.[14] On 28 June, several young men studying medicine under Dr. Taylor warned him of imminent danger as the Boxers were approaching. They pleaded with him to leave the city, but Dr. Taylor declined. That afternoon the storm broke and a mob seized and beheaded the pastor of the Congregational Church (ABCFM). The next day the Presbyterian missionaries made plans to leave but were assured by a city official that there would be no further trouble. On 30 June, a mob attacked the mission compound. Dr. Taylor was in the house he shared with Walter Lowrie. He seized a rifle that belonged to Lowrie, and warned the mob not to come nearer. They pressed on. Taylor, "alone, and with the traditions of a Quaker ancestry strong within him, chose rather to die himself than to inflict death upon the people he had come to save."[15] The Boxers set the house on fire and Taylor perished in the flames.

The Simcox and Hodge families were gathered together in the Simcox house. Here the two men, attempting to defend their wives and the children, fired on the oncoming mob and witnesses say that two of the Boxers were killed in the attack. All of the missionaries and children were either put to death or died when the house was set on fire. At least five loyal Chinese servants, hospital employees and church workers were beheaded.

The Boxers then attacked the compounds of the American Board and the CIM. Some missionaries were killed in the initial assault and the others imprisoned in a city temple. A mock trial was held and all were beheaded the next day. In all 191 Chinese Christians, 15 missionaries and their children died in the Baoding massacre.[16]

It was the same throughout much of North China. Chinese Christians suffered many more losses than the missionaries. The worst massacre occurred in Taiyuan, capital of Shanxi Province. Yuxian, who had been appointed governor after his ouster from Shandong, summoned all missionaries to the provincial headquarters promising protection. Then a mock trial was held and forty-four missionaries and their children were beheaded. But it should be noted that a number of Chinese officials, at great risk to themselves, ignored the order of the Empress Dowager and offered protection to the foreigners.

When the declaration of war was issued in Peking, the governors of the southern provinces refused to recognize the legality of the action. Such insanity could only have taken place if the Boxers had seized control of the court. In some cases the message "to kill" was changed to "to protect" the foreigner. To further defuse the situation the Western powers announced that they were not at war with China and had dispatched the expeditionary force only to suppress the rebels. Thus most of the southern provinces avoided the destructive forces unleashed in the north.

In Jiangsu Province, most of the Southern Presbyterian missionaries evacuated their stations but there was little damage to property. In Xuzhou the telegraph operator who received the message from Peking to kill the foreigners was Samuel Shen, a young Christian graduate of St. John's University. He gave Mark and Nettie Grier advance warning of the impending storm. The local magistrate urged their immediate departure and provided his official carts to get them out of the city. When a mob of Boxers arrived the next day at the compound they dared not enter, for long strips of paper bearing the characters "CONFISCATED" had been fastened across the gate with the seal of the magistrate.[17]

The Boxer Protocols

With the court in exile both Chinese and foreign troops continued the extermination of the Boxers. Yuan Shikai fought them tooth and nail in Shandong. Foreign troops were sent on punitive expeditions to root them out of the countryside. Many of the Boxers, disillusioned and leaderless, simply dissolved back into the peasant masses from which they had come.

But the international force was not yet willing to call it quits. China had to be "taught a lesson." A Shandong missionary reported that German forces killed two hundred men from what were suspected Boxer villages and then burned the villages down.[18] Dr. A. J. Brown investigated many atrocities and concluded that

> the great Christian nations of the world are being represented in China by robbing, rapine, looting soldiery.... With what show of consistency is the Occident to denounce the barbarity of the Chinese, when Occidental soldiers go to China and perpetrate the very acts which constitute the very basis of barbarity?[19]

But mercifully, it was finally time to make peace. Once again the Manchu court recalled the indomitable Li Hongzhang, who had adamantly opposed the Boxers from the beginning, to negotiate a peace settlement. There was much bickering among the foreign powers, who could not agree on the terms. Germany and Britain favored a harsh line. Russia and Japan, seeking concessions, opted for leniency. The United States warned against the dismemberment of China into spheres of influence.

The final settlement, known as the Boxer Protocols, was signed in January 1901 with the following terms: (1) punishment of officials most responsible for the atrocities: Some were banished, several committed suicide and a few, including Yuxian, were executed; (2) China would pay a staggering indemnity of 67 million pounds sterling over a period of thirty-nine years at 4 percent per annum;[20] (3) foreign troops would be stationed permanently in Peking as legation guards. The one provision won by the Chinese negotiators was that the Empress Dowager would remain in power.

In September 1901 the foreign troops evacuated Peking. In January 1902 the Empress Dowager and her court returned to the capital. In Shandong, where it all had begun, Governor Yuan Shikai invited the missionaries to return, and personally guaranteed their safety.[21]

Aftermath

It was all over but what did it mean? It would be easy to quote the dictum of Tertullian: "The blood of the martyrs is the seed of the church." But it was not that simple. The Boxer Uprising had decimated the Christian movement in northern China. Latourette estimates that 30,000 Chinese Roman Catholic Christians, 5 bishops, 31 European priests and 9 sisters were put to death. Estimated Protestant losses were 1,900 Chinese, 134 missionaries and 52 missionary children.[22]

Presbyterians were dealt a crippling blow in Hebei and Shandong provinces. Three mission stations at Peking, Baoding and Weixian were completely destroyed. In Peking out of 460 baptized members on the roll, 174 had been killed.[23] Grace Newton wrote of her sense of personal loss:

> My work is destroyed. The boarding schools and the day schools have been wiped out. Four Peking teachers massacred. Of the girls in the Girls' School I know of only six who are living.[24]

In Baoding the Presbyterian church — just five years old — suffered the loss of one third of its members.[25] In Weixian over two hundred Christian families had been robbed, looted or burned out.[26] In Jinan, one-third of the Chinese pastors had been killed and many more had been flogged and stoned.[27] In many cases it was the best church workers who were lost. Buildings demolished included three major hospitals, five dispensaries, six academies, fifteen missionary residences and scores of churches and chapels. The total financial loss incurred by the Board of Foreign Missions was approximately $200,000.[28]

Damage to morale is difficult to calculate. After so many years in China how could such a thing happen? The Presbyterian Mission had been in Peking for forty years. In Weixian the damage had been done, not by marauding bands from afar, but by local people. The brutality of the foreign troops had only increased the hatred and suspicion for the foreigner. Most of the leaders that had permitted the outrage were still in power.

But along with the heartaches was encouragement. The Chinese Christians had held up well under the ordeal. True, some had recanted under pressure. But the great majority had remained faithful even under threat of life and limb to themselves and to family. The Rev. Ting Li Mei, later to distinguish himself as the Qingdao pastor and well-known evangelist, remained with his flock, was flogged a hundred times and left for dead.[29] The *Annual Reports* contain many accounts of those who kept the faith.

> One Truth Hall [Academy] student died pleading with, and praying for, his murderers. One helper, Mr. Tu, was tortured for forty-eight hours, and while fully conscious of the fact that the burning of a single stick of incense would save his life, he died true to his faith. Boys who could have escaped by saying they were not Christians when taken by the "Boxers" said, "I cannot say otherwise. You can kill my body, but you cannot kill my soul.

I am a Christian." ... Another old Christian, who had been robbed, and his house almost destroyed during his absence ... returned to the wreck and said to the crowd who had gathered to see the fun, that he was a Christian still, that when they heard singing they might know that he was conducting worship as of old.[30]

At a joint meeting of the East and West Shandong Missions held 1 December 1900 a resolution was adopted

expressing our joy and gratitude to God that so many of our native brethren, though placed for a time in imminent peril or subjected to actual distress, have remained steadfast and immovable, witnessing a good profession.[31]

In the case of those who had recanted, an inquiry would be held "in a spirit of tenderness rather than severity, remembering ourselves lest we also be tempted."[32]

Appraisal

The Boxer Uprising turned the spotlight of world opinion on the China missionary in both the religious and secular press. How did the missionary movement fare? Board executives painted in vivid details the heroic actions of missionaries and Chinese Christians sometimes in overly sentimental and melodramatic terms. But the secular press reacted quite differently. They picked out statements of missionaries that were labeled "vindictive," "bellicose" and "vengeful."[33] Presbyterians Dr. W. A. P. Martin, Rev. Gilbert Reid and Rev. J. Walter Lowrie were chided for arguing that American treatment of the Chinese had been too lenient. Some claimed that missionaries had taken part in the looting. In an article for the *North American Review* Mark Twain linked the China missionaries with American imperialism in the Philippines. In a subsequent article he launched a devastating satirical attack on his "Missionary Critics."[34]

It was partly to investigate these charges that Dr. Arthur Judson Brown, board secretary of the BFM, visited China from May to September 1901. Brown wrote that Presbyterian missionaries had suffered reproach from the "furious onslaught of criticism" and that he felt obligated to investigate the matter.[35]

While in China he interviewed British and American diplomats, army generals, Chinese officials and a host of missionaries. These included Sir Robert Hart, Major General Chaffee and Governor Yuan Shikai. Brown dealt at length with three specific charges: revenge, looting and the indemnity.

Revenge. It was readily admitted that some missionaries gave way to outbursts of anger but Brown reminded his readers of the emotional strain they were under. Missionaries and Chinese colleagues had been murdered in cold blood. In Brown's words: "It is grossly unjust to treat such excited utterances as representative of the great body of missionary opinion."[36] After sober reflection some had second thoughts about what they had said earlier. Rev. Paul Bergen of Qingdao retracted statements he made while he was hearing each day of new atrocities. Missionaries would have been nearer the truth, he wrote the Board, if they had "acted as peace makers rather than advocates of severer measures."[37] As to charges that Lowrie had used his authority as interpreter to get even with his enemies, nothing could be further from the truth:

> It would have accorded with Chinese custom if Mr. Lowrie had availed himself to the utmost of his extraordinary opportunity to punish the antagonists. . . . Profound was their amazement when they saw the man whom they had so grievously wronged acting not only with moderation and strict justice, but in a kind and forgiving spirit.[38]

Lowrie's personal testimony is convincing:

> In all my relations . . . I endeavored myself, and exhorted our little flocks, to act upon the principle of overcoming evil with good, and refrained from utilizing in the slightest degree the foreign troops to secure the punishment of those who had wrought havoc in our work.[39]

Looting. As to charges of looting, Brown's findings were that when the siege was lifted some missionaries had exhausted their meager supplies of food and had taken the necessities of life from whatever source was available as did all the others who were liberated. In many cases they felt obligated to find food for Chinese Christians whose plight was worse than their own. Nothing could be bought for the simple reason that there was no one to do the selling. Half the population had fled in terror and shops had been abandoned. In many cases missionaries had left their names with promises to pay full market value when normal times returned. Brown denied "point blank that our Presbyterian missionaries took any part in the looting of Peking."[40]

Indemnity. Missionaries were divided as to whether indemnities should be sought. Some felt that although payment for losses was authorized by the Protocols, the renunciation of such rights would emphasize the difference between the missions and the "foreign powers." This was the position taken by the China Inland Mission and some Presbyterian missionaries. The BFM took the position that security for the future required some payment. But indemnities were claimed only for the actual destruction of property so that hospitals, churches, schools and residences could be rebuilt. Claims were compensatory, not punitive. Reparations were claimed for personal losses of missionaries, although some missionaries declined to receive them. Funds were sought for the destruction of the property of Chinese Christians according to a carefully worked out formula. Although the Protocols authorized the payment of $15,000 for each loss of life, the BFM declined such payments as they could "place no money value upon the lives of our martyred dead."[41] Governor Yuan Shikai personally expressed appreciation to Dr. Brown for the constraint used in Presbyterian requests in comparison with indemnity demands by other bodies.[42]

Dr. Brown's exoneration of the charges of which the missionaries were accused is convincing. Yet some of his language does identify the missionary enterprise too closely with the "manifest destiny" of the United States:

When the Main was blown up in Havana Harbor and Lawton was killed in Luzon, did we demand withdrawal from Cuba and the Philippines? When the gallant Luscum fell under the walls of Tientsin, did we insist that our troops should be recalled? Or did not the American people, in every one of these instances, find in the very agonies of struggle and defeat a decisive reason for advance? ... And shall the Church of God weakly, timidly run away because the very troubles have occurred which Christ himself predicted?[43]

One of the tragedies of the Boxer Uprising was that the cause of Christian missions was linked anew with the fortunes of the Western powers.

The Boxer Uprising forced some second thoughts about the advisability of intervention on behalf of Christians before magistrates and foreign consuls. For it was clear that one reason for the hostility was the interference of the foreigner in lawsuits. Dr. Brown recorded this conversation:

I asked the magistrate of Paotingfu why the people had killed such kindly and helpful neighbors as our missionaries. He replied: "The people were angered by the interference of the Catholics in their lawsuits. They felt they could not obtain justice against them and in their frenzy they did not distinguish between Catholic and Protestants."[44]

Missionary opinion was beginning to change. The Rev. Paul Bergen of Qingdao sent a questionnaire concerning this vexing question to two hundred missionaries representing a number of Protestant denominations. In the seventy-three responses there was widespread difference of opinion but the majority believed intercession on behalf of Chinese Christians was justified only in a very limited number of cases. Only a very few favored making an appeal to the consul and that only as a last resort.[45]

Withdrawal or Advance?

It was decision time for missionaries, the Board at home and the church. Christian missions were not welcome in China. How could it have been said any plainer? What to do?

One decision had to be made rather quickly. The destruction of three stations in North China forced a consideration as to future plans for this area. Both the ABCFM and the Methodist missions were at work in Peking and Hebei Province. Rather than rebuild in Peking and Baoding, would it be wise to transfer this work to the other missions in the interest of ecumenical cooperation? All with whom Dr. Brown consulted urged the Presbyterians not only to continue but to strengthen their work in the province. Chinese Christians could never understand a withdrawal. It would dishonor the "martyred dead." The links formed with the Chinese Christian community after thirty-eight years of working together simply could not be broken.[46]

What effect did the events of 1900 have on missionary morale? Would many want to leave? Could new missionaries be recruited? Except for a small drop in the number of China missionaries for the year 1901, the number continued its upward climb. There was no discernable increase in resignations from among either the northern or southern missions. The depleted ranks at Baoding were quickly made up. Remarkably, the Boxer Uprising probably aided the recruitment of new missionaries.

One by one, decisions were made. In Peking the Douw Hospital would be rebuilt. The former two compounds would be consolidated and enlarged. The mission would proceed with the plans for establishing a new station at Shunde (Shunteh) south of Baoding on the rail line. At Baoding a new piece of property, more conveniently located than the old one, had been donated by the city magistrate. Here rebuilding would take place. A closer working relationship with the ABCFM and the Methodist Mission would be established.

In Weixian the entire compound would be rebuilt and enlarged. The plan to move Dengzhou College to Weixian would be put into effect. A massive new building program and recruitment of faculty would begin.

Missionaries from Lianzhou in the South China mission had successfully entered the province of Hunan, long a stronghold of anti-foreign sentiment. Here a major new enterprise would begin. Dr. Brown felt that one deficiency in the program was the Western style of architecture. This had accentuated the foreign nature of the enterprise, which had not helped during the Boxer crisis. "Architecture should conform as nearly as practicable to that of the country in which the building is situated." A professional architect would be enlisted to supervise the extensive building program which was envisioned.[47]

All this would need new personnel and new money. An urgent appeal was made to the home church to undergird the new advance with volunteers, financial support and prayer.

By the fall of 1901 most missionaries were back at their stations. In the words of one of them: "In spite of everything, siege, massacres, looting, atrocities, newspapers reports and Mark Twain, I believe the work is going on."[48]

1. Rev. Walter M. Lowrie,
1819–1847

2. Divie Bethune McCartee, M.D.,
1820–1900

3. Rev. John Livingston Nevius,
1829–1893

4. Rev. Calvin Wilson Mateer,
1836–1908

5. Rev. J. Linton and Mrs. Mary Stuart, Hangzhou, 1916

6. Rev. Hampden Coit DuBose, 1845–1910

7. Mary West Niles, M.D., 1854–1933

8. Eleanor Chesnut, M.D., 1868–1905

9. George Clarkson Worth, M.D. (1867–1936), Mrs. Emma Chadbourn Worth, and their son Charles, Jr.

10. Rev. Henry Winters Luce, 1868–1940

11. Rev. John Leighton Stuart, 1876–1962

12. Pearl Sydenstricker Buck, 1892–1973

13. Southern Presbyterian Mission Meeting, Shanghai, 1902

14. Presbyterian Mission Press, Shanghai, about 1904

15. Ruins of the Presbyterian Church of Peking, destroyed in the Boxer Rebellion

16. Survivors of the Boxer Rebellion meet with Dr. and Mrs. Arthur Judson Brown, 1901

17. Baoding Martyrs' Memorial Pavilion, erected to honor missionaries and Chinese Christians killed in the Boxer Rebellion

18. Lianzhou church (dedicated 1 March 1905, burned in mob violence, 28 October 1905)

19. The Centenary Missionary Conference in session, Shanghai, 1907

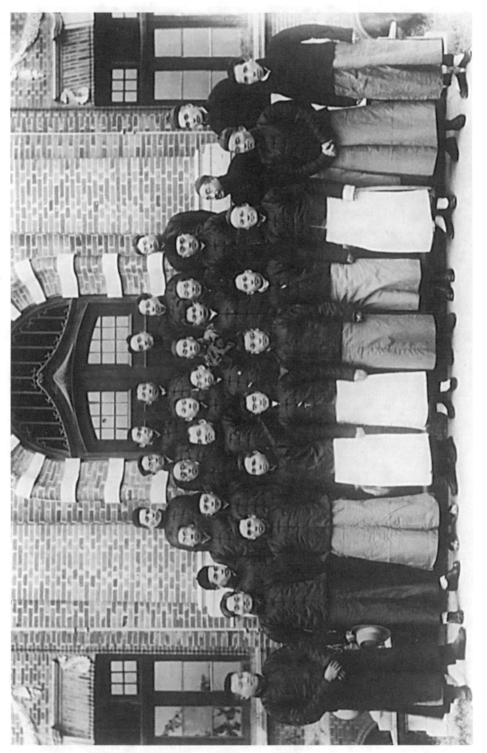

20. Graduating Class of the Nanjing Theological Seminary, 1916

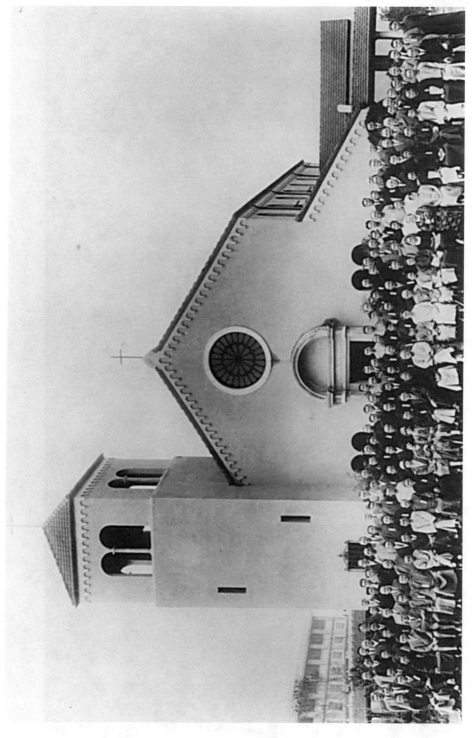

21. Organizational Meeting of the General Assembly of the Church of Christ in China, Shanghai, 29 September 1927

22. School for Missionary Children, about 1915. Mrs. Margaret Baxter teaches the ten children of Xuzhou station.

23. A primary school meeting in an ancestral hall in the country near Zhenjiang, Jiangsu

24. War relief committee of Presbyterian missionaries (from left to right) Bird Talbot, Nettie D. Grier and Frank A. Brown with Buddhist Red Cross, Xuzhou, about 1939

25. General George C. Marshall gives a reception for American missionaries in Xuzhou during his efforts to bring about a cease fire between Communist and Nationalist forces, 1946. From left to right, Martin Hopkins, unidentified, Bishop Cote, Gen. Marshall, Rev. and Mrs. Frank A. Brown.

The Twentieth Century

War Lords, Nationalism and the Emerging Church

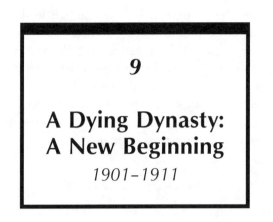

9

A Dying Dynasty:
A New Beginning
1901–1911

The New Century

The first decade of the new century witnessed the death throes of a dynasty and the birth pangs of a republic. Winds of change swept across the land that were equally traumatic for Chinese society and the Christian movement. According to Latourette the changes gave to Christian missionaries

> a greater opportunity to imprint their message upon its people than they had had in all the centuries of their presence in the Empire. The changes were so profound that they were to introduce little less than a revolution in Chinese culture in all its phases, intellectual, political, economic, social and religious.[1]

A marked change was noted in the attitude toward Christianity among the upper classes. Instead of being relegated to the fringes, missionaries now operated within the mainstream of Chinese society. Anti-foreign incidents decreased. The American treaty of 1903 put an end to the protection of foreign laws that had been given to converts:

> Converts . . . being Chinese subjects, shall . . . conform to the laws of China, and shall pay due respect to those in authority; and the fact of being converts shall not protect them from the consequences of any offense . . . or exempt them from paying legal taxes levied on Chinese subjects generally.[2]

With the new century an explosion took place in the number of missionaries, the variety of their work and the number of their institutions. This will necessitate a change in the way this history is written. A greater selectivity must be used in telling the story. Another change: It will become less "Presbyterian" and more "ecumenical" as Presbyterian hospitals and schools merged with those of other denominations to form the great medical centers and universities of the twentieth century. Slowly, as the century progressed, the dominant role shifted from that of the foreigner to that of national church leadership. So the story will become less "missionary" and more "Chinese."

In this chapter the story will be told through the last decade of the Qing dynasty. In Chapter 10 we deal with the period from the Revolution of 1911 through the time of the War Lords. In Chapters 11 and 12 a closer look will be given, first to the medical institutions and then to the educational work, which were at their peak in 1926. This will bring us down to the pivotal year, 1927, when again a major shift in direction occurred.

Last Chance at Reform

On 29 January 1901, at the dictation of the Empress Dowager, the emperor issued an edict calling for fundamental reforms in the administration of the state.[3] It was a complete reversal for Cixi and her cohorts. On returning to the capital after the debacle of the Boxer Uprising, she received the diplomatic corps who were duly impressed by her not insignificant grace and charm. At a tea party given for the wives of the ambassadors she explained why she had left Peking and how much she regretted the inconveniences the recent incident had caused her dear friends.

Reform was now a matter of national survival. Anti-Manchu agitation was on the rise. Reform was demanded by the foreign powers. The surprising victory of Japan over Russia in 1905 advanced the reformers' cause. Japan had become a constitutional monarchy through the reforms of the Meiji Era and had defeated a major Western power. Why could not China do the same thing?

The reform edicts of special significance to the Christians were an edict against footbinding (1902), reforms in the marriage laws (1902), prohibition against opium (1906), a new criminal code (1908) and the far-reaching abolition of the thirteen-hundred-year-old examination system based on the Confucian classics. Appointment to public service would no longer depend on the rote memory of ancient texts but on a university degree.

This signaled a massive popular movement toward Western-style education. Mission schools were now "in" and enjoyed a popularity they had not previously known. But now there was competition as they were no longer the sole dispensers of Western learning. In 1904 the total number of schools throughout the Empire was 4,222 with 92,169 students. In 1909, the number of schools had leaped to 52,348 with 1,560,270 pupils.[4]

Constitutional reforms were promised in the edict of 1906. Provincial assemblies were elected in 1909. The timetable called for the election of a national assembly in 1917. But the electorate was carefully limited to males over twenty-five years of age and drawn from the scholarly and land-owning class. In Shandong, with a population of 38 million, only 119,000 people voted for the provincial assembly.[5]

Paradoxically, efforts to protect the dynasty contributed to its downfall. Attempts to prohibit the free discussion of political issues among the students abroad only succeeded in alienating all the intellectuals. The result was that practically all of the overseas students joined the opposition. The first provincial assemblies clamored for the convening of a national assembly in 1910. But time was running out.

The Empress Dowager died in 1908. One day before the "Old Buddha" passed away, the Guangxu Emperor died mysteriously in seclusion in the confines of the Forbidden City. Was the timing of his death a coincidence? Or had the crafty old woman given instruction that he was to be poisoned before she died?

The line of succession was murky. The Emperor had died without leaving an heir and the three-year-old Puyi, great nephew of the Dowager, was chosen to mount the dragon throne. The regent was Prince Chun, father of the child and no friend of the reform movement. Puyi "reigned" from 1909 to 1911 and was the last royal occupant of the Forbidden City. This tragic, elusive figure is known to history as the "last emperor of China."[6]

A Fresh Start

Protestant missions began the decade with the exhilaration of a new beginning. The expectant mood of advance was highlighted by the great Centennial Conference held in Shanghai in 1907 to commemorate the arrival of Robert Morrison. Almost without exception all Protestant missions were represented by the eleven hundred delegates who came together to worship, study, debate and plan for the future. It was a great demonstration of the essential unity of the Protestant missionary enterprise. The conference made marked progress in cooperation, regional councils and training for the ministry. There was also one conspicuous failure: Only seven voting delegates were Chinese.[7]

One distinctive change in methodology was the marked increase in institutional work. Missionary medicine and education had been vindicated. New buildings were built and modern equipment was added. This increased the scope and the effectiveness of the program but the emphasis on raising standards made self-support more difficult and led to other dangers that would become more apparent in the next decade. With the shift of emphasis to education, by 1911 less than half of the Protestant missionaries were engaged in direct evangelistic work.[8]

But the Presbyterian program called for expansion into new territory and for this evangelistic effort missionaries were all important. In 1911 the number of NPM and SPM missionaries engaged in evangelistic work was close to two-thirds of the work force.

For both northern and southern missions there was a sustained, steady increase in personnel. By the end of the decade there were 464 Presbyterian missionaries in China — a 45 percent gain.

Communicant membership for the churches related to the NPM nearly doubled in the ten-year period — rising from 11,000 in 1901 to 18,470 in 1911.[9] For the SPM the increase was even more astonishing. In 1900 the total number of communicant members was under four hundred. By 1911 it had increased to 2,516.[10] But the rate of increase was uneven. As a general rule the church grew more rapidly in the country than in the city. The degree to which responsibility was turned over to Chinese pastors also seemed to have had an impact on the rate of growth.

Both missions continued the expansion of their work. The Northern Presbyterians organized two new missions to initiate work in the provinces of Hunan and Anhui. Shunde, the station on the railroad south of Peking that had been delayed by the Boxer Uprising, was begun in 1904.[11] Yixian (Yihsien) in southern Shandong Province was started the next year.[12] Southern Presbyterians began four new stations in northern Jiangsu.

During the decade hospitals were upgraded and formalized training of doctors and nurses was begun. Mission colleges achieved university status. The Sunday school, unknown in previous years, came into its own. Famine relief, orphanages, schools for the blind and the dumb and an asylum for the insane were begun. The northern and southern missions cooperated in union schools, a Christian college, a united seminary and, at long last, the establishment of a united Synod.

But all was not smooth sailing. The small increase in the number of ordained pastors was disappointing.[13] The problem of self-support continued to plague both missions. How could the church support an educated clergy on the meager salaries paid by local congregations? Churches had difficulty replacing the older pastors, who were passing from the scene, with younger men.

There were tragic missionary losses. Two young men, Rev. Henry Faries of Linyi and Rev. John Jones of Nanjing, died of typhus while engaged in famine relief. Rev. and Mrs. George Cornwell of Yantai died of cholera within a few days of each other. The Southern Presbyterian mission at Dongshang was destroyed in a riot in 1908. The *Annual Reports* indicate encounters with river pirates and bandits and the looting of missionary homes by armed brigands. The second massacre in the history of Presbyterian China missions took place when four missionaries and one child suffered martyrdom when a mob attacked and burned to the ground the mission station at Lianzhou.

Forward Movement at Home

The expansion of the China missions would have been impossible except for a remarkable advance that took place in the church at home. During the last decade of the nineteenth century, giving to missions had not kept up with the expansion of the program. In 1894 the BFM reported a debt of $102,000.[14] In 1895 Dr. Speer wrote:

> The fiscal outlook is bad...there is a kind of growing discontent in the churches. I have gone up and down the land for twenty-five years preaching the cause of foreign missions. It has never been harder than now.[15]

In 1897 a 30 percent cut in the China appropriations for the northern church forced a massive reduction in programs.

But the downward trend was dramatically reversed with the beginning of the new century. The reason, wrote Dr. James Bear, was due to "new methods of promotion."[16]

These new methods emphasized the systematic appeal to donors for designated causes and the support of individual missionaries. One example of the new methods was the Forward Movement launched in 1902 by the southern church. Three missionaries then on furlough, J. L. Stuart and L. I. Moffett from China and J. F. Preston of Korea, began a carefully planned visitation of churches, enlisting pledges for the support of specific missionaries who had volunteered for the foreign field but were unable to go because of lack of funds. The venture met with considerable success and in 1903 the plan was adopted by the General Assembly. By the year 1910, 888 congregations were making annual pledges for the support of specific missionaries or projects.[17] Under the impetus of the Forward Movement, The PCUS General Assembly of 1907 adopted a "missionary platform" that "accepted responsibility" for the evangelization of certain areas of the world. This included an estimated population of 12 million in China. The plan had an enormous impact on the church and its missionary commitment as evidenced by these figures: In 1901 receipts for missions were $164,883. Receipts for the year 1912 were $501,412 — a fourfold increase in ten years![18]

But more was happening than just a change in methodology. There was a groundswell of grassroots support for the mission enterprise. The interdenominational Laymen's Missionary Movement was organized in 1906 by a group of laymen in New York City to support the work of missions abroad through prayer and financial support. Called by Dr. John R. Mott "the most significant development in world missions during the first decade of the present century," the movement was soon endorsed by both Northern and Southern Presbyterian Assemblies.[19] During these years the Laymen's Missionary Movement became the primary vehicle for enlisting men in the cause of missions. Salary support for new missionaries and capital funds for the building of hospitals and schools came from designated gifts contributed by individual donors and churches. For example, of the twenty-one missionary members of Shanghai station in 1912, only five were listed as being supported by the general fund. The rest were supported by women's societies, specific congregations, mission guilds and the mission press.[20]

The Hunan Mission

A striking example of the new advance was the initiation of the Hunan Mission. It began when Rev. W. H. Lingle, a young missionary at Lianzhou in the South China Mission, crossed the mountain passes into Hunan during the late 1890s and started two churches. There was intense persecution but the churches grew. From this small beginning grew Lingle's vision of a Hunan Mission in the province where the gospel had not yet penetrated.[21]

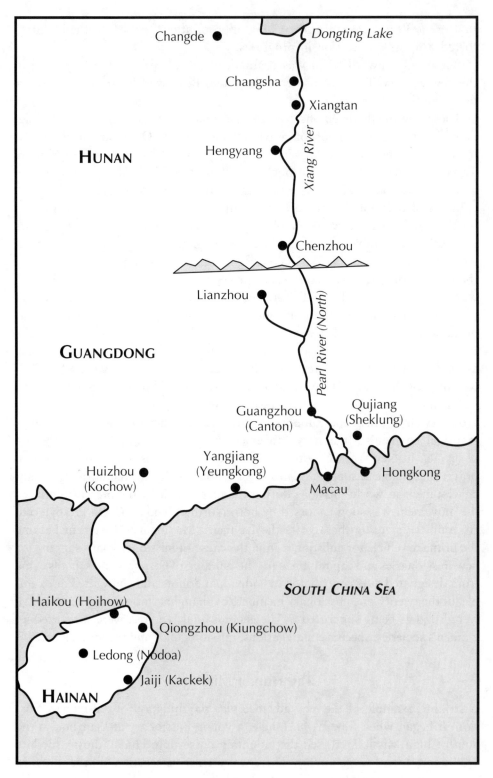

South China and Hunan Missions 1900–1912

Hunan ("South of the Lake"), with a population of 20 million people, was strategically located in central China. It was Mandarin-speaking, which linked it to the northern provinces. It was also linked with the south through navigable lakes and rivers. It was known for its fiery hot peppers and for the fierce independence of its people. It was the home of Mao Zedong and its people are described by Mao's biographer in these words:

> Other Chinese have to watch out for the fire and obstinacy of the Hunanese. But they do not deny that the fieriness goes along with courage. "China can be conquered," runs a saying known over the country, "only when every Hunanese is dead." The people...fight and curse and state their views with gusto. [They]...are China's Prussians.[22]

Hunan was the last of the eighteen provinces to admit the foreigner. Attempts to gain entrance from the north by Roman Catholic and Protestant missionaries had failed. Its anti-Christian stance was accented by the vitriolic propaganda written by Hunanese literati and circulated throughout the empire.

In the summer of 1899 Mr. Lingle started out on a 250-mile trek to cross Hunan from south to north. His destination was the capital city of Changsha, where he hoped to start a station. Once over the mountains he traveled downstream along the Xiang River, preaching along the way. People were curious about the lone foreigner traveling without a retinue but were not unfriendly. He arrived at Changsha, was forbidden to enter and returned to Lianzhou by the same route he had come.

Xiangtan (Siangtan)

Lingle returned the next year with Board approval for starting a new mission and was soon joined by two new appointees, Mrs. Louise Judson Doolittle and her daughter, Dr. Leila L. Doolittle.[23] Changsha was still closed but Lingle was able to rent quarters in the city of Xiangtan, fifty miles south on the Xiang. Dr. Doolittle began a clinic and one of her first patients was the daughter-in-law of Mr. Shu, a Confucian gentleman and rice merchant. The family had sent for the foreign doctor with much trepidation but were overcome with joy when the young woman was cured. A few months later, when the fury of the Boxer Uprising swept over the province, Mr. Shu smuggled the foreigners over the city wall into a junk at midnight and they sailed out to safety.

In March 1901 Lingle was back at Xiangtan and soon was joined by Mrs. Lingle, their two children, Dr. Doolittle and her mother.[24] Mrs. Lingle, having served in Mandarin-speaking Shandong before her marriage, was of great help in getting started. A boys' school was begun with twelve scholars each paying $2.00 a month for board and tuition. Mrs. Lingle and Mrs. Doolittle began visiting the women. Fifty people regularly filled the small room where preaching services were held. In 1902 there were four baptisms, the "first fruits" of the Hunan Mission.

Hengyang (Hengchow)

In 1902 property was purchased in the city of Hengyang, fifty miles further upstream on the Xiang. Here the pioneers were Rev. and Mrs. George Gelwicks, who were later joined by Rev. and Mrs. David Crabb. With two stations in operation the Hunan Mission was officially organized.

Chenzhou (Chenchow)

In 1903 a third center was opened at the city of Chenzhou, a fifteen-day trip further up the river by junk. Here Lingle rented quarters for a residence, began house repairs and selected a site for a chapel. Rev. T. W. Mitchell and Dr. Stephen C. Lewis soon joined him. Added responsibilities came in 1904 when the London Missionary Society withdrew from the area and asked the Presbyterians to take over their work.

Thus, in rather quick succession stations had been established in the three principal cities along the Xiang River. Evangelistic work proceeded in much the same way as it had in the other missions — daily preaching at street chapels, classes for inquirers, distribution of tracts and visitation among the women. In each place medical work helped to break down suspicion. In Xiangtan, the medical pioneers were Drs. E. D. Vanderburgh and F. J. Tooker. A generous grant from Mr. Nathaniel Tooker, father of the medical missionary, made possible the construction of a hospital in 1907. Dispensary work at Chenzhou was started by Dr. Stephen Lewis on his arrival in 1904. A new hospital building was completed just before Chinese New Year, 1909, and the dedication service was accompanied by the din of firecrackers and bugles, the presentation of banners by the gentry, a proclamation by the governor and a banquet prepared by the ladies of the station.[25]

In these early days the missionaries dressed in Chinese clothes, and the men braided their hair into queues in order to be less conspicuous. This could have created a problem for Thomas Mitchell when he traveled to Shanghai to meet his fiancée, Miss McAfee, who had come all the way across the Pacific to marry him. His fellow missionaries in Shanghai were shocked by his shabby appearance, his Chinese clothes and his queue. They lent him a suit for the wedding and insisted that his hair be cut. True love was equal to the occasion.

An astonishing change took place in the attitude of the people. Hunan became one of the most open and progressive provinces. But this popularity led to problems not yet encountered. In 1902 five chapels were begun by men who knew nothing of Christianity, but who claimed a connection with the missionaries in order to gain political advantages and extort money. The Hunan mission insisted that all be closed.[26]

Changde (Changteh) and Changsha

The enlargement of the mission came about in other ways. About the same time that Lingle entered Hunan from the south, Rev. T. J. Preston and Dr. and Mrs. O. T. Logan of the Cumberland Presbyterian Church began work in Changde in the northwest sector of the province. In 1906 the union of the Cumberland Church with the PCUSA united this work with that of the PCUSA Hunan Mission. Their work had been well developed and consisted of a girls' school, a twenty-five bed hospital, a street chapel and a church of about forty members.

In 1912 Changsha became the fifth mission station in the province when the London Missionary Society withdrew its missionaries and requested the Presbyterians to take over their work. The mission debated the issue at some length as some felt they were already overextended. But finally the responsibility was accepted and the LMS property was transferred to the NPM.[27] Presbyterian work in Changsha consisted primarily of union work, which included the Union Theological School, the Fuxiang Union School for Girls, the Yali Union Boys' School, the Women's Bible School, the YMCA and the Hunan Educational Union.

Hunan took the lead in inter-mission cooperation. In 1903 thirty-two representatives of twelve Protestant missions at work in the province met in Changsha to form an advisory committee, which took steps toward avoiding duplication and competition. All agreed to avoid entanglements in Chinese litigation. A baptized member of one church would not be received or employed by another mission without prior consultation.[28]

These years were remarkably free from anti-foreign agitation but in April 1910 the "rice riots" broke out in Changsha. Floods had devastated the countryside and the calamity was blamed on the foreigners, who had disturbed the spirits of the air and the water. The governor's decisive action undoubtedly saved many lives. He sent his personal launch up the river to Xiangtan and evacuated all missionaries except for Mr. Lingle, who elected to stay. All were back in their stations by the fall.

Mission reports for the year 1911 indicate some of the "ups" and "downs" encountered during these first ten years. In Xiangtan fifteen members were added to the church roll but two members died, two were expelled for opium-smoking, four dropped for nonattendance and five suspended because of involvement in Taoist funeral rites, leaving a net increase of two. An effort to put finances into the hands of the Christians had not been successful. They would try again next year.

In Hengyang thirty country towns were regularly visited and special services held for the women. Four evangelists completed the five-year training course (three months each winter), and had been assigned churches. Problems were encountered with the Seventh Day Adventists and their proselytizing activities.

Chenzhou reported seventy-three baptisms, fifty-two adults and twenty-one infants. The general expenses of the church were being met by contributions from the Christian community. Regular medical itineration had begun and was very successful. Boys from eight counties were attending the Boys' Academy. The Girls' School was eagerly awaiting their move to the new building.

Statistics for the year 1910 indicate the progress made in the ten-year period since the mission began: 36 missionaries, 4 organized churches, 436 communicant members, 60 Chinese teachers and evangelists, 15 schools and 345 students enrolled.[29] As yet there were no ordained pastors, no fully self-supporting churches and no presbytery. All this lay in the future.

South China

Canton

During these years Canton grew to become one of the largest, most influential and prosperous cities of the Empire. It was also the hot spot for the revolutionaries and the home of most of the Chinese immigrants to the United States. This meant it was open to influences from abroad, which had both positive and negative effects on the Christian movement. Immigrants converted to Christianity in America were generous contributors to the building of churches in their home villages. But the oppressive treatment of Chinese in the United States resulted in frequent demonstrations against Americans.[30]

Canton did not escape the devastation of the Boxer Uprising but it was less than that suffered further north. Missionaries were evacuated from interior stations. Some work was relocated temporarily in Macau. Twenty-four chapels destroyed during the Boxer unrest were rebuilt almost entirely by contributions received from Chinese immigrants in California.[31]

Quickly rebounding from the Boxer year, the Christian community entered a period of rapid growth and expansion. The year 1906 was described as the "most fruitful in the history of the mission" with 1,564 new members received, many new churches organized and the steady development of educational and medical institutions.[32] Rev. Andrew Beattie's report for the year 1904 is breathtaking: He spent 118 days in itineration, conducted over 300 meetings, administered the Lord's Supper 82 times, examined over 500 candidates, baptized 270, traveled by boat over 1,200 miles, on foot another 500 and on bicycle about 400 more.[33]

Rev. A. A. Fulton, writing in 1907, contrasts the changes that had taken place in his field:

> I began fourteen years ago with six narrow shops and about three score of converts and five native helpers in the four districts in the southern part of the Province...I have now twelve churches, six self-supporting, and thirty-nine chapels, and forty native helpers, including four ordained ministers, and have received over 3,000 men and women on confession.[34]

He credits the large increase to three factors: (1) "steadfast preaching and increased watchfulness over converts on the part of native preachers," (2) the work of "capable Bible women," and (3) the increase in self-support.[35]

The *Annual Reports* for these years abound with accounts describing the vitality of church life. In the city of Canton there were five organized congregations, four of which were self-supporting. The church in a "leper village" became a showpiece in its growth, devotion and liberality. The lepers spoke of themselves as outcasts from home and friends but beloved of Christ. The church at Chung Lau was a fine example of tenacity in prosecuting evangelistic work. For twenty years there had been little progress. Then with the appointment of an exceptionally able evangelist the work began to blossom. In one year seventy-five members were added. The church grew to a membership of two hundred and became entirely self-supporting.

Total communicant membership increased from 2,991 in 1900 to 7,397 in 1909 — a doubling in eight years. After 1909 the rate of increase flattened out and then showed some decline because of the transfer of several churches to the Hunan mission and the transfer of others to the Canadian Presbyterian Mission. The number of ordained Chinese ministers increased from three in 1900 to eight in 1909. During this decade Christian education was significantly strengthened. The number of schools operated by the mission increased from 36 in 1900 to 54 in 1910, and the number of students from 722 in 1900 to 2,031 in 1910. Sunday school scholars increased from 300 to 1,847.[36]

Another characteristic of this period was the development of Christian institutions in Canton, a distinctive feature of which was the care of those who were outcasts of society. The John G. Kerr Refuge for the Insane, the Hackett Medical School for Women, the Ming Sum School for the Blind and the Canton Christian College are covered in later chapters.

Among the Canton institutions, the *True Light Academy* became one of the premier institutions in the country for the training of women. In addition to primary and intermediate departments, the school had a separate section for older women, who were trained as teachers and religious workers. In 1911 the enrollment numbered 312 girls and women in all departments. They came from many missions including the Church of England, the London Mission, the Wesleyans, Scandinavians and Canadian Presbyterians. During these years the academy sent out more than four hundred trained workers as teachers and Bible women. For many years Miss Harriet Noyes served as principal assisted by Misses Butler, Lewis and Patton and a staff of Chinese teachers.[37]

Leadership training developed at the *Fati High School* with a threefold purpose: (1) to "raise up a native ministry," (2) to give a "good solid Christian education to sons of Christians" and (3) to "train teachers of mission schools."[38] The theological department had a two-year course of study for high school graduates and a short course for men who could not meet this requirement. In 1911 the enrollment had grown to 157 students. Graduates served as teachers and pastors from as far away as the Chinese church in Honolulu. The student body was made up of Presbyterians, Methodists, Congregationalists and United Brethren. Generous support from Mr. L. H. Severance provided funds for a building and scholarships.[39]

Qujiang (Sheklung)

In 1904 the work along the East River developed to such an extent that a station was opened at Sheklung, a railroad station between Canton and Hong

Kong. Rev. and Mrs. A. J. Fisher were the pioneers. The work expanded rapidly and by 1906 eleven hundred communicant members were reported in four organized churches and a number of chapels. Because of its proximity to the metropolis, in later years Qujiang was considered a substation of Canton.[40]

Yangjiang

This mission station south of Canton near the South China coast had a turbulent history. Missionaries were evacuated in 1894 when the property was destroyed by rioters and again during the Boxer year.

With the construction of the Foreman Memorial Hospital in 1902 the outlook for the station took a turn for the better. The hospital, the only one within a radius of 150 miles, won the support of the local magistrate, who participated in the hospital's opening ceremony. During the first year Dr. William Dobson treated 6,178 patients and performed 216 operations.[41] The hospital reported a variety of unusual medical cases:

> Here is an old man who feels his way along.... He has cataract and it gladdens his heart to hear he can be cured. The next is an old woman who wants the doctor to pull the worm out of her ear, because it kicks and causes pain.... She will not be convinced that there is no worm there. We secretly send out for an angle worm and while washing her ear allow it to slip into the dish. Ah! wonderful doctor, you have captured the worm. Do you feel all right now, Madame? Yes, quite well; it does not kick now. Afterwards we tell her that we caught the worm in the garden and that it did not come out of her ear.... Here is another woman who has a snake in her leg.... Another has swallowed a toad; another has an alleged worm in his tooth.[42]

A breakthrough was achieved in 1904 when 174 adults were baptized bringing the total communicant membership of the church to 435 members. A theological class for the training of lay preachers was opened with seven students. The "True Light Chinese English Learning Hall" enrolled forty-three students from the "literati class." Mrs. Dodson's visitation among the women resulted in the baptism of twenty-five women.

Because of the scattered membership an innovative plan called "the groups of ten" was initiated, which divided the members up in districts with a lay leader chosen for each. The leader was provided with the Sunday School lesson and a study guide and led the group each Sunday in a convenient location — often the home of a member. On the fourth Sunday all came to worship at the central chapel. Twenty-two groups were organized the first year. In 1911 the station reported nine chapels, four lay preachers, four Bible women, three school teachers and a blind girl who drilled the women in their memory work.[43]

Huizhou (Kochow)

In 1912 a new station was opened 183 miles southwest of Canton on the Ko Chau River by Rev. and Mrs. Charles E. Patton. Huizhou was the district capital and a special effort was made to reach the gentry and officials. Some were attracted to the new faith but felt it was beneath their dignity to sit beside barefoot farmers in the crude street chapels. Patton tried everything: a special section in the church for visiting officials, a men's association, a reading room, social events, lectures and civic projects. In 1914 Mrs. Isabella Patton, M.D., established a small hospital for women and children. The intensive activity produced results: three city chapels and a baptized membership of 955.[44]

Lianzhou

The most isolated of Presbyterian mission stations was reached after a seventeen day trip up the river from Canton. By the year 1905 steady progress was being made. A new church able to accommodate 700 people had been built. This same year the men's hospital under Dr. Edward Machle and the women's hospital under Dr. Eleanor Chesnut treated 13,056 patients with 195 operations. Three patients with leprosy who had been driven from their village attached themselves to the hospital, which built a shed for them just outside the compound. A young Princeton seminary graduate, Rev. John Peal, and his wife, Rebecca, had just arrived. Dr. Machle reported that "the bitter anti-foreign feeling is passing away."[45]

Then without warning disaster struck. The Presbyterian Board in New York first heard the news through an Associated Press dispatch of 1 November 1905 stating that Lianzhou station had been attacked by a mob, that Mrs. Machle, her eleven-year-old daughter, Amy, Dr. Chesnut and Rev. and Mrs. Peale had been killed and all buildings had been destroyed. On November 10 a U.S. naval flotilla accompanied by the American Consul General, several Presbyterian missionaries and Chinese officials departed Canton for the trip up river to investigate what had happened. The following account follows the report that was made.[46]

On the morning of 28 October Dr. Machle encountered celebrants of Ta Tsiu ("All Souls Day") from the nearby temple parading with their images through the hospital grounds amid great noise and confusion. A dispute followed over a mat shed that the temple officials had erected on hospital grounds. Dr. Machle picked up three six-inch "joss cannon" (incense burners) that were being fired by some boys, adding to the confusion. Elders from the temple and Dr. Machle agreed that the shed would be removed when the festival ended later that day. Dr. Machle returned the cannon and it seemed that all had been resolved.

But at this point a rabble led by armed young men appeared and refused to disperse even when assured by the older men that the issue had been settled. When they began to pelt the hospital with stones, Dr. Machle sent a message to the magistrate asking for protection. The mob forced its way into the hospital building and came across certain anatomical specimens that were used for teaching. The specimens were paraded through the street as evidence of the evil practices of the missionaries. This enraged the crowd which was now intent on doing deadly harm. The officials arrived, tried to disperse the crowds but could do little except offer sanctuary in the *yamen* across the river. Leaving the burning buildings the missionary party became separated from the officials who were seeking to protect them and made their way out of the city where they were offered refuge by the priest at the Lung Tau (Dragon Cave) Temple. Here they hid in the recesses of the cave. Machle was the last to enter the cave, was separated from the others and hid himself in an obscure recess by submerging himself partly under water. Miss Elda Patterson was hidden in another part of the cave by a kind-hearted Chinese gentleman. When the mob arrived the other five (Mrs. Machle, Amy, Dr. Chesnut, Rev. and Mrs. Peale) were found, taken to the front of the cave and killed. Eyewitnesses related that "the last act of Dr. Chesnut...was to tear off a portion of her skirt and bind up an ugly gash on the head of a Chinese boy who had been accidentally struck by a stone."[47]

Reparations were demanded by the U.S. government and promptly paid by the provincial authorities. As in the case of the Boxer indemnity, the BFM made no claims for the missionary deaths, but accepted payment for the replacement value of the buildings ($45,000).[48] Dr. Machle was transferred to the Philippines for a time to get him away from the scene of such poignant personal tragedy.

The South China Mission began to make plans to return to the scene of the tragedy and rebuild. But the return was delayed by the Consul General, who insisted that certain conditions had to be met: that those guilty be prosecuted, that the small temple that was the hotbed for the mob violence be turned into a school and that a memorial tablet be erected on the site of the massacre. The mission disassociated itself from these demands and Dr. A. J. Brown wrote the Chinese ambassador in Washington making it clear that they had not pressed for punitive damages. He also expressed regret at the unjust treatment of Chinese in the United States. A gracious reply was received stating that "America had lost a noble son [John Peale] and China a true friend."[49]

By February 1907, all conditions had been met and the mission was ready to reopen the station. A farewell service of prayer and praise was held in Canton for the missionary party as they boarded two boats and started up the river. When they were still some distance from Lianzhou, a boatload of Christians appeared from up river to welcome the missionary party back.[50] Dr. and Mrs. Robert Ross took the place of the Machles. Taking the place of Eleanor Chesnut was Dr. Elizabeth Carper and for the Peales, who had died one day after arriving in their new station, there was Rev. J. S. Kunkle. The work of rebuilding began. Soon to be constructed was the city church, the Van Norden Hospital for Men and the James H. A. Brooks Hospital for Women.

Central China

In 1901 the Central China Mission of the PCUSA consisted of five stations in rapidly growing cities of the Empire: Ningbo (population 400,000), Shanghai (600,000), Hangzhou (800,000), Suzhou (500,000) and Nanjing (500,000).[51] A number of Protestant missions were now engaged in the provinces of Jiangsu and Zhejiang but the adjacent interior province of Anhui had scarcely been touched. The Central China Mission made this territory its next priority.[52]

Huayuan (Hwai Yuan)

In the late 1890s missionaries from Nanjing had entered the province and had chosen the walled city of Huayuan, 150 miles northwest of Nanjing, as their next station. Huayuan was at the junction of the Hwai and Ko rivers and could be reached from Nanjing in five days of travel overland or in two weeks by launch and houseboat on the Yangtze, the Grand Canal and the Hwai River. The city had a population of thirty thousand and was located in the center of a thickly populated region in which there were no other missions at work.

The first sustained Christian witness was done by Chinese evangelists dispatched from Nanjing. In 1901 Rev. Edwin C. Lobenstine and Rev. Dubois S. Morris succeeded in renting property and moved in. Dr. Samuel Cochran arrived the next month by boat, bringing furniture and supplies. Somewhat later the wives joined them. These families were the first foreigners in the area and were the subject of great curiosity.[53] They found one Christian in the city, Mr. Liu, a doctor of Chinese medicine, who had been baptized earlier in Nanjing. Liu had studied the books of the Buddhists and the Taoists but was still searching for the truth when a copy of the Bible fell into his hands. He proved to be a loyal friend and leader in building the church. Evangelistic efforts began with what the missionaries called "guest room work." Visitors were invited to the missionary homes at the rate of a hundred a day. At the time of the "fifth moon" festival the numbers swelled to fifteen hundred. Tea was served, followed by a round of sightseeing as the guests examined every nook and cranny. A separate opportunity was provided the women as custom prohibited them from attending with the men. "We observed Chinese etiquette," the report read, "and tried in every way to make them feel at home and forget that we were foreigners."[54]

A reading room and a loan library were opened where young men could browse and check out books on travel, history and geography as well as Christian literature. Dr. Cochran opened his dispensary in a room back of the chapel. Among his first patients were a number of "opium suicide" cases. Itineration in the country area began soon after the missionaries arrived.

The Central Presbyterian Church of New York City provided funds to build all the buildings. Huayuan probably became the best equipped station in China.

Those interested in becoming members were enrolled as "inquirers." This required abstinence from opium, drunkenness and gambling. During a six-month period of probation, the candidate was expected to learn the Lord's Prayer, the Apostles Creed and the Ten Commandments, and to study the life of Christ and attend church regularly.

Before baptism, heads of households were required to get rid of the paper idols from their homes. This could be a traumatic experience for those who had put their trust in those paper images for many years. On such occasions, other Christians would gather at the home to lend their support:

> Hymns were sung, the family exhorted to obey the Supreme God and to fear none but Him, and prayer was offered.... The idols, mostly of paper, were then torn down from the walls and doors and burned before the eyes of all.[55]

The first baptism came in 1903. In 1908 the first church in northern Anhui Province was organized with over sixty members. The missionaries spoke in glowing tones of their superb Chinese staff consisting of six graduates of the Shandong College, two Chinese doctors and a woman teacher.

In 1909 construction of the Hope Hospital was completed. At the dedication 500 invited guests were served the customary sixteen-course Chinese feast. Total patients treated the first year were 5,800. Many of those treated came from accidents on the nearby railroad as peasants simply could not adjust to the velocity of the "fire carts" speeding down the track.

After 1910, which was a famine year, the work became more difficult. Mr. Lobenstine wrote in his report for 1911:

> It is with the deepest humility that we come to this part of the report. The results do not seem to be commensurate with the work done. The city of Hwai-yuen is still cold and unresponsive.... Sometimes it seems as if the very smallness of the town... increases the difficulty of a person's becoming a Christian.... All of the progressive young men are drawn to the larger cities.[56]

In 1907 the Central China Mission was divided, with Nanjing and Huayuan forming a new "Kiangan Mission."[57] The reasons: distances and dialects. Nanjing and Huayuan were Mandarin-speaking while each of the other cities had its own local dialect.

A rapid review of the work of Presbyterians in central China will bring this portion of the survey up to date.

Ningbo

Presbyterians had been engaged in work in Ningbo for fifty-five years. Mature, stable leadership was provided ten organized churches by ordained pastors and elders trained by the early pioneers. But progress in self-support had been disappointing. The educational work of the station included the academy for boys, a girls' boarding school and ten elementary day schools. Sunday schools were a new emphasis.

Shanghai

Here were three strong city churches: South Gate, Lowrie Memorial and Hongkew. Each had its own ordained minister, was governed by its session and was entirely self-supporting. Miss Emma Silver itinerated in country areas unreached by the gospel even though they were not far from the heart of the city. Missionary "sidelines" included the seamen's mission, the city jails and the preparation of Christian literature. The mission office provided logistical support for the whole enterprise.

In 1907 Shanghai station passed two memorable milestones. The Lowrie Boys' School alumni, many of whom had become well-to-do leaders in the business community, took over the financial support of their alma mater. A joint board, composed of five members elected by the mission and five by the "Old Student Society," took responsibility for the administration of the school. In 1910 the school celebrated the fiftieth anniversary of its founding by Dr. Farnham with the dedication of a new chapel and lecture hall. Lowrie Institute was the first successful transfer of an institution to Chinese control and financial support.[58]

Also in 1907 the Presbyterian Mission Press passed the 100 million mark in the number of pages printed annually. It is hard to overemphasize the magnificent contribution the press made to the Christian cause in the publication of Bibles, commentaries, hymnbooks, textbooks, tracts and religious periodicals. Printing was done in Chinese, English, Greek, Japanese, Manchu and a number of Chinese dialects. The press was entirely self-supporting. For twenty-six years Rev. George Fitch served as superintendent of a staff that in 1910 numbered 12 internationals and 208 Chinese.[59]

Hangzhou

Here there was growing cooperation between the Northern and Southern Presbyterian missions. In the city were six strong self-supporting churches. In 1911 the two missions merged their two girls' schools with an enrollment of 105 girls and a faculty of 3 missionaries and 16 Chinese. It soon became one of the largest and best equipped girls' schools in the land.

Suzhou

The work here was described as "the hardest and least fruitful field in the Central China Mission."[60] By 1911 five congregations had been organized by the NPM and SPM missions but none were self-supporting. Not until 1911 was there an ordained pastor. A special ministry to over one hundred "brothel girls" is reported in the PCUSA *Annual Report* for 1906. In 1899 Dr. James Richard Wilkinson built the first SPM hospital in the northern part of the city. In south Suzhou Dr. Hampden DuBose became known for his white beard, his booming voice and his daily preaching at the Yang Yoh Hang Chapel.

Nanjing

During this decade Nanjing became the center for cooperative mission work in the lower Yangtze Valley. Five Protestant missions (Methodists, Presbyterians, Disciples, Adventists and Friends) cooperated in a number of union projects. One of these was the Women's Training Institute which provided year-round training for women church workers and an annual short-term training institute for pastors, evangelists and lay workers. Three major union institutions — Nanjing University, the University Hospital, and the Presbyterian Seminary — are covered in later sections.

During this decade the mission noted the passing of a number of the Chinese pastors who had been trained by the early pioneers. Success in great measure was dependent on these loyal disciples of Christ, who often endured ridicule and shame even from their own families.

Rev. Bao Kwong-hyi of Ningbo was born in 1828, attended the Presbyterian Academy and was baptized by Dr. Nevius at the age of seventeen. At the age of twenty-nine he was ordained as pastor of the Yu Yiao church. In his thirty-one years of service he baptized over three hundred persons. He became quite blind in his old age but still engaged in daily chapel preaching until his death.[61]

Rev. Taung of Shanghai was the beloved and honored pastor of the South Gate Church for twenty-seven years. He was well known throughout the community for his "uprightness of life," which gave weight to his preaching. He loved to preach, and during later years would rise "from days of weakness and nights of pain to stand before his people on the Sabbath."[62]

Peng Shen-ts'ai served as an elder of the church in Nanjing for nineteen years and died of cholera in 1903. Mrs. Abbey wrote of this godly man:

> He was the one man that everyone, Chinese or foreigner, turned to in any difficulty.... More than a hundred looked to him as their father in Christ, and I have known few men who blended love and firmness, wisdom and simplicity in due measure, as he did.[63]

This passing of the "old guard" created a crisis as the church had great difficulty in replacing them. Many of the more recent graduates of the mission schools sought higher-paying commercial employment in the large cities.

North Jiangsu

The work of the PCUS Mid-China Mission evolved in close cooperation with that of the PCUSA Central China Mission and is covered somewhat sketchily in the preceding section. No new stations were begun because the area was compact and enjoyed the work of other missions. But the situation in the North Jiangsu Mission was quite different. The geographical area was estimated at thirty thousand square miles (twice that of Mid-China) with a population of thirteen million. There were few major cities and practically no other Protestant missions at work in the area.[64]

The years 1906–1911 were famine years in north Jiangsu. Dr. Henry Woods wrote that during these times "all regular mission work is crowded out by the pressing needs of the famine."[65] A new missionary, Miss Mary Thompson, who had just arrived in the famine area wrote home: "I never even imagined such suffering and misery."[66] The Shanghai Famine Committee raised funds for the purchase of grain, which was shipped to the famine area. Here missionaries were enlisted in the urgent task of distribution. On trips into the famine areas, tickets would be given to those most destitute irrespective of whether they were Christians or non-Christians. Ticket holders were then given grain at distribution points. In January 1906 a correspondent of the *North China Daily News* visited Huaiyin and filed this report:

> I have now counted forty-eight camps, averaging from 1,000 to 1,200 families each. I estimate the total number of refugees at 450,000.... The women and children for miles are grubbing for roots, grass and every conceivable thing that might serve for food or fuel. In the camps one sees people eating mixtures of cooked leaves, grass and twigs with a little cereal and rice.[67]

In 1907 the North Jiangsu mission, with the help of Dr. Klopsch, editor of the *Christian Herald,* began two orphanages for children left homeless by the famine. Dr. Klopsch's committee provided $20.00 (U.S.) per orphan per annum, and the mission provided workers and buildings. The orphanage in Xuzhou reached a capacity of 180 boys and girls under Mr. and Mrs. Thomas Grafton. The Huaiyin (TKP) orphanage took in 55 boys and girls under Rev. and Mrs. James Graham. After seven years the orphanages were discontinued as the worst of the famine had passed.

But the great priority of these years continued to be the extension of the mission into unevangelized area between the Grand Canal and the Yellow Sea. The area was impoverished, isolated and resistant to change.

Huaian (Hwaianfu)

In 1898 Dr. Henry Woods was preaching on the main street of Huaian, a prefectural city on the Grand Canal, about ten miles south of the mission station at Huaiyin (TKP).[68] An unruly gang crowded around the tall, dignified foreigner who was dressed in the long robes of a Chinese gentleman. At this point Mr. Ku, a Confucian gentleman appeared on the scene and asked Dr. Woods, "Foreign gentleman, are you not afraid to be here alone among so many strangers?" Dr. Woods shook his head and pointed upward. Mr. Ku understood the gesture and was so impressed that he invited him to his home to rest and talk. A close friendship between the two developed and led to the opening of a mission station in this aristocratic and conservative city.

In 1903 Dr. Woods secured a desirable piece of property, which was "haunted by a weasel," and thus available for foreign purchase. He and his family moved to the new location the next year. The Woods kept "open house," welcoming guests to wander through all the rooms and examine the strange items of equipment. Curiosity was stronger than suspicion and over a thousand took the tour during the first month. Daily preaching began in the street chapel. The doctors from the hospital in Huaiyin (TKP) came regularly to hold clinic.

Why two mission stations just ten miles apart? The rationale was often debated by the mission. But the two cities were very different. Huaiyin (TKP) was a commercial city on the canal whereas Huaian was the prefectural capital and home of a number of wealthy scholars. Dr. Woods, with a scholarly bent, believed that by moving there, he could gain an entry into this prestigious community. In recent years, Huaian's fame has been enhanced by its most illustrious son — Zhou Enlai — who grew up in the city during the time the missionaries were there. But there is no evidence that they ever met. Today, the city has a strong church and is the center of Christian activity.

But in the beginning it was rough going. Dr. Woods's friends in the scholarly community treated him well but there were few conversions. In 1908 Dr. Woods was joined by Rev. Orville Yates, who married Ellen Baskerville the next year. The first converts were baptized in 1909. A girls' school was opened in 1916, followed by a boys' school in 1919. By 1923 the number of communicant members had grown to eighty-seven.[69]

Lianyungang

In 1904 Rev. and Mrs. A. D. Rice were assigned the task of opening a station at Haichow, an important harbor city on the Yellow Sea. In time it would take the name of Lianyungang and become the eastern terminus of the Lunghai Railroad, which runs from the coast through Xuzhou to Kaifeng and on westward to Xian and beyond. Efforts to purchase property were rebuffed. Owners willing to sell were arrested and beaten. Not until Christmas 1908 was a house rented and the Rices moved in. Mrs. Rice described the city to which they had moved:

> Haichow is a high, well drained city.... With the mountains on one side and the sea only ten miles distant on the other, we hope it will be more healthful than are most of the cities.... We are very much pleased with our new home and surroundings. Our home is strictly Chinese, but the addition of doors and windows has made it quite comfortable.[70]

In 1910, the Rices were joined by Rev. and Mrs. J. W. Vinson, and Dr. and Mrs. L. S. Morgan. After prolonged negotiations, property was purchased and a dispensary was opened. With the beginning of medical work, a marked change was observed in the attitude of the people. A day school opened with 14 pupils. Attendance at the street chapel was encouraging and 7 baptized members were reported in 1911. By the year 1923 places of regular worship numbered 24 with 378 communicants.[71]

Taizhou (Taichow)

In 1906 Rev. C. N. Caldwell visited the area southeast of Huaiyin (TKP) in search of a good location for a new station. Taizhou, he wrote, was the ideal location:

> I have made since May 15th five trips of three weeks each...and have sold about 7,000 books and portions of Scripture....I have just, after much effort, secured in Taichow a very desirable chapel in a splendid location where crowds of people come whenever it is opened and pay good attention to the preaching by my helper and myself.[72]

However, Caldwell's initial optimism was ill-founded. The Chinese evangelist working with him was nearly beaten to death.[73] The property deal fell through, a residence could not be secured and Caldwell, his family far away in the United States, lived alone on a houseboat for months. Help was slow in coming. Dr. and Mrs. R. M. Stephenson were assigned to the station but these plans fell apart when Mrs. Stephenson died in Zhenjiang. Rev. Frank A. Brown was next but after a year he was transferred to Xuzhou.[74] Mr. Caldwell became thoroughly discouraged and at the annual meeting in 1911 petitioned the mission to discharge the building committee, sell the property and withdraw from the field. Caldwell's motion was postponed until later in the meeting and then a resolution was adopted to wholeheartedly support the continuation of the station and give it high priority. In 1912 Rev. and Mrs. Thomas Harnsberger were assigned there. This was a turning point for ten years later the station reported these encouraging statistics: 2 organized congregations, 7 places of regular worship, 199 communicants, 6 day schools with 214 students, and 6,238 patients treated.[75]

Yancheng (Yencheng)

Rev. and Mrs. Hugh White were transferred from Xuzhou to open work in the prosperous city of Yencheng, which lay between Taizhou and Lianyungang and was reached by a branch of the Grand Canal. Some itineration had been done in the area by CIM and Methodist missionaries. Land was purchased in 1910 but the deal fell through because of the opposition of the officials. Unexpectedly, when all doors were closed, Buddhist priests offered Rev. White a refuge in their temple and a place to preach. Permanent property was secured after the 1911 revolution when opposition to the foreigner had faded away. Rev. and Mrs. Harold Bridgman arrived in 1920. During the first ten years five congregations were organized with a membership of 1,030 and a Christian constituency of over 1,500.[76]

Nanjing Theological Seminary

In 1901 a joint conference of Presbyterian missionaries adopted a plan for the establishment of a union seminary at Nanjing. The Central China Mission

(PCUSA), Mid China and North Jiangsu Missions (PCUS) each appointed members to the board and were asked to contribute $6,000 each for property and buildings.

The new Presbyterian Theological Seminary opened in Nanjing in 1906 with twenty-two students. The faculty consisted of Dr. J. C. Garritt (PCUSA) and Dr. J. W. Davis (PCUS). Rev. J. Leighton Stuart (PCUS) joined the seminary as a third professor in 1908 and introduced the teaching of Greek.

Two courses of instruction were offered: a seminary course for those with a college degree and a training class for those without this qualification. In the report for 1908–1909, forty-three students were enrolled. The first class of four students graduated in 1908. In 1910, two Chinese professors joined the faculty.[77] Also, in this year the seminary board voted to ask the recently formed union synod to appoint four advisory members. In 1911 Dr. P. Frank Price (PCUS) took the place of Dr. Davis, who desired to returned to the evangelistic work in Suzhou.

The issues that dominated the seminary in its early years were the struggle to secure capital investment for the buildings, the lack of candidates for the ministry and a continuing debate about academic standards. Should the seminary insist on the high standards of the home churches, or should it lower the qualification to fit the China scene? Students graduating from mission colleges were reluctant to enter the ministry.[78] The North Jiangsu Mission expressed concerns about "doctrinal differences" and voted against broadening the seminary constituency to include other missions. Yet, strangely, the majority of the students came from the North Jiangsu area.[79]

A United Synod

After years of discussion and debate the formation of a united Chinese Presbyterian church finally became a reality. But the breakthrough did not occur until it had been debated at great length by the PCUS General Assembly.

In 1902 the Mid China Mission overtured the PCUS General Assembly to permit them to organize a Chinese presbytery independent of the church at home with missionaries holding a dual relationship with both churches according to the Amoy Plan.[80] The General Assembly rejected the overture on the grounds that it was incompatible with the Presbyterian system of government. In 1903 a similar overture was presented to the General Assembly by the PCUS Korea Mission and was again rejected by the Assembly. But this time a committee was appointed to study the issue and report to the next General Assembly.

The Assembly of 1905 noted that the request, which had been made repeatedly by missionaries from Korea and China, had been declined by three different assemblies. But the Assembly cited with approval the concept of establishing union native churches with the PCUSA and authorized its missionaries to take all such steps as may be necessary, and in their judgement in conformity with Presbyterian principles, to secure the independence of the proposed United Presbyterian churches in Korea and China.[81]

The action of the Assembly was remarkably vague and somewhat contradictory. Without expressly saying so, it reversed the decision of three assemblies and gave the missionaries on the field the final authority for the decision as long as it was, in their opinion, in accordance with "Presbyterian principles."

The Mid China Mission lost no time in organizing the "Kiang Cheh" (South of the River) Presbytery along the lines of the Amoy Plan. The organizational meeting was held at the Dongshang Church on 4 April 1906 with ten missionary ministers, four missionary elders, one Chinese ordained pastor and seventeen Chinese elders who comprised the initial membership of the presbytery. The roll call of the churches numbered 14 organized congregations and 985 communicant members. Each signed a solemn covenant to be true to the faith and to render obedience to one another in the Lord.[82] Missionary members had the right to vote and hold office. Although they were subject to the authority of the American church, the presbytery, by a two-thirds vote, could expel any missionary who "behaved disorderly."[83]

The meeting was held in a mood of celebration. Three hundred lay workers attended a three-day workers' conference held along with the meeting of presbytery. A separate meeting was held for the women. It was a picturesque scene. The district magistrate attended arrayed in his official robes. More than sixteen hundred meals were served to delegates and visitors. The church was adjacent to the canal and some delegates, Chinese and missionaries alike, stayed in their boats, which were tied up at the front door.[84]

The way was now open for the organization of a union synod. The PCUSA Synod of Central China extended an invitation to other Presbyterian bodies to unite in the formation of such a body. The synod was organized at Nanking, 26 May 1906. The name chosen was the "Wu Song Synod" (Synod of the Five Provinces); it was composed of the presbyteries of Ningbo, Shanghai, Hangzhou and Nanjing of the PCUSA and the newly organized Kiang Cheh Presbytery of the PCUS. Attending the organizational meeting were 20 ordained missionaries, 14 Chinese pastors, 16 Chinese elders, representing 33 organized churches, and 3,259 communicants. The synod was constituted as "having ultimate jurisdiction over the churches within its bounds."[85]

Opinions within the North Jiangsu Mission were divided on the issue of joining the union synod. A small minority led by Rev. Hugh White protested the action of the Mid China Mission in an appeal to the PCUS General Assembly in 1905. White's appeal was rejected. Sydenstricker and Paxton of the North Jiangsu Mission attended the union synod and reported favorably on it. In 1909 the mission recommended that Xuzhou and Suqian stations, with their three organized churches and five hundred communicant members, organize a presbytery, which would be placed under the union synod. Kiang Pei Presbytery

(North of the River) was duly organized in March 1910 and became a member of the union synod.[86]

The Goforth/Ting Revivals

During the years 1907–1910 a far-reaching evangelistic movement swept across the country that breathed new vitality into the Christian church. The names associated with the movement were Rev. Jonathan Goforth, a Canadian Presbyterian from Manchuria, and Rev. Ting Li Mei, a young graduate of the Shandong College. Significantly, both had suffered terribly during the Boxer Uprising. Goforth had been seriously wounded by the Boxers and barely escaped with his life. Rev. Ting Li Mei had remained with his congregation when the Boxers entered his city and had been so badly beaten he had been left for dead.

Goforth visited Korea in 1908 to learn firsthand of the spiritual movement sweeping that country. Returning to China, he told of the spiritual manifestations that had taken place: the public confession of sin, the freedom experienced in forgiveness and the fresh vitality that had touched every phase of church life. Goforth was invited to speak to groups of missionaries at their summer vacation centers. From there the movement spread throughout the church. During the year 1909, Goforth spoke in twenty-eight different cities with his simple, fervent message. Many Chinese pastors took part in his services.

Typical of the meetings was the one held in Nanjing in March 1909. A great tent was set up with a seating capacity of twelve hundred. For months the Christian community of Nanjing had been much in prayer. All Protestant churches of the city supported the movement. Initially Goforth's preaching was directed at the Christians. The first several days were fairly routine. Then there was an abrupt break. Men and women, boys and girls, began to confess their sins with weeping and deep contrition. Gambling, impurity, unfilial treatment of parents, abuse of wives, falsification of grades, misuse of church funds and smuggling were all confessed. Missionaries were not immune and confessed sins of pride, temper and lack of faith. The preaching schedule had to be cancelled as the confessions went on and on. Goforth ended the meeting with words of encouragement and united prayer for the Christian movement throughout the Empire.[87]

As a follow-up, the tent meetings continued with services for non-Christians, which were attended by two thousand or more people. Singing was a prominent part of the services. Four hundred people expressed the desire to "study" the Christian faith and were organized into classes. Over one hundred applied for baptism.

In Suzhou fifteen hundred people signed cards expressing a desire to know more about "the doctrine."[88] In Jiangyin and Jiaxing Southern Presbyterians reported the same evidences of divine grace: "We have passed through experiences which can be accounted for only by the working of an irresistible Divine power, and it was all in answer to prayer."[89]

Rev. Ting Li Mei participated in the meetings and was especially effective with young people and college students. He led services at Weixian where classes at the college and the girls' high school were suspended so the students could attend the services. Pastor Ting held interviews with students who desired to talk to him and the number who came exceeded all expectations. Here, unlike the meetings at Nanjing, there was little excitement but all "were conscious of a strong, deep steady current of conviction."[90] Ting Li Mei continued his meetings in Peking and Tianjin, where two hundred students made decisions to enter the ministry.

The revival movement brought reconciliation between factions, a deepening of spiritual life and a sharp increase in the number of new believers. It also left a deep impression on the general public. People in the streets were heard to say: "The Christians' God has come down."[91]

10

Revolution and War Lords

1911–1926

On 9 October 1911 a premature bomb explosion in Wuhan triggered the beginning of the national uprising against the Qing dynasty.[1] On the morning of the tenth the Eighth Engineer Battalion mutinied and seized the ammunition depot and by nightfall the city was firmly in control of the revolutionaries. This date — the tenth month, the tenth day — became known as the "double tenth" and the national day of independence.

By the end of October six provinces were in open rebellion. Qing officials acted belatedly to convene a provisional national assembly but swiftly moving events outpaced the deliberations of the court reformers. Manchu forces suffered a staggering defeat at Nanjing in early December at the hands of a loose confederation known as the Revolutionary Alliance. Sun Yat-sen, then in the United States on a fund-raising campaign, arrived in Shanghai on Christmas Day to a tumultuous welcome. Four days later he was elected provisional president of the Republic of China by delegates from sixteen provinces.

In the meantime the Qing dynasty turned to Yuan Shikai as the only personage with enough prestige to restore confidence in the Manchus. Yuan commanded the loyalty of the powerful Beiyang (North China) army, the only force that could counteract the revolutionary armies in the south. Yuan was elected premier by the provisional national assembly in Peking but the reforms came too late. The final blow came when the senior commanders of the Beiyang army signed an appeal for the establishment of a republic. The Emperor's mother and court officials frantically negotiated a settlement that guaranteed the boy Emperor's continued residence in the Forbidden City, protection of the Manchu ancestral temples and an annual stipend. The court then announced the abdication of the boy Emperor, Puyi, on 12 February 1912. Just four months after the insurrection had begun, two thousand years of China's imperial history came to an end.

But China now had a president in Nanjing elected by the Revolutionary Alliance and a premier in Peking elected by the National Provisional Assembly. The impasse was broken when Sun resigned his post in favor of Yuan. Sun, who had immense popular support, had no military strength to match

Yuan's northern army. The compromise provided for the holding of national elections for a legislative body that would elect the new president. It was also agreed that Yuan would move the capital from the Manchu bastion of Peking to Nanjing where Sun's Revolutionary Alliance, renamed the National People's Party (Kuomintang [KMT]), was strong. But Yuan reneged on the agreement, claiming that civil strife demanded his presence in the north.

China's first national election, held in January 1913, resulted in a clear victory for the KMT. But the victory was short-lived. Sun's candidate for premier, Song Jiaoren, an able and popular administrator, was assassinated at the Shanghai railroad station as he began his trip to Peking to take office. In all likelihood, Yuan was involved. Pro-KMT provincial governors were dismissed. In heavy fighting in the summer of 1912, troops loyal to the KMT were routed by the Beiyang army. In October, Yuan forced the legislature to elect him to a five-year term. At the end of November, Sun Yat-sen, once more an exile, sailed for Japan.

Yuan gained the support of the foreign powers, who were impressed by his show of strength and his promises to support reform causes. In 1913 the United States granted full diplomatic recognition. But Yuan had little popular support and tax revenue from the provinces virtually ceased. To take their place, massive foreign loans were negotiated but for the indebtedness a price had to be paid. Great Britain sought autonomy for Tibet, and Russia the same for Outer Mongolia. Even worse was Japan's Twenty-one Demands, which claimed concessions in the north.

Chinese patriots felt betrayed and organized anti-Japanese riots and the boycott of Japanese goods. As Yuan's popularity plummeted he became more despotic. The legislature was dissolved. In 1915 Yuan rode to the Temple of Heaven in an armored car and offered the annual sacrifices, which in previous days had been the Emperor's prerogative. Many interpreted this as the first step toward establishing a new dynasty with Yuan as Emperor. But Yuan had badly miscalculated. Province after province declared independence of Peking. Yuan's prestige was shattered and he died six months later of natural causes — probably compounded by humiliation and disgrace. He was fifty-six years old.

The War Lords

The death of Yuan Shikai and the rapid disintegration of his short-lived administration brings us to the period of the "war lords." It is one of the most confused and chaotic times in Chinese history. The political scene became a continuing power struggle between three main factions.

In Peking, the presidency was occupied by a figurehead elected in accordance with the constitution. This preserved the semblance of a republic recognized by Western powers anxious to preserve their interests and the repayment of their loans. But the constitutionality of the Peking government was largely a facade as it rarely controlled more than a few provinces.

In Canton, there remained the remnants of the revolutionary party, which was loyal to Sun Yat-sen and refused to recognize the legitimacy of Peking.

In between Peking and Canton, the real power lay with what became known as the war lords (Chinese: *dujun*). For the most part these were provincial military commanders who had consolidated their power when the central government collapsed.

The war lords can be characterized by the following features: (1) *Militarism.* War lords held power because they could muster, control and pay local armies whose primary loyalty was to them. (2) *Provincialism.* Local concerns, rather than national interests, were in control. Power was maintained through heavy taxation, smuggling and tariffs on goods crossing provincial borders. (3) *Shifting alliances.* Since no one war lord was strong enough to dominate the scene, coalitions were constantly being formed. Smaller war lords offered their services to whichever major player promised the most. (4) *A variety of ideologies.* Some were rightist and fought for the reestablishment of the dynasty. Some were anarchists. Some had sold out to Japan, which provided weapons and support. Some undoubtedly were genuine patriots, and struggled to reestablish the republic.

One characteristic of the era that had a direct effect on missionary activity was *banditry.* The breakdown of law and order, the dire poverty of the people and the recruitment of mercenaries resulted in the proliferation of armed bands that roamed the countryside and thrived on extortion, plunder and kidnapping. Soldiers became bandits and bandits became soldiers. Hardest hit were the provincial border lands, which offered easy escape from one jurisdiction to another. A case in point was southern Shandong and northern Jiangsu, where Presbyterian missionaries were at work. A British consul traveling through the area in 1913 estimated that "80 percent of the male population had been bandits for some length of time at one period or another."[2]

Three of the most durable and colorful war lords are worth noting. *Zhang Zuolin* was a former bandit chieftain who rose to power under Yuan and gained control of Manchuria. During many of these years he dominated the Peking government. He was killed by a bomb that blew up his train near Shenyang (Mukden) in 1928. In all likelihood, the Japanese military, who had supported him earlier, were behind the assassination.

Wu Peifu, a Confucian scholar who chose a military career, became the dominant war lord in the Yangtze Valley. Wu and Zhang were sometimes colleagues, sometimes at each other's throats.

The third figure in the trilogy and the most interesting for our story is *Feng Yuxiang.* Feng enlisted in the army as a common soldier. Stationed in Baoding in 1900, he was deeply moved by the martyrdom of the missionaries at the hands of the Boxers. He rose through the ranks, made a public profession of his Christian faith and was baptized. Later he became known as the "Christian General" and the treatment of his troops reflected his change in character. Gambling and prostitution were forbidden and his command was noted for discipline and the absence of graft. Christian chaplains were appointed. His troops were taught to read and write and were instructed in a useful trade. Some say he became lukewarm in his Christian faith later in life, but those who knew him well stoutly defended his character.[3]

The Chinese Renaissance

Paradoxically, this period of chaos and confusion was also a time of economic and intellectual growth and is known as "China's Renaissance." Chinese manufacturing surged as the British and French competition was busy at home during the First World War. Chinese capitalism flourished as cotton production, the silk industry, banking and shipping companies prospered. The period saw the rise of labor unions and the outburst of strikes protesting low wages and miserable working conditions.

Another contradiction was the role of the treaty ports. On the one hand they exemplified the humiliation China experienced at the hand of the colonial powers. Yet on the other hand, they provided the security for China's burgeoning commercial strength and became a sanctuary for the new intellectual movement. Fairbank notes that the period constituted

> two areas and two regimes — warlord China and treaty-port China...
> Chinese patriots had to confront the paradox that the unequal treaties,
> while humiliating in principle were often of material help in fact.[4]

Intellectuals were bitterly disappointed with the failure to establish a republic. The old Qing dynasty had passed but nothing had taken its place. Lu Xun, the foremost writer of the day, gave up his medical training in Japan, returned to Shanghai and chose literature as a means of social reform. At Peking University the intellectual ferment was ignited by two dominant personalities: Chen Duxiu and Hu Shih. Chen founded the journal *Young China* (La Jeunesse) in 1915, which engaged in the wholesale repudiation of Chinese cultural values and advocated the study of Western science and democracy. Hu Shih also advocated Western science and democracy but was less radical in his political views. For Hu Shih the point of attack was reform of the language. Instead of the stilted, terse *Wen Li* used by classical scholars Hu advocated the use of Mandarin *(Bai Hua)*, the spoken language of the north China masses. *Bai Hua* quickly became the medium of instruction in schools and the literary medium of the rising student class.

Initially the new intellectuals were supportive of Christianity. Although Chen Duxiu later became one of China's first advocates for Marxism, in his earlier years he wrote of his great admiration for Jesus Christ:

> We must foster within our very blood the great and noble personality
> of Jesus, his profound and ardent feelings, to save us from the abyss of
> cruelty, darkness and filth into which we have fallen.[5]

A Christian leader of the times, Timothy T. Lew, noted the contributions the intellectual "renaissance" made and the new opportunity this gave the Christian movement:

> It developed a critical, inquiring attitude of mind. It inspired the race with new hope and courage. It taught the people the value and absolute necessity of science and scientific procedure. It gave the people a new tool for expression — the *Bai Hua* or conversational style of speaking and writing.[6]

A Christian intellectual, Y. C. James Yen, led the attack against illiteracy through his Mass Education Movement. Yen went to France with the YMCA to aid Chinese laborers during World War I and introduced a system of teaching that used only a basic number of one thousand characters. The results were encouraging and Yen returned to China to introduce his methods on a national scale.[7]

Missionaries and the Revolution

The revolution came as a shock to the foreign community in China. Diplomats and business interests feared the loss of their loans and urged a policy of nonsupport for the revolutionary cause. The missionary reaction was quite different; they urged the Western powers to support the revolution. Sun himself was a baptized Christian. Many of the leaders of the revolution had been educated in mission schools. A contemporary authority credits the missionary influence with changing the policy of the Taft administration from that of nonrecognition to one of support.[8] General Huang Hsing, Minister of War in Sun Yat-sen's provisional government, attributed the swift, near bloodless success of the revolution to the influence of the missionaries:

> Christianity is far more widespread in its influence than you missionaries realize. Its ideals have largely pervaded China. Along with its ideals of religious freedom it brings a knowledge of western political freedom, and along with these it inculcates everywhere a doctrine of universal love and peace. These ideals appeal to the Chinese; they largely caused the revolution, and they largely determined its peaceful character.[9]

On the first anniversary of the Republic, the *Assembly Herald* reported on the viewpoint of Presbyterian missionaries from across China. All were ecstatic in their support of the revolution and the opportunities it brought. This response from George Fitch is representative of many others:

> For Christianity the decisive hour would seem to have come. There are open doors such as never existed before. There are opportunities which are simply glorious in their possibilities, provided the Christian Church is prepared to enter in with needed men and means, and a faith that will move mountains.[10]

Missionaries applauded the election of Yuan Shikai to the presidency. Although not a Christian, he had supported the missionary cause during the Boxer Uprising. Yuan created quite a sensation in the United States when he asked Americans to pray for China when the new Chinese parliament convened in 1913.[11] Missionaries were instrumental in getting President Woodrow Wilson to adopt a more favorable China policy.[12] John R. Mott was asked by the president to become the China ambassador. He declined but the nomination illustrates the influence of the Protestant missionary establishment.

Professor Fairbank has drawn attention to the degree of cooperation between the new reformers and the missionaries:

> This era of Christian cooperation was marked by signal achievements such as the road-building and rural credit work of the Chinese International Famine Relief Commission, the research and training of the Rockefeller-supported Peking Union Medical College... growth of Yenching University and other Christian colleges, including agricultural research at Nanjing University, and the Mass Education Movement under Yan Yangchu (Jimmy Yen).[13]

The collapse of the Yuan Shikai government brought disillusionment but did not end missionary-inspired attempts to bring reform through their educational and social welfare institutions. Mission institutions in the treaty ports were immune to the ravages of the civil strife sweeping across the land. In the hinterland missionaries made their peace as best they could with the prevailing war lord. Remarkably, relations of friendship often developed as each had something the other needed. Missionaries needed stability for themselves and their people. War lords needed the national and international recognition that came with the friendship of the foreigners.

In Lianyungang the local war lord, General Bei Bao Shan, became a warm friend of the Southern Presbyterians. Missionaries gave him high marks for the good behavior of his troops.[14] In 1924, when banditry was rampant, the general provided the Rev. Thomas Grafton with an escort of thirty heavily armed soldiers on his country trips. Grafton expressed appreciation for the protection after seeing the heads of nineteen bandits prominently displayed on the city wall.[15]

Missionaries in Changde, Hunan, reported the arrival of the "Christian General" (Feng Yuxiang) in their city in 1920:

> Probably in all the long centuries of her history there has never been witnessed the sight which became comparatively commonplace to our eyes — of a thousand Chinese soldiers marching through the city streets, singing "Onward Christian Soldiers..." as they marched. [Here is] a Chinese city where no opium could be smoked, where the city streets were clean, where vice was compelled to hide its hideousness, where the church was invited to preach to those in prison... and where reform was the order

of the day.... We gladly bear this testimony to the genuine Christianity of General Feng U Hsiang [Feng Yuxiang] and his officers.[16]

Rev. O. V. Armstrong's story of General Feng's visit in their home in Xuzhou is a commentary on missionary life during these times. The general arrived in the city in his private train and became ill. The pastor of the West Gate Presbyterian Church suggested that the Armstrongs invite the general to stay in their home while he was recuperating. Mr. Armstrong thought it highly unlikely that the invitation would be accepted but it was sent. To their surprise, General Feng soon arrived accompanied by his retinue of doctors, secretaries, cooks and bodyguards. The Armstrongs turned over the upstairs of their home to the general and his party. The cooks took over the kitchen to prepare the general's meals. The general's wife soon joined him. Ten days later the party departed by special train after profuse thanks, gifts and Mr. Armstrong's invitation to return.

Two weeks later the marshal again visited Xuzhou and sent word they would like to accept the Armstrong's invitation. Again, the upstairs of the house was turned over to them. One Sunday evening the general came downstairs and said "Mr. Armstrong, I have come down because I feel hungry and thirsty." Mr. Armstrong replied that Mrs. Armstrong would be glad to prepare tea and refreshments. "No, I am thinking of spiritual hunger and thirst," he said. "I want you to read to me and interpret your favorite Bible passages." Armstrong replied that he knew the marshal was a student of the Bible and it would be presumptuous to teach him but suggested that each read their favorite passages and share their spiritual insights. This they began to do.

The marshal had been offered the seat of honor, which was the treasured Montgomery Ward rocking chair. But the general was a large man weighing over 250 pounds. Rocking back and forth, the chair collapsed under the weight, and the marshal fell backwards. It took some time and effort to extract him from the remnants of the broken chair but neither the missionary nor the marshall changed expression. Neither mentioned the embarrassing incident. A second chair was offered and the conversation continued as if nothing unusual had happened.[17]

During the tumultuous year of civil war, famine, and banditry, missionary compounds and hospitals became havens for refugees. During the summer of 1913, Nanjing became a storm center with opposing sides battling for control of the strategic city. The PCUSA *Annual Report* cites the relief work for the refugees and the impression this made on the populace:

> The fact that 5,000 helpless women and children found refuge within the walls of the missionaries' homes, hospitals and schools during those awful days made a profound impression on the hearts of the people.... The assistance which the missionaries were able to give the Chamber of Commerce, before and after the capture of the city, and the relief to all classes of the community has meant more than years of preaching could have done, in removing prejudice and showing the people what Christianity means.[18]

The most dramatic form of intervention came when missionaries served as peacemakers between warring factions. The city fathers in Suqian asked Rev. William Junkin to intercede on their behalf when a large band of looting soldiers besieged the city. Ransom money was offered. Mr. Junkin went out to meet the chiefs of the besieging force and pleaded for peace. But the ransom money was less than the amount demanded. Junkin returned at midnight and reported the failure. The next day the city was shelled and looted. There was a mass exodus into the mission compound which was the safest place in town.[19]

Missionaries in Jiangyin were more successful. In 1925 southern forces took possession of the city and were then besieged by northern troops supported by six hundred Russians. After intense fighting the fort commanding the Yangtze river narrows was taken by the Russians and the guns turned against the city. The gentry asked the three senior members of the mission (Lacy Little, George Worth and Lacy Moffett) to intervene in order to save the city from bombardment and looting. The three first visited the general of the southern troops in the city and then the northern commander and his Russian allies outside the walls. Terms for a truce were proposed but were first rejected. For four days the missionary men visited the two camps back and forth, sometimes under sniper fire. Finally an agreement was reached and the two opposing generals met in one of the missionary homes. After a five-hour session of intense negotiations, terms of peace were drawn up. The next day the generals returned to the compound and signed formal surrender documents. The northern army marched into the East Gate to accept the surrender of the defeated southerners. The city was spared.[20]

"The Golden Years"

Historians have called the years following the Revolution of 1911 "the golden years" of the missionary enterprise.[21] For a few brief years, China seemed to be moving toward reform. The new intellectual climate was supportive of Christianity. Christians held high positions in the government. Christian schools were filled to overflowing. In spite of the turbulent years of the war lords, the prestige and influence of the missionary was high.

But the term "golden years" should be used with caution. Banditry and the movement of revolutionary armies caused the repeated evacuation of mission stations in the interior. Presbyterian missionaries in Jiangsu, Shandong, Anhui, Hainan, Zhejiang and Yunnan were all caught in the middle of the furious fighting between rival factions.[22] During such times all normal activity came to a halt. Latourette cites the names of thirty Protestant missionaries abducted by brigands during the sixteen years from 1911 to 1926. Of this number seven were murdered.[23] Among these was the Rev. George Byers of Jiaji (Kachek), Hainan, in June 1924.

But in spite of the disorder these were the peak years for missionary numbers. Between 1911 and 1926 the BFM sent 522 new missionaries to China. The peak was reached in 1926 when 576 missionaries were on the roll of the China missions.[24] The numbers for the Southern Presbyterians were comparable. New appointments for the period came to 149. The peak year was 1925, when 214 missionaries were under appointment.

Aiding in the expansion of the missionary force was the favorable exchange rate, which meant that the purchasing power of the dollar was high. This facilitated the paying of salaries and the building of schools, hospitals and churches. Existing programs were strengthened and new stations were opened.

Church membership increased dramatically. Communicant members of congregations related to the Northern Presbyterians increased from 18,470 in 1911 to 49,985 in 1926. This represented a 10 percent increase per year for fifteen years. For the Southern Presbyterians the increase was an astonishing fourfold — from 2,516 in 1911 to 11,986 in 1926. Clearly, the Christian church was becoming a vital and self-sustaining community.

During these years a gradual shift took place in the nature of mission activity. Note the following comparisons in work assignments for the Northern Presbyterians:

Work Assignments	1910	1926
Evangelism	134	183
Medical Work	67	116
Education	78	195
Theological/Leadership Training	5	16
Other	6	66
Totals	290	576[25]

Increases are observed in all areas of the work. But the educational program outstrips all others as the number of those in school work doubles. Much of this represented the new commitment to higher education. Some expressed fears that the shift would lead to a neglect of the primary goal of evangelism.[26]

The figures for the two Southern Presbyterian missions show the same increase in education:

Work Assignments	1912	1926
Evangelism	67	87
Education	25	55
Medicine	22	36
Theological/Leadership Training	6	10
Other	8	8
Totals	128	196[27]

These years are characterized by other changes and new emphases. More and more, the work was done by Chinese pastors, evangelists, Bible women, teachers and medical personnel. In 1924, Chinese workers associated with the

Northern Presbyterian Mission numbered 2,976 or three times the total number of missionaries.[28] Work responsibilities were transferred from the missions to the presbyteries.[29] A new "Evangelize the Cities Campaign" begun by the Shandong Mission was carried out entirely by well-qualified Chinese leadership.[30] More attention was given to problems of literacy. The curriculum of mission schools was standardized. The North Jiangsu Mission appointed a committee to survey the field in order that a plan could be made for its "ultimate evangelization."[31] Famine relief was a continuing necessity for North Jiangsu and Shandong. Mass evangelistic campaigns were launched in the big cities. In 1913 the Shandong Mission turned over responsibility for an area of their work to missionaries of the Korean Presbyterian Church.[32]

The enlarged number of missionaries and programs necessitated administrative changes. In 1910 the BFM created the China Council to coordinate the work of the eight Presbyterian China missions and the twenty-four stations where missionaries resided. The Council, made up of two representatives from each mission, met annually to approve personnel and budget requests, and give general oversight to the work. The Rev. James W. Lowrie was unanimously elected chairman — a position he held until 1925 when he was succeeded by Rev. Ralph C. Wells.

In 1924 the Executive Committee of Foreign Missions proposed that its two China missions establish a council similar to that of the Northern Presbyterians. Plans were proposed but were voted down by the North Jiangsu Mission.[33]

Central China

The increased number of new missionaries made it possible to open new work in southern Shandong and Anhui along the route of the newly constructed Tianjin-Pukou railroad.

Tengxian (Tenghsien)

In 1912 the Shandong Mission invited the SPM North Jiangsu Mission to cooperate in the establishment of a training school for Christian workers at a new station to be started at Tengxian somewhat equidistant between the two mission areas. Rev. and Mrs. H. G. Romig moved to the new location in December 1913. In 1918 the North Jiangsu Mission assigned Rev. and Mrs. George Stevens to this work.[34]

A gift of $10,000 (U.S.) from the estate of Calvin Mateer provided funds for the new school, which was named the Mateer Memorial Institute. Mateer trained evangelists and teachers who because of age, family or academic preparation were unable to attend a four-year college or seminary. The school attracted men from all over Shandong and North Jiangsu. In 1919 it enrolled 80 students in its Bible and Normal School departments. The school was one of the first to operate under a Chinese principal (Rev. Liu Si I) with a board of directors jointly appointed by the Synod of Shandong and the two Presbyterian missions.[35]

Nanxuzhou (Nanhsuchow)

Missionaries at Huayuan were at work in northern Anhui, a largely unreached area as large as the state of Maine. The area was made more accessible by the construction of the railroad line on which the Kiangan Mission opened a station at the city of Nanxuzhou in 1912. Rev. George C. Hood and Rev. and Mrs. Thomas F. Carter were welcomed by the city officials who, incredibly, provided the use of two old Buddhist temples. Soon they were put to new use:

> The one, an old ancestral temple, is full of boys in school uniform, hard at work at geography or arithmetic or Bible.... The temple of the God of War ... used for a reading room and lecture hall, is much more of a building, and with its new coat of paint looks quite distinguished. As long as the old sign, "Buddhist Association," stands over the door (and we are in no hurry to take it down) the priests are delighted to have us do anything we want with their temple, and let them get part credit for the good deeds. We have even covered over all their idols, though at the suggestion of the head priest we left a hole in front of each idol for him to look out, so that the poor old idols would not lose face completely.[36]

Here, instead of burning incense to the God of War, a day of prayer for the nation was observed. Here also an inquirers' class was begun with twenty men from country villages attending for a week. Dispensary work was begun by a Chinese Christian doctor. Slowly the nucleus of a Christian community began to form.[37]

During this period the Southern Presbyterians started no new mission stations but assigned mission personnel to a number of cooperative programs. In Shanghai the mission treasurer, Maxcy Smith, was a member of the Associated Mission Treasurers, S. I Woodbridge was editor of the ecumenical Chinese magazine, the *Intelligencer,* and from time to time teachers were assigned to the Shanghai American School (for missionary children).[38] In Nanjing they cooperated in the Nanjing Theological Seminary, the Union Women's Bible School, and University Hospital and the Nanjing Language School. In Jinan, Dr. Randolph Shields served as dean of the Shandong Christian University Medical School. In Tengxian, they cooperated with the Shandong Mission of the PCUSA in the Mateer Memorial Institute, the North China Theological Seminary and the North China Women's Theological Seminary. Dr. W. H. Venable was attached to the Kuling Hospital.[39]

The Isle of Palms

In spite of the strenuous efforts of missionaries and Chinese workers, results had been slow on Hainan island. In 1900, nineteen years after the work had been initiated, there were only 106 baptized Christians, no organized churches and no ordained ministers.[40] Why the slow growth? Perhaps the polyglot nature of the island's culture made it difficult to weld the various factions into a Christian community. Ledong was a veritable "modern day Babel," with eight different language groups within a thirty-mile radius. The insular culture of the island made it more difficult for them to relate to any outsider — foreigner or mainlander alike.

But the years of witness and service began to have their effect. Year after year the mission schools in Ledong and Qiongzhou (Kiungchow) continued to graduate boys and girls. The Hainan Bible Institute turned out well-trained church workers. The seed sown in the preaching in the street chapels sometimes fell on fertile soil. And Dr. Henry McCandliss's forty years medical practice left an indelible impression.

Above all else it was personal relationships that broke down suspicion. Rev. Frank Gilman said that the antidote to the persistent rumors that foreigners "ate the livers and dug out the eyes of people" was to simply mingle with them to "show yourself friendly with them, chat about the common things of life." If this was done "ill natured gossip would soon die down."[41]

Jiaji

In 1901 a new station was started at Jiaji, a large market town one-third the way down the east coast. Isolated from the rest of the island, it was reached by a two-day trip on a small boat and then two more days overland. When Mr. Gilman began construction there was great agitation because of the chimney, the likes of which none had seen. It reached so high it would surely upset the good luck of the region. Gilman explained its workings and assured them it would not rise higher than thirty feet. After the explanation all went well. Street chapel preaching, the McCormick School for Boys, the "Daughters School" for Girls and Kilbourne Hospital soon followed.[42]

By the year 1910 there was a sharp upturn in missionary numbers and the growth of the church. The first pastor was ordained and called to the Ledong Church — the Rev. Deng Tui Vang from the Hakka tribe.[43] Seven new missionaries arrived in 1913 and five more the next year. Between the years 1909 and 1917 Hainan church membership increased fourfold — from 375 to 1,642.

In 1914 the Ledong church membership passed 500. But more remarkable than the growth was the make-up of the congregation: 240 from the Limko Tribe, 197 Hakkas, 48 Hainanese, and 24 Mandarin-speaking mainlanders.[44] Each had a different tongue and culture! But in Christ there was neither "Greek nor Jew, circumcised nor uncircumcised, barbarian, Scythian, slave or free" (Col. 3:11).

In 1916 a Christian mass movement took place among the Miao tribe. The chief had a dream in which he saw his house in black darkness, suddenly illuminated by a great light. He came to the Jiaji Mission station saying his people were in darkness and asked that they be brought into the light. The missionaries told him that Jesus was the light of the world and could bring light to his tribe. Those visiting the chief's village brought back an astonishing report:

> After our first visit to his village, his people built a thatched chapel and our Chinese evangelist soon reported throngs of these people, from many miles around, coming every Sunday to learn of the Christian's God. Some days nearly a thousand Miao would meet, and it was very hard to hold any orderly meeting with people so new and strange. When they had learned a few lessons in the worship of the true God they returned home, and village after village built a chapel of their own, and assembled every morning and evening to sing hymns, read the New Testament and pray. I asked one village chief how many families in his village worshiped God. "All of them," he replied; "when we built the chapel two families refused to join with us and so they moved to another village."[45]

The first communion service for the Miao was held on Easter Sunday, 1919. It was "a sight never to be forgotten — the little groups...departing in the evening, each group its flaming torch lighting up the surrounding darkness."[46]

A unique custom of the Hainan Christians was the holding of what they called "Big Sunday." The festivities would be held twice a year when all the Christians in the area would gather at a central church for several days of instruction, inspiration and fellowship. On one occasion a Taoist priest, seeking baptism, turned over his books of incantation to the church elders.[47] Margaret Moninger has described a typical Big Sunday:

> It is indeed an inspiration to see the Christians come in — men, women and children — some by boat and some by road, some having walked twenty-five or thirty miles. Services are held in the chapel morning and evening, special classes for women are carried on, and the members of the session are kept busy examining candidates. In fact all of us are kept busy finding places for the crowds to sleep, hearing of the sorrows and joys of our flock, giving a word of warning here or of encouragement there.... The climax, to us all, is the baptism of the new members of the Church of Christ and the tiny babies of the Christian families, and then the communion together.[48]

During these perilous times when the island was devastated by competing war lords and bandits, the Rev. George D. Byers was killed by brigands. He was returning to his home after attending evening vespers at the Jiaji hospital on 24 June 1924. Four armed men, seeking ransom money, were waiting in the shadows and seized him as he was walking up the steps to his home. He was dragged down the road with a rope around his neck to prevent an outcry. When the Byers's ten-year-old son, Robert, heard the incessant barking of his dog, he went out to investigate. Fearing the commotion would bring the police the brigands began firing. Mr. Byers was mortally wounded. Another shot grazed Robert's leg but he escaped to sound the alarm. But by the time help had arrived, Mr. Byers was dead. He was buried in the foreign cemetery in Qiongzhou not far from the grave of the pioneer, Jeremiassen. The tribute in the mission minutes describes him as

> quiet, conscientious, standing with unwavering fidelity for the right as it was given him to see it, devoted to the task of bringing the Good News of the Kingdom to the people of Hainan, a man of prayer and of deep spiritual discernment.[49]

He had served in Jiaji for eighteen years and was the spiritual father of the Miao people. Following the murder the American consul advised the evacuation of Ledong and Jiaji as the marauding band responsible for the attack was still at large.[50]

The success on the island was due in large measure to the long years of service of a number of the pioneers:

Rev. Frank P. Gilman, thirty-two years (1886–1918). Mr. Gilman pioneered in the founding of each of the four stations. In his lifetime he saw the work grow from practically no adherents to hundreds of members in central churches and small congregations. He was described by his colleagues as the "best known and the best beloved Hainan missionary."[51]

During the intermittent fighting for control of Haikou by rival war lords, Gilman and McCandliss sought to disarm soldiers who were hiding in the hospital. In the confusion, Gilman fell while climbing the compound rock wall. He died two weeks later from injuries sustained in the fall.[52]

Dr. and Mrs. Henry M. McCandliss, forty years (1885–1925). Dr. and Mrs. McCandliss were the first missionaries to serve a full forty years in Hainan. He was as well known for his preaching as for his medical practice. On his retirement, the *Shanghai North China Daily Herald* published this tribute:

> Dr. McCandliss began work when foreigners were objects of superstitious dread and fear, and when western medicine was considered a black art. Patiently, faithfully, skillfully, Dr. McCandliss has carried on his ministry of healing, and has seen the work grow from a tiny dispensary in Kiungchow to a hospital for 150 in-patients in Hoihow. The Chinese greatly regret his leaving. In the invitations they gave to attend the farewell gathering in Hoihow, which they planned in honor of the doctor, they mentioned 388,518 patients and 2,395 maternity cases as the number of those who have come under his care.[53]

Mrs. Olivia McCandliss was the daughter of Dr. John G. Kerr and grew up in Canton. She was known for her gracious hospitality, her work in the day schools for girls and boys, her fluency in the Hainanese dialect, her work for lepers and for country itineration when her children were grown.[54]

Mrs. Margaret Rae Melrose, forty-three years (1890–1933). Mrs. Melrose arrived in 1890 with her husband, the Rev. John C. Melrose. After his early death in 1897, Mrs. Melrose went home with her two young sons but later returned and for years was the senior member of the mission, loved and admired by Chinese throughout the island. The following resolution was adopted by the mission upon her retirement:

> With iron physique and will to match, she has moved mountains, crossed oceans, suffered the deepest sorrows and loneliness, counted discomforts as nothing — all to make known the Kingdom of God in Hainan. No one can estimate the villages that are changed nor the lives she has touched because she has left all and followed Him to the uttermost parts.[55]

In 1927 statistics for the Hainan Mission were as follows: 3 ordained ministers, 8 organized churches, 4,075 communicant members, 24 primary schools, 2 high schools, 3 hospitals (240 beds), 1,707 in-patients, and 22,127 out-patients.[56]

South of the Clouds

The Presbyterian Mission in Yunnan ("South of the Clouds") was located in what must certainly be one of the most isolated spots on the face of the earth. It would be a good candidate for the proverbial "ends of the earth" to which Jesus directed his disciples. The Rev. Ralph C. Wells, Chairman of the China Council and the only mission executive to ever visit the area, described the trip he made in 1932:

> Twenty-two days of steamer travel on five steamers ranging in size from a Pacific liner to a tiny steamer on the 6,400 foot elevation lake south of Yunanfu [Kunming], thirty-two days of mountainous journey by sedan chair (with plenty of walking and climbing included), six and a half days of mule back riding through wild mountain country, four days of railway journey, and three days of bus travel through tropical jungles, mountains and plains were involved in making the journey from Shanghai and return.[57]

How did the Presbyterians become involved in a mission so distant from the rest of the China work? It all began with the explorations of Siam (Thailand) missionaries among the Tai people along the Mekong and Red rivers. The travels of Rev. and Mrs. W. Clifton Dodd took them across the border into the Yunnan Province of China. Here they were warmly welcomed by northern Tai people who were non-Buddhist, for the most part illiterate, but otherwise closely related to the Tai people of Siam with whom the Dodds had been at work. Dodd estimated these tribal people numbered over 5 million and pled with the BFM for permission to open a mission station among them. The result was the founding in 1917 of a mission station at Jiulongjiang (Kiulungkiang) on the Mekong river just across the border in Yunnan. It was a journey of sixteen days, on foot, by mule or sedan chair from the nearest mission station in Siam. The Dodds were soon joined by Dr. and Mrs. Charles E. Park and

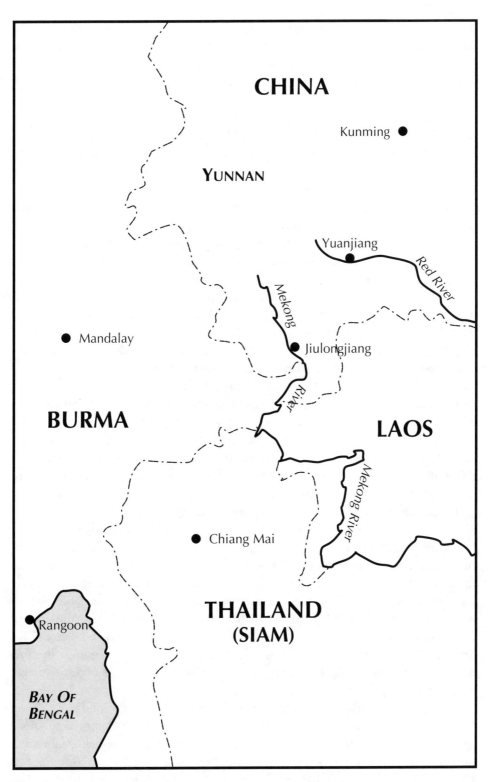

Yunnan Mission 1917–1932

Rev. and Mrs. Charles R. Callender. Tai Christians from Siam enthusiastically took part in this mission to their kinfolk to the north. In the early years they furnished all the ministers, evangelists and teachers for the enterprise. The work was most encouraging and resembled a mass movement: "Whole villages have turned to the Lord."[58]

Mr. Dodd died two years after the mission was founded at the age of sixty-two "worn out by the toil and strain of his strenuous life."[59] But his widow, Mrs. Isabel Dodd, continued indefatigably in the pioneer work. In 1921 she undertook an expeditionary tour further north and arrived with a party of Tai Christians from Siam at Yuanjiang (Yuankiang) on the Red River.

The mission minutes report that here two providential things happened that determined the future direction of the enterprise. First, the Chinese magistrate warned that a large company of bandits was on the road they were traveling. The foreign woman could not stay. Second, a Tai convert who had returned to his native home came to the inn where they were staying and asked that they stay and teach his kinsmen the new doctrine. The party decided that Mrs. Dodd would proceed on to Kunming, the provincial capital, a distance of seven travel days. Two elders from Siam would stay in the town and begin classes for those interested. Initially eight families came every evening to study. In three months over nine hundred villagers expressed their desire to become Christians.

The Chinese officials then became alarmed at the popularity of the new faith and prohibited its teaching until Mrs. Dodd returned from the capital with official documents stating that the new religion was lawful and was not to be molested. With a nucleus of Christians and the tacit consent of the authorities, "Red River Valley" (Yuanjiang) became the second station of the mission.[60] Early missionaries enjoyed the abundance of the valley's tropical fruit — pineapple, papaya and grapefruit. But the other side of the coin was the prevalence of malaria, swarms of termites and an abundance of rats.[61]

Because the two stations were in China proper, the BFM decided to transfer the work from Siam to China and establish the new Yunnan Mission. Everything had to start "from scratch." Logs had to be dragged several days' distance from the forest. They were sawed into planks for residences, schools, chapels and hospitals. Tiles for roofs were constructed on the site. Pipes and plumbing were imported from French Indo-China. Wells had to be dug. Yunnan had its own currency into which Chinese "Mex" dollars had to be converted. Tai literature came from the Bible Society in Siam. Schools were begun at the primary school level. Public health began with simple instructions about hygiene, mosquitoes and the taking of pills.

Families who became Christian were forced to move out of their village. Many congregated at what was called the "Christian village" near the missionary compound. Initially, this was an advantage as it helped provide for Christian nurture and fellowship. Later a breakthrough was achieved when a number of Christian families at the village of Ban Met resisted attempts to drive them out and were allowed to stay.

Two practices of the local culture were problematic. In "bride purchases," wives were chattel and could be bought and sold; in funeral feasting for the dead, the more animals that were killed the more the departed would have for the future state. But the practice wasted the resources of the village and increased the debt of the bereaved family. As progress was made in eliminating such practices, living conditions improved not only for the Christian community but for the general public.

In 1926 bandits in the area came to the missionaries with a most strange request:

> They would put themselves under Christian discipline, using an old temple for a Chapel and asked for three teachers to come and assist them.... We talked the proposition over frankly with our magistrate who expressed himself heartily in sympathy with their accepting Christianity and with our going to teach them, admitting that as converts they would be better citizens.[62]

As evangelists and teachers from Siam completed their terms of service and returned to their homeland, more reliance was placed on local leadership. In 1926 the first elders were elected in the Red River Valley. The process had to proceed with great care as the people had never elected anybody to anything. After several weeks of explanation a congregational meeting was held at which four men were chosen unanimously. The newly elected session then conducted the examination for new members which was much more rigorous than that given by the missionaries. Fifty applicants were baptized and two hundred received communion.[63]

During the disturbances that threatened many parts of the republic in 1926–1927, all missionaries in Yunnan were advised to leave the province by the American consul. In Jiulongjiang the magistrate pleaded with them not to leave and guaranteed an escort to the Siam border should the need arise. The missionaries stayed and were never in danger. In the Red River station, all seemed peaceful until April 1927 when an urgent message was received from the American Legation in Peking warning of trouble. "Reluctantly and regretfully we bade these converts of five years goodbye, asking them to follow their appointed leaders."[64] It was two years before the missionaries could return.

When they did return they noted great strides had been taken in self-government and self-support. The report read:

> A self-governing nationalist church is making some real strides.... Every matter of importance to the Kingdom's work is first considered and passed upon by the committees... and they are shouldering responsibilities in a commendable way. We, the missionaries are co-workers with them in Christ Jesus, and we rejoice in the privilege.[65]

During the next several years progress was marked by the organization of a Women's Bible School, the establishment of a colony for leprosy patients and the dedication of the new hospital. The three organized churches had a total of twenty-six ordained elders who in most cases conducted the services and administered the business of the congregations.

Christian villages spread up and down the Red River and the extent of the progress is seen in this 1929 report:

> The total number received into the churches since the inception of the work under Mrs. Dodd and the Tai evangelists in 1921, exclusive of death and some who have returned to demons, is 452.... Present membership of the three churches is 411 of which 84 were received this year.[66]

As more Chinese people moved into the area, an effort was made to reach these Mandarin-speaking folk. Day schools were started in Chinese. In 1929 the Red River Church called the Rev. Edward S. Kao, a young Chinese minister from Shandong, to be its pastor. In 1932 Rev. and Mrs. Arthur Romig, fresh from the Peking language school, arrived to strengthen the Chinese work.[67]

In 1932 an event that "overshadowed everything else" was a new mass movement among the Ka Do tribe, who lived in the high mountains west of the Red River. An incredible number of eight hundred households took the first step toward church membership by destroying their spirit shrines and appealed to the mission for help.[68] Missionaries, elders, lay evangelists, school teachers and Christian students were sent to the mountains to "strike while the iron was hot." They went out two by two with an experienced evangelist being paired with a novice, and the experience of one such team is recounted in the station report:

> They cleansed 553 houses of demons by holding Christian services in the houses and tearing down their spirit shrines. Sixty villages were reached by these two, embracing 2,838 persons, including children. The lad said they were at it from morning to night. They got weary but God sustained them; foot sore but God gave them power of endurance. Many times they thought they could go no longer, but they could not resist the lure of the call of these hungry people. So they would keep on until utterly exhausted, and darkness came upon them.[69]

The mass movement of the Ka Do people brought new opportunities but also an increased work load for the Yunnan mission. They were spread too thin. In 1933 five missionary couples and fourteen children made up the mission. The Mekong Valley station (Jiulongjiang) was seventeen days by foot or sedan chair from the Red River Valley station (Yuanjiang), which was another seven days travel by foot to the provincial capital.

The support of these pioneers at the ends of the earth simply could not be sustained over the long distances. The worldwide depression ruled out the appointment of any new missionaries. After much soul-searching, the Yunnan Mission proposed a plan for transferring the work at Yuanjiang to the German Vandsburger Lutheran Mission. Vandsburger was a new missionary society that was concentrating its work in Yunnan. The mission to the Tai and Ka Do people could be strengthened by the Lutherans in ways the Presbyterians could not do. Jiulongjiang, so near the Siam border, would revert to the Siam Mission.

In 1932 Rev. Ralph Wells made the long trek to Yunnan to discuss the transfer. It was a bitter decision to give up a task that had been started and sustained with so much sacrificial effort. But Christian comity and the spiritual welfare of the people made the transfer the only right course of action.[70]

But before the transfer could take place one more traumatic episode took place. Dr. Charles Park, one of the original members of the Tai mission team, heard rumors of a plague in the mountains some three days journey from Yuanjiang and set out to determine the truth behind the reports and see if he could help. On the way he was thrown from the mule he was riding and struck his head. He returned to the station with a raging headache and died a few days later. His patient Helen Romig was pregnant, had a high fever and needed medical attention. The nearest medical facility was in Kunming. Somehow, Art Romig managed the seven-day trek over the mountain trails with Helen. Soon after they arrived in Kunming, a healthy little girl, Elizabeth Ann, was born at the London Missionary Society hospital.[71]

The Tai Christians had come to love the Presbyterian missionaries and their ways of working and begged them not to leave. But the transfer was accomplished in true Presbyterian fashion — "decently and in order." The last report of the Yunnan Mission closes with these words:

> The Presbyterian Church can look back on twelve years of work in the Red River valley. Many people have had a share in the development of this work, for as each one came and lived there he left his print in the lives of these people. Those who have been here through the entire history of the place as a mission station, can see the changes and results among the people most clearly. There were no Christians when the work began; but the Tai opened their homes to the missionary and to the Siamese workers. First through the medium of healing the bodies, and then through the healing of the soul the church has grown to five hundred baptized Christians. Numerically the Presbyterians need not be ashamed. We cannot judge the full influence of the church in this valley nor dare we attempt to measure it. We only know that light has been brought to many dark lives.[72]

Theological Crosscurrents

The history of Presbyterians in China had been happily free from theological controversy for the better part of eighty years. This changed in the 1920s. The "fundamentalist-modernist" controversy was raging back home and inevitably this had its effect on the missionary effort abroad.

The occasion that launched the controversy in China was a series of lectures on the dangers of "modernism" given by Dr. W. H. Griffith Thomas of Philadel-

phia at the Kuling Missionary Conference during the summer of 1920.[73] Later
he wrote an article for the *Princeton Theological Review* entitled "Liberalism
in China" in which he charged Dr. J. Leighton Stuart, newly elected president
of Yenching University, with having "unsound views."[74] Soon after the Thomas
lectures some of the missionaries who championed the fundamentalist cause
organized under the name of "The Bible Union." The Union's statement of
faith expressed unqualified adherence to the deity of Christ, the virgin birth,
atonement, personality of the Holy Spirit, the miracles of the Old and New Testaments and the Bible as the inspired Word of God. By 1921 the Union had
enrolled seventeen hundred members.

The Union's statement of faith was not new. The majority of Protestant missionaries in China were evangelical and had always adhered to such beliefs.
What was new was the formation of an organization that undertook to root
out those suspected of "modernistic" leanings and who did not agree with the
Bible Union's interpretation. The controversy could not have come at a worse
time, as Latourette's incisive comment indicates:

> The result was discord: Protestants were at odds with each other during
> the years when they were facing the most difficult situation which had yet
> confronted them in China.[75]

Fuel for the conflagration was added by agitators back home as both mission boards came under attack.[76] Central Mississippi Presbytery overtured the
PCUS General Assembly to investigate the theology taught in union institutions
abroad.[77] Nanjing Theological Seminary was the intended target.

Nanjing Theological Seminary

Cooperation between the PCUSA and PCUS missions at the Nanjing Seminary
had gone well until a new constitution was proposed in 1912 that broadened
the basis for union to include Methodists and Disciples. The North Jiangsu Mission, which had been suspicious of the seminary all along, withdrew its support
by a vote of eleven to seven. The reason given was the dilution of Presbyterian standards by the inclusion of non-Presbyterian bodies. Oddly enough,
two years later with little debate the mission voted to rescind its previous action and reestablished its support of the seminary. But it would continue to
view the school with a jaundiced eye and the issue again surfaced when the
fundamentalist-modernist controversy broke.

For five years (1921–1925) the theology of the Nanjing Theological Seminary was debated by the board of the Seminary, the two SPM missions, the
PCUS Executive Committee and the PCUS General Assembly.[78] Criticism of
the seminary revolved around the following issues: "liberal" textbooks, "destructive" views of Old Testament criticism taught by one professor, laxity in
enforcing the seminary requirement that faculty be in accord with the seminary's conservative statement of faith and the use of foreign and Chinese faculty

who lacked pastoral experience in the Chinese church. The problem was compounded by the position of the United Christian Missionary Society (Disciples) against subscribing to any creed except that of the New Testament.

The PCUS Executive Committee sought to keep the loyalty and support of the church at home and at the same time to keep peace between its two China missions, which were at odds over the matter.[79] In the end, North Jiangsu voted to withdraw from the seminary while Mid China voted to continue its support. Opinions from leaders of the Chinese church — the body most affected by the outcome — are hard to come by. The debate was between American missionaries on issues that had originated in North America.

In spite of the controversy the seminary continued to grow and prosper. In 1924 the enrollment numbered 116 students. The next year the alumni were given representation on the Board of Managers. The report for 1925–1926 stated that "the faculty is harmonious and the student body increasing."[80]

One factor that lay behind the divergent action of the two missions was probably nontheological:

> North Jiangsu was poor and culturally backward. Students sent south of the River to Nanking found an area higher in standard of living, salaries paid, and culture. It was not easy for them to return to their homes "up country" and work happily. North Jiangsu came to feel that it was better for them to have schools in their own cultural and economic area, where their students might receive their training.[81]

Furthermore, partnership in a new conservative theological school in Shandong was beckoning.

The North China Theological Seminary

In 1905 the PCUSA Shandong Mission began the training of its ministerial candidates at the Gotch-Robinson Theological College of the newly created Shandong Christian University located at Tsingchow on property provided by the English Baptist mission. Rev. J. Percy Bruce of the English Baptists was president. Rev. Watson B. Hayes, the distinguished China scholar of the Presbyterian mission, was one of the leading professors.

In 1919, the Shandong Mission took the following action expressing dissatisfaction with the union seminary:

> While thoroughly approving of the principle of union in higher educational work...we wish to reiterate the emphatic disapproval, expressed at various times by our representatives, of the operation of the union which especially in the theological department has brought about the dissatisfaction of the mission and is causing the alienation of the Chinese church.[82]

There appeared to have been three areas of dissatisfaction: (1) the theological content of the teaching, (2) the need for greater cooperation with the Chinese church and (3) disagreement over control of the School of Theology, which was the crux of the matter. The British Baptists believed that the theology department should be an integral part of the university while the Shandong Mission believed its primary relationship should be to the Christian church. The Shandong Mission stated that unless some reorganization took place they would "take steps looking toward the immediate withdrawal of its students and faculty members" and would explore with the Southern Presbyterians the possibility of establishing a Presbyterian seminary elsewhere.[83]

In the fall of 1919 the seven Presbyterian students withdrew from the seminary and appealed to the Shandong Mission to continue their theological education under Presbyterian auspices. At a called meeting of the Executive Committee the Mission took the following action in regard to the crisis:

> While regretting exceedingly the action of the Presbyterian students in leaving the University School of Theology against the repeated advice and earnest solicitations of the teachers and officers of the University, and the members of the Mission, we nevertheless feel that we cannot escape a certain amount of responsibility for their future.[84]

In view of the earlier criticism of the seminary by the mission, one wonders how much the students were acting on their own. Whatever the case, the mission authorized Dr. Hayes to continue their education at the Weixian Bible School on a temporary basis.

The presbyteries of Shandong then took matters into their own hands and began to raise funds for the establishment of their own seminary. A mission committee conferred with them and the university officials to see if any compromise could be worked out. This apparently failed. In 1920 the mission made the decision to cooperate with the presbyteries in the establishment of a "conservative Theological Seminary mainly under Chinese control" and to invite the Southern Presbyterians to take part in the union. Tengxian, where the two missions were already cooperating, was the logical location for the new school.[85]

In 1921 the seminary moved to the new location. In 1922 the North Jiangsu Mission voted to cooperate and assigned the Rev. B. C. Patterson and Rev. George P. Stevens to teach.[86]

From the beginning the Synod of Shandong assumed the major responsibility for the new school, which was named the North China Theological Seminary. The five Shandong presbyteries raised an initial $11,000 for buildings. All members of the board and faculty, including missionaries, were appointed by the Synod.[87]

In 1923 the North China Women's Theological Seminary was established under a separate board of directors, which included several women. Women students took courses at the men's seminary and the surprised faculty reported that the women "could take the same work as the men and do as well as the average man."[88]

The seminary experienced rapid growth. In 1926 enrollment reached 130 students from nine provinces with 50 more in the affiliated women's seminary. Reasons given by a church leader for the school's popularity: Its teaching was conservative, it was under Chinese church control and most of the faculty were Chinese.[89] Other reasons could be cited: lower fees, lower academic standards and a schedule that permitted students to spend five months a year in church employment. The PCUSA China Council noted that the seminary was a step forward "in the development of initiative and interest in the Chinese Church not reached in any other of the institutions with which our Mission is related."[90]

The Church of Christ in China

The crowning event of these years was the establishment of a united national Protestant church. The first step was taken in 1906 with the establishment of the Synod of the Five Provinces — an autonomous Chinese church with relationships to PCUSA and PCUS missions, which was described in Chapter 9. This led to the formation of the Council of Presbyterian Churches, which includes representatives from churches related to the following missions:

- Presbyterian Church, USA

- Presbyterian Church, US

- Reformed Church in America

- Church of Scotland

- United Free Church of Scotland

- Presbyterian Church in Canada

- Presbyterian Church in Ireland

- Presbyterian Church of England

The "Declaration and Resolution of Union of the Presbyterian Church of Christ in China" was adopted, which noted the substantial doctrinal agreement of the eight denominations but affirmed that

> the Presbyterian Church of China, being autonomous, will have the prerogatives of formulating its own standards. But these will, we believe, in the Providence of God, and under the teaching of His Spirit, be in essential harmony with the creeds of the parent churches.[91]

The agreement stated that the goal was not a Presbyterian union in any exclusive sense, but the first step toward forming a united church. Until such time as a General Assembly could be established the Council would act as the coordinating body for the new church that was coming into being.

The third meeting of the Council convened in Jinan in 1914 with delegates representing sixty thousand communicant members in Manchuria, Hebei, Shandong, Henan, Anhui, Jiangsu, Zhejiang, Fujian and Guangdong. The Chinese delegates were in favor of establishing a General Assembly as soon as possible. The question was presented to the presbyteries for vote with a report of the outcome to be made at the next meeting in 1915.

At the fourth meeting of the council, held in Shanghai, the overwhelming number of presbyteries reported in favor of the establishment of a General Assembly and a committee was appointed to work on a proposed constitution.

The General Assembly of the new church met in Shanghai in April 1922 representing six synods, 26 presbyteries and 77,000 communicant members. The assembly elected as its first presiding officer the Rev. P. Frank Price of the Southern Presbyterian Mission.[92] An extensive debate was held on the name for the new church. The Chinese delegates were strongly opposed to including any denominational name and also opposed including the word "united" on the "grounds that the new church was to be in its own right a Chinese church and not just a union of Western denominations."[93] The name chosen was "The Church of Christ in China" (Chung Hua Chi Tu Chiao Hui; CCC). An invitation was extended to other church bodies to join in this union.

As the momentum for church union continued to build, two of the oldest and most prestigious mission boards — the London Missionary Society and the American Board of Commissioners — expressed the desire to enter the negotiations. Later the English Baptists, the Disciples, the Swedish Missionary Society, the United Brethren, the American Friends Mission, some indigenous Chinese churches and some churches affiliated with the China Inland Mission expressed interest in joining.

But undertaking a wider union so soon after the Presbyterian merger was risky business. The broader the union became, the more difficult it would be to include churches with different views on theology and polity. The Rev. Asher R. Kepler, with a long commitment to cooperative enterprises, was asked to serve as organizing secretary to explore the possibility of a wider union. For the next five years Kepler traveled all over China visiting church leaders and mission agencies in the interest of the union. It was a courageous venture at a time of theological discord, political disturbance and anti-Christian feelings.

Kepler's work was consummated with the convening of the First Assembly of the Church of Christ in China held in Shanghai in October 1927. Eighty-eight commissioners, sixty-six of whom were Chinese, were present representing eleven synods and forty-six district associations with 120,000 communicant members. They represented approximately one-third of the Protestant Christians of China bringing together a variety of communions: Presbyterian, Reformed, Baptist, Congregational and independents. At the time it was considered the largest and most diverse church union that had taken place in mission lands. Dr. C. Y. Cheng, pastor of an independent church in Peking associated with the London Missionary Society, was elected moderator. Cheng had suffered during the Boxer Uprising and was one of the three Chinese delegates to attend the Edinburgh World Mission Conference of 1910. Kepler was elected General Secretary and when Cheng was elected to that position, served as his Associate.[94] For fifteen years they worked together harmoniously. Kepler's work for the CCC involved travel throughout China and abroad, fund raising and the delicate art of diplomacy.

Church polity in the CCC followed the historic Presbyterian form. Local congregations were governed by either elders or deacons. District associations corresponded to presbyteries. Synods, based on geographic areas covering one or more provinces, formed the basic structure of the CCC. Each synod had the freedom to organize itself — in many cases following the denominational polity of the dominant church in that area. The assembly met every three or four years.

> In effect the Church of Christ in China lived a double life. On the one hand it was a national church representing a variety of denominational traditions and carrying on programs in the name of the total church. On the other hand it was a group of regional churches in loose association with a central staff and not very close relations with each other.[95]

Matters such as infant or believers baptism, sprinkling or immersion and ministerial ordinations were left to each synod. The constitution included a brief statement of faith, which affirmed: (1) faith in Jesus Christ as Redeemer and Lord, (2) the Holy Scriptures of the Old and New Testaments as the divinely inspired word of God and the supreme authority in matters of faith and duty and (3) the Apostles' Creed.[96] A committee was appointed to work on a fuller statement of faith, but this was never completed due to the turbulent nature of the times.

All PCUSA- and PCUS-related presbyteries joined the union except for five conservative presbyteries related to the North Jiangsu and Shandong missions. They gave these reasons for not joining: too many diverse doctrinal elements, an insufficient creed, and a concern that the union was imposed from the top down.[97]

The next year in the city of Tengxian a continuing Presbyterian denomination was organized with the support of the North China Seminary. The union included the five presbyteries from Jiangsu and Shandong plus some congregations of the Canadian Presbyterian Mission and the Christian Reformed Mission. This assembly represented 80 congregations and 88 ministers (62 Chinese and 26 missionaries) with a constituency of 17,766 church members.[98] Eventually, the continuing Presbyterian church was received into the CCC as the Kianghuai Synod and was officially welcomed at the Fifth General Assembly in 1948.[99]

Some major communions chose to remain separate: the Episcopal Church, most Methodists, Southern Baptists, Lutherans and most churches related to the China Inland Mission.[100]

While it [the CCC] never achieved the hope of bringing together the bulk of Protestant Christianity in China, the Church of Christ in China represented a substantial proportion of the whole. It sought to establish an identity as an indigenous Chinese church and with the exception of distinctively Chinese sects . . . came nearer to that goal than any other church in China.[101]

The National Christian Council

Another ecumenical venture in which the Presbyterians played a leading role was the National Christian Council. The concept of regional councils was proposed at the great Edinburgh Missionary Conference of 1910. John R. Mott visited China in 1913 to promote this ecumenical venture, the result of which was the formation of the China Continuation Committee. The Committee called two full time secretaries, the first of which was Dr. C. Y. Cheng, who later became the General Secretary for the Church of Christ in China. As Cheng's missionary counterpart, the committee called Rev. Edwin C. Lobenstine of the Kiangan Mission.

The Continuation Committee's assignment was to lay the groundwork for the 1922 National Christian Conference. A major part of this preparation was the publication of a comprehensive survey of the Protestant missionary endeavor under the unfortunate English title *The Christian Occupation of China*.[102] The title in Chinese was less offensive: *China for Christ*.

The 1922 conference was a milestone in the history of the ecumenical movement in China. It was a continuation of the series of missionary conferences held in 1890 and in 1907 but in three respects differed sharply from the earlier meetings.

1. While the earlier conferences were primarily planned by missionaries for the missionary community, the leadership of the 1922 conference was Chinese as was the majority of the delegates. It was described as "the first really representative gathering of Chinese Christians."[103]

2. The conference moved decisively toward a fuller expression of unity than the mere cooperation of missionary societies. Note this taunting quip by a Chinese participant: "We have no objection to the missionaries worshipping their ancestors [Luther, Calvin, Wesley]. But they are not *our* ancestors."[104]

3. The conference authorized the formation of a continuing body to be known as the National Christian Council of China (NCCC), which held its first meeting in Shanghai 10–16 May 1923. Of the sixty-four delegates, thirty-eight were Chinese. The major addresses were given by Chinese leaders. Cheng and Lobenstine were continued as general secretaries. Actions of the Council were only advisory, and doctrine and polity lay beyond its purview. Nevertheless, the Council did engage in the study of many issues facing the church and in making recommendations to its constituent bodies.

From the beginning the Council had rough going. For some it was too radical; for others, far too conservative. The Southern Baptists, the Lutherans and the SPM North Jiangsu Mission never joined. In its fourth year, the China Inland Mission and the Christian Missionary Alliance withdrew. To continue at all during these years of theological controversy and political turmoil was a remarkable achievement.

The survey produced in 1922 provides an interesting update of the Protestant Christian movement:[105]

Membership: Communicant members numbered 366,500. This was a fourfold increase in twenty years, which far exceeded the population growth. The Protestant constituency (catechumens, inquirers, children) would be two or three times this number.[106]

Missionary societies. Protestant missionary societies numbered 130. There were 6,250 missionaries of whom 30 percent were single women. Missionaries resided in 675 cities of the nation.[107]

Chinese workers. For every missionary there were approximately four Chinese workers. One-fourth of the Chinese salaried workers were women. Foreign ordained men (1,310) still outnumbered Chinese ordained workers (1,065).[108]

Schools. Mission schools numbered 7,046 with 212,819 students. There were 14 Christian colleges with 2,017 students, of which only 150 or 7.5 percent were women.[109]

Hospitals. Protestant hospitals numbered 326 with 16,737 beds. The figures for total in-patients treated that year was given as 144,477. Almost the entire nursing profession was Christian.[110]

Influence of Christianity on the national life. The following contributions were listed: literacy, one day of rest in seven (sabbath), uplift of womanhood, the monogamous ideal, reform of public vices (opium, gambling, footbinding, prostitution), religious liberty, intellectual awakening.[111]

Weaknesses of the Chinese church. The following shortcomings were acknowledged: small number of voluntary (nonpaid) workers, dependence on foreign funds and leadership, disunity and failure to reach the intellectual classes.[112]

Weaknesses of the missions. These were listed: race prejudice, sectarianism, failure to adapt to a Chinese culture, unwise use of money, domineering attitude, disunity.[113]

Missionary Culture

Our understanding of missionary life has been helped considerably by the insights gained from cross-cultural studies in recent years. Such studies refer to expatriates who live abroad for long lengths of time as "Third Culture People" (TCP). Such expatriates are no longer at home in the American culture from which they came. But neither are they assimilated into the culture of the people among whom they live. They create for themselves a "third culture" that borrows elements both from the home culture and the host culture in which they now live.[114]

Thus missionaries, as TCP people, developed a third or missionary culture over the years they lived in China. Some aspects of this culture were those of nineteenth-century America — language, ethical values, democratic institutions, holidays, furniture, dress. But other aspects of the missionary culture were taken from the Chinese environment — words and phrases, servants, the role of the "amah" (or nurse), courtesy, Chinese delicacies, family values, love of antiquities. Some elements were a blending of both. Children were bilingual. Food was purchased on the Chinese market but prepared as Western dishes. The missionary compound had elements that were both Chinese and Western. Some aspects of their culture were neither "American" nor "Chinese" but distinctively "missionary." In *Minor Heresies* John Espey gives a delightful description of the ambiguities of a missionary child growing up in the "missionary culture" of the South Gate compound in Shanghai.[115] For example, one of the customs at South Gate and other missionary communities was that adult missionaries were given the title of "courtesy aunts and uncles." But the Chinese background also played a part. "Western directness" was augmented by "Chinese practicality." The Chinese culture "worked a gentle miracle" on the spiritual descendants of John Calvin: "It brought gaiety to Presbyterians."[116]

One could wish that the missionaries had been completely assimilated into the Chinese culture but this was seldom possible. Single women missionaries did it the best. But for most, the "third" or "missionary culture" provided an environment in which East and West could meet and productive activity could be carried out. For missionaries in inland stations the missionary culture within the compound walls provided a degree of normalcy where family life and work could go on in the midst of the violence and turmoil that were tearing China apart.

By the 1920s a certain pattern of life and work that could be considered somewhat normal had developed among the Protestant missions. Annual meetings, attended by all voting members of the mission, provided the time for mission business to be transacted. Here personnel assignments for the coming year would be made, budgets adopted, language exams given to new members and requests transmitted to the home board. Mission meetings, often held in one of the major cities, provided time for shopping and an opportunity to lay in supplies for the coming year. Ecumenical retreat centers were developed in the mountains (Kuling, Mokanshan) or the beach (Qingdao, Peitaiho). Here families and children, isolated for most of the year, could spend time during the hot, humid summer months. It was a time for spiritual renewal, Bible conferences and socializing with members of other missions. Missionary children were taught during their early years by their mothers — many using the lesson plans of the Calvert School of Baltimore, Maryland. One event, dreaded by the mothers but looked forward to by the young people concerned, was the ritual of leaving home for one of the boarding schools (Kuling, North

China, or Shanghai American School or the Pyongyang Foreign School in Korea).

It has been customary to view the missionary life as one of sacrifice. And undoubtedly this it was. There were physical danger, health hazards, family separation, and the constant pressures of living and working in a cross-cultural environment. But it would be a mistake to think of the missionary vocation solely in these terms. Missionary salaries during this period were comparable to those of religious workers at home. The Board provided travel, housing, all medical and dental expenses, furniture and outfit allowances. There was considerable job security and the pension benefits after forty years of service were far better than for home missionaries. From research on the Hainan Mission, Kathleen Lodwick concludes:

> If one was seeking a very secure job situation with benefits few other positions offered, plus the opportunity to travel to foreign countries, becoming a foreign missionary was an excellent career choice.[117]

It would also be a mistake to set the missionary on a pedestal as a super-pious saint. Note Lodwick's comment:

> If the traditional view of missionaries has been that they were "holier than thou" individuals, research suggests that this simply was not the case, at least as far as the Presbyterian Church was concerned, and it was not true of the Hainan Mission in particular.[118]

Missionaries wrote home exhaustively about their work activities but seldom of their religious experiences. Perhaps this was so basic it was taken for granted. Or perhaps their Calvinist tradition made the "gushy" type of religious expression difficult. But Sabbath observance was strict. Playing cards was taboo. The game of Rook, known as "missionary bridge," took its place. One missionary confessed, "We meet as a station to play Rook once a week but can't find time for station prayers."[119]

Life within the compound varied greatly. On the whole it became a mutually supportive fellowship that was closer than family or kin. But when it went sour, it could be very bad indeed. In an example of missionary humor of the times, the story is told of the new appointee going to China thinking

> he would have a wonderful and loving time with his fellow missionaries, that he would be able to get along agreeably with the Chinese Christians, but that he would have a very difficult time with the "heathen" Chinese.... He later confessed that he had a wonderful time with the non-Christians; that he was able in a way to have fellowship with the native Christians; but that he had a terribly difficult time living and working with the other missionaries![120]

Missionary life revolved about two foci: "The Home" and "The Work." The missionary home was a combination residence, nursery, school, chapel, office and guest house. Elisabeth Luce Moore, daughter of Henry Winters and Elizabeth Root Luce, has described in a vivid fashion her early life on the Presbyterian Weixian compound which was in some ways unique yet was characteristic of many other missionary families.[121]

There was *the compound wall:*

> The college compound was a couple of miles out from Weihsien which was a walled city — and so was our compound a walled city....On top was cement with sharp pieces of glass imbedded in it to keep robbers from coming over....I remember as a child [hearing] the wonderful, comforting sound of the watchman going around at night beating his gourd. It was a hollow "click, click, click" sound.

Celebrations both Chinese and American:

> I do have memories of the 1911 Revolution...the "Double Ten..." celebration which was way outside the compound on a great big open field with bands and flags and all kinds of excitement....Father was thrilled and he kept telling us, "This is the Fourth of July for China."...We had huge Fourth of July celebrations on our compound. When Americans are abroad they are far more patriotic than when they're at home.

The missionary cemetery:

> We had a charming little missionary cemetery in the compound and the cedar trees there had tiny little cones which we were allowed to collect from the ground but could not pick off the trees. There was another person who loved to walk in the cemetery, perhaps to visit his first wife's grave, but when I saw him coming I always went the other way. He was a great tall man in a long black coat, leaning forward with his hands behind his back, with a long white beard. Quite a terrifying figure to a little girl, and I had identified him with Yahweh, so I stayed clear of him. And this was Calvin Mateer, a great force among the China missionaries.

Dinner conversations:

> We were so fortunate to be in a community of people who were interested in ideas. Father was a great believer that there should be interesting conversation at the meal table. And we often put up a visiting guest, because there were no hotels and the visitor added to the lively discussion.

Servants and afternoon tea:

> Father's salary was only $100 a month, but we had six servants. Mother organized all the labor for the house and it was probably the best kept house on the whole campus. Marketing had to be done every day. Laundry was done by hand, and this was a full-time job for one man, especially since we had great damask tablecloths at breakfast, lunch and dinner, to

say nothing of tea. And Mother served a delicious tea. It just happened that quite a few of the faculty people came to see Father at tea time.

Cooking:

Our cook made the best ice cream on the compound. He must have cooked wonderful Chinese dishes, but we almost never had Chinese food. Instead we had an elaborate Victorian menu, exactly what Mother's family had served in Utica, New York.... We had our own vegetable garden, and a very skillful gardener, and stored the vegetables in a big underground cellar in the late summer.

Home schooling and Sunday worship:

Mother was really the one who taught us reading, writing, and arithmetic. We were brought up on Shakespeare, the Bible and Dickens.... Reading was a major pastime because there was no radio or television then, not even electricity. Mother played the piano and Father the violin.... There would be an entertainment gathering at someone's house about once every month. Every Sunday the foreign community had their own church service at four o'clock in the afternoon in somebody's parlor, a different house each week. We would have prayers, lots of hymns, and a sermon. It was taken very seriously and everyone attended.

Outside the walls, the real China:

One day — without my parents' knowledge — I went to a hanging in a nearby village. There was terrific excitement and such a crowd that although I was perched on top of old Chang's shoulders, I didn't see a thing. Our great interest, however, was over the local funeral processions which Mother would sometimes let us go out to see. There was plenty of noise, banging of gongs and drums, and I was fascinated by the elaborate bamboo and paper models of whole houses and temples with animals and servants and concubines.

Family prayers:

We all went downstairs to the sitting room for prayers. Mother played the hymns on the piano. Then we had a little Bible reading. Then we would kneel down with our heads on the chairs. I liked the one with the cane bottom. I was always putting my little finger in the holes.[122]

Superiority Complex?

I think we did have a feeling of scorn for the squalor and filth of the Chinese markets and towns, and the terrible problems with disease.... But the question of superiority was very different on the intellectual level. Father revered his Chinese associates in their scholarly endeavors. He knew that they knew a lot more than he did, and in the process he became fascinated by the great heritage of Chinese culture that these men had inherited.

Something of value:

> We never felt threatened or unwelcome in China. We had a real sense
> that the Americans were bringing something that the Chinese desperately
> need....Father was so enthusiastic that you really felt that China was his
> favorite world...He was a passionate Christian and wanted to educate
> young Chinese in a Christian life of service. The terrible living conditions
> didn't bother him so much as the fact that all these thousands of people
> had never heard of Jesus Christ.

The other focus for missionary life was "The Work." This could be itineration among the villages, the girls' school or the hospital. But it was much
more than the mission or church assignment. Often it was the challenge of
some need discovered after arrival in China. "The Work" was the niche in
which the missionary found fulfillment for time and talents. It was the cause
for which the missionary returned to China again and again after furlough. It
was the special piece of the action with which one could identify, which one
could call one's own and which claimed one's loyalties. It was the cause for
which one solicited special funds, or used one's tithe account, or fought over
at mission meetings when budgets were adopted. It was John G. Kerr's refuge
for the insane, Annetta Mills's school for the deaf, Charlotte Brown's class of
old country women, Frank Chalfant's oracle bones, Hunter Corbett's science
museum, Henry Woods's conservative Bible encyclopedia or Asher Raymond
Kepler's vision of a united Christian church. For others it was simply "the call
of Christ."

This strong sense of missionary calling provided the fuel that drove the missionary enterprise. But it was not without its problems. Once a project became
one's own it was difficult to give up. Sometimes the missionary became indispensable. This could hinder the transition to national leadership. The work
ethic made it difficult not to take oneself or one's calling too seriously. But without its force and drive the endeavor could not have been sustained for the long
haul. Here were exemplified both the strengths and weaknesses of the Calvinist
tradition.

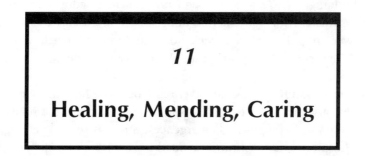

11

Healing, Mending, Caring

Before proceeding to the next period in this history, it would be well to pause and take a closer look at the institutional work that the Presbyterian missions had brought into being and that had a great impact not only on the church but on Chinese society. In 1926 the institutions were at their peak. In this chapter we will look at the medical related institutions and in the next the schools and colleges.[1]

The first professional survey of modern medical practice in China was made in 1914 by the China Medical Commission of the Rockefeller Foundation. Government hospitals were so few in number that the Commission report "resolves itself almost completely into a consideration of the mission hospitals."[2] Mission hospitals in all of China numbered 244. They were staffed by 446 physicians (117 women) and 140 nurses.[3] Most of the above were missionaries as medical education for Chinese was just beginning. As to the proficiency of missionary health workers, the Commission commented:

> On the whole the standard both of medical and of general efficiency is high, and not a few would have made their mark professionally anywhere in the world. The day of the half-trained medical missionary is rapidly drawing to a close.[4]

By the year 1926 great strides had been made in mission medical institutions. American Presbyterians were engaged in the administration and support of 49 hospitals and 50 dispensaries throughout the republic. These institutions were served by 78 missionary physicians and 34 registered nurses. Of the physicians, 16 were women — a high percentage for that day. If one adds to this number doctors' wives and others engaged in some form of medical service, the total number of medical missionaries would come to about 165 or 20 percent of the total missionary force. Chinese doctors numbered about the same as the missionaries while there were two or three times as many Chinese trained nurses. During the year, 640,000 patient visits were recorded.[5]

The years between 1910 and 1926 saw a surge in hospital construction. A PCUSA Mission Architects Bureau in Shanghai provided technical assistance. The exchange rate was favorable and a grant of $10,000 would provide an

221

adequate building. In 1920 the Weixian hospital received a grant of $26,000, which was sufficient for constructing and equipping an entire hospital plant.[6] Hospitals were popular projects back home as "medical needs were tangible, vivid, and concrete."[7] Many hospitals were given as memorials and named accordingly.

Most of the hospitals were small, averaging between fifty and sixty beds. The seventy-eight missionary doctors were spread thin to cover the forty-nine hospitals. Considering furloughs and emergences, this was scarcely enough for one doctor per hospital. Each institution tended to revolve about the personality of the missionary doctor, who often had sole responsibility for its administration.

Ten of the hospitals were exclusively for women. In the early days this was an unavoidable duplication as Chinese women simply would not come to a hospital where men were treated. Another more subtle reason for separate institutions was the opportunity this gave missionary women physicians to exercise their leadership potential. Also, hospitals for women were popular projects back home. However, the cost of duplicating facilities meant that over the years the trend was for mergers. In 1926 all hospitals had missionary superintendents except for the small Tooker Memorial Hospital of Suzhou, which was operated "very successfully" by Chinese women physicians.[8] All hospitals were under mission control. This would change in the next decade.

Missionary Medicine

Sophie Montgomery Crane, in her history of Southern Presbyterian medical missions, to which the author is heavily indebted, has described the characteristic stages of missionary medicine, which were virtually the same for both missions.[9]

Stage One might be called "pillbox medicine." In the beginning untrained missionaries dispensed medicines and simple remedies in the course of their evangelistic ministry. For example, Miss Helen Kirkland of Hangzhou started out each morning

> with a basket on her arm which contained her Chinese Bible and hymn-book, [going] from home to home of the Chinese whether rich or poor, distributing simple remedies, relieving pain, sharing with the women their many sorrows, and telling of the Savior that she loved.[10]

Stage Two began with the appointment of professionally trained medical doctors as it was soon recognized that only fully trained and licensed practitioners should carry on this ministry. In 1898 the PCUS mission adopted a resolution that prohibited the distribution of medicine except by "Doctors of Medicine, male or female."[11] The professional practice of medicine proved of great help in breaking down suspicion and became "a powerful tool of evangelism." It was variously described as a "wedge," "the bait," "a magnet" that could lead to conversion.[12]

In Stage Three medical work became recognized in its own right as a ministry to those in pain and suffering. The evangelistic motive was not dropped but healing in and of itself came to be seen as a necessary component of the Christian mission if it was to faithfully represent the compassion of Jesus Christ. Such a ministry required the highest quality of medical care.[13]

The logical extension of such a ministry led to Stage Four, which was the training of nationals for medical leadership. Thus came the emphasis on teaching hospitals, medical schools and nursing education. As early as 1890 Dr. John G. Kerr called for making "the education of physicians and surgeons for the people of this great empire" a matter of utmost importance and urgency.[14]

As mission hospital personnel reached out to the surrounding community, a new phase was begun. Stage Five was the recognition that the chronic problems affecting the welfare of the community could not be met within the institutional walls. There was a call for an emphasis on preventative medicine and public health. Medical teams itinerated with evangelistic missionaries throughout the countryside and set up temporary clinics in schools and churches for well-baby clinics, prenatal care, teaching of hygiene, nutrition and vaccinations.

A prime example of missionary public health work was that of Dr. Charles Lewis of Baoding. In addition to his practice at the Taylor Memorial Hospital, Dr. Lewis became known throughout the province for his itinerating trips into hundreds of towns and villages. "Fairs" were organized where simple medical practice was combined with religious and educational exhibits.

In 1910 the deadly pneumonic plague broke out and threatened to overrun Manchuria and North China. The provincial officials asked Dr. Lewis to take charge of the anti-plague campaign. He did it in a big way, enlisting the entire staff of his hospital in a massive effort to keep the plague from spreading further south. For three months the hospital was closed as doctors, nurses and other workers traveled to the plague-infected areas and engaged in a systematic effort to disinfect the houses where plague victims had died. Dr. Lewis "toiled incessantly in oilcloth overalls and masks saturated with carbolic acid until the plague was stamped out."[15] When the plague broke out again in 1921 in a neighboring province, the president of the Red Cross asked Lewis to take responsibility for anti-plague work, and under his leadership it was again checked. Lewis and his hospital were showered with praise and memorial scrolls. One read: "A Foreigner in Nationality, A Brother in Kindness." Another came from the president of China and read: "Medical Skill Equal to the best of the Ancients. Worthy of all praise!" After thirty-five years of strenuous service, Lewis returned to America in broken health in 1932 and died a few months later.[16]

Each new stage did not displace the previous one but built upon it. Public health did not take the place of institutional medicine but was added to it. The emphasis on evangelism and treating the poor and needy continued after the training of national health workers became a high priority. Together the five stages illustrate the full scope of missionary medical practice.

Sophie Crane has commented on the high qualifications and superb training of the China missionary doctors. The medical schools most frequently
attended by members of the southern church were Medical College of Virginia, Johns Hopkins and Tulane University.[17] Medical schools attended by
the four missionary doctors on the staff of the Yantai Temple Hill Hospital
in 1926 were Johns Hopkins, University of Pennsylvania, Western Reserve and
the College of Physicians and Surgeons of Columbia University.[18] The Rockefeller Foundation report characterized the medical missionary as having the
highest professional training but "invariably overworked" and "underpaid."[19]
The missionary physician gained experience in a wider variety of diseases than
would have been possible back home. Regular furloughs provided opportunities
to keep abreast of the latest scientific developments. In due time many became
board certified in their specialty. The high standard of practice at the "Love and
Mercy Hospital" at Huaiyin (TKP) was recognized when an accredited program
for American interns was initiated in 1929.[20]

Nevertheless the transition from medical training in the United States to
a small mission hospital in China could be quite a shock. Dr. Philip B.
Price arrived in 1926 to take charge of the Elizabeth Blake Hospital in
Suzhou and described the gap between his ideals and the reality of the China
scene:

> I brought out a boat-load of ideals.... Actual conditions have awakened
> me with a series of jolts. My dream-hospital has to be modified almost
> past recognition to fit into cheerless Chinese buildings, or antiquated,
> inappropriate "foreign" buildings. My dream equipment is in the hazy
> future.... The "eager and devoted" assistants are keener on prestige than
> on routine work and self-giving service. My dream-clinic is contracted into
> inadequate quarters, where a small crowd of the poorest and most igno-
> rant come to give the foreign doctor a chance to cure in a single visit their
> long-standing ailments.[21]

In spite of such frustrations, many doctors enjoyed long years of service. Of the
first eleven PCUS appointments, seven served in China for over thirty years.[22]
The four doctors at the Temple Hill Hospital in 1925 served an average of
twenty-four years.[23]

The nursing profession, which was gaining recognition in the United States,
was soon recognized as a priority as mission hospitals initiated training programs modeled after the Florence Nightingale pattern. "The missionary nurse
may have had a higher professional standing than her counterpart in the United
States" as her work was supervisory in nature.[24] The Rockefeller Foundation
commission was "profoundly impressed" with the role of the missionary nurse
whose influence in maintaining standards of cleanliness was a more important
factor than that of the doctor.[25] Her contribution, writes Ms. Crane, cannot
be overestimated:

In addition to supervision of nursing care in the hospitals, they operated dispensaries and well-baby clinics, handled supplies, and when the physician was unavailable found themselves thrust into all kinds of challenging situations. A prime accomplishment was the establishment of nursing schools; the training of young women in the nursing profession helped to revolutionize the status of women with results that were far-reaching.[26]

In recent years missionary physicians have been criticized for their hostility to traditional Chinese medicine. But, writes Sophie Crane, there were understandable reasons for this: (1) The medical profession in the United States out of which they had come was going through a period of putting "quacks" out of business and it was intolerant of any deviation in what was perceived of as the scientific basis for medicine; (2) "the missionary doctor encountered many tragic examples of patients who had suffered at the hand of traditional practitioners;" (3) their busy schedules and language limitations gave them little opportunity to communicate with traditional healers who felt threatened by the foreign competition.[27] It should be noted, however, that what little was known of Chinese medicine in the West was researched by missionary physicians. Dr. John Kerr did some of the earliest research. The Presbyterian Press published one of the first works on "Chinese Materia Medica."[28] Grudgingly:

> Experienced medical missionaries often came to appreciate the fact that in the field of psychosomatic problems the traditional healer's success rate was sometimes equal to, if not superior to, Western approaches. The traditional healer was better able to navigate in the cultural milieu than the neophyte from an alien culture.[29]

Except for the salaries of the missionary staff and the capital investment in buildings and equipment, hospitals were expected to be self-supporting. Special gifts helped provide for charity patients. The operating budget for the Temple Hill Hospital in 1922 was the equivalent of $15,000 (U.S.). Of this amount $11,900 came from hospital fees, $1,200 from board appropriations, and $1,900 from special gifts.[30]

Surgery was the "drawing card." Often the results were dramatically successful and had an electrifying effect on the community. Dr. Ernest Vanderburgh of the Xiangtan Hospital in Hunan told of the successful removal of an 11-pound tumor from a woman's breast which created quite a sensation. An immense crowd gathered as news of the operation spread and soldiers were called to keep the crowd in order. The tumor was on exhibition for hours.[31] Another hospital reported the successful removal of a record-setting 121-pound tumor from a woman.[32]

The hospitals treated all kinds of divers diseases and afflictions. Those most often mentioned were tuberculosis, diseases of the eye, tumors, malaria, demon possession, attempted suicide, opium addiction, diphtheria, cholera, typhoid fever, typhus, gunshot wounds, venereal diseases, dysentery and malnutrition.

Mission hospitals were incredibly crowded:

> Stand at any hospital gate as it is opened today and watch the faces of
> the crowd as they stream in. They come by rowboat, by wheelbarrow,
> by donkey. Some are carried on their beds, and little children are carried
> in baskets swung from poles, but most of them have walked the weary,
> painful miles; and now and then one crawls on hands and knees. When
> you remember that this hospital is the only one of its kind ministering to
> the needs of about two million people, you are not surprised at the vast
> numbers.[33]

The regular routine of Dr. Nettie D. Grier of the Xuzhou Women's Hospital
stretches the imagination:

> Caring for inpatients in the Women's Hospital, where often it is so
> crowded that patients have to lie on the floor. There are operations...
> eye trouble...stones in the bladder...tumors...cancer of the breast...
> gunshot wounds...obstetrical cases...would be suicides...every other
> day a *Kala-Azar* clinic...epidemics [such as] scarlet fever...cholera...
> country clinics...treating one hundred to two hundred sick in a day.[34]

An example of the evangelistic program of mission hospitals is that of the
Jiaxing Hospital, which is described in the report for 1924: (1) a warm welcome
was extended to every patient upon their admittance to make them feel at home
in the strange new environment; (2) the chaplain took time to listen patiently
to each patient's "story" of sorrow and heartache; (3) a gospel tract was given
to each one who could read; (4) for all who requested it, a full account of the
gospel message was shared; and (5) on discharge each was given the name and
location of the nearest church to their home village.[35]

In these chaotic times, the mission hospital was often the first to answer
the call for emergency help. In this account a mission hospital responds to a
bandit raid:

> "Come on let us go pick up the wounded...." One of our villages had
> been shot to pieces by bandits and twenty-three people were killed.... We
> took stretcher bearers, went seventeen miles, and brought in thirteen badly
> wounded people. The doctor looked them over and said, "We can save
> twelve of them" and he did. About midnight soldiers brought forty of their
> wounded comrades and stormed the hospital gate. They were all cared for
> at once. One dreadful November day, fifty-four children were kidnapped
> near one of our hospitals, some were slain to hurry up the ransom, and
> others died of exposure in the bitter winter weather. After paying an enor-
> mous ransom, they were released a month later, and our doctors hurried
> to that village to render free aid.[36]

A closer look must now be given to certain key institutions that are
representative of the larger whole.

The John G. Kerr Refuge for the Insane

During the late 1890s Dr. John G. Kerr, superintendent of the Canton Hospital, felt a call to start work for the insane, whose needs were not then being addressed by any government or mission agency. The asylum he proposed to start would be the first in all of China. Long and at times heated correspondence with the BFM resulted in their refusal to endorse or fund the project. Dr. Kerr appealed the decision to the PCUSA General Assembly of 1893 but again it was rejected.

Dr. Kerr refused to give up, started the asylum on his own and secured contributions from friends in America and Canton. The financing and managing of an independent institution by a PCUSA missionary "resulted in some embarrassment" in relationship to the Board and in 1901 he submitted his resignation.[37] He died the next year after an illustrious career of forty-seven years.[38]

But Mrs. Kerr took over where her husband had left off, serving as administrator and fund raiser for the asylum. Dr. Charles Selden, a physician of independent means, served as medical superintendent. The Refuge for the Insane prospered. It received patients from all classes of society and its ministry extended to the relatives and family of those afflicted. Fifteen acres of land was purchased in 1921, which added to its capacity.

In this year the Refuge promoted a campaign that must be unique in the annals of mental health promotion. During the New Year celebrations the public was invited to the Refuge for five days of lectures, drama, wrestling matches and acrobatic shows. But the greatest attraction was the insane patients. "We wished to show the people what could be done for the insane and to teach them something in the line of preventive measures." Fifty thousand people attended the event![39]

Heart-rending stories were told in the hospital's reports. One was reminiscent of the apostle Paul's encounter with the soothsayers of Philippi. A girl of seventeen was brought in by a man who said she was his daughter. On a later visit he confessed she was not his daughter but he had "bought her for business." In her present condition she was a worthless commodity and he threatened that "if she is not well by the end of the month I will take her out and drown her." When police were informed they ended the control of her cruel master. The girl recovered fully, learned to read and write, developed into a bright young woman and in time became a Christian.[40]

Morning prayers were held for staff and patients who could sit quietly. On the Sabbath there was Sunday school and church. Singing and prayer were recognized as part of the therapy.

During the two-year period 1920–1921, 11,781 out-patient visits were recorded. In this year a total of 439 in-patients were received and 380 were discharged. Of those discharged, 22 percent were pronounced cured, 21 percent were improved to some extent, 27 percent were not improved, and 25 percent had died. There had been at least 125 baptisms.[41] Finally convinced of its value, the BFM took the institution under its care in the year 1922.[42]

The Hackett Medical School for Women

Dr. Mary Fulton arrived in 1884 and soon took charge of the women's wards in the Canton Hospital. To meet the shortage of women physicians Dr. Fulton offered to teach a training course and eleven young women were "brave enough to present themselves as students."[43] It was an astonishing beginning at a time when there were few career opportunities for women in China. In 1903 the David Gregg Hospital for Women was built through the generosity of the Lafayette Avenue Presbyterian Church in Brooklyn. The first graduates of the Hackett Medical School for Women completed the course in 1904 and were immediately in demand in mission hospitals and a few government institutions. Associated with the hospital was the Julia Turner School of Nursing. These three institutions developed into the largest medical complex for women in China. Students came from as far away as Honolulu.[44]

The prestige of the school and the cause for women's education was enhanced by the presence of the Mayor of Canton and the American Consul-General at the graduation exercises in 1909 when seven young women received medical degrees. The Mayor made a notable address congratulating the Americans for establishing such a hospital just for women and for teaching "virtuous ladies" "the method of delivering the people of the world." He urged the ladies to "pluck up their courage" and "make good use of their profession and be brilliant lights among the females."[45]

In 1919 Hackett became a union institution that was supported by a number of mission boards. In 1922, Dr. John A. Hofmann, with special training in medical education, was appointed college president and superintendent of the hospital. He presided over an international staff of twenty-nine, half of whom were Chinese including the dean and nursing school director.[46]

Three-fourths of the medical students were Christians and were actively engaged in Christian witness and service in rural areas. In its first twenty-five years the medical school reported 177 graduates. Of these, 27 were serving in mission hospitals, 13 in government hospitals, and 80 were in private practice.[47]

The Ming Sum School for the Blind

In 1889 five little blind girls were brought to the Canton Hospital. Dr. Mary West Niles tells what happened next:

> They had been brought as patients but when found incurable and their friends were proposing to commit them to worse than useless lives we rescued them from this fate.... Friends in America moved to compassion by my mother's recital of their woes, furnished their support.... A blind teacher educated at the Berlin Foundling House was employed to teach them Braille and knitting.[48]

The plight of the blind girls of Canton was wretched, indeed. Called "sing-song girls," they were led through the streets at night with their musical instruments.

They sang and begged but others often took the money they had collected. Frightened half to death, they lived as slaves in the singing homes, which were filthy with dirt and vermin and riddled with disease.[49]

Dr. Niles was determined to provide a place to care for these waifs and in 1892 wrote to the Board secretary requesting assistance. Dr. Speer's response was negative. Such a school was not a part of the Board's design. Mary Niles continued her one woman campaign on behalf of her blind girls. An article she wrote for the journal *Woman's Work for Woman* entitled "The Blind Girls of Canton" touched the hearts of benefactors at home. How could the Board reject such a cause? The appeals of many in the home church were heard, and in 1894 the Board gave its blessing to Mary Niles's school for blind girls.

The school that Mary Niles started was the first such institution in all of China. The course of study ran from kindergarten through junior high. Music was an important part of the course with classes in piano, organ and chorus. In 1906 two and a half acres were purchased along the river. The sale of knitted goods made by the girls helped to provide support. "Ming Sum" (The School of the Understanding Heart) became a beautiful place "with beloved old banyans and many other trees, bricked and meandering paths, and tidy and light classrooms."[50]

In 1912 the enrollment of the school multiplied three-fold when the Canton Chief of Police brought sixty-five singing girls to enroll. The Chief said the Police Department would pay for their room and tuition and money for a school building. Some months later the Chief suddenly dropped dead. The Police Department repeatedly declined to honor the commitments he had made. But the building program was in progress and debts had to be paid. Chinese recognize an obligation to pay off old debts on the last day of the year, and on the last day of 1915, Dr. Niles presented her case one more time at police headquarters. She sat calmly and with great dignity for over six hours in the waiting room. A few hours before the beginning of the new year, the debt was paid in full — in wads of $5.00 Canton bills.[51]

Dr. Niles attributed the success of the school to her Chinese associate Miss Chau Sin Shang. Miss Alice Carpenter joined them in 1922.[52] A monumental achievement was the translation of the Braille system of writing into the Cantonese language, for which Mary Niles's alma mater, Elmira College, conferred on her the degree of LL.D.

A survey of the graduates of the school for the thirty-year period 1908–1938 gives these statistics:

Evangelistic work in schools, hospitals, churches	27
Teachers in schools for the blind	21
Teachers in schools for the seeing	9
Massagers in hospitals	4
Industrial work (knitting, etc.)	30
Married, housework	22

Dr. Niles retired in 1928 after forty-six years of service. Her colleagues paid her this tribute:

Into dark places, full of pain and suffering she went, taking light and relief and beauty, and most of all, a loving heart.[53]

The Chefoo School for the Deaf

The founding of the first school for the deaf in the Chinese empire came about through tragic circumstances. Rev. and Mrs. Charles R. Mills were among the first missionaries to arrive at the mission station at Dengzhou in 1862. Three of the Mills children died during the cholera epidemic of that year. A fourth child was deaf and Mr. Mills educated the little boy himself so that the child could read and write simple sentences. Mrs. Mills died in 1874 and Mr. Mills placed his little boy in the School for the Deaf in Rochester, New York. Several years later Mr. Mills married Miss Annetta Thompson, one of the teachers at the Rochester School. She returned with him to Dengzhou and became deeply moved by the plight of the deaf mutes, who were shunned by society as it was believed that they were possessed by evil spirits. In 1887 she gathered a little group of these helpless children and began to teach them the language of "lips and fingers."[54] The numbers grew from two to eleven. Mrs. Mills taught a Chinese colleague the skills for deaf teaching. Mr. Mills provided encouragement and support. His death in 1895 was a severe blow, which cast a shadow over the future of the school. Mrs. Mills had no independent income and the financially strapped Presbyterian Board declined to take on support for a new project. Yet Mrs. Mills felt she could not abandon the bright little boys and girls "on whose lips God had placed the seal of silence — into whose soul comes no ray of light."[55] Help came from an unexpected source. Benefactors from the Rochester School raised Mrs. Mills' salary. Contributions for land and buildings began coming in. Dr. E. M. Gallaudet, the influential president of the college for the deaf in Washington, added encouragement and support.

In 1897 a difficult decision had to be made. Isolated Dengzhou, the school's home for the first ten years, was not a good location. Mrs. Mills struck out in faith and moved the school to Yantai. Land was purchased and buildings were erected on a beautiful site overlooking the bay. The managers of a Chinese bank provided a loan on very favorable terms.[56]

But more important than the physical plant was the development of teaching methods. Mrs. Mills had to adapt Western techniques to fit the Chinese tonal language and the use of characters. Finger spelling, pantomime, gestures and picture cards were used. Texts had to be printed. Teaching staff, both deaf and hearing, had to be trained.

Results were phenomenal. The transformation wrought in the mind of a deaf child imprisoned by silence and loneliness was profound. A wonderful new world of companionship and knowledge brought a change of personality. When the deaf child acquired the use of language it was like "giving him a soul."[57] Always there were more boys than girls. Manual work was begun. Boys were taught carpentry and gardening. Girls were taught knitting, lace making and fashioning hairnets. Silkworm culture was introduced. Students came from rich and poor families alike. A third were supported fully by their families. Others received scholarships from friends in Europe, America and China. After hard years of privation, recognition came in 1910. Mrs. Mills wrote "we have justified our existence...and had the pleasure of being received back under the care of the Board."[58]

One mission of the school was to educate the public about the teachability of deaf-mute children. During the closing weeks of the school in June guests would be invited to the special exercises to demonstrate what the children had learned in speech, lip-reading and the writing of characters. High city officials were astonished at what had been learned. The session of the Temple Hill Presbyterian Church examined students for baptism and were amazed that the students could answer all the questions.[59]

A major undertaking was to find employment for the boys and husbands for the girls upon graduation. A number of graduates found employment with the great Commercial Press of Shanghai, which was under Christian auspices. A number of girls were married to hearing men and were happy home-keepers.[60]

A heartwarming story was told of a deaf mute girl whose father had tried to sell her into slavery. She had been rescued for two dollars. A picture taken at the time showed her in rags with matted hair and dirty face. She became a bright, educated young woman who read lips with ease and became one of the teachers in the school. But one thing more was needed. Could the school find her a husband? A match was made with a young man, a former student in the employ of the Commercial Press.[61]

The Chefoo School became the pioneer in furthering the cause of deaf/mute education through the "colonization" of its program. A teacher would travel to another city with one of the bright students to form the nucleus of a new school. In this way schools were started in Peking, Hangzhou and Shenyang. By 1931 ten such schools had been started throughout the country. These cared for four hundred deaf children, but at the time it was estimated that the deaf population of China was not less than four hundred thousand.[62]

Mrs. Mills retired in 1924 and her place was taken by Miss Anita Carter. The work could not have been accomplished without the superb staff of Chinese teachers. The school continued to grow and in spite of the turbulent times reported its most successful year in 1937 with sixty-one pupils.[63]

Shandong Christian University School of Medicine

In the early 1900s medical doctors were being trained in a number of institutions in different parts of the country. In 1914 a historic conference was called by the Rockefeller Foundation which was then considering a major commitment to medical education in China. An outcome of the conference was the appointment of the China Medical Commission, which visited China, surveyed the existing medical schools and hospitals and urged the consolidation of medical schools in order that higher standards could be maintained. This resulted in the establishment of the famous Peking Union Medical College (PUMC).[64]

The missionary medical community welcomed the Rockefeller expertise and money but reacted strongly against one feature of the PUMC model, which was that instruction was given in English. Missionaries in the hinterland needed their own institution in which the instruction was in Chinese. The Rockefeller Foundation recognized this need and helped establish a School of Medicine in 1916 as part of the Shandong Christian University. It was formed by the union of four medical colleges which moved to the Jinan site.[65] Dr. Randolph Shields and other faculty from the East China Medical School in Nanjing formed the nucleus of the new school.

The Medical School became a cosmopolitan institution with faculty from China, the United States, Great Britain and Canada.[66] The three "ideals" of the school were (1) high professional standards, (2) instruction in Chinese and (3) development of Christian character. Admission to the school required six years of high school plus two years of college. The medical course took five years, the last of which was an internship. In 1919 the student body numbered ninety, including seventy-two young men and eighteen young women from thirteen of the twenty-one provinces of China. About 90 percent were Christians.[67]

The school was administered by a board of governors with offices in New York and London and a local board made up of mission representatives.[68] Dr. Shields served for many years as dean. In 1924 the medical institution received a charter from the Canadian Parliament which authorized the granting of the M.D. degree. This "Western degree" was of great importance to the graduates.[69] Other degrees were given by the School of Nursing and the School of Pharmacy and for courses in physiotherapy and laboratory science.[70]

Alumni of the school have had a distinguished record of service to China and the cause of medical missions. Of the 304 living graduates in the year 1935, 22 were serving the medical school in Jinan and 86 in other mission hospitals representing 24 missionary societies.[71]

"The Love and Mercy Hospital," Huaiyin (TKP)

Typical of the "up country" mission hospital off the beaten track was the "Love and Mercy Hospital" at Huaiyin (TKP). Located on the Grand Canal in north Jiangsu it was in an area that was desperately poor and devastated by bandits, famine and flood.

A new eighty-bed hospital on spacious newly acquired grounds was completed under the leadership of Dr. James Baker Woods, Sr., during the summer of 1914 at the cost of $9,500.

In the early days the people had been suspicious. Terrible tales were told of what the foreign doctors did behind their high walls. But by the time the new hospital was constructed, suspicion had given way to curiosity. At the opening ceremonies the doors were thrown wide open and the populace was invited to inspect the premises. They were astonished at the iron beds, the microscope, the sterilizer and the elevator that took whoever was brave enough for the ride up to the exalted heights of the third floor from which a view of the whole city could be seen.

In 1916 Dr. and Mrs. L. Nelson Bell arrived. Bell was described as a "human dynamo" and both he and Dr. Woods had strong personalities. Because of his age and experience, Woods was enormously respected by the Chinese. He had been director of the hospital since the time when Nelson was a child. Bell had new ideas that sometimes clashed with those of his senior. Bell thought the hospital should have screens. Woods believed the money could be better used elsewhere.[72] Sophie Crane's comment:

> It is to the credit of both that...[they] were able to work together in harmony. In spite of differences in age and temperament, these two men provided dynamic leadership to the TKP [Huaiyin] General Hospital. Both men were dedicated to providing the highest possible quality of professional care along with the proclamation of the gospel of Jesus Christ.[73]

Drs. Woods and Bell were joined by two Chinese physicians. In 1922 Cassie Lee Oliver, R.N. (Mrs. Addison A. Talbot) arrived and began a nursing school. In 1921 an electrical power plant was installed. The next year a tuberculosis unit was added. Dr. Woods gave special attention to the treatment of leprosy.[74]

This period of rapid expansion coincided with times of turmoil. The years 1907, 1910 and 1912 were famine years. War lords fought around the hospital compound for possession of the city and control of the Grand Canal. Hospital cases reflected the turbulent times: gunshot wounds, attempted suicides, opium addiction, venereal diseases and cholera.

In 1921 the hospital was compared to a small boy whose "britches were too small." Bell found twenty-six people sleeping in a room in the men's ward with ten beds.[75] Help came in 1924 from the First Presbyterian Church of Houston, Texas, which raised $20,000 for hospital expansion. Construction was completed in record time when the contractors heard the ominous news that a war lord army was approaching the city.[76] The new addition, called the "Houston Unit," added a women's building and an administration unit with a nine-room operating suite and a chapel.

Three characteristics of the hospital stand out. First was the emphasis on *charity.* How could it be otherwise with the name "Love and Mercy"? Woods held special clinics for beggars in a nearby temple. None were turned away. Yet those with means were expected to pay the full amount. "A jovial battle of wits" developed as the administrator tried to determine whether old clothes or tales of grief were genuine. Satin slippers were a sure indication of one's ability to pay.[77]

Another characteristic was the *close identification with the evangelistic work.* Doctors accompanied missionary evangelists on their preaching missions into the country. Dr. and Mrs. Bell made periodic visits to the city jail to treat the prisoners for the itch, to give out Gospel portions and to preach. Almost without exception they were enthusiastically welcomed. On one occasion Bell was invited to preach at the home of wealthy parents whose son had been treated in the hospital. Like the case of Cornelius of old, a crowd of family and neighbors had gathered. Bell found the concept of redemption was all too familiar as many of his listeners had to redeem their loved ones by paying a ransom.[78]

A third emphasis was *research and treatment of kala azar.* This tropical disease, caused by a parasite in the bloodstream that enlarged the spleen, was epidemic in north Jiangsu. If not treated it is almost always fatal. Whole villages were affected. Not until 1930 was the carrier identified as the sandfly through research partly carried out at the Love and Mercy Hospital.[79] Scientists in Germany developed the drug "stibosan," which proved highly effective in treating the disease in three weeks time. But the drug was highly toxic and required careful supervision. The nearby boys' school was made into a fifty-bed kala azar unit. The number of kala azar patients treated rose to 3,283 in 1932 and 4,717 in 1940.[80] With the addition of the kala azar unit, the Love and Mercy Hospital reached a capacity of 380 beds and was described as "the world's largest Presbyterian hospital."[81]

The Medical Profession

The influence of missionary medicine had a profound effect on China's medical profession. In fact, it can be said that the modern medical profession in China was a creation of the missionary enterprise. In 1930 the Directory of the National Medical Association of China listed the names of 2,950 doctors. Of these 325 were missionaries and another 530 were Chinese doctors in mission institutions.[82] Added to this number were Christian doctors in government hospitals or private practice. It is safe to say that over 50 percent of the medical profession were Christians or had been trained in Christian institutions.

The number of hospitals practicing Western medicine in China in 1943 was estimated at 310. Of these, 235 were Protestant mission hospitals, 60 government hospitals and 15 Roman Catholic or private hospitals.[83] In the early 1930s there were six Protestant medical schools:

- Lingnan University Medical School (Canton)

- Shandong University School of Medicine (Jinan)

- Mukden Medical College (Shenyang)

- Women's Union Medical College (Shanghai)

- St. John's University (Shanghai)

- West China Union University Medical School (Chengdu)

Two other schools were mission-related: Yale-in-China at Changsha and Peking Union Medical College. Aurora University Medical School in Shanghai was the one Roman Catholic school. Most of the doctors of the realm were trained in these schools. Of the 249 Peking Union Medical College graduates between the years 1931 and 1943, all but 5 did their premedical work at mission colleges.[84] There is ample evidence that before 1941 the medical profession in China was dominated by mission institutions.

In the case of nursing, the missionary influence was even greater. Nursing as a profession was unknown in China prior to the coming of missionaries. Dr. Shields wrote that when he went to China in 1905 "it is doubtful that there was one Chinese nurse." In 1935 there were a thousand Chinese graduate nurses, and four thousand student nurses training in mission institutions.[85] Over 90 percent of the graduate nurses in China were Christians.

Missionary physicians established the Chinese Medical Missionary Association in 1887. Dr. John G. Kerr was elected the first president. The Association was the pioneer in the standardization of medical nomenclature and the translation of medical and scientific texts. In 1915 the National Medical Association was formed by Chinese physicians who had been educated abroad. In 1932, in a fine example of cooperation, the two associations joined to become the China Medical Association. This organization, which traces its history back 190 years to its missionary origins, has continued to function as the premier medical association in the People's Republic of China.

12

Teaching, Training, Schooling

After the abolition of the thirteen-hundred-year-old examination system based on the Confucian classics in 1905, mission schools came into their own. Western education had been exonerated and was now accepted as the norm. For a few short years the mission schools had a near monopoly on Western education. Consequently their enrollment exploded with the number doubling every six years. In 1921 the number of students enrolled in all Protestant mission schools numbered 218,819 in 7,046 different schools from kindergarten through university.[1]

For Presbyterians, the peak was reached in the school year 1924–1925. In that year Northern and Southern Presbyterians were engaged in the operation of 1,108 schools of all grades. There were 42,755 students with twice as many boys as girls. The teaching force consisted of a national staff of 2,232 and 250 missionaries. Over 90 percent of the Chinese teachers were Christians.[2] The schools could be divided in these categories: kindergarten — 35 schools, primary — 995 schools, middle (high) — 72 schools, colleges and universities — 6 schools.

A Christian School System

These are impressive figures. But after a slow start government schools too were increasing at a rapid rate. Students enrolled in mission schools probably represented only 5 percent of the number in government primary and secondary schools, and 12 percent of those in government colleges.[3] China had a long tradition that venerated education. Was it necessary, or even possible, for the foreigners to maintain a competitive educational system? Protestant educators believed that Christian schools were of critical importance for the following reasons:

Schools were agents for evangelism. Dr. Speer reported that in 1926, out of 3,657 new members received by churches related to PCUSA missions, 793 attributed their conversion to their mission school experience.[4] Often schools furnished one of the few contacts with the upper classes.

236

Schools were needed by the Christian constituency for the education of their sons and daughters. Rural congregations lacked the facilities or leadership to provide Christian nurture. For the Christian constituency the mission school was all-important because Confucian ceremonies, which were considered idolatrous, were required in the government schools.[5]

Schools were necessary for the training of the clergy and other leaders. For Presbyterians an educated clergy was a must. This began with the primary and secondary schools that were the feeders for the colleges and seminaries.

Mission schools provided educational opportunities for those otherwise excluded. China's long educational tradition was elitist while mission schools provided upward social mobility. As late as 1935, out of a population of 436 million, only 67 million were literate.[6] Mission schools gave women the opportunity for education that was lacking in the general society.

Initially schools were begun by individual missionaries who ran them on their own with little coordination. But with the increased government competition it became essential to standardize practices. The first attempt to do so came in 1890 with the establishment of the Educational Association of China. A uniform school curriculum and standard text books were adopted.

Presbyterians operated a three-tier educational system: (1) primary schools, (2) station middle (high) schools or academies and (3) union colleges and universities.[7]

Primary Schools

Often these schools were in rural areas and attached to the church in the village. Teachers were local Christians who worked as valuable members of the church team teaching Sunday School and leading in worship. The policies established by the North Jiangsu Mission in 1908 for their primary schools were probably similar to those of other missions. The mission would provide one-third of the expense as long as the other two-thirds was raised locally. A majority of the students should be baptized Christians or come from Christian homes. Each grade should include some form of Christian instruction. All teachers should be Christian.[8]

An example of many mission primary schools is the *Yuanjiawa Village School.* The village name, "the Yuan Family Puddle," tells something of its despicable condition — a desperately poor hamlet of some five hundred people — often flooded by the silt-laden Yellow River. Only one man in the village could read and write. He was Hu Youting, a prominent member of the Hu family clan. Hu had married a lady of means from a higher social class and was "endlessly under her thumb." One day after a furious row with his wife, he left home for the nearby city of Xuzhou and roamed the streets until evening. He was tired and hungry but too proud to go home. In tears, he sat down to rest by the West Gate of the city near the Presbyterian mission hospital. Mr. Xu, evangelist at the hospital, chanced to come by and asked him why he was so sad.

After hearing his tale, Mr. Xu took him home, gave him supper and late into the night told him the message about the Christ. The message struck home and Hu returned to Yuanjiawa the next morning feeling like a free man. He became an enthusiastic Christian and was determined to spread the gospel to his village. He donated a piece of land on the outskirts of the village for a school and church. Teachers from the Xuzhou mission came to teach. The school began with a two-year course and each year another grade was added. When students finished the seventh year they could enroll in the mission school in Xuzhou.

A steady stream of Yuanjiawa boys and girls graduated from the village school, went on to the middle school in Xuzhou and from there to various colleges. They became medical doctors, ordained ministers, high school teachers, engineers and nurses. My friend Peter Hu became a professor of agriculture. Hu Shiu Ying, a protegée of Miss Lois Young who was principal of the Xuzhou Girls' High School, went on to earn her B.A. from Ginling College for Women, a Master's degree from Lingnan University, and a Ph.D. from Radcliffe. Later she joined the faculty of Harvard University as professor of botany and researcher at the Arnold Arboretum. Dr. Hu, now retired and living in Boston, writes: "If in 35 years, Christianity can change Yuanjiawa into a very prosperous Christian village, it can save China."[9]

Station Academies

The next level was the middle school, sometimes known as the station academy. Such schools required higher standards. Dormitories were needed so that students from the countryside could attend. Each mission station wanted to have such a school but resources were limited and so it was often a struggle as to which school would be upgraded.

Inevitably the schools tended to follow the North American model, which was what was known to the missionary principal. Mission policy recognized this danger and dictated that insofar as possible the schools should follow the Chinese government education policies "especially in the adoption of curricula and methods of instruction more adequately adapted to the psychology of the Oriental mind."[10] They should teach service to one's country and were warned not to isolate their students from the wider Chinese community.

The teaching of English was controversial. It was one of the most popular subjects but some felt it would further alienate the students from their own culture. In the North Jiangsu Mission schools it could only be elected in the last two years for college preparation.[11] Courses in Bible were required at each level. Attendance at chapel services was compulsory. A majority of the students should be baptized Christians or from Christian families but as the years progressed there was some erosion in this principle. Nevertheless, a number of students each year were received into the church. Vocational training was introduced at some schools but with mixed results. Presbyterians were better at professional training (medicine, teaching, the ministry) than in manual skills. Schools were encouraged to organize advisory boards in order to gain the cooperation of the community.[12]

The impact these schools had on the molding of character and on the training of church workers is hard to exaggerate. Some achieved a reputation known far and wide. Among these were:

- The True Light School, Canton
- Lowrie Institute, Shanghai
- Truth Hall, Peking
- The Yali (Yale) Union Boys' School, Changsha
- Fuxiang Girls' School, Changsha
- The James Sprung Academy, Jiangyin
- The Mary Thompson Stevens School for Girls, Xuzhou
- Riverside Academy for Girls, Ningbo
- Pitkin School for Girls, Qiongzhou
- The Chinkiang Boys School, Zhenjiang

The Hangzhou Union Girls' School

One example of a station academy that achieved excellence was the Hangzhou Union Girls' School. The school also illustrates the transition from mission control to Chinese management under an interdenominational board.

In 1911 the Mid China Mission (PCUS) and the Central China Mission (PCUSA) merged their two girls' schools and agreed to share alike in the support of the new union institution. The school opened with 105 girls, and a faculty of 3 missionaries and 16 Chinese. The next year the American Baptists asked that their school be included in the merger. Each mission supplied two missionary teachers, an annual grant of $1,800 and capital funds as needed. Dr. Jane V. Lee was chosen as the first principal.

By pooling resources the school became one of the best equipped schools in central China. The Southern Presbyterian "Children's Day Offering" of 1907 provided $10,000 for a new administration building. A new primary school and dormitory was built by the Baptists. Later came an open-air gymnasium.[13]

In the first ten years, the school more than tripled its enrollment, which reached 346 in 1921. Grades ran from kindergarten through middle (high) school. A normal school for primary and kindergarten teachers was added. Music, household science, physical training, social studies, a school magazine and religious education were distinctive features of the program. The school compared favorably with the best government schools in the city and graduates had no difficulty getting teaching jobs.[14]

In 1923, the faculty reported: "We are not satisfied with the spiritual condition of the school" and engaged in a struggle to maintain a Christian atmosphere. This was a common challenge for all mission schools during the 1920s. Efforts to improve the situation were made through the YWCA and evangelistic services. In 1927 the school reported that 35 percent of the students and 75 percent of the faculty were Christian.[15]

The school board was composed of missionaries appointed by each mission. Later, three Chinese members were added. In 1925 Miss Myi Sih-Me became the first Chinese principal.

The China Colleges

The establishment of a college required a much heavier commitment in personnel and finances. It also required a degree of expertise the missions lacked. Once organized, a college did not easily fit into the mission structure. Yet all across China there was a clamor for Western education now that the old model had been proved inadequate.

And so Protestant missions plunged into unknown waters and began to establish "Christian colleges" just like the ones they had known back home. In many cases the mission academy provided a platform on which to build. At first they were "colleges" in name only. Soon it became apparent that to succeed they would have to be union institutions. Even the strongest denomination did not have the resources to go it alone. Extensive fund raising beyond the normal mission board channels became necessary.

The general pattern that emerged was the establishment abroad of a board of trustees made up of denominational representatives. In order to raise funds the body had to be incorporated in the United States or Canada. The college would then apply for a charter as an educational institution under the regulations of New York or some other state. A local Board of Managers would be established at the site of the college with representatives from the cooperating missions.

Such a pattern dictated that the school would have a foreign flavor. It was under foreign management and supported by foreign funds, and its educational policies followed a foreign design. Dr. William P. Fenn, historian of the China Christian colleges, wrote that "at the beginning this foreignness was unavoidable. There simply were too few Chinese with a modern education."[16] It would be different once a later generation of scholars had been graduated from these pioneering institutions.

The development of the colleges took place during a time of political and social turmoil. At times their campuses were overrun by competing war lords and looting soldiers. During the intense nationalism of post-1911 China the colleges provided students the opportunity for self-expression and at the same time became lightning-rods that attracted student protests and demonstrations. St. John's University was closed in 1925 during the May 30 Incident when British police fired on demonstrators. Shandong Christian University was forced to close in 1928 when employees under the control of radical elements seized control of the campus and threatened to burn down the buildings. Lingnan

University was overrun by Cantonese troops fighting an invading army from Yunnan in 1925.[17] Hangzhou College was forced to close during demonstrations following the signing of the Versailles treaty in 1919 by the Allies.[18] Nanking University was overrun by southern troops in 1927. Its buildings were ransacked and its vice-president, John E. Williams, was killed by looting soldiers.

Throughout these troubled times the colleges made valiant attempts to retain their Christian character. After all, this was the reason for their existence. But there was no general agreement on the best way to do this. Some had required Bible courses but for others this was voluntary. It was the same with chapel attendance. Christian student organizations such as the YMCA and YWCA engaged in activities of witness and community service. Special evangelistic services were held. The colleges tried to insist that 50 percent of the student body be made up of baptized Christians and those from Christian homes. But with a Christian constituency of less than 1 percent of the population, this was difficult to do. Yet, most colleges reported a significant number of students who became Christians during their college years. Invariably, the number of Christians in the senior class was much higher than that for the freshman year.

North American and British mission boards found it impossible to provide the necessary resources for all the institutions striving to achieve college status. So in 1921 they appointed the China Educational Commission headed by Professor Ernest D. Burton of the University of Chicago to survey the situation and make recommendations. The Burton Commission recommended a sharp reduction in the number of Christian colleges and greater cooperation in their administration. This led to various mergers and the establishment of what became known as the United Board for Christian Colleges in China, which had support for the following eleven colleges:

- Fujian Christian College (Fuzhou)

- Ginling College for Women (Nanjing)

- Hangzhou Christian College

- Hwa Nan College for Women (Fuzhou)

- Huachung University (Wuhan)

- University of Nanjing

- West China Union University (Chengdu)

- St. John's University (Shanghai)

- Suzhou University

- Shandong Christian University (Jinan)

- Yenching University (Peking)[19]

During the roughly seventy-five years of the history of the China Colleges, some 26,000 students were graduated. An additional 35,000–40,000 attended but did not receive diplomas.[20]

Presbyterians cooperated in the support of a number of the colleges of which four will now be given a closer look.[21]

Hangzhou Christian College

Hangzhou Christian College had its origins in the Ningbo Boys' School which was established in 1844 and moved to Hangzhou in 1867. A new era began in 1908 when the school purchased for $1,000 (U.S.) sixty acres on a beautiful new site overlooking the Qiantang River about six miles outside the city walls. Southern Presbyterians joined the venture in 1910, provided $1,600 (half the school budget) and appointed the Rev. Warren Stuart to serve on the faculty. Tuition fees were set at approximately $40.00 (US) for non-Christians and $20.00 (US) for Christians.

Two outstanding educators contributed to the school in the early years: Rev. Junius H. Judson and Rev. Elmer L. Mattox. Both were experienced educators and did much to develop the science department of the school, which laid the foundations for the future College of Engineering. Incredible teaching assignments were given the early faculty. Mattox taught Plan of Salvation, Analytical Chemistry, General History, English and Political Economy. Stuart taught English, Geology, Ethics, Logic, Comparative Religions, and New Testament History. "Obviously," wrote Dr. Fenn, "over-specialization was at that time no threat."[22] Other missionaries associated with the college were Dr. Robert Fitch and Dr. Robert J. McMullen, both of whom served as president, and Dr. Clarence B. Day, who served for twenty-three years as professor of philosophy and head of the English Department.[23]

The college was constantly hard pressed financially, yet a beautiful campus was developed: Severance Hall, an observatory on the peak of the hill, Tooker Memorial Chapel and dormitories. Alumni raised $40,000 for a gymnasium.

A memorable occasion was the visit of Dr. Sun Yat-sen in 1912 when he addressed the faculty and students. In 1920 the college obtained a charter under the laws of the District of Columbia as a four-year college and from this date began to grant degrees. The strongest department of the college became that of civil engineering. In 1924 the college had an enrollment of 256, a foreign staff of 16 and a Chinese staff of 20.[24] In 1927 Dr. Fitch resigned as president in order that the college could elect a Chinese, Dr. Chu Ching-Nung, to that position.

University of Nanjing

Nanjing University had its beginning in 1910 with the union of Methodist, Disciples and Presbyterian schools. Each of the founders agreed to provide $40,000 in cash for land and buildings, and to share in providing faculty. Dr. Arthur

Bowen of the Methodist Mission was elected president. Dr. John E. Williams of the Presbyterian Mission became vice-president.

The great famine of 1911 brought thousands of destitute farmers to Nanjing. The university began a program of clearing land, planting fruit trees, building roads and planting potatoes and beans. Out of this effort came the founding of the School of Agriculture in 1914. The next year forestry was added. Soon thereafter the government closed its own school of agriculture and sent its students to the mission institution. In 1917 the distinguished agriculturalist Dr. John H. Reisner became head of the school. Under his leadership it became the leading school of its kind with departments of Agricultural Economics, Agronomy, Botany, Forestry, Horticulture, Rural Education and Sericulture. The catastrophic flood of 1931 provided another challenge. At the request of the National Flood Relief Commission, the School of Agriculture and Forestry undertook a survey of the affected area under the leadership of Dr. J. Lossing Buck. People in the area affected by the flooding of the Yangtze and Hwai rivers were equivalent to the entire farm population of the United States! The survey documented the extent of the damage, the causes of flooding, relief efforts that should be undertaken and preventative measures for the future.[25]

The university included a School for Missionary Training which in 1919 had thirty-five in residence.[26] Here missionaries from many denominations received training in the Mandarin dialect and were introduced to Chinese culture.

The university's religious activities centered in the YMCA. One of the "Y" projects was the sending of books and supplies to the Chinese Labor Corps at work with the Allied armies in France. At religious services held in 1918–1919 over 100 students signed cards for full-time Christian service; some 20 "decided for Christ for the first time."[27] The university received students from twelve of the provinces of China and from thirty-six different mission schools. The 1917–1918 university bulletin reported that "of the 145 graduates since 1896...96 percent have been Christians; 74 percent entering mission work as teachers, preachers and doctors."[28]

Ginling College for Women

Higher education for women was practically non-existent during the years of the Manchu dynasty. As late as 1919 girls constituted only 5 percent of government primary schools. A male-dominated society saw little need for educated women.

With this background one can readily understand the revolutionary nature of an event that took place in 1915. In that year representatives of five mission boards (Northern Baptists, Disciples, Northern and Southern Methodists and Northern Presbyterians) opened a college for women. It took as its name Ginling, the literary name for Nanjing where the college was located. Mrs. Lawrence Thurston, with wide experience in college administration, was

elected president. Thirteen students were enrolled. Four years later five of these
became the first women to receive a B.A. degree from a China institution.

In 1923 a major $300,000 building program was completed on a new
twenty-seven acre campus near the University of Nanjing. Ginling College was
among the first mission schools to adopt Chinese architecture to Western educational needs. In 1924 enrollment had reached 133. In 1928 Dr. Wu Yi-fang,
a member of the first graduating class, was elected president.[29]

Yenching University

In 1915 the Methodists, the London Missionary Society and the Northern Presbyterians put together their several denominational schools to form a union
college in Peking. The union was a fragile one with different departments occupying separate locations. In 1918 the trustees elected as president Dr. John
Leighton Stuart, then on the faculty of the Nanjing Theological Seminary. Stuart
was born in Hangzhou of Southern Presbyterian parents, spoke fluent Mandarin
and gave inspired leadership to the university for the next thirty years.[30]

The first issue to be addressed was the name. A committee of prominent Chinese scholars recommended "Yenching" — the ancient literary name for Peking.
Next came a new site. A sixty-five-acre estate five miles northeast of the city was
secured, and later expanded to over a hundred acres. In 1926 the university
moved to the new campus.

The university had ambitious plans for development but the mission boards
did not have the funds for a major capital funds drive. A breakthrough was
made when the Rev. Henry Winters Luce of Shandong was invited to become
vice-president with responsibility for fund raising and development.[31] For the
next eight years Luce's time, talent and energy were spent in the formation of a
foundation in New York, the raising of millions of dollars and the development
of the Peking campus.

At Luce's insistence, the building of the campus followed an architectural
style that matched the stateliness and grandeur of the Forbidden City — even
to the water tower, which was disguised as a pagoda. What was called Luce's
"Chinese Castles in the Air" became the reality of the "great Yenching." A lake
and pavilion in the center of the university was donated by Henry Robinson
Luce, founder of *Time* magazine, in honor of his father.

During Stuart's presidency the university experienced rapid growth and development. Student enrollment grew from 103 in 1913 to 1,156 in 1941.
Faculty appointments grew from 25 to 137.[32] The university was organized into
three colleges: Arts and Letters, Natural Science and Public Affairs. The North
China Union College for Women joined Yenching in 1920. Yenching's School
of Journalism achieved a national reputation. Endowment increased from half
a million to 3 million dollars. In 1925, the Yenching School of Religion was
added. However it attracted a disappointing number of students in spite of
distinguished faculty members such as Drs. T. T. Lew and T. C. Chao.

Stuart's educational philosophy at Yenching can be summarized in his phrase "a synthesis of the abiding values in two [Western and Chinese] confluent civilizations."[33] Stuart's specific interests lay in practical vocational training, rural life and service, and the molding of Christian character. In order to permeate Yenching with the Christian faith he established the "Yenta" [short for Yenching University] Christian Fellowship. Requirement for admission to Yenta was a declaration "to grow in the knowledge of our Lord Jesus and to live according to the way which He taught and lived." During Stuart's years at the university membership in the fellowship ranged from one-fourth to four-fifths of the student body. This was no mean achievement considering the anti-Christian spirit of the times.[34] In 1928 Vice-President Wu Lei-Chuan was elected chancellor with Dr. Stuart continuing as president.[35]

Critique

The China colleges were not without their critics. For some they were too foreign. For others they cost too much money. Some felt that their Christian influence was too weak.

The PCUSA China Council, while consistently affirming its support of the colleges, repeatedly expressed its concern about the direction higher education was taking. Attempts to create standards to match those of North America were too expensive. The massive capital grants and expenditures were out of proportion to the emphasis placed on other areas of the work.[36] The colleges had too large a foreign staff.[37] In 1926 there were seventy-six PCUSA personnel assigned to six of the China colleges.[38] There was the danger that evangelistic personnel were being lost to the institutions.[39] Incorporation of universities in the United States raised many problems: It accentuated their foreignness and tended to separate the institution from mission or church influence and control.[40] Policies were set by the university boards that met in New York rather than by mission or church bodies in China. Fund raising for the colleges had a glamor lacking in the more humdrum aspects of church development.

Mr. Xu Yi Hua, a Ph.D. candidate at Princeton University, gives this scathing criticism of his alma mater, St. John's University, in his dissertation:

> The native church workers trained by the Christian colleges usually had a better education in western learning than in their own. . . . It was much easier for Chinese Christians to take over the support of any other Christian institution than a college. It hindered Christianity from becoming indigenous. Since the 1920's, the Christian colleges have been a liability rather than an asset to the church in China.[41]

Although the universities were created, in part, to train pastors, their departments of theology attracted few candidates for the ministry. Most of the Protestant clergy continued to be trained in Bible schools or seminaries unrelated to the universities. Note the following statistics taken from a survey of students preparing for the ministry in 1933–1934:

Institution	*Total Enrollment*
Canton Christian College	29
Lutheran Theological Seminary	34
Shandong University School of Theology	32
Nanjing Theological Seminary	62
Shanghai Baptist Theological Seminary	13
West China School of Religion	10
St. John's School of Religion	3
Yenching School of Religion	30
North China Theological Seminary	133
Peking Theological Seminary	29
Central Theological School	17[42]

The three schools that were related to the Christian universities (Shandong, Yenching and St. John's) attracted few students. The two schools with the largest enrollment were Nanjing Theological Seminary and the North China Theological Seminary, both of which were church-related rather than university-related. The conservative North China seminary had twice as many students as the three universities combined! For the training of ministers, a school with a close relationship to the church was more important than the higher standards a university could provide.

The Christian colleges did a better job at training lay men and women for professional leadership positions. With smaller classes the colleges provided opportunities for experimentation, practical teaching experiences, physical education, sports and debating societies. A survey made in 1933 of the 6,930 living graduates of the Christian colleges gives these statistics: 1,764 teachers and administrators of Christian colleges, 1,075 teachers and administrators of government schools, 919 medical practices, 823 business enterprises, 436 in public life, 430 social and religious work other than the ministry, 308 ordained clergy, 262 in law, agriculture, forestry, engineering, 461 in postgraduate study.[43]

Dr. Fenn's assessment:

> It is impossible to avoid the conclusion that, in spite of weaknesses, the Christian colleges contributed significantly, and clearly out of proportion to their numbers to the awakening of China to the modern world.[44]

An interesting phenomenon in recent years has been the emergence of alumni associations, which have sought to perpetuate the identity of their alma maters. Former students at Yenching have petitioned the government to establish a Yenching Institute. In 1987 the Ginling College for Women was reestablished as a part of Nanjing Normal University.[45] In 1987 four hundred alumni and former faculty of Hangzhou Christian College held a mass meeting on their former campus to celebrate the school's 140th anniversary.[46] Such activities bear witness to the reservoir of good will the colleges left.

Several years ago I sent a questionnaire to the 26 members of the Hangzhou Alumni Association residing in the United States.[47] All respondents wrote positively about their college experience. All felt that they had been well prepared academically. Most of the respondents had gone on to graduate study in China or the United States. Two of the eight respondents were Christians when they enrolled, one was baptized while at the college and one became a Christian after leaving. Two others, though not members of a Christian denomination, described themselves as deeply religious and appreciative of the religious instruction they had received. One was and remained a Buddhist. One question asked for opinions as to the foreignness of the college. Several respondents indicated that while at the college they were indifferent to such issues. Several thought that the college combined Western knowledge with Chinese cultural values in a helpful way. Only one felt that the college was too much of a foreign institution. The chief contributions the college had made to their lives were moral integrity and high academic standards. Missionaries who had made a lasting impression were Dr. R. J. McMullen and Dr. and Mrs. Clarence B. Day.

The greatest tribute to the enduring contribution of the China colleges is the fact that the four most influential leaders of the church in China today were graduates of these schools:

- *Bishop K. H. Ting,* President of the China Christian Council, President of Nanjing Seminary, President of the Amity Foundation, was a graduate of St. John's University.

- *Bishop Shan Yifan* (deceased), former Vice President and General Secretary of the China Christian Council, was a graduate of St. John's University.

- *Rev. Wen Hao (Peter) Tsai* (deceased), former Vice President of the China Christian Council, and President of the Zhejiang Province Christian Council, was a graduate of Shanghai Baptist College, Yenching University, and chaplain at Hangzhou Christian College.

- *Dr. Wenzao Han,* General Secretary of the Amity Foundation and the China Christian Council, was a graduate of Hangzhou Christian College and was baptized while a student there.

It is hard to imagine what the Christian movement in China would be like today without the leadership of these men who received their education in the China Christian colleges.

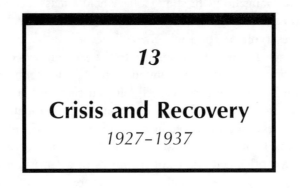

13

Crisis and Recovery

1927–1937

The year 1927 was the low point for Christian missions in China. The year is described in the PCUSA *Annual Report* with these words: "tragedy, disillusionment, disappointment, discouragement, doubt, uncertainty, perplexity."[1] Latourette's usual optimistic tone changes to one of profound pessimism: "The middle of 1927...found Protestantism in China in the worst plight in its history."[2]

After the decade of the "golden years" of 1915–1925, what had happened to reverse so suddenly the fortunes of the China mission? China had been hit by the convergence of three forces that threatened to undo the work of the previous century of mission progress: (1) nationalism, (2) the Great Depression, and (3) the anti-Christian movement. But to understand what was happening we must first consider the phenomenon of Chinese nationalism.

Nationalism

After the death of Sun Yat-sen of cancer in March 1925, the Chinese revolution entered a new phase. For a decade the war lords had kept China in turmoil and division. But now a new factor — nationalism — became the dominant force in China's public life. Nationalism had its inception in the frustrations of a great nation with a proud history that had for too long been humiliated by powers abroad and betrayed by leaders at home. Its flames had been fanned by the ignominious treatment China received at Versailles in 1919.

One faction in the nationalistic movement was the Kuomintang Party (KMT) founded by Sun Yat-sen. Earlier, Sun had approached the Western powers for assistance but they were uninterested. Britain and the United States continued to recognize the Peking regime, then under the control of the northern war lords. Sun then turned to the Soviets and Stalin was only too glad to supply rifles, machine guns, artillery and military advisors.

The other faction was the Chinese Communist Party (CCP) which had its organizational meeting in the Shanghai International Settlement in 1921. One of the twelve party members was a young library assistant from Peking University named Mao Zedong. He would be the only one to have any influence on the future course of events. The CCP was under Russian tutelage as it was too inexperienced and small in numbers to chart an independent course. The CCP was urged by its Russian advisors to make common cause with the KMT, infiltrate the party apparatus, organize labor unions in the cities and bide its time.

Chiang's "Northern Expedition"

After Sun's death Chiang Kai-shek inherited the leadership of the KMT and began to build up his power base in Guangdong and plan for the long-awaited campaign which would rout the war lords and reunite the nation.[3] The armies would sweep north along three lines of advance: (1) on the west, an assault on Wuhan following the railroad; (2) in the center, a thrust into Jiangxi toward Nanchang and (3) along the east coast an attack aimed at Fuzhou. Preceding the military advance, political cadres would infiltrate the cities and organize the workers. "Silver bullets" (bribes) would be used to win over uncommitted war lords.

In July 1926 the "Northern Expedition" was launched and initial victories routed the army of Wu Peifu and captured Changsha. After heavy fighting, the tri-city area of Wuhan was seized. The Nationalist capital was moved here from Canton.

Chiang shifted his attention to the Nanchang offensive. City after city fell in heavy fighting and by November Nanchang was taken. The campaign along the coast was made easier by the defection of provincial armies and naval units. By December Fuzhou and most of Fujian Province was in Nationalist hands. The Nationalists now controlled seven provinces and a population of 170 million. The initial victories were attributed to the discipline of the troops, their political indoctrination, support given by peasants and workers and timely defections.

The campaign now shifted to the ideological front as the various factions jockeyed for positions of influence. Communist elements in the KMT gained control of the Wuhan headquarters and seized the British concession, provoking an international uproar.

The intensely anti-foreign Wuhan faction favored the continued advance northward toward the capital. On the other hand, Chiang, who had remained in Nanchang, favored an assault on the lower Yangtze valley aimed at the industrial powerhouse of Shanghai where he could count on the support of the business community. He visited Wuhan in January but was rebuffed and publicly insulted by the Russian advisor, Michael Borodin. An open break was narrowly averted. Surprisingly, the Soviet Union threw its weight behind Chiang. Cooperation with the KMT must continue. Shanghai and Nanjing would be the next target.

In December Hangzhou fell to the Nationalist forces. On 24 March 1927 KMT armies entered Nanjing. There was little resistance as the Northern troops evacuated the city, fleeing across the great river. But quite unexpectedly one of the divisions launched a vicious attack on the foreign community. The British, Japanese and American consulates were ransacked; property was looted and burned and a number of foreigners were killed. Missionaries and other internationals took refuge on American and British gunboats anchored in the river. The "Nanjing Incident," as it was called, created an international crisis and precipitated the evacuation of missionaries from the interior.

Shanghai fell to the Nationalist armies a few days later. They were aided by six hundred thousand striking workers who had been organized by the Communist party. To the relief of the foreign community Chiang promised that foreign property would be respected. The issue of the Unequal Treaties would be settled by negotiation, not by armed conflict.

With the northern armies in full retreat, the schism between the two factions in the KMT grew more ominous. General strikes, inspired by communist labor unions, erupted in urban areas. A basic difference in ideology was laid bare. Was the goal to defeat the war lords and unite the country or was it to bring about revolution through class struggle?

In Shanghai during the predawn hours of April 12 the final break occurred. Heavily armed men in civilian clothes launched a surprise attack on the headquarters of the city labor union known to be under communist domination. It was said that thugs in the Shanghai underworld took part in the attacks. They were assisted by troops loyal to Chiang Kai-shek. Hundreds of workers were killed and hundreds more arrested. Simultaneously, known communists within the party were rounded up. The alliance between the CCP and the KMT was in shambles.

In July 1928, Michael Borodin and his staff departed Wuhan on the long overland trek across central Asia to Russia in disgrace. The Russian enterprise in China had ended in total failure. Communist leaders who escaped the clutches of the KMT took to the hills of Guangxi and began to rebuild the party on an agrarian base. We will hear from them again.

The Northern Expedition pushed north along the lines of the Tianjin Pukou railroad in the summer of 1927 and stalled. Chiang's overextended armies suffered defeat at the strategic railroad junction of Xuzhou and retreated to the Yangtze. For a while the safety of Nanjing, which had been named the new capital, was in doubt. But in a decisive six-day battle the northerners were defeated.

Before the campaign to the north could be continued, other matters had to be settled. The purge of communists continued. Shanghai businessmen were pressured into bankrolling the KMT finances, which had been depleted by the military campaign. Chiang made a quick trip to Japan on private business. He wanted the approval of Madame Soong, widow of the Americanized trader, Charlie Soong, to marry her youngest daughter, Soong Meiling, a Wellesley College graduate. The Soong family was Christian and it was reported that Madame Soong agreed to the marriage on the condition that the Generalissimo "study Christianity."[4] The marriage took place in Shanghai in December 1927 and helped cement ties with the Shanghai elite. Meiling's two elder sisters were the widow of Sun Yat-sen and the wife of financier H. H. Kung. Meiling's brother was T. V. Soong, a business tycoon who was brought on board to run the government's finances.

Late in 1927, the Northern Expedition was resumed. Alliances were forged with the remaining war lords in preparation for the final assault on Peking. Only Zhang Zuolin of Manchuria was left. Xuzhou was retaken after a major battle in November. Jinan fell to the Southerners in April 1928. Here they encountered Japanese troops, who had entered the city to protect their nationals. Chiang, seeking to avoid a confrontation, bypassed the city and continued the advance north.

Zhang Zuolin returned to his home base in Manchuria where he had assurances of Japanese support. But on the morning of 4 June 1928 he was killed when his railway car was demolished by a bomb as his train was approaching Shenyang. It is thought the perpetrators were junior Japanese officers unhappy with the decision to support Zhang.

On 6 July 1928 Chiang entered Peking and declared the end of the Northern Expedition and the country unified under the three principles of Sun Yat-sen: Nationalism, Democracy, and People's Livelihood. But years of fighting lay ahead.

Mass Evacuation

The year 1927 was the year of the mass missionary evacuation. As the revolution worked its way up from the south, American consuls first warned and then strongly urged missionaries to leave the interior. For Presbyterians, the evacuations started with the island of Hanoi, moved to the interior cities of Guangdong Province and then followed the military campaign as it moved north.

For the most part the missionary sympathies were with the southerners, who seemed to offer the best chance for a unified China. But the Nanjing Incident, with its unprovoked attack on foreign civilians, sent shock waves throughout the missionary community. The story of the evacuation is best told by those who experienced it in their own words. *Eliza Lancaster* with her children went to the American gun boat when strongly urged to do so by the consul:

> There were about 150 women and children that got on the gun boats Tuesday, March 22....All afternoon we could hear the guns and could see the northerners fleeing crossing the river in little boats that were very crowded....On Thursday we were told not to go on the deck of the gun boat so we had to stay down all day....At about 3:40 one of the men on the boat came and said the gun boats were going to fire and for us to put cotton in our ears and not to worry....I felt that my whole attention

should be given to the children.... We talked with them and told them stories and sang with them all the songs that they knew.... The children were not frightened although I can still feel Page's arm around me every time they shot.... Of course we were all worried sick over our husbands not knowing a thing.[5]

Lewis Lancaster returned to the seminary compound after getting his family on the gun boat. The next morning:

A squad of soldiers entered our gate firing as they came. I met them at the front door of the house, holding a small American flag in my hand.... They demanded money, arms, and ammunition.... Then another larger group of soldiers came in.... These men searched me more thoroughly, having me open all my clothing down to my underwear....

In a very few minutes everything was plundered... all movable furniture... books and papers.... The soldiers who still held me demanded $400.... When I insisted that all my ready money had been taken... they threatened to shoot me.... After a number of shots had been fired close to my head I was taken aside from the crowd and told I would be shot. Just at this time Dr. Goodwin... came out and the soldiers turned to search him....

One of our servants... managed to get us away through the crowd and hid us in a straw hut not far away.... Dr. Chen of the Seminary brought a jar of stewed peaches and gave me his sweater.... We heard the firing of the U.S. destroyers and the British cruiser in the afternoon but did not know what it meant. Things did become strangely quiet....

Sometime near eight o'clock several students of the Methodist Boys' school came with a note from Mr. Pryor, principal of the school, saying that he and four others were in the school under the protection of the major whose troops were quartered in the school and that it would be safe to join them.... At the gate of the school they produced military passes and took us to the room where the five foreigners were. Of the seven in that room Dr. Price had suffered most, having been in the hands of those brutal soldiers nearly nine hours.... After a prayer all round the group, we lay down to get what sleep we could.... Early in the morning... under escort of the soldiers and accompanied by some of our students we went to the University where all the foreigners were being gathered.... The greeting received from those already gathered at the university is never to be forgotten. We could not trust ourselves to speak but clasped hands with deep emotions of joy and thanksgiving....

Late Friday afternoon nine carriages came, arranged for by the Red Swastika Society [Buddhist Red Cross].... [We were] escorted all the way by a squad of soldiers and some students. We reached the gunboats about eight.[6]

Pearl Sydenstricker Buck and her family (her husband, Lossing, father, Absalom Sydenstricker, and children) had decided not to seek refuge on the ship because they did not believe that foreign gun boats had any business in Chinese waters:

> Wednesday night rumors came that the city gates were opening to allow the retreating Northern soldiers to come through the city. Immediately our Chinese neighbors and friends came to ask if they might sleep in our house, because they thought the retreating soldiers would not trouble foreigners. We were glad to help in this way, and about forty people came in. All night some one of the missionary men patrolled the neighborhood....
>
> Just after breakfast as I was taking the children upstairs, our coolie came running in with a white face crying, "Oh, Mistress, I hear the Southerners are after the foreigners, and some foreign man has already been killed." Immediately our other servants came running in ... saying that we must hide if we were to save our lives.... So we all hurried out of the back gate and across a field into a little group of thatched houses and then into a little back room.... It was a tiny place not more than six by eight feet ... but we were thankful indeed for its shelter.... We waited there in perfect silence while we heard the crowd come and begin to break into our home and loot it.... I cannot well describe to you the horror of that moment.... It was as keen a moment of pain as I had ever known. Something I had created was being wantonly torn to pieces....
>
> From time to time our faithful servants came in to do what they could for us, telling us with tears of the horrible devastation that was going on.... All that day we stayed without stirring in the tiny dark hut. The three children were wonderfully patient and good.... Just when the noise and havoc was at its height we heard a sinister sound. The American destroyer began to send shells into the city.... Soon after a bugle began to blow, and almost instantly the mobs began to quiet down.... At last Mr. Chou came in [to get us].... Under his protection then and that of a Southern guard, we proceeded, a sorry little procession to Bailie Hall. There we found the other foreigners assembled in one room on the third floor....
>
> What a sight it was! All our friends, with the exception of some who had not yet been found, were gathered there, worn and haggard ... most of them had had to face the mobs, had been fired at again and again, had everything torn from them, rings, watches, even spectacles, and had to submit to degrading searches of their bodies for money.... But in every case there was the same testimony of gratitude for our Chinese friends who exerted themselves at the cost of their own lives to get us protection and aid. Very humble people, women, and ricksha coolies and servants, as well as professors and students.... Hearing of the stories of others ... made me think with special tenderness of Mrs. Williams.... At

last I found her sitting a little apart from the others. I went to her at once, and could only hold her tight, sensing a little of what the day had been for her. But she was very calm and brave, and told me gently what had happened.[7] ... About midnight Miss Anna Moffet, the secretary of our station, came in. She had been shot twice by a soldier, once in the knee and once in the thigh.... They had hidden all day in a workman's hut beneath a pile of straw.... Dr. Price, vice-president of the theological seminary, had been beaten again and again with the butts of guns, and some half dozen times had been stood up and guns cocked ready to fire, and each time some devoted Chinese friend had interposed his own body.... At last word came that arrangements had been made that we were to be taken through the city to the Bund and put on board the destroyer....

The city as we went through it was like a city of the dead. Shops were burned and there were no civilians in sight.... we finally reached the destroyer where our American marines received us, and did everything they could to make us comfortable.[8]

How does one account for the behavior of the southern troops, who had gained a reputation of being well disciplined? There was probably no more sympathetic group to the Nationalist cause than the Nanjing foreign community. The most probable explanation is that it was a well-orchestrated, deliberate attack ordered by the radical wing of the KMT party and carried out by the 6th Division which was under their control. An effort was made to excite the general populace of Nanjing against the foreigner but this attempt failed. All accounts emphasize the friendship shown by the people of Nanjing — Christians and non-Christians alike. Missionaries were hidden; food was provided; emergency care was given; ransom money was raised.[9]

When news of the Nanjing Incident spread throughout north China, American consuls ordered the immediate evacuation of missionaries from the interior. Presbyterian mission stations were squarely in the path of the advancing southern armies. Twenty-six of the thirty Presbyterian mission stations in central and north China were evacuated. Foreign property was seized, looted, and occupied by one army or the other. Nanjing University, Ginling College for Women, Nanjing Seminary, Shandong Christian University and Hangzhou Christian College were all closed.

At Huaiyin (TKP) Dr. Nelson Bell turned his radio on at noon, 29 March, in time to hear the announcer say:

I have a very important message for Southern Presbyterians listening in at TKP. It is imperative that you evacuate immediately — travel north via Haichow and Tsingtao ... notify Hwaian, Sutsien, Hsuchowfu and Haichow.[10]

In Suqian the elders of the church insisted that the missionaries leave and promised to keep the school open and continue the work as best they could.[11]

In Lianyungang General Bei, the friend of the missionaries, was defeated by Zhang Zuolin and his "white Russian" mercenaries. The terrified people of the city flooded the mission compound and begged for protection while the soldiers looted and ravished the city. After Zhang's men were defeated and had withdrawn, a committee of "merchants, gentry, farmers, and students" sent a message to Consul John K. Davis at Nanking expressing heartfelt thanks for the assistance rendered by missionaries Morgan, Grafton, Vinson, McLauchlin and Currie in protecting and calming the distraught Lianyungang people at a time of great peril.[12]

The important rail junction of Xuzhou was a prize coveted by all. Missionaries there had received the Nanjing consul's warning but had paid it little attention. But when a telegram arrived from the ambassador in Peking, the station realized something serious had happened. Christian leaders urged their American colleagues to leave. All normal rail service had been suspended but word was received that a special train would be leaving for the north in two hours. "Fourteen adults, twelve children — with baskets, bedding rolls, water bottles, and what not, made a wild rush through the darkness to the train."[13] The normal eighteen-hour trip to Tianjin took two days because of delays waiting for troop trains moving south. Later most families went to Qingdao to wait for the time when they could return.

I was a boy of six, and I well remember the 1927 evacuation and the ride through the night to the station in rickshaws. Qingdao, with its wonderful beaches and friendly U.S. Navy ships in the harbor was not a bad place to "refugee." "Uncle Ben" (Dr. Benjamin Harding) was the favorite of the boys as he had a boat. There were great fourth of July celebrations when we were invited aboard the American ships to eat hot dogs and watch the submarines make their practice dives. When cold weather came, the missionary families took over the top floor of Castle Inn, the Qingdao hotel on the waterfront. Missionary kids had a hilarious good time. But for our fathers, who returned to mission station in Shandong and north Jiangsu, it was a time of danger, uncertainty and despair.

Rev. Frank Brown and Dr. Nettie Grier returned to Xuzhou several times during the intermittent battles for the control of the city. Everything was in turmoil, hospitals crowded to overflowing, refugees everywhere, mission residences looted and occupied by soldiers.

The same thing was happening all over north China. Missionary families were waiting it out in coastal cities. Medical personnel and the men were making every effort to return to their work. Some took emergency furloughs; some, leaves of absence to relieve the boards of financial responsibility; some were transferred to other lands. In 1927, the two Presbyterian boards reported that half of the 727 missionaries under appointment were in the United States or temporarily assigned to other countries. But by the time of the *Annual Report* a year later, most missionaries were back at their posts.[14]

Chaos and Confusion

For the Chinese people and the foreign missionaries in their midst the civil war was a disaster. It had a far more devastating effect on the countryside than either the Boxer Uprising, which was violent but short lived, or the 1911 Revolution, which had little loss of life. Militarism became the dominant way of life.

> The sense of moral community — the broad and pervasive consensus regarding the values and proper relationships of culture and social life, which had so richly contributed to the stability of traditional China — had disintegrated and in its place were confusion and contention.[15]

In 1930 there were 2.6 million men in the Nationalist armies.[16] Attempts to disband them simply made them into bandits. "All the bandits were ex-soldiers, and all soldiers were ex-bandits."[17] Traditionally, bandits preyed on the rich and left the common peasants alone. But the "Soldier banditry" of the late 1920s became predators of rich and poor alike and engaged in savage acts of cruelty if their exorbitant demands for ransom were not met. It is against this background of violence that the life and work of missionaries during this decade can be understood.

One positive result of the forced departures was the acceleration of the transfer of responsibilities to Chinese leaders. As missionaries prepared for evacuation they appointed committees to take over the station's work in their absence. An example was Xuzhou, where a hastily organized Committee of Eighteen (city pastors, elders, heads of hospitals and schools) was appointed just before the missionaries departed. It was given full authority for making all decisions: supervising the work, paying salaries, hiring and firing. The committee was subject to the same rules that had applied to the missionaries: financial statements, care of property, audits. Checks were mailed each month to the Committee by the mission treasurer in Shanghai.

Frank A. Brown reported on his first return to Xuzhou that all departments of the work were functioning well: hospitals overflowed with military and civilian patients; all twenty-nine primary schools were open; regular worship services were being held at all twenty-five country preaching points. Salaries were all paid on time. Accounts were carefully kept and audited. One new subcommittee had been organized — the "Red Cross Corporation" — to respond to calls for help from the battlefields.[18]

When the station was reactivated with the return of most of its members in September 1928, the chairman of the Committee of Eighteen made his final report, gave thanks for God's gracious care during the bad times and asked the missionaries to again take over.[19] A North China missionary reported some unexpected results of the missionary withdrawals:

> The temporary withdrawal of foreign staff has been a humbling and salutary experience for all of us. The foreign staff found that their Chinese

colleagues could get along perfectly well without them, and the Chinese found that they couldn't. . . . We each got a higher opinion of the other.[20]

In the early autumn of 1927 amid the intermittent clash of opposing armies, Jining station was reoccupied by Dr. and Mrs. W. F. Seymour, Rev. Charles M. Eames and Miss Mary Stewart. The hospital was reopened and the evangelistic work resumed. By April most of the northern soldiers had left and on 16 April the vanguard of southern soldiers entered the city and approached the mission. Dr. Seymour assured them there were no northern soldiers in the compound. Under circumstances difficult to understand, he was attacked by a soldier, who shot and killed him. The unit commander called to express regret and promised protection. No anti-foreign or anti-Christian motivation was apparent.[21]

In October 1931, John Walker Vinson visited one of his favorite churches at the village of Yang-Djia-Gee, some eighteen miles away from the mission station of Lianyungang. Bandits were active throughout the area but the trip was considered safe as the village was protected by a wall and one hundred militia. Saturday night six hundred bandits descended on the village, overwhelmed the militia and burned and looted everything in sight. Sunday evening they left the town with about 150 hostages including John Vinson. The next day, 4 November, government troops were in hot pursuit, and Vinson, who was not well, had difficulty keeping up with the escaping bandits. Vinson was offered his freedom if he would write a letter to the commanding officer of the government troops telling them to withdraw. Vinson asked if they would release all the other hostages as well. The bandit chief replied: "Certainly not." Vinson then declined his freedom. A bandit pointed a rifle at him and asked if he was afraid. Vinson, according to the story in the *New York Times,* replied, "If you shoot me I'll go straight to heaven." The bandit fired and Vinson was killed instantly.[22] Vinson's decapitated body was found by Rev. Edward Currie, who led the search party. His body was taken to Lianyungang where he was buried in the small missionary cemetery.

But his death did not end the story. John Vinson and his wife, Jeanie, had three children. Twin boys — Chal and Jack — both became missionaries and served in China. Their daughter, Jean Vinson Urquhart, served with her husband, Bob, as a missionary in Korea. John Vinson's colleague, Rev. E. H. Hamilton of Xuzhou, penned this poem in memory of the martyr's death:

> Afraid? Of what?
> To feel the spirit's glad release?
> To pass from pain to perfect peace,
> The strife and strain of life to cease?
> Afraid of that?
>
> Afraid? Of what?
> Afraid to see the Saviour's face,
> To hear His welcome, and to trace

The glory gleam from wounds of grace?
Afraid — of that?

Afraid? Of what?
A flash — a crash — a pierced heart;
Darkness — light — Oh, Heaven's art!
A wound of His a counterpart!
Afraid of that?

Afraid? Of what?
To enter into Heaven's rest,
And yet to serve the Master blest,
From service good to service best?
Afraid — of that?

Afraid? Of what?
To do by death what life could not:
Baptize with blood a stony plot,
Till souls shall blossom from the spot?
Afraid — of that?[23]

The Great Depression

The second calamity that struck the China missions was the Great Depression. Giving to missions and all church causes plummeted. For the Southern Presbyterian Church, the giving to the worldwide mission cause crested in the year 1928 ($1,490,922) and then began a steady decline for the next six years.[24] The bottom was reached in 1934 when $572,143 was received. For the Northern Presbyterians, mission giving reached its peak in 1929 ($4,149,188) and its bottom in 1936 ($2,030,966.)[25]

This drop of over 50 percent in income together with the emergency expenses of the 1927 evacuation had a crippling effect on the China missions. For the PCUSA the number of China missionaries declined each year for the next thirteen years. In the year 1940 there were two hundred fewer missionaries than in the peak year, 1924. Qujiang and Huizhou stations were closed and the Yunnan Mission transferred to the Lutheran Vandsburger Mission.

The effects of the depression for the Southern Church were probably even more severe. The home board went into debt from which it did not recover until the year 1942. Missionary salaries were cut by 20–30 percent. New appointments were curtailed. Furloughs were delayed. The China missionary force declined from a record 214 in the year 1925 to 126 in 1940.

A contributing factor to the drop in mission giving was the "fundamentalist-modernist" debate that was raging at home. Both PCUSA and PCUS mission boards suffered attacks from both the liberal and fundamentalist sides.

In 1930 an unofficial commission representing seven Protestant denominations, including the PCUSA, initiated an investigation of mission work called the

"Laymen's Inquiry of Foreign Missions." The commission, chaired by William Ernest Hocking, published its report in 1932 under the title *Re-Thinking Missions*.[26] The report, which was given wide publicity in the secular press, was highly critical of many phases of mission administration and activity. Its theological presuppositions caused most of the storm. These were "not those of traditional Christian orthodoxy" and regarded the Christian message as "based on universal rational principles...with a very uncertain place left for the historical Jesus."[27] The report had instant repercussions for all mainline Protestant denominations. The two Presbyterian boards expressed agreement with some of its suggestions but denounced in no uncertain terms its Christological basis. Dr. Robert E. Speer "was vigorous in his repudiation of the theology of the report."[28]

It was unfortunate that the storm over the Laymen's Inquiry occurred the same year that Pearl Buck was awarded the Pulitzer Prize for her novel *The Good Earth*. Pearl Buck, the most famous — and controversial — missionary to be appointed by the PCUSA Board was catapulted into being a world celebrity. In an article in the *Christian Century* she praised the Laymen's Inquiry and severely criticized the mission board and her fellow missionaries. This thrust her into the midst of the fundamentalist-modernist debate. J. Gresham Machen, who several years earlier had withdrawn from Princeton Seminary in a storm of theological controversy, used the Laymen's Inquiry and Pearl Buck's writings to show that the Board was guilty of "modernist tendencies" since it had in its employee a missionary with unorthodox views. When Pearl Buck sent in her resignation, Machen was furious that it was accepted "with regret," saying she should have been fired.[29]

Machen failed to win the support of either his presbytery or the General Assembly and proceeded in 1933 to organize the Independent Board of Foreign Missions for "Bible-Believing" Presbyterians. Efforts to win the support of missionaries largely failed. In 1933 the PCUSA China Council expressed its strong support of the Board then confronting "financial depression" and "critical attacks from various sources."[30] Only one missionary couple, Rev. and Mrs. Albert B. Dodd, resigned from the China mission to join the new body. But the controversy created an uproar in the home church that inevitably weakened its mission cause.

The Anti-Christian Movement

The third calamity that struck the China missions was the Anti-Christian Movement and of the three it is the most difficult to analyze. To understand it we must go back to the year 1919 and the origins of what came to be called the May Fourth Movement.

At the Versailles Peace Conference China's representatives were pressured into conceding to Japan's demands for German concessions in Shandong. When word of the agreement reached Peking, three thousand students assembled on

4 May 1919 at the Tiananmen (Gate of Heavenly Peace), held a massive demonstration and issued a manifesto protesting the action. Patriotic Chinese felt betrayed. China, too, had supported the Allied cause and had contributed a hundred thousand laborers for work on the docks and trenches in France. Strikes broke out all over China. The concessions were repudiated and China never signed the Versailles treaty.

The movement released the pent-up fury of China's youth, who lashed out at China's betrayers (government officials) and China's exploiters (Western powers). Their list of grievances included the ineptness of the bureaucracy, the Unequal Treaties, China's male patriarchy and special privileges for the foreigners. China should free itself both from the stranglehold of Confucian conservatism and the shackles of the foreign colonial system.

The movement created a new class of citizens — the students — who became the self-appointed custodians of the nation's honor. They were a force that would have to be reckoned with by every aspirant for China rule — Chiang Kai-shek, the Japanese military, Mao Zedong and Deng Xiaoping.

Initially the movement was not primarily anti-Christian or anti-missionary. Indeed, most students in mission schools supported the crusade. But inevitably, many Chinese youth came to identify the foreigner with the governing elite. They saw the missionary as the principal of the school, the president of the college, the dispenser of discipline or the paymaster who had control over huge sums of money that came from abroad. This was only a caricature but from the students' perspective it is the one that fit. Fairbank has this remark on the changing role of the missionary after 1900:

> To get a balance sheet on this problem, I would suggest first of all that the missionaries began as subversives, undermining and attacking an old order that was overdue for change.... But if the first impact of Christianity was a tremendous stimulus to change, gradually after 1900 another phase began.... The missionary contribution in the twentieth century continued to be one of leadership toward reform, but at the same time the missionary institutions and their administrators became part of the established order.[31]

The first missionary confrontations with the May Fourth Movement came at Yenching University. Dr. Leighton Stuart had just begun his tenure as president when the city and the university were plunged into the crisis created by the demonstrations. Most of the students did not hear Stuart's inaugural address as they were locked up in Peking prisons. Most of the university administrators of the day took the side of law and order. But in a bold move, Stuart sided with the students. He declared that the May Fourth Movement had given Yenching "a great opportunity for service in this important crisis" and in an open letter to missionaries wrote "I hope you can feel with us the thrilling import of this student movement."[32]

Confrontation between Christianity and the students came when the World

Student Christian Federation scheduled a conference in Peking in 1922. This worldwide gathering of Christian students resulted in the outbreak of anti-Christian demonstrations. Meetings scheduled for the provincial capitals had to be cancelled because of the threat of disturbances.[33]

Most Westerners probably did not take the May Fourth Movement with enough seriousness. But another incident in 1925 provoked a new wave of public outrage that could not be ignored. On 30 May British police in Shanghai fired on Chinese students who were demonstrating against the killing of a Chinese workman by Japanese guards at a textile mill. Eleven demonstrators were killed. Dr. Hawks Potts, the president of St. John's University, prohibited his students from demonstrating. A strike was called and classes were suspended.[34] Demonstrations broke out in twenty-eight other cities. Japanese and British goods were boycotted.

The principal target of the anti-foreign movement was the Unequal Treaties which granted special privileges to foreigners. On this matter the missionary community was coming to a consensus. Whatever its necessity in the past, its usefulness had passed. James Bear wrote from Shanghai in 1929:

> All missionaries (and I might say practically all foreigners), favor the doing away with the "unequal treaties" as soon as possible.[35]

The issue was one of timing. "As soon as possible" meant when there was a strong central government with which a treaty could be made. In 1925 the Shandong Mission sent to the American consul a resolution that "strongly advocated the progressive revision of the so-called unequal treaties."[36]

Some progress was being made in treaty revisions. Great Britain gave up a number of concessions. Japan was forced to give up the German concessions in Shandong. In a significant revision of the treaties in 1928, China achieved tariff autonomy.

The May Fourth Movement affected the activity of the missions in a number of ways. Mission schools were the hardest hit. The Hunan Mission reported that all their "schools felt the effects, more or less, of the anti-Christian agitation."[37] School enrollment dropped. Discipline became more difficult. Student-initiated strikes forced the suspension and in some cases the closing of schools. Issues were seldom related to religion but to local matters such as the firing of a favorite teacher or the boycott of Japanese goods. Candidates for the ministry applying to Nanjing Seminary declined by 50 percent.[38] Anti-Christian literature made outreach to non-Christians more difficult.

In the larger cities, labor unions provoked strikes at mission establishments. Three venerable institutions had to be closed: the Canton Hospital, the Kerr Asylum for the Insane, and the Shanghai Presbyterian Mission Press. Issues were confused but administrators believed the agitation was initiated by radical groups that had infiltrated the working force.[39]

Most to be feared was that the anti-foreign agitation would drive a wedge between the Chinese Christians and the missionaries. For the anti-Christian movement put Chinese Christians in an awkward position. As Christians, they could not but reject the fundamental tenets of a movement that opposed Christianity. But as Chinese, they could not but agree that some of the criticisms of the movement were valid. Dr. Timothy Tingfang Lew, theologian, hymn-writer and fifth-generation Christian, warned mission board members in America of the danger of "post mortem first aid" — instigating measures that bring temporary relief rather than permanent solutions.[40] R. Leung Siu Choh, chairman of the Guangdong Christian Council, spoke for many of his Chinese colleagues in his address to missionaries:

> While we all agree that the great bulk of criticism made by the recent Anti-Christian Movement against the Christian Church is unreasonable and unjust, we Chinese Christians, however, find ourselves in a very awkward situation for the fact that we cannot make a satisfactory reply to some of the criticisms in the light of the present organization of the Church and of Missions.[41]

Mr. Choh had some specific suggestions for his missionary colleagues. All mission activities and programs should be expressed through the Chinese church. The Chinese church should then deal directly with the overseas mission boards. Except for salaries and allowances for missionary maintenance, all other funds should be turned over to the Chinese church council.[42]

Most of these principles would be readily accepted today. But in the mid-1920s they were considered revolutionary. And in the chaotic state of revolutionary China in 1927 it is difficult to see how they could have been implemented. Yet the questions they raised were of such critical importance that the future of the missionary enterprise depended on their resolution.

Devolution

"Devolution" it was called — "the process of transferring authority and responsibility for mission work from the foreign missionaries to the Chinese Christians."[43] In the mid-1920s it became the number-one agenda item for North American missions.

In 1926 Robert E. Speer, Secretary, and Hugh T. Kerr, Chairman of the Board of Foreign Missions, arrived in China for a series of conferences at Ji-nan, Nanking and Canton to resolve some of these issues. The meetings were held with open and frank discussions. Two divergent trends were debated:

> In some regions mission and church plan to move along parallel but somewhat independent lines though with mutual consultation and hearty cooperation. In other regions the missionary relaxes his relation to the mission to strengthen his relation to the church which assumes almost complete control over his location and activities.[44]

Each of the China missions chose its own direction but sought some middle ground between the two extremes — the independence of the mission organization apart from the church and its absorption by the church. In general the following principles were followed:

Presbyteries. The work assigned and done by presbyteries would be enlarged and strengthened. As the presbyteries were all male preserves, it was agreed that women would be added to their work committees.

Joint Boards. Middle schools and hospitals would be governed by joint boards of church leaders and missionaries. For the union schools and colleges this had already taken place.

Missions. The China missions and their stations would continue their function of providing logistical support for the missionary, maintaining relationships with the home church and dealing with matters not yet undertaken by the Chinese church. The mission was considered a "temporary agency" whose functions would be transferred to the church as speedily as possible.

The China Council. The Council would continue to represent the home board and coordinate the work of the PCUSA missions.[45]

The Missionary. Missionary assignments for evangelistic work would normally be made by the presbytery. Assignments to other forms of service would be made by the committee or board responsible for that activity. Dr. Andrew Roy, who arrived in China with his wife, Margaret, in 1930, wrote that "in all our years in China, we worked by invitation and under the direction of Chinese colleagues, with occasional advice from older missionaries and friends."[46]

At the consultations, Dr. Speer expressed his deep concern about the lack of self-support. It was the same concern he had expressed thirty years earlier on his visit in 1897. "So long as the Church is economically dependent it is not and cannot be independent."[47] He was frustrated by Chinese Christians and missionaries alike who "dragged their feet on self-support."

> There were times when Dr. Kerr and I were driven nearly to despair in discussing the ideal of self-support with Chinese groups. And there were many missionaries, too, who have grown so accustomed to the use of money in the work ... that even some of them relax the pressure, which is relaxed only at the peril of the life of the Church itself.[48]

Speer called attention to the disappointing record of self-support reached by the Chinese churches. Statistics for the year ending 30 June 1926 indicated that there were only 32 self-supporting Churches in all the China Missions. "Clearly, something must be done."[49]

In 1928 the PCUS Executive Committee directed its two China missions to each appoint its own evaluation committee to visit each station and interview missionaries and Chinese. A thorough evaluation of the work was to be made in the light of the anti-foreign agitation and the necessity for budget reductions.

The plan outlined by the Evaluation Committee of the Mid-China Mission indicates that they operated in much the same way as that of the PCUSA

Central China Mission with which they closely worked. Evangelistic funds were allocated to presbyteries. A cooperative committee in each station had "full authority over the various forms of educational, evangelistic and medical work."[50] Joint boards operated the schools. The hospitals followed three different plans of administration. The Elizabeth Blake Hospital in Suzhou was under direct mission control. The Jiaxing Hospital was under a board chosen by the Synod with one-fourth missionary and three-fourths Chinese representation. The Jiangyin Hospital was under a local joint committee. All three plans seemed to be working with a fair degree of success under different local conditions.[51]

The Evaluation Committee of the North Jiangsu Mission took a different tack. The Committee viewed mission and church as two separate entities. The mission would operate its programs separate from the church until the church was able to support them. This, they believed, was the best way to develop an independent, self-supporting church. It did not look on the establishment of joint committees with favor.[52]

However, with some reluctance, it gave Xuzhou Station permission to experiment locally on its own plan for a cooperative committee. So in 1928 the station formed a cooperate committee of ten members — five elected by the Christian community and five elected by the mission. The committee had oversight of all the evangelistic, educational and medical work. The plan worked well and was continued into the 1930s.[53]

To Register or Not to Register

The most divisive issue to arise in the late 1920s was the matter of school registration. In earlier days, only government run schools were registered and the mission schools were on their own. But in 1925 regulations were issued by the Peking government that required all private schools to register. But due to the unsettled conditions these regulations could not be enforced.

In 1929 when the Nationalists had succeeded in "unifying" most of the country, the demand again was made that all private schools be registered. This time the issue could no longer be ignored. The requirements for registration were: (1) certain conditions relating to property and income had to be met; (2) schools had to follow the prescribed curriculum; (3) the school principle had to be a Chinese citizen; (4) membership of school board had to be two-thirds Chinese; and (5)

> A private school founded by a religious body is not permitted to give religion as a required subject, nor is religious propaganda permitted in the class instruction. If there are any religious exercises, students should not be compelled or induced to participate. No religious exercises should be allowed in primary schools.[54]

Requirements 1–4 gave no difficulty and were readily accepted. The crux of the matter lay in regulation number 5, which missionaries and Chinese Christians believed was an infraction of the principle of religious freedom. How would the regulation prohibiting "religious propaganda" be interpreted? Particularly disturbing was the provision that no "religious exercises," even on a voluntary basis, could be given in primary schools. Some provinces (Hunan) had additional requirements that were even more obnoxious: The government would determine the school budgets and assign a teacher to teach revolutionary philosophy.[55] Another concern was the requirement that there would be weekly services where all students would stand, bow and meditate before a portrait of Sun Yat-sen.

In an attempt to resolve the issue, fifteen Chinese church denominations united in presenting a petition to the Ministry of Education in July 1930. The petition was "to allow all grades of church schools to have elective religious courses and to permit the primary grades to have the privilege of worship." The reply was courteous but a decisive no — "Let this be considered final and not subject to further review."[56]

It was now decision time. Opinions differed widely among the missionaries. Most Chinese Christians favored registering the schools rather than closing them and then working out the best conditions they could get. The education of their sons and daughters in a Christian environment was at stake. There were no easy options, but in the end the missions and schools chose one of the following courses of action:

1. Continue the school but delay registration as long as possible, hoping for a more opportune time when the government would relax its restrictions.[57]

2. Register the school and comply with all the regulations but make the Christian statement of purpose explicit. The school would continue to bear witness to its Christian character in every way it could — through Christian faculty, extracurricular activities and religious services where possible.[58]

3. Turn the school property over to the presbytery or board of Chinese Christians under a renewable contract from one to three years. The Chinese board would manage the school, deal with the government and make whatever compromises were necessary. Missionaries would still teach but would have no administrative responsibility. Mission subsidies would be continued but at a considerably reduced amount.[59]

4. Close the schools outright. If Christian instruction and worship could not be assured, why should the mission use personnel and funds to run secular schools according to the dictates of the state?[60]

To some extent all of the above options were followed as local situations differed widely. As some schools were closed the number of mission schools declined by about a third.[61]

For several years the universities and colleges supported by the Presbyterian missions were battered by strikes, occupation by revolutionary armies, declining budgets, the anti-Christian movement and the government requirements for registration. Yet, surprisingly, by 1933 all had weathered the storm, were in the process of registering and were open for classes.

Recovery

By the year 1932 there were signs of recovery. The Nationalist government had strengthened its control over the countryside. The war lords had not been eliminated but were gradually being subdued by the central government. Bandit raids had become less frequent. The anti-Christian movement of the 1920s had began to fade. In 1931 Frank Rawlinson, editor of the *Chinese Recorder,* noted that "Christian activity had risen...work is again moving forward...the spirit of violent antagonism to Christianity has notably subsided."[62] By the year 1933 the change of climate was even more noticeable:

> Japan had replaced Westerners as a prime target for national hostility....
> The spring of 1933 brought reports of a shift in national attitudes....
> [There was] a growing pro-Christian attitude on the part of the national
> government.[63]

Mission schools were able to continue their Christian witness with less interference than had been feared. In Changde "every student elected a Bible course and attended worship."[64] In Nanxuzhou "the Senior Middle School was registered but the entire school was present at chapel services on a voluntary basis."[65] In North China the primary schools did not register but were not interfered with by the government.[66] Ming Deh Girls' School reported an increased enrollment (483) and almost 100 percent attendance at voluntary chapel and Bible classes.[67]

These were years of expansion for the Christian colleges. Ginling, Nanking University, Hangzhou College, Shandong Christian College and Yenching all reported high enrollments and satisfactory participation in campus worship and elective classes in religion. For the Nanjing Theological Seminary it was the "Period of Great Development." The astonishing Wendel-Swope bequest of $2.5 million provided new opportunities for development.[68]

Church membership reversed its decline and started moving up again. The Mid China Mission reported a net loss of 1,300 church members between the years 1927 and 1930 but then membership began to rise and reached an all-time high of about 5,000 communicant members by the year 1931.[69] In the North Jiangsu Mission the reversal of the downward trend came in 1932 and membership reached a high of 10,500 members in 1937.[70] Beginning in 1930 PCUSA church membership statistics are included within the Church of Christ in China and become more difficult to track.

By the early 1930s the worst of the depression years had passed. In the three years 1930–1932, the PCUSA sent sixty-two new missionaries to China. This was scarcely enough to make up for the losses but it did indicate a more stable situation at home.

New Initiatives

The Nanjing regime of the KMT that ruled China for the 1927–1937 decade has been much maligned by history. Its shortcomings have been well documented. Yet for the missionary community the degree of security and peace "exceeded anything China had known since the brief republican interlude of 1912."[71]

Political stability and a more or less peaceful countryside provided an environment for new opportunities. George Hudson of Jiaxing pioneered in tent evangelism. Revival services were led by nationally known evangelists. Ten-day Bible classes for country Christians during the slack winter months became the norm. The publication of Christian literature exceeded all expectations.

The Nanjing regime made overtures to mission and church organizations to cooperate with the government in various social reform programs. The church's response was not without some ambivalence. It wished to take advantage of the new opportunities but was wary of developing too cozy a relationship with the KMT. Yet the various missions and Christian agencies did engage in many cooperative efforts aimed at national reconstruction and reform. The disastrous Yellow River floods of 1936 initiated a partnership between the missionaries and the China International Famine Relief Commission. Frank Brown put to work three thousand starving refugees from the flooded areas near Xuzhou to work on improving the dirt roads. Agencies such as the YMCA, YWCA, the National Christian Council, the Guangxi Christian Rural Service Union, Christian colleges, the North China Christian Rural Service Union and Jimmy Yen's Tinghsien Institute all became involved in national reconstruction. Missionary George Shepherd served for some years as advisor for the KMT New Life Movement. All tried, with varying degrees of success, to bring reform through education, social service and community development.

During these years two features of the Presbyterian program stand out.

Women's Work

The 1930s was the decade of the women. Women missionaries steadily gained ground in exercising positions of leadership as they now made up two-thirds of the mission body. Women missionaries of the PCUSA were given the right to vote at mission meetings around the year 1915. Voting rights for women of the Southern Presbyterian missions came a few years later in the 1920s. The issue of a separate department for women's work within the PCUSA China Council was first proposed in 1920. It was first rejected but in 1923 the issue came up again and Miss Margaret A. Frame was elected to the position of Secretary for Women's Work and served for many years in this capacity.[72] Miss Margaret Moninger was elected by the Hainan Mission to various positions of leadership — mission secretary, treasurer, board correspondent and representative on the China Council.

Single women missionaries, with no family of their own, were able to penetrate cultural boundaries, "adopt" Chinese young people and immerse themselves in the Chinese society. The impact they made on individuals — young and old, men and women, rich and poor — will never be known.

An example of many such women was Marguerite Mizell of Taizhou. At a young people's fellowship she met a young middle school teacher named Wang Weifan. Through Miss Mizell, Weifan heard the word of the Lord. Then came baptism and a call to the ministry which Weifan first rejected. But through tumultuous years of hardship during the Cultural Revolution, the mysterious "call" received through Miss Mizell persisted until it was claimed. Today Professor Wang, hymn-writer, poet and professor at the Nanjing Theological Seminary, is engaged in the task of constructing a Chinese Christian theology.[73]

During the decade, training schools for "Bible women" came into their own. These did not require registration and in a number of cases utilized the property of middle schools that had been closed. Bible Schools provided simple training for older women, often widows, who became indispensable in starting new churches. They were the "shock troops" able to penetrate a new village and begin services in homes — before it was possible to secure the services of an ordained minister.

During the decade strides were made in improving women's rights. The incessant campaigns against footbinding that had been launched by missionary women were finally showing results. In 1936 a survey of rural communities reported that the practice was "decreasing rapidly."[74] The survey also reported that great strides were being made in raising the social standing of women. All Christian colleges had become co-educational except for Ginling, one of the few all-women colleges in the country.

The Rural Church

During the decade there was a growing realization that special attention needed to be given to the country church and the rural community. Two-thirds of the Christians of China lived in the country. Piecemeal efforts in literacy or public health were not enough. An integrated effort needed to be made, first to understand the nature of rural society and second, to develop an integrated model of ministry.

One of the most successful programs was started by the Nanjing Theological Seminary's Rural Training Center at the market town of Shunwachen in 1933 under the direction of Dr. Frank W. Price. Eight acres of farm land and the erection of simple buildings got the program started. Here in a typical rural environment students learned how the rural church could participate in programs of literacy, health, youth clubs and cooperatives.[75]

During the years 1933–1937 Dr. Price conducted an extensive survey of the rural church in China. Teams visited all rural congregations in three nearby provinces — Anhui, Jiangsu, and Zhejiang. Questionnaires were sent to 122 representative rural churches all over China.[76]

From this survey, conducted on the eve of the Japanese invasion, a remarkable picture of a vibrant rural church emerged. "Protestant Christianity was taking root in the villages."[77] There were ten thousand rural churches in China, one-third of which had resident pastors. Twenty percent said that they were entirely self-supporting. The rural church was growing faster than the church in the cities. Significantly, the Wenzhou area of southern Zhejiang was noted as having the strongest concentration of churches.[78] This is the area in China today in which the rural churches are probably the strongest.[79]

The Maturing of the Mission

Professor Daniel Bays has spoken of the period from 1925 to 1950 as "Missions on the Decline."[80] But perhaps a better title would be "The Maturing of the Mission." The decade of the 1930s marks the transition from mission to church. In 1937 the Presbyterian enterprise in China was one hundred years old. It was high time that the mission should decrease in order that the church might increase.

But this did not happen without pain and anguish. For it meant giving up control, which is never easy. Some missionaries left China during the 1927 general evacuation and never returned. They could not make the necessary adjustments.

Nevertheless, the transition was made. As the number of ordained missionaries plummeted, the number of ordained Chinese leaders rose sharply.[81] Statistics of the Shandong Mission in 1938 reported twenty-four ordained missionaries and eighty-one ordained Chinese pastors. Rev. John Minter (PCUS) and Rev. Paul Lindholm (PCUSA) were the only missionary members of Kiangan Presbytery, with twenty-six ordained Chinese pastors.[82]

It was the same with the hospitals. In 1927 there were more missionary physicians than nationals. By 1937 there were twice as many Chinese doctors as missionaries. Patient load increased but more of the work was being done by national staff.[83]

During the decade the management of schools and hospitals shifted to Chinese boards. Joint committees were taking over. Ecumenical cooperation was being strengthened through the Church of Christ in China and the National Christian Council of China. Church — Mission relationships were entering a new phase.

But the time was cut short. The year 1937 was the last "normal" year for Protestant missions during the Nanjing regime. After that came the great war of Japanese aggression.

14

Under Fire

1937–1952

On 7 July 1937 a company of Japanese garrison troops on maneuvers fired on a Chinese patrol at the "Marco Polo Bridge" near Peking. Chinese troops returned the fire. This minor military engagement initiated a major Japanese offensive and became known as the first battle of World War II.[1]

A number of events led up to the outbreak of the conflict. Japan's march toward the conquest of East Asia had begun six years earlier with the "Manchurian Incident" of 18 September 1931. Japanese militarists had become alarmed at China's growing strength and decided that if Manchuria was to be incorporated into the Empire they would have to act soon. Units of Japan's Kwantung Army, probably acting independently of the civilian authorities in Tokyo, blew up a portion of the railroad tracks north of Shenyang. The bomb explosion was blamed on a nearby Chinese garrison and served as an excuse for the mobilization of Japanese troops. The vacillating civilian government in Tokyo was unable to restrain their military forces, which were soon on the way to taking over southern Manchuria.

Events followed in quick succession. The League of Nations appointed a commission to investigate Japan's act of aggression. Japan announced the establishment of the puppet state of "Manchukuo" with Puyi, the last Emperor of the Manchu dynasty, as its head. In January 1932 Japanese marines landed at Shanghai and ruthlessly bombed Chapei, the crowded Chinese area of the city. Worldwide public opinion was outraged by photographs of the carnage. The Chinese Nationalist Nineteenth Route Army fought the Japanese to a standstill and won international acclaim. In February 1933 the League of Nations censured Japan for its aggression in Manchuria. Japanese delegates walked out of the League, never to return. Shaken by the turn of international events and dissent at home, Japan offered China peace terms. Chiang Kai-shek, unable to stop Japan's aggression, felt he had no recourse but to accept Japan's offer. The terms of the Tanggu Truce, signed in May 1933, were humiliating for China and virtually gave up Manchuria. In turn, Japan agreed to seek no further territorial ambitions in China. The truce bought China three years of time.

Chiang's first priority was the elimination of the Communist base area in

Jiangxi through a series of "extermination" campaigns. But in October 1934 the Communists succeeded in breaking through the encircling armies, and began their "Long March" — a six-thousand-mile trek through China's hinterland into Shaanxi, where they established their headquarters in the city of Yanan. It is hard to overestimate the importance of the Long March for the CCP. It delivered them from the inept bungling of Russian advisors, established Mao Zedong as undisputed leader and became a national epic comparable to the children of Israel's exodus from Egypt. With the Communists isolated in the remote northwest the warfare between Chiang and Mao was put "on hold."

Chiang's truce with the Japanese was not popular. In particular it rankled one of Chiang's generals, Zhang Xueliang, whose father had been assassinated by the Japanese. In one of the bizarre incidents of the times, Zhang seized the generalissimo while he was inspecting troops in Xian and held him captive for thirteen days. During this tense period Mao Zedong's deputy Zhou Enlai helped negotiate Chiang's release on the grounds that a united front against Japan needed a live Chiang and KMT support. On Christmas day 1936 Chiang was released and flew back to the capital. Spontaneous celebrations broke out all over China. Terms reached between Chiang, his captors and the Yanan Communists have remained a mystery. Whatever they were, Chiang's resistance to Japan stiffened and cooperation with the CCP was initiated to prepare for the inevitable conflict with Japan.

The War of Japanese Aggression

It was in this context of national and international events that Japan launched the sweeping attack on north China following the Marco Polo Bridge incident. Was the incident provoked with the deliberate intent of starting an all-out war or was it an unplanned accident? What seems most likely is that Japan miscalculated China's response. The earlier settlement in Manchuria had come easily and the Japanese military thought they could "bully" China into one more concession. But Chiang refused to surrender another inch of territory and prepared for an all-out war. This time the nation was solidly behind him.

As hostilities began, Chiang, in a risky gamble, shifted some of his best armies from North China to Shanghai. Initially the Chinese outnumbered the Japanese and fought well. But when the Japanese landed a force in Hangzhou Bay to the rear of the Chinese army, the Chinese retreated in disorder toward Nanjing.

The Japanese captured the Nationalist capital in December 1937 and there followed the notorious "rape of Nanjing." Japan expected Chinese resistance to collapse with the taking of the capital. But China fought on as the capital was moved to Wuhan. Following Chiang's "scorched earth" strategy, the armies retreated westward into the mountainous regions of China's vast hinterland.

Japanese forces moved down the railroads to seize control of north China. At the southern Shandong town of Taierzhuang they fell into a trap and their army was decimated with a loss of forty thousand men. The victory, although an isolated one, demonstrated the fact that Japan was not invincible and that Chinese troops could fight and win battles.

The strategic rail junction of Xuzhou fell in May 1938. Kaifeng was next but here the defenders of the city opened the dikes of the Yellow River, sending an avalanche of water across the path of the invaders. The advance was halted for a time but at enormous cost to Chinese villages in the path of the river.[2] Wuhan, the new capital, fell in October. Again Japan expected the Chinese to capitulate, but again Chiang refused to surrender. The capital was moved to Chongqing, beyond the Yangtze gorges.

By the end of 1938 the war had been in progress for eighteen months. Some of Chiang's armies had fought well. But many of the Chinese commanders "were hesitant and cowardly . . . and had enjoyed regional autonomy too long to risk their lives and power at Chiang Kai-shek's command."[3] But the national will to resist had not collapsed. Under KMT control were the provinces in the far west and southwest. The Communist's Eighth Route Army held Shaanxi and its newly organized Fourth Army much of Shanxi. The Chinese strategy was to wage a war of attrition and wear down the invader by attacking Japan's long lines of communication.

The Japanese controlled the eastern seaboard, the major cities and the railroads. Casualties had been much higher than expected. Realizing that a continued westward advance would exhaust their armies, they were content to tighten the economic blockade and bomb the inland cities into submission. For the next three years there was little change in the battle lines.

Missions in the Path of Destruction

About 350 Presbyterian missionaries were in China in 1937 when hostilities began. They were at work in forty-one mission stations, of which thirty-one were in the path of the Japanese onslaught. The immediate question facing them and the home boards was whether a general evacuation was in order. Would it be like 1927 all over again? Then the presence of the foreigner was a liability. This time the presence of American missionaries would undoubtedly be encouraging to the Christian community and the nation. Dr. Nelson Bell spoke for many: "If missionaries stay out now they will miss the grandest chance God ever gave them for winning the confidence and love of the people."[4]

For the first time, the missionary endeavor was perceived by Chinese patriots as being on the side of Chinese nationalism. The threat to China's sovereignty came no longer from Western but from Japanese imperialism. The Unequal Treaties had become a moot issue. The presence of British and American navy ships in the harbors and rivers served as a deterrent to the invaders.

As the Japanese war machine rolled south, one by one the mission compounds were overrun. Missionaries were advised by their consuls to leave but were told that if they insisted on staying they should display the American flag prominently on the gates, walls and roofs of American property.

At Shunde the gates to the mission compound were flung open as fifteen hundred women and children poured in to escape the ravages of the Japanese soldiers.[5] It was a scene that was repeated again and again in the coming months.

When Yixian in southern Shandong was overrun, three thousand refugees flooded the Catholic and Protestant compounds. They occupied mission buildings, slept on church benches and built shelters from straw mats. During the day foraging parties went out to gather food. Nettie Junkin has described the cooking procedure:

> Food thus gathered was put into huge caldrons in the yards — everything dumped into a stew. It was not too appetizing but it was nourishing and no one went hungry. We all shared.[6]

The Japanese air force subjected Jiangyin, with its strategic forts guarding the narrow point of the Yangtze, to an intense air bombardment in preparation for an attack on the city. The Christian leaders and missionaries (Rev. and Mrs. Andrew Allison, Marion Wilcox, Katheryne Thompson) met and decided it was time to evacuate the city. They would remain together as a group in order to provide mutual support. Three houseboats bearing eighty Chinese Christians and the four missionaries sailed up a little-used canal and took refuge in a small village some fifteen miles out of the city. The missionaries remained on their houseboats and the others found lodging in the homes of villagers. Here they established a refugee Christian community that remained intact for the next six months. Not only did they survive but they used their time well — in setting up a school for children, holding Bible classes and preaching in nearby temples. Later they were offered an abandoned school building on the condition that they would start a clinic. This they did with the help of a Chinese Christian doctor and Dr. Alex Moffett, who joined the group.

A few days after the compound was evacuated Japanese aircraft bombed it in broad daylight despite the clear marking of the U.S. flag. What the bombers did not destroy, the troops did. Household furnishings, hospital beds and school equipment were piled up, doused with kerosene and set on fire.[7]

The Elizabeth Blake Hospital in Suzhou was filled to overflowing as the Japanese army approached the city. Five hundred wounded were received in one day from the aerial bombardment. Dr. Mason Young went out to meet the Japanese commander under a flag of truce to plead for the people of the city. The commander was noncommittal. When the city fell the city and hospital were systematically looted and destroyed. Dr. Young's responsibility included forty-five inmates in the mental wards of the hospital. These he could not abandon. As the bombs were falling and night approaching, he and Lucy Grier, R.N., shepherded the distraught mental patients some fifteen miles along the canal tow path to safety. The patients remained quiet and obedient. Not one was lost.

Later travel passes were secured for travel to Shanghai, where the patients were admitted to a hospital.[8]

After Suzhou came the Rape of Nanjing:

> Nanking fell to the Japanese on 12–13 December 1937, after which the Japanese offensive slowed while their troops engaged in the most shameful episode of the war, the "rape of Nanking." During seven weeks of savagery, at least 42,000 Chinese were murdered in cold blood, many of them buried alive or set afire with kerosene. About 20,000 women were raped.[9]

But it could have been even worse if it had not been for the heroic efforts of an international committee that negotiated with the Japanese Embassy in Peking for recognition of a five-square-mile area within the city walls as a Safety Zone that the Japanese would refrain from bombing or occupying with their troops. A German layman was elected the chairman of the Zone and George Fitch, YMCA secretary, its director. Before leaving, the mayor of the city turned over administrative responsibility for the Zone to the committee along with two thousand tons of rice, ten thousand bags of flour and $50,000 in cash. The zone was cleared of all military personnel and anti-aircraft guns. Twenty-five refugee camps using the University of Nanjing, Ginling College and public buildings were set up. Seventy-five thousand refugees, mostly women and children, were received into the zone. On 14 December Japanese troops arrived. What followed next is described by George Fitch:

> Complete anarchy reigned for ten days — it has been a hell on earth. Not that my life has been in serious danger at any time; though turning lust-mad, sometimes drunken soldiers, out of houses where they are raping women is not altogether a safe operation. Nor does one feel too sure of himself when he finds a bayonet at his chest or a revolver at his head and knows it is handled by some one who heartily wishes him out of the way. For the Japanese is anything but pleased at our being here.... They wanted no observers.[10]

Some order was maintained within the Zone, but apparently the Japanese army did not recognize the agreements made by their embassy. All accounts mention the heroic service to protect the women and children by the missionary ladies at Ginling. The University Hospital, with a depleted staff, was the only one in operation during those terrible days.

Following the Rape of Nanking refugees streamed northward toward the city of Huayuan. The Chinese troops evacuated the city without a fight but the "non-combatant population suffered the same fate as had been the case in almost every other city occupied and the only places of even comparative safety were the compounds of our mission and the Catholic mission."[11] The task of guarding the compound gates and turning away the rampant soldiers was done by the missionary women and Dr. Robert McCandliss, for any Chinese in this role would have been shot. Dr. McCandliss described the scene:

> Picture our street, a long walled alley with heavy wooden gates opening into half a dozen compounds of our schools and hospitals. If you come from the south, you will see Helen Boughton, sitting on a bench outside the gate, rising and bowing to each group of soldiers.... Further on to the right is the Girls' School where Mabel Hall is busy at the gate receiving refugees.... Next on the left is the Woman's School gate where Hattie MacCurdy remains inside, waiting for the gateman to inform her of approaching soldiers. Further on ... is the Men's Hospital where I am meeting all comers.... Diagonally opposite is the Women's Hospital, where Betty Turner is on guard.[12]

For three days Dr. McCandliss sat by the gate of the compound, and dared not leave even for his meals. As time went on the Japanese guards became more friendly and gave reasonably good protection. Japanese officers were appreciative of the treatment provided some of their comrades by Dr. McCandliss.[13]

On 19 May 1938 Japanese troops entered the strategic railroad junction of Xuzhou after extensive bombing for nine months. Dr. Nettie D. Grier, Dr. and Mrs. A. A. McFadyen and Rev. and Mrs. Frank A. Brown were in the city at the time. They had prepared as best they could. At the bank's suggestion, all funds were withdrawn. American flags were put on the compound gates. Frank Brown wrote of the events of the next two days:

> *May 19.* About 7 A.M. five Japanese tanks pass within three hundred yards of our house — no firing; — then the Japanese infantry appear. Then we heard the heaviest bombardment that we have heard by Japanese planes over the East Suburb.... Fires everywhere.... ALL IS OVER. Two Japanese appear at our gate but do not molest us. We are much relieved. We hear the Japanese have killed the twenty or more wounded Chinese soldiers they found in the military hospital I visited the other night — bayonetted them. Looting began.

> *May 20.* called on the West Suburb to see how our two doctors [Grier and McFadyen] are doing. All safe.... Called on the Japanese General and was well received and promised protection. A dead city; not a Chinese seen; but many Japanese soldiers. The city has been 100 percent looted — we couldn't find a single door unbroken, though travelled over the city in the car with an American flag on it.... Called on the Catholics. Their compound like ours to be protected.

> *May 20–June 12.* We have 2,600 refugees and the Catholics 1,700 more. ... Japanese soldiers search men and women and rob them of even ten cent pieces. The atrocities against women are frightful.... Women stand at our gates begging to be taken in. We are doing our best.[14]

Far to the south, Canton underwent 250 air raids and finally fell in October 1938 when an attacking force landed on the unprotected coast. Mission schools and the Synod of the Church of Christ in China moved to the protection of Hong Kong. The refugee story was the same as in the other cities. Ten thousand were protected in the mission compounds. The Hackett Medical Center "was the only place where surgical attention could be given to the numerous casualties of fires, bombings, and shooting."[15]

The Japanese began bombing the island of Hainan in 1937 and landed on the island in February 1939. Haikou and Qiongzhou were very quickly taken. But Ledong in the interior was a different matter. Fighting broke out every evening between the guerrillas and the invaders. The mission compound was overrun with refugees — who climbed the walls to get in. Mrs. Edric Burkwall and Ms. Margaret Moninger stood at the gate trying to limit those who came in to women, children, boys under fourteen and men over sixty. Every evening Mr. Melrose would "rout out the men and lock the gate." Both sides respected the neutrality of the compound and its refugee population. On one occasion the Japanese commander presented the missionaries with a case of forty-eight small tins of sweetened condensed milk. The missionaries responded as best they could with a pair of live rabbits.[16]

The "Occupied" Territories

Life and work in the "occupied" territories slowly regained a semblance of normalcy. Mission activity continued unabated. Language study, new missionary appointments, furloughs and committee meetings went on. War rehabilitation funds provided help in repairing destroyed property. As one mission station reported in 1939, "We are slowly emerging out of chaos."[17]

In interior stations, there were three "governments" to deal with. Each demanded allegiance, exacted taxes, issued its own currency and exercised swift retribution. There was the Japanese army of occupation in the cities and along the railroad lines. In the countryside there were pockets of resistance still held by the Nationalist government. A third entity in the north were guerrilla bands loyal to the Communist regime of Yanan.

In the cities only Japanese occupation currency could be used. In the country areas only Chinese currency was accepted. It was dangerous and "illegal" to exchange one into the other or to be caught with the wrong "brand." Missionaries often discussed among themselves the ethics of smuggling. But sometimes it couldn't be helped. Hospitals had no choice but to receive payment of fees in whatever local currency the patient presented, but they needed silver or Japanese currency to pay for drugs and equipment in Shanghai. Missionaries delighted in telling tales about how they hoodwinked the Japanese inspectors.

Ms. Nettie Junkin told of hiding a supply of Chinese money on her body. She was stopped and searched by a Japanese guard. Nothing was found in her purse or pockets. Then the guard wanted to search her body. Nettie protested and said it was uncivilized for men to search women and demanded that they summon a woman policeman to do the job. The guard had no way of doing this, and not wanting to be considered uncivilized, let Nettie off with two hard blows on her back with the butt of his gun![18]

Rev. Houston Patterson's problem was how to carry a supply of silver dollars from Tengxian to Shanghai. He knew he would be searched by inspectors along the way. He took a two-gallon bucket, put his silver dollars in the bottom and on top put various spare parts of his motorcycle engine. Then he filled his bucket with thick black engine oil. He was inspected four times but in each case the inspector passed up the gooey looking mess.[19]

War experiences heightened the spirit of cooperation. The East China Mission (PCUSA) and the Mid China Mission (PCUS) merged their medical, educational and evangelistic work in Hangzhou and Suzhou.[20] Rev. John Minter (PCUS) and Rev. Paul Lindholm (PCUSA) visited their country churches together.

Mission hospitals were filled to beyond their capacity. They now specialized in gunshot wounds, victims of air raids, malnutrition and bandit atrocities. The Temple Hill Hospital in Yantai and the Shadyside Hospital in Weixian reported record patient admissions. All the Kiangan Mission hospitals reported "crowded clinics, every available bed space being taken...and over-worked staff."[21] Since the Elizabeth Blake Hospital had been destroyed by the Japanese, Dr. Mason Young operated five clinics throughout the city of Suzhou. In 1938 the Love and Mercy Hospital in Huaiyin (TKP) broke all previous records: 6,076 in-patients and 96,674 out-patients.[22] Charlotte Dunlap reported that the Goldsby King Hospital had had "the biggest and best year in its history in point of patients cared for; preaching the gospel; finances; cooperation and harmony among our staff."[23]

Surprisingly, mission schools were filled to overflowing. With the collapse of the government school system, the people again turned to the mission schools. Many reported the highest enrollment of their history.[24] The seminary in Tengxian received 170 students from 13 provinces using every available space to capacity.[25] By careful diplomacy Dr. Leighton Stuart kept Yenching University open for four years "as a little oasis of freedom against Japanese oppression."[26]

The International Settlement of Shanghai became an "island of refuge" in the midst of chaos. Hangzhou Christian College, with Dr. Robert McMullen as temporary president, moved to the settlement and occupied rented buildings. Branches of Ginling College and Nanjing Theological Seminary did the same. The Hangzhou Union Middle School for Girls, Lowrie Institute and the Farnham Girls' School moved to the Settlement until it was safe for them to return to their former campuses. Rev. John Minter, unable to return to Suzhou, was called to serve as pastor of the English-speaking Community Church with five hundred members, fifteen nationalities and thirty or more denominations.[27] Shanghai become a haven for three hundred thousand refugees, of whom seventy-five thousand were little children who did not know whether their fathers and mothers were dead or alive.

It is more difficult to evaluate the evangelistic work. From the mission reports of these years, two distinct pictures emerge. On the one hand the reports speak of the near collapse of the institutional structures. Church buildings had been burned, looted and occupied by opposing armies. Congregations had been scattered. Previously strong city churches in Nanjing and Hangzhou had lost so many members that they practically had to start all over again. Missionary itineration into the country was greatly restricted as travel passes had to be obtained from the Japanese military. The countryside was divided into "occupied territory" and "free China," making it difficult for Christians to get together. Presbyteries met infrequently or not at all.

Yet on the other hand, the mission reports abound with accounts of the responsiveness of people previously uninterested in the gospel. The scattering of Christians, like the dispersion of the disciples in the book of Acts, brought the Christians new opportunities to share their faith. Government officials, students, merchants and soldiers — previously resistant to the gospel — now showed a new openness. The reports speak of crowded churches, a record number of Bible sales and an increase in the number of inquirers. The Shandong Mission reported:

> the largest number of inquirers in its history, the figure being three times that of five years ago.... The sales of Bibles and Christian literature reached an unprecedented record.... Weihsien [Weixian] Presbytery added 3,035 members.... Churches are crowded. Many a service has been held in open courts because the buildings were too small.... The congregations in Yihsien [Yixian] and Ichow [Linyi] number over a thousand.... New churches have been organized, new buildings erected, old divisions healed.[28]

A new boldness in witnessing to the faith came about through the organization of "evangelistic bands." A pastor and several elders or lay people would visit as a group, distributing tracts, entering places of business, stopping to pray in homes.[29]

Of necessity there were gains in self-support. In Ningbo twelve independent churches were reported as entirely self-supporting. Dr. Wilfred McLauchlin reported that fifty churches of the Lianyungang field fully supported the twenty-four preachers who ministered to them without the use of mission funds.[30] Two churches in Peking finally broke the bonds of dependency on the mission and began a new life by electing elders and deacons and beginning the support of a pastor.[31]

The North Jiangsu Mission's report for 1940 was the most optimistic in years:

All spoke of the great crowds attending church services and other meetings, and the wide opportunities for preaching and teaching....[Zhenjiang] Station reports the best year in its history.[32]

The Mid China Mission summed it all up by saying that "a topsy-turvey, chaotic situation" had become a "great open door."[33]

A key to understanding the new situation was the fact that the opinion of the foreign missionary had changed. Instead of being perceived as a representative of an alien colonial power, the missionary was now seen as a true friend of China. Chinese newspapers that in the past were strongly anti-missionary now praised the missionary for standing by the people at a time of national crisis. In the darkness of the hour the church was seen as "the one, good, vital constructive factor in utterly evil conditions."[34] For the first time in one hundred years, the missionary enterprise and Chinese nationalism were on the same side.

As the war wore on, Chinese Christians increasingly faced the wrath of the Japanese military. American missionaries were officially neutral but everyone knew where their sympathies lay. They had broadcast to the world eyewitness accounts of the Rape of Nanjing. On furloughs they had been instrumental in introducing legislation to prohibit the sale to Japan of scrap iron and high octane gas. Americans could hide behind their neutrality but Chinese Christians had no such protection. Their heroism in facing persecution kept the faith alive.

One young pastor saved his village from being burned because he stood at the door of his little church and met the invaders face to face after all the villagers had fled. Another pastor had the courage to go alone to the Japanese commander and explain how the people in his village had been compelled to beat and bind two Japanese soldiers who had tried to rape their women. He asked the officer in charge to come and get them.[35] Another pastor stayed with his congregation when Japanese soldiers came into the village looking for guerrillas and was bayonetted for no reason at all.[36] An elder of a country church remarked that whenever he saw the Japanese soldiers coming, he "kneeled and prayed and then sicked the dogs on them!"[37]

In 1939 four pastors and fifteen elders from the churches in Xuzhou and Suqian were arrested in the middle of the night on fabricated charges of "secret plotting." No one could see them or send clothes or food. At times they were tortured. The missionaries did everything possible to secure their release — intercession with local police, appeals to the Japanese high command, and a visit to the Foreign Office in Tokyo. Dr. Nettie Grier "kowtowed" — prostrating herself on the floor before the Japanese commander pleading for their release. Finally, after seventy days all charges were dismissed and they were released.

On the first Sunday after his release, Rev. Wang Heng Hsin preached on lessons learned from his prison experience: (1) a new appreciation of the Bible,

(2) how to live without the so called necessities of life, (3) progress in prayer, (4) appreciation of freedom and (5) a new sympathy for those in prison. Once when almost overcome with despondency and despair he heard the church bells ringing on Sunday. It was *his* church, and he knew that *his* congregation was gathering for worship and would be praying for him. His heart was strengthened and his faith renewed.[38]

"Free China"

While a new chapter in the history of Christian missions was being written in the Japanese-occupied regions, an equally dramatic epic was being acted out in unconquered West China. A migration of unprecedented proportions took place as government offices, factories, schools, laboratories, hospitals, universities, banks and Christian organizations moved westward. The goal was to build a social and economic base that could outlast the invaders. Dr. Frank Price has estimated that the equipment of 452 factories, 120,000 tons of machinery, was moved up the Yangtze or over mountain roads.[39] When the Japanese blockade became more effective, West China was reached by the narrow-gauge railroad from Haiphong in French Indo-China to Kunming. Later when this route was blocked, the only access was the famed Burma Road.

With the Chinese migrants went the missionaries. They traveled with the universities to which they had been assigned. Nanjing University, Shandong Christian University with its School of Medicine, and Ginling College found a home on the campus of the West China Union University in Chengdu. West China provided the missionary with new ways to relate to Chinese society. In the context of the wartime frontier environment friendships were formed with leaders in government, education, business and the military.

Two Presbyterian missionaries, Frank Price and Andrew Roy, have left accounts of their life and work as "exiles" in West China. Dr. Price, with his wife, Essie, was the only Southern Presbyterian missionary in West China. He served on the faculty of the Nanjing Theological Seminary, and as corresponding secretary for the Church of Christ in China. He wrote of the following opportunities for the church and the "evacuee missionary":

War relief. Missionaries served on a host of international relief committees and organizations. The Christian missionary interpreted the relief needs of China and added "the touch of Christly concerns and a message of hope."[40]

Social rebuilding. China was in the midst, not only of war, but of a mighty social revolution. The missionary with special skills in cooperatives, public health, agriculture or child welfare was in great demand.

International service. West China was no longer an isolated backward area. Chongqing and Chengdu became the crossroads of international diplomacy. The missionary was a "bridge builder...an interpreter of East to West and West to East, a mediator between different civilizations...a minister of reconciliation in a world of tension and war."[41] The missionary residence was a place where American servicemen could reaffirm Christian faith and renew ties with church and home.

Christian literature. Since the war began, more than 20 million adults had learned to read. Christian literature was much in demand. An ambitious project was launched by Roman Catholic and Protestant scholars for translating a hundred of the great Christian classics into modern Chinese.[42]

Training ministers. Nanjing Theological Seminary had been invited by the West China Union Theological Seminary to share its campus at Chengdu. Students came from fourteen provinces. Provincialism was broken down. An extension service provided correspondence courses to two hundred preachers and laymen. Religious music and art were emphasized.[43]

Dr. Andrew Roy had been assigned to the exiled University of Nanjing.[44] He and his wife, Margaret, entered West China by "the back door" — up the narrow-gauge railway from Hanoi to Kunming and by plane to Chengdu. But before beginning work with the university he was asked by the Church of Christ in China to join a team carrying medical supplies to isolated hospitals serving wounded Chinese soldiers in the northwest.

They traveled on a Dodge truck named "Eva," which had a habit of balking in awkward circumstances — such as on the fourteen-thousand–foot Qinling Pass. Roy was greatly impressed with the ability of Chinese mechanics to improvise. Carburetors, broken springs, axles and feed lines could all be replaced with local products.

They visited small hospitals carved out of the loess caves high in the hills. On one arrival they were greeted with the banner: "We Welcome the Christian Service Council for Wounded Soldiers.... America is a nation that holds fast to righteousness for mankind and peace." Morale was high, equipment was primitive and medical supplies badly needed.

The trek took Roy's party to Yanan, the Communist headquarters. Roy's account of the trip is the only one we have of any PCUSA missionary visit to the Communist capital. They were given rooms in the "Northwest Hotel," which they found was just a series of caves. They were courteously entertained at dinner by the highest military commander then in the camp. He claimed there was no discrimination as to religious belief but this was difficult either to confirm or deny. Roy was impressed with the model hospital, sanitation, public health and the "Resist Japan University." But the fanaticism of the leaders was troubling. They left with reservations and criticisms but also with admiration for the "honest willingness to sacrifice."[45]

On returning to Chengdu Roy began his assignment as director of religious activities for the university. This included conferences, chapel services, summer service projects, and whatever else seemed to be useful. They experienced constant air raids but had a bomb shelter in the yard where Margaret often sat, calmly reading stories to their two sons.

On one occasion the missionary community was invited to meet Chiang Kai-shek at a reception given by the governor. Roy was well dressed with coat and tie. A colleague, Norman, had come in an open khaki shirt and shorts. As they were waiting for the Generalissimo to arrive, it became obvious from the expression on the governor's face that he disapproved of Norman's casual garb. What to do? Roy suggested that he would go through the reception line first, shake hands with the Generalissimo, and then meet Norman in an empty office room. Here they would change clothes and Norman would put on the suit, shirt and tie and go through the line well dressed. All went well until a security guard surprised them as they were undressing! Roy explained their predicament, and the guard cooperated by escorting Norman, now in the one suit of clothes, back to the reception line, while Roy waited in his underwear![46]

The war with Japan brought new opportunities for the National Christian Council of China (NCCC). In its role as the national voice for Chinese Protestants, it issued "A Call to a Forward Movement" with the motto "The Lord is Our Refuge Camp." The "Call" was a ringing affirmation of faith addressed to the Christians of China and the world. In the midst of its "outcry against the injustice and cruelty of the invasion" it asks for a spirit of tolerance toward the Japanese people.[47]

The NCCC maintained offices in Shanghai and West China. Foremost among its wartime activities was the War Relief Commission. This became the channel through which worldwide organizations sent their relief funds. Another activity of the Council was its support of twenty-one "orphaned" European missions and two hundred missionaries who were cut off from the support of their home boards because of the war.[48] A committee of the NCCC assisted Europeans, mostly Jewish, who came to Shanghai in large numbers to flee from Hitler's reign of terror. The Council's medical office placed a number of Jewish refugee doctors in Christian hospitals. One of these, Dr. E. M. Lippa, ran the Jiangyin hospital in the absence of a missionary.[49]

For the Church of Christ in China the war years were times of testing, of growing maturity and of expanding opportunities. The scheduled meetings of the General Assembly were cancelled but synod conferences were held. Offices were maintained both in Shanghai and in West China. The CCC lost two of its pioneer founders during the war years: Dr. C. Y. Cheng died after a long illness in 1939, and Rev. A. R. Kepler of a heart attack while on furlough in 1942.[50] New leadership took over as Dr. H. H. Tsui was appointed General Secretary.

One of the extraordinary services the CCC performed for the nation was the organization of the National Christian Service for Wounded Soldiers in Transit. As Chinese armies retreated westward, the care of wounded soldiers became a national crisis. Chinese armies were simply unable to provide for their care in transit. Volunteers were recruited, organized into mobile teams and stationed along the roads, rail centers and river ports. The teams provided care for the wounded as best they could by bathing them, dressing wounds, providing food, drink and comfort. In two years over nine hundred workers had been trained and put to work.[51]

Julia Bradley has described one team of missionary women at work at the Yangtze river port of Jiujiang:

> I wish you could have seen some of the patients who came from Nanking and were from eight to twelve days on little slow sailboats coming up the river...caked with dirt, their hands and faces black, barefoot and wounded leaning on each other.... We went to work to clean them up. ...Most of you will wonder how in the world I could be doing medical dressing with a degree in religious education only, but, believe me, I've been through rigid practical training the last two months, and of course had a trained nurse to show me.[52]

At a time when their backs were to the wall and the nation was facing disaster, the CCC initiated work in three new "home mission fields" in the far west. It is one of the most stirring and less well known stories of wartime China.

The *Guizhou Mission* was begun in May 1939 among tribespeople in this backward and neglected province. At its height the mission operated seven churches and schools with a staff of fourteen evangelists and seven educators. Initially all personnel and funds were Chinese. Later as missionaries were forced to leave their posts in the east a number, including Rev. and Mrs. John D. Hayes of Peking, joined the Guizhou Mission.[53]

A second and more ambitious venture was the *Border Mission*. A mission was organized to work in the vast region along the Tibetan, Xinjiang, Gansu and Qinghai borders where 40 million people lived. It did its work in cooperation with many different groups — the China Inland Mission, the Christian universities in Chengdu and even the U.S. Air Force "in teaching the Lolos [tribal people] how to take care of the American airmen who bailed out in their regions."[54] The unsung heroes of the war years were the Chinese "home missionaries" who served far from home, endured opposition from minority tribes, suffered from illness and received inadequate salaries. Later, the Rev. and Mrs. Archie Crouch joined the mission with Mr. Crouch serving as English language secretary.

The third endeavor was the *Yunnan Mission*, which was an "experiment which sought to begin new work on the basis of a joint effort of mission boards with the Chinese Church."[55] Nine mission boards cooperated in the mission, to which they assigned personnel and funds. An urgent need was Kunming, a backward provincial capital, which had become a center of refugees, military airfields and universities that had migrated from the east. Here the Rev. W. H. Clark was assigned to work with refugee students. Another ministry was begun among the tribal people of southern Yunnan. Rev. and Mrs. Kenneth J. Foreman were appointed to the mission in 1949 and were the last of the western missionaries to leave Yunnan.[56] By 1949 five hundred members had been received by the churches founded by the Yunnan Mission.

Pearl Harbor

In the fall of 1940 relations between Tokyo and Washington took an ominous turn for the worse. The State Department urged women with small children to leave and made arrangements for the *S.S. Washington* to evacuate American families. The home boards authorized emergency furloughs for all who wished to leave, but the final decision was left to each missionary. It was not easy to decide. Some transferred to the Philippines. Some with small children were obligated to leave. Others needed to stay.

The Japanese army of occupation continued to tighten its controls. Travel passes became harder to obtain. Nine PCUS missionaries and one child in Huaiyin (TKP) were confined in the hospital quarters where they were harassed, insulted and given insufficient food, and their homes were looted. After a week and the strenuous objections of the American consul, they were released. In Hainan missionaries were placed under house arrest, their bank accounts frozen and the hospital financial records seized.[57]

The "Day to Remember" for Americans in China, and for all Americans of that generation, came on 7 December 1941 with the Japanese attack on Pearl Harbor. Missionaries first heard the news on the morning of 8 December when Japanese officers called at mission compounds across the land and announced that Japanese planes had destroyed the American fleet, that Japan and America were now at war and that American citizens were under arrest.

The attitude of the Japanese commanders varied. Some were belligerent, some were stiffly formal, some made the effort to be friendly. The commander at Xuzhou solemnly announced: "Our two countries are now at war." And then he added: "But this does not mean, Mr. Brown, that you and I have to be enemies."[58]

In Hainan all missionaries were moved to Haikou, where they were confined with other foreigners. Scarce food items were confiscated. But Christmas was approaching and the little group of evacuees began to make preparation. Mrs. Elva Bercovitz trimmed the tree, which was the "top of a horsetail pine." Invitations were sent to the Japanese officers for an afternoon tea. It was an odd gathering of "official" enemies on foreign soil, meeting to celebrate the birth of the Prince of Peace! In attendance were the commander-in-chief of military forces on the island, the Japanese consul, interpreters and others. Apologies were made for one officer who had had too much "saki" (rice wine) and could not make it. Boxes of candy were given out and the Japanese seemed to enjoy the occasion. "Ironically, at nearly the same moment the missionaries were entertaining the Japanese, their families [in the U.S.A.] were reading in newspapers that the Japanese had massacred all the Hainan missionaries."[59]

Treatment given missionaries varied greatly. In most cases they were confined to a compound. Bank accounts were frozen and only very limited allowances could be drawn each month. Unauthorized visitors were prohibited. Shortwave radios were confiscated. A few missionaries were beaten. More were robbed of personal possessions. Many, however were treated with kindness and dignity within the limits imposed from higher headquarters. Later they were gathered into concentration camps.

Most hospitals and schools continued for a while under missionary control before the Japanese took over their management.[60] Yenching University was closed but loyal teachers and alumni reopened the university in Chengdu. Most churches continued to worship without serious restrictions. Later the Japanese army tried to force the churches into a kind of political-ecclesiastical union similar to the United Church (KYODAN) in Japan. But this did not prove to be successful.

A diplomatic exchange took place during the summer of 1942 for American citizens in the Far East. A half-century of missionary effort was represented by the 750 missionaries and children from 60 different agencies who were included in the exchange. The major denominational groups were the following:

Presbyterians (North and South)	208
Roman Catholic (9 agencies)	117
Baptists (North and South)	54
Lutheran Missions (6 agencies)	44
American Church Mission (Epis.)	29
Methodists	25[61]

The passengers embarked on 29 June from the Shanghai Bund on the Italian ship *Conte Verde*. As the ship passed through the straits at Singapore it met the *Asama Maru,* carrying some nine hundred American evacuees from Japan and Korea. The two ships sailed together, arriving 21 July at Lourenço Marques in Mozambique, where they met the Swedish ship M.S. *Gripsolm,* which arrived from the United States with a boatload of Japanese nationals. There in neutral Portuguese East Africa the exchange was made. The *Gripsolm,* with its American evacuees, sailed around the Cape of Good Hope, stopped once at Rio and then sailed on to New York, where joyful family reunions took place.

But as one repatriate expressed it, "Christ was not repatriated on the *Gripsolm.*" Life went on in the civilian concentration camps. The most famous of these was located at the Presbyterian compound in Weixian. Here some two thousand men, women and children were confined. They included missionaries, businessmen, professors, tobacco salesmen, adventurers, junkies and prostitutes. The largest contingent was made up of missionaries — 400 Protestants and 430 Roman Catholic priests and nuns. The internees organized their own activities and were responsible for food preparation, sanitation, medical care, education, sports, entertainment and religious services. The story of the compound community is graphically told by Dr. Langdon Gilkey, then a young teacher at Yenching, in his *Shantung Compound.*[62] It is a story of saints and sinners living in close confinement under constant pressure from their Japanese masters. In the camp all social distinctions disappeared. It was "as if a ruthless but whimsical fate had sought to bring the mighty of the treaty ports low and to mingle them with those of lesser degree."[63]

In 1943 an event of unique significance for the China missions took place halfway around the world in Cairo, Egypt. There, on 11 January at the meeting of Roosevelt, Churchill and Chiang Kai-shek, new protocols were signed that repealed the despised Unequal Treaties, ended extraterritoriality, agreed to the return of Manchuria and Taiwan to China, and promised the independence of Korea "in due course."[64] The United States also repealed the Chinese Exclusion Act, which removed a "sixty-year-old source of infectious ill will and resentment."[65]

The entry of the United States into the war did not bring any immediate improvement to the situation. Chiang Kai-shek was reluctant to commit his troops to a new offensive since the eventual defeat of Japan was now assured. Japan seized the initiative and launched its Ichigo ("Number One") offensive early in 1944 to destroy the air bases in south-central China from which General Chennault's Fourteenth Air Force had begun to launch air raids on Japan. Changsha was taken. Hengyang fell after a heroic forty-seven-day siege when most of the city, and the mission compound, were destroyed. The Japanese invaders overran most of the province.

This meant the evacuation of four of the Hunan mission stations: Changsha, Hengyang, Xiangtan and Chenzhou. Dr. Edith Millican has told the epic story of the evacuation of the Hengyang Hospital 690 miles westward in advance of the Japanese army. The hospital staff took with them delivery tables, beds, surgical instruments, drugs and supplies. They traveled by train, hand carts, horse carts, ferry boats, nondescript vehicles and occasionally U.S. Army trucks over icy roads, mountain passes and muddy stream beds. Somewhere behind them were the advancing Japanese. Along the route the hospital was called on to treat those wounded from air attacks:

> What we found was enough to keep us busy for a full twenty-four hours, but we were racing against the return of the day. We had strict orders to be out of there before dawn. We worked furiously.... Some of them were hopeless. We did what we could to relieve pain. There seemed to be no end to them. Two large rooms of a school building were filled and the court outside and beyond the walls, a large vacant lot from which cries for help and moans and groans kept reaching our ears. One at a time, one at a time, no use going over to answer that cry until you've finished here. Then the order to load those that could be moved into the cars.... Our time was almost up. We kept working up to the last minute. Then we had to turn a deaf ear on the rest. The cars were full. No more could go. I looked off into the darkness on either side of us... bodies as far as I could see.[66]

Lianzhou was the one Presbyterian Mission station that was never occupied by the Japanese. The city overflowed with refugees who crowded the Presbyterian compound, which became a "brotherhood of sufferers in a common cause."[67] The Synod of Guangdong, the Union Theological Seminary of Canton, the True Light Middle School, were all welcomed. Dr. and Mrs. J. S. Kunkle never knew how many were sleeping on the first floor of their house. Neither did they know how many would come in late at night needing breakfast in the morning. Those who came in after nine o'clock had to be careful not to step on those already stretched out on the floor, asleep. By November 1944 the Japanese had taken the American air base at Guilin. They advanced to the outskirts of Lianzhou but that was as far as they got. Events elsewhere in the Pacific were dictating the course of the war.

Langdon Gilkey has graphically described the end of the war as it looked to the internees at the Weixian Internment Camp after the two long years of waiting:

> The day, August 16, 1945, was clear, blue and warm as such a day should have been. We all began our chores of cooking, stoking, and cleaning up slops as usual. About the middle of the morning, however, word flashed around camp that an Allied plane had been sighted....A boy [came in] screaming in an almost insane excitement, "An American plane, and headed straight for us!" We all flung our stirring paddles down beside the cauldrons, left the carrots unchopped on the tables, and tore after the boy to the ballfield....This miracle was true: there it was, now as big as a gull and headed for us from the western mountains.... "Why, it's a big plane, with four engines! It's coming straight for the camp — — Look, look, they're waving at us! They know who we are. They have come to get us!"...At this point, the excitement was too great for any of us to contain. It surged up within us, a flood of joyful feeling, sweeping aside all our restraints....It was pandemonium...proper middle-aged Englishmen and women were cheering or swearing. Others were laughing hysterically, or crying like babies....This plane was *our* plane. It was sent here for *us,* to tell us the war was over.[68]

The Return

At the end of the war the roll call of PCUSA China missionaries and their places of service was as follows: West and South China, 29; "Special War Service," 8; Internment Camps — China, 15; Internment Camps — Philippines, 18.[69] One PCUS couple, the Rev. and Mrs. Frank W. Price, was stationed in Chengdu. Six PCUS missionaries were interned in the Philippines.[70] Dr. J. Leighton Stuart, president of Yenching University, had been confined with two companions to a residence in Peking for three years and eight months.[71] The reason he was not repatriated may have been that the Japanese were holding him for possible use as a diplomatic channel in case peace negotiations became necessary. Dr. Watson Hayes died at the Weixian camp on 2 August 1944. Rev. J. Hillcoat Arthur died aboard the *Gripsolm* on 20 October 1943.

Those interned in the Philippines suffered the most. Mrs. Jessie Junkin gave birth to a baby boy six weeks after they were interned in a civilian concentration camp near Baguio in northern Luzon. Billy's first bath was from a Chase and Sanborn coffee tin and the cotton used by the nurse was put in the oven and resterilized so it could be used again. It was a miracle, says Jessie, that her baby survived. For the first year, all the men were kept separated from the women and children by two fences six feet apart. For three years there never was a time that the prisoners and little children did not know acute and painful hunger. Grown men got down on their hands and knees and picked on scrap bones like dogs. When William Junkin served as dishwasher, he would carefully scrape the plates to collect the garbage which he stored for his wife and baby. For months no form of group activity was permitted. Later church services and Sunday Schools were begun. Jessie made her little boy a teddy bear out of a brown canvas suitcase cover and Bill carved for it a wooden head. In December 1944 all in the camp were moved to the Bilibid prison in Manila just a week before the Americans landed at Lingayen Gulf. Freedom and food came on 4 February 1945 when the camp was liberated. For the Junkins the meaning of the terrible experience was clear: They had been "delivered out of the mouth of the lion" (II Tim. 4:17) in order that they could return to China:

> We thought we had learned all about suffering and hunger the first six months, but after three years and six weeks, we feel we have had better training and understanding in so many of the problems of China. And we have absolute proof that God is a source of strength and power when our physical selves are weak and feeble.[72]

Rev. and Mrs. Paul Lindholm took refuge with resistance forces in the mountains of Negros Island. For a thrilling account of their adventures see Lindholm's *Shadows from the Rising Sun*.[73] They were eventually evacuated by a U.S. Navy submarine.

When the doors of the concentration camps swung open, missionaries began returning to their stations. What they found in the eastern provinces was utter devastation. Dr. Frank Price, one of the first to return, estimated that at least 10 million soldiers and civilians were killed in battle. Many more died of wounds. More still died of famine. Fifty million people had been uprooted. At least one-third of the mission schools, hospitals, churches and residences had been destroyed. In the first two years of war 150 mission compounds had been hit by bombs or shells. Most of the property not destroyed had been occupied by Japanese occupation forces, Chinese soldiers or refugees. Getting back possession of it would be a delicate task.[74]

The first returnees received an overwhelming welcome by Christians and non-Christians alike. When Dr. W. C. McLauchlin arrived at the hospital gate at Huaiyin (TKP) he was greeted by a multitude of people with the firing of firecrackers and a scene of general jubilation.[75] Everywhere the mood was one of exhilaration and thanksgiving to God for deliverance. The Guangdong Synod took as its motto Nehemiah 2:18: "Let us arise and build."[76] Missionaries were thrilled by stories of courage, loyalty and triumphant witness. Church leaders urged them to resume the work they had done before the war.

A deputation from the New York Board arrived, surveyed the situation, made recommendations and set priorities. Of first importance was the return of personnel, recovery of property and the restoration of buildings. In spite of severe difficulties of arranging travel on U.S. military transports, within eighteen months, two hundred PCUSA missionaries, including fifty-seven new appointees, were back in China.[77] A campaign for raising $23 million for the War Restoration Fund had been launched. The first postwar meeting of the PCUSA China Council was held in Shanghai in August 1947. The seven China missions (North China, Shandong, Kiangan, East China, South China, Hunan, Hainan) were reconstituted but urged "not to administer the work that rightly belongs to the church."[78] Former stations fell into three classes:

1. *Stations discontinued:* Dengzhou, Yixian, Shouzhou and Huizhou.

2. *Stations temporarily unoccupied:* (in Communist-dominated areas) Shunde, Yantai, Weixian, Jining, Tengxian, Linyi, Kachek and Ledong.

3. *Stations now functioning:* (with resident missionaries) Peking, Baoding, Jinan, Qingdao, Shanghai, Suzhou, Hangzhou, Ningbo, Nanjing, Huayuan, Nanxuzhou, Changsha, Changde, Xiangtan, Hengyang, Chenzhou, Canton, Lianzhou, Yangjiang, Haikou and Qiongzhou.[79]

For the Christian colleges, 1946 was the "Year of Return from Exile." The travel back was by trucks, ox-carts, river steamer and train. By the fall of 1946 all but two of the mission middle schools had been reopened and the Ming Sum School for the Blind was back in business.[80]

Fifteen hospitals were soon back in operation. Some had never shut down. But it was clear that with limited staff and funds, not all could be continued. The medical policy adopted by the China Council was that six hospitals and medical schools were given high priority: Shandong University School of Medicine, Hackett Medical Center, Hunan Medical Center in Xiangtan, the University Hospital at Nanjing and the hospitals at Baoding and Haikou.[81]

The Executive Committee in Nashville appointed a Survey Committee composed of six missionaries that sailed for China in January 1946. They were charged with visiting all former stations and making recommendations for the future. One of their first decisions was to combine North Jiangsu and Mid China into one China Mission. Another decision: Chinese church leaders would be consulted as to the return of former missionaries.

Dr. C. Darby Fulton, Executive Secretary, and Dr. William M. Elliott, chairman of the Executive Committee, went to China in December 1946 to review the situation and make recommendations. They traveled in the dead of winter in unheated trains, open trucks and river barges. To keep them warm Mrs. Stacy Farrior provided "an abundance of garments, many of a strange and astonishing design." Dr. Fulton's impressions of the visit: "fantastic inflation which made planning impossible;...the isolation and rigorous nature of missionary life;...the physical destruction of mission property;...surprise at the extent of activities under way;...concern that the old structures were being revived and that missionaries were paying the bills." He provided these highlights of the Southern Presbyterian mission stations:

- *Hangzhou* — the city churches were alive....Hangzhou College had a record enrollment....The union girls school was doing excellent work.

- *Jiaxing* — Hospital under Dr. Mason Young; high school under William Koo; city and country churches assisted by Rev. and Mrs. George Hudson; all carrying on with vigor.

- *Suzhou* — Fine relationship between John Minter and Chinese leaders... clinic in operation.

- *Jiangyin* — Despite the near total destruction of the station, the country work was strong...hospital was operating under a Chinese doctor... middle school was crowded.

- *Nanjing* — The Seminary and Training School for Women were operating at full capacity.

- *Taizhou* — Marguerite Mizell and Gussie Fraser are our only missionaries....Hospital continues in badly damaged building under a Chinese doctor...boys and girls schools are open.

- *Huaian* — Lillian Wells is carrying on alone, teaching and working with women.

- *Huaiyin (TKP)* — Margaret Woods, R.N., is alone....Hospital is operating at half capacity under a United Nations doctor. Country work was badly in need of an ordained missionary.

- *Suqian* — City churches have suffered greatly under the ruthless opposition of the communist regime. Country churches are in better shape.

- *Xuzhou* — Probably our strongest center....Middle schools, operated by presbytery, have an enrolment of 1,800....Hospital is functioning well under Chinese doctors and Mrs. McFadyen....Country churches are reviving under F. A. Brown....North China Seminary with 45–50 men and women and Martin Hopkins have moved here from Tengxian.

- *Lianyungang* — Hospital going well under a Chinese doctor. Dr. McLauchlin carrying on evangelistic work.[82]

One is struck with the speed with which the programs of both PCUSA and PCUS missions were resumed and the way in which they settled back into the old patterns. After a long absence and with such radical changes sweeping across the country, was it not unfortunate that the same old mission structures resumed?

And yet, could it have been any different? Chinese Christian leadership had been decimated and scattered. Many had been exhausted by the long years of carrying on alone. Much of the property was in such sorry shape as to be unusable without extensive renovation. Under such circumstances how could missionaries have refused the earnest petitions of former colleagues? Overwhelmed by the immediate tasks at hand, few realized how little time was left. Charles West's comment is to the point: "Most did not grasp the enormity of events that overwhelmed us."[83] Radical restructuring was necessary but was postponed until a more stable situation arrived. But the political and economic situation had begun to unravel.

Civil War

Peace came suddenly in Asia with the dropping of the bomb on Hiroshima. No one had expected the end to come so suddenly. But with the surrender of the Japanese on 10 August 1945, both Nationalist and Communist forces made a rush to move their troops into the liberated areas to take over Japanese garrisons and seize their arms and equipment. The Nationalists were aided by U.S. planes and ships. The Red Army had the support of the Soviet armies in Manchuria who had entered the war just days before the end. Very quickly the coalition between the KMT and the CCP broke down as each attempted to gain the upper hand.

The United States tried in vain to bring about a genuine coalition government. General George C. Marshall was dispatched to China as President Harry Truman's personal envoy to make this effort. At General Marshall's recommendation, Dr. J. Leighton Stuart was appointed ambassador to assist in the peace negotiations. Stuart was a superb choice because of his personal integrity, knowledge of the Chinese scene and association with Chinese leaders on both sides. But from the first Stuart's hands were tied by irreconcilable differences between the Chinese personalities and by Washington politics.[84]

Civil war broke out and grew in intensity during 1947. Communist armies increased their hold on rural area in Manchuria and North China. By the fall of 1948 they were ready to attack Nationalist garrisons in key cities. Jinan fell in September 1948. Mukden surrendered in October. Communist armies launched their Huai-Hai campaign aimed at the railroad junction of Xuzhou. For this decisive engagement each side committed upwards of half a million men. The sixty-five day encounter ended in disaster for the Nationalist armies. My seventy-two year old father, Frank A. Brown, was in Xuzhou with fellow missionaries Rev. and Mrs. Deane Walter when the city fell and told of a night of waiting at the airfield for an evacuation plane that never arrived:

6:00 p.m. Mrs. Stella Walter arrived at the airport in our car with some of the baggage. An American pilot is just leaving for Nanking and assures her he will be back in two hours to take us all to Shanghai. By ten o'clock we hope to see the lights of Shanghai.

7:00 p.m. Walter and I arrive with plenty more trunks, bedding and what not. A Catholic priest joins our party....

11:00 p.m. A sound of rushing planes, for everything that has wings on this big air field is leaving for the south loaded down with the high command and every soldier that can climb on board.

Midnight. Walter and I explore the control tower. Lights all on, but instruments and utensils all left in disorder....

Daybreak.... Gasoline drums have been placed all around the field.... It may be that the nationalists are about to bomb with incendiaries.... We move out of range and wait for our plane that never comes. So back we go homeward. Evidently the Lord still has a work for us to do here.

The roads are crowded with huge retreating armies — trucks, tanks, infantry.... A doomed army is in full retreat. The private soldier is brave enough.... But many of the higher officers are cowardly, selfish and inefficient, with the result that the army has no will to fight.... Am anxious tonight for this old city. "THEY" arrived before midnight.... Came to our hospital gate and said they knew there were three foreigners here, but not to fear.[85]

After the fall of Xuzhou, the Nationalist defenses began to crumble. Peking and Tianjin were taken in January 1949. Nanjing fell in April. Chiang Kai-shek began the move of his government to Taiwan in July. On 1 October 1949 Mao Zedong made his historic proclamation from Tiananmen Square in the new capital of the People's Republic: "The Chinese People have stood up."

A thorough analysis of the causes for the fall of the KMT is beyond the scope of this study. Various reasons have been proposed among which the following are noted: failure to deal with agrarian reform, failure to develop a unifying ideology, failures in military strategy, corruption within the KMT leadership, war weariness and fatigue, rampant inflation, and American policy, which was "hesitant and wavering."[86]

Revolution and Mission

Initially the sympathies of the missionary community were overwhelmingly with the Nationalist government. There had been little or no contact with the CCP before their military victories in North China. Rumors of violence and the persecution of Christians were rampant. But by 1947 the high hopes for the KMT had changed to disillusionment.

First impressions of the Red armies in the liberated zones were favorable. Soldiers were well disciplined and orderly. There was surprise at the "degree of tolerance the Church has enjoyed" and it was said that the Communist authorities "looked with special favor on Christian medical work."[87]

The first reactions of the Protestant Church leadership was guardedly optimistic. In December 1949 a group of Christian leaders representing most of the major denominations issued a significant document entitled "Message from Chinese Christians to Mission Boards Abroad." It stressed the radical nature of the revolution that was taking place. As Christians they felt the "urgent necessity of re-examining our work and our relationships with the older churches abroad in the light of this historical change." However, "our fundamental faith in Christ is not to be shaken." The Communist view that Christianity had been implicated with imperialism and capitalism was admitted. But the authors of the letter went on to say:

> We do realize and wish to assert that missionary work in China never had any direct relationship with government policies.... Missionaries have been sent here for no other purpose than to preach the Christian gospel of love, and to serve the needs of the Chinese people. The central Christian motivation will not and can never be questioned.[88]

Specifically, three points were made as to future policy: (1) Policy determination and financial administration should pass to Chinese leadership wherever this had not yet been done. (2) There was "nothing in principle which makes the future position of the missionary untenable, or render his service unnecessary." An open mind toward the new political environment would be necessary. The future contribution would not be along administrative lines: "To BE, to SHARE, and to LIVE will be a significant contribution." (3) Financial support would still be welcomed, provided there were no strings attached, but should be considered temporary in nature.[89]

The response of the Presbyterian mission boards was favorable. The PCUS Executive Committee of Foreign Missions issued the following "Statement on Policy" in early 1950:

> It is the earnest desire of the Presbyterian Church, in full cooperation with the Church of Christ in China, to continue its Christian service under the Communist regime. The Christian people of the United States are eager to maintain the close bonds of friendship with the people of China and to express that friendship concretely in a continued program of cooperation with the Chinese church and to assist... Christian hospitals and Christian universities, that are an essential part of the Church's ministry.... As evidence of this continuing policy, missionaries are remaining at their posts of service in China and new missionaries have already gone or are preparing to go.[90]

Although missionary service would soon become impossible, it is significant that the attempt was made. Missionaries had lived in and given their loyalty to many different regimes and governments during the long tumultuous years in China. They were prepared to do the same with the People's Republic of China (PRC).

In spite of many signs of approaching disaster China missionaries were incurably optimistic:

> It is true that the fall of the capital of Shantung, Tsinan, 200 miles to the north has shattered the morale somewhat.... It is true that our railroads, north, south, east, and west are being cut and repaired every few days. And it is true that last summer, the American Consul "alerted" us and advised women and children to leave, but the situation has improved since then. We don't feel that we have a call from the Lord to leave his work yet.[91]

"We Cannot Quit in China" was the title of an article by Stanton Lautenschlager.[92] Missionary tenacity was remarkable. Were they just stubborn or was it because they were Presbyterians and believed in the sovereignty of God?

> Our wish to stay is still unchanged. It's partly Scotch stubbornness... partly because I'd like to find out for myself what can be done for Christ in Communist territory.[93]

But on 25 June 1950 an event took place that eliminated any possibility of missionary service. North Korean troops crossed the thirty-eighth parallel in force into South Korea. Soon Chinese "volunteers" and U.S. Marines were killing each other in the frozen hills of North Korea. The United States froze Chinese assets in America. China retaliated. On 29 December 1950 The State Administrative Council of the PRC demanded that all Christian churches, hospitals and schools break their relationships with American mission boards.[94] The CCC sent a statement to overseas mission boards citing the action of the State Council and declined further financial support. The statement, however, reiterated their loyalty to the faith, the Word of God, the teachings of Christ and the eternal Gospel.[95]

One by one mission institutions were taken over by the government. Christian universities and schools were nationalized. The Church of Christ in China held its last meeting in Suzhou in 1948. It had been thought that medical missions that benefited the peasants would have been welcomed but this was not the case. All benevolent programs had to be dispensed by the state, which would receive credit for such philanthropy.

A much more politicized statement was published in July 1950 under the title "Christian Manifesto." The author was Y. T. Wu, the emerging leader of the Three-Self Movement, who had conferred with Premier Zhou Enlai and secured his endorsement of the first draft. Initially there was considerable opposition by Christian leaders and some changes were made. In the end forty prominent Christians endorsed the statement and a campaign was launched to get all Christians to sign it. By 1952 it was reported that four hundred thousand signatures had been obtained.[96]

The Manifesto acknowledges the contribution Protestant Christianity had made to China. Nevertheless, since missionaries came from imperialistic countries, "Christianity consciously or unconsciously, directly or indirectly, became related with imperialism." All Chinese Christians should support the "Common Political Platform" and "oppose imperialism, feudalism, and bureaucratic capitalism." The United States was singled out for denunciation. Churches should discontinue all relations with Western imperialistic agencies in the shortest period of time.[97]

Exodus

One by one they left. Each made his/her own decision. But in the end there was no other option. Travel restrictions brought to an end church visitation. Enormous taxes were imposed on mission property. For those who waited too long, leaving was no simple matter. Applications for departure had to be filed. Some individuals were subject to "denunciation meetings." A few were imprisoned or held on house arrest. For all, the weeks before departure were "days of intense spiritual crisis and growth."[98]

In reviewing this painful period, it is well to remember the nature of the times. Chinese volunteers were fighting American soldiers in Korea. Chinese casualties were estimated at nine hundred thousand. The Chinese people knew only what the government told them. The United States had pledged support for a regime in Taiwan that claimed sovereignty over all of China and had vowed to return. We have only to remember what happened to loyal Japanese on the West Coast during World War II to understand war hysteria.

Rev. Sam Moffett was taken to the Nanking police station and charged with embezzlement because as treasurer he had paid missionary salaries instead of turning the funds over to Chinese Christians. He was given a public trial, found guilty and ordered to leave within a few days as an "enemy of the people."[99]

My father, Frank A. Brown, spent three months in Xuzhou after the Communist armies had taken the city. Having reached the years of mandatory retirement, he applied for an exit permit and was given a pass by the mayor of the city, who urged that he leave at once before the army cut off all transportation south. But first he visited the Catholic compound to say good-bye to friends who had elected to stay. Father Cossett gave him a letter of introduction to Catholic missions in the areas through which he would pass. It was written in Latin, which would cover any nationality. He traveled with a band of refugees in an old, creaky army truck. They followed the course of the Grand Canal. When they reached the Yangtze, they took to two small boats traveling along the banks of the great river. The last Communist sentry was passed. Then they were in "no-man's land." Father got out of the boat and walked along the tow-path with hands held high. Then the cry "Halt" from a Nationalist sentry. They were through the lines at last.[100]

Dr. Joseph L. Wilkerson, alone in Jiaxing without much fluency in the Chinese language, continued to treat patients and perform operations until late 1950. His wife, Estelle, and newborn baby had been evacuated to the United States. Later Wilkerson was placed under guard and confined to his room, but on several occasions he operated on Communist soldiers brought to his hospital. The Christians were told they had to present a missionary for criticism at a public denunciation meeting. They selected a missionary lady who had long since departed this world and called her an "imperialist warmonger." One of the Christians explained: "In Heaven she will know and understand. . . . It can't hurt her." Wilkerson suffered from malnutrition until money for a supplementary diet was received from Hong Kong. With the money he was able to pay his taxes and place an advertisement in the paper saying he was leaving and was prepared to pay all debts.[101]

Dr. Lalla Iverson arrived at the Shandong University School of Medicine at Jinan as the Communist armies were approaching the city. The hospital voted to accept the invitation to join three Christian hospitals in Fuzhou on the south China coast. Three DC-3 transport planes were chartered to fly them to Qingdao where they boarded a former U.S. Navy LST for the trip south. Lalla played a major role in negotiating the necessary transportation for the successful one-thousand-mile move.[102]

Dr. Henry Nelson was determined to keep the Sarah Walkup Hospital in Taizhou open as long as possible. Katie Nelson, who was seven months pregnant, departed in November 1948, leaving Henry and Pete and Agnes Richardson to hold things together. When the Communist authorities announced they were taking over the hospital, Henry agreed to give them one building. To their surprise in three days time Nelson had gotten a brick wall built dividing the compound in two, keeping a section of the hospital for the mission. Relations with the new regime remained cordial and on some occasions Nelson was called in for consultations. On one critical case no blood donor could be found for a Communist soldier. Nelson gave his own blood. This created a sensation and the presentation of gifts and profuse thanks on the part of the patient. But the incident caused the hospital administrator to be fired. No more "fraternization" was permitted.[103] Finally, the exit permits arrived. Agnes Richardson has described the day of departure:

> The hundreds of friends who dared to come out in public and see us off at the bus station truly brought tears to our eyes. . . . Taichow friends sent two of the elders of the church to Shanghai to bid us farewell. Their tear-stained faces as our train pulled out, is something I'll never forget.[104]

The 1949–1950 academic year at Nanjing University finished surprisingly well. Dr. Andrew Roy and Mr. Lee Swann were officially invited to stay by the Communist administration. Mr. Swann, a new appointee and the first black

Presbyterian missionary to China, got along well with the students and was appointed head of the English Department. Roy's assignment was to teach the controversial course on dialectical materialism. Roy protested on the grounds that he was not a Marxist and thus not qualified to teach such a course. The department head insisted. After much persuasion Roy agreed:

> Why did I agree to the plan? We loved China and wanted to be with the Chinese people through this period of upheaval and change.... We had promised not to interfere with whatever political and economic system the Chinese might adopt.... That left room, I thought, for Christian insight and witness.[105]

Suddenly, on 1 December 1950, the university was covered with posters denouncing Dr. Roy. Twelve charges were made based on things Roy had said in his course. Two mass accusation meetings were planned. Roy explained what happened next:

> On the day of the first mass meeting a police guard was at our gate. We were later told that the emotional intensity of the meetings was unbelievable. Students wept on the platform. Accusations quickly went beyond quoted words into realms of imaginative venom.... The meeting was broadcast by loudspeakers over the whole section of the city.[106]

But there was the other side. One Christian professor came late at night to apologize for the denunciation he would make the next day. A mass meeting of Christian students was called and urged to denounce Roy but refused to do so. The head of the Student Labor Corps asked for baptism at a city church, stating that the attacks on the missionaries had led him to this decision.

Roy was told he had to write "confessions." Altogether he wrote seven of them, the first six of which were rejected. He apologized for living on a higher standard than many Chinese friends. He apologized for any "insulting behavior or words, which I, inadvertently, may have been guilty of." Finally, enough was written. Permission to leave came in February 1951.[107]

Dr. Frank Price was a special target. He had been an advisor to Chiang Kai-shek and a member of the Chinese delegation at the inaugural meeting of the United Nations in San Francisco. Among the accusations was that Dr. Price had once arranged for fifty Chinese students to go to America and stay in American homes where their minds had been poisoned.[108] For months Dr. and Mrs. Price kept a small suitcase packed in case police should arrive to take him to prison. He heard mob slogans against him broadcast over the radio. After two years of house arrest they received permission to leave in October 1952.

Dr. and Mrs. Nathaniel Bercovitz were detained in cramped quarters on the upper floor of the hospital in Haikou, Hainan until March 1953 after three years of detention.[109]

The last Presbyterian missionaries to leave were Dr. and Mrs. Homer Bradshaw and Miss Sarah Perkins of Lianzhou. Their release was negotiated by representatives of the United States and the People's Republic of China in Geneva during the summer of 1955. They were set free after nearly five years of prison life during which time they suffered severe malnutrition.[110]

For the first time in 113 years there was no American Presbyterian missionary in China.

15

Epilogue

Forty years after the last Presbyterian missionaries were expelled from China, Bishop K. H. Ting, President of the China Christian Council, came to the United States to take part in two events that symbolically bridged the gap of time and the events of history and once again linked American missionaries to the church in China. He met with Methodist missionaries at Lake Junaluska in North Carolina and with the Presbyterians at Columbia Seminary in Decatur, Georgia. He came with a special message for China missionaries.

The Presbyterian gathering was attended by 160 China missionaries and sons and daughters of missionaries who had grown up in China. The number exceeded all expectations and was striking evidence that, even after forty years, the China mission was alive in the hearts of many. Many of the old China names and families were represented. They had come to remember the past, renew acquaintances, celebrate the vitality of the church in China and hear what Bishop Ting wanted to say to them.

In a moving address Bishop Ting gave thanks for the missionary endeavor and expressed an apology on behalf of Chinese Christians for those forced to leave China over forty years ago:

> I want to apologize to former China missionaries and their families for all the suffering wrongly imposed on them forty years ago. I would be glad if you take my presence here as a token of healing and reconciliation in Christ.[1]

The missionaries responded by adopting the "Message to Chinese Christians," which they asked Bishop Ting to take back with him. In it they gave thanks for the gracious hospitality and friendship they had experienced from individual Chinese and for the church that had "adapted a gospel from abroad ...to a style that is essentially Chinese." Then they added:

> We also must apologize. We confess that we have not always been faithful in our calling to share your journey in the Lord. We have not always been sensitive and open enough to the work of the Spirit in your midst. We have not always been strong enough in our hope or insightful enough in our witness to God's work among you. In our pride we have sometimes

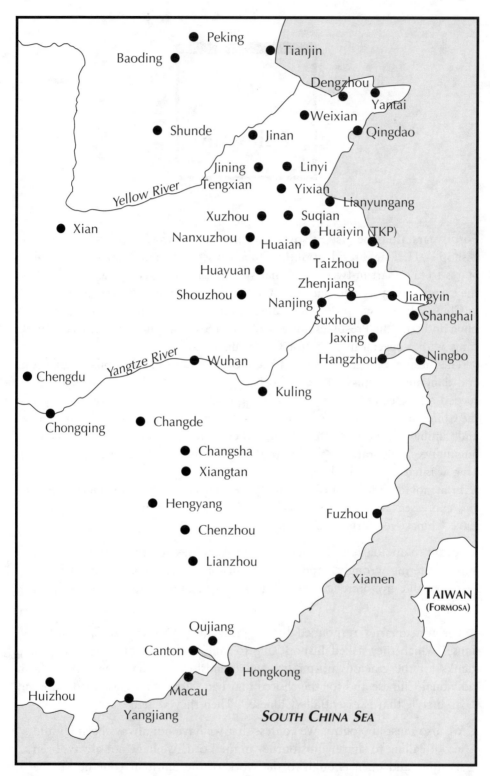

Presbyterian Mission Stations and Principal Cities 1934

been judges when we should have found ourselves before God among the judged.[2]

For many the China experience had ended on a note of rejection as they, or their parents, had been forced to leave China under difficult and painful circumstances. The memory of those events had left scars. Bishop Ting's presence and his words brought healing and wholeness. The reunion was a historic event that helped to seal the relationship between Chinese and American churches, members and missionaries.

This could be the fitting point at which to end our history. The story of these American missionaries in China has now been told. But the forty-year gap between the time it ended and the present compels us to ask some further questions. After all these years what remains of the old missionary order? After the anti-rightist campaigns, the Great Leap Forward and the Cultural Revolution can we still find any links with the past? Or have the ravages of time, the changes in the political system and the persistent campaign to discredit foreign imperialism eliminated any possibility of tracing the connections between the pre-1949 church and the church of today?

Astonishingly one discovers that there are a great number of links with the past. Certainly there is profound discontinuity. But there is also continuity. For it is the same church, the same gospel and the same people. The best metaphor of mission and church in China is Jesus' parable of the seed that fell into the ground and died and, in dying, produced much fruit (John 12:24). And that fruitfulness has exceeded all expectations in ways the missionary could not have imagined. But fruit and seed are of the same substance. The identity with the past is unmistakable.

An account of the Christian movement during these forty years is beyond the scope of this history.[3] But what we can and must do is to search the present scene for links with the past. In what ways did the missionary movement contribute to the character, vitality and growth of the Christian movement today? When that has been done it will be possible to offer a tentative assessment of the China missionary enterprise.

Links with the Past

Many of the former mission stations have been revisited by missionaries, family members or others who knew it in the pre-1949 days. I have visited China ten times between the years 1981 and 1993. Other information comes from reports published by the China Christian Council[4] and the Amity Foundation. Another source of information is the journal *Bridge: Church Life in China Today,* whose roving reporter has traveled all over China, visiting "Three-Self" churches, house congregations and sectarian groups and interviewing Christians of all persuasions as well as officials of the Religious Affairs Bureau.[5]

From these bits and pieces we can put together a picture of the church in

China. There are sharp contrasts between the various regions. All are different from the past. In this "post-denominational" era, Presbyterian churches are not to be found. Yet the impact of the Church of Christ in China is everywhere evident.

Two differences would be applauded by the missionaries: (1) The church is *Chinese* — in its leadership, culture, financial support, loyalties and ideology; (2) the church is experiencing *explosive growth*. Generations of missionaries tried to achieve these goals but with mixed success.

One surprise: In spite of all the anti-foreign, anti-missionary talk and propaganda of the 1950s and 1960s, whenever missionaries and their sons and daughters have returned, they have been overwhelmed by the welcome they have received.

Now for a cursory exploration of those places of missionary service. What are the links with the past?

Zhejiang

It is fitting that the city where the first Protestant church on China's soil was established would be the place for the first reopening of the churches at the end of the Cultural Revolution. In *Ningbo* on 8 April 1979 a group of Christians opened the doors of a church and held a service of Christian worship — the first such service held in all of China in ten years.[6] In 1984 800 new believers were baptized. By 1986 there were 250 churches and meeting points in the area but only 27 pastors. The church at Yu Yiao, where the Presbyterian revivals occurred in 1857, is again open.[7]

Zhejiang has the second largest number of Christians of any province of China. In 1996, the number of Christians was estimated at between 1.25 and 1.4 million, which would make up 2.5 percent of the population.[8] Throughout the province there were 2,000 churches, of which more than half were newly built. But there were only 96 pastors and 160 seminary graduates.[9]

Much of the increase has been in the southern district of Wenzhou, which has been called the "Jerusalem of China." More than 500 new churches have been built in Wenzhou over the past ten years. All were built with local resources.[10]

At the center of this activity has been *Hangzhou*, the capital city of the province, where there is a seminary, offices of the provincial Christian council, a distribution point for Bibles and Christian literature and the strong Sicheng church. Here a mass baptismal service was held in 1992 that reflected the various denominational traditions of today:

> In a grand service of July 5, the first group of 308 people out of 700 new converts who had applied for baptism were baptized at Sicheng Church in Hangzhou. Of the 308 baptismal candidates, 206 chose baptism by sprinkling and 102 were baptized by immersion.[11]

The Rev. Peter Tsai, grand old man of the Presbyterians in the pre-1949 years and chairman of the provincial Christian Council until his death in 1993, was the leader in the resurgence of the church. He bridged the gap between the leadership of the old Church of Christ in China of which he had been a part and that of the emerging Three-Self Movement. He had been deeply moved by the simple faith of the lay Christians during the Cultural Revolution and served as a bridge-builder between grassroots Christians and the national Christian council.

> Rev. Tsai was nurtured in the Reformed Tradition, but he was instrumental in bringing people from diverse Christian backgrounds together. He worked tirelessly for reconciliation with groups outside the CCC [China Christian Council] and TSPM [Three-Self Patriotic Movement].[12]

The number of Buddhists and Taoists in the province is dropping. Reasons for the rapid growth of Christians are difficult to determine but it should be remembered that this area was one of intensive missionary activity from the mid-nineteenth century.

Shanghai

Shanghai, the location of many ecumenical offices in the pre-1949 days, is again a thriving center of Christian activity. The valuable property on Yuen Ming Yuan Road that housed the Associated Mission Treasurers and related ecumenical offices is now the headquarters for the Three-Self Patriotic Movement. The city of 11 million people has 23 churches and 33 meeting points — the largest number of any city in China.[13] The number of Christians is estimated at between 100,000 and 127,000. Among the best known of the churches are the Mo-en Church (former Methodist), the Pure Heart Church (former Presbyterian) and the International Church (formerly the English-speaking Community Church). Adventists meet on Saturday at the Mo-en Church.

The author visited the Pure Heart Church in 1993 and talked with the pastor and members of the session. Their records go back to the early beginnings of the South Gate Presbyterian Church, established in 1860 — making it one of the oldest churches in China. The church, remodeled and beautifully equipped, has had a continuous record of Christian worship and service for 135 years, except for the "lost years" of the Cultural Revolution.

Anhui

Estimates of the number of Christians in the province run from 1 to 1.2 million. Although one of the smaller provinces with no big cities, it is the third or fourth largest in terms of the concentration of Christians. Officials have been at a loss to explain the rapid growth and a study of the phenomenon was made by the Chinese Social Science Publishing Company. The movement was started by women in their seventies. Many were illiterate. Of the Christians in the province, 92 percent were converted after 1976. Two principal reasons were given for becoming Christians: result of a healing incident in the family and the breakdown of family values after the Cultural Revolution. Christianity appealed to people because of its high ethical values, its respect for elders and love of children.[14]

Dr. Horace H. Whitlock visited *Nanxuzhou* and his old hospital in 1987, and received a most warm reception. The hospital staff wanted to make him the "honorary director" and petitioned the government to give the hospital back its old name of "Goodwill."[15] Dr. Christina Yates Parr, M.D., daughter of Dr. and Mrs. Theodore Yates of *Huayuan,* returned to her old home in 1991. The mission compound and hospitals had long since disappeared but "a lovely new church" had a congregation of about one thousand. The "struggling chapel" at the railroad junction of Bengbu was now a large church of twelve hundred members. She was reminded of the churches she had known as a child:

> close rows of wooden benches, raised platform with central pulpit, cross and verses on the wall, a communion table with artificial flowers below and plain undecorated windows. Their glory is the congregation — crowded to the doors…three times on Saturdays and Sundays.[16]

Jiangsu

Rev. Peter Han, general secretary of the Jiangsu Christian Council, reported in 1994 that there are 800,000 Protestant Christians in the province and 1,400 churches and meeting points. All churches are self-supporting and 95 percent of them have been built since 1980. On an average there are 30,000 adult baptisms annually. Infant baptisms are not performed. In the province there are only 85 ordained pastors and 65 seminarians preparing for ordination. The seminary is unable to train enough pastors, so a new Bible School for lay workers is being planned.[17] One problem: The True Jesus Church, the Little Flock and the Seventh Day Adventists want to worship separately and are stretching the limits to which they can go while remaining under the umbrella of the Christian Council.[18]

The church headquarters for Protestant Christians in the province (and the nation) is at *Nanjing.* Here are the offices of the China Christian Council, the Amity Foundation, the printing press and the Nanjing Union Theological Seminary. In the city there are seven Protestant churches with a membership of 8,000. There is one Roman Catholic church and two mosques.

In 1991 a significant event took place that illustrates the ecumenical linkage of the Chinese church:

> On April 28, 1991 Philip Wickeri [PCUSA missionary] the overseas coordinator of the Amity Foundation was ordained to the Christian ministry of the Chinese Church at St. Paul's in Nanjing. Ordination was conducted by Bishop K. H. Ting on behalf of the Jiangsu Christian Council. Methodist, Presbyterian, Baptist, and Anglican-Episcopal clergy participated. This was the first foreigner to be ordained in China in over 40 years.[19]

Another event illustrates the link with the past. The Drum Tower Hospital, begun by Disciples of Christ, Methodists and Presbyterians, celebrated its centennial in May 1993. The hospital, which is the oldest and one of the largest hospitals in the city, invited representatives of the founding missions to attend the celebration. City officials paid high tribute to the early missionaries. The PCUSA made a donation of ophthalmology equipment some years ago and provided opportunities for hospital staff to study in the United States.

The Amity Foundation, an organization founded by Chinese Christians, has served as a channel through which overseas churches and friends can help. Two projects should be noted. The Amity Press was established in 1985 with the co-operation of the United Bible Societies. The press printed and distributed 2.5 million copies of the Bible in 1995.[20] Amity sponsors the support of overseas English teachers and other volunteers in universities and technical schools. Included among these were 15 PCUSA young people who served in China in 1995.[21]

In both *Jiangyin* and *Suzhou* churches are thriving. The *Bridge* reporter visited Jiangyin in 1985 and reported nine thousand Protestant Christians in the city, 20 percent of whom had been baptized within the last three years.[22] Ms. Pat Johnson, daughter of Dr. and Mrs. Felix Welton who served at the Elizabeth Blake Hospital, visited Suzhou and the Church of the Apostles which was founded by Dr. Hampden DuBose in 1874. She has described her visit:

> The Apostles' Church...has 1,000 people worshipping in its two sanc-
> tuaries each Sunday (the lower sanctuary is serviced by closed circuit
> TV...). After the service about 150 people from the countryside are fed.
> The pastors...estimate there are 4,000 Christians in Suzhou's 1 million
> population. The services are basically Presbyterian in form.[23]

Relationships have been reestablished with the Christian community at *Zhen-jiang* through the former Goldsby King Hospital — now the Number One People's Hospital of the city. The superintendent asked the author about establishing a relationship with the PCUS mission board — which they acknowledge as the founder of the hospital. Through the Amity Foundation Dr. and Mrs. Henry Nelson were assigned there for a two-year period from 1986 to 1988.[24] Dr. Nelson located four of the old churches of the city — Baptist, Methodist, Presbyterian and China Inland Mission. One church had been reopened. City authorities want to preserve the old home of Pearl Sydenstricker Buck as a museum.

While in Zhenjiang, Dr. and Mrs. Nelson were able to visit the Sarah Walkup Hospital in *Taizhou* where they had served before 1949. They received a very warm welcome from twenty former colleagues who were still actively employed at the hospital. Sarah Walkup is now known as the Number One People's Hospital, and with an expanded 350-bed capacity is the largest hospital in the city.

The Christian church at Taizhou meets each Sunday in the former Lancaster residence. Between four hundred and five hundred people attend the services. The names of the early missionaries (Richardson, Lancaster, Mizell, Price and Bridgman) were all well remembered. The church has ambitious plans to build a new sanctuary as soon as negotiations for the return of property can be completed.[25]

Church growth in northern Jiangsu has been phenomenal. In one county there are seventy-eight meeting points, thirteen of which have congregations in excess of one thousand![26] Visitors to the former mission stations in the area underline the fantastic increase in the organization of new congregations and church attendance.

Ruth Bell Graham has described her visit to her old home in *Huaiyin* (TKP) in May 1980:

> It was small, gray, dilapidated. It was still of service, but the new oc-cupants, unused to the awkward "foreign architecture," had made the best of an inconvenient situation. Our home served them apparently as a dormitory for teachers. Between wars and revolutions and the inevitable looting the house had fared badly.... But over the front steps hung a large red-and-white banner: "American friends, your coming is warmly welcomed by the people living in your birthplace."[27]

The Love and Mercy Hospital, where Dr. L. Nelson Bell practiced, is now op-erated as a center for Chinese herbal medicine. Hospital staff were friendly and spoke with pride of their relationship with the Bell family and with Billy Graham, who had visited them.

Rev. Don and Jessie Junkin McCall visited Huaiyin (TKP) in October 1994 and both were invited to preach at the regular Tuesday afternoon service, which meets in the former Graham residence. All three floors were filled as well as the courtyard. "I was told there were 1,000 people present — the usual crowd." The Huaiyin church is the "mother church" to more than one hundred chapels and churches of various sizes. Elderly church members told stories of their friendship and recollections of early missionaries.[28]

The *Amity News Service* has reported that construction of a new church sanctuary has begun:

> Construction work has begun on what will be the largest church in Jiangsu Province. The church in Huaiyin will seat more than 3,000 people and is being built at a cost of more than three million Yuan.... It is estimated that there are more than 400,000 Christians in Huaiyin Prefecture wor-shipping in 1,200 churches and meeting points.... There is currently no proper church building in Huaiyin city and worship services are being held at a former missionary residence, in extremely cramped conditions.[29]

The neighboring city and mission station of *Huaian* on the Grand Canal is the county seat for an area that has sixty-one churches and preaching points. Jessie and Don McCall were asked to preach at Sunday morning and evening services held in the former Yates home. Every room of the old two story gray brick building was filled, and several hundred were seated under a large canopy in the courtyard. Because of steady rain the attendance was not as large as the usual one thousand, but there were at least seven hundred people present. Christians are building a new sanctuary that will seat two thousand and will be the center for the numerous Bible classes and training sessions for the other churches in the area.[30]

The long and fruitful years of service by Dr. and Mrs. William F. Junkin, Sr., at *Suqian* are well remembered by the Christian community. One old gentleman told the McCalls the stories he had heard about "Dr. Junkin kneeling in the mud outside the city gates, pleading with bandit leaders to relinquish their attacks on the city."[31] Today about 4 percent of the 1.2 million people in the county are Christian. Christians in the Suqian area now outnumber the Buddhists.[32] The large church building had not been returned but the city gave the Christians a smaller plot in an outlying district on which they were preparing to build.[33]

Readers will remember the account of the martyrdom of John Walker Vinson in 1932 at the village of Yang-Djia-Gee near the mission station of *Lianyungang*. Jean Vinson Urquhart, daughter of the martyred missionary, has kept in touch with the Christian congregation in the village down through the years. Recent letters have told of the rebuilding and enlargement of the sanctuary in 1988. The Christian community now numbers about two thousand with another two thousand in the countryside.[34]

The author has visited his home at *Xuzhou* on two recent occasions. The girls' school was still open but was coeducational and run by the government. The former mission hospital is now the Number Two People's Hospital and enjoys a fine reputation of caring for the poor and needy. But the big surprise was the fantastic number of people that packed the old West Gate Church, built by Rev. O. V. Armstrong in 1914. In order to reach the seats reserved for foreign visitors one had to step over those seated or squatting in the courtyard to listen to the service broadcast over the public address loudspeakers.

Churches in the area now number 30 organized congregations, 200 meeting points and 150 church buildings. There have been 3,000 adult baptisms since 1980.[35] Because of the near impossible congestion at the West Gate Church, the Christians have finally obtained possession of the South Gate Church, founded by Rev. E. H. Hamilton years ago. One elderly lady, who worked with the missionaries in starting rural churches, made this comparison: "In the olden days, the shepherds (pastors) would seek the sheep, while today it is the sheep that seek the shepherd."

Shandong

The Shandong Provincial Christian Conference, meeting in 1993, reported that there were 460,000 Protestant Christians in the province, 851 churches and more than 3,000 preaching points. At a festive service 31 pastors (including 6 women) were ordained and assigned to work in their respective churches.[36]

The largest number of Christians are in the southern part of the province and are enjoying the extremely rapid growth that has been noted in northern Jiangsu. *Linyi* has become the central location for the many churches in that area. In the district are more than one hundred thousand Christians, mostly in the rural areas. Because of the large number seeking church membership, a three-year study period is required before baptism.

One problem has been the growth of bizarre Christian sects known as "The Sect of Rebirth" and the "Sect for Truth."[37] Another problem has been the slowness of the authorities to return church properties seized during the Cultural Revolution. Churches have become more aggressive in pursuing lawsuits against work units that have refused to return such property.[38]

Dr. Norval Christy, longtime missionary ophthalmologist and cataract surgeon in Pakistan, visited Linyi in 1990 in connection with a survey of eye clinics in North China. He reported that the Floyd D. White General Hospital was now known as the "People's Hospital of Linyi District," had been expanded to a six-hundred-bed capacity and was responsible for medical care in the surrounding thirteen counties. He reported that the hospital was proud of its Presbyterian mission heritage.

In *Jinan,* the capital of the province, five churches are now open but are unable to accommodate the four thousand Christians in the city. "To discourage enthusiastic believers from running from one place to another to hear the word of God on Sundays, all churches in Jinan hold their worship services at the same time."[39]

In *Qingdao* two buildings stand out on the city's skyline: the Catholic cathedral and the Lutheran church. It is said that the oldest church in the city was built by the Presbyterians in 1873. It was not used for many years but has recently been renovated and put back in service.[40]

Peking

In 1993 there were eight Protestant churches in the capital and another three in the surrounding area. Meeting points numbered two hundred, most of which were affiliated with the Peking Christian Council. Church membership of the city probably numbers thirty thousand and two hundred thousand in the surrounding province of Hebei. The two most prominent churches in the city are the Gangwashi and the Chongwenmen. The political climate in Peking has had a detrimental effect on church growth as problems have persisted with the government over the registration of churches and the appointment of pastors.[41]

The Douw Hospital, founded by Presbyterians in 1885, is now known as the Number Six Hospital of Peking. Today it is a modern medical center with five hundred beds, thirty clinics, and a staff of nearly a thousand. It celebrated the 110th anniversary of its founding in 1995 and sent an invitation to the Presbyterian Church (USA) to send a representative. The hospital would like to establish a relationship with a Presbyterian hospital in the United States.[42]

In the early 1950s the PCUSA Board of Foreign Mission received a check for $1 million from an anonymous Chinese donor. He said he was a graduate of the Truth Hall Academy in Peking, founded by W. A. P. Martin in 1864. He was grateful for the education he had received, which had enabled him to make his fortune in the import-export trade. He had noted that missionaries, when they reached retirement age, had no place to call home since they had spent the better years of their lives abroad. The gift was designated for a missionary retirement home, and was used to establish Westminster Gardens in Duarte, California.

Hunan

The reopening of the churches in Hunan was slower than it was in provinces along the eastern seaboard and did not really get started until after 1985. Churches have now been reopened in all the cities of the Hunan Presbyterian Mission: Changsha, Hengyang, Xiangtan, Changde and Chenzhou. Christians in the province now number at least sixty thousand with a growing number of young people. The church is becoming active in social service projects — with a home for the aged and disabled and a rehabilitation center for the hearing and speech impaired in Changsha.[43]

In 1994 the Fuxiang Girls' School, now the Number Two Middle School of Changsha, celebrated the eightieth anniversary of its founding in 1914 by Miss Annie R. Morton of the Hunan Mission. A history of the school was published, which expressed great appreciation to the Presbyterian Church for its contribution to women's education. At the school reunion, 160 alumnae met and as they sat down to dinner they sang their school hymn of thanksgiving. One alumna remarked: "What God has taught us in those years is kept deep in our hearts." In the celebration recognition was given to the founder, Annie Morton, and to the school's most illustrious graduate and national hero, Yang Kaihui, the first wife of Chairman Mao Zedong who was captured and executed by the KMT in 1930.[44]

Yunnan

Nobody knows how many Christians are in the province. Estimates begin at 640,000 and go as high as 900,000. Minority tribal people make up 90 percent of the Christian numbers.[45]

The two former mission stations among the Dai (Tai) people at Jiulongjiang and Yuanjiang are difficult to identify because places and roads have changed. But the *Bridge* roving reporter found one village that claimed all their members were Christians and linked their history with the coming of the Presbyterians:

> An old woman said that at the turn of the century, missionaries of the American Presbyterian Mission came to Xishuangbana from North Thailand. Altogether they built three churches in the prefecture.[46]

There were now sixteen churches or meeting places among the Dai.

Hainan

In 1985 a delegation from the Guangdong Christian Council made a tour of the island. They reported that thirty-one churches and meeting points were in operation. New places of worship were being built and a training course for Christian leaders had been held. Three pastors were ordained by the delegation.[47]

Most encouraging was the work among the Miao tribe. Over eight hundred of these tribal people met for worship with the delegation and told of their history. The church had been planted among them by Presbyterian missionaries. They had suffered unjust persecution in 1945 as they had been suspected of collaboration with the Japanese. Whole villages had been slaughtered. In more recent years new churches have been built. One village reported that all of their 150 members were Christians. The Miao Christians have retained many of their pre-Christian customs such as the exorcism of evil spirits and "spiritual dancing."[48]

Ms. Marie Melrose and the Rev. Robert Thomas, who lived on the island in early years, have visited their old homes and received a warm welcome. Churches in the four mission centers of Ledong, Haikou, Qiongzhou and Jiaji are all in operation. The two hospitals at Ledong and Haikou are operated by the government. Estimate of the number of Christians on the island is between ten thousand and thirty thousand.[49]

Guangdong

Church membership throughout the province is said to be between 160,000 and 200,000. Relationships with Christians in Canton have been numerous and cordial. But possibly because of commercialization, church growth has not been as rapid as in the rural areas further north.

The church in *Lianzhou* where the massacre of five missionaries took place in 1905 is again open after passing through most difficult times. The *Bridge* reporter visited the city and gave an account of the founding of the church, of the massacre, of steady growth. Then came double trouble:

> Immediately after the liberation of Lian Xian [Lianzhou] in December, 1949, however, the Double Happiness Hill Incident occurred, which resulted in the incarceration of all foreign missionaries, Chinese pastors, evangelists, doctors and even the matron of the hospital for two years. Church work was brought to a total halt.[50]

What was the "Double Happiness Hill Incident"? We do not know. The missionaries in Lianzhou who were there at the time are no longer with us. Neither the mission nor board records give any clue to what happened. Obviously, it had something to do with the imprisonment of Dr. and Mrs. Homer Bradshaw and Miss Sarah Perkins, who were not released until 1955. But the details of the trouble are shrouded in silence.

Nevertheless, the Christian community has rebounded from the adversity. After years of negotiation, the property on Double Happiness Hill has been exchanged for another plot of land on which a church has been built. The dedication service was held in 1986 and attended by 130 brave souls who had remained faithful throughout the times of adversity.[51]

And so the church...had peace and was built up; and walking in the fear of the Lord and in the comfort of the Holy Spirit it was multiplied. (Acts 9:31).

Assessment

The story of the Presbyterian China missions would be incomplete without some attempt at an appraisal of these 117 years of history. A total of 1,730 missionaries from the two American boards served in China. Of this number approximately 210 died and were buried there. At least 250 of their children also died there.[52] The author owes it to his readers to offer an assessment of this costly investment. Some of the observations will meet with near universal acceptance. Some will be debated. Some will need to be revised in the light of other studies.

This assessment is primarily that of the author. However, the conclusions are supported by recent surveys, interviews and questionnaires. Four should be mentioned: (1) the survey made of returning China missionaries by the National Council of the Churches of Christ in the USA (NCCCUSA), Division of Foreign Mission in 1951;[53] (2) a questionnaire prepared by the author and mailed to all Presbyterian (North and South) China missionaries in 1988;[54] (3) the China Missionaries Oral History Project conducted by the Claremont Graduate School in 1973;[55] and (4) interviews with Chinese Christian leaders in May 1993.[56]

Contributions

To begin with there is a general consensus as to the many contributions made by Protestant missionaries in China. In more recent years this appreciation has been growing as Chinese scholars probe the history of the missionary era. Recently published works in China give prominent space to the work of the missions.[57] Although still critical, they are far more sympathetic than the accounts available fifteen years ago.

Viewed by secular scholars, the primary contribution lay in the educational and medical institutions. The missionary was the catalyst that initiated the modernization of the country. Movements for reform (literacy, public health, democracy, the medical and nursing professions, education for women) were closely associated with the coming of the missionary.

As viewed by the Christians, the chief contribution of the missionaries was that they brought the gospel of Jesus Christ to China and planted the church in their land. The format of the worship services, the content of the preaching and the hymn book all reflect the missionary presence. Most of the present church leaders were trained in mission institutions.

Were there specific "Presbyterian" contributions? Three areas are listed by those interviewed and in the surveys:

1. *The unity of the Church*. Presbyterians took the lead in most of the ecumenical institutions and programs. "We were a part of the Church of Christ in China, heart, soul, and money. We supported interdenominational hospitals, schools, universities and programs....Praise God we served the work of Christ, his mission and his church, not something with the label 'Presbyterian.' "[58]

2. *Leadership training*. Higher education, the training of ministers, short-term institutes for laypeople, and schools for women were areas of substantial achievement.

3. *Health ministries*. This included medical institutions but also ministry to marginalized peoples neglected by Chinese society such as the blind, the deaf and the insane.

Failings

There is also general agreement on the part of both Chinese Christians and missionaries as to the flaws and failures of the missionary movement. Those most often mentioned:

1. *Foreignness*. "The church as it developed remained too western in character — not sufficiently indigenous as to thought patterns, worship, architecture....Too many missionaries had an inadequate understanding of the Chinese language...culture";[59] "...our inability to indigenize theology and the traditions of the church."[60] "...an overemphasis on European cultural aspects of church life."[61]

2. *Life-styles*. "Too much foreign owned and controlled property...large houses in high-walled isolated residence compounds."[62] "We were unable to truly identify with the Chinese...use of Chinese style clothes, food or shelter was only superficial."[63] "Our huge houses were deplorable."[64] Yet "I still don't see how [changes in life-style] could have been done without sacrificing our children."[65]

3. *Control*. "Too many missionaries kept too much control too long over institutions, funds, policies, methods, and activities."[66] "The governing theory was we must control what we pay for."[67] "We were always taught that a mission was a 'scaffolding' within which the Chinese Church should emerge, but we kept the scaffolding up too long."[68]

4. *Denominationalism*. "Too much denominational emphasis."[69] "The numerous denominations and sects brought in by the mission societies transplanted among us a variety of denominations and sectarian groups which were greatly detrimental to the communion and unity of church members and the growth of the true church."[70]

Continuity and Discontinuity

Although there is general agreement on these shortcomings, the viewpoint of present-day church leaders and former missionaries does differ in one respect. Chinese Christian leaders tend to emphasize the discontinuity between the missionary era and that of the Three-Self church while former missionaries stress the continuity. Some Chinese leaders say that it was only after 1949 that a true Three-Self autonomous church emerged. Note this statement of the Chinese viewpoint:

> Christians in China as a whole regarded the individual missionary workers with high esteem and good will because they were such fine people and they brought us the Gospel — for which fact we shall remain grateful always. But the resentment was quite prevalent for the way the church, instead of being governed by ourselves, was managed primarily the similar way the branch offices of foreign business firms in China were controlled by their parent organization.[71]

Presbyterian missionaries serving in China would question whether this would be an accurate description of their church relationships after 1927, although it might have been applicable in an earlier period. Two factors are pointed out: (1) There were great differences in policy between the various mission boards and it would be a mistake to lump them all together. (2) Great strides were made in the decade 1927–1937, and criticisms that would be more than valid for an earlier period would not be true for that last decade. In contrast to the Roman Catholics, who by 1926 had only one Chinese bishop, "Protestants had already placed Chinese in the majority on the National Christian Council, and were making them district superintendents, secretaries of boards, and principals of schools."[72] There is ample evidence that during the decade 1927–1937 Presbyterian missions had taken genuine strides toward establishing a Three-Self church. The Church of Christ in China was the capstone of these efforts.[73] "It would be a terrible mistake," writes Paul Lindholm, "to conclude, as some present day Chinese leaders say, that there was no truly 'Chinese indigenous Three-Self Church' until the Communist era."[74] The issue seems to be one of perception rather than reality. The Church of Christ in China, by its doctrinal confession, its constitution, its elected leadership, its program and budgets and its interchurch relationships, was an autonomous Chinese church. Yet the perception of Chinese leaders and the public was that it, along with other denominations, was still a foreign institution. Although Chinese served as moderators, presidents and chairmen, they felt constrained by age, seniority or friendship with missionaries to follow the "missionary line." In many cases minutes were still printed in English. Because of the necessity for foreign funding, it was assumed that the "missionary club" made the decisions behind the scenes. Missionaries speak of their efforts in getting Chinese leaders to take over, but their Chinese colleagues were reluctant to do so as long as their seniors in age and experience were still around.

It is understandable that the present Christian leadership emphasizes the discontinuity of the two periods, for it was only after the departure of the missionaries in 1949 that the public perception of the church changed from one of foreign dependence to one of self-determination. This radical shift was certainly one of the major reasons for the rapid growth and vitality of the church in the "New China." But it would be wrong to underestimate the degree of real progress toward independence and selfhood that was made prior to 1949.

In fact a case could be made that the Church of Christ in China laid the groundwork for today's Three-Self church. Certainly the similarities are striking: the national aspirations for a "Chinese church," the acceptance of different theological traditions, the decentralized style of administration, the role of the elder and the nonliturgical style of worship. Even the slogan of the "three-selfs" was articulated in a popular hymn of the Church of Christ in China.[75]

The Christian Constituency in 1949

How many Christians were in China at the time of the missionary withdrawal? An estimate of 700,000 Protestants and 3,000,000 Catholics has often been given.[76] But this figure almost certainly underestimates the number of Protestants. Statistics in the *World Christian Handbook* of 1952 give the baptized Protestant membership as 902,821.[77] But note the following: (1) These figures are based on a survey made by the National Christian Council in China in the year 1950 — during a time of social upheaval and civil war and just when the Communist forces were coming to power. Almost certainly reports from some areas were incomplete. The number of adherents would be minimized as Christian groups waited to see the attitude of the new regime. (2) The figures do not include statistics for the "Little Flock" and some other indigenous Chinese Christian groups. (3) The figures are for baptized adult members. They do not include children of Christian families, inquirers or others under Christian instruction. In all probability the Protestant Christian constituency in 1950 numbered at least 3 million. And the influence of the Christian movement on the China of the day was out of all proportion to the number of adherents. The 1931 edition of *Who's Who of China* shows that 35 percent of those listed had been educated in Protestant schools and colleges.[78] A high percentage of government officials and professionals were Christians.[79] In 1930 over 50 percent of the medical profession were either Christians or had been trained in mission medical schools.[80]

Protestant Denominations in 1949

The seven largest Protestant denominations in 1949, listed in order of communicant membership, were the following:

Church of Christ in China	206,000
The True Jesus Church	125,000
The Methodist Church	102,000
China Inland Mission churches	85,000
Anglican/Episcopal Church	76,000
Baptists	65,000
Lutheran	65,000[81]

The denominations can be grouped in the following categories.

1. *The Church of Christ in China.* The history and organization of this church have been treated earlier.

2. *Other "Mainline" denominations.* These included Anglicans, Methodists, Lutherans and some Baptists. Most were members of the National Christian Council of China and were cooperative. Denominational emphases were observed but methods of work were broadly similar.

3. *The China Inland Mission.* This nondenominational "faith" mission had the largest number of missionaries in China. It had the best record in distancing itself from the colonial system and made a concerted effort to adapt to Chinese customs and dress. The mission worked in remote areas of China with emphasis on evangelistic outreach rather than on schools and hospitals.

4. *Chinese indigenous or independent churches.* Some of these developed along Western models but separated themselves from the missionary movement, usually around their own Chinese charismatic leader. Other indigenous churches developed completely apart from Western influence. Often these rejected the practice of a professional clergy and were communal in nature. These included the True Jesus Church, the Jesus Family and the Little Flock. Some of these sects have grown rapidly in the new China; they are accepted under the umbrella of the Three-Self church but insist on their own distinctive practices.[82]

5. *The YMCA and YWCA.* Although not denominations as such, they were quite influential in the development of Christianity in China. Their work was limited for the most part to the major cities and the better-educated classes. Perhaps for these reasons they were quite successful in achieving self-support for programs and Y secretaries. They were more liberal in theology, more actively engaged in social service and very influential in the Three-Self leadership of the "new China."[83]

Chinese Workers

Mission records tend to overemphasize the work done by missionaries, and do not give sufficient credit to the many Chinese workers who served as pastors

and staffed the medical and educational institutions. Professor Daniel H. Bays
has made this critical observation:

> Mission records seriously understate the Chinese role, and often don't even
> have the names of Chinese participants, but they were there. They played
> key roles in religious activities, as assistants, preachers, translators. They
> staffed the thousands of stations with no resident missionaries.[84]

Missionaries wrote for home consumption. Americans found Chinese names
strange, hard to pronounce and soon forgotten. To raise support, it was important that the results of missionary activity be appreciated. All mission histories,
including this one, tend to overemphasize the deeds of the missionary. But a
mission history cannot tell the whole story of the Christian movement. This is
why it is so important for Chinese scholars to write the history of the Christian
movement from their perspective.

Anti-foreign Movements

How serious was the outbreak of anti-foreign and anti-Christian movements
in China? In the 1988 questionnaire the following question was asked of missionaries who had served between the years 1921 and 1951: "How serious was
anti-foreignism in your China experience?" Surprisingly, twenty-four missionaries said it was never a problem; ten said it was sometimes a problem, but
not serious. Only five said that it was, indeed, a serious problem. The Claremont Oral History Project's report was the same: "After 1928 the missionaries
were not bothered by overt anti-foreignism."[85] Many said that in China personal relationships made all the difference and that their acquaintances were
little concerned with national politics. Aside from the Boxer Uprising in 1900
and the May Fourth Movement (1922–1927), anti-foreignism was negligible.
But students were probably an exception. After the Communist victory in 1949,
there was a change, but missionaries felt that the anti-Americanism expressed
at that time was forced and not spontaneous.

Martyrs

Fourteen Presbyterian missionaries and four of their children met violent deaths
during the 117 years of this history. The remarkable fact, however, is that there
were not more of them. These were violent times in China and the places of
missionary residence made them vulnerable. Yet the violence of the anti-foreign
riots should not be overestimated. Most missionaries lived out their lives or
terms of service in peace and friendship with their Chinese neighbors. Compared to the treatment Americans were giving Chinese immigrants in America,
missionaries were treated very well indeed. Chinese officials kept the Unequal
Treaties with the United States far better than Americans kept their treaties with
China. The China missions and the home boards repeatedly protested the treatment of Chinese immigrants in America to the President and the Congress but
to little avail.

Self-Support and John L. Nevius

The NCCCUSA Survey found general agreement among missionaries about the failure to achieve self-support: There was "much *talk* about self-support but not enough *action* in that direction."[86] In retrospect, missionaries often referred to John L. Nevius and the methods he proposed for developing self-supporting churches.[87]

Would the outcome have been different if the methods he proposed had been followed? It's hard to say. Certainly the adoption of the Nevius methods by the Presbyterian missions in Korea was one reason for their success.[88]

Yet more progress was made in this area than is often recognized. The Nevius methods, while never fully accepted, nevertheless had their influence. Shandong, where Nevius worked, became the strongest synod for the Presbyterians and the one that most clearly exemplified a Three-Self church. In 1932, the Presbytery of Weixian became entirely self-supporting.[89] This meant that the presbytery of 7,645 communicant members raised sufficient funds within its own bounds to support its 12 ordained ministers, 36 organized churches, and 15 chapels without any financial support from abroad.[90]

Mission/Church Property

One of the legacies of the missionary era that is often overlooked is the large amount of valuable property left to the churches. For example, millions of dollars worth of property was left by the missions in Shanghai alone.[91] The government recognizes the right the Christians have to this property. In a number of cases where the property was damaged or vandalized by the Red Guards, the government has provided funds for rehabilitation. The Nanjing Union Theological Seminary was able to swap a valuable piece of property for the construction of a new modern dormitory. Where the church does not have possession of the property, substantial rental fees are collected. These fees have been a valuable and continuing source of revenue.

People Movements

For the most part the growth of the Christian movement in China was through the conversion of individuals and their families. In a few significant occasions there were what might be called "people movements" — the San Poh revival near Ningbo, the breakthrough at Lingwu near Hangzhou, the mass movements among the Miao tribe in Hainan and the Ka Do people in Yunnan. What can be learned from these experiences? First, that they cannot be planned or anticipated. When fire strikes, great care should be taken not to "quench the spirit." When such a phenomenon occurs, the missionary should stay in the background and work through local Christian leadership. And one should be prepared to accept changes as it should not be surprising if the movement takes on characteristics that are not entirely in keeping with the polity and traditions of the West.[92]

Dilemmas in Theological Education

For Presbyterians the training of ministers has always been a matter of great importance. But in China they were caught in a dilemma. Their church tradition emphasized the development of an educated ministry. Another basic principle was that of having self-supporting churches. And the two goals collided with each other. Raising the standards of the ordained ministry to that of a college education plus a theological degree meant developing a clergy that small churches and rural congregations could not support. A highly educated clergy could be supported only through substantial subsidies from abroad. It was a dilemma never solved. There was a second dilemma: Should theological education be ecumenical or indigenous? Missionaries, often at the strong urging of the Home Boards, established theological colleges that were departments of their universities. Such institutions related admirably to the ecumenical milieu of the university campus, but had difficulty gaining the loyalty and acceptance of the denominational churches that provided ministerial candidates. For example, the Home Boards made a considerable investment in funds and faculty for the theological departments of Yenching and Shandong Christian University. But such schools attracted few candidates for the ministry. On the other hand, the ultra-conservative North China Theological College, established by the Synod of Shandong and the presbyteries of North Jiangsu with little support from the home boards, had twice the student body of the theological departments of Yenching and Shandong Christian University combined.[93]

Missionaries and Their Boards

In the early days the missionaries were pretty much left on their own. They received little guidance (or interference) and mission policies were adopted by trial and error. A new day began in 1875 when regular mail service was initiated by steamers that crossed the Pacific in sixteen days. Home Boards began to exercise a far greater degree of management and control. For the most part relationships between Boards and missionaries were cordial and respectful. But in perhaps a dozen or so cases, there was a sharp dissent from the Board's ruling and a protest lodged with the General Assembly. In almost all cases, the Assembly, as would be expected, sided with the Board.

Responses to the 1988 questionnaire regarding Board relationships were overwhelmingly favorable. Typical responses were: "excellent," "very supportive," "very cordial and sympathetic." Missionaries spoke of the "spiritual giants" of their times — Robert E. Spear, Arthur J. Brown, Egbert W. Smith, and C. Darby Fulton.[94]

The one criticism of the New York Board that surfaced from time to time was that the Board or one of its secretaries sometimes took actions precipitously without consulting the field body. The Executive Committee in Nashville was faulted for the opposite reason: It did not act with sufficient decisiveness in settling controversial issues. For example, disagreements between the North

Jiangsu and Mid China missions over support of the Nanjing Theological Seminary continued over a decade with the board unwilling or unable to resolve the matter one way or the other.

Local Initiatives

Significantly, many of the initiatives launched by the China missions did not come about as the result of the carefully orchestrated selection of goals and priorities by long-range planning committees. The creative incentive for new undertakings often came from an individual missionary who became obsessed with some critical human need and then endeavored to move heaven and earth to fill that need. Often the venture was first opposed by the home Board. For example, the first school for the deaf in the Chinese Empire was started by Mrs. Annetta Thompson Mills, the first school for the blind by Dr. Mary West Niles and the first asylum for the insane by Dr. John G. Kerr. All met initial Board resistance. Funds came from gifts given by individuals or churches as a result of missionary appeals. From the standpoint of a unified program of setting priorities, it was a decidedly "messy" way of doing business. Yet this is the way the "great advance" in China missions took place.

This is not to say that the role of the Board was unimportant. At some point for the project to survive it needed to be "baptized" by the Board and incorporated into the ongoing program. Often the Board, as a referee, had to make judgment calls between projects that were in competition.

Missionaries and the Revolution

China missionaries have been faulted for not having perceived more clearly the meaning of the Communist revolution. The Rev. Donald MacInnis points to this omission in the NCC 1951 Survey, which summarized the replies of 152 American missionaries recently returned from China:

> Nowhere do these missionaries, recently living in the midst of the greatest revolutionary upheaval in modern history, refer to that cataclysmic event, or to the social forces that brought it about, nor do they point to the need to understand and relate to such events in the future.[95]

The NCC statement of returning missionaries speaks obliquely of the "immense revolution of China." Perhaps this was all they could say at the time for they were writing in 1951, all too close to their experience to see it clearly.

A year later Dr. Frank W. Price spoke of "the end of an era" after his release from house arrest and return home:

> Communism is a judgement, a warning and a challenge. It may in unexpected ways bring about what we have long hoped for — a Christian church rooted in the soil of China, and not dependent on the missionary finances and personnel of Western countries. . . . I would say to missionaries in every land — work as if this were your last year; prepare the church where you are for the storm that may come.[96]

But how does one prepare for a revolution? Humanly speaking there is nothing that the missionary movement could have done to change the course of events leading up to 1949.

Perhaps the greatest lesson from the Chinese Revolution for the world mission enterprise is that the goal can never be reduced to short-term ends or easy solutions. We are involved in a long-term enterprise that looks to the distant horizon of history and the consummation of the age. Only now, forty-five years after the end of the mission, are we able to see the amazing results of the seeds that were sown.

Influence back Home

China missionaries changed the way Americans thought about the Chinese people. For most of these years they were the primary interpreters of the "Middle Kingdom." They heavily influenced American foreign policy toward China.[97] W. A. P. Martin (consul), Hampden Coit DuBose (nemesis of the opium trade), Pearl Sydenstricker Buck (novelist), Henry Winters Luce (educator and father of the founder of *Time*), John Leighton Stuart (ambassador), all took part in shaping U.S.-China relations.

The Claremont interviewers found that "living in China exercised a subtle influence on the personal attitudes and behavior" of their missionaries who believed they had "returned to the United States as better individuals."[98] They had found much to admire in the Chinese character: industriousness, friendliness, family orientation, optimism in face of adversity, personal dignity, pragmatism, tolerance and politeness.[99] They were eager to tell their experiences to their home churches. One of the learnings repeated by the Presbyterians was the "increasing realization of the absolute necessity of linking evangelism with social concern and with the preservation of the unity of the church in Christ."[100]

For the southern church, it could be said that the China mission had as much impact on the home church as it did on China. It provided the means by which Presbyterians in the South became internationalized. The Civil War and slavery had isolated the South from the world scene. The China mission changed all this. China was the bridge that led to a broader commitment to worldwide mission, social service and the ecumenical movement.

The world mission enterprise, in which China played such a leading part, helped to shape the identity of Presbyterians (North and South) as members of a "connectional" church. The cause of "Foreign Missions" mandated a strong General Assembly structure, for missions could not be done any other way. "Presbyterians were members for life of a missionary society, the object of which was the conversion of the world."[101]

Faith in the China Mission

One of the striking characteristics of the missionary responses to their experience was their conviction that their China mission would one day come to fruition. In spite of the bitter experience through which they had passed, their faith was unshaken. The message of the returned missionaries at the 1951 NCCC conference ends with this ringing challenge:

> The taking of the Christian Gospel to China and the establishing of the Church of Jesus Christ among the Chinese people, we believe to be the plan and work of God, ultimately triumphing over all the human weakness of the missionary movement.[102]

The Claremont China Oral History Project report is much the same:

> Few of the missionaries expressed any regret over their decision to become a China missionary.... This abrupt ending to a century of effort on the part of many thousands of Catholic and Protestant missionaries ... seems not to have destroyed their faith that Christian moral and spiritual values have taken root.[103]

Presbyterian missionaries speak of their continued commitment to missions and to China. Many of them have returned to visit their places of service and to talk with former colleagues. They have been enthusiastic about the renewal of PCUSA relationships with China, and in support of Amity Foundation projects. Many are deeply involved in ministries to Chinese congregations and students in the United States.[104]

Earthen Vessels and Transcendent Power

We return once again to the theme expressed at the beginning of this history:

> We have this treasure in earthen vessels to show that the transcendent power belongs to God and not to us. (2 Cor. 4:7)

The missionaries were the "earthen vessels" or "clay pots" — common, fragile and flawed. The gospel they proclaimed was the treasure — precious and powerful beyond measure. Time and again the fragile humanity of the missionary has been contrasted with the "transcendent power" of the gospel they brought.

The results of the enterprise exceeded all expectations. Yet the course of events was not what was expected. The transforming power of the gospel did its work but followed no human timetable. It accomplished its purpose but in so doing shattered the human hopes and desires of its carriers. And in the end the missionary movement had to die in order that its mission could be accomplished.

The mantle of the clay pots passed to the Chinese Christians. Their experience has been the same as that of the missionaries, power in the midst of weakness, life in the midst of death. Bishop Ting wrote of this experience during the darkest days of the Cultural Revolution:

> We thought of the Gospel as something precious, but the Red Guards ... thought of it as nothing but a poisonous weed.... Not a single church

remained open.... We were very weak indeed, a little flock. By all human reckoning Christianity, perhaps for the fourth time in Chinese history, was again breathing its last breath. What we were blind to was that when we were weak and dying, life was in the offing.[105]

We "have this treasure" and yet our full understanding of it remains incomplete until the Christians of China have added their insights and their wisdom.

Appendix A

Presbyterian Mission Hospitals in China

City names are given in Pinyin with Wade-Giles spelling in parenthesis. Figures in parenthesis following the name of the city indicate the year missionary residence occurred. Figures following the hospital's name are the approximate date of opening. A "(U)" indicates the hospital was a union institution. The hospital's name in Chinese was often quite different from the one in English. Information about present state of hospitals is often incomplete.

Peking (1863)

An Ting ("Tranquility") Hospital for Men (1883)
Douw Memorial Hospital for Women (1887)
    Later merged. Today known as "Number 6 Hospital of Peking."

Hebei

Baoding (Paoting) (1893)
    Taylor Memorial Hospital — Men (1893)
    Hodge Memorial Hospital — Women (1893)
        Later merged. No record since 1951.
Shunde (Shunteh) (1903)
    Hugh O'Neill Memorial Hospital — Men (1905)
    Grace Talcott Hospital — Women (1905)
        Not reopened after World War II.

Shandong

Jinan (Tsinan) (1872)
    McIlvaine Hospital — Men (1892)
    Louisa Y. Boyd Hospital — Women (1900)
        Became dispensaries. Not reopened after World War II.
    Cheeloo Medical School (U) (1917)
        Now part of the Shandong Medical College.
Jining (Tsining) (1892)
    Rose Bachman Hospital for Women (1892)
    Annie Hunter Memorial Hospital for Men (1893)
        Later united. Not reopened after World War II.
Linyi (Ichow) (1890)
    Floyd D. White General Hospital (1889)
        Now known as the "People's Hospital of Linyi District."

Weixian (Weihsien) (1883)
  Shadyside Hospital (1922)
      Not reopened after World War II.
Yantai (Chefoo) (1862)
  Temple Hill Hospital (1914)
      Not reopened after World War II.
Yixian (Yihsien) (1905)
  Raymond Memorial Hospital (1906)
      Not reopened after World War II.

Jiangsu

Huaiyin (TKP) (1887)
  Love and Mercy Hospital (1914)
      Burned during the Nationalist/Communist Civil War.
Jiangyin (Kiangyin) (1895)
  Kiangyin Hospital (1904)
      Not reopened after World War II.
Lianyungang (Haichow) (1908)
  Ellen Lavine Graham Hospital (1914)
      Has continued as a general hospital under the PRC.
Nanjing (Nanking) (1874)
  Drum Tower Hospital, University of Nanjing (U) (1892)
      Has continued as a major city hospital under the PRC.
Suqian (Suchien) (1894)
  Suqian Hospital (1912)
      Burned during World War II.
Suzhou (Soochow) (1871)
  Elizabeth Blake Hospital (Southern Presbyterian) (1899)
      Today is an affiliate of the Suzhou Medical School.
  Tooker Memorial Hospital (Northern Presbyterian) (1899)
      Merged with Elizabeth Blake. Burned down during World War II.
Taizhou (Taichow) (1908)
  Sara Walkup: ("Fuyin Yiyuan" — Good News Hospital) (1922)
      Has continued in operation under the PRC.
Xuzhou (Suchow, Hsuchowfu) (1897)
  Mary Erwin Rogers Memorial Hospital for Women (1915)
  Bennie Blue Memorial Hospital for Men (1916)
      Merged by the PRC. Now "Number 2 People's Hospital."
Yancheng (Yencheng) (1911)
  Yencheng Hospital (1916)
      Destroyed during World War II.
Zhenjiang (Chinkiang) (1883)
  Goldsby King Memorial Hospital (1923)
      Now known as the "Number 1 Hospital of Zhenjiang."

Anhui

Huayuan (Hwaiyuan) (1901)
  Hope Memorial Hospital — Men (1909)
  Cragin Memorial Hospital — Women (1917)
      Later merged. Destroyed during the Cultural Revolution.

Nanxuzhou (Nanhsuchow) (1913)
  Goodwill Hospital (1915)
    Now known as the "Suhsien District Hospital."

Zhejiang

Jiaxing (Kashing) (1892)
  Benjamin Morgan Palmer Memorial Hospital (1908)
    Now known as the "Number 2 People's Hospital of Jiaxing."

Hunan

Changde (Changteh) (1897)
  "Kwang Teh" Hospital For Men (1898)
  Women's Hospital (1911)
    Founded by the Cumberland Presbyterians. Later merged.
    Reopened after World War II. No record since 1951.
Chenzhou (Chenchow) (1903)
  "Hwei Ai" Hospital (1909)
    Reopened after World War II. No record since 1951.
Hengyang (Hengchow) (1902)
  "Ren Chi" Hospital (1910)
    Badly damaged during World War II. Reopened in 1946. No record since 1951.
Xiangtan (Siangtan) (1900)
  Nathaniel Tooker ("Hwei Ching") Hospital (1903)
    Reopened after World War II. No record since 1951.

Guangdong

Guangzhou (Canton) (1845)
  Canton Hospital 1835 (U)
  Hackett Medical College for Women (1901) (U)
  David Gregg Hospital (1901)
  Turner School of Nursing (1901)
    Merged into Lingnan University in 1934.
  Kerr Hospital for the Insane (1899)
    Closed in 1927 because of labor strikes.
Lianzhou (Linchow) (1890)
  Van Norden Hospital for Men (1890)
  Brooks Memorial Hospital for Women (1894)
    Reopened after World War II. No record since 1951.
Yangjiang (Yeungkong) (1892)
  Forman Memorial Hospital (1902)
    Reopened after World War II. No record since 1951.

Hainan

Haikou (Hoihow) (1914)
  Hoihow Hospital (1896)
    Now known as the "People's Hospital of Haikou."

Jiaji (Kachek) (1900)
  Kilbourne Hospital ("Christ Hospital") (1900)
       Rebuilt as a part of the PRC hospital.
Ledong (Nodoa) (1886)
  Mary Henry Memorial Hospital (1902)
       Rebuilt as a part of the PRC hospital.

Yunnan

Kiulungkiang Hospital (1924)
       Transferred to the Siam Presbyterian Mission, 1933.
Yuankiang Hospital (1924)
       Transferred to the Vandsburger Lutheran Mission, 1933.

Appendix B

Presbyterian Mission Schools in China

Schools listed are middle schools (U.S. High Schools), higher level Bible Institutes, and colleges. Not all the schools were open during all these years. Chinese names were usually different from the names in English which often memorialized a benefactor in the United States. City names are given in Pinyin with Wade-Giles spelling in parenthesis. Spelling of the schools' Chinese names follows the usage at the time — usually Wade-Giles. Dates in parenthesis after the city indicate the year in which the station was opened. Dates in parenthesis after the name of the school indicate the approximate date of its opening. A (U) after the name indicates it was a union institution. An asterisk (*) indicates the school is known to still be in operation under the PRC government. A double asterisk (**) indicates the school was closed after the 1927–30 crisis over the government registration requirements.

Peking (1863)

Truth Hall Academy (Boys) (1864)
School of Gentleness (Girls) (1876)
Bible Training School for Women (U) (1914)
Yenching University* (U) 1917

Hebei

Baoding (Paotingfu) (1893)
    Hero Hall Boarding School for Boys** (1904)
    True Aim Boarding School for Girls (U) (1904)
Shunde (Shunteh) (1903)
    Hugh O'Neill, Jr., Memorial School for Boys (1910)
    T'ao Shu Girls' School (1911)

Shandong

Jinan (Tsinan) (1872)
    Clara Linton Hamilton Memorial Academy (1903)
    Murray Girls' School (1913)
    Shandong Christian University (Cheeloo) (U) 1904
Jining (Tsining) (1892)
    Laughlin Academy for Boys (1894)
    Kenarden School for Girls (1909)
    Women's Bible and Training School (1910)
Linyi (Ichow) (1890)
    McPherson Academy for Boys (1907)
    Hwei Ying Middle School for Girls (1908)
    Louise Junkin Comegys Women's Bible Institute (1906)

Qingdao (Tsingtao) (1898)
    Wen Deh Girl's High School (1919)
    Hugh O'Neill Jr. (Chung Te) Boys High School (1911)
Dengzhou (Tengchow) (1861)
    Tengchow Boys' School/College (1865) — moved to Weixian (1902)
    Tengchow Girls' School (1862)
    Tengchow Boys' (Wen Hwei) Academy (1906)
Tengxian (Tenghsien) (1913)
    Tengxian Girls' School (1920)
    Mateer Memorial Institute (U) (1914)
    North China Theological Seminary (U) (1922)
    North China Bible Seminary for Women (U) (1923)
Weixian (Weihsien) (1883)
    Point Breeze Academy for Boys (1884)
    Wen Mei Girls' High School (1895)
    College of Arts & Science/Shandong Christian University (1902) — moved to Jinan 1917
Yantai (Chefoo) (1862)
    Chefoo Boys' School (1866)
    Chen Kwang Girls' High School (1867)
    Temple Hill English School (1887)
    Charles Rogers Mills School for the Deaf (1887)
    Yih Wen Commercial College (1897)
Yixian (Yihsien) (1905)
    Cheng Teh Girls' Boarding School (1911)
    Boys Industrial School (1914)

Jiangsu

Huaian (Hwaianfu) (1904)
    Martha Riddle School for Girls (1916)
    Hwaianfu Boys' School** (1917)
Huaiyin (TKP) (1887)
    Tsing Kiang Pu Boys School** (1906)
    Tsing Kiang Pu Girls School** (1910)
Jiangyin (Kiangyin) (1895)
    James Sprung Academy for Boys (1906)
    Luola Murchison Academy for Women and Girls (1909)
Lianyungang (Haichow) (1908)
    Jewell Link Lucket School for Girls** (1917)
    Haichow Middle School for Boys** (1918)
Nanjing (Nanking) (1874)
    Ming Deh Girls' School (1893)
    Nanking Theological Seminary* (U) (1906)
    Bible Teachers' Training School for Women (U) (1912)
    Ginling College for Women* (U) (1915)
    University of Nanjing* (U) (1910)
Shanghai (1850)
    Mary Farnham School for Girls (1861)
    Lowrie Institute (1860)
Suqian (Suchien) (1894)
    Suchien Boys Middle School** (1906)
    Suchien School for Girls** (1907)
Suzhou (Soochow) (1871)
    Vincent Miller Academy for Boys (1893) (NPM)

George C. Smith School for Girls (1907) (SPM)
Soochow Boys' School (1907) (SPM)
Taizhou (Taichow) (1908)
Wichita Falls Academy for Boys** (1921)
Marietta Hunt School for Girls** (1922)
Xuzhou (Suchow, Hsuchowfu) (1897)
Julia Farrior Stanford School for Boys* 1902
Mary Thompson Stevens School for Girls* 1911
Yancheng (Yencheng) (1911)
Hwai Mei Middle School for Boys (1920)
Zhenjiang (Chinkiang) (1883)
Burton Memorial School for Boys** (1907)

Anhui

Huayuan (Hwaiyuan) (1901)
Han Mei School for Boys (1904)
Chi Hwei School for Girls (1908)
Nanxuzhou (Nanhsuchow) (1913)
Han Kuang Boys' School (1914)
Ch'i Hsiu Girls' School (1815)

Zhejiang

Hangzhou (Hangchow) (1859)
Hangchow Union Girls' School (U) (1912)
Hangchow Christian College* (U) (1908)
Jiaxing (Kashing) (1892)
Kashing Axing Memorial School for Boys (1900)
Kashing Girls' High School (1923)
Ningbo (Ningpo) (1844)
Ningbo Boys School (1845) — moved to Hangzhou in 1867
Riverbend Boys' Middle School (U) (1922)
Riverside Academy for Girls (U) (1922)

Hunan

Changde (Changteh) (1897)
I Deh Girls' School (1904)
John Miller Boys' Middle School** (1906)
Changsha (1912)
Yali Union Boys' High School (U) (1906)
Fuxiang (Fuhsiang) Union Girls' High School* (U) (1914)
Union Theological College (U) (1914)
Chenzhou (Chenchow) (1903)
New China Middle School for Boys (1905)
Chenchow Girls' School (1905)
Hengyang (Hengchow) (1902)
Kwang Teh Academy for Boys (1905)
Hwei Wen Girls' Boarding School (1906)
Xiangtan (Siangtan) (1900)
Sunnyside Girls' School (1904)
John D. Wells School** (1901)

Guangdong

Guangzhou (Canton) (1845)
>   True Light Middle School & Women's Seminary (1872)
>   Pui Ying (Noyes Memorial) Middle School for Boys (1878)
>   Ming Sum ("Understanding Heart") School for the Blind (1899)
>   Lingnan University* (1904)
>   Union Theological College (U) (1914)
>   Union Normal School (U) (1916)

Lianzhou (Lien Chow) (1890)
>   People's Hope Boys' School* (1899)
>   Kwong Wai Girls' School* (1899)

Yangjiang (Yeungkong) (1892)
>   Loving Light School for Girls** (1922)
>   Beacon Light Academy for Boys** (1923)

Hainan

Jiaji (Kachek) (1900)
>   McCormick Boys' School (1904)
>   Daughters' School (1913)

Ledong (Nodoa) (1886)
>   Ling Kang Boys' School (1891)
>   Kittanning Girls' School (1891)

Qiongzhou (Kiungchow) (1895)
>   Albert J. Pitkin Memorial School for Girls (1903)
>   Hainan Christian Middle School (1919)
>   Hainan Bible Institute (1923)

Appendix C

Presbyterian Missionaries in China, 1837–1953

For PCUSA missionaries, Arthur Judson Brown, *One Hundred Years* (New York: Revell, 1936) was the basic source for those appointed prior to 1937. For later appointments, a supplement to Brown's listing entitled "The Crisis Decade" was used for the years 1937–1947. For PCUS missionaries the basic sources were: Sophie Montgomery Crane, *Missionary Directory, 1867–1987* (Atlanta: PCUS Division of International Mission, 1987) and P. Frank Price, *Our China Investment* (Nashville: Exec. Committee of Foreign Missions, 1927).

Names. Names are listed alphabetically, then by date of their arrival in China. Married women are listed immediately following their husbands. Maiden names are given wherever these are know. A woman's name in parenthesis indicates either an earlier or later married name. An asterisk (*) indicates the person is listed both in the PCUSA and PCUS lists because of transfer.

Dates. The first date is the time of appointment by the home board which usually coincides with the date of arrival in China. However, in some cases the appointment predated the arrival in China by a year. Normally, the second date is the time of the last departure from China. In some cases it represents the termination of the board relationship which could be one or more years after leaving China.

End of Term. Most regular appointments were for life. But in many cases service was ended for a number of reasons. In this column the reason for the end of the term of service is given. The designation (D) indicates death and burial on the field, or in a few cases death in the United States following a terminal illness. The designation (DS) indicates the death of the spouse resulting in the necessity for a return to the homeland. Retirement (RT) came only after thirty-five to forty years service. Resignations (RS) could be for any number of reasons. One of the most common was a health breakdown (H) of one kind or another. (TR) indicates a transfer to another country or mission. (M) indicates a woman's marriage which resulted in a transfer to another mission. (EV) indicates evacuation because of revolution or war. (ET) indicates the end of a short-term appointment.

Years in China. These years do not necessarily coincide with the time between the two dates because service in China could have been interrupted by a leave of absence and a second appointment.

Work Assignment. It would be difficult to limit the work of many missionaries to any one category. Whatever they did, most would consider they were engaged in evangelism. Leadership training cut across all categories. However, in this column one specific category of service is indicated which, in the opinion of the author, best exemplified the primary work assigned. In most cases both spouses were given assignments. Where records do not indicate a specific assignment for the missionary wife, it was assumed that, along with homemaking, her energies were directed toward the husband's assignment. Assignment categories, with their abbreviations are indicated below. Since all were expected to engage in language study this is not shown.

EVA	Evangelism	ED	Education
MED	Medical	HED	Higher Education
NUR	Nursing	WW	Work with Women
LIT	Literature/Literacy	IND	Industrial Arts
AG	Agriculture	PRI	Printing/Publishing
TRA	Translation Work	ARC	Architectural Service
ADM	Administration	SEC	Secretarial Work
THE	Theological Educations/	TMC	Teacher, Missionary
	Leadership Training		Children
PAS	Pastor, Internat. Church	MUS	Music
UNK	Unknown	MT	Medical Technician
UNA	Unassigned	STU	Student/Youth Work

Places of Service. Missionary assignments were often shifted from one city to another. Usually, these were within the bounds of that particular China mission. No attempt has been made to list all the locations where a missionary served. In these columns one primary station (ST 1), and where needed, a secondary, or subsequent, station (ST 2) are shown. Note the list of city abbreviations on the following page which shows both the current Pinyin spelling as well as the older Wade-Giles spelling (in parenthesis.)

PCUSA & PCUS Mission Stations with Abbreviations

AMO	Xiamen (Amoy), Fujian
CAN	Guangzhou (Canton), Guangdong
CHA	Changde (Changteh), Hunan
CHE	Yantai (Chefoo), Shandong
CHN	Chenzhou (Chenchow), Hunan
CHS	Changsha, Hunan
HAI	Lianyungang (Haichow), Jiangsu
HAN	Hangzhou (Hangchow), Zhejiang
HEN	Hengyang (Hengchow), Hunan
HOI	Haikou (Hoi How), Hainan
HUA	Huaian (Hwaianfu), Jiangsu
HWA	Huayuan (Hwai Yuan), Anhui
ICH	Linyi (Ichow), Shandong
JAX	Jiaxing (Kashing), Zhejiang
JIA	Jiangyin (Kiangyin), Jiangsu
KAC	Jiaji (Kachek), Hainan
KAN	Kang Hau, Guangdong
KIL	Jiulongjiang (Kiulungkiang), Yunnan
KIU	Qiongzhou (Kiungchow), Hainan
KUL	Lushan (Kuling), Jiangxi
LNC	Lianzhou (Linchow, Lien Chow, Linhsien), Guangdong
MAC	Macau
NAH	Nanxuzhou (Nanhsuchow), Anhui
NAN	Nanjing (Nanking), Jiangsu
NIN	Ningbo (Ningpo), Zhejiang
NOD	Ledong (Nodoa), Hainan
PAO	Baoding (Paoting, Paotingfu), Hebei
PEK	Beijing (Peking)
SHA	Shanghai
SHE	Qujiang (Sheklung), Guangdong
SHO	Shouzhou (Showchow), Anhui
SHU	Shunde (Shunteh), Hebei
SIA	Xiangtan (Siangtan), Hunan
SIN	Singapore
SNG	Sinchang (Tunghiang), Zhejiang
SOO	Suzhou (Soochow), Jiangsu
SUQ	Suqian (Suchien)
TAI	Taizhou (Taichow)
TEN	Dengzhou (Tengchow), Shandong
TKP	Huaiyin (Tsing-Kiang-Pu), Jiangsu
TNG	Tengxian (Tenghsien), Shandong
TSI	Jinan (Tsinan), Shandong
TSN	Jining (Chining, Tsining), Shandong
TST	Qingdao (Tsingtao), Shandong
WCH	West China
WEI	Weixian (Weihsien), Shandong
WUX	Wuxi (Wusi), Jiangsu
XUZ	Xuzhou (Suchow, Hsuchowfu), Jiangsu
YEN	Yancheng (Yencheng), Jiangsu
YEU	Yangjiang (Yuankiang), Guangdong
YIH	Yixian (Yihsien), Shandong
YUA	Yuanjiang (Yuankiang), Yunnan
ZHE	Zhenjiang (Chinkiang), Jiangsu

(I) Presbyterian Church, U.S.A.

DA=Date of Arrival in China;　　　　YC=Years in China;
DP=Date of Departure;　　　　　　　ST1=First station location;
TM=Reason for term ending;　　　　　ST2=Second station location (if needed).
　　　　　WP= Primary Work Assignment

Last Name	First Name	DA	DP	TM	YC	ST1	ST2	WP
Abbey	Rev Robert E.	1882	1890	D	8	NAN		EVA
Abbey (Whiting)	Mrs Louise Parsons	1873	1920	RT	40	NAN		EVA
Abbott	Rev Paul R.	1910	1945	RS	35	HEN		EVA
Abbott	Mrs Bessie Stone	1910	1945	RS	35	HEN		EVA
Abbott	Rev Paul R., Jr.	1936	1950	EV	14	NAN		EVA
Abbott	Mrs Laura Phillips	1936	1950	EV	14	NAN		EVA
Abraham	Miss Julie D.	1923	1928	RS	5	CAN		ED
Adolph	William H., PhD	1915	1950	TR	35	PEK		HED
Adolph	Mrs Katherine Witmer	1915	1950	TR	35	PEK		HED
Ady	Rev Merrill S.	1923	1950	TR	30	YEU	CAN	EVA
Ady	Mrs Martha Meloy	1923	1950	TR	30	YEU	CAN	WW
Alf	Miss Mildred E., RN	1932	1935	RS	3	CAN		NUR
Alger	Miss Edna C.	1910	1926	RS	16	SHU		ED
Allen	Horace N., MD	1883	1884	TR	1	NAN		MED
Allen	Mrs Frances Messenger	1883	1884	TR	1	NAN		MED
Allison	Rev Roy M.	1911	1948	RT	37	TNG		EVA
Allison	Mrs Edith Early	1911	1948	RT	37	TNG		WW
Allured	Rev Paul J.	1911	1916	RS	5	LNC		EVA
Allured	Mrs Helen Strange	1911	1916	RS	5	LNC		EVA
Allyn	Miss Harriett M., PhD	1913	1923	RS	10	CAN		MED
Althaus	Mr Christian P.	1911	1928	RS	17	SIA		ED
Althaus	Mrs Laura Wilson	1911	1928	RS	17	SIA		ED
Anckner	Miss Ada	1921	1935	RS	14	TSI		ED
Anderson	Miss Sarah J., MD	1877	1879	H	2	TSI	SOO	MED
Anderson	Miss Emma	1887	1896	RS	9	WEI	CHI	WW
Anderson	Miss Elizabeth E., MD	1907	1916	D	9	TSI	SOO	MED
Anderson	Miss Grace, RN	1920	1924	RS	4	TSI		NUR
Anderson	Rev Benjamin Johnson	1946	1949	EV	3	PAO		UNA
Anderson	Mrs Louise Gaillard	1946	1949	EV	3	PAO		UNA
Armentrout	Miss Lois L.	1932	1951	EV	19	CAN		WW
Armstrong	Rev George A.	1902	1913	RS	11	TSN		EVA
Arthur	Rev James Hillcoat	1912	1943	D	31	HAN	SHA	EVA
Arthur	Mrs 1 Eliz. Walker	1912	1924	D	12	HAN		WW
Arthur	Mrs 2 Lelia Droz	1926	1943	DS	17	HAN	SHA	WW
Arthurs	Miss Ann C.	1913	1922	RS	9	CAN		THE
Atterbury	Boudinot C., MD	1879	1899	H	20	PEK		MED
Atterbury	Mrs Mary Lowrie	1883	1899	H	16	PEK		WW
Atterbury	Miss Marguerite	1920	1922	RS	2	PEK		HED
Ayer	Miss Mary A., MD	1897	1901	RS	4	SOO		MED
Bailie	Rev Joseph	1890	1919	RS	15	SOO		EVA
Bailie	Mrs Effie Worley., MD	1892	1898	RS	6	SOO		MED
Baird	Miss Margaret	1883	1888	RS	5	CAN		WW
Balm	Mr James H.	1922	1927	RS	5	CAN		ADM
Bankes	Miss Mary T.	1910	1928	RS	18	CAN		ED
Bannan	Rev Edward J.	1922	1951	EV	29	CHA		EVA
Bannan	Mrs Phyllis Kurtz, RN	1917	1951	EV	34	CHA		NUR
Bannon	Mr Peter L.	1937	1942	RS	5	NAN		HED
Bannon	Mrs Ruth Sparling	1938	1942	RS	5	NAN		HED
Barker	Rev Joseph E.	1921	1922	RS	1	HWA		EVA
Barkman	Rev Charles P.	1922	1928	RS	6	HAN		HED
Barkman	Mrs. Rebecca Hammond	1922	1928	RS	6	HAN		HED
Barnes	William J., MD	1919	1923	RS	4	HWA		MED
Barnes	Mrs Grace Wheeler	1919	1923	RS	4	HWA		MED
Barnes	Miss Margaret	1924	1951	EV	27	PEK		WW

Barr	Miss Mary E.	1877	1883	RS	6	PEK		ED
Bash	Miss Cora C., MD	1913	1941	D	28	PEK		MED
Bayless	Miss Gertrude R.	1923	1950	EV	27	CHS		MUS
Bayley	Miss Margaret Hamer	1946	1950	EV	4	SIA		EVA
Beattie	Rev Andrew	1889	1909	H	20	YEU	CAN	EVA
Beattie	Mrs Ellen Hartwell	1891	1909	H	18	YEU	CAN	EVA
Beattie	David, MD	1893	1895	RS	2	YEU		MED
Beattie	Mrs David	1893	1895	RS	2	YEU		MED
Beebe	Rev Lyle J.	1923	1935	TR	12	KIL		EVA
Beebe	Mrs Mary Neiderhauser	1923	1935	TR	12	KIL		WW
Beegle	Miss Caroline D., RN	1917	1951	RT	36	CHE		NUR
Bell	Miss Rosa, RN	1920	1950	RT	30	TSI		NUR
Bell	Miss Miriam, MD	1924	1934	RS	10	CAN		MED
Bent	Rev Rufus H.	1892	1900	RS	8	TSN		EVA
Bent	Mrs Sarah Poindexter, MD	1893	1900	RS	7	TSN		MED
Bercovitz	Nathaniel, MD	1915	1953	EV	38	HOI	KAC	MED
Bercovitz	Mrs Elva Higgins	1915	1953	EV	38	HOI	KAC	MED
Bergen	Rev Paul D.	1883	1915	D	30	TST	WEI	EVA
Bergen	Mrs Mary McKinney	1883	1918	RS	33	TST	WEI	EVA
Berger	Miss Electa M., RN	1923	1930	RS	7	SIA		NUR
Berry	Miss Minnie L.	1882	1885	RS	3	CHE		ED
Berry	Miss Mamie L., RN	1932	1933	RS	1	HWA		NUR
Berst	William L., MD	1907	1946	RT	35	CHE		MED
Berst	Mrs 1 Mary Venable	1905	1908	D	3	CHE		ED
Berst	Mrs 2 Leada Newman	1909	1946	RT	33	CHE		WW
Bible	Rev Frank W.	1904	1919	RS	15	HAN		HED
Bible	Mrs Henrietta Caskey	1904	1919	RS	15	HAN		HED
Bickford	Rev John T.	1920	1950	EV	30	PAO		EVA
Bickford	Mrs Margaret Millar	1920	1950	EV	30	PAO		EVA
Birkel	Rev Augustus H.	1918	1950	EV	32	CHS		EVA
Birkel	Mrs Lulu Francis	1913	1950	EV	32	CHS		EVA
Bischoff	Miss Mary, RN	1928	1949	EV	21	LNC	CAN	NUR
Bisson	Mr Thomas A.	1924	1928	RS	4	HWA		ED
Blackstone	Rev William T.	1931	1949	EV	18	CAN		EVA
Blackstone	Mrs Elizabeth Shirk	1931	1949	EV	18	CAN		EVA
Blanford	Rev Carl Edwin	1947	1950	EV	3	KIU		EVA
Blanford	Mrs Muriel Ausink	1947	1950	EV	3	KIU		EVA
Blick	Miss Virginia	1925	1934	RS	9	CAN		ED
Bliss	Solon C., MD	1873	1874	RS	1	TEN		MED
Bliss	Miss Margaret S.	1911	1916	RS	5	YEU		WW
Bocker	Mr Leon M.	1919	1922	RS	3	SHA		ADM
Boehne	Miss Emma S.	1903	1940	RT	37	TSI		EVA
Boggs	Rev John J.	1894	1919	RS	25	CAN		ED
Boggs	Mrs Ruth Bliss, MD	1892	1919	RS	27	CAN		MED
Boone	Rev Wilmot D.	1912	1949	D	37	SHA	TSI	ED
Boone	Mrs Nelle Burgess	1912	1949	RT	37	SHA	TSI	ED
Boone	Miss Mary Muriel	1917	1950	EV	33	CHN		WW
Booth	Mr William C.	1903	1948	RT	45	CHE		ED
Booth	Mrs Elsie Harrod	1905	1948	RT	43	CHE		ED
Boughton	Miss Emma F.	1889	1903	H	14	WEI		WW
Boughton	Miss Helen E.	1925	1950	TR	25	HWA		SEC
Bousman	Rev Henry H.	1925	1930	TR	5	KAC		EVA
Bousman	Mrs Noma Stimmel	1925	1930	TR	5	KAC		EVA
Boyd	Harry W., MD	1899	1923	RS	15	SIA		MED
Boyd	Mrs Margaret Fullwood	1899	1923	RS	16	SIA		MED
Brack	Miss Edna M.	1914	1916	D	2	WEI		WW
Brack	Miss Ruth A., RN	1914	1943	RS	29	WEI		NUR
Braden	Rev Samuel R.	1913	1915	RS	2	KIU		EVA
Braden	Mrs Mary Altman	1913	1915	RS	2	KIU		EVA
Bradshaw	Homer, MD	1928	1955	EV	27	LNC		MED
Bradshaw	Mrs Wilda Hockenberry	1928	1955	EV	27	LNC		MED
Braskamp	Miss Christina J.	1911	1929	RS	18	CHE		WW
Braskamp	Rev Otto J.	1911	1930	RS	19	ICH		EVA
Brewer	Francis, MD	1923	1930	RS	7	CHE		MED
Brewer	Mrs Ester Irwin	1926	1930	RS	4	CHE		MED

Broady	Robert A., MD	1932	1937	RS	5	HEN		MED
Broady	Mrs Ellen Cox	1932	1937	RS	5	HEN		MED
Brogden	Rev Ura	1921	1924	RS	3	KIU		EVA
Brogden	Mrs Della Peek	1921	1924	RS	3	KIU		EVA
Brown	Rev Hugh A.	1844	1848	H	4	AMO		EVA
Brown	Miss Mary, MD	1889	1900	D	11	WEI		MED
Brown	James W., MD	1915	1919	RS	4	CAN		MED
Brown	Mrs Laura Smith	1915	1919	RS	4	CAN		MED
Brown	Mr John Warner	1918	1923	RS	5	CAN		ADM
Brown	Mrs Maude Hubbard	1918	1923	RS	5	CAN		ADM
Brown	Chauncey F., MD	1921	1934	D	13	HEN		MED
Brown	Mrs Callie Wright	1921	1934	DS	13	HEN		MED
Browne	Rev George F.	1913	1950	RT	37	CHE		EVA
Browne	Mrs Irene Cowen	1913	1950	RT	37	CHE		ED
Browne	Rev George Chalmers	1943	1950	EV	7	CHN		EVA
Browne	Mrs Polly Landes	1943	1950	EV	7	CHN		EVA
Bruce	Rev George G.	1903	1904	H	1	YEU		EVA
Bruce	Mrs Eliz. Davies	1903	1904	H	1	YEU		EVA
Bryan	Herman, MD	1902	1944	RT	42	NOD	CHE	MED
Bryan	Mrs Esther Love	1920	1944	RT	22	CHE		MED
Bryant	Rev Richard Whitney	1945	1950	EV	5	PEK		EVA
Bryant	Mrs 1 Adeline Fox	1946	1947	D	2	PEK		EVA
Bryant	Mrs 2 Evelyn C., RN	1949	1950	EV	1	PEK		NUR
Bryars	Mr James H.	1917	1931	RS	14	SHA		ED
Bryars* (Sykes)	Mrs Anna	1919	1931	RS	12	SHA		ED
Bryon	Rev Adelmer R.	1929	1935	RS	6	HWA		EVA
Bucher	Rev Henry Hale	1934	1949	EV	15	KIU	NOD	THE
Bucher	Mrs Louise Scott	1934	1949	EV	15	KIU	NOD	EVA
Buck	John Lossing, PhD	1915	1942	RS	27	NAH	NAN	AG
Buck* (Sydenstricker)	Mrs Pearl	1917	1933	RS	16	NAH	NAN	LIT
Bullock	Rev Amasa A.	1909	1929	RS	20	NAN		HED
Bullock	Mrs Ruth Beckwith	1909	1929	RS	20	NAN		HED
Burkwall	Herman F., MD	1932	1951	EV	19	HOI		MED
Burkwall	Mrs Edric Porter, RN	1932	1951	EV	19	HOI		NUR
Burkwall	Miss Margaret, RN	1932	1951	EV	19	HOI		NUR
Burkwall	Miss Edna, RN	1937	1944	RS	7	CAN		NUR
Burnham	Miss Mary L., MD	1897	1917	RS	11	TSI		MED
Bushnell	Rev Paul P..	1923	1930	RS	7	HEN		ED
Buswell	Calvin E., MD	1919	1928	RS	9	KUL		MED
Buswell	Mrs Adah Boxell	1919	1928	RS	9	KUL		MED
Butler	Rev John	1868	1885	D	17	NIN		EVA
Butler	Mrs Frances Harshberger	1875	1892	RS	17	NIN		ED
Butler	Miss Electa M.	1881	1923	RT	42	CAN		ED
Butler	Mr David C.	1924	1930	RS	6	TSI		ED
Butler	Mrs Mary Goodman	1924	1930	RS	6	TSI		ED
Byers	Rev John	1852	1853	D	1	SHA		EVA
Byers	Mrs John	1852	1853	DS	1	SHA		EVA
Byers	Rev George D.	1906	1924	D	18	KIU		EVA
Byers	Mrs Clara Primm	1912	1925	DS	13	KIU		EVA
Bynon	Miss Margaret H., MD	1903	1912	RS	9	WEI		MED
Byrns	Miss Marion L.	1923	1925	RS	2	CHS		UNK
Caldwell	Miss Doris Eliz.	1946	1951	EV	5	SOO		EVA
Callender	Rev Charles R.	1923	1935	TR	12	YUA		EVA
Callender	Mrs Winella Marks	1923	1935	RS	12	YUA		EVA
Campbell	Rev Wilbur M.	1898	1932	RT	34	KIU		THE
Campbell	Mrs Lilian Park	1898	1932	RT	34	KIU		WW
Campbell	Rev Kenneth	1923	1950	EV	27	YUA	HWA	EVA
Campbell	Mrs Dorothy Davis	1923	1950	EV	27	YUA	HWA	EVA
Capp	Rev Edward P.	1869	1873	D	4	TEN		EVA
Capp	Mrs Maggie Brown	1867	1882	D	15	TEN		ED
Carlson	Miss Minnie E.	1926	1929	RS	3	HAN		UNK
Carpenter	Miss Alice Margaret	1922	1945	RS	23	CAN		ED
Carper	Miss Elizabeth R., MD	1907	1910	M	3	LNC		MED
Carrow	Fleming, MD	1875	1878	RS	3	CAN		MED
Carrow	Mrs Fleming	1875	1878	RS	3	CAN		MED

Carson	Arthur L., PhD	1921	1938	RS	17	TSI		HED
Carson	Mrs Edith Scott	1921	1938	RS	17	TSI		ED
Carter	Rev Thomas F.	1910	1922	RS	12	NAH		EVA
Carter	Mrs Dagny Olsen	1910	1922	RS	12	NAH		EVA
Carter	Miss Anita Eunica	1913	1942	RT	29	CHE		ED
Carter	Miss Alice	1920	1926	M	6	SIA		WW
Cassat	Rev Paul C.	1913	1925	RS	12	TST		ED
Cassat	Mrs Rowena Wilson	1915	1925	RS	10	TST		ED
Cattell	Frances F., MD	1897	1908	RS	11	SOO		MED
Chaffee	Rev Clifford Earl	1944	1950	EV	6	HWA		EVA
Chaffee	Mrs Mary Koper	1944	1950	EV	6	HWA		EVA
Chalfant	Rev William P.	1885	1917	D	32	ICH	WEI	HED
Chalfant	Mrs 1 Louise Boyd	1887	1903	D	16	ICH	WEI	WW
Chalfant	Mrs 2 Ada Gilbert	1907	1923	D	26	ICH	WEI	WW
Chalfant	Rev Frank H.	1887	1914	D	27	WEI		EVA
Chalfant	Mrs Jennie Martin	1887	1914	DS	27	WEI		WW
Chalfant	Archibald S., MD	1926	1931	RS	5	TSN		MED
Chalfant	Mrs Julia Merriken	1926	1931	RS	5	TSN		MED
Chandler	Rev Horace E., PhD	1908	1949	RT	41	WEI	TSI	HED
Chandler	Mrs Chloe Edgerton	1908	1949	RT	41	WEI	TSI	HED
Chandler	Rev James R.	1928	1932	H	4	NAN		EVA
Chandler	Mrs Emily Gordon	1928	1932	H	4	NAN		EVA
Chaney	Miss Florence J.	1912	1919	RS	7	HWA		ED
Chapin	Rev Oliver H.	1882	1886	RS	4	SHA		EVA
Chapin	Mrs Oliver H.	1882	1886	RS	4	SHA		EVA
Chapin	Rev Dwight C.	1906	1911	RS	5	PAO		EVA
Chapin	Rev Edward D.	1913	1927	RS	14	CHA		ED
Chapin	Mrs Eva Brunner	1913	1927	RS	14	CHA		ED
Chapin	Miss Mae	1913	1935	TR	22	KIU		ED
Chaplin	Rev Maxwell	1919	1926	D	7	SHO		EVA
Chaplin	Mrs Edith Kingman	1920	1927	DS	7	SHO		EVA
Chapman	Rev William C.	1910	1927	RS	17	CHA		EVA
Chapman	Mrs Agnes Leith	1912	1927	RS	15	CHA		EVA
Charles	Miss Neva I.	1918	1919	RS	1	CAN		UNA
Chase	Miss Cora, RN	1924	1925	RS	1	SHO		NUR
Chesnut	Miss Eleanor, MD	1894	1905	D	11	LNC		MED
Chester	Miss Ruth Miriam, PhD	1947	1951	EV	4	NAN		HED
Christmann	Miss Helen E.	1913	1948	RT	35	TST		WW
Churchill	Miss Elizabeth A.	1901	1921	RS	20	CAN		EVA
Clark	Rev William H., PhD	1925	1950	EV	25	CHS	WCH	EVA
Clark	Mrs Antoinette Black	1932	1950	EV	18	CHS	WCH	EVA
Clawson	Miss Dorothy L., RN	1927	1950	TR	23	HWA		NUR
Clemons	Mr Harry	1913	1920	RS	7	NAN		HED
Clemons	Mrs Jennie Jenkins	1918	1920	RS	2	NAN		HED
Cliness	Miss Lulu, RN	1921	1924	RS	3	CAN		NUR
Cochran	Rev James B.	1899	1920	RS	21	HWA		ED
Cochran	Mrs Margaret Jenkins	1899	1912	D	13	HWA		WW
Cochran	Samuel, MD	1899	1926	H	27	HWA	TSI	MED
Cochran	Mrs Margaret Watts	1899	1926	H	27	HWA	TSI	MED
Cochran	Miss Anne	1925	1950	EV	7	PEK		HED
Cochran	Miss Margaret W., RN	1925	1926	RS	1	TSI		NUR
Cochran	Williams, MD	1933	1950	RS	17	PAO		MED
Cochran	Mrs Mary Williams	1933	1950	RS	17	PAO		MED
Cogdal	Miss Mary E.	1890	1932	D	42	SHA		WW
Cole	Mr Richard	1843	1847	RS	4	CAN	NIN	PRI
Cole	Mrs Richard	1843	1847	RS	4	CAN	NIN	PRI
Coleman	Rev Delbert L.	1913	1914	RS	1	WEI		EVA
Coltman	Robert, Jr., MD	1885	1898	RS	13	TSI	PEK	MED
Coltman	Mrs Robt.	1885	1898	RS	13	TSI	PEK	MED
Condit	Rev Ira M.	1860	1865	TR	5	CAN		EVA
Condit	Mrs Laura Carpenter	1860	1865	TR	5	CAN		WW
Cooley	Miss Alice S.	1878	1879	M	1	SOO		WW
Coonradt	Rev Ralph G.	1912	1950	RT	38	TST		EVA
Coonradt	Mrs Marie Woodward	1913	1950	RT	37	TST		EVA
Cooper	Miss Effie B., MD	1899	1912	RS	13	CHE	TSI	MED

Corbett	Rev Hunter	1863	1920	D	57	CHE		EVA
Corbett	Mrs 1 Lizzie Culbertson	1863	1873	D	10	CHE		EVA
Corbett	Mrs 2 Mary Nixon	1875	1888	D	13	CHE		WW
Corbett	Mrs 3 Harriet Sutherland	1889	1922	RS	33	CHE		EVA
Corbett	Rev Charles H.	1908	1926	RS	18	PEK		HED
Corbett	Mrs Minnie Webster	1908	1926	RS	18	PEK		HED
Cornwell	Rev George	1892	1909	D	17	CHE		EVA
Cornwell	Mrs Mary Meade	1892	1909	D	17	CHE		WW
Coulter	Rev Moses	1849	1852	D	3	NIN		PRI
Coulter	Mrs Caroline Crowe	1849	1854	RS	5	NIN		PRI
Cowles	Rev Ben Thomas	1943	1949	EV	6	NAN		STU
Cowles	Mrs Maxime Brittell	1943	1949	EV	6	NAN		MUS
Crabb	David E.	1905	1937	RT	31	HEN	CHA	ED
Crabb	Mrs 1 Eliz. Lauren	1905	1915	D	10	HEN		EVA
Crabb	Mrs 2 Myrtle Mccubins	1916	1937	RT	21	HEN		EVA
Craft	Miss Ruth J.	1922	1930	RS	8	CAN		ED
Craig	Miss Mary I.	1913	1920	RS	7	CAN		ED
Crawford	Rev Oliver C.	1900	1939	D	39	SOO		EVA
Crawford	Mrs Varina Scott	1900	1941	RT	41	SOO		EVA
Crawford	Miss Eliz Loretta	1927	1945	RS	18	SOO		EVA
Creighton	Rev John W., PhD	1907	1930	RS	23	CAN	TSI	ED
Creighton	Mrs Lois Jameson	1910	1930	RS	20	CAN	TSI	ED
Creighton	Mr Roy L.	1915	1927	RS	12	SHA		ARC
Creighton	Mrs Clara Linn	1915	1927	RS	12	SHA		ED
Crossett	Rev Jonathan F.	1870	1879	RS	9	TSI		EVA
Crossett	Mrs Mary Merrill	1870	1910	RS	29	TSI	WEI	EVA
Crothers	Rev James M.	1942	1950	EV	8	PEK		STU
Crothers	Mrs Elizabeth Hopkins	1942	1950	EV	8	PEK		WW
Crouch	Rev Archibald R.	1936	1946	RS	7	NIN	WCH	ED
Crouch	Mrs Ellen Gibbs	1936	1946	RS	7	NIN	WCH	ED
Crozier	Rev William N.	1891	1900	RS	9	NAN		EVA
Crozier	Mrs Sue Blake	1894	1900	RS	6	NAN		EVA
Culbertson	Rev Michael S.	1844	1862	D	18	NIN	SHA	TRA
Culbertson	Mrs Michael	1844	1862	DS	18	NIN	SHA	EVA
Cunningham	Rev Alexander M.	1890	1933	RT	43	PEK		EVA
Cunningham	Mrs Mary Neely	1890	1933	RT	43	PEK		EVA
Cunningham	William R., MD	1904	1928	RS	14	YIH		MED
Cunningham	Mrs Helen Ward, RN	1923	1928	RS	5	YIH		NUR
Curtis	Mr Gordan A.	1923	1927	RS	4	CHN		AG
Curtis	Mrs Gertrude Sibley	1923	1927	RS	4	CHN		AG
D'Olive	Rev Walter C.	1916	1949	D	33	TSN		EVA
D'Olive	Mrs Lottie Haehle	1916	1949	RT	33	TSN		
Danforth	Rev Joshua A.	1859	1863	RS	4	SHA	TEN	EVA
Danforth	Mrs Joshua	1859	1861	D	2	SHA	TEN	EVA
Daniels	John H., MD	1919	1950	RS	31	NAN		MED
Daniels	Mrs Helen Dunn	1919	1950	RS	31	NAN		MED
Darling	Miss Grace	1922	1951	TR	31	SHA		ED
Davenport	Rev Silas A., MD	1874	1874	RS	1	NIN		MED
Davenport	Miss Dorothy	1914	1915	RS	1	NAH		UNA
Davies	Rev Llewellyn J.	1892	1935	RT	37	TST	TSI	HED
Davies	Mrs Helen Goodsill	1892	1935	RT	37	TST	TSI	HED
Davis	Miss Ethel L.	1916	1952	RT	36	CHS		EVA
Davis	Rev William W.	1918	1927	RS	9	SIA		EVA
Davis	Mrs Eva Williams	1918	1927	RS	9	SIA		EVA
Day	Rev Clarence B., PhD	1915	1953	TR	38	HAN		HED
Day	Mrs Ethelwyn Colson	1916	1953	TR	37	HAN		HED
Day	Miss Isabella	1917	1925	RS	8	NAN		HED
De Jong	Miss Nettie R.	1914	1949	RT	35	CHA		EVA
Dean	Mr Samuel M.	1925	1949	EV	24	PEK		HED
Dean	Mrs Ruth Eldridge, RN	1925	1949	EV	24	PEK		HED
Derr	Rev Charles H.	1904	1938	D	34	HEN		EVA
Derr	Mrs Mysie Stump	1904	1939	DS	35	HEN		EVA
Dickey	Miss Elizabeth S.	1873	1875	H	2	TEN		ED
Dickie	Miss Edith C.	1906	1928	RT	22	NIN		EVA
Dickson	John R., MD	1915	1933	D	14	SHO		MED

Dickson	Mrs 1 Josephine McConnel	1915	1928	D	13	SHO		MED
Dickson	Mrs 2 Rachel Newton	1932	1948	RS	16	SHO		EVA
Dieterich	Frederick H., MD	1916	1917	RS	1	UNA		MED
Dilley	Frederick E., MD	1907	1937	D	30	CHE		MED
Dilley	Mrs Mary French	1907	1944	RT	37	CHE		WW
Dilworth	Rev David Edgar	1945	1951	EV	6	YEU		EVA
Dilworth	Mrs Eliz. Barker	1945	1951	EV	6	YEU		EVA
Dinkelacker	Miss Bertha L., RN	1916	1923	RS	7	TSI		NUR
Dobson	William H., MD	1897	1940	RT	43	YEU		MED
Dobson	Mrs Effie Moore	1899	1916	D	17	YEU		MED
Dodd	Rev Samuel	1861	1878	RS	17	NIN	HAN	EVA
Dodd	Mrs Samuel Green	1864	1878	RS	14	NIN	HAN	WW
Dodd	Rev Albert B.	1903	1935	RS	32	TNG		THE
Dodd	Mrs Mabel Mennie	1904	1935	RS	31	TNG		THE
Dodd	Mrs Isabel Eakin	1923	1926	RT	3	YUA		EVA
Dodds	Miss Alma D.	1910	1942	RT	32	TNG		ED
Dodds	Rev Walter A.	1925	1932	RS	7	SHA		EVA
Dodds	Mrs Ina Secor	1925	1932	RS	7	SHA		EVA
Doherty	Miss Carrie R.	1923	1928	RS	5	SOO		EVA
Donaldson	Miss Lucile F.	1917	1939	D	22	WEI		WW
Donaldson	Miss Mary L.	1924	1949	EV	25	TSI		EVA
Donaldson* (Grier)	Miss Henrietta, MD	1893	1895	TR	2	TSN		MED
Doolittle	Rev Justus	1872	1873	H	1	SHA		LIT
Doolittle	Mrs Louise Judson	1872	1904	RS	12	SHA	SIA	EVA
Doolittle	Miss Leila L., MD	1899	1903	M	4	SIA		MED
Douglas	Mr Clarence W.	1898	1932	RT	35	SHA		PRI
Douglas	Mrs Josie Silver	1898	1932	RT	35	SHA		PRI
Douglas	Richmond, MD	1923	1930	RS	7	NAH		MED
Douglas	Mrs Margaret Erskine	1923	1930	RS	7	NAH		MED
Douglas	William C., MD	1929	1933	RS	34	SIA		MED
Douglas	Mrs Ruth Earp, MD	1929	1933	RS	34	SIA		MED
Dowling	Mr Philip H.	1913	1927	RS	14	CHN		ED
Dowling	Mrs Blanche Klebo	1913	1927	RS	14	CHN		ED
Downing	Miss Calista B.	1866	1880	RS	14	CHE		ED
Dresser	Miss Ellen E.	1894	1931	RT	37	NAN		THE
Drummond	Rev William J.	1890	1934	RT	44	NAN		EVA
Drummond	Mrs Emma Lane	1889	1928	D	39	NAN		EVA
Drummond	Miss Ellen Lane	1925	1946	RS	21	NAN		EVA
Duncan	Miss Margaret B.	1903	1941	RT	37	NIN		WW
Dungan	Rev Irvine M.	1928	1948	RS	20	SHA		ED
Dungan	Mrs Gertrude Peterson	1928	1948	RS	20	SHA		ED
Dunlap	Robert Weyer, MD	1909	1928	RS	18	CHE		MED
Dunlap	Mrs Alice Logan	1912	1928	RS	16	CHE		ED
Durham	Miss Lucy	1909	1929	RT	20	CAN		WW
Eames	Rev Charles M.	1907	1946	RT	39	TSN		EVA
Eames	Mrs Carrie Johnston	1914	1946	RT	32	TSN		WW
Eames	Miss Susie Frances	1909	1946	RT	37	CHE		ED
Eckard	Rev Leighton W.	1869	1874	H	5	CHE		EVA
Eckard	Mrs Eliz. Longstreth	1869	1874	H	5	CHE		WW
Eddy	Miss Elsie S.	1915	1923	RS	8	SHA		ED
Edwards	Rev Rees F.	1898	1936	RT	35	LNC		EVA
Edwards	Mrs Margaret Edwards	1898	1936	RT	35	LNC		WW
Edwards	Miss Margaret J.	1930	1938	RS	8	LNC		WW
Ellington	Miss Minta	1910	1919	RS	9	CHA		ED
Elterich	Rev William O.	1889	1929	D	40	CHE	ICH	EVA
Elterich	Mrs Anna Berger	1889	1930	RT	41	CHE	ICH	EVA
Elterich	Miss Helen B.	1913	1930	RS	17	CHE		ED
Ensign	Rev Samuel J. R.	1924	1930	RS	6	KIU		ED
Ensign	Mrs Martha Whitlock	1924	1930	RS	6	KIU		ED
Espey	Rev John M.	1905	1934	RT	29	SHA		ED
Espey	Mrs Mary Jenkins	1909	1934	RT	25	SHA		ED
Eubank	Rev Bransford	1930	1937	RS	7	CHE		HED
Eubank	Mrs Martha Fenn	1932	1937	RS	5	CHE		HED
Ewers	Ernest M., MD	1916	1928	RS	12	WEI		MED
Ewers	Mrs Ruth Schaefer	1916	1928	RS	12	WEI		MED

Faries	William R., MD	1889	1903	H	14	WEI		MED
Faries	Mrs Priscilla Chittick	1890	1903	H	13	WEI		MED
Faries	Rev Henry G.	1922	1927	RS	5	SHU		EVA
Faris	Rev Wallace S.	1896	1907	D	11	ICH		EVA
Faris	Mrs Ellen Asper	1896	1907	DS	11	ICH		EVA
Faris	Rev Paul P.	1905	1914	RS	9	YIH		EVA
Faris	Mrs Mary Alexander	1905	1914	RS	9	YIH		WW
Faris	Miss Margaret	1906	1914	RS	8	YIH		WW
Faris	Miss Sarah	1911	1938	RT	26	TEN		EVA
Farnham	Rev John M. W.	1859	1917	D	58	SHA		ED
Farnham	Mrs Mary Scott	1859	1913	D	54	SHA		ED
Farnham	Miss Lizzie D.	1882	1885	RS	3	SHA		ED
Farr	Miss Elsie Elizabeth	1948	1949	EV	1	CAN		UNA
Fenn	Rev Courtenay H.	1893	1932	RT	39	PEK		THE
Fenn	Mrs Alice May	1893	1932	RT	39	PEK		EVA
Fenn	Mr Henry C.	1920	1950	RS	13	PEK		HED
Fenn	Mrs Constance Sargent	1925	1950	RS	8	PEK	SHA	ED
Fenn	William P., PhD	1932	1950	RS	18	NAN	SHA	HED
Fenn	Mrs Frances Cocks	1932	1950	RS	18	NAN	SHA	HED
Field	Rev Frank C.	1905	1934	RS	29	CHE	TSN	HED
Fildey	Rev Harold W.	1940	1948	RS	8	TST		EVA
Fildey	Mrs Vadna Shelton	1940	1948	RS	8	TST		EVA
Fine	Miss Mary D.	1919	1921	RS	2	SHO		UNK
Fisher	Rev Edward P.	1895	1897	H	2	YEU		EVA
Fisher	Rev Alzo J.	1902	1947	RT	45	CAN		EVA
Fisher	Mrs 1 Arminda Elliott	1901	1929	D	28	CAN		WW
Fisher	Mrs 2 Dorothy Mackeon	1920	1947	RT	27	CAN		WW
Fisher	Mr J. Elliott	1947	1949	EV	2	CAN		ED
Fisher	Mrs Gladys Erickson	1947	1949	EV	2	CAN		ED
Fitch	Rev George F.	1870	1923	D	53	SOO	SHA	PRI
Fitch	Mrs Mary McLillan	1870	1918	D	48	SOO	SHA	EVA
Fitch	Rev John A.	1889	1930	RT	41	WEI		EVA
Fitch	Mrs Mary Richardson	1889	1930	RT	41	WEI		EVA
Fitch	Rev Robert F.	1898	1943	RT	44	HAN		HED
Fitch	Mrs 1 Isadore Kloss	1898	1936	D	38	HAN		HED
Fitch	Mrs 2 May Robson	1937	1943	RT	5	HAN		LIT
Flaniken	Miss Sarah A.	1919	1925	RS	6	CAN		ED
Fleming	Miss Emma, MD	1898	1936	RT	38	ICH		MED
Flower	Miss Edythe M.	1920	1926	RS	5	WEI		ED
Folsom	Rev Arthur	1863	1868	RS	5	CAN		EVA
Folsom	Mrs Mary Thomas	1863	1868	RS	5	CAN		EVA
Forbes	Miss Velma R., RN	1926	1931	RS	5	HOI		NUR
Foreman	Rev Kenneth Joseph	1949	1952	EV	3	WCH		EVA
Foreman	Mrs Mary Frances Ogden	1949	1951	EV	2	WCH		EVA
Forsythe	Miss Francis Irene	1926	1951	EV	25	TST		EVA
Fouts	Frederick, MD	1905	1912	RS	7	ICH		MED
Fouts	Mrs Nellie Boring	1905	1912	RS	7	ICH		MED
Fowler	Miss Eva G., MD	1917	1919	RS	2	CAN		MED
Frame	Miss Margaret A.	1910	1949	RT	39	SHA		ADM
Franklin	Miss Rachel G.	1922	1930	RS	8	CHS		ED
Franz	Miss Anna K. M.	1902	1924	RS	22	WEI		WW
French	Rev John B.	1846	1859	D	13	CAN		EVA
French	Mrs Mary Ball	1851	1859	DS	8	CAN		ED
French	Miss Hazel M.	1915	1923	RS	8	HAN		WW
French	Rev Arthur E.	1930	1941	EV	11	KAC		EVA
French	Mrs Evelyn Winger	1930	1941	EV	11	KAC		EVA
Friedericks	Carl Williams, MD	1946	1950	TR	4	CAN		MED
Friedericks	Mrs Elizabeth Lutz	1946	1950	TR	4	CAN		MED
Fulton	Rev Albert A.	1880	1922	RT	42	CAN		EVA
Fulton	Mrs Florence Wishard	1882	1922	RT	40	CAN		WW
Fulton	Miss Mary H., MD	1884	1918	RS	34	CAN		MED
Fulton	Philip R., MD	1914	1922	RS	8	CAN		MED
Fulton	Mrs Evelyn Manful	1917	1922	RS	5	CAN		MED
Fulton	Miss Grace	1917	1935	RS	18	CAN		ED
Fuson	Chester G., PhD	1917	1949	RT	32	CAN		HED

Fuson	Mrs Phebe Meeker	1917	1949	RT	32	CAN		ED
Gailey	Miss Helen	1919	1925	RS	6	CHS		ED
Galt	Curtis M., MD	1923	1935	TR	12	KIL		MED
Galt	Mrs Florence Moore	1923	1935	TR	12	KIL		WW
Gamble	Mr William	1858	1869	RS	11	SHA		PRI
Gammon	Rev George U.	1917	1918	RS	1	CHE		EVA
Gammon	Mrs Helen Smith	1912	1918	RS	6	NAN	CHE	WW
Gardner	Miss Marian W.	1915	1919	RS	4	NAH		UNK
Garritt	Rev Joshua C.	1889	1922	RS	33	HAN		THE
Garritt* (McDannald)	Mrs Nannie	1891	1922	RS	31	HAN		EVA
Garside	Mr Bettice A.	1922	1929	RS	7	TSI		HED
Garside	Mrs Margaret Cameron	1922	1929	RS	7	TSI		ED
Gates	Rev M. Halsted	1940	1949	EV	9	LNC		EVA
Gates	Mrs Wanda Edwards	1940	1949	EV	9	LNC		EVA
Gault	Arabella Sangster, MD	1926	1946	D	20	TSI		MED
Gauss	Miss Esther M.	1911	1949	RT	38	NIN		ED
Gayley	Rev Samuel R.	1856	1862	D	6	SHA	TEN	EVA
Gayley	Mrs Sara Mills	1856	1862	DS	6	SHA	TEN	EVA
Gelwicks	Rev George L.	1901	1922	D	21	HEN		EVA
Gelwicks	Mrs Lida Galt	1901	1944	RT	43	HEN		WW
Gernhardt	Miss Ella M.	1922	1950	EV	28	HEN	TST	EVA
Gernhardt	Miss Lucinda S.	1923	1951	EV	28	HEN		EVA
Gill	Rev Charles O.	1895	1897	H	2	PEK		EVA
Gill	Mrs Mary Nelson	1895	1897	H	2	PEK		EVA
Gilman	Rev Frank P.	1885	1918	D	33	NOD	KAC	EVA
Gilman	Mrs 1 Marian McNair	1885	1899	D	14	NOD		WW
Gilman (White)	Mrs 2 Mary Martin	1880	1917	D	37	CAN	KAC	ED
Gilman	Miss Janet	1917	1920	M	3	KIU	CAN	TMC
Gleysteen	Mr William Henry	1905	1946	RT	41	PEK		ED
Gleysteen	Mrs 1 Alice Carter	1903	1917	D	14	PEK		ED
Gleysteen	Mrs 2 Theodora Culver	1917	1946	RT	29	PEK		ED
Goerzen	Miss Elisabeth M.	1925	1928	H	3	TST		ED
Goodenberger	Rev Ernest C.	1923	1935	TR	12	KIL		EVA
Goodenberger	Mrs Hilda Longstaff	1923	1935	TR	12	KIL		EVA
Gordon	Mr Simeon M.	1916	1927	RS	11	PEK		AG
Gordon	Mrs Jessie Winchester	1918	1927	RS	9	PEK		WW
Gordon	Mr Karl M.	1920	1926	RS	6	YIH		AG
Gordon	Mrs Mabel Kersey	1920	1926	RS	6	YIH		AG
Gould	Miss Orpha B., RN	1921	1950	RS	29	PAO		NUR
Gowans	Miss Annie H.	1901	1926	RS	25	PEK		EVA
Gray	Rev Alfred V.	1907	1924	RS	17	NAN		EVA
Gray	Mrs Minnie Moore	1907	1924	RS	17	NAN		EVA
Green	Rev David D.	1859	1872	D	13	NIN	HAN	EVA
Green	Mrs David	1859	1872	DS	13	NIN	HAN	EVA
Greene	Theodore C., MD	1926	1951	RS	24	TSI	PEK	MED
Greene	Mrs Phoebe Cutler	1926	1950	RS	24	TSI	PEK	MED
Griggs	Joseph F., MD	1902	1906	RS	4	PEK		MED
Griggs	Mrs Alice Van Gorder	1902	1906	RS	4	PEK		MED
Groves	Rev Samuel B.	1891	1895	H	4	TEN		HED
Groves	Mrs Clara Anderson	1891	1895	H	4	TEN		EVA
Guffin	Miss Alice I.	1912	1917	RS	5	PEK		HED
Gumbrell	Miss Edith E.	1911	1922	D	11	PAO		EVA
Gunn	Mr Charles A.	1921	1938	RS	17	SHA	PEK	ARC
Gunn	Mrs May Borden	1921	1938	RS	17	SHA	PEK	ED
Guy	Rev Thomas R.	1902	1905	RS	3	TSI		EVA
Hacker	Miss Frances L., MD	1919	1920	RS	1	SOO		MED
Hackett	Miss Martha, MD	1913	1923	RS	10	CAN		MED
Hadley	Rev Lindsay S. B.	1914	1922	RS	8	PEK		EVA
Hadley	Mrs Mary Humphrey	1914	1922	RS	8	PEK		EVA
Hall	Francis J., MD	1906	1913	D	7	PEK		MED
Hall	Mrs Anna Hoffman	1908	1921	RS	8	PEK		ED
Hall	Miss Mabel Seymour	1920	1938	RS	18	HWA		ED
Hallock	Rev Henry G. C., PhD	1896	1905	RS	9	HAN		EVA
Hallock	Miss Adelia Cobb	1923	1942	RS	19	NAH		WW
Hamilton	Rev William B.	1888	1912	D	24	TSI		ED

Hamilton	Mrs 1 Clara Linton	1888	1889	D	1	TSI		ED
Hamilton	Mrs 2 Margaret Woods	1892	1934	RT	42	TSI		WW
Hamilton	Guy W., MD	1903	1930	RS	27	SHU		MED
Hamilton	Mrs Alice Ernst	1903	1930	RS	27	SHU		ED
Hamilton	Miss Mary L.	1917	1920	RS	3	TSI		ED
Hamlin	Rev Earl John	1947	1951	EV	4	TSI		STU
Hamlin	Mrs Frances Jane Cade	1947	1951	EV	4	TSI		STU
Hand	Miss Katherine W.	1920	1950	TR	30	SHA		ED
Happer	Rev Andrew P.	1844	1894	D	50	CAN		HED
Happer	Mrs 1 Elizabeth Ball	1847	1865	D	18	CAN		EVA
Happer	Mrs 2 A. L. Elliott	1869	1873	D	4	CAN		EVA
Happer	Mrs 3 Hannah Shaw	1870	1894	DS	24	CAN		ED
Happer	Miss Lucy A.	1869	1870	M	1	CAN		UNK
Happer	Miss Lilly	1871	1879	M	8	CAN		ED
Happer	Miss Alverda	1878	1888	RS	10	NIN		WW
Happer	Miss Mary	1879	1884	M	5	CAN		ED
Harding	Benjamin O., MD	1913	1949	RT	36	ICH		MED
Harken	Mr Charles William	1947	1949	EV	2	HEN		ED
Harken	Mrs Hazel	1947	1949	EV	2	HEN		ED
Harkness	Mr Harold W.	1915	1920	TR	5	WEI	TSI	HED
Harkness	Mrs Eva Brownlee	1916	1920	TR	4	WEI	TSI	HED
Harvey	Joseph L., MD	1915	1926	RS	11	CAN		MED
Harvey	Mrs Ella Kenney	1915	1926	RS	11	CAN		MED
Harvey	Rev Earle Rolston, Jr.	1945	1949	EV	4	NIN		EVA
Harvey	Mrs Berneita Cornell	1945	1949	EV	4	NIN		EVA
Hawes	Miss Charlotte E.	1897	1917	RS	17	WEI		WW
Hawley	Rev Edwin C.	1904	1913	RS	9	SHU		ED
Hawley	Mrs Winifred Gold	1904	1913	RS	9	SHU		ED
Hayes	Rev John N.	1882	1923	RT	41	SOO		EVA
Hayes	Mrs Mercie Briggs	1882	1923	RT	41	SOO		EVA
Hayes	Rev Watson M.	1882	1933	RT	41	TEN	WEI	HED
Hayes	Mrs Margaret Young	1882	1933	RT	41	TEN	WEI	HED
Hayes	Rev John D.	1917	1952	TR	36	PEK	WCH	STU
Hayes	Mrs Barbara Kelman	1917	1953	TR	36	PEK		STU
Hayes	Miss Grace C., RN	1921	1927	RS	6	CHN		NUR
Hayes	Rev Ernest M.	1923	1935	RS	12	SHA		ADM
Hayes	Mrs Dorothy Drew	1923	1935	RS	12	SHA		ADM
Hayne	Miss Jemmima Hester, MD	1944	1950	EV	6	HEN		MED
Hays	Rev George S.	1886	1895	RS	9	CHE		EVA
Hays	Mrs Fanny Corbett	1886	1895	RS	9	CHE		EVA
Heeren	Rev John J., PhD	1911	1940	D	29	TSI		HED
Heeren	Mrs Edith Weeks	1912	1945	RT	33	TSI		STU
Heimburger	Leroy F., MD	1913	1934	RS	21	TSI		MED
Heimburger	Mrs 1 Louise Corbett	1914	1930	D	16	TSI		MED
Heimburger	Mrs 2 Margaret Smith, RN	1926	1934	RS	8	TSI		NUR
Henke	Harold E., MD	1927	1950	RS	23	PEK		MED
Henke	Mrs Jessie Paddock, RN	1927	1950	RS	23	PEK	PEK	NUR
Henry	Rev Benjamin C.	1873	1900	H	27	CAN		EVA
Henry	Mrs Mary Snyder	1873	1898	D	25	CAN		EVA
Henry	Miss Julia V.	1896	1900	RS	4	CAN		ED
Henry	Rev James M.	1909	1919	RS	10	CAN		HED
Henry	Mrs Natalie F. Brown	1909	1919	RS	10	CAN		HED
Hepburn	James C., MD	1841	1846	H	5	SIN	AMO	MED
Hepburn	Mrs Clara Leete	1841	1846	H	5	SIN	AMO	MED
Hermann	Mr Adolph	1926	1927	RS	1	CHN		UNK
Hermann	Mrs Emma Hicks	1904	1927	RS	6	CHN		EVA
Herring	James H., Jr., MD	1931	1939	RS	8	YEU		MED
Herring	Mrs Mary Eliz Shoesmith	1931	1939	RS	8	YEU		MED
Herriott	Rev Clarence D.	1903	1911	RS	8	HAN		EVA
Herriott	Mrs Lilian Taylor	1906	1911	RS	5	HAN		EVA
Herriott	Miss Anna G.	1914	1920	RS	6	HEN		ED
Hicks	Rev Walter W.	1902	1921	D	19	PEK		EVA
Hicks	Mrs 1 Agnes Hubbard	1902	1906	D	4	PEK		EVA
Hicks	Mrs 2 Cora Small	1908	1940	RT	32	PEK		HED
Highberger	Rev William W.	1913	1928	RS	15	HEN		EVA

Highberger	Mrs Emily Patterson	1913	1928	RS	15	HEN		WW
Hill	Miss Mary J., MD	1895	1899	RS	4	TSN		MED
Hill	Miss Ethel Gertrude	1920	1946	RT	26	CAN		SEC
Hille	Miss Bessie M.	1913	1952	RT	39	SHA		ADM
Hills	Oscar F., MD	1907	1924	RS	17	CHE		MED
Hills	Mrs Euphemia Pomeroy	1907	1924	RS	17	CHE		MED
Hilscher	Rev Harris G.	1923	1950	EV	27	TEN	NAH	EVA
Hilscher	Mrs Gladys Jones	1923	1950	EV	27	TEN	NAH	ED
Hinkhouse	Miss Myrtle J., MD	1916	1948	RT	32	PAO		MED
Hodge	Cortland Van R., MD	1899	1900	D	1	PAO		MED
Hodge	Mrs Elsie Sinclair	1899	1900	D	1	PAO		MED
Hoffman	Stanley L., MD	1946	1948	EV	9	SIA		MED
Hoffman	Mrs Mary Kepler	1941	1950	EV	9	SIA		MED
Hofmann	John A., MD	1922	1933	D	11	CAN		MED
Hofmann	Mrs Margaret Jones	1913	1933	RS	15	CAN		TMC
Hogan	Rev Milo A. V.	1919	1926	RS	7	LNC		EVA
Hogan	Mrs Emily Beach	1919	1926	RS	7	LNC		EVA
Holland	Mr Ira H.	1943	1950	EV	7	TSI		HED
Holland	Mrs Beverly Myers	1943	1950	EV	7	TSI		HED
Holt	Rev William S.	1873	1885	TR	12	SHA		PRI
Holt	Mrs Frances Pratt	1873	1885	TR	12	SHA		PRI
Hood	Rev George C.	1911	1936	RS	25	NAH		EVA
Hood	Mrs Mary Preston	1913	1936	RS	23	NAH		WW
Hosler	Rev Paul M.	1920	1926	RS	6	SHE		EVA
Hosler	Mrs Sarah Crothers	1920	1926	RS	6	SHE		EVA
Houston	Miss Bessie	1878	1879	RS	1	NIN		WW
Houston	Rev Thomas W.	1891	1899	RS	8	NAN		EVA
Houston	Mrs Zula Suydam	1891	1899	RS	8	NAN		EVA
Howe	Mr Edwin C.	1914	1929	RS	15	CAN		ED
Howe	Mrs 1 Almeda Baird	1914	1915	D	1	CAN		ED
Howe	Mrs 2 Eliz. Faries	1913	1929	RS	16	CAN		ED
Howe* (McGinnis)	Miss Anna	1896	1899	M	3	NAN		ED
Howell	Miss Elsie M.	1923	1928	RS	5	CAN		ED
Hoy	Miss Mabel R.	1914	1916	RS	2	CHS		UNA
Huebener	Mr Eugene C.	1941	1950	EV	9	SHA		ADM
Huebener	Mrs Evelyn Davey	1946	1950	EV	4	SHA		ADM
Hughes	Miss Freidda	1921	1928	RS	7	CHN		ED
Humphreys	Miss Anna F., MD	1913	1915	RS	2	SOO		MED
Hunter	Rev Stephen A., MD	1879	1892	RS	13	TSI		MED
Hunter	Mrs Sarah	1879	1892	RS	13	TSI		MED
Hyde	Miss Jane Adelaide	1905	1942	RT	37	NAN		EVA
Inglis	John, MD	1898	1903	H	7	PEK		MED
Inglis	Mrs Martha Marshall	1898	1903	H	5	PEK		MED
Inslee*	Rev Elias B.	1857	1861	RS	4	NIN		EVA
Inslee	Mrs Euphemia Ross	1857	1861	RS	4	NIN		ED
Irwin	Rev John P.	1894	1934	RT	40	TEN		ED
Irwin	Mrs Martha Archibald	1894	1934	RT	40	TEN		ED
Irwin	Rev Donald A., PhD	1920	1950	EV	30	CHE	HAN	STU
Irwin	Mrs Mary Totten	1920	1950	RS	30	CHE	HAN	STU
Irwin	Rev Charles L.	1922	1937	RS	15	NAH		EVA
Irwin	Mrs Vera McCormick	1922	1937	RS	15	NAH		TMC
Irwin	Miss Anita R.	1925	1950	EV	25	NAH		ED
Isett	Rev William C.	1906	1907	RS	1	YIH		EVA
Isett	Mrs Gertrude Johnston	1906	1907	RS	1	YIH		EVA
Jackson	Rev Frederick W., Jr.	1892	1895	RS	3	CHE		EVA
Jacobson	Miss Josephine E., RN	1921	1930	RS	9	HEN		NUR
Jacot	Mr Arthur P.	1920	1931	RS	11	TSI		HED
Jacot	Mrs Lydia Jaccard	1920	1948	RS	11	TSI		HED
Jenkins	Rev George F.	1903	1934	RS	31	CHA		EVA
Jenkins	Mrs Edna McCuan	1903	1934	RS	31	CHA		WW
Jenness	Rev Richard E.	1916	1941	D	25	SHU		THE
Jenness	Mrs Lillian Keyes	1916	1950	RS	34	SHU		ED
Jeremiassen	Mr Carl C.	1885	1898	RS	13	NOD		EVA
Jeremiassen	Mrs Jeanne Sutter	1891	1904	RS	13	NOD		EVA
Jillson	Miss Mary A., RN	1923	1926	RS	3	PEK		NUR

Johnson	Charles F., MD	1889	1931	D	42	ICH		MED
Johnson	Mrs Agnes Elliot	1889	1933	RT	44	ICH		MED
Johnson	Rev Erving L.	1905	1949	RT	37	PEK		EVA
Johnson	Mrs Esther Emery	1905	1949	RT	37	PEK		EVA
Johnson	Miss Margaret E.	1914	1917	RS	3	TSI		ED
Johnson	Hosmer F., MD	1928	1948	RS	20	WEI		MED
Johnson	Mrs Cora Hoffman, RN	1932	1948	RS	16	WEI		NUR
Johnston	Miss Louise H.	1889	1903	RS	4	LNC		WW
Johnston	Rev William W.	1907	1925	RS	18	TSI		EVA
Johnston	Mrs Mary Harding	1908	1925	RS	17	TSI		EVA
Johnston	Robert H., MD	1930	1936	RS	6	CHN		MED
Johnston	Mrs Annie Vanderslice	1930	1936	RS	6	CHN		ED
Jones	Miss Margaret J.	1901	1905	RS	4	HAN		ED
Jones	Rev John R.	1905	1907	D	2	NAN		EVA
Jones	Mrs Amanda Risher	1905	1927	RS	22	NAN	NAN	WW
Jones	Miss Anita M., RN	1923	1928	RS	5	CAN		NUR
Jones	Rev Henry David	1947	1950	EV	3	SHA		EVA
Jones	Mrs Maurine Fink	1947	1950	EV	3	SHA		EVA
Judd	Rev Laurence Cecil	1947	1949	TR	2	NIN		UNA
Judd	Mrs Virginia Moffat	1947	1949	TR	2	NIN		UNA
Judson	Rev Junius H.	1879	1923	RT	44	HAN		HED
Judson	Mrs Jennie Filley	1879	1923	RT	44	HAN		EVA
Judson	Miss Marjorie M.	1910	1950	RT	40	SHU		WW
Judson	Herbert A., MD	1919	1927	RS	8	LNC		MED
Judson	Mrs Ruth McCandliss	1919	1927	RS	8	LNC		MUS
Junkin	Miss Nettie D.	1933	1948	TR	15	YIH	WCH	EVA
Karcher	James F., MD	1926	1948	RS	22	CAN		MED
Karcher	Mrs Mary Sanner	1926	1948	RS	22	CAN		MED
Karr	Mrs Effie Dunn, RN	1922	1927	RS	5	SHU		NUR
Keator	Miss Louise H., MD	1903	1922	RS	15	SHU	WEI	MED
Kelly	Rev Jonathan C.	1896	1899	RS	3	LNC		EVA
Kelly	Mrs Ella Cunningham	1896	1899	RS	3	LNC		EVA
Kelly	John F., MD	1904	1921	RS	17	KIU		MED
Kelly	Mrs Lillian Marks	1904	1921	RS	17	KIU		MED
Kelsey	Miss Adeline D.H., MD	1878	1884	RS	6	TEN		MED
Kennedy	Rev Edward B.	1894	1898	H	4	NIN		EVA
Kepler	Rev Asher Raymond	1901	1942	D	41	SIA	SHA	EVA
Kepler	Mrs Jeanette Fitch	1902	1942	RT	40	SIA	SHA	EVA
Kepler	Rev Kenneth M.	1930	1948	RS	18	CHN	TNG	EVA
Kepler	Mrs Kathleen Neale	1930	1948	RS	18	CHN	TNG	EVA
Kepler	Rev Raymond F.	1930	1949	EV	19	HEN	CHS	EVA
Kepler	Mrs Margaret Blain	1930	1949	RS	19	HEN	CHS	EVA
Kerr	John G., MD	1854	1901	D	47	CAN		MED
Kerr	Mrs 1 Abby Kingsley	1854	1855	D	1	CAN		MED
Kerr	Mrs 2 Isabella Moseley	1858	1885	D	27	CAN		MED
Kerr	Mrs 3 Martha Noyes	1873	1923	RT	50	CAN		MED
Kerr	Harold D., MD	1920	1928	RS	8	HWA		MED
Kerr	Mrs Eleanor Smith	1920	1928	RS	8	HWA		MED
Kidder	Rev Jonathan Edward	1920	1945	RS	25	CHE		EVA
Kidder	Mrs Florence Howe	1920	1945	RS	25	CHE		WW
Killie	Rev Charles A.	1889	1916	D	27	ICH	PEK	EVA
Killie	Mrs Louise Scott	1889	1916	DS	27	ICH	PEK	ED
Knickerbocker	Rev Edgar F.	1909	1916	RS	7	NIN		EVA
Knickerbocker	Mrs Minnie May	1909	1916	RS	7	NIN		EVA
Kolfrat	Miss Mary E.	1902	1924	RS	22	SIA		ED
Kunkle	Miss Hannah E.	1911	1920	D	9	LNC		ED
Kunkle	Rev John S.	1906	1949	RT	43	LNC	CAN	THE
Kunkle	Mrs Julia Mitchell	1916	1949	RT	33	CAN		THE
Lair	Rev Howell P.	1914	1950	RT	36	TSI		HED
Lair	Mrs Kathryn Stephens	1914	1950	RT	36	TSI		NUR
Lane	Rev William	1889	1896	D	7	TSN		EVA
Lane	Mrs Lucy Kenyon	1889	1896	DS	7	TSN		EVA
Langdon	Rev William M.	1888	1891	H	3	PEK		EVA
Lanning	Mr Roy A.	1914	1950	TR	36	CHE		ED
Lanning	Mrs Wilhelmina Mitray	1914	1950	TR	36	CHE		ED

Larson	Miss Anna, MD	1892	1897	D	5	ICH		MED
Lasell	Sidney L., MD	1899	1930	RS	31	HAN	NAN	MED
Lasell	Mrs Ruth Lyon	1912	1930	RS	18	HAN	NAN	MED
Latimer	Miss Nannie M., MD	1911	1913	D	2	LNC		MED
Lattimore	Miss Mary	1888	1917	D	29	NAN		ED
Laube	Paul Julius, MD	1944	1949	EV	5	TSI		MED
Laube	Mrs Lavon Dunlea	1944	1949	EV	5	TSI		MED
Laughlin	Rev John H.	1881	1903	TR	22	WEI	TSN	EVA
Laughlin	Mrs 1 Annie Johnson	1881	1884	D	3	WEI		WW
Laughlin	Mrs 2 Jennie Anderson	1878	1899	D	21	WEI	TSN	WW
Lautenschlager	Rev Stanton	1920	1950	D	30	TSI		HED
Lautenschlager	Mrs Sarah Herner	1920	1950	RT	30	TSI		HED
Lautenschlager	Mr Roy S.	1922	1953	RS	31	HAN		HED
Lautenschlager	Mrs Harriet Miller	1922	1953	RS	31	HAN		HED
Lawson	Chester W., MD	1939	1948	RS	9	CAN		MED
Lawson	Mrs Doris Haswell	1939	1948	RS	9	CAN		MED
Lazear	Mr Edwart T.	1913	1917	RS	4	WEI		HED
Lazear	Mrs Grace Fairman	1913	1917	RS	4	WEI		HED
Leaman	Rev Charles	1874	1920	D	46	SHA	NAN	EVA
Leaman	Mrs Lucy Crouch	1873	1910	D	37	SHA	NAN	WW
Leaman	Miss Mary A.	1901	1935	RT	34	NAN		WW
Leaman	Miss Lucy A.	1909	1923	RS	14	NAN		ED
Lee	Miss Mary E.	1912	1916	RS	4	UNK		UNK
Lee	Miss Mabel L.	1912	1930	RS	18	NAN		WW
Lefever	Rev Rufus H.	1923	1926	RS	3	WEI		ED
Lefever	Mrs Mary Daugherty	1923	1926	RS	3	WEI		ED
Lehman	Miss Mary A.	1932	1936	RS	4	CAN		ED
Leiper	Rev Henry Martyn W.	1945	1950	EV	5	PAO		EVA
Leiper	Mrs Jane Crichton	1946	1950	RS	4	PAO		EVA
Leonard	Miss Eliza E., MD	1895	1924	D	29	PEK		MED
Leverett	Rev William J.	1894	1925	RT	29	NOD		ED
Lewis	Miss Harriette	1883	1922	RT	39	CAN		ED
Lewis	Charles, MD	1896	1932	D	36	PAO		MED
Lewis	Mrs 1 Alice Davis	1896	1897	D	1	PAO		MED
Lewis	Mrs 2 Cora Savige	1902	1936	RT	34	PAO		MED
Lewis	Stephen C., MD	1902	1927	RS	25	CHN		MED
Lewis	Mrs Mary Land, RN	1918	1927	RS	9	CHN		NUR
Lewis	Miss Elizabeth F., MD	1906	1931	RS	25	SHU		MED
Lewis	Rev Charles H.	1916	1950	RT	34	YEU	CAN	EVA
Lewis	Mrs Hary Hudson	1920	1950	RT	30	YEU	CAN	EVA
Lewis	Ralph C., MD	1933	1952	EV	19	SHU	PAO	MED
Lewis	Mrs Roberta Taylor	1933	1952	EV	19	SHU	PAO	MED
Leyenberger	Rev Joseph A.	1865	1896	D	31	NIN	WEI	ED
Leyenberger	Mrs Susan Fugate	1865	1896	DS	31	NIN	WEI	EVA
Leynse	Rev James P.	1920	1950	RT	30	PEK		EVA
Leynse	Mrs Anna Groenendyke	1920	1950	RT	30	PEK		EVA
Lindholm	Miss Elfrida A.	1895	1910	RS	15	SHA		ED
Lindholm	Rev Paul R.	1931	1949	EV	18	SOO		THE
Lindholm	Mrs Clara Malbon	1931	1950	EV	19	SOO		THE
Lingle	Rev William H.	1890	1932	RT	42	LNC	SIA	EVA
Lingle	Mrs 1 Martha Smith	1890	1893	D	3	LNC		EVA
Lingle (Ritchie)	Mrs 2 Jean Richardson	1889	1932	RT	43	TEN	SIA	EVA
Lloyd	Rev John	1844	1848	D	4	AMO		EVA
Lobenstine	Rev Edwin C.	1898	1937	RT	39	HWA	SHA	EVA
Lobenstine	Mrs 1 Rose Hoffman	1902	1908	D	6	HWA		EVA
Lobenstine	Mrs 2 Susan Clark	1916	1937	RT	21	SHA		ADM
Locke	Rev William T.	1903	1924	RS	11	CHN	CHA	EVA
Locke	Mrs 1 Emma Roehl	1903	1910	D	7	CHN		ED
Locke	Mrs 2 Agnes Crother, MD	1909	1924	RS	15	CHN	CHA	MED
Logan	Oliver T., MD	1897	1919	D	22	CHA		MED
Logan	Mrs Jennie Manget	1897	1920	DS	23	CHA		WW
Logan	Miss Florence L.	1921	1951	TR	26	PAO		WW
Logan	Miss Elsa M.	1935	1950	EV	15	SHA		ED
Long	Miss Helen Lucille, RN	1947	1950	EV	3	YEU		NUR
Loomis	Rev Augustus W.	1844	1849	RS	5	NIN		EVA

Loomis	Mrs Augustus	1844	1849	RS	5	NIN		ED
Lovell	Rev Gilbert	1904	1920	RS	16	CHA		EVA
Lovell	Mrs Florence Bell	1904	1920	RS	16	CHA		ED
Lowrie	Rev Walter M.	1842	1847	D	5	CAN	NIN	EVA
Lowrie	Rev Reuben	1854	1860	D	6	SHA		EVA
Lowrie	Mrs Amelia Tuttle	1854	1907	D	30	SHA	PEK	WW
Lowrie	Rev James W.	1883	1930	D	47	PAO	SHA	ADM
Lowrie	Miss Mary L.	1924	1928	M	4	PEK		WW
Lucas	Miss Grace M.	1906	1917	D	11	NAN		ED
Luccock	Rev Emory W.	1921	1938	RS	17	SHA		PAS
Luccock	Mrs Lois Maddock	1924	1938	RS	13	SHA		WW
Luce	Rev Henry W.	1897	1928	RS	31	WEI	PEK	HED
Luce	Mrs Elisabeth Root	1897	1928	RS	31	WEI	PEK	HED
Lynch	Miss Grace D.	1907	1907	D	1	WEI		UNK
Lynn	Robert B., MD	1940	1945	RS	5	YEU		MED
Lynn	Mrs Gladys Oanes	1940	1945	RS	5	YEU		MED
Lyon	Rev David N.	1869	1904	RS	30	HAN	SOO	EVA
Lyon	Mrs Mandana Doolittle	1869	1910	RS	36	HAN	SOO	EVA
Lyon	Charles H., MD	1900	1918	RS	18	TSN		MED
Lyon	Mrs Edna Van Schoick	1902	1918	RS	16	TSN		MED
Lyon	Miss Lois D.	1903	1943	RT	34	HAN		ED
Lyons	Rev John R.	1913	1922	RS	9	SHU		EVA
Lyons	Mrs Mary Lippincott	1913	1922	RS	9	SHU		EVA
MacCurdy	Miss Harriet R.	1913	1948	RT	35	HWA		WW
Macdonald	Miss Grace	1921	1948	RT	27	HOI		ADM
Machle	Edward C., MD	1889	1929	RT	40	LNC	CAN	MED
Machle	Mrs 1 Ella Wood	1889	1905	D	16	LNC	CAN	MED
Machle	Mrs 2 Jean Mawson	1911	1929	RT	18	CAN		ED
Mackey	Miss Maud A., MD	1899	1940	RT	41	PAO		MED
MacKubbin	Miss Mary E.	1919	1925	RS	6	NAN		EVA
MacLeod	Rev Alexander Napier	1929	1949	EV	20	ICH	TNG	THE
MacLeod	Mrs Dorothy Miles	1930	1949	EV	19	ICH	TNG	MUS
MacMillan	Miss Margaret Ainsle	1941	1944	RS	3	NAN		ED
Madelaire	Miss Hilma C. H., RN	1924	1950	EV	26	TSI		NUR
Maggi	Miss Minnie B.	1908	1910	RS	2	PAO		UNK
Mahy	Rev George G., Jr.	1935	1950	EV	15	WEI	TST	ED
Mahy	Mrs Helen Scott	1935	1950	EV	15	WEI	TST	ED
Manus	Miss Frieda	1941	1950	EV	9	KIU		EVA
Marcellus	Rev Algernon	1869	1870	H	1	CAN		EVA
Marcellus	Mrs Algernon	1869	1870	H	1	CAN		EVA
March	Mr Arthur W.	1907	1950	D	43	NAN		HED
March	Mrs Mary Herriott	1909	1950	RT	41	NAN		HED
Marshall	Rev George W.	1895	1935	D	36	SHE	CAN	EVA
Marshall	Mrs Edmonia Sale	1899	1936	RT	37	SHE	CAN	WW
Martin	Rev Samuel N.D.	1850	1858	RS	8	NIN		EVA
Martin	Mrs Margaret Wylie	1850	1858	RS	8	NIN		EVA
Martin	Rev William A. P.	1850	1868	RS	18	NIN	PEK	ED
Martin	Mrs Julia Vansant	1850	1868	RS	18	NIN	PEK	ED
Martin	Rev Walter Burton	1945	1950	EV	5	TSI		ED
Martin	Mrs Barbara Blackstone	1945	1950	EV	5	TSI		ED
Mason	Claud W., MD	1923	1926	RS	3	KIL		MED
Mason	Mrs Anna Anderson	1923	1926	RS	3	KIL		MED
Mason	Miss Marian C.	1914	1919	RS	5	PAO		UNK
Mateer	Rev Calvin W.	1864	1908	D	44	TEN	WEI	HED
Mateer	Mrs 1 Julia Brown	1864	1898	D	34	TEN		HED
Mateer	Mrs 2 Ada Haven	1900	1924	RT	24	WEI	PEK	HED
Mateer	Rev Robert M.	1881	1921	D	40	WEI		EVA
Mateer	Mrs 1 Sadie Archibald	1881	1886	D	5	WEI		EVA
Mateer	Mrs 2 Madge Dickson, MD	1889	1933	RT	44	WEI		MED
Mateer	Miss Lilian	1881	1883	M	2	TEN		WW
Mather	Rev William Arnot	1902	1945	RT	43	PAO		EVA
Mather	Mrs Grace Burroughs	1904	1938	D	34	PAO		ED
Mather	W. Brewster, MD	1940	1945	RS	5	HEN		MED
Mather	Mrs Brewster	1940	1945	RS	5	HEN		MED
Mather	Rev Richard B.	1941	1946	EV	7	UNA		EVA

Mather	Mrs Virginia Temple	1941	1946	EV	7	UNA			EVA
Matthewson	J. M., MD	1883	1887	RS	4	WEI			MED
Mattox	Rev Elmer L.	1893	1934	RT	41	HAN			HED
Mattox	Mrs Emma King	1893	1934	RT	41	HAN			HED
McAfee	Rev Wallace T.	1924	1928	RS	4	NAN			EVA
McAfee	Mrs Edna Clark	1924	1928	RS	4	NAN			EVA
McAulay	Rev John R.	1933	1934	RS	1	NAN			UNA
McAulay	Mrs Edith Bishop	1933	1934	RS	1	NAN			UNA
McBryde	Rev Thomas L.	1840	1843	H	3	SIN	AMO		EVA
McBryde	Mrs Thomas	1840	1843	H	3	SIN	AMO		EVA
McCandliss	Henry M., MD	1885	1925	RT	40	KIU	HOI		MED
McCandliss	Mrs Olivia Kerr	1885	1925	RT	40	KIU	HOI		MED
McCandliss	William K., MD	1919	1927	RS	8	YEU			MED
McCandliss	Mrs Maybelle Taylor	1919	1927	RS	8	YEU			MED
McCandliss	Robert J., MD	1923	1941	RS	18	CAN			MED
McCandliss	Mrs Tirzah Roberts	1923	1941	RS	18	CAN			MED
McCartee	Divie B., MD	1844	1872	RS	28	NIN	CHE		MED
McCartee	Mrs Juana Knight	1852	1872	RS	20	NIN	CHE		ED
McChesney	Rev William E.	1869	1872	D	3	CAN			EVA
McChesney	Mrs William	1869	1872	DS	3	CAN			EVA
McClain	Miss Helen B.	1938	1948	RS	10	TSI			HED
McClintock	Rev Paul W.	1892	1916	RS	24	KIU			EVA
McClintock	Mrs Rebecca Ewing	1892	1916	RS	24	KIU			EVA
McCoy	Rev Daniel C.	1869	1891	RS	22	PEK			EVA
McCoy	Mrs America Pollock	1869	1891	RS	22	PEK			EVA
McCoy	Miss Bessie C.	1896	1939	D	43	PEK			ED
McCreery	Miss Caroline I., RN	1922	1953	EV	31	HOI			NUR
McCullough	Rev Malcolm S.	1944	1950	EV	6	CHA			EVA
McCullough	Mrs Ruth Strandness	1944	1950	EV	6	CHA			EVA
McDonald	Miss Dorothy	1949	1951	EV	2	KIU			UNA
McGaffin	Rev Andrew, Jr.	1931	1937	RS	6	NIN			EVA
McGaffin	Mrs Katherine Wilson	1931	1937	RS	6	NIN			EVA
McIlvaine	Rev Jasper S.	1868	1881	D	13	PEK	TSI		EVA
McIntosh	Mr Gilbert	1890	1933	RT	43	SHA			PRI
McIntosh	Mrs 1 Mary Harper	1891	1917	D	26	SHA			PRI
McIntosh	Mrs 2 Jane Kniep	1920	1933	RT	13	SHA			PRI
McIvor	Miss Ruth, RN	1916	1921	RS	5	CHE			NUR
McKee	Rev William J.	1878	1894	D	16	NIN			EVA
McKee	Mrs Abbie Ketchum	1876	1894	DS	16	NIN			ED
McKee	Rev Samuel C.	1910	1927	RS	17	HEN			EVA
McKee	Mrs 1 Catherine List	1910	1919	D	9	HEN			EVA
McKee	Mrs 2 Mildred Jenks, MD	1918	1927	RS	9	HEN			MED
McKee	Rev Sidney	1911	1923	RS	12	SHA			EVA
McKee	Miss Elizabeth S.	1921	1948	RT	27	CHS			ED
McKillican	Miss Janet C., RN	1888	1926	RT	38	PEK			NUR
McMillen	Rev Olin W.	1915	1933	RS	18	CAN			ED
McMillen	Mrs Mary Wallace	1915	1933	RS	18	CAN			ED
Mead	Miss Frederica R.	1914	1923	RS	9	NAN			HED
Melrose	Rev John C.	1890	1897	D	7	KIU	NOD		EVA
Melrose	Mrs Margaret Rae	1890	1933	RT	43	NOD			EVA
Melrose	Rev Paul C.	1916	1951	EV	35	KIU			AG
Melrose	Mrs Esther Agnew	1916	1951	EV	35	KIU	NOD		ED
Merwin	Miss Caroline S., MD	1905	1923	D	14	TSI			MED
Merwin	Rev Wallace C.	1931	1951	TR	20	PAO	SHA		ADM
Merwin	Mrs Signe Stenberg	1933	1951	TR	18	PAO	SHA		WW
Metzler	Rev Carl P.	1902	1906	RS	4	TST	TEN		EVA
Meyer	Miss Erna, RN	1916	1919	RS	3	PAO			NUR
Meyer	Rev William Lawrence	1946	1948	RS	2	CHN			EVA
Meyer	Mrs Ruth Andrews	1946	1948	RS	2	CHN			EVA
Miller	Rev James A.	1894	1930	RT	36	SHU			EVA
Miller	Mrs Mary McGaw	1894	1930	RT	36	SHU			WW
Miller	Miss Rebecca Y.	1893	1900	RS	7	TEN	WEI		ED
Miller	Rev Robert C.	1945	1951	EV	6	PEK			EVA
Miller	Mrs Anabel Schlosser	1945	1951	EV	6	PEK			EVA
Millican	Rev Frank R.	1917	1950	RT	33	SHA			LIT

Millican	Mrs Aimee Boddy	1917	1950	RT	33	SHA		LIT
Millican	Miss Mary M.	1920	1933	RS	13	HAN		EVA
Millican	Miss Edith Francis, MD	1943	1948	RS	5	HEN		MED
Mills	Rev Charles R.	1857	1895	D	38	TEN		ED
Mills	Mrs 1 Rose McMaster	1857	1874	D	17	TEN		EVA
Mills	Mrs 2 Annetta Thompson	1884	1923	RT	39	TEN	CHE	ED
Mills	Rev Frank V.	1882	1890	RS	8	HAN		EVA
Mills	Mrs Frank	1882	1890	RS	8	HAN		EVA
Mills	Mr Samuel J.	1911	1933	RS	22	NAN		HED
Mills	Mrs Mary Shipley	1917	1933	RS	16	NAN		ED
Mills	Rev Wilson P., PhD	1932	1950	EV	18	NAN		HED
Mills	Mrs Harriet Seyle	1932	1950	EV	18	NAN		EVA
Mitchell	Rev John A.	1837	1838	D	1	SIN		EVA
Mitchell	Rev Thomas W.	1902	1944	RT	42	SIN		EVA
Mitchell	Mrs Elizabeth McAfee	1903	1944	RT	41	SIA		EVA
Moffet	Miss Anna Elizabeth	1920	1944	M	24	NAN		SEC
Moffett	Rev Samuel Hugh, PhD	1947	1951	RS	4	PEK	NAN	THE
Moffett	Mrs Eliz. Tarrant	1947	1951	RS	4	PEK	NAN	THE
Moninger	Miss Mary Margaret	1915	1944	RT	29	NOD		ED
Montgomery	Miss Henrietta	1894	1917	RS	23	KIU		WW
Montgomery	Rev Thomas H.	1909	1922	RS	13	TST		EVA
Montgomery	Mrs Florence Powers	1909	1922	RS	13	TST		EVA
Montgomery	Rev Robert	1912	1923	RS	11	SHA		ED
Moomau	Miss Antoinette	1899	1907	RS	8	SOO		ED
Moore	Miss Mary C.	1903	1906	M	3	WEI		UNK
Morgan	Rev Fred Bruce, Jr.	1945	1951	TR	6	TST		EVA
Morgan	Mrs Ruth McNamee	1945	1951	TR	6	TST		EVA
Morris	Rev Dubois S.	1898	1928	RS	30	HWA		EVA
Morris	Mrs Alice Buell	1910	1928	RS	18	HWA		EVA
Morrison	Rev William T.	1860	1869	D	9	NIN	PEK	EVA
Morrison	Mrs Mary Arms	1860	1876	RS	16	NIN	PEK	WW
Morrison	Miss Charlotte	1922	1926	RS	4	PEK		HED
Morse	Miss Esther M., MD	1930	1951	EV	23	HOI		MED
Morton	Miss Annie R.	1890	1924	D	34	NIN	CHS	ED
Morton	Miss Manuella D.	1903	1933	RT	30	SHA		ED
Murdock	Miss Agnes Gordon, MD	1908	1945	RT	37	HWA		MED
Murdock	Miss Margaret F., RN	1908	1948	RT	40	HWA		NUR
Murdock	Miss Mary Cole	1908	1942	RT	34	HWA		EVA
Murray	Rev John	1876	1926	RT	50	TSI		EVA
Murray	Mrs Sarah Rue	1876	1902	D	26	TSI		EVA
Murray	Miss Effie M.	1908	1926	RS	18	CHS		ED
Murray	Everett E., MD	1923	1949	EV	23	WEI	SHA	MED
Murray	Mrs Lucy Booth	1923	1949	EV	26	WEI	SHA	ED
Myers	Rev Charles M.	1906	1945	RT	39	SHA		ADM
Myers	Mrs Mary Macphail	1909	1945	RT	36	SHA		ADM
Myers	Miss Hazel H.	1936	1951	TR	17	TSI		STU
Neal	James B., MD	1883	1923	RT	40	TSI		MED
Neal	Mrs Eliz. Simonton	1883	1923	RT	40	TSI		WW
Nevius	Rev John L.	1854	1893	D	39	NIN	CHE	EVA
Nevius	Mrs Helen Coan	1854	1910	D	56	NIN	CHE	LIT
Newman	Frank W., MD	1936	1950	EV	14	HEN	SIA	MED
Newman	Mrs Eliz. Anderson, RN	1936	1950	EV	14	HEN	SIA	NUR
Newton	Miss Grace	1887	1915	D	28	PEK		ED
Newton	Rev Charles H.	1896	1920	RS	24	KIU		EVA
Newton	Mrs Rusella Anderson	1896	1918	D	22	KIU		EVA
Nicholas	Miss Mildred, MD	1932	1934	RS	2	CAN		MED
Niles	Miss Mary W., MD	1882	1928	RT	46	CAN		MED
Niles	Rev Frank S.	1913	1930	RS	17	HWA		ED
Niles	Mrs Margaret Beebe	1915	1930	RS	15	HWA		ED
Norman	Rev Bertil V.	1945	1948	RS	3	HWA		ED
Norman	Mrs Dorothy Thompson	1945	1948	RS	3	HWA		ED
Norton	Rev Richard Burdge	1945	1950	TR	5	HAN		EVA
Norton	Mrs Mary Klein	1945	1950	TR	5	HAN		EVA
Noyes	Miss Harriet N.	1868	1923	RT	55	CAN		ED
Noyes	Rev Henry V.	1866	1914	D	48	CAN		EVA

Noyes	Mrs 1 Cynthia	1866	1867	D	1	CAN		EVA
Noyes	Mrs 2 Arabella Anderson	1876	1916	RT	40	CAN		EVA
Noyes	Rev William D.	1903	1922	RS	19	CAN		EVA
Noyes	Mrs Mary Stevensen	1907	1922	RS	15	CAN		EVA
Null	Miss Miriam E.	1923	1950	EV	27	NAN		EVA
Ogilvie	Rev Charles L.	1911	1919	D	8	PEK		EVA
Ogilvie	Mrs Abbie Miller	1911	1922	RS	11	PEK		EVA
Orr	Rev Robert W.	1837	1841	H	4	SIN		EVA
Orr	Mrs Eliza Carter	1837	1841	H	4	SIN		EVA
Owens	Rev Arthur C.	1921	1953	RS	32	SIA	TST	EVA
Owens	Mrs Rachel Wood	1921	1953	RS	31	SIA	TST	EVA
Park	Charles E., MD	1923	1933	D	10	YUA		MED
Park	Mrs Celia Collins	1923	1935	RS	12	YUA		WW
Park	Miss Florence, RN	1941	1944	RS	3	KIA		MED
Parker	Rev Albert G.	1920	1928	RS	8	TSI		HED
Parker	Mrs Katherine McAfee	1920	1928	RS	8	TSI		HED
Partch	Rev Virgil F.	1888	1900	RS	12	NIN		EVA
Partch	Mrs Jennie Childers	1888	1900	RS	12	NIN		ED
Partch	Rev George Enos	1895	1937	RT	42	SHA		EVA
Partch	Mrs 1 Hannah Taylor	1895	1905	RS	10	SHA		WW
Partch	Mrs 2 Julia Wood, MD	1918	1937	RT	19	SHA		MED
Patrick	Miss Mary M	1869	1871	M	2	TEN		UNK
Patterson	John P., MD	1871	1872	RS	1	TEN		MED
Patterson	Mrs John P.	1871	1872	RS	1	TEN		MED
Patterson	Rev John C.	1899	1904	H	5	NOD		EVA
Patterson	Mrs Eleanor Mundi	1899	1904	H	5	NOD		EVA
Patterson	Miss Elda G.	1903	1937	RT	34	LNC		ED
Patterson	Miss Florence B.	1923	1948	RT	25	HWA		ED
Patton	Rev Charles E.	1899	1937	RT	38	YEU	SHA	ADM
Patton	Mrs 1 Edith Carswell	1899	1902	D	3	YEU		WW
Patton	Mrs 2 Isabella Mack, MD	1905	1937	RT	32	YEU	SHA	MED
Patton	Miss Lulu R.	1908	1932	D	24	CAN		ED
Patton	Rev Millard Harmer	1940	1946	RS	6	NAH		EVA
Patton	Mrs M. H.	1940	1946	RS	6	NAH		EVA
Peale	Rev John R.	1905	1905	D	1	LNC		EVA
Peale	Mrs Rebecca Gillespie	1905	1905	D	1	LNC		EVA
Perkins	Miss Sara E., RN	1926	1953	EV	27	PEK	LNC	NUR
Perry	Rev Edward W.	1917	1925	RS	6	HAN		EVA
Perry	Mrs Martha Taylor	1918	1925	RS	7	HAN		EVA
Pike	Miss Florence F.	1915	1951	RT	38	YEU		EVA
Pommerenke	Rev Herbert H.	1930	1950	RS	20	CAN		HED
Pommerenke	Mrs Jean Macpherson	1920	1950	RS	30	CAN		HED
Posey	Miss Mary A.	1888	1914	RS	26	SHA		ED
Pratt	Rev Alonzo A.	1913	1922	RS	9	SHE		EVA
Pratt	Mrs Grace Beeks	1915	1922	RS	7	SHE		EVA
Preston	Rev Charles F.	1854	1877	D	23	CAN		EVA
Preston	Mrs Mary Byrne	1854	1877	DS	23	CAN		EVA
Preston	Rev Thomas J.	1907	1928	RS	21	CHS		THE
Preston	Mrs Clara Beekley	1907	1928	RS	21	CHS		THE
Primrose	Miss Adelaide, RN	1913	1916	RS	3	CHE		NUR
Quarterman	Rev John W.	1846	1857	D	11	NIN		EVA
Ramsay	Rev Hugh C.	1913	1921	DS	8	SHU		EVA
Ramsay	Mrs Ada Ransom	1913	1921	D	8	SHU		EVA
Ramsay	Miss Mary M.	1930	1936	RS	6	SOO		EVA
Rankin	Rev Henry V.	1848	1863	D	15	NIN	CHE	EVA
Rankin	Mrs Mary Knight	1848	1864	DS	16	NIN	CHE	EVA
Rankin	Mr Carl S.	1912	1917	RS	5	WEI		ED
Rankin	Miss Marjorie	1912	1929	RS	17	WEI		ED
Rauch	Miss Chloe B., RN	1920	1935	RS	15	YEU	CAN	NUR
Reed	Charles E., MD	1896	1901	RS	5	CAN		MED
Reed	Mrs Edith Robinson	1896	1901	RS	5	CAN		MED
Reed	Miss Anna G.	1913	1916	D	3	PAO		ED
Reed	Miss Dorothy D.	1923	1929	RS	6	CAN		ED
Reeder	Rev Charles V.	1916	1949	RS	37	WEI		EVA
Reeder	Mrs 1 Frances Abernethy	1919	1925	D	6	WEI		EVA

Reeder	Mrs 2 Barbara Lorenz	1928	1949	RS	21	WEI		WW
Refo	Henry B.	1939	1950	EV	11	CAN		HED
Refo	Mrs Sarah Flaniken	1939	1950	EV	11	CAN		ED
Reid	Rev Gilbert	1882	1894	RS	12	TSI	PEK	EVA
Reisner	Mr John H.	1919	1931	RS	12	NAN		AG
Reisner	Mrs Bertha Betts	1919	1931	RS	12	NAN		AG
Rhoda	Miss Ethel S.	1916	1917	RS	1	UNK		UNK
Rhodes	Rev Paul Brown	1941	1949	EV	8	HEN	EVA	EVA
Rhodes	Mrs Kathryn Napp	1941	1949	EV	8	HEN		EVA
Richards	Miss Laura M., RN	1921	1929	RS	8	PAO		NUR
Ricketts	Miss Juniata	1901	1941	RT	40	HAN		EVA
Riddle	Rev Charles Wainwright	1946	1948	TR	4	PEK		ED
Riddle	Mrs Katherine Parker	1946	1948	TR	4	PEK		ED
Ritchie	Rev Ellsworth G.	1889	1890	D	1	TEN		ED
Ritchie (Lingle)	Mrs Jean	1889	1932	RT	43	TEN	LNC	EVA
Ritchie	Miss Minnie B.	1893	1896	H	3	PEK		UNK
Ritter	Rev Richard H.	1923	1937	RS	14	PEK		STU
Ritter	Mrs Emma Lueders	1926	1937	RS	11	PEK		STU
Roberts	Rev John S.	1862	1878	RS	7	SHA		EVA
Roberts	Mrs John S.	1862	1878	RS	7	SHA		EVA
Roberts	Mr Ray C.	1912	1927	RS	15	CHS		STU
Roberts	Mrs Eva Rewalt	1912	1927	RS	15	CHS		WW
Robertson	William E., MD	1906	1928	RS	22	HEN		MED
Robertson	Mrs 1 Minnie Smith	1906	1917	D	11	HEN		MED
Robertson	Mrs 2 Lavinia Ewers	1916	1928	RS	12	HEN		MED
Robinson	Miss Mary, MD	1913	1917	RS	4	LNC		MED
Rollestone	Miss Lavinia M.	1894	1926	RT	32	NIN		ED
Romig	Rev Harry G.	1901	1944	RT	43	TNG	TST	EVA
Romig	Mrs Lucy Alexander	1901	1944	RT	43	TNG	TST	EVA
Romig	Rev Arthur Mathes	1931	1942	EV	11	YUA	HWA	EVA
Romig	Mrs Helen Anderson	1931	1942	EV	11	YUA	HWA	EVA
Romig	Rev Theodore F.	1937	1950	RS	17	HEN	NAN	EVA
Romig	Mrs Harriet Statler	1937	1950	RS	17	HEN	NAN	EVA
Ross	Robert M., MD	1906	1932	RS	26	LNC		MED
Ross	Mrs 1 Nellie Read	1903	1923	D	20	LNC		MED
Ross	Mrs 2 Marg. Taylor, MD	1922	1932	RS	10	CAN		MED
Rowley	Miss Grace M.	1910	1950	RT	40	HWA		EVA
Roy	Andrew T., PhD	1930	1951	EV	21	NAN	WCH	HED
Roy	Mrs Marg. Crutchfield	1930	1951	21	21	NAN	WCH	WW
Roys	Charles K., MD	1904	1920	D	16	WEI	TSI	MED
Roys	Mrs Mabel Milham	1904	1920	DS	16	WEI	TSI	MED
Ruch	Mr Harold G.	1948	1949	EV	1	SHA		ADM
Ruch	Mrs Harold	1948	1949	EV	1	SHA		ADM
Ruland	Rev Lloyd S.	1915	1927	RS	12	NAN		STU
Ruland	Mrs Margaret Haywood	1921	1927	RS	6	NAN		ED
Rupert	Miss Grace M.	1921	1950	RT	27	CAN		MED
Russel	Miss Emily G.	1932	1938	RS	6	CHE		EVA
Russell	Miss Ada Culperna	1912	1942	RT	30	HAN		EVA
Russell	Miss Myrtle L.	1914	1917	RS	3	HAN		EVA
Rustin	Miss Marie, RN	1916	1934	RS	18	PAO		NUR
Sailer	Randolph C., PhD	1924	1950	EV	26	PEK		HED
Sailer	Mrs Louise Egbert	1924	1950	EV	26	PEK		HED
Salsbury	Clarence G., MD	1914	1929	RS	15	HOI		MED
Salsbury	Mrs Cora Burrows	1914	1929	RS	15	HOI		SEC
Sargent	Mr Clyde B.	1932	1943	RS	11	TSI		HED
Sargent	Mrs Elizabeth Sweet	1932	1943	RS	11	TSI		HED
Sargent	Miss Lola I.	1919	1923	RS	4	NAH		WW
Sauer	Mr Francis	1947	1949	TR	2	KIU		UNA
Sauer	Ms Ernestine Juckett, RN	1947	1949	TR	2	KIU		UNA
Savige	Miss Bertha L.	1916	1919	RS	3	PAO		ED
Schaefer	Miss Alice H.	1938	1951	TR	12	CAN		ED
Schaeffer	Miss Katherine L.	1894	1931	D	37	KAC		ED
Scheirer	Rev Edward M.	1902	1904	D	2	LNC		EVA
Schmucker	Miss Alice J.	1878	1879	M	1	SOO		WW
Schopmeier	Miss Beatrice J., RN	1933	1938	RS	5	HEN		NUR

Schulz	William M., MD	1909	1919	RS	10	TSI		MED
Scott	Rev Charles E.	1906	1941	RT	35	TSI	TST	EVA
Scott	Mrs Clara Heywood	1906	1941	RT	35	TSI	TST	EVA
Scott	Mr Frank D.	1916	1920	RS	4	HAN		HED
Scott	Mrs Jane Hook	1916	1920	RS	4	HAN		HED
Scott	Miss Annie V., MD	1920	1951	EV	33	TSI		MED
Scott	Rev Francis H.	1937	1948	RS	11	CHN		EVA
Scott	Mrs Helen Rhodes	1937	1948	RS	11	CHN		EVA
Scovel	Frederick G., MD	1930	1950	RS	20	HWA		MED
Scovel	Mrs Myra Scott	1930	1950	RS	20	HWA		MED
Scribner	Miss Eleanor D.	1923	1927	RS	4	KIU		ED
Seaton	Stuart P., MD	1924	1950	RS	20	HOI		MED
Seaton	Mrs Myrtle Foster	1924	1950	RS	20	HOI		MUS
Sellers	Miss M. R.	1874	1876	RS	2	NIN		ED
Seymour	Walter F., MD	1893	1928	D	35	TSN		MED
Seymour	Mrs Mary Gochenour	1894	1929	RT	35	TSN		MED
Seymour	Miss Ida M., RN	1920	1927	RS	7	TSN		NUR
Shannon	Mr James V.	1915	1922	RS	7	KIU		ED
Shannon	Mrs Grace Poling	1915	1922	RS	7	KIU		ED
Shaw	Rev James M.	1874	1876	D	2	TEN		EVA
Shaw	Mrs James	1874	1886	RS	12	TEN		WW
Shoemaker	Rev Jonathan E.	1894	1935	RT	41	NIN		EVA
Shoemaker	Mrs Mary Condit	1894	1935	RT	41	NIN		EVA
Silsby	Rev John A.	1887	1928	RT	41	SHA		EVA
Silsby	Mrs Anna Moore	1890	1928	RT	38	SHA		WW
Silsby	Miss Helen C.	1917	1921	RS	4	SOO		WW
Silver	Miss Emma	1895	1934	RS	39	SHA		ED
Simcox	Rev Frank E.	1893	1900	D	7	PAO		EVA
Simcox	Mrs May Gilson	1893	1900	D	7	PAO		EVA
Sinclair	Miss Mariam E., MD	1888	1894	RS	6	PEK		MED
Sindles	Miss Ethel L.	1920	1923	RS	3	SHA		SEC
Skilling* (Armstrong)	Miss Helen	1929	1931	M	2	NAN		ED
Skinner	Miss Alice Hannah	1903	1942	RT	39	KIU		ED
Sloan	Thomas D., MD	1912	1921	RS	9	NAN		MED
Sloan	Mrs Marg. Dunnington	1915	1921	RS	6	NAN		MED
Small	Miss Elizabeth	1912	1946	RT	34	ICH		ED
Smawley	Miss Eva L.	1918	1936	RS	18	NAN		THE
Smith	Rev John N. B.	1881	1899	RS	18	SHA	NIN	EVA
Smith	Mrs Fannie Strong	1882	1899	RS	17	SHA	NIN	EVA
Smith	Horace R., MD	1881	1884	RS	3	WEI		MED
Smith	Mrs Horace	1881	1884	RS	3	WEI		MED
Smith	Mr Harold F.	1910	1930	RS	20	TSI		HED
Smith	Mrs May Corbett	1914	1930	RS	16	TSI		HED
Smith	Rev Elleroy M.	1916	1950	RT	34	NIN		EVA
Smith	Mrs Maybelle Conquist	1916	1950	RT	34	NIN		EVA
Smith	Mr Harry L.	1916	1920	RS	4	TSI		HED
Smith	Mrs Celestine Brown	1916	1920	RS	4	TSI		HED
Smith	Miss Christina M., RN	1917	1924	RS	7	CAN		NUR
Smith	Rev C. Stanley, PhD	1917	1949	EV	32	NAN		THE
Smith	Mrs Dorothea Zaenglein	1917	1949	EV	32	NAN		TMC
Snodgrass	Miss Mary A.	1892	1916	D	24	TEN		ED
Snyder	Mr James P.	1925	1950	RS	15	CAN		HED
Snyder	Mrs Dorothy Terry	1925	1950	RS	15	CAN		HED
Speake	Miss Margery M.	1931	1939	RS	8	TEN		ED
Speer	Rev William	1846	1850	RS	4	MAC	CAN	EVA
Speer	Mrs Cornelia Breckenridge	1846	1847	D	1	MAC		EVA
Speer	Miss Margaret B.	1925	1948	RS	23	PEK		HED
Speers	Mr James M., Jr.	1920	1929	RS	9	NAN		HED
Speers	Mrs Margaret Campbell	1920	1929	RS	9	NAN		HED
Spencer	Selden P., Jr., PhD	1915	1930	D	15	CAN		HED
Spencer	Mrs Julia Lyman	1915	1931	DS	16	CAN		HED
Stearns	Thornton, MD	1916	1934	RS	18	TSI		MED
Stearns	Mrs Caroline Taber	1919	1934	RS	15	CAN	TSI	MED
Steinbeck	Mr Clark C.	1921	1941	RS	20	PEK		ADM
Steinbeck	Mrs Minnie Robbins	1921	1941	RS	20	PEK		ADM

Steiner	Rev John F.	1913	1943	D	30	HOI		EVA
Steiner	Mrs Madelene Hubscher	1913	1943	RT	30	HOI		ED
Stevenson	Rev Merle Q.	1919	1926	RS	7	PAO		EVA
Stevenson	Mrs Hortense Salsbury	1919	1926	RS	7	PAO		ED
Stevenson	Theodore D., MD	1934	1950	EV	16	CAN		MED
Stevenson	Mrs Beatrice Scott	1934	1950	EV	16	CAN		MED
Stewart	Miss Mary J.	1911	1943	RS	32	TSN		ED
Stewart	Miss Rosabel	1920	1934	RS	14	NIN		WW
Stinson	Rev William V.	1917	1924	D	7	KIU		EVA
Stockton	Miss Helen I., RN	1912	1922	RS	10	CAN		NUR
Stoddard	Rev Ross E.	1922	1925	RS	3	PEK		EVA
Stoddard	Mrs Georgia Luccock	1922	1925	RS	3	PEK		EVA
Street	Rev Alfred E.	1891	1904	H	9	NOD		EVA
Street	Mrs Jannie Montgomery	1901	1904	H	3	NOD		EVA
Stringham	James A., MD	1933	1940	RS	7	CHN		MED
Stringham	Mrs Charlotte Wild	1933	1940	RS	7	CHN		MED
Stroh	Miss Harriet	1919	1942	RS	23	HWA		EVA
Stuart*	Rev Warren H.	1926	1929	RS	3	NAN		THE
Stuart*	Mrs Annie Chesnutt	1926	1929	RS	3	NAN		THE
Stubbert	J. E., MD	1881	1883	H	2	NAN	NIN	MED
Sutherland	Miss Catherine E.	1918	1925	RS	7	NAH		ED
Swan	John Myers, MD	1885	1910	RS	25	CAN		MED
Swan	Mrs Araminta Hickman	1885	1910	RS	25	CAN		MED
Swan	Rev Charles W.	1893	1901	RS	8	KAN	LNC	EVA
Swan	Mrs Rhuy Wilson, MD	1893	1901	RS	8	KAN	LNC	MED
Swann	Rev Darius Leander	1948	1951	EV	3	NAN		HED
Tappan	Rev David S., Jr.	1906	1950	RT	44	KIU		EVA
Tappan	Mrs Luella Rice	1921	1950	RT	29	KIU		STU
Taylor	George Y., MD	1887	1900	D	13	PAO		MED
Taylor	Miss Mary H.	1918	1950	RS	22	HOI		ED
Terrill	Charles S., MD	1893	1895	RS	2	NOD		MED
Terrill	Mrs Charles	1893	1895	RS	2	NOD		MED
Terry	Rev Myron E.	1925	1948	TR	21	SHA		LIT
Terry	Mrs Harriet Collins	1925	1948	TR	21	SHA		LIT
Tewksbury	Rev Malcolm G.	1921	1950	TR	29	SHA	TST	STU
Tewksbury	Mrs Ruth Savage	1921	1950	TR	29	SHA	TST	STU
Thomas	Rev David H.	1918	1950	RT	35	HOI		EVA
Thomas	Mrs Meta Oelfke	1918	1950	RT	35	HOI		EVA
Thompson	Rev Thomas N.	1901	1935	D	34	YIH		EVA
Thompson	Mrs Mabel Hall	1902	1940	RT	38	YIH		EVA
Thompson	Mr Kenneth K.	1911	1934	RS	20	TSI		ADM
Thompson	Mrs Bernice Archer	1911	1934	RS	20	TSI		TMC
Thompson	Miss Edith Pauline, MD	1939	1942	RS	3	LNC		MED
Thomson	Rev Joseph C., MD	1881	1894	RS	13	LIE	YEU	MED
Thomson	Mrs Agnes Dornin	1881	1894	RS	13	LIE	YEU	MED
Thomson	Rev George D.	1909	1923	RS	14	YEU		EVA
Thomson	Mrs Margaret Everall	1909	1923	RS	14	YEU		EVA
Thomson	Mr Herbert F.	1914	1951	RT	37	CAN		ED
Thomson	Mrs Eleanor Logan	1914	1951	RT	37	CAN		ED
Thomson	Rev James C.	1917	1950	RS	33	NAN		HED
Thomson	Mrs Margaret Cook	1917	1950	RS	33	NAN		HED
Throop	Rev Frank H.	1909	1926	RS	15	SOO		EVA
Throop	Mrs Elsie McKenzie	1909	1926	RS	15	SOO		STU
Thurston	Mrs Matilda C.	1913	1942	RT	29	NAN		HED
Thwing	Rev Edward W.	1892	1899	H	7	LNC		EVA
Thwing	Mrs Lulu Burniston	1892	1899	H	7	LNC		EVA
Thwing	Miss Gertrude	1892	1894	RS	2	KAN		WW
Tiffany	Miss Ida	1881	1882	M	1	CHE		WW
Tinkham	Miss Catherine A.	1922	1927	RS	5	PAO		ED
Todd	Paul Jerome, MD	1902	1908	RS	6	CAN		MED
Todd	Mrs Margaret Strathie	1905	1908	RS	3	CAN		MED
Tooker	Frederick J., MD	1901	1921	RS	20	SIA		MED
Tooker	Mrs Mary Fitch, MD	1901	1921	RS	20	SOO	SIA	MED
Tootell	George T., MD	1913	1950	RT	37	CHA		MED
Tootell	Mrs Anna Kidder	1913	1950	RT	37	CHA		MED

Tootell	Miss Jennivieve, RN	1943	1945	RS	2	UNK		UNK
Torrance	Mr Andrew A.	1910	1943	D	33	TSI		ED
Torrance	Mrs 1 Fannie Wysor	1910	1928	D	18	TSI		ED
Torrance	Mrs 2 Mercie MacHayes	1921	1945	RS	24	TSI		ED
Torrey	Rev Reuben A., Jr.	1913	1950	EV	27	TSI	SHA	EVA
Torrey	Mrs Janet Mallary	1913	1950	EV	27	TSI	SHA	EVA
Toulmin	Miss Marian P.	1923	1926	RS	3	SHA		SEC
Towne	Miss Edith E.	1914	1917	RS	3	NAN		ED
Turner	William H., Jr., MD	1927	1934	RS	7	NAH		MED
Turner	Mrs Edna Wood	1927	1934	RS	7	NAH		MED
Twinem	Mrs Mary D.	1919	1931	RS	10	SHO		ED
Van Deusen	Rev Cortland C., Jr.	1914	1948	RT	34	TST		EVA
Van Deusen	Mrs Mary Lorenz	1915	1948	RT	33	TST		EVA
Van Dyck	Rev David B.	1919	1950	RS	31	HWA		EVA
Van Dyck	Mrs Anna Booraem	1919	1950	RS	31	HWA		WW
Van Etten	Rev Albert H.	1925	1940	D	15	LNC		EVA
Van Etten	Mrs Florence King	1925	1941	DS	16	LNC		ED
Van Evera	Rev Kepler	1912	1951	RT	39	HAN		EVA
Van Evera	Mrs Pauline Wurster	1912	1951	RT	39	HAN		WW
Van Schoick	Isaac L., MD	1890	1899	H	9	TSN		MED
Van Schoick	Mrs Louise Hess	1890	1899	H	9	TSN		MED
Van Wagenen	Miss Kathrina H.	1912	1916	RS	4	CHS		ED
Vanderbilt	Miss Mary E., RN	1926	1930	RS	4	TSI		NUR
Vanderburgh	Ernest D., MD	1894	1930	RT	36	SIA		MED
Vanderburgh	Mrs Eleanor Beeman	1894	1930	RT	36	SIA		MED
Vanderburgh	Alexander, MD	1925	1930	RS	5	CHA		MED
Vanderburgh	Mrs Ruth Ferguson	1925	1930	RS	5	CHA		MED
Vaughan	Miss Mary L. B.	1902	1913	RS	11	CHE	TST	ED
Vaughn	Miss Helen C.	1921	1927	RS	6	CAN		MED
Veghte	Miss Adeline Hollister	1929	1938	RS	9	PEK		MUS
Vincent	Rev Howell S.	1920	1928	RS	8	PEK		HED
Vincent	Mrs 1 Nellie Nesbit	1920	1923	D	3	PEK		HED
Vincent	Mrs 2 Agnes Sinclair	1924	1928	RS	4	PEK		HED
Waddell	Miss Susan S., MD	1921	1934	RS	13	TSI		MED
Wagner	Miss Maria Margaret, RN	1913	1946	RT	33	YIH		NUR
Wagner	Miss Dorothy Caroline	1944	1950	TR	7	HWA		WW
Waite	Rev Alexander	1902	1907	RS	5	TSN		EVA
Waite	Mrs Edna Parks, MD	1899	1907	RS	8	TSN		MED
Waite	Rev James	1902	1907	RS	5	TSN		EVA
Waite	Mrs Emma Stanley	1902	1907	RS	5	TSN		EVA
Walline	Rev Edwin E	1917	1951	TR	36	CAN	SHA	ADM
Walline	Mrs Ruth Hinshaw	1917	1951	TR	36	CAN	SHA	ADM
Walmsley	Miss Evelyn M.	1916	1934	RS	18	NAN		ED
Walter	Rev Deane C.	1926	1951	EV	25	TSN		EVA
Walter	Mrs Ethel McKee	1926	1951	EV	25	TSN		EVA
Ward	Miss Fannie E.	1884	1888	RS	4	PEK		UNK
Warner	Miss Sarah O.	1878	1890	RS	12	NIN		ED
Warner	Miss Bertha	1934	1937	M	3	HWA		NUR
Way	Rev Richard Q.	1844	1859	RS	15	NIN		EVA
Way	Mrs Susan Quarterman	1844	1859	RS	15	NIN		EVA
Weekes	Rev Ernest J.	1914	1924	RS	10	CAN		EVA
Weekes	Mrs Jessie Angell	1917	1924	RS	7	CAN		EVA
Welles	Henry H. 3rd, PhD	1925	1937	RS	12	SHA		ED
Welles	Mrs Josephine Sailer	1921	1937	RS	16	SHA		ED
Welles	Marshall P., MD	1938	1949	TR	11	ICH	TST	MED
Welles	Mrs Helen Antisdale	1938	1949	TR	11	ICH	TST	MED
Wells	Mr Mason	1899	1918	RS	19	TEN		HED
Wells	Mrs Margaret Grier	1899	1918	RS	19	TEN		HED
Wells	Mr Ralph C.	1902	1947	RT	45	SHA		ADM
Wells	Mrs Harriet Corbett	1904	1947	RT	43	SHA		ADM
West	Rev Donald Kirkland	1930	1948	RS	18	TST		EVA
West	Mrs Helen Fraser, MD	1930	1948	RS	13	TST		MED
West	Rev Charles C., PhD	1947	1950	EV	3	PEK	NAN	HED
West	Mrs Ruth Carson	1947	1950	EV	3	PEK	NAN	HED
Westling	Miss Tyra M.	1936	1951	RS	14	CHE		ED

Westra	Miss Rena D., RN	1936	1951	EV	15	CAN			NUR
Whallon	Rev Albert K.	1912	1940	D	28	PAO			EVA
Whallon	Mrs Marion Oskamp	1912	1940	RT	28	PAO			EVA
Wheeler	Rev W. Reginald	1915	1937	RS	22	NAN			HED
Wheeler	Mrs Constance Hayes	1915	1937	RS	22	NAN			HED
Whelpley	Frank R., MD	1921	1924	RS	3	KIU			MED
Whelpley	Mrs Florence Fairban	1921	1924	RS	3	KIU			MED
Wherry	Rev John	1864	1918	D	54	SHA	PEK		EVA
Wherry	Mrs Sara Brandon	1864	1908	D	44	SHA	PEK		EVA
Whitaker	Miss Helen E.	1926	1939	RS	13	CHS			ED
White	Rev Wellington J.	1880	1891	D	11	CAN	LNC		EVA
White (Gilman)	Mrs Mary Martin	1880	1917	D	37	CAN	KAC		EVA
White	Mr Ralph M.	1913	1950	RT	37	SOO			ED
White	Mrs Blanche Howard	1913	1950	RT	37	SOO			ED
White	Mr Henry H.	1922	1927	RS	5	NAN			ED
White	Mrs Irma White	1922	1927	RS	5	NAN			ED
Whiting	Rev Joseph L.	1869	1906	D	37	PEK			EVA
Whiting	Mrs Lucy Jackson	1869	1914	RS	45	PEK			EVA
Whiting	Rev Albert	1873	1878	D	5	SOO	NAN		EVA
Whiting (Abbey)	Mrs Louise Parsons	1873	1920	RT	40	SOO	NAN		EVA
Whiting	Harry S., MD	1924	1931	RS	7	TEN			MED
Whiting	Mrs Marjorie Scott	1924	1931	RS	7	TEN			MED
Whitlock	Horace H., MD	1931	1943	EV	12	NAH			MED
Whitlock	Mrs Edna Moore	1931	1940	EV	9	NAH			MED
Wight	Rev Joseph K.	1848	1857	RS	9	NIN	SHA		EVA
Wight	Mrs Elizabeth VanDyke	1848	1857	RS	9	NIN	SHA		EVA
Wight	Miss Fannie E.	1885	1898	D	13	CHE	WEI		WW
Wight	Mrs Ida Emerick	1900	1937	RT	37	TEN			ED
Wilcox	Miss Vella M.	1904	1941	RT	33	YEU			ED
Wilds	Miss Mamie C.	1918	1924	RS	6	SOO			EVA
Williams	Rev John E.	1899	1927	D	28	NAN			HED
Williams	Mrs Lilian Caldwell	1899	1928	DS	29	NAN			HED
Williams	Miss Ruth C., RN	1920	1930	RS	10	NAH			NUR
Wilson	Rev Kenneth W.	1930	1950	EV	20	ICH			EVA
Wilson	Mrs Eleanor Blackstone	1930	1950	EV	20	ICH			EVA
Wilson	Miss Nellie, RN	1946	1950	EV	4	SIA			NUR
Wiltsie	James W., MD	1915	1918	RS	3	NAH			MED
Wiltsie	Mrs Marion Webb	1915	1918	RS	3	NAH			MED
Winchester	Miss Margaret, RN	1919	1922	RS	3	PEK			NUR
Winfield	Mr Gerald F.	1932	1948	RS	16	TSI			HED
Winfield	Mrs Lida Parks	1932	1948	RS	16	TSI			HED
Winn	Rev Gardner L.	1938	1948	EV	5	YIH	NAN		EVA
Winn	Mrs Viola Schuldt	1938	1948	RS	10	YIH	NAN		EVA
Winn	Rev Paul R.	1939	1943	EV	5	SOO	NIN		EVA
Winn	Mrs Ann Lewis	1939	1941	EV	3	SOO			EVA
Winslett	Miss Margaret L.	1926	1950	EV	14	NAN			THE
Winter	Mr William E.	1912	1928	RS	16	YIH			IND
Winter	Mrs Allie Reeves	1912	1928	RS	16	YIH			ED
Wisner	Miss Jessie	1885	1889	RS	4	CAN			UNK
Wisner	Rev Oscar F.	1885	1894	RS	9	CAN			ED
Wisner	Mrs Sophie Preston	1887	1894	RS	7	CAN			WW
Witmer	Miss Minnie C., RN	1920	1951	EV	31	PAO			NUR
Wolferz	Louis E., PhD	1917	1951	RT	34	PEK			HED
Wolferz	Mrs Katharine King	1918	1951	RT	33	PEK			WW
Woodberry	Rev Earle J.	1930	1948	RS	18	ICH			EVA
Woodberry	Mrs Ada Pierce	1930	1948	RS	18	ICH			EVA
Woods	Miss Catherine Trimm	1910	1946	RT	36	SIA			EVA
Wright	Rev Harrison K.	1902	1923	D	21	NIN			EVA
Wright	Mrs 1 Mary Miller	1902	1904	D	2	NIN			EVA
Wright	Mrs 2 Edwina Cunningham	1891	1935	D	44	NIN			EVA
Wright	Rev John V.	1919	1927	RS	8	TNG			EVA
Wright	Mrs Mildred McCrory	1919	1927	RS	8	TNG			EVA
Wright	Miss Ruth P.	1920	1924	RS	4	NAN			MUS
Wright	Miss Eleanor M.	1926	1939	D	13	NAN			ED
Wright	Miss Elizabeth C.	1926	1948	RT	22	NAH			ED

Wylie	John H., MD	1915	1940	D	25	PAO	PEK	MED
Wylie	Mrs Mary Bushell	1915	1940	RS	25	PAO	PEK	MED
Wylie	Miss Martha E., RN	1925	1950	EV	25	WEI	TSI	NUR
Wylie	Miss Sarah Elizabeth	1943	1947	TR	4	NAN		ED
Yates	Theodore M., MD	1923	1941	EV	20	HWA		MED
Yates	Mrs Jean Kammarer	1923	1941	EV	20	HWA		SEC
Yerkes	Rev Carroll H.	1904	1927	RS	23	YIH		EVA
Yerkes	Mrs Helen Eckard	1904	1927	RS	23	YIH		WW
Young	Rev John N., Jr.	1891	1893	D	2	PEK		EVA
Young	James L. R., MD	1938	1950	EV	12	TSI		MED
Young	Mrs Marguerite Luce, RN	1932	1950	EV	18	CHE	TSI	NUR
Zimmerman	Rev Donald Eugene	1941	1945	EV	4	UNA		UNA
Zimmerman	Mrs Donald	1941	1945	EV	4	UNA		UNA
Zink	Lalah, RN	1924	1927	RS	3	CHA		NUR

(II) Presbyterian Church, U.S.

Last Name	First Name	DA	DP	TM	YC	ST1	ST2	WP
Abbott	Miss Helen Raymond	1925	1928	ET	3	HUA		TMC
Albaugh	Miss Ida McKay, RN	1908	1919	RS	11	JIA		NUR
Alderman	Miss Flora S., RN	1904	1904	D	1	SOO		NUR
Allison	Rev Andrew	1910	1950	RT	40	JIA		ED
Allison	Mrs Ella Ward	1910	1950	RT	40	JIA		ED
Armstrong	Rev Oscar Vance	1908	1933	RS	25	ZHE	XUZ	ED
Armstrong	Mrs 1 Lena Stutzman	1908	1929	D	11	ZHE	XUZ	ED
Armstrong*	Mrs 2 Helen Skilling	1932	1933	RT	1	XUZ		ADM
Bailey	Miss Helen	1923	1936	RS	13	SUQ		ED
Baxter	Mrs Margaret McB.	1921	1926	ET	5	XUZ	ZHE	TMC
Bear	Rev James Edwin, Sr.	1887	1903	D	16	ZHE		EVA
Bear	Mrs Laura Devault	1892	1903	DS	11	ZHE		EVA
Bear	Rev James Edwin, Jr.	1923	1929	H	6	ZHE		ED
Bear	Mrs Margaret I. White	1923	1929	H	6	ZHE		ED
Bell	L. Nelson, MD	1916	1948	EV	32	TKP		MD
Bell	Mrs Virginia Leftwich	1916	1948	EV	32	TKP		MED
Bissett	Miss Mary Stuart, RN	1919	1929	RS	10	HAI		NUR
Blain	Rev John Mercer	1897	1932	D	35	JAX	HAN	EVA
Blain	Mrs Claude Grier	1897	1941	RT	44	JAX	HAN	ED
Boardman	Miss Emma	1894	1925	RT	31	HAN		EVA
Bracken	Miss Ruth A., RN	1925	1934	RS	9	XUZ	HAI	NUR
Bradley	John Wilson, MD	1899	1929	D	30	SOO	SUQ	MED
Bradley	Mrs 1 Mamie McCollum	1901	1903	D	2	SUQ		MED
Bradley	Mrs 2 Agnes Junkin	1904	1944	RT	40	SUQ		EVA
Bradley	Miss Lina Elizabeth	1920	1942	RS	17	SOO	TKP	SEC
Bradley	Miss Julia Junkin	1935	1944	RS	9	TNG		ED
Bridgman	Rev Harold Thomas	1920	1948	EV	28	YEN	TAI	EVA
Bridgman	Mrs Eleanor Galbraith	1920	1948	EV	28	YEN	TAI	NUR
Brown	Rev Francis Augustus	1910	1949	RT	39	TAI	XUZ	EVA
Brown	Mrs Charlotte Thompson	1909	1949	RT	40	XUZ		EVA
Brown	Frank Augustus, Jr., MD	1947	1950	TR	3	XUZ	SHA	MED
Brown	Mrs Ann Vertovsek, RN	1947	1950	TR	3	XUZ	SHA	NUR
Buckingham	Edwin Wheeler, MD	1920	1929	RS	9	JAX		MED
Buckingham	Mrs Bessie Kenniger, RN	1921	1929	RS	8	JAX		NUR
Caldwell	Rev Calvin Norris	1889	1927	RT	38	TAI	SHA	ADM
Caldwell	Mrs Mary Tippett	1889	1927	RT	38	TAI	SHA	WW
Caldwell	Miss Mary White, RN	1926	1927	H	1	TAI		NUR
Campbell	Miss Anna	1920	1923	ET	3	JAX		ED
Carmichael	Miss Janet	1901	1904	RS	3	SOO		NUR
Conover	Miss Lula	1922	1927	ET	5	JIA		TMC
Converse	Rev Thomas E.	1868	1870	H	1	HAN		EVA
Converse	Mrs Eliza Leyburn	1868	1870	H	1	HAN		EVA
Corriher	Miss Elizabeth, RN	1908	1927	EV	19	JAX	SOO	NUR
Cox	Mr Warren Murdock, Jr.	1924	1928	ET	4	HAN		HED
Cox	Mrs Rubye Diehl, RN	1923	1928	ET	5	JAX	HAN	NUR
Craig	Rev Augustus R.	1925	1938	EV	13	HAN	TKP	EVA
Craig	Mrs Mary Bellingrath	1925	1938	EV	13	HAN	TKP	EVA

Crawford	Francis Randolph, MD	1914	1932	RS	18	JIA	JAX	MED
Crawford	Mrs Martha P. Paxton	1916	1932	RS	16	JIA	JAX	WW
Crenshaw	Rev John Crawford	1911	1927	EV	16	ZHE		EVA
Crenshaw	Mrs May Moffett, RN	1911	1927	EV	16	ZHE		NUR
Cumming	Rev William Cooper	1923	1927	EV	5	JIA		EVA
Cumming	Mrs Maude C. Carson	1923	1927	EV	4	SOO	JIA	EDS
Currie	Rev Edward Smith	1920	1952	TR	32	HAI		EVA
Currie	Mrs Gay Wilson	1920	1952	TR	32	HAI		EVA
Currie	Miss Mabel Claire	1919	1926	RS	7	SOO		ED
Davis	Rev John W.	1873	1917	D	44	SOO	NAN	THE
Davis	Mrs Alice Schmucker	1878	1906	D	28	SOO		WW
Davis	Rev Lowry	1910	1949	RT	39	JAX		ED
Davis	Mrs Mary Barnett	1910	1949	RT	39	JAX		ED
Dixon	Miss Margaret, RN	1921	1927	RS	6	SOO	JIA	NUR
Douglas	Rev Rhodas Clyde	1920	1927	EV	7	JAX		EVA
Douglas	Mrs Eliz. Leybu, RN	1920	1927	EV	7	JAX		WW
DuBose	Rev Hampden Coit	1872	1910	D	38	SOO		EVA
DuBose	Mrs Pauline McAlpine	1872	1914	D	42	SOO		EVA
DuBose	Rev Palmer Clisby	1906	1927	H	21	SOO		EVA
DuBose	Mrs Elizabeth Zemp	1906	1927	H	21	SOO		EVA
Dunlap	Miss Charlotte, RN	1922	1949	TR	27	SUQ	ZHE	NUR
Embery	Miss Doris	1930	1931	ET	1	HUA		TMC
Emerson	Miss Ellen	1888	1904	D	14	TKP	HAN	EVA
Evans	Mr Edward, Jr.	1920	1927	RS	7	HAN		HED
Evans	Mrs Jean McLachlan	1920	1927	RS	7	HAN		HED
Farmer	Mrs Nancy Smith, RN	1917	1918	H	1	SOO		NUR
Farr	Miss Grace	1920	1948	RS	28	TAI		EVA
Farrior	Rev Stacy Conrad	1912	1951	RT	39	HAN	ZHE	ED
Farrior	Mrs Kitty McMullen	1910	1951	RT	41	JAX	ZHE	ED
Farrior	Miss Ruth	1948	1951	EV	3	SHA		EVA
Fishburne	Richard Baxter, MD	1881	1883	H	2	HAN		MD
Fleming	Miss Elizabeth	1893	1916	D	23	SOO		ED
Fletcher	Miss Lucy Allena	1930	1942	RS	12	YEN		ED
Franklin	Rev Benjamin H.	1893	1899	H	6	HAN		EVA
Fraser	Miss Gussie Louise	1923	1951	TR	28	YEN		EVA
French	Miss Eliza Byrneside	1888	1923	RT	35	SOO	HAN	EVA
Ghiselin	Rev Charles, Jr.	1915	1926	RS	11	TAI		EVA
Gieser	Paul Kenneth, MD	1934	1949	EV	15	TKP	ZHE	MED
Gieser	Mrs Catherine Kirk	1934	1949	EV	15	TKP	ZHE	ED
Grafton	Rev Thomas Buie	1904	1927	EV	23	XUZ	HAI	EVA
Grafton	Mrs 1 Letty Taylor	1904	1925	D	21	XUZ	HAI	EVA
Grafton	Mrs 2 Mary Woods	1923	1927	EV	4	HAI		EVA
Graham	Rev James Robert II	1889	1937	RT	48	TKP		EVA
Graham	Mrs Sophie M Peck	1889	1937	RT	48	TKP		EVA
Graham	Miss Sophie Peck	1916	1943	RS	27	HAN	HAI	ED
Graham	Rev James Robert III	1921	1937	RS	16	YEN	ZHE	ED
Graham	Mrs Louise Garret	1921	1937	RS	16	YEN	ZHE	ED
Grier	Rev Mark Brown	1891	1917	D	26	SUQ	XUZ	EVA
Grier*	Mrs Nettie Donaldson, MD	1896	1940	RT	44	SUQ	XUZ	MED
Grier	Miss Isabel	1919	1927	RS	8	XUZ		ED
Grier	Miss Eliz. Hemphill	1930	1936	RS	6	XUZ		ED
Grier	Miss Lucy Henrietta, RN	1933	1941	EV	8	SOO		NUR
Haden	Rev Robert Allen	1891	1917	D	26	WUX	JIA	EVA
Haden	Mrs 1 Julia McGinnis	1893	1894	D	1	WUX		EVA
Haden	Mrs 2 Eugenie Hilbold	1897	1917	DS	20	JIA		EVA
Hall	Miss Jessie Dalziel	1907	1948	RT	41	TKP		EVA
Hall	Miss Margaret Sprunt	1925	1927	ET	2	TKP		TMC
Hamilton	Rev Evelyn Harrison	1923	1951	TR	28	XUZ		EVA
Hamilton	Mrs Estelle McAlpine	1923	1951	TR	28	XUZ		EVA
Hancock	Rev Charles Frederick	1907	1927	H	20	YEN		EVA
Hancock	Mrs Mary Penick	1907	1927	H	20	YEN		EDS
Harnsberger	Rev Thomas Lyttleton	1912	1942	EV	27	TAI		EVA
Harnsburger	Mrs 1 Lanie Gillespie	1912	1917	D	5	TAI		EVA
Harnsburger	Mrs 2 Agnes Woods	1914	1942	EV	14	TKP	TAI	ED
Hawkins	Miss Irene Anna	1909	1925	H	16	JAX		ED

Head	Walter Hobson, MD	1926	1927	RS	1	HUA		MED
Head	Mrs Lora Lee Nabers	1926	1927	RS	1	HUA		MED
Helm	Rev Benjamin	1868	1878	RS	10	HAN		EVA
Hewett	Julius Winch, MD	1915	1926	RS	11	YEN		MED
Hewett	Mrs Dorothy Conyers	1915	1926	RS	11	YEN		MED
Hill	Miss Alma Lucile	1921	1926	H	5	SOO		ED
Hopkins	Rev Martin Armstrong	1917	1951	EV	34	ZHE	TNG	THE
Hopkins	Mrs Bessie Atkinson	1917	1951	EV	34	ZHE	TNG	EVA
Houston	Rev Matthew Hale	1868	1897	RS	13	HAN		EVA
Houston	Mrs Evelyn Withrow	1871	1882	D	6	HAN		EVA
Howe	Mr James L.	1921	1924	ET	3	HAN		HED
Hudson	Rev George	1891	1911	H	20	HAN		EVA
Hudson	Kate (nee Hudson)	1893	1911	H	18	HAN		EVA
Hudson	Rev Waddy Hampton	1894	1940	RT	46	SNG	JAX	EVA
Hudson	Mrs Maude Chapin	1894	1935	D	41	SNG	JAX	EDS
Hudson	Rev George Alexander	1923	1951	TR	28	JAX		EVA
Hudson	Mrs Katherine Hodgson	1924	1951	TR	27	JAX		EVA
Hutcheson	Allen Carrington, MD	1908	1927	EV	19	JAX	NAN	MED
Hutcheson	Mrs Straussie McCaslin	1908	1927	EV	19	JAX	NAN	MED
Innes	Miss Agnes Violet, RN	1905	1906	D	1	SOO		NUR
Inslee*	Rev Elias B.	1867	1870	D	4	HAN		EVA
Inslee	Mrs Eugenia Young	1867	1870	DS	4	HAN		ED
Iverson	Miss Lalla, MD	1947	1949	EV	2	TSI		MED
Johnson	Rev James Francis	1882	1888	D	5	HAN		EVA
Johnston	Miss Mary Melrose	1897	1942	RT	45	SUQ		EVA
Jones	Miss Hattie (McIlwaine)	1889	1891	TR	2	SOO		EVA
Jourolmon	Miss Rida	1905	1927	RT	23	JIA		EVA
Junkin	Rev William Francis, Sr.	1897	1943	RT	46	SUQ		EVA
Junkin	Mrs Nettie DuBose	1897	1943	RT	46	SOO	SUQ	EVA
Junkin	Miss Lila Elizabeth	1924	1929	ET	5	SUQ		TMC
Junkin	Rev William Francis, Jr.	1940	1951	TR	9	HAN		EVA
Junkin	Mrs Jessie McElroy	1940	1951	TR	9	HAN		EVA
Kirkland	Miss Helen	1874	1895	D	11	HAN		ED
Kok	Miss Annie (Brady)	1948	1948	EV	1	HAN		EVA
Lacy	Miss Sallie McGavock	1910	1923	H	13	TKP	YEN	EVA
Lancaster	Rev Richard Venable	1887	1892	H	5	HAN		EVA
Lancaster	Ms Littlepage Holladay	1889	1892	H	3	HAN		EVA
Lancaster	Rev Lewis Holladay	1916	1950	RT	34	NAN	XUZ	EVA
Lancaster	Mrs Eliza Neville	1917	1950	RT	33	NAN	XUZ	EVA
Lee	Miss Jane Varenia, MD	1899	1936	RT	37	HAN	JIA	ED
Lee	Miss Caroline Virginia	1917	1927	ET	10	JIA		ED
Little	Rev Lacy LeGrand	1895	1942	RT	41	JIA		ED
Little	Mrs 1 Pauline DuBose	1896	1897	D	1	JIA		ED
Little	Mrs 2 Ella Davidson	1891	1916	D	16	HAN	JIA	ED
Little	Mrs 3 Nellie Sprunt	1911	1942	RT	25	TKP	JIA	ED
Lynch	Miss Rusella Elinore	1910	1950	RT	40	JAX		WW
Malcolm	William, MD	1910	1913	RS	3	HUA		MED
Malcolm	Mrs Lyle Pringle	1909	1913	RS	4	HUA		MED
Matthes	Miss Hazel Lee, RN	1921	1948	RS	27	ZHE		NUR
Matthews	Miss Mary Susan	1897	1915	RS	18	HAN		EVA
McCain	Miss Elizabeth Irene	1915	1922	D	7	SOO		ED
McCollum	Miss Bess	1921	1924	RS	3	SHA	SOO	ADM
McCormick	Mrs Minnie Pearson	1896	1929	RT	33	TKP	SOO	WW
McCown	Miss Mary Wilson	1920	1948	RS	24	TKP		ED
McCutchan	Rev James Trimble	1908	1909	H	1	TAI		EVA
McCutchen	Mrs Mary Wilson	1908	1909	H	1	TAI		
McCutchen	Mr Hugh Walker	1908	1948	RT	33	SUQ		ED
McCutchen	Miss Mada Isabel	1911	1948	RT	34	SUQ		ED
McDannald*	Miss Nannie (Garritt)	1889	1891	M	2	SOO		EVA
McFadyen	Archibald A., MD	1904	1942	RT	38	XUZ		MED
McFadyen	Mrs 1 Catherine Williams	1905	1914	D	9	XUZ		EVA
McFadyen	Mrs 2 Helen Howard, RN	1912	1949	RT	37	SOO	XUZ	NUR
McGinnis	Rev James Young	1893	1941	RT	46	JAX		EVA
McGinnis*	Mrs Anna Howe	1896	1941	RT	43	JAX		ED
McIlwain	Miss Annie Orene	1922	1929	RS	7	SOO		ED

McKnight	Miss Emma	1896	1900	RS	4	JAX		EVA
McLauchlin	Rev Wilfred Campbell	1916	1949	TR	33	SUQ	HAI	EVA
McLauchlin	Mrs Elizabeth Wilson	1916	1949	TR	33	SUQ	HAI	EVA
McMullen	Rev Robt Johnston	1911	1950	RT	39	HAN		HED
McMullen	Mrs Emma Moffett	1911	1950	RT	39	HAN		ED
McMullen	Miss Nettie Johnston	1915	1928	H	13	HAN		EVA
McRoberts	Miss Bella	1897	1924	D	27	SUQ		EVA
Miller	Samuel Houston, MD	1915	1916	D	1	TKP		MED
Minter	Rev John Perrin	1937	1950	EV	14	SOO		EVA
Minter	Mrs Elizabeth Manget	1937	1950	EV	13	SOO		EVA
Mizell	Miss Marguerite	1921	1948	TR	27	TAI		EVA
Moffett	Rev Lacy Irwine	1904	1948	RT	44	SOO	JIA	EVA
Moffett	Mrs Kate Rodd	1904	1948	RT	44	SOO	JIA	WW
Moffett	Miss Carrie Lena	1907	1941	RT	34	SOO	JIA	ED
Moffett	Rev Lyle Moore	1910	1916	RS	6	TKP		EVA
Moffett	Miss Natalie Crawford	1922	1940	EV	18	HAN		ED
Moffett	Alexander Stuart, MD	1935	1950	RS	15	JIA		MED
Moffett	Mrs Virginia Billing	1935	1950	RS	16	JIA		MED
Montgomery	Rev James Nelson	1917	1949	TR	32	HUA		EVA
Montgomery	Mrs Aurie Lancaster	1917	1949	TR	32	HUA	TKP	EVA
Montgomery	Virginia (McCall)	1948	1948	EV	1	UNA		EVA
Mooney	James Potter, MD	1911	1915	RS	4	SOO		MED
Mooney	Mrs Annie Wilkerson	1911	1912	D	1	SOO		MED
Moore	Rev Lynford L., MD	1897	1904	H	5	XUZ		MED
Moore	Mrs Mary Torrence	1897	1904	H	4	XUZ		EVA
Moore	John William, MD	1922	1925	H	3	SOO		MED
Moore	Mrs Laura Venabale, RN	1922	1925	H	3	SOO		NUR
Morgan	Lorenzo Seymour, MD	1905	1934	RS	29	TKP	HAI	MED
Morgan	Mrs Ruth Bennett, MD	1905	1934	RS	29	TKP	HAI	MED
Morton	Miss Esther	1908	1910	H	2	TKP	SOO	MED
Mosley	Kirk Thornton, MD	1931	1939	RS	8	TKP	YEN	MED
Mosley	Mrs Corinne Daigle, RN	1931	1939	RS	8	TKP	YEN	NUR
Nelson	Henry Sperry, MD	1947	1951	TR	4	TAI		MED
Nelson	Mrs Kathryn Wolff, RN	1947	1951	TR	4	TAI		NUR
Nesbit	Miss Sade A	1914	1929	RS	15	JAX	JIA	ADM
Newman	Henry Wade, MD	1924	1926	RS	2	ZHE		MED
Newman	Mrs Ethel Smith	1924	1926	RS	2	ZHE		MED
Nickles	Miss Florence Eugenia	1915	1950	TR	32	JAX	NAN	THE
Painter	Rev George Whitfield	1873	1904	RT	31	HAN		EVA
Patterson	Rev Brown Craig	1891	1939	RT	45	SUQ	TNG	THE
Patterson	Mrs Annie Houston, MD	1891	1939	RT	45	SUQ	SUQ	MED
Patterson	Rev Craig Houston	1923	1941	EV	18	SUQ	TNG	EVA
Patterson	Mrs Frances Glasgow	1923	1941	EV	18	SUQ	TNG	EVA
Patterson	Norman Guthrie, MD	1929	1939	EV	10	TKP	SUQ	MED
Patterson	Mrs Athalie Hallum	1929	1939	EV	10	HWA	SUQ	MED
Paxton	Rev John Wardlaw	1891	1929	RT	33	SOO	ZHE	ED
Paxton	Mrs Una Hall	1896	1941	RT	30	SOO	ZHE	EVA
Price	Rev Philip Francis	1890	1941	RT	51	JAX	NAN	THE
Price	Mrs Esther Wilson	1888	1941	RT	53	JAX	NAN	ED
Price	Robt Black, MD	1915	1941	EV	26	TAI		MED
Price	Mrs Sarah Armstead	1915	1941	EV	26	TAI		MED
Price	Rev Frank Wilson, PhD	1923	1952	EV	29	NAN	WCH	THE
Price	Mrs Essie McClure	1923	1952	EV	29	NAN	WCH	WW
Price	Philip Barbour, MD	1925	1940	EV	15	SOO	TSI	MED
Price	Mrs Octavia Howard, RN	1925	1940	EV	15	SOO	TSI	NUR
Randolph	Mrs Anna Edgar	1872	1888	TR	16	HAN		ED
Reaves	Rev Henry Lide	1917	1936	H	19	SOO		EVA
Reaves	Mrs Claudia Brown	1918	1936	H	18	SOO		EVA
Reed	John Hobart, MD	1931	1941	EV	10	HAI		MED
Reed	Mrs Sallie Childrey	1931	1941	EV	10	HAI		MED
Rice	Rev Archibald Dean	1899	1919	D	20	TKP	HAI	EVA
Rice	Mrs Emma Bissett	1899	1937	RT	38	TKP	HAI	EVA
Richardson	Rev Donald William	1910	1929	RS	19	ZHE	NAN	THE
Richardson	Mrs Virginia McIlwain	1910	1929	RS	19	CHI	NAN	ED
Richardson	Rev Robert Price	1923	1951	EV	28	TAI		EVA

Richardson	Mrs Agnes Rowland	1923	1951	EV	28	TAI		EVA
Rodd	Miss Florence Smith	1902	1906	M	4	HAN		WW
Roe	Miss M.Dickson	1909	1911	H	2	JAX		SEC
Rowland	Miss Wilmine Maltbie	1929	1933	ET	4	TAI		TMC
Safford	Miss Anna C.	1873	1890	D	17	SOO		LIT
Satterfield	Miss Ruby	1920	1942	RS	22	JAX	SOO	ADM
Sells	Miss Margaret	1938	1949	TR	11	HAI	HAN	EVA
Sheldon	Rev Charles Augustus	1940	1942	EV	2	HAN		EVA
Sheldon	Mrs Nell Allison	1940	1942	EV	2	HAN		EVA
Shields	Randolph Tucker, MD	1904	1942	RT	37	NAN	TSI	MED
Shields	Mrs Ella Page	1904	1941	RT	37	NAN	TSI	EVA
Shires	Mr Wilbur S.	1925	1927	EV	1	JAX		ED
Shires	Mrs Grace Nicholson	1926	1927	EV	2	JAX		ED
Sloan	Miss Addie	1896	1939	RT	43	SOO		EVA
Sloan	Miss Gertrude Lee	1908	1929	EV	21	SOO		ED
Sloan	Miss Mary Lee	1920	1941	EV	19	XUZ		ADM
Smith	Miss Belle	1893	1900	RS	7	SOO		WW
Smith	Rev Hart Maxcy	1901	1941	RT	40	SNG	SHA	ADM
Smith	Mrs Margaret Jones	1905	1941	RT	36	SNG	SHA	EVA
Smith	Rev Cecil Hiawatha	1911	1941	EV	30	YEN		EVA
Smith	Mrs 1 Millie Beard	1914	1919	D	5	SOO	YEN	MUS
Smith	Mrs 2 Minna Amis	1920	1941	RT	21	NAN	YEN	EVA
Smith	Mr Walter E.	1921	1922	ET	1	HAN		HED
Smithwick	Miss Laura Gladys, MD	1929	1936	H	7	XUZ		MED
Stephenson	Robt Mills, MD	1910	1912	DS	2	ZHE		MED
Stephenson	Mrs Allene Gwin	1910	1911	D	1	ZHE		MED
Stevens	Rev George Phifer	1909	1941	RT	32	TNG	YEN	EVA
Stevens	Mrs Mary Thompson	1908	1919	D	11	XUZ	TNG	ED
Stribling	Miss Frances	1917	1951	TR	30	HAN		ED
Stuart	Rev John Linton	1868	1913	D	45	HAN	SOO	EVA
Stuart	Mrs Mary Horton	1874	1925	D	51	HAN	SOO	EVA
Stuart	Rev John Leighton	1904	1925	TR	21	HAN	NAN	THE
Stuart	Mrs Aline Rodd	1904	1925	D	21	HAN	NAN	ED
Stuart	David Todd, MD	1907	1909	D	2	SOO		MED
Stuart*	Rev Warren Horton	1906	1927	TR	21	HAN	NAN	HED
Stuart*	Mrs Annie Chesnut	1907	1927	TR	20	HAN	NAN	ED
Sydenstricker	Rev Absalom	1880	1931	D	51	SUQ	ZHE	EVA
Sydenstricker	Mrs Caroline Stuling	1880	1921	D	41	SUQ	ZHE	EVA
Sydenstricker	Miss Grace (Yaukey)	1921	1923	M	3	ZHE		ED
Sydenstricker*	Miss Pearl (Buck)	1915	1917	M	2	ZHE		ED
Sykes	Mrs Anna McGinnis	1893	1928	RT	35	WUX	JIA	EVA
Sykes*	Miss Anna (Bryars)	1916	1919	M	3	SHA		
Talbot	Miss Elizabeth	1895	1939	RT	44	JAX		EVA
Talbot	Rev Addison Alexander	1905	1947	RT	42	TKP		EVA
Talbot	Mrs 1 Katherine Bird	1905	1937	D	32	TKP		EVA
Talbot	Mrs 2 Cassie Lee Oliver, RN	1923	1951	RT	28	TKP		NUR
Talbot	Rev George Bird	1935	1949	EV	10	XUZ	TKP	EVA
Talbot	Mrs Mary Alice Wade	1935	1949	EV	10	XUZ	TKP	EVA
Taylor	Rev Hugh Kerr	1917	1933	DS	16	TKP		EVA
Taylor	Mrs Fanny Bland Graham	1917	1933	D	16	TKP		EVA
Terrill	Charles S., MD	1899	1900	D	1	SUQ		MED
Terrill	Mrs Charlotte Neven	1899	1900	DS	1	SUQ		MED
Thompson	Miss Katheryne Luella	1921	1951	TR	30	JIA		ED
Tidball	Miss Lily	1886	1889	H	3	HAN		EVA
Van Hook	Mr J. O.	1925	1926	ET	2	KAS		ED
Van Putten	Rev James Dyke	1925	1927	RS	2	HAN		HED
Van Putten	Mrs Frieda Gunneman	1925	1927	RS	2	HAN		HED
Van Valkenburg	Rev Horace Bulle	1908	1913	ET	5	JAX		ED
Van Valkenburg	Mrs Beulah Williams	1908	1913	ET	5	KAS		ED
Venable	Wade Hampton, MD	1893	1927	EV	34	JAX	KUL	MED
Venable	Mrs Eliza Talbot	1893	1927	EV	34	JAX	KUL	MED
Vinson	Rev John Walker	1907	1931	D	24	SUQ	HAI	EVA
Vinson	Mrs Jeanie Junkin	1904	1923	D	19	SUQ	HAI	EVA
Vinson	Rev John Walker, Jr.	1940	1949	EV	9	JAX		EVA
Vinson	Mrs Mary Lucy Boone	1941	1949	EV	8	JAX		EVA

Vinson	Thomas Chalmers, MD	1940	1949	EV	9	TKP		MED
Vinson	Mrs Olivert Castile	1940	1949	EV	9	TKP		MED
Voss	Charles H., MD	1922	1929	RS	7	SUQ		MED
Voss	Mrs Mathilda Easley	1923	1929	RS	6	SUQ		MED
Watkins	Miss Mildred Cabell	1911	1922	D	11	JAX	SHA	TMC
Wayland	Rev John Edwin	1920	1927	EV	7	TKP		EVA
Wayland	Mrs Rosa Lee Clark	1920	1927	EV	7	TKP		EVA
Wells	Miss Lillian Crowell	1912	1949	TR	37	HUA		EVA
Welton	Felix Burwell, MD	1930	1937	RS	7	SOO		MED
Welton	Mrs Lelia Gardner	1930	1937	RS	7	SOO		MED
White	Rev Will. Breckeridge	1892	1897	H	5	SNG		EVA
White	Rev Hugh Watt	1894	1940	D	46	XUZ	YEN	EVA
White	Mrs Augusta Graves	1893	1940	RT	47	XUZ	YEN	EVA
White	Rev Locke	1922	1927	EV	5	XUZ		EVA
White	Mrs Emma Edwards	1922	1927	EV	5	XUZ		EVA
Wilcox	Miss Marion	1923	1951	TR	28	JIA		EVA
Wilkerson	Joseph Leyburn, MD	1948	1951	EV	3	JAX		MED
Wilkerson	Estelle Isenhour, RN	1948	1951	EV	3	JAX		NUR
Wilkinson	James Richard, MD	1894	1920	RS	26	SOO		MED
Wilkinson	Mrs Annie Barr	1894	1920	RS	26	SOO		MED
Williams	Miss Carrie Knox, RN	1916	1918	RS	2	SUQ		NUR
Wilson	Miss Rebecca Elizabeth	1899	1941	RT	42	JAX	HAN	EVA
Wilson	Miss Annie Randolph	1908	1941	RT	33	HAN		EVA
Wilson	Mr James Morrison	1912	1925	RS	13	HAN		HED
Wilson	Mrs Martha Cecil	1912	1925	RS	13	HAN		HED
Womeldorf	Rev George Raymond	1923	1942	EV	19	HUA	ZHE	EVA
Womeldorf	Mrs Mary Goetchius	1923	1942	EV	19	HUA	ZHE	EVA
Wood	Miss Margaret P., RN	1935	1951	TR	16	SUQ	TKP	NUR
Woodbridge	Rev Samuel Isett	1882	1926	D	44	ZHE	SHA	LIT
Woodbridge	Mrs 1 Jeanie Woodrow	1884	1913	D	19	ZHE	SHA	EVA
Woodbridge	Mrs 2 Mary Newell, MD	1915	1929	H	14	SHA		MED
Woodbridge	Caspar Lignon, MD	1922	1929	RS	7	HAI		MD
Woodbridge	Mrs Elizabeth Wilson	1922	1929	RS	7	HAI		MED
Woods	Rev Henry McKee	1883	1928	RT	44	HUA	SHA	LIT
Woods	Mrs 1 Jos. Underwood	1883	1920	D	37	HUA	SHA	EVA
Woods	Mrs 2 Grace (Taylor)	1923	1928	RT	5	SHA		LIT
Woods	Edgar, Jr., MD	1888	1899	RS	11	TKP		MED
Woods	Mrs Frances Smith	1888	1899	RS	11	TKP		MED
Woods	James Baker, Sr., MD	1894	1941	RT	47	TKP		MED
Woods	Mrs Bessie Smith	1894	1941	RT	47	TKP		MED
Woods	Miss Josephine	1907	1947	RT	40	HUA		WW
Woods	Miss Lily Underwood	1915	1936	H	21	HUA		ED
Woods	James Baker, Jr., MD	1924	1941	EV	17	ZHE		MED
Woods	Mrs Elizabeth Blain	1935	1941	EV	6	SHA	ZHE	MED
Woods	Rev Edgar Archibald	1931	1941	EV	10	SUQ	HAI	EVA
Woods	Mrs Lydia Daniel	1931	1941	EV	10	SUQ	HAI	EVA
Woods	Rev John Russell	1930	1941	EV	11	TKP		EVA
Woods	Mrs Elinor Myers MT	1931	1941	EV	10	TKP		MED
Worth	George Clarkson, MD	1895	1936	D	41	WUX	JIA	MED
Worth	Mrs Emma Chadbourn, RN	1895	1926	D	31	WUX	JIA	MED
Worth	Rev Charles William	1922	1947	RS	22	JIA		EVA
Worth	Mrs ElizabethMcAlpine	1922	1942	D	20	JIA		EVA
Worth	Miss Ruth MT	1932	1951	EV	19	JIA	ZHE	MED
Yates	Rev Orville Ford	1908	1941	EV	33	HUA		EVA
Yates	Ms Ellen Baskerville, RN	1909	1941	EV	32	TKP	HUA	NUR
Young	Mason Pressly, MD	1916	1949	EV	33	SOO	JAX	MED
Young	Mrs Louise Oehler	1916	1949	EV	33	SOO	JAX	MED
Young	Miss Flora Lois	1917	1941	EV	24	XUZ		ED

Notes

Introduction

1. "Forty-five New Pastors Ordained," *Amity News Service* (Hong Kong: newsletter published by the Amity Foundation Overseas Coordinating Office) 1:1 (Jan. 1992): 4.

2. "Mass Baptisms in Hangzhou, Zhejiang," *Amity News Service* 1:4 (July 1992): 2.

3. "1994 Bible Production in China Higher than ever," *Amity News Service* 3:4/5 (Oct. 1994): 1.

4. Rev. Peter Han, Vice-Chairman of the Jiangsu Provincial Christian Council, interview with the author, Nanjing, 29 May 1993. A "meeting point" is defined at a place of regular worship but not yet organized as a church with an ordained pastor.

5. *China News Update*, Jan. 1997, 1.

6. "How Many Christians Are There in China?" *Amity News Service* 96.5.4 (Sept. 1996): 14.

7. Edmond Tang and Jean-Paul Wiest, eds., *The Catholic Church in Modern China: Perspectives* (Maryknoll, NY: Orbis, 1993), xvii.

8. Paul A. Cohen, "Christian Missions and Their Impact to 1900" in *Cambridge History of China*, Denis Twitchett and John K. Fairbank, eds., vol. 10 *Late Ch'ing 1800–1911, Part I* (Cambridge: Cambridge University Press, 1978), 10:543.

9. *Chinese Around the World* (Hong Kong: Newsletter published by the Chinese Church Research Center), Dec. 1990.

10. For example: Leonard Outerbridge, *The Lost Churches of China* (Philadelphia: Westminster Press, 1952); "First Thoughts on the Debacle of Christian Missions in China by a China Missionary," *International Review of Missions* 40/60 (Oct. 1951): 411.

11. Conversations of the author with scholars of the Shanghai Academy of Social Science, 3 June 1993; and of the Beijing Academy of Social Science, 8 June 1993.

12. Bishop K. H. Ting, interview with the author, Nanjing, 29 May 1993.

13. The Beijing *China Daily*, 6 July 1987.

14. Chen Guanfeng, "Hospital Centenary Plea for Caring Values," *China Daily*, 23 Oct. 1985.

15. Bishop K. H. Ting, interview with the author, Nanjing, 29 May 1993. The Bishop cited the attention given the Drum Tower Hospital celebration by the secular press as evidence of the change that has taken place in the official views of the missionary era.

16. Marvine Howe, "Christian Churches Still Play a Role in Education in China," *The New York Times*, 29 Apr. 1987.

17. Letter from Ye-toh and Bei-sih to Rev. and Mrs. John Minter, 3 Dec. 1985, which was referred to the author for reply.

18. Wang Yu-hua to the author, 24 Jan. 1991.

19. For the PCUSA: Hunter Corbett (1906); for the PCUS: Hampden C. DuBose (1891), P. Frank Price (1936), Donald W. Richardson (1943), Frank W. Price (1953), and L. Nelson Bell (1972).

20. Suzanne Wilson Barnett and John King Fairbank, eds., *Christianity in China: Early Protestant Missionary Writings* (Cambridge: Harvard University Press, 1985), 2.

Chapter 1: Foundations

1. H. McKennie Goodpasture, "150 Years in Global Mission," *Mission Yearbook for Prayer and Study, 1987* (New York: Presbyterian Church USA, 1987), 6.

2. John C. B. Webster, "American Presbyterian Global Mission Policy: An Overview of 150 Years," *AP* 65 (1987): 72.

3. Ibid., 71. For a history of the Western Foreign Missionary Society see Ashbel Green, *Presbyterian Missions* (New York: Anson D. F. Randolph & Co., 1893), 173–245. At the 1837 Assembly the rupture between the two factions resulted in the formation of the "Old School" and "New School" assemblies.

4. 5th Annual Report, Western Foreign Missionary Society, May 1837, Green, *Presbyterian Missions*, 173–174.

5. 1st Annual Report of the BFM, PCUSA, May 1838, in James E. Bear, Jr. "The Mission Work of the Presbyterian Church in the United States in China: 1867–1962," 5 vols., unpublished manuscript in Union Theological Seminary in Virginia, 1963, 1:50. Bear's work, which has been used extensively, is abbreviated as "Bear, *History.*"

6. Ibid., 51.

7. Charles W. Forman, "A History of Foreign Mission Theory in America" in R. Pierce Beaver, ed., *American Missions in Bicentennial Perspective* (Pasadena: William Carey Library, 1977), 71–72.

8. Valentine Rabe, "Evangelical Logistics: Mission Support and Resources to 1920" in *The Missionary Enterprise in China and America*, John K. Fairbank, ed. (Cambridge: Harvard University Press, 1974), 89.

9. Arthur Schlesinger, Jr., "The Missionary Enterprise and Imperialism," in ibid., 346.

10. Jean Chesneaux, Marianne Bastid, and Marie-Claire Bergere, *China from the Opium Wars to the 1911 Revolution* (New York: Pantheon Books, 1976), 59.

11. Cohen, "Christian Missions and Their Impact to 1900," in *The Cambridge History of China*, 10:565.

12. Kenneth Scott Latourette, *A History of Christianity in China* (New York: Macmillan, 1929), 154.

13. Chesneaux, *China from the Opium Wars to the 1911 Revolution*, 38–57.

14. The consideration of "Confucianism" as a religion is debatable. But the fact that it is linked with Buddhism and Taoism in this ancient saying would indicate that in the popular mind it did have at least some of the characteristics of religion.

15. W. E. Soothill, *The Three Religions of China* (London: Oxford University Press, 1929), 13.

16. John K. Fairbank and Edwin O. Reischauer, *China: Tradition and Transformation* (Boston: Houghton Mifflin Co., 1978), 44.

17. Soothill, *The Three Religions of China*, 172.

18. Fairbank and Reischauer, *China: Tradition and Transformation*, 88.

19. Soothill, *The Three Religions of China*, 48.

20. Donald E. MacInnis, *Religions in China Today: Policy and Practice* (Maryknoll, NY: Orbis, 1989), 204.

21. Fairbank and Reischauer, *China: Tradition and Transformation*, 243.

22. Samuel Hugh Moffett, *A History of Christianity in Asia. Volume I: Beginnings to 1500* (New York: HarperCollins Publishers, 1992), 1:313.

23. Jonathan D. Spence, *The Memory Palace of Matteo Ricci* (New York: Viking, 1984), 9.

24. Latourette, *History*, 91–130.

25. Bob Whyte, *Unfinished Encounter: China and Christianity* (Harrisburg, PA: Morehouse Publishing, 1988), 49, citing a lecture by Bishop Ting at Doshisha University in Japan in Sept. 1984. The author wrote to Bishop Ting in an effort to trace the authenticity of the Kangxi quote. In his response of 16 Feb. 1995 the bishop referred to Hymn #170 "From

the Cross the Crimson Flows" in *Hymns of Universal Praise*, attributed by the hymnbook editors to Kangxi.

26. Latourette, *History*, 131–151.

27. Ibid., 183.

28. Eliza A. Morrison, *Memoirs of the Life and Labours of Robert Morrison, D.D.* compiled by his widow, 2 vols. (London: Longman, Orne, Brown, and Green, 1839) 1:409.

29. Ibid., 2:2. Morrison used portions of early Roman Catholic translations and a version made by J. C. Marshman, of India. See Latourette, *History*, 210–212.

30. Daniel H. Bays, "Christian Tracts: The Two Friends" in *Christianity in China: Early Protestant Missionary Writings*, 19–34.

31. Fred W. Drake, "Protestant Geography in China: E. C. Bridgman's Portrayal of the West" in Barnett and Fairbank, *Christianity in China: Early Protestant Missionary Writings*, 89–106.

32. D. W. C. Olyphant has been described as "The Canton Merchant who Said 'No' to Opium." From missionary letters of the times he can be characterized by an intense hatred of the opium trade, a strong Christian character, generosity in the support of mission causes, wise counsel to missionaries and board officials and a lasting friendship for China. He was convinced that it was possible to operate a shipping business at a profit by engaging in trade that would be mutually beneficial for both America and China. His unashamed witness to his Christian faith made him an oddity among the Canton merchants and the Olyphant office in the Canton factory was named, somewhat in derision, "Zion's Corner." Olyphant's support of missionary causes became legendary. He offered free passage on his ships to all Protestant missionaries irrespective of their denomination. At least fifty-one free passages were given in the space of the next twenty-five years. Olyphant engaged in some missionary exploration of his own. In 1837 he dispatched his ship the *Morrison* on a goodwill venture to take back to Japan a number of shipwrecked Japanese seamen marooned in Macau. But the voyage ended in failure as the Japanese refused to allow their countrymen to land. A more lasting contribution was made in his support of Elijah Bridgman's publications. Olyphant became an elder in the Bleecker Street Presbyterian Church of New York City and a member of the Presbyterian Board of Foreign Missions. On business trips to China he took time to visit mission work in Canton and Shanghai, offering sound advice and financial support. Olyphant died in Cairo in 1851. See Robert Charles, "Olyphant and Opium: A Canton Merchant Who Just Said 'No,'" *IBMR* 16 (Apr. 1992): 67; Thatcher Thayer, *A Sketch of the Life of D. W. C. Olyphant* (New York: Edwin O. Jenkins, 1852).

33. Jonathan Spence, "Peter Parker: Bodies or Souls" in *To Change China: Western Advisers in China 1620–1960* (Boston: Little, Brown and Company, 1969), 34–56.

34. Noah Webster, *An American Dictionary of the English Language* (New York: White, Gallaher and White, 1831).

Chapter 2: First Encounters

1. Bear, *History*, 1:50–55.

2. For the account of Lowrie's sea voyages see Walter Lowrie, *Memoirs of the Rev. Walter M. Lowrie, Missionary to China*, edited by his father (New York: Robert Carter and Bros., 1849), 165–173.

3. One chest of opium weighed about 75 pounds.

4. Sources used on the opium war: Jonathan D. Spence, *The Search for Modern China* (New York: W. W. Norton, 1990), 147–158; Fairbank & Reischauer, *China: Tradition and Transformation*, 271–285; Chesneaux, *China from the Opium Wars to the 1911 Revolution*, 61–80. Chesneaux gives the text of an extraordinary letter from Lin ZeXu, to Queen Victoria in 1839 pleading with great earnestness that the opium trade be curtailed as it was doing enormous damage to the Chinese people. Tragically, the letter was probably never delivered. See *China: Tradition and Transformation*, 279.

5. Latourette, *History,* 229. Fairbank has a most interesting interpretation of the treaty port system. The Qing dynasty was following its traditional way of dealing with foreigners and acting in its own interests. The terms of the Treaty of Nanking are remarkably similar to those made with the Kokand traders of Central Asia a few years earlier: designated foreign settlements where the foreigners managed their own affairs and were subject to the laws of their own country. John King Fairbank, *The Great Chinese Revolution: 1800–1985* (New York: Harper and Row, 1986), 92–93.

6. Michael H. Hunt, *The Making of a Special Relationship: The United States and China to 1914* (New York: Columbia University Press, 1983), 31.

7. George B. Stevens, *The Life, Letters, and Journals of the Rev. and Hon. Peter Parker* (Boston: Congregational Sunday School Publishing Society, 1896), 253, 328–329.

8. McBryde, Letters dated 30 June and 27 July 1842, in *MC* 11 (1843): 44, 46, 54, 114–116.

9. Walter Lowrie, *Memoirs of the Rev. Walter M. Lowrie, Missionary to China,* 214–230.

10. After Dr. Hepburn's health was restored, he resumed his medical practice in New York City. Learning that the Board was planning to start a mission to Japan, he again volunteered for missionary service. The Hepburns were reappointed in 1859 and sailed for Japan where they engaged in the opening of Protestant mission work, serving in that country for over half a century. Arthur Judson Brown, *One Hundred Years: A History of the Foreign Missionary Work of the Presbyterian Church in the U.S.A., with Some Account of Countries, Peoples and the Policies and Problems of Modern Missions* (New York: Fleming H. Revell, 1936), 691.

11. For the opening of Ningbo see J. C. Garritt, ed., *Jubilee Papers of the Central China Presbyterian Mission, 1844–1894* (Shanghai: APMP, 1895), 1–34.

12. A. W. Loomis, ltr. in *FM* 9 (1850): 102–103.

13. Dr. D. J. MacGowan and Mr. and Mrs. Edward C. Lord of the American Baptist Mission began work soon after McCartee's arrival. Hudson Taylor arrived in 1857. The first Roman Catholics (Lazarists) arrived in 1846. Latourette, *History,* 234, 238, 251–252.

14. *AR,* 1845, 23.

15. *MC* 14 (1846): 169.

16. Ibid.

17. See A. W. Loomis, *Scenes in Chusan: or Missionary Labors by the Way* (Philadelphia: Presbyterian Board of Publications, 1859) for an interesting account of his service as a chaplain for the British garrison on the island of Chusan.

18. Divie Bethune McCartee was one of the most versatile missionaries ever appointed by the BFM. In addition to his skill as a medical practitioner, McCartee was linguist, writer, preacher, and diplomat. Every aspect of the mission program claimed his attention: the chapel preaching, the press, the schools, and the writing of Christian literature and hymns. He made friends easily. His medical practice brought him into contact with high mandarin officials, Portuguese traders, the Roman Catholic bishop, British mercenaries and Buddhist monks. In 1853 he married Miss Juana Knight, who was the first single woman appointed by the Board. McCartee resigned from the mission in 1872 but his years of service in China were far from over. He served as American consul in Shanghai, as Professor of Law and Natural Science in Tokyo and as advisor to the Chinese legation to Japan. He resumed his connection with the Board in 1888 engaging in teaching and translating tracts. He died in San Francisco at the age of eighty in 1900. See Robert E. Speer, ed., *A Missionary Pioneer in the Far East: A Memorial of Divie Bethune McCartee* (New York: Fleming H. Revell, 1922).

19. Walter Lowrie, *Memoirs of the Rev. Walter M. Lowrie,* 322.

20. Latourette, *History,* 248; Garritt, *Jubilee Papers,* 5.

21. *MC* 14 (1846): 296. See also Garritt, *Jubilee Papers,* 115.

22. Walter Lowrie, *Memoirs of the Rev. Walter M. Lowrie,* 324.

23. Speer, *A Missionary Pioneer in the Far East,* 16.

24. *MC* 16 (1848): 36.

25. Ibid., 16 (1848): 171. See also Bear, *History*, 1:90.

26. *AR,* 1848, 39–40. No reason was given for the action. Mr. Cole was employed by the London Missionary Society (LMS) to supervise their printing press in Canton after his work with the Presbyterians was terminated.

27. A number of Lowrie's papers were deposited in the Historical Foundation (Department of History) in Montreat, NC. Among these was a small, well-worn Hebrew, Greek and English Bible with the notation that it was the one he threw back on the boat when he was thrown overboard.

28. See Lowrie, *Memoirs of the Rev. Walter M. Lowrie,* 456–500. A memorial stone to Lowrie's memory was erected in Ningbo. The translation of the Chinese characters on the stone reads: "The American teacher of the religion of Jesus, Low-le-wha, Seen Sang [Teacher Lowrie]. Born in the reign of Kea-King, 24th year . . . died in the reign of Taou-Kwang . . . 27th year. . . . In the 25th year of Taou-Kwang . . . he reached Ningpo in order to propagate the holy religion. How can we know whether a long or a short life is appointed for us? He had but attained the age of twenty-nine years, when traveling by sea, he was drowned by pirates. Of all his associates there is none who does not cherish his memory, and they have accordingly erected this stone as a testimony of their affection."

29. Quarterman, a native of Georgia and a graduate of Columbia Seminary, died of smallpox in 1857. He served faithfully in the boys' school. Henry Rankin's health failed after fourteen years. He was assigned to Dengzhou in Shandong because of the climate but died in 1863 shortly after his arrival. He was remembered for his preaching, his writing of hymns and his wise counsel of young pastors. *FM* 22 (1863): 70–71; Garritt, *Jubilee Papers,* 18.

30. Garritt, *Jubilee Papers,* 21–22.

31. Ibid., 22.

32. "Helper" was a technical term in missionary parlance for an unordained church worker who was employed by the mission as a catechist, evangelist or colporteur (Bible salesman).

33. *AR,* 1855, 71.

34. Mr. Speer returned to the United States in 1849. When gold was discovered in California, the Board appointed him a missionary to work with the large number of Chinese laborers who were brought to America to work in the mines under very harsh circumstances.

35. Mrs. Elizabeth Happer, the mother of four daughters and two sons, died in 1865. Happer's second wife, whom he married in 1869 on furlough, was Miss A. L. Elliott. She returned to Canton with him but died four years later. His third wife was Hannah J. Shaw, who had come to China as a single missionary.

36. C. F. Preston, "Date and Events Connected with the Opening of the Canton Mission of the Board of Foreign Mission, PCUSA," *CR* 7 (1876): 185–195.

37. R. E. Speer, *Presbyterian Foreign Missions* (Philadelphia: Presbyterian Board of Publications, 1901), 109.

38. Ibid.

39. Parker was one of the most impressive, colorful and controversial of early missionaries in China. His fame as an ophthalmologic surgeon and his charming personality catapulted him into the high echelons of government both among Chinese and American officials. For a number of years he was employed by the United States in diplomatic service in China and retired in 1857. See Jonathan Spence's account of Parker's China years in his *To Change China: Western Advisers in China 1620–1960,* 34–56.

40. *AR,* 1856, 78.

41. Quoted in Pan Ling, *In Search of Old Shanghai* (Hong Kong: Joint Publishing Co., 1983), 13.

42. Both British and French concessions gradually expanded over the years until the British, or International Settlement, reached a size of 8.35 square miles and the French, just

under 4 square miles. By 1885 the Chinese population, which paid taxes at a higher rate, outnumbered the foreigners by nearly 35–1. Ibid., 18.

43. Walter Lowrie, *Memoirs of the Rev. Walter M. Lowrie*, 438.

44. See J. M. W. Farnham, "Historical Sketch of Shanghai Station," *Jubilee Papers of the Central China Presbyterian Mission*, J. C. Garritt, ed. (Shanghai: APMP, 1895), 35–77.

45. *HFR* 13 (1862): 270. Animosity between the British and American delegates played a part in the debate. See Farnham, *Jubilee Papers*, 37. There were other differences: The Bridgman/Culbertson version aimed for accuracy and was written in a simpler style more easily understood by those of little education. The Medhurst/Milne version sacrificed accuracy for literary grace and was favored by Chinese scholars. Latourette, *History*, 262–263.

Chapter 3: Treaty Ports and the Long-Haired Rebels

1. Sources used for this section: Spence, *The Search for Modern China*; Chesneaux, *China from the Opium Wars to the 1911 Revolution*; Fairbank and Reischauer, *China: Tradition and Transformation*; Fairbank, ed., *The Cambridge History of China*.

2. *AR*, 1856, 88.

3. The war began without the approval of Parliament. Lord Palmerston, the Prime Minister, was censored and his party lost on a vote of confidence. Parliament was dissolved. In the subsequent elections, the government won an endorsement of its China policy and hostilities continued.

4. The priest, Auguste Chapdelaine, was traveling in the interior where he had no legal rights, far from any treaty port. He was arrested by Chinese authorities, given a trial and executed.

5. Those of interest for this history were: Tianjin (Tientsin), Hankou (Hankow), Dengzhou (Tengchow), Zhenjiang (Chinkiang), and Haikou (Hoi-How on Hainan Island). Dengzhou was later changed to Yantai (Chefoo). Suzhou (Soochow) and Hangzhou (Hangchow), both early Presbyterian mission stations, became treaty ports by the Treaty of Shimonoseki in 1895.

6. In 1898 the New Territories were leased to Britain for ninety-nine years. Without the New Territories Hong Kong and Kowloon would not be a viable self-sustaining area. After protracted negotiations between the British and Chinese an agreement was reached in 1984 that transfered the sovereignty of the island and adjacent territories to the PRC in 1997. It has become a "Special Administrative Region" with a high degree of local autonomy.

7. Text of the religious clause is from Ralph Covell, *W. A. P. Martin: Pioneer of Progress in China* (Washington, DC: Christian University Press, 1978), 93. Covell's source is *The Life and Letters of Samuel Wells Williams* (New York: G. P. Putnam Sons, 1889), 273. Six years before the treaty, the Emperor had issued an edict of religious toleration for Catholics. In 1845 a subsequent edict made it applicable to Protestants as well.

8. The Yuan Ming Yuan is not to be confused with the extant summer palace built in 1888 by the Empress Dowager Cixi, which is a major tourist attraction in Peking today.

9. *AR*, 1857, 65.

10. News item, *HFR* 10 (1859): 215.

11. *AR*, 1858, 83–84.

12. K. H. Ting, "Facing the Future or Restoring the Past?" (Address delivered in Toronto, Nov. 1979.)

13. Latourette, *History*, 410.

14. J. H. Morrison, *William Carey: Cobbler and Pioneer* (London: Hodder and Stoughton, 1924), 53.

15. Stephen Neill, *Colonialism and Christian Missions* (New York: McGraw-Hill Book Company, 1966), 134.

16. John King Fairbank, *The United States and China*, 4th ed. (Cambridge: Harvard University Press, 1978), 162.

17. Covell, *W. A. P. Martin*, 104.

18. Dr. Robert E. Speer suggests that the toleration clauses were encouraged by the representatives of the Chinese government and supports this view with a quotation from Wm. B. Reed, the framer of the treaty. See his article "Missionaries and Their Rights" in *CR* 33 (1902): 50. But this may have been a misunderstanding of remarks made years later by Reed at the Shanghai Conference of 1877. See Covell, *W. A. P. Martin*, 105.

19. Covell, *W. A. P. Martin*, 90.

20. W. A. P. Martin, *A Cycle of Cathay: or China South and North with Personal Reminiscences,* 3rd ed. (New York: Revell, 1900), 193.

21. Kenneth Scott Latourette, *The Chinese, Their History and Culture,* 3rd ed. (New York: Macmillan Co., 1946), 352.

22. In a history of the Maryknoll Mission in China, Jean-Paul Wiest wrote of their French predecessors: "A series of treaties between 1844 and 1860 granted foreign missioners the right to reenter China and placed them and their converts under the protection of France. During the remainder of the century, the Catholic Church relied on the French civil and military representatives to obtain compensation for real as well as alleged wrongdoings. Hard feelings arose when missioners, eager for converts, accepted into the Church unsavory characters who had no religious convictions but wanted to stay beyond the reach of Chinese law." Jean-Paul Wiest, *Maryknoll in China: A History, 1918–1955* (Armonk, NY: M. E. Sharpe, 1988), 46.

23. Woh Cong-Eng, "The Man [McCartee] as an Oriental Christian Saw Him," in Speer, *A Missionary Pioneer,* 207–208.

24. Inslee, ltr. to BFM staff, 30 July 1858. See Bear, *History,* 2:26.

25. The other two large missionary societies were the London Missionary Society (LMS) and the American Board of Commissioners for Foreign Missions (ABCFM). Elijah Bridgman, *FM* 18 (1859): 125–126. The China Inland Mission (CIM), which was to become the largest Protestant mission in China, was not organized until 1865.

26. *HFR* 7 (1856): 57.

27. Ibid., 10 (1859): 106.

28. J. M. W. Farnham, "Historical Sketch of Shanghai Station," and Gilbert McIntosh, "Historical Sketch of the Presbyterian Mission Press," *Jubilee Papers,* 60, 112.

29. McIntosh, *Jubilee Papers,* 114.

30. *AR,* 1858, 87.

31. Ibid., 1857, 70.

32. *FM* 16 (1857): 326.

33. *HFR* 13 (1862): 113.

34. John L. Nevius, ltr. in *FM* 16 (1857): 185–186.

35. Ibid., 185–186. See discussion by Bear, *History,* 1:173–176.

36. Ibid., 187.

37. *HFR* 11 (1860): 41–42.

38. Bear, *History,* 1:257, 266–267.

39. Samuel Dodd, ltr. of 2 Nov. 1863, *FM* 23 (1864): 222 (emphasis in original).

40. Farnham, *Jubilee Papers,* 45.

41. Mrs. J. L. Nevius, ltr., *FM* 23 (1864): 14.

42. J. S. Roberts, ltr. of Jan. 1863, *FM* 22 (1863): 9.

43. The presbytery is the body composed of both ordained ministers and lay elders that has jurisdiction over the congregations in the district.

44. Henry V. Noyes, Stated Clerk of Canton Presbytery, handwritten manuscript (circa 1884 or 1885), PDH(Phil). The manuscript lists the first Chinese ministers of the presbytery as U-Sik-Kau, Kwan-Loy, and Lai-Po-Tsun. All three were ordained 22 Jan. 1884.

45. *HFR* 2 (1851): 181.

46. Presbytery minutes for 1851, 1852 and 1853 appear in *HFR* 5 (1854): 118. See discussion in Bear, *History,* 1:135.

47. Samuel Dodd to Walter Lowrie, 26 Jan. 1864, BSF (Incoming).

48. Bear, *History,* 1:287–290. The Presbytery of Shanghai was organized in 1861, and as in the case of Canton and Ningbo, its first members were all missionaries. The first two ordained ministers were Bau Tsih-dzae and Wang Vung-lan. Both came to Shanghai as employees of the mission press.

49. Hunter Corbett, "The American Presbyterian Mission in Shantung During Fifty Years: 1861–1911." (Pamphlet published by the APMP in Shanghai, circa 1914.)

50. Ibid., 2–3. *AR,* 1863, 36–37.

51. Corbett served fifty-seven years in China and was elected moderator of the PCUSA General Assembly. Mateer served forty-four years, and Nevius thirty-nine years. Corbett's first wife, Lizzie Culbertson, died after ten years in China. Corbett's second wife, Mary Nixon, died after thirteen years. His third wife, Harriet Sutherland, outlived him and retired from the field in 1922. Mateer's first wife, Julia Brown, died after thirty-four years; his second wife, Ada Haven, outlived him and retired in 1924. Nevius's wife, Helen Coan, suffered all her life from poor health but died in service after fifty-six years in China!

52. *AR,* 1862, 42.

53. Corbett, "American Presbyterian Mission in Shantung," 10.

54. Sources for the Taiping Rebellion: Eugene Powers Boardman, *Christian Influence upon the Ideology of the Taiping Rebellion 1851–1864* (Madison, WI: University of Wisconsin Press, 1952); Latourette, *History;* and Spence, *The Search for Modern China.* Jonathan D. Spence's *God's Chinese Son: The Taiping Heavenly Kingdom of Hong Xiuquan* (New York: W. W. Norton, 1996) was published after the completion of this chapter. Spence has some new archival sources and gives a fascinating account of previously unknown details of the movement. However, it does not substantially change the assessment given in this chapter.

55. The Historical Museum of the Taiping Heavenly Kingdom in Nanjing has numerous displays that call attention to the similarities between Communist ideology and Taiping practices. These include: common ownership of land, equality of the sexes, opposition to foreign rule, elimination of land taxes, etc. However no attention was given to the religious roots of the rebellion or the founder's use of the Christian scriptures.

56. The Hakkas ("guest people") originally came from north China and settled in the southern provinces centuries ago. They are fiercely independent and have preserved their distinctive cultural characteristics wherever they have migrated.

57. See P. Richard Bohr, "Liang Fa's Quest for Moral Power," in Barnett and Fairbank, eds., *Christianity in China: Early Protestant Missionary Writings,* 40–44.

58. Boardman, *Taiping Rebellion,* 12–13.

59. Nicknamed "Chinese Gordon," the general was one of the most colorful personalities of British colonial rule. A devout Christian, he banned all looting, prostitution, drunkenness and trading in opium throughout his command. He was fearless in battle and received the highest award from the Manchu government for his victory in suppressing the Taipings. He later served in Egypt and the Holy Land, where he was a patron for the excavation of the holy places. He died in the siege of Khartoum in 1885 when the British garrison was overrun by the forces of the Mahdi. For the exploits of Ward and Gordon see Spence, *To Change China,* 57–92.

60. Chesneaux, *China from the Opium Wars to the 1911 Revolution,* 125.

61. Latourette, *History,* 298.

62. Boardman, *Taiping Rebellion,* 114.

63. Covell, *W. A. P. Martin,* 82–88.

64. Speer, *A Missionary Pioneer in the Far East,* 117–124.

65. Farnham, *Jubilee Papers,* 48–49.

66. Boardman, *Taiping Rebellion,* 50; Latourette, *History,* 293–294.

67. Richards is quoted in Latourette, *History,* 301.

Chapter 4: To the Heart of the Empire

1. Sources used for the Restoration Period: Fairbank and Reischauer, *China: Tradition and Transformation*; Fairbank, *The Great Chinese Revolution: 1800–1985*; Chesneaux, *China from the Opium Wars to the 1911 Revolution*; Latourette, *History.*

2. *CHA* 19 (Feb. 1896): 144.

3. Paul A. Cohen, *China and Christianity: The Missionary Movement and the Growth of Chinese Anti-foreignism, 1860–1870* (Cambridge: Harvard University Press, 1963), 127–148, 275–281.

4. Arthur Judson Brown, *New Forces in Old China* (New York: Revell, 1904), 239.

5. Irwin T. Hyatt, Jr., *Our Ordered Lives Confess: Three Nineteenth-Century American Missionaries in East Shantung* (Cambridge: Harvard University Press, 1976), 151.

6. For a full account of the Miao incident, which profoundly affected Mateer's later relationship with American consuls and Chinese officials, see Hyatt, ibid., 153–157.

7. Hunt, *The Making of a Special Relationship*, 81.

8. The Geary Act "stripped Chinese in the United States, whether citizens or not, of substantial legal rights....Under the law any person of Chinese descent found in the United States was subject to imprisonment at hard labor followed by deportation unless the Chinese could produce positive proof of legal residence." Hunt, *The Making of a Special Relationship*, 94.

9. Ernest Trice Thompson, *Presbyterians in the South*, 3 vols. (Richmond: John Knox Press, 1973): 2:13–14.

10. Lowrie, letters to missions, 1861–1863, BSF (Outgoing).

11. Prior to 1861 China missionaries known to have been from southern states were: Rev. and Mrs. Thomas McBryde (South Carolina), Mrs. Clara Leete Hepburn (North Carolina), Rev. and Mrs. Richard Way (Georgia), Rev. John Quarterman (Georgia), Mrs. Isabella Moseley Kerr (Virginia), Rev. and Mrs. Joshua Danforth (Mississippi), and Rev. and Mrs. Elias Inslee (Mississippi).

12. Lowrie, letter to Siam mission, 11 Oct. 1862, BSF (Outgoing). One attempt was made to preserve the unity of the missionary effort during the war. See Cornelia K. Hudson, "Daniel McGilvary in Siam: Foreign Missions, the Civil War, and Presbyterian Unity," *AP* 69 (1991): 12.

13. Lowrie to Siam Mission, 14 Nov. 1863, BSF (Outgoing).

14. John C. B. Webster, "American Presbyterian Global Mission Policy: An Overview of 150 Years" in *AP* 65 (1987): 73.

15. Arthur Judson Brown, *One Hundred Years*, 1092.

16. For this important change in the *Missionary Manual*, see Andrew T. Roy, "Historical Overview of the Overseas Mission Policies of the UPCUSA" (Paper prepared for the General Assembly Mission Council, UPCUSA, 1977), 14.

17. Clifton J. Phillips, "The Student Volunteer Movement and Its Role in China Missions, 1886–1920," Fairbank, *The Missionary Enterprise in China and America*, 106.

18. Latourette, *History*, 406, 479.

19. All the deaths appear to be because of sickness. Most resignations were for health causes, but this included a wide range of afflictions including physical, mental and adjustment problems. Most of the transfers were due to the marriage of a single woman to a man of another mission. There were no retirements as the BFM required forty years of service before retirement benefits were given.

20. Statistics are from Brown, *One Hundred Years,* 1100–1110.

21. Kathleen L. Lodwick, "Women at the Hainan Presbyterian Mission: Ministry and Diversion," *AP* 65 (1987): 19.

22. "The Board will insist on language examinations for new missionaries....The more they resist, the more the Board will insist....Too many men and women have never gotten the language." Frank F. Ellinwood to B. C. Henry, 23 Dec. 1886, BSF (Outgoing).

23. The most prolific missionary writers were: Calvin Mateer, John G. Kerr, John L. Nevius, Michael Culbertson, Hampden DuBose, W. A. P. Martin, Anna Cunningham Safford, Mary West Niles, Samuel I. Woodbridge, and Henry Woods. See Alexander Wylie, *Memorials of Protestant Missionaries to the Chinese: Giving a list of their publications, and obituary notices of the Deceased, with copious indexes* (Shanghai: Presbyterian Mission Press, 1867; reprinted in Taipei, Taiwan by the Chengwen Publishing Co., 1967).

24. "Comity" was a formal agreement by which specific geographical areas were assigned to different denominations.

25. *Missionary Manual,* 1889, par. 38. The *Manual* is quoted by Webster, in his "American Presbyterian Global Mission Policy," *AP* 65 (1987): 74.

26. Latourette, *History,* 362.

27. Nanjing missionaries were rebuked for engaging in expenditures without Board approval. W. W. Eddy to John Butler, 23 Oct. 1883, BSF (Outgoing).

28. Ellingwood to Mateer, 13 July 1887, BSF (Outgoing). See also the revised *Missionary Manual* of 1888.

29. The Board expressed dismay over the scarcity of Chinese pastors in Nanjing after so many years of work (W. W. Eddy to George F. Fitch, 4 Mar. 1886, BSF [Outgoing] and concern over Corbett's control over unordained native helpers (John Gillespie to Hunter Corbett, 10 Nov. 1888, BSF [Outgoing]).

30. "There should be more supervision by the mission, less each working out his own plans" (John C. Lowrie to Calvin Mateer, 27 Aug. 1884, BSF [Outgoing]).

31. The Board modified its position recognizing "the propriety of consulting the missions before final action" was taken. See Brown, *One Hundred Years,* 80–82; *General Assembly Minutes,* 1891, 79.

32. Gillespie to Farnham, 6 Sept. 1887, BSF (Outgoing).

33. Covell, *W. A. P. Martin,* 69.

34. Happer attributed the lack of success in Canton to "strife within the mission." Ltrs. from Happer to Board Secretaries, 29 Nov. 1870 and 9 Apr. 1872, BSF (Incoming).

35. Statistics for Ningbo and Shanghai from "Summary of the Annual Reports of the Central China Mission of the PCUSA, for the year ending Sep. 30th, 1893," Archives, PDH(Phil).

36. Sources used for the opening of the Presbyterian Mission in Hangzhou: D. N. Lyon and J. H. Judson, "Historical Sketch of the Hangchow Station" in *Jubilee Papers;* Pauline Van Evera "A Historical Sketch of the American Presbyterian Mission, Hangchow, China" (Unpublished paper, 1936 Archives PDH[Phil]); Helen S. Coan Nevius, *Life of John Livingston Nevius,* 164ff.

37. Green's service in Hangzhou was short-lived. He returned with his family on furlough in 1869 and died of pneumonia as he was packing up for the return to China.

38. Van Evera, "Historical Sketch," 2.

39. McCartee ltr. to Board Secretary, 7 Aug. 1867, BSF (Incoming).

40. "Annual Report of the Central China Mission, 1893."

41. Albert B. Rawlinson, "Historical Sketch of the Missions in China," pamphlet in the Archives PDH(Phil).

42. G. F. Fitch, "Historical Sketch of Soochow Station," *Jubilee Papers,* 98–101.

43. *AR,* 1887, 134.

44. D. N. Lyon, "Riot at the Door," *CHA* 12 (1892): 122.

45. "Annual Report of the Central China Mission," 1893.

46. M. Geraldine Guinness, *The Story of the China Inland Mission,* 2 vols. (London: Morgan and Scott, 1900) 1:341–346.

47. Sources used in this section on Nanjing were: *Annual Reports;* Mrs. R. E. Abbey, "Historical Sketch of Nanking Station," *Jubilee Papers* 102–109; C. Leaman, "Presbyterian Mission Work in Nankin [sic]," *CR* 16 (1885); Emma Lane, "Fresh Glimpses of the Ancient City of Nanking" *WWW,* Feb. 1892, 39–41.

48. *AR,* 1884, 104.

49. "Annual Reports of the Central China Mission, 1893."

50. Lowrie to W. A. P Martin, 10 Sept. 1859, BSF (Outgoing).

51. Covell, *W. A. P. Martin,* 136.

52. *AR,* 1864, 37. The first Protestant missionary to initiate work in the city was Dr. William Lockhart of the London Missionary Society who arrived in 1860 as a medical officer of the British legation. Latourette, *History,* 364.

53. For a summary of the *Evidences,* see Covell, *W. A. P. Martin,* 108–125.

54. Covell, ibid., 1. For the extensive literature about Martin see: Covell, *W. A. P. Martin;* Covell's "The Legacy of W. A. P. Martin," *IBMR,* 17 (1993): 28–31; Jonathan Spence, "Martin and Fryer: Trimming the Lamps," in *To Change China: Western Advisors in China 1620–1960;* Peter Duus, "Science and Salvation in China: The Life of W. A. P. Martin (1827–1916)" in Kwang-Ching Liu, ed., *American Missionaries in China: Papers from Harvard Seminaries* (Cambridge: Harvard University East Asian Research Center, 1970); Mei-xiu Wang, "Chinese Religions in the Eyes of W. A. P. Martin with Regard to Christianity" (Beijing: Academy of Social Science, unpublished paper, 1993). Martin's books in English, *The Lore of Cathay* and *The Cycle of Cathay,* did as much as any writings of his day to present the "enigmatic" people of China to the West in a more favorable light. Martin died in Peking in 1916 at the age of eighty-nine. He was eulogized by the President of the new Republic of China whose message read: "The passing away of a figure which has been regarded by scholars of this country as the T'ai Mountain and the North Polar star, fills me with particular sorrow and grief." Covell, *W. A. P. Martin,* 266.

55. *AR,* 1893, 59.

56. Ibid., 1887, 131.

57. Sources used for the Peking hospital: The *Annual Reports;* "The 'An Ting' Hospital and Medical Mission in Peking," *CHA* 3 (1888): 183–186; "The Hospital at Peking," *CHA* 1 (1887): 172.

58. *MR* 33 (1882): 15.

59. *AR,* 1893, 59–60.

60. *AR,* 1895, 74.

61. W. M. Hayes, "Secrets of Success in Shantung," *CHA* 15 (1894): 122–123.

62. Brown, *One Hundred Years,* 281–283.

63. *AR,* 1893, 66.

64. Gilbert Reid, "The Shantung Mission — Its Progress and Promise," *CHA* 15 (1894): 118–119.

65. William P. Fenn, *Christian Higher Education in Changing China: 1880 — 1950* (Grand Rapids, MI: Eerdmans, 1976), 28.

66. Hyatt, *Our Ordered Lives Confess,* 164–165.

67. Fenn, *Christian Higher Education in China,* 28.

68. Hyatt, *Our Ordered Lives Confess,* 185.

69. Ibid., 170.

70. Daniel W. Fisher, *Calvin Wilson Mateer: Forty-five Years a Missionary in Shantung, China* (Philadelphia: Westminster Press, 1911), 233. Next to the Shandong College, Mateer's chief contribution was the Mandarin version of the Bible on which he worked for ten years. His passion was to do for the three hundred million people of North China who spoke Mandarin what Wycliffe had done for the people of England.

71. John Murray, "Tsinanfu Station in the Earlier Years" in Corbett, *The American Presbyterian Mission in Shantung,* 29–36.

72. Ibid., 14.

73. The property dispute is described by Hunt, *The Making of a Special Relationship,* 160, and by Philip West, "The Tsinan Property Disputes (1887–1891): Gentry Loss and Missionary Victory" in *Papers on China* (1970) Vol. 23. Hunt places considerable blame on Reid, who is described as having "neither the wisdom of the serpent nor the harmlessness

of a dove." The assessment is unfair. Later, Reid's relationships with Confucian scholars, the governor and Peking intelligentsia were cordial and effective. See *AR*, 1893, 64–65.

74. J. Neal, "The McIlvaine Hospital," *CHA* 17 (1895): 138.

75. *AR*, 1886, 137–138.

76. Fannie Wight, "The Luxuries of Itinerating," *CHA* 11 (1892): 548.

77. *AR*, 1894, 93–94.

78. See "The History and Work of Ichowfu Station" in Corbett, *The American Presbyterian Mission in Shantung,* 36–42. The six new missionaries assigned to Linyi were: Rev. and Mrs. C. A. Killie, Rev. and Mrs. W. O. Elterich, and Dr. and Mrs. C. F. Johnson.

79. *WWW*, Oct. 1893, 261–262; *AR*, 1894, 94–95.

80. References used in this section were: *Annual Reports;* and Corbett, *The American Presbyterian Mission in Shantung,* 14, 42–47.

81. Mr. Laughlin married Jennie Anderson after his first wife's death.

82. Mary Lane, "Our New Home in Chiningchow, China," *WWW,* Apr. 1893, 107–108.

83. Ibid., 107–108.

84. *AR*, 1894, 99–100.

85. Quoted in Helen Nevius, *The Life of John Livingston Nevius,* 381.

86. For the Nevius methods see: John L. Nevius, *Planting and Development of Missionary Churches,* 4th ed. (Grand Rapids, MI: Baker Book House, 1958); Charles Allen Clark, *The Nevius Plan of Mission Work in Korea* (Seoul, Korea: Christian Literature Society, 1937); G. Thompson Brown, "Why Has Christianity Grown Faster in Korea than in China?" *Missiology,* 22 (1994): 77–88; Everett Hunt, "The Legacy of John Livingston Nevius," *IBMR* 15 (July 1991): 124.

87. *AR*, 1889, 139.

88. *CR* May 1886, 201–202.

89. Henry Noyes, Stated Clerk, "The Presbytery of Canton, China," unpublished paper in Archives, circa 1890, PDH(Phil). Statistics for 1895 come from *AR,* 1895, 36–37.

90. Statistics are from *AR,* 1893, 32–34, and *AR,* 1894, 54–55.

91. B. C. Henry, "The Projection of the Christian College in China located at Canton" (Proposal for the BFM, Jan. 1885), 8–13.

92. For a brief sketch of the life of Dr. Andrew P. Happer see William Rankin, *Memorials of Foreign Missionaries* (Philadelphia: Presby. Board of Publication, 1895), 145ff.

93. *AR*, 1890, 43.

94. Ibid., 1889, 140–141.

95. Ibid., 1892, 35.

96. Gillespie to A. A. Fulton, Apr. 1889, BSF (Outgoing).

97. B. C. Henry, "Strategic Importance of Lien Chow," *CHA* 6 (1889): 244.

98. *CHA* 15 (1894): 114.

99. *AR*, 1891, 33.

100. Ibid., 1895, 35–36.

101. Principal sources for Hainan: *Fifty years in Hainan: American Presbyterian Mission 1881–1931* (Committee of the mission on the occasion of the 50th anniversary of its founding, *circa* 1931). For this description of Jeremiassen see p. 1. For the description of Hainan Island and other pioneers, see pp. 2–5.

102. *AR*, 1894, 65–66.

103. Ibid., 1894, 67–68.

Chapter 5: Along the Grand Canal

1. Extensive use has been made of James E. Bear, Jr., "The Mission Work of the Presbyterian Church in the United States in China, 1867–1952." The terms "Northern" (NPM) and "Southern" (SPM) Presbyterian Missions, although not technically correct, will be used for convenience and because this is how the two missions were distinguished in China.

2. Hampden C. DuBose, *Memoirs of Rev. John Leighton Wilson* (Richmond, VA: Presby. Committee of Publication, 1895), 247.

3. Thompson, *Presbyterians in the South,* 2:22–23.

4. Ibid., 2:23.

5. Wilson wrote a paper opposing the removal of the British squadron, which had been highly effective in deterring slave traders along the coast of West Africa, which may have come to the attention of Lord Palmerston and influenced his decision to strengthen the squadron. DuBose, *Memoirs of Rev. John Leighton Wilson,* 219–227.

6. Wilson inherited two slaves from his parents. He wrote that he "used every means, short of coercion, to induce them to go where they could safely accept their freedom." But they were opposed to leaving the place of their nativity, continued "in voluntary servitude" and were paid for their work. By marriage Wilson became the legal owner of thirty slaves. They were offered their freedom to go to the North or to Liberia. They chose Liberia and Wilson provided the expenses for them to emigrate. Ibid., 97–105.

7. S. H. Chester, *Behind the Scenes* (Austin, TX: Press of Von Boeckman-Jones, 1928), 11.

8. DuBose, *Memoirs of Rev. John Leighton Wilson,* 281–282.

9. In 1875 the office was transferred to Baltimore, which provided better financial facilities for the overseas work. In 1889 seemingly irreconcilable differences arose between the executive secretary (Dr. Houston) and members of the Executive Committee, all of whom resided in Baltimore. The General Assembly deemed the easiest way to solve the problem was to move the offices to another city! The move was made to Nashville, Tennessee, where it remained until all General Assembly agencies moved to Atlanta in 1973.

10. Samuel Isett Woodbridge, *Fifty Years in China* (Richmond, VA: Presby. Committee of Publication, 1919), 30–31.

11. For Inslee's life and work see Bear, *History,* 2:3–53.

12. *FM* 17 (1858): 185.

13. Bear, *History,* 2:45–49.

14. Ibid., 2:7–9.

15. Ibid., 2:53.

16. Eugenia Inslee, "Missionary Life in China Thirty Years Ago," *TM* 31 (1898): 281.

17. *TM* 1 (1868): 131.

18. Inslee, ltr. of 6 Aug. 1868, *TM* 1 (1868): 139.

19. Bear, *History,* 2:71–73.

20. Ibid., 2:99.

21. Dr. Wilson was completely vindicated by the General Assembly. Bear, *History* 2:107–112.

22. *TM* 4 (1871): 86; Bear, *History,* 2:84.

23. Eugenia Inslee, "Missionary Life," *TM* 31 (1898): 280.

24. Bear, *History,* 2:91.

25. P. Frank Price, *Our China Investment* (Nashville: Executive Committee of Foreign Missions, circa 1927), 165; P. Frank Price, "A Sturdy Path-Breaker," *PS* 32 (1942): 405.

26. Source for the early life of Mrs. Stuart is Mrs. Charles K. Hartwell, "Mobile to China: A Valiant Woman's Mission," in *The Alabama Review* 31 (1978): 243–255. Mary Horton Stuart served in China for fifty years, became known as "Mother Stuart" and is buried in Hangzhou. Note this tribute from a fellow missionary: "No ordinary words fit her.... She was a woman of unusual mental and social gifts. Her voice was such that she was advised to go to Germany for its training. She preferred however to come to China and teach the illiterate to sing 'Jesus Loves Me....' She seemed to never lose her temper or fail in kindness to a fellow missionary. There is no record on earth of all the lives she touched." Price, *Our China Investment,* 174.

27. W. Milne, quoted by Woodbridge, *Fifty Years in China,* 51.

28. Price, *Our China Investment,* 8–9.

29. "Bible woman" is the term used for the unordained Chinese woman who was given simple Christian instruction and employed as Bible teacher, visitor or evangelist.

30. After sixteen years as principal of the Girls' School in Hangzhou, Mrs. Randolph transferred to Japan, where she founded the Kinjo School for Girls in Nagoya.

31. Bear, *History*, 2:214.

32. Ibid., 2:200.

33. Nettie DuBose Junkin, ed., *For the Glory of God: Memoirs of Dr. and Mrs. H. C. DuBose* (Lewisburg, WV: Published by the children of Dr. and Mrs. DuBose, n.d.), 16.

34. Ibid., 17–18.

35. Bear, *History*, 2:190.

36. Ibid., 2:191.

37. Ibid., 2:205. Note Mrs. Stuart's tribute to this pioneer for women's causes: "Miss Safford was one of the most brilliant women I ever knew. Flashes of wit and humor sparkled from her lips, mingled with weighty thoughts and words of deepest pathos, interspersed with anecdotes and reminiscences of her varied life, thus making her one of the most delightful companions.... Being a woman of strong convictions and independent spirit, she early took the ground that single women in China should have homes of their own." *TM* 24 (1891): 102.

38. Bear, *History*, 2:194.

39. Ibid., 2:250.

40. Ibid.

41. Ibid., 2:279.

42. Ibid., 2:176.

43. Woodbridge, *Fifty Years in China*, 149; Bear, *History*, 2:176. See also S. I. Woodbridge, *A Short History of Chinkiang* (Chinkiang: Chinkiang Literary Association, 1898), 31–41.

44. Bear, *History*, 2:291.

45. From the minutes of the meeting, it is hard to say what the problem was. Bear believed it to have involved the appropriations for a residence. Bear, *History*, 2:302.

46. *TM* 22 (1889): 195–196.

47. Bear, *History*, 2:531.

48. Mrs. P. Frank Price, ltr. in *TM* 26 (1893): 134.

49. Extract from P. Frank Price, *The Opening of Sinchang* (pamphlet, 1894), 25–28. See Bear, *History*, 2:385.

50. Samuel Hall Chester, *Memories of Four-Score Years* (Richmond, VA: Presby. Committee of Publication, 1934), 145.

51. Bear, *History*, 2:477. Because of health reasons, Dr. and Mrs. Venable moved from Jiaxing to the hospital at Kuling where the climate was better. He had a reputation as a skillful physician, scholar and teacher of the Bible. From 1915 to 1917 he served as president of the China Medical Missionary Association. Price, *Our China Investment*, 43.

52. Waddy Hampton Hudson, Personal Report for 1896. See Bear, *History*, 2:447.

53. Note should be made of Lawrence D. Kessler's *The Jiangyin Mission Station: An American Missionary Community in China 1895–1951* (Chapel Hill: University of North Carolina Press, 1996). Unfortunately, this important addition to the SPM history in China had not been printed when this chapter was written. Dr. Kessler draws on a number of sources from the First Presbyterian Church in Wilmington and papers from the Charles W. Worth family.

54. Lacy L. Little, *"Rivershade": A Historical Sketch of Kiangyin Station, China* (pamphlet prepared by the Station, n.d.), 2.

55. Pauline DuBose was the daughter of H. C. DuBose, the veteran missionary of Suzhou. She died in Japan a year later and is buried in Yokohama. In 1900 Little married Ella Davidson, who had been assigned to the Girls' School in Hangzhou. She died in 1916. In 1919 Little married Nellie Sprunt, who came to China in 1911 to take charge of the Girls'

School in Huaiyin (TKP). Mr. Haden's first wife was Julia McGinnis, who came to China in 1893 with her mother, sister and brother. Julia died in less than a year and is buried in Shanghai. Haden's second wife, Eugenie Hilbold of France, was a missionary of the Methodist Mission. In 1908 she went to Switzerland for the education of the children. In 1917 Haden was on his way to join his family when his ship was torpedoed by a German submarine. Haden lost his life "endeavoring to save some Chinese passengers." Price, *Our China Investment*, 160, 166, 172.

56. Bear, *History,* 2:528.

57. Ibid., 2:291–292.

58. Liao Pin, ed., *The Grand Canal: An Odyssey* (Beijing: Foreign Language Press, 1987), 3.

59. *TM* 31 (1898): 458–460.

60. Huaiyin (Tsing-Kiang-Pu) was known in missionary parlance as "TKP." This designation has been used to help distinguish this city from two other mission stations with similar names: Huaian, which was ten miles further south on the Grand Canal, and Huayuan in Anhui Province.

61. *TM* 20 (1887): 70. George Duncan of the CIM was the first Protestant missionary to visit the city in 1859. Later several single women missionaries of the CIM arrived. Relations with the Presbyterians have been cordial. Guinness, *The Story of the China Inland Mission,* 1:383–384.

62. Richard Baxter Fishburne, M.D., arrived in 1881 and was assigned to Hangzhou, but resigned two years later.

63. Each of the three had sons and daughters who served as China missionaries: Josephine and Lily were daughters of Henry McKee and Josephine Underwood Woods; Mary (Mrs. Thomas Grafton) and Rev. Edgar A. Jr. were children of Edgar and Francis Woods; Agnes (Mrs. Thomas Harnsberger), James Baker Woods, Jr., and John Russell were children of James Baker, Sr., and Bessie Woods.

64. Crane, "PCUS Overseas Medical Missions," 99–100.

65. *AR,* 1894, xv.

66. Price, *Our China Investment,* 176.

67. In 1900 Junkin married Nettie DuBose, daughter of Hampden DuBose of Suzhou.

68. Henry Woods, ltr. spring of 1899, *TM* 32 (1899): 484.

69. *TM* 32 (1899): 361–362.

70. Ibid., 216.

71. Quoted in Bear, *History,* 2:534.

72. Dr. Houston's personal report for the years 1895 and 1896. See Bear, *History,* 2:428, 443.

73. Ibid.

74. For a fair presentation of Houston's "trial" before the Presbytery of Louisville, see Bear, *History,* 2:490–506.

75. Chester, *Behind the Scenes,* 25–26.

76. Bear, *History,* 2:562.

77. Ibid., 2:460.

Chapter 6: Toward a Common Witness

1. Latourette, *History,* 406.

2. In 1891 Miss Nannie McDannald of the SPM married J. C. Garritt of the NPM and was received into the northern mission. In 1896 Dr. Nettie Donaldson of the NPM married Rev. Mark Grier of the SPM and joined the southern mission. In 1899 Miss Anna Laurena Howe of the NPM married Rev. J. Y. McGinnis of the SPM and joined the Southern Presbyterians.

3. DuBose, *Memoirs of John Leighton Wilson,* 231.

4. Bear, *History,* 3:588.

5. Ibid., 2:586.

6. D. MacGillivray, ed., *A Century of Protestant Missions in China (1807–1907) being The Centenary Conference Historical Volume* (Shanghai: American Presbyterian Mission Press, 1907), 1.

7. The inclusion of the "Presbytery of Foochow" (Fuzhou) is strange as no PCUSA missionaries had labored there. The inclusion of Japan and Siam in the Synod of China is even stranger. The minutes of the PCUSA General Assembly list Japan as a presbytery of the Synod of China for a number of years but it sent no representatives and had it done so it would have been a disaster. The composition of the Synod of China seems to reflect more on the convenience of those keeping the records in New York than the political, geographic and cultural realities in Asia.

8. Samuel Dodd, Stated Clerk, "Statistics of Religion in the Synod of China for the Year 1873," unpublished paper, PDH(Phil).

9. *Minutes of the General Assembly, PCUSA,* 1897, 131.

10. Paul Berger, "Minutes of the Synod of North China, May 19–23, 1898," unpublished paper, PDH(Phil).

11. M. H. Houston, ltr. 23 July 1874 to J. L. Wilson, *TM* 7 (1874): 248–249. See discussion of the issue in Bear, *History,* 2:230–231.

12. *Minutes of the General Assembly (PCUS),* 1876, 299, 303.

13. *TM* 30 (1897): 544.

14. Ibid., 32 (1899): 316–317; see also Bear, *History,* 2:541.

15. Chinese synods were under the General Assembly of the PCUSA until 1906. During this period, the American General Assembly was the final arbiter of disputes involving Chinese culture and customs. For example, the issue of whether rice wine could be used for communion services in locations where grape wine was unknown or unobtainable was appealed to the PCUSA General Assembly. See *Minutes of the General Assembly (PCUSA), 1889,* 91.

16. Gibson is quoted in George A. Hood, *Mission Accomplished? The English Presbyterian Mission in Lingtung, South China* (Frankfurt am Main: Verlag Peter Lang, 1986), 140.

17. Ibid., 139–140.

18. D. MacGillivray, ed., *A Century of Protestant Missions in China (1807–1907),* 370.

19. Gerald F. De Jong, *The Reformed Church in China, 1842–1951* (Grand Rapids: Eerdmans, 1992), 62–77.

20. *TM* 8 (1875): 44–46; see also Bear, *History,* 2:242.

21. See Bear, *History,* 2:580–584 for text of the Plan of Union.

22. Bear, *History,* 3:309–314. Chwen Sheng succeeded Woodbridge as editor and was noted for his literary style and scholarship.

23. *Records of the General Conference of the Protestant Missionaries of China held at Shanghai, May 7–20, 1890* (Shanghai: American Presbyterian Mission Press, 1890).

24. Ibid., 625.

25. Ibid., 203–205.

26. John L. Nevius, "Historical Review of Missionary Methods," *Records of the General Conference,* 167–177.

27. *Records of the Conference,* lvi.

28. Ibid., lvii.

29. Ibid., 732–733. The column "Presbyterian" includes the eight Presbyterian and Reformed missions mentioned in the earlier part of this chapter.

30. Ibid., 1.

31. Latourette, *History,* 415.

Chapter 7: Advocates of Reform

1. *AR*, 1896, 43.
2. Ibid., 1895, 60.
3. Ibid., 1897, 76.
4. Ibid., 35.
5. See *Annual Reports* for 1896, 41, 78; and for 1899, 75.
6. *AR*, 1896, 51, 56.
7. Ibid., 1897, 74.
8. As in the case of the Taiping Rebellion, the Tonghak ("Eastern Learning") movement was an eclectic mixture of religious fanaticism and agrarian reforms. It combined certain features of Roman Catholicism with native Korean religions.
9. Immanuel C. Y. Hsu, "Late Ch'ing Foreign Relations" in *The Cambridge History of China*, 11:108.
10. Fairbank, *The United States and China*, 320–327, and Hunt, *The Making of a Special Relationship*, 152–154.
11. Hunt, *The Making of a Special Relationship*, 159.
12. Ibid., 162.
13. U.S. Consular Files for Chefoo (microfilm) 1866-1901, National Archives, Washington, DC.
14. Fowler, report dated 8 Mar. 1897, U.S. Consular Files for Chefoo.
15. Bear, *History*, 2:560–561. Northern Presbyterians took the same position. See Latourette, *History*, 499.
16. Hao Chang, "Intellectual Change and the Reform Movement, 1890–8," in *The Cambridge History of China*, 11:274–280.
17. Jessie G. Lutz, "Protestant Christian Education in China, 1850–1950" in *China Notes* 21 (1985): 363–367. See also Lutz, *China and the Christian Colleges, 1850–1950* (Ithaca: Cornell University Press, 1971).
18. "The Young Men's Christian Association in China" in D. MacGillivray, ed., *A Century of Protestant Missions in China, 1807–1907* (Shanghai: American Presbyterian Mission Press, 1907), 597–608.
19. Bear, *History*, 2:336.
20. "Letters from Mary Thompson Stevens to her mother from China, 1910–1919." Entry of 22 Nov. 1912.
21. *AR*, 1896, 52.
22. Paul Berger, "Minutes of the Synod of North China, May 19–23, 1898," unpublished paper in PDH(Phil).
23. Fairbank, *China: A New History*, 234.
24. Palmer C. DuBose, "Rev. Hampden C. DuBose and the Anti-Opium Movement in China" in *For the Glory of God*, edited by Nettie DuBose Junkin (Lewisburg, WV: Published by the children of Dr. and Mrs. DuBose, n.d.), 51.
25. Ibid., 56. Hampden DuBose was "in his day the most widely known missionary of the Southern Presbyterian Church in China and one of the picturesque figures of the missionary body" (Price, *Our China Investment*, 170). Chinese far and wide identified him as the commanding foreigner with the long flowing white beard who spoke their language with eloquence. He was a prodigious writer of sermons and biblical commentaries in Chinese. His books in English include *Preaching in Sinim* (1873) and *The Image, the Dragon, and the Demon* (1887). He was honored by the church at home by being elected moderator of the PCUS General Assembly in 1891 and by his congregation, the Yang Yoh Hang Church, where he preached for thirty-seven years, by the erection of a stone tablet, from which these words are translated: "Mr. DuBose was the first preacher of the Gospel who came to Soochow and opened a chapel.... [He] spared not himself in his work but was daily in the pulpit in cold or heat, preaching Jesus Christ as the only Way of life.... From this church have grown twelve churches in the country around Soochow.... He was called from the midst of his labors to

rest in his Heavenly Home on the 22nd day of March, 1910....We, the members of his church, will always remember him with love and thanksgiving." Ibid., 73–75.

26. Hao Chang, *The Cambridge History of China*, 11:278. See also Paul Bohr, *Famine in China and the Missionary: Timothy Richards as Relief Administrator and Advocate of National Reform, 1876–1884* (Cambridge, MA: Harvard University Press, 1972), 175.

27. "A Reform Club in China," *CHA* 19 (1896): 100.

28. Hao Chang, *The Cambridge History of China*, 11:278.

29. *AR*, 1899, 54.

30. DuBose, "Progress in China," *TM* 19 (1886): 56.

31. The rail line was completed to Baoding by 1900 and to Wuhan by 1907.

32. Amelia Lowrie was the widow of Reuben Lowrie, who died in Shanghai in 1860. She and her son, James, returned to China in 1883.

33. The *New York Sun* article is quoted in *AR*, 1895, 63.

34. Quoted by Charles E. Scott, "Tsingtao Station: Its Life and Work" in Corbett, *The American Presbyterian Mission in Shantung*, 47.

35. *AR*, 1900, 78.

36. Ibid., 1899, 71.

37. Scott, "Tsingtau Station: Its Life and Work," 48.

38. Dr. and Mrs. L. L. Moore, *TM* 33 (1900): 89–91.

39. *TM* 30 (1897): 121–122.

40. Quoted in Bear, *History*, 2:459.

41. This episode and others relating to the Griers and the opening of Xuzhou are from E. H. Hamilton, "Nettie Donaldson Grier: A Mender of Broken China" in Hallie Paxson Winsborough, ed., *Glorious Living* (Atlanta: Committee on Woman's Work, 1937), 35–36.

42. *TM* 39 (1906): 299.

43. Mary Thompson married Rev. George P. Stevens in 1912. Charlotte Thompson, the mother of the author, married Rev. Frank A. Brown in 1914.

44. *TM* 40 (1907): 229.

45. Catherine Williams, who married Dr. McFadyen in 1906, died in 1914; Rev. Mark Grier died in 1917; Mary Thompson Stevens in 1919. Missionary children who died in these early years were Linford Moore, who died of smallpox in 1900, Donaldson Grier of diphtheria in 1908 and Gertrude White of heat stroke in 1909.

46. Hao Chang, *The Cambridge History of China*, 11:288. See also Fairbank, *China: A New History*, 228.

47. *AR*, 1899, 54.

48. It was said that Emperor Guangxu was introduced to Western learning "under the indirect supervision of W. A. P. Martin." Kang Youwei "is said to have told a reporter in 1898 that he owed his conversion to reform chiefly to the writings of [Timothy] Richard and [Young J.] Allen." See Paul A. Cohen, "Christian Missions and Their Impact to 1900," *The Cambridge History of China*, 10:587–588.

49. The circumstances of the coup d'etat of 1898 are shrouded in mystery. Some of the unanswered questions: Was the dowager's coup precipitated by a plot on the part of the Emperor to have her assassinated? What was the role of Yuan Shikai, commander of the Tianjin garrison, without whose help the coup could not have taken place? Did he double-cross the Emperor when he turned his support to the dowager? See J. O. P. Bland and E. Backhouse, *China under the Empress Dowager: Being the History of the Life and Times of Tsu Hsi* (London: William Heinemann, 1910).

50. Statistics from *Annual Reports* for 1898, 1899, and Arthur J. Brown, *Report of a Visitation of China Missions, May 22–Sept. 19, 1901*, 3rd. ed. (New York: Board of Foreign Missions, 1902), 23.

51. Bear, *History*, 2:250.

52. Robert E. Speer, *Report on the China Missions of the Presbyterian Board of Foreign Missions*, 2nd ed. (New York: Board of Foreign Missions, 1897), and S. H. Chester, *Lights*

and Shadows of Mission Work in the Far East: Being the Record of Observations Made during a Visit to the Southern Presbyterian Mission in Japan, China and Korea in the Year 1897. (Richmond, VA: Presby. Committee on Publication, 1899).

53. Speer, *Report,* 62.

54. Ibid., 26, 28, 36, 63.

55. Quotation from Dr. Divie McCartee, Speer, *Report,* 29.

56. Ibid., 29, 37.

57. Ibid., 33.

58. Ibid., 32–35.

59. Ibid., 29–33.

60. Ibid., 40.

61. Ibid., 58.

62. Ibid., 62.

63. Chester, *Lights and Shadows,* 66–68.

64. Ibid., 126–129.

65. Ibid., 130.

66. Bear, *History,* 2:541–542, 565.

67. Chester, *Lights and Shadows,* 65–66.

68. Speer, *Report,* 22–23.

69. Ibid., 22.

70. Ibid., 24.

71. Ibid., *Report,* 24.

72. Rev. Mark Grier's letter of 20 Oct. 1906 to Dr. Chester describing the incident is worth noting: "This is a man fifty odd years of age, who took his second wife years before he became acquainted with the Gospel. He lives about sixty miles from this city. When our evangelists visited this place in their preaching tours, he became interested in the Gospel and as he is a man of some means, he came at intervals of several years to our station, remaining several weeks at a time, at his own expense, for the sole purpose of studying the Bible. He applied for baptism and was repeatedly refused on the ground of his polygamous relations.... Through all this time we were able to discover absolutely no unworthy motive in his desire to enter the church. Finally, not being able to justify myself, either on Scriptural or other grounds, either in compelling him to discard the woman he had taken, or in longer refusing him the rite of baptism, I did, with the approval of Mr. Grafton and Dr. McFadyen...administer the same." Bear, *History,* 3:477.

73. Ibid., 44–45.

74. Statistics for the Southern Presbyterian Mission are more difficult to evaluate. The most complete report is for the year 1895 and given at the end of Chapter 5.

Chapter 8: The Boxer Year

1. Sources used for the Boxer Uprising: Hsu, "Late Ch'ng foreign relations, 1866–1905" in *The Cambridge History of China,* 11:115–127; Spence, *The Search for Modern China,* 231–235; Bland and Blackhouse, *China Under the Empress Dowager;* Latourette, *A History of Christian Missions in China,* 501–526.

2. Joseph Esherick, *The Origins of the Boxer Uprising* (Berkeley: University of California Press, 1987), 299–300, quoted by Spence, *The Search for Modern China,* 232.

3. Charles Killie to BFM staff, 27 Mar. 1899, BSF (Incoming).

4. *AR,* 1900, 71.

5. John Fowler, dispatch of 23 Mar. 1900 to State Department, U.S Chefoo. Consular Files (Microfilm), National Archives, Washington, DC.

6. Fowler, dispatch to David H. Hill, Assistant Secretary of State, 9 Aug. 1900, Chefoo Consular Files.

7. George Cornwell, report to Consul Fowler, 29 June 1900, Chefoo Consular Files.

8. Frank Chalfant, report to Consul Fowler, 6 July 1900, Chefoo Consular Files. The BFM never mentioned the killing of the Chinese attacker in its public announcements of the incident. Chalfant defended his use of arms in a letter to the Board: "The revolver was just as much a part of the providential means of escape as the ladder on the front porch. Our forefathers went to church with their rifles." Chalfant, 18 Oct. 1990, BSF (Incoming).

9. The foreign embassies were clustered in what was called the "Legation Quarter," which had as its southern boundary the great wall of the city and defensible lines to the north, east, and west.

10. *AR*, 1901, 86–87.

11. Ethel Daniels Hubbard, *Under Marching Orders* (Young People's Missionary Movement, 1906), quoted by Tess Johnson and Deke Erh, *God and Country: Western Religious Architecture in Old China* (Hong Kong: Old China Hand Press, 1996), 33.

12. *AR*, 1901, 86–87. For a description of life within the legations during the siege, see Mrs. A. H. Mateer, *Siege Days* (New York: Fleming N. Revell, 1903).

13. J. Walter Lowrie, "The Story of Paotingfu," ltr. of 29 Oct. 1900; *AH*, 4–5 (1901): 61.

14. Arthur J. Brown, *Report of a Visitation of the China Missions, May 22–September 19, 1901*, 3rd ed. (New York: Board of Foreign Missions, 1902).

15. Ibid., 4.

16. Ibid., 2; Latourette, *History*, 514.

17. Hamilton, "Nettie Donaldson Grier," *Glorious Living*, 50–52.

18. W. O. Elterich to Board staff, 14 Nov. 1900, BSF (Incoming).

19. Brown, *Visitation of the China Missions*, 151. Brown cites the *Japan Weekly Mail*, Rev. D. Z. Sheffield of the ABCFM, and Bishop D. H. Moore to substantiate the charges of brutality. He quoted the *New York Times*: "Every outrage perpetrated on foreigners in China has been repaid tenfold by the brutalities perpetrated by the allied armies." He had a higher regard for the behavior of the American and Japanese troops. The Germans were the worst.

20. In 1908 the United States returned $10,000,000 of its share of the indemnity and waived payment of the remainder. The refund was designated for educating Chinese students in the United States.

21. This extract of the governor's letter is of interest: "You, reverend sirs, have been preaching in China for many years, and without exception, exhort men concerning righteousness.... You have been careful to see that Chinese law was observed." Brown, *Visitation of the China Missions*, 31.

22. Latourette, *History*, 512–513, 517.

23. *AR*, 1902, 78.

24. Grace Newton to BFM staff, 10 Sept. 1900, BSF (Incoming).

25. Brown, *Visitation of the China Missions*, 87.

26. *AR*, 1901, 109.

27. W. M. Hayes to A. J. Brown, 1 Aug. 1900, BSF (Incoming).

28. Estimate based on Brown, *Visitation of the China Missions*, 41–47. Replacement value would be higher. Figure includes personal losses by missionaries, although some declined to be reimbursed.

29. Latourette, *History*, 517.

30. *AR*, 1902, 78, 105.

31. Brown, *Visitation of the China Missions*, 79.

32. Ibid.

33. Stuart C. Miller, "Ends and Means: Missionary Justification of Force in Nineteenth Century China" in Fairbank, ed., *The Missionary Enterprise in China and America*, 273–282; and James Hevia, "Leaving a Brand on China: Missionary Discourse in the Wake of the Boxer Movement," *Modern China*, 18:3 (July 1992): 304–331.

34. Mark Twain's articles appear in *North American Review*, 172 (1901): 161–176 and 520–534.

35. Brown, *Visitation of the China Missions*, 32.

36. Ibid., 61.

37. Paul Bergen, to BFM staff, 26 Dec. 1900, BSF (Incoming).

38. Brown, *Visitation of the China Missions*, 8.

39. *AR*, 1902, 84. Latourette wrote that Lowrie "saved hundreds of lives from the vengeance of the punitive expedition." *History*, 520.

40. Brown, *Visitation of the China Missions*, 33–35.

41. Ibid., 39–59.

42. Ibid., 47, 49.

43. Ibid., 158.

44. Ibid., 70.

45. Ibid., 73–74.

46. Ibid., 80–89.

47. Ibid., 126. Mr. H. B. Gordon, a professional architect, arrived in 1902 to supervise the building program.

48. W. O. Elterich to Board staff, 24 May 1901, BSF (Incoming).

Chapter 9: A Dying Dynasty: A New Beginning

1. Latourette, *History*, 527.

2. Miner Searle Bates, "The Protestant Endeavor in Chinese Society, 1890–1950" (Ms. in the Day Mission Library, Yale University), Series II (1890–1906) 13–214, 13. Bates's source is the *Treaty Series* of the Maritime Customs, 1:557. Professor Bates was engaged in a major research and writing project when he died unexpectedly in 1978, leaving his papers somewhat in disarray. File designations are not consistent. Page numbers are not always used. See Melville O. Williams and Cynthia McLean, *Gleanings from the Manuscripts of M. Searle Bates* (New York: China Program, NCC, 1984).

3. See Chuzo Ichiko, "Political and Institutional Reforms, 1901–11" in *Cambridge History of China*, vol. 11; Jean Chesneaux et al., *China from the Opium Wars to the 1911 Revolution*, Chapter 10; and Jonathan D. Spence, *The Search for Modern China*, Chapter 11.

4. Ichiko, *Cambridge History of China*, 11:379.

5. Chesneaux, *China from the Opium Wars to the 1911 Revolution*, 351.

6. Puyi emerged briefly as the figurehead for Japan's puppet state of Manchukuo. He was arrested and tried by the Communist government, served a prison term and then was reinstated as a private citizen. Note Columbia Pictures film *The Last Emperor*, and the biography with the same name by Edward Behr (New York: Bantam Books, 1987). Puyi tells his own story in *From Emperor to Citizen* (Peking: Foreign Language Press, 1964).

7. Latourette, *History*, 665–666; MacGillivray, ed., *A Century of Protestant Missions in China, 1807–1907*.

8. Latourette, *History*, 619.

9. *Annual Reports* for these years.

10. For Mid-China statistics, see Bear, *History*, 3:291(a) and 305; for North Jiangsu, see Bear, *History*, 3:390, 419(a), 446, 473.

11. Rev. J. L. Whiting and Dr. Guy W. Hamilton, M.D., moved to Shunde early in the year and began the arduous task of property purchasing and house building. They encountered no opposition. Later in the year they were joined by their wives. Hamilton wrote that he "made a formal call upon the first local officials to pay our respects and inform him of our intentions. He received us kindly.... The next day His Excellency, carried in his sedan chair by four liveried bearers, and attended by quite a retinue of underlings, made us a return visit" (*AR*, 1905, 109). Preaching was begun in the street chapel. Dr. Hamilton began medical work in the dispensary and made country trips. Dr. Louise M. Keator, M.D., arrived the next year. The Fifth Avenue Church of New York City provided the funds for the opening

of the station. A gift from Mrs. Hugh O'Neil of New York of $20,000 provided funds for the construction of both the hospitals for men and women.

12. Yixian was an important city on a rail line that carried coal from nearby mines to the Grand Canal. Rev. and Mrs. C. H. Yerkes and Dr. and Mrs. W. R. Cunningham, M.D., were the pioneers. Medical work was begun in 1906, a day school in 1907, a women's training institute in 1913 and an industrial school in 1914.

13. Statistics from the PCUSA *Annual Reports* list thirty-nine ordained ministers in 1901, and only forty a decade later in 1911.

14. R. E. Speer, communication to missions, June 1894, BSF (Outgoing).

15. R .E. Speer to W. M. Hayes, 20 Sept. 1895, BSF (Outgoing).

16. Bear, *History,* 3:99.

17. Ibid., 3:101.

18. Ibid., 3:99. Professor Lawrence D. Kessler of the University of North Carolina pays tribute to this advance: "Within a decade, among the nine major American Protestant churches, the Southern Presbyterians ranked first, on a per member basis, both in number of missionaries ... and in the amount of support for foreign missions." "A Helping Hand — Southern Presbyterians in Republican China" in *American Asian Review,* Summer 1991.

19. Bear, *History,* 3:101. Initially, the movement met with some resistance on the part of the mission boards. See Chester, "The Laymen's Missionary Movement" in *Behind the Scenes.* See also Ostrom, ed. *The Modern Crusade: Addresses and Proceedings of the First General Convention of the Laymen's Missionary Movement* (Athens, GA: Laymen's Missionary Movement, 1909).

20. *The Central China Mission, PCUSA, Reports for 1912–13,* 14.

21. See *Brief Historical Sketch of the Work of the Presbyterian Church of America in Hunan Province, China* (Hankow: The Religious Tract Society, circa 1936); PCUSA *Hunan Mission Station Reports, Mission Minutes* and BFM *Annual Reports.*

22. Ross Terrill, *Mao: A Biography* (New York: Harper, 1981), 7.

23. Mrs. Doolittle had served with her husband, Rev. Justus Doolittle, with the ABCFM in Fuzhou and with the PCUSA in Shanghai until her husband's death. She was later reappointed by the BFM. For Justus Doolittle's distinguished career in Christian literature see Susan Wilson Barnett, "Justus Doolittle at Foochow: Christian Values in the Treaty Ports" in Barnett and Fairbank, eds., *Christianity in China: Early Protestant Missionary Writings.*

24. Leila Doolittle resigned from the mission in 1903 to marry Mr. Berkin of the Kuling Sanatorium.

25. *AR,* 1909, 83–84.

26. Ibid., 1903, 89; 1905, 92.

27. *Hunan Mission Minutes,* 1911, 9.

28. *AR,* 1904, 84.

29. Ibid., 1911, 124.

30. Ibid., 1907, 140.

31. A. A. Fulton to BFM staff, 12 Apr. 1900, BSF (Incoming).

32. *AR,* 1906, 45.

33. Ibid., 1904, 46.

34. A. A. Fulton, "The Mighty Problem and the Grand Opportunities in China," *AH,* 13 (1907): 70.

35. *AR,* 1904, 44.

36. Statistics from the *Annual Reports* for these years.

37. *AR,* 1902, 44; 1911, 93–95.

38. Ibid., 1911, 94.

39. Ibid., 1903, 52; 1911, 95–96.

40. Ibid., 1906, 57–58.

41. Ibid., 1904, 53.

42. Ibid., 1905, 55.

43. Ibid., 1911, 103.

44. Ibid., 1912, 141; 1917, 186.

45. E. C. Machle to BFM staff, 3 Feb 1904, BSF (Incoming).

46. Arthur J. Brown, *The Lien-Chou Martyrdom,* pamphlet (New York: BFM, PCUSA, circa 1905).

47. Ibid., 11.

48. The report of the commission placed the responsibility for the deaths of the missionaries on the Chinese officials who did not act promptly enough in disbursing the mob. It also cited as a contributory cause Dr. Machle "interference with the native ceremony" and the most unfortunate discovery of the anatomical specimens. Indirect causes cited were the general anti-foreign sentiments in South China, the hostility to Americans because of the ill treatment of Chinese in the United States, the purchase of land by the missionaries in the interior and their erection of foreign style buildings. See Brown, *The Lien-chou Martyrdom,* 12. Also ltr. of H. V. Noyes to staff, 12 Dec. 1905, BSF (Incoming).

49. A. J. Brown correspondence for 22, 23 Nov. 1905, BSF (Incoming) and *AR,* 1907, 151–152.

50. Dr. Machle returned for a short time to visit the grave of his wife and daughter. Later he was reassigned to the hospital in Canton and probably never returned to Lianzhou.

51. These statistics, probably nothing more than rough estimates, are taken from *AR,* 1905, 60.

52. Sources for this section: Central China and Kiangan Mission reports; *Kiangan Mission Minutes,* 1909 and 1911; Dubois S. Morris, "The New Station in Central China Mission," *AH,* 9 (1903): 105–107.

53. The first Roman Catholic priest arrived in 1909 — a French Jesuit with whom the Presbyterians established very cordial relationships. *AR,* 1909, 97.

54. Morris, "The New Station," 107.

55. *AR,* 1909, 95.

56. Ibid., 1911, 140.

57. The name was taken from the first syllables of the two provinces "Kiangsu" and "Anhui."

58. *AR,* 1912, 163. See also the pamphlet "Lowrie Institute, Shanghai, China" (Shanghai: PCUSA Mission Press, circa 1916).

59. George F. Fitch served an incredible fifty-two years in China from 1870 to 1923. He died in Shanghai 17 Feb. 1923. He was the patriarch of a remarkable "missionary dynasty" of four generations. One son, Robert, served as president of Hangzhou Christian College. Another son, George, was with the YMCA. One daughter, Mary, came as a medical missionary, served briefly in Suzhou and then married Dr. Frederick J. Tooker, who "took her" to Hunan. Another daughter, Jeanette, married Rev. Asher Raymond Kepler who was the architect behind the united Church of Christ in China. Two of Asher and Jeanette's sons served in China: Raymond in Hunan and Kenneth in Shandong, and later with the SPM in Taiwan. One daughter of Kenneth Kepler, Mary Kay, is presently serving with her husband, Rev. S. Franklin Sapp, as a Presbyterian missionary in Japan.

60. *AR,* 1899, 48.

61. Ibid., 1908, 48.

62. Ibid., 1909, 52.

63. Ibid., 1903, 70.

64. *Half Our Burden: A Statement and An Appeal through its Executive Committee of Foreign Missions to the Southern Presbyterian Church* (Shanghai: Commercial Press, 1915).

65. In Bear, *History,* 3:94.

66. In ibid., 3:97.

67. In ibid., 3:92.

68. Annie L. Montgomery, "Beginning of Mission Work in Hwaianfu," pamphlet (Nashville: ECFM, n.d.).

69. Williams, *In China,* 65.

70. In Bear, *History,* 3:483.

71. Ibid., 3:483–486; Williams, *In China,* 69.

72. C. N. Caldwell, "The Opening of Taichow," *BMB* 1 (1906): 137.

73. Williams, *In China,* 66.

74. Why the transfer? I have often wondered, but the minutes give no hint of the reason. Could it have been because of his interest in Charlotte Thompson, my mother, who had recently arrived in Xuzhou, and whom he married in 1914?

75. Bear, *History,* 3:480–483; statistics are from Williams, *In China,* 67.

76. Williams, *In China,* 72.

77. Rev. Chen Gying-yung, Professor of Bible Study and History, and Mr. Chen Deh-gwang, Instructor of Music. Bear, *History,* 3:323.

78. "…it is a very significant fact that not one of those who last year graduated from our Mission institutions has as yet decided to give his life to the Christian ministry." J. Leighton Stuart, *BMB* 4 (1910): 49.

79. Bear, *History,* 3:315, 319, 324. See also Frank Wilson Price, *History of Nanjing Theological Seminary, 1911–1961,* mimeographed paper (New York: Board of Founders of Nanking Theological Seminary, 1961). This seminary is not to be confused with the Nanjing Union Theological Seminary, which included a number of other denominations and was established in the 1950s.

80. For the Amoy Plan see Chapter 6 above, "Toward a Common Witness."

81. *Minutes of the General Assembly, PCUS,* 1905, 35–36. For Bear's discussion of the action of the Assembly, see his *History,* 3:351.

82. *BMB* 1 (1906): 60.

83. Bear, *History,* 3:355–356.

84. *BMB* 1 (1906): 56.

85. The "five provinces" of the synod were: Jiangsu, Zhejiang, Hubei, and Henan. The inclusion of Hubei and Henan, where there was no Presbyterian work, was an open invitation for others to join. For PCUSA General Assembly actions approving the separation of the synod from the mother church in America see *Minutes of the General Assembly* 1906, 102, and 1908, 172. See also Garritt, "The Formation of the Union Synod," *BMB* 1 (1906): 86–87. See also *AR,* 1907, 45.

86. Bear, *History,* 3:351, 362–364.

87. "Showers of Blessing in the Chinese Empire," *AH,* 16 (1910): 86–87; J. Leighton Stuart, "Memorable Meetings at Nanking," *BMB* 3 (1908): 200–204.

88. Bear, *History,* 3:231.

89. P. Frank Price, *TM* 42 (1909): 402.

90. "Showers of Blessing," *AH,* 16 (1910): 87–88.

91. Ibid., 88.

Chapter 10: Revolution and War Lords

1. Major source for this account of the revolution: Spence, *The Search for Modern China,* 262–299.

2. R. G. Tiedemann, "The Persistence of Banditry: Incidents in Border Districts of the North China Plain," *Modern China* 8 (1982): 398.

3. Marshall Broomhall, *General Feng: A Good Soldier of Christ Jesus* (London: CIM, 1923); Latourette, *History,* 777–779.

4. Fairbank, *China: A New History,* 260.

5. Quoted in Wang Weifan, "The Word Was Here Made Flesh," lecture at the conference *China and Culture: A Sino-American Dialogue,* Columbia Theological Seminary, 23–25 Oct. 1992, 5.

6. Timothy T. Lew, "Chinese Renaissance — the Christian Opportunity," *CR* 52 (1921): 301–323; Bear, *History*, 4:12.

7. Latourette, *History*, 781–782; Spence, *The Search for Modern China*, 292.

8. Yang Yongyi, "U.S. 'Missionary Mind Set' Impact on the 1911 Revolution," *Beijing Review*, 27 (1988): 32–34. Mr. Yang is staff member of the Foreign Affairs Bureau, National People's Congress.

9. Quoted in Bates, "The Protestant Endeavor in Chinese Society," Series III (1907–1922), 120–1058, 3.

10. George F. Fitch, *AH*, 18 (1912): 26–27.

11. Spence, *The Search for Modern China*, 282.

12. Hunt, *The Making of a Special Relationship*, 293.

13. Fairbank, *China: A New History*, 261.

14. *BMB* 10 (1914): 466–467; Bear, *History*, 4:322.

15. Bear, *History*, 5:293.

16. *AR*, 1921, 127–128.

17. O. V. Armstrong, "Marshall Feng Yu Hsiang a Guest in our home," unpublished MSS, 1932, courtesy of Oscar Armstrong, Jr.

18. *AR*, 1915, 109–110.

19. C. Houston Patterson, *From the Boxer Rebellion to Pearl Harbor: My China That Was* (Harrisonburg, VA: privately printed, 1990), 36.

20. The author's conversation with Mrs. Nell Allison Sheldon, who remembers the incident as a child. See also Lacy L. Little, *"Rivershade": A Historical Sketch of Kiangyin Station*, 55–57. See also Kessler, *The Jiangyin Mission Station*, 58–62.

21. Hunt, *The Making of a Special Relationship*, 293; Daniel H. Bays, "Missions and Christians in Modern China, 1850–1950" (Address at the Northwest Regional China Council symposium "American Missionaries and Social Change," Linfield College, July 1994), 8.

22. Examples: river pirates attacked Presbyterian missionaries traveling from Canton to Lianzhou in 1922 (*AR*, 1922, 29); the Ledong mission compound was occupied by Cantonese troops in 1924 (*Hainan Newsletter*, Summer 1925, 19–20); a furious battle was fought around the mission compound at Huaiyin (TKP) in 1925 (Nelson Bell, ltr. of 10 Nov. 1925; Bear, *History*, 5:22).

23. Latourette, *History*, 815–816.

24. *Monthly Cycle of Prayer for China Missions of the PCUSA* (Shanghai: APMP, 1926).

25. Figures are from the 1910 *Annual Report* and the 1926 *Cycle of Prayer*. Wherever possible separate assignments for both husbands and wives are shown. Where there is no separate assignment for the wife, she is given the assignment of her husband. "Affiliate" and "Corresponding" missionary appointments are not included. The figures for "theological/leadership training" are deceptively low. Institutions for formal theological training were few but most ordained missionaries were engaged in some form of leadership development. The "Other" column includes administrators, secretaries, printers, architects, those engaged in language study and those whose assignments are not listed.

26. The China Council and its chairman, J. W. Lowrie, repeatedly warned against the transfer of missionaries from evangelistic to educational work and the costly support of too many colleges. See China Council Minutes (CC), 1912, 4; 1916, 75; 1918, 13.

27. PCUS *Annual Reports* for 1912 and 1927, supplemented by data from James Bear's *History* for the years 1911–1927.

28. *AR*, 1924, 45.

29. CC, 1912, 71; 1913, 46; 1914, 18; 1915, 19; 1923, 101.

30. CC, 1913, 5.

31. North Jiangsu Mission, *Half Our Burden: A Statement and an Appeal* (Shanghai: Commercial Press, 1915), 1.

32. CC, 1913, 55; 1914, 4. For work of the Korean church in Shandong see Charles

Allen Clark, *The Nevius Plan of Mission Work in Korea* (Seoul: Christian Literature Society, 1937), 176–179.

33. Bear, *History,* 5:415–418. North Jiangsu's reluctance to approve the council plan was probably because of an inherent distrust of any centralized decision-making body, and concern that the Mid China Mission's cooperation in union projects had resulted in dangerous doctrinal compromises. Also, with only two missions, instead of eight, there was not the same degree of compulsion.

34. Mary Thompson Stevens, "Some New Work of Yours," *MS* 9 (1919): 232. Tragically, Mrs. Stevens died in childbirth in 1919 shortly after moving to the new location and Mr. Stevens took his two young children back to the United States but returned later.

35. *Mateer Memorial Institute Catalogue, 1920–21; Shandong Mission Minutes,* 1923, 1924.

36. Thomas F. Carter, "Station Report for Nanhsuchow," *Another Year in Changing China, Kiangan Mission, 1913,* 52.

37. The Kiangan Mission opened a small station at Shouzhou (Showchow) fifty miles southwest of Huayuan on the Hwai River in 1919. Rev. and Mrs. Maxwell Chapin and Miss Mary Fine began the work, which initially consisted of a chapel and school. In 1926 a small eighteen-bed hospital treated thirty-four hundred patients. *AR,* 1927, 59.

38. Also stationed in Shanghai were Dr. and Mrs. Henry Woods, who moved here to edit a conservative Bible encyclopedia, based on James Orr's *International Standard Bible Encyclopedia.* This work was begun in 1918 and published in 1925.

39. This listing is given by Bear, *History,* 5:333.

40. Mary Margaret Moninger, ed., *The Isle of Palms: Sketches of Hainan, The American Presbyterian Mission on the Island of Hainan* (Shanghai: Commercial Press, 1919; reprinted, New York: Garland Press, 1980), Appendix D.

41. Hainan Presbyterian Mission, *Fifty Years in Hainan,* 13.

42. Moninger, *Isle of Palms,* 71; *Fifty Years in Hainan,* 12–13.

43. *Hainan Newsletter, American Presby. Church,* Sept. 1912, 1.

44. *Hainan Newsletter,* Dec. 1914, 6.

45. George D. Byers, *Hainan Newsletter,* June 1921, 13–14.

46. Hainan Presbyterian Mission, *Fifty Years in Hainan,* 18–19.

47. George D. Byers, *Hainan Newsletter,* Nov. 1919, 9.

48. Quoted in Moninger, *Isle of Palms,* 83–84.

49. *Hainan Mission Minutes,* 1925, 9. See *Hainan Newsletter,* Summer 1924, for a full account of Byers's death and obituary.

50. Hainan Mission asked the American consul to help secure an indemnity for Mrs. Byers. The China Council was ambiguous in its support of the mission's request, and noted that "it is the policy of the Board because of its effect upon the work to seek no indemnity for loss of life nor to encourage such steps by individuals concerned." But the Council reminded the BFM that this policy "lays a special responsibility upon the board to assure in some manner a reasonable support" for Mrs. Byers and her four children, all under the age of twelve. Ultimately an indemnity of US $10,000 was paid by the general then in control of the island to the bereaved family. See *Hainan Mission Minutes,* 1925, 9–10, 14–15; 1926, 1; CC, 1924, 111–112; Latourette, *History,* 818.

51. George Byers, *Hainan Newsletter,* Mar. 1919, 3.

52. For Mr. Gilman's obituary and tribute see *Hainan Newsletter,* Mar. 1919, 1–3. Mrs. Gilman died on furlough in 1917.

53. Quoted by Margaret Moninger, *Hainan Newsletter,* Summer 1926, 10. Note also in this issue the article by Dr. McCandliss, "Medical Experiences during 40 Years in China," 4–10.

54. Katherine L. Schaeffer, "Mrs. McCandliss: An Appreciation by a Co-Worker," *Hainan Newsletter,* Summer 1926, 13–14. Three of the four children of Dr. and Mrs. Mc-

Candliss returned to China as missionaries: Dr. W. K. McCandliss of Yangjiang, Mrs. Herbert Judson of Lianzhou, and Dr. R. J. McCandliss of Canton.

55. *Hainan Newsletter,* Autumn 1933, 1. Mrs. Melrose's son, Paul, returned to the land of his birth in 1916 with his wife, Esther, and served on the island until it was occupied by the Communist armies in 1951. Marie Melrose, daughter of Paul and Esther, continued the missionary tradition of parents and grandparents by serving as a missionary to Korea and an Amity Foundation English teacher in China.

56. *AR,* 1928, 42.

57. Ralph C. Wells, "Those Furthest Two Dots on the Map of China," *Yunnan Mission Station Reports,* 1932–1933, 39.

58. Brown, *One Hundred Years,* 966.

59. Ibid.

60. Yunnan Mission, PCUSA, "The Beginnings of the Yunnan Mission," MSS extracted from the First Annual Report of the Mission, PDH(Phil).

61. Arthur Romig, ltr. to author, 8 June 1995.

62. *Yunnan Mission Station Reports,* 1927, 16.

63. Ibid., 1927, 21–22, 24.

64. Ibid., 1927, 18.

65. Ibid., 4.

66. Ibid., 1929–1930, 18.

67. For description of missionary life and work in Yunnan, see Arthur and Helen Romig, *To Bend and Rise as the Bamboo: Letters from China. 1931–42* (Albuquerque, NM: Franklin Press Masters, 1992).

68. *Yunnan Mission Station Reports,* 1932, 2.

69. Ibid., 1932, 5–6. Rev. Arthur Romig wrote of his experiences in similar activities: "I participated a few times in cleaning a home of the spirits which were, in my estimation, the elements of Nature Worship which had to be placated in order to rid themselves of the fear that dominated their lives. A whole household, not just an individual became Christian" (Ltr. to author, 8 June 1995).

70. Wells, "Those Furthest Two Dots on the Map of China," *Yunnan Mission Station Reports,* 1932–1933, 41.

71. Romig, *To Bend and Rise as the Bamboo,* 37–39.

72. *Yunnan Mission Station Reports,* 1933–1934, 9.

73. For the controversy, see Bear, *History,* 4:390–402, 5:366–386.

74. *Princeton Theological Review,* Oct. 1921. The basis for Dr. Thomas's charge was a series of lectures Dr. Stuart had given at a YWCA conference explaining the basic Christian beliefs in God, Christ, the Holy Spirit and the Bible using language that would be understood by Chinese intellectuals. The controversy concerning Dr. Stuart's teachings became so intense that he requested a "trial" by his home presbytery (East Hanover in Virginia), which gave him a unanimous vote of confidence. The *Presbytery of the South* editorialized in its 29 Sept. 1926 issue: "No man has had his views on theology more carefully gone into by a Presbytery...and no man ever more fully convinced a Presbytery of his holding the faith held by the Southern Presbyterian Church." For Dr. Stuart's response to the charges, see his autobiography, *Fifty Years in China: The Memoirs of John Leighton Stuart, Missionary and Ambassador* (New York: Random House, 1954), 45–48.

75. Latourette, *History,* 796.

76. *Minutes of the General Assembly, PCUSA,* 1922, Part III, ix; and 1924, Part II, vii.

77. *Minutes of the General Assembly PCUS,* 1921, 53; Bear, *History,* 5:362.

78. This summary follows the analysis of Dr. Bear in his *History,* 4:390–402; 5:366–386.

79. The controversy was intensified by the Rev. Hugh White of the North Jiangsu Mission who, in the words of Dr. James Bear, acted as a self-appointed "champion of orthodoxy" and waged an attack not only on the Nanjing Seminary but on colleagues and the

Executive Committee through writings circulated through influential members of the church back home. See Bear, *History,* 5:380–385.

80. Bear, *History,* 5:354; CC, 1924, 74.

81. Ibid., 4:398.

82. *Shandong Mission Minutes,* 1919, 6.

83. Ibid., 1921, 29; 1919, 47.

84. Ibid., 1919, 59.

85. Ibid., 1920, xii.

86. Dr. B. C. Patterson has this account of the matter in his *Autobiographical Notes* (Montreat: Historical Foundation, 1952), 51–52: "Union was in the air. The Northern Presbyterians had a going school of their own, fine men teaching. When Dr. Brown of the Northern Presbyterian Board came to China he forced the Mission into a union in a great university, with complete medical and full theological schools as two of its departments. The missionaries warned him against the Canadian mixed church and the English Baptists, but he was determined to accomplish this great, good thing.... He put Dr. W. M. Hayes, one of the greatest educators in China, in to teach. It was not long till he [Dr. Hayes] taught one thing and they taught the contrary. He resigned and seven Northern Presbyterian students resigned also. He went back to his old station ... opened a class in the basement of a dwelling, and carried on.... Dr. Hayes consulted with us, and Mr. Stevens and I persuaded the North Jiangsu Mission to unite in this seminary work."

87. *Tenghsien Station Report,* 1923, 14; *AR,* 1923, 23.

88. *Shandong Mission Minutes,* 1924, 62.

89. Ibid., 1924, 61.

90. CC, 1923, 80.

91. Presbyterian Church of Christ in China, *Minutes of the Council, First Meeting Including Act of Union,* 1907, 8.

92. Bear, *History,* 4:434.

93. Wallace Merwin, *Adventure in Unity: The Church of Christ in China* (Grand Rapids, MI: Eerdmans, 1974), 33.

94. Ibid., 54–55.

95. Ibid., 69.

96. Ibid., 214.

97. Rev. Martin Hopkins, who opposed the union, gives his reasons in *The Presbyterian Survey,* 19 (1928): 90. Rev. P. Frank Price, who favored the union, responds in his article in *The Presbyterian Survey,* 19 (1928): 310.

98. Bear, *History,* 5:404.

99. Merwin, *Adventure in Unity,* 63.

100. The ecumenical vision of the Methodists was for a world Methodist union rather than a union with other Protestants in a national Chinese church. Bishop Bashford, who consistently opposed the union, wrote: "I depreciate encouragement of the Chinese to form entirely independent Chinese churches. The New Testament ideal is not national churches but world-wide churches" (Bates, "The Protestant Endeavor in Chinese Society," Series III [1907–1922] 122–1089, 8). The bishop was not entirely successful in his opposition as the South Fujian Conference of the Methodist Episcopal Church did in later years become a part of the CCC. Merwin, *Adventure in Unity,* 36–37.

101. Merwin, *Adventure in Unity,* 67.

102. The term "occupation" was severely criticized as denoting a military occupation of China by foreign forces.

103. Merwin, *Adventure in Unity,* 27.

104. Bates, "The Protestant Endeavor in Chinese Society," Series III (1907–1922), 120–1058, 36.

105. *The Chinese Church as Revealed in the National Christian Conference held in Shang-*

hai, May 1922. Report of Commission I, L. H. Roots, Chairman (Shanghai: Oriental Press, 1922).

106. Ibid., 82, 89.

107. Ibid., 95. In some ways the large number of Protestant missionary societies is misleading. Over 95 percent of the missionaries were supported by the largest fifteen societies.

108. Ibid., 95, 101.

109. Ibid., 112, 116.

110. Ibid., 124.

111. Ibid., 173–183.

112. Ibid., 184–198.

113. Ibid., 198–204.

114. An example: The culture of "Chinatown, San Francisco" is not the same as that of native China or America. A third or "Chinatown" culture has emerged.

115. John Espey, *Minor Heresies* (New York: Alfred Knopf, 1945).

116. Ibid., 4, 66.

117. Kathleen L. Lodwick, *Educating the Women of Hainan: The Career of Margaret Moninger in China, 1915–1942* (Lexington: University Press of Kentucky, 1995), 4.

118. Ibid., 2.

119. Ibid., 157.

120. E. H. Hamilton, 1988 Questionnaire.

121. All quotations except as noted from Terrill E. Lautz, *"Shantung Girl," Elisabeth Luce Moore: A Spoken History* (Hastings-on-Hudson, NY: privately printed, 1989), 5–16. By permission.

122. Ralph G. Martin, *Henry and Claire: An Intimate Portrait of the Luces* (New York: G. P. Putnam and Sons, 1991), 42.

Chapter 11: Healing, Mending, Caring

1. For a listing of all hospitals, medical schools and related institutions, see Appendix A.

2. Rockefeller Foundation, China Medical Commission, *Medicine in China* (New York: Rockefeller Foundation, 1914), 54.

3. Ibid., 113.

4. Ibid., 65.

5. PCUSA and PCUS Statistical Reports for the year 1927.

6. *Weihsien Hospital Report*, 1920, 21.

7. Sophie Montgomery Crane, *PCUS Overseas Medical Missions*, unpublished MSS, 1993, 20.

8. CC, 1921, 21.

9. Crane, *PCUS Overseas Medical Missions*. See also her article "A Century of PCUS Medical Mission, 1881–1983," *AP* 65 (1987): 135–146.

10. Crane, *PCUS Overseas Medical Missions*, 25, 48.

11. Ibid., 26.

12. Ibid., 18.

13. Ibid.

14. In ibid., 36, 142. See also Randolph Shields, "Medical Education in China," *PS* 26 (1936): 465.

15. Brown, *One Hundred Years*, 370; see also *AR*, 1912, 218.

16. Brown, *One Hundred Years*, 369.

17. Crane, *PCUS Overseas Medical Missions*, 7.

18. *Temple Hill Hospital*, Report for 1925.

19. China Medical Commission, *Medicine in China*, 66–67.

20. Crane, *PCUS Overseas Medical Missions*, 105.

21. Ibid., 60–61. The quote is from Philip B. Price, a letter to the "Embryo Medical Missionary" titled "What to Expect."

22. Annie Houston Patterson, Wade Hampton Venable, James Baker Woods, Sr., George C. Worth, Nettie Donaldson Grier, John W. Bradley, Jane Varenia Lee. Ibid., 50.

23. R. W. Dunlap (eighteen years), Herman Bryan (forty-two years), F. E. Dilley (thirty years), Francis Brewer (seven years). See *Temple Hill Hospital,* Report for 1925.

24. Crane, *PCUS Overseas Medical Missions,* 9.

25. China Medical Commission, *Medicine in China,* 70–71.

26. Crane, *PCUS Overseas Medical Missions,* 9.

27. Ibid., 31–32.

28. Latourette, *History,* 460.

29. Crane, *PCUS Overseas Medical Missions,* 8.

30. *Temple Hill Hospital,* Report for 1922, 34–35. Figures are approximate based on exchange rate of $1.00 (U.S.) equal $2.00 (Mex).

31. *AR,* 1905, 92.

32. *Weihsien Station Report,* 1921, 25.

33. Frank A. Brown, "The Preaching Missionary Looks at the Medical Missionary," *PS* 23 (1933): 479.

34. E. H. Hamilton, "Nettie Donaldson Grier, M.D.: A Mender of Broken China" in *Glorious Living,* 82–83.

35. J. Y. McGinnis, *Annual Report of the Kashing Hospital,* Apr. 1923–Apr. 1924, 8.

36. Brown, "The Preaching Missionary Looks at the Medical Missionary," 479.

37. Brown, *One Hundred Years,* 364.

38. Dr. Kerr was one of the foremost medical missionary pioneers of China. At his death his colleagues paid him a high tribute: "No man in all that empire, and perhaps no medical missionary in any mission field had accomplished so great a professional work as Dr. Kerr. One hundred and fifty well-instructed Chinese physicians were among the results of his labors.... He was a man of decided evangelistic interests and labored from the beginning to the end, always embracing opportunities for proclaiming the Gospel." *AR,* 1902, 40.

39. *The John G. Kerr Hospital for the Insane,* Reports for the Years 1918–1921 (Canton: Wai Hing Printing Co., 1921), 4–5.

40. Ibid., 3.

41. Ibid., 7, 9, 15.

42. Brown, *One Hundred Days,* 364. A second psychiatric service was started in 1911 by Dr. James R. Wilkinson at the Southern Presbyterian Elizabeth Blake Hospital in Suzhou. Crane, *PCUS Overseas Medical Missions,* 72. See also Bear, *History,* 3:235–243.

43. *AR,* 1902, 46.

44. Ibid., 1903, 55.

45. Ibid., 1909, 157.

46. Others who served at Hackett: Physicians: Miriam Bell, Joseph Harvey, James F. Karcher, Theodore Stevenson, Chester Lawson. Nurses: Chloe B. Rauch, Anita M. Jones, Rena Westra, Mary Bischoff.

47. Bulletin of the David Gregg Hospital for Women and Children, Hackett Medical College for Women, Julia Turner School of Nursing, Canton, 1929, 14.

48. *Ming Sum School for the Blind,* 50th Anniversary Report, 1889–1939 (Hong Kong: Standard Press, 1939), 13.

49. Heng You, "Alice Carpenter and the Chinese Ming Sum School for the Blind," *AP* 58 (Winter 1990): 259.

50. Ibid., 261.

51. *Ming Sum School for the Blind,* 50th Anniversary Report, 14.

52. The work of Alice Carpenter at Ming Sum is told by Ms. Heng You, a graduate student at Temple University, Philadelphia. Her research led her to question the association of missionaries with the concept of "imperialistic culture," which had been advanced by

American historian Arthur Schlesinger, Jr.: "Looking at her (Alice Carpenter) life and values, I arrived at a different conclusion." See Carpenter, "Alice Carpenter and the Chinese Ming Sum School for the Blind," 259.

53. *Ming Sum School for the Blind,* 50th Anniversary Report, 11.

54. Brown, *One Hundred Years,* 371.

55. Sara Entrican, *The Story of the Chifu [Chefoo] School,* pamphlet (Trenton, NJ: The Silent Worker, n.d.), 18.

56. Ibid., 7–8.

57. Ibid., 28.

58. Brown, *One Hundred Years,* 371–372.

59. *Chefoo Station Annual Reports,* 1922, 18; 1924, 16.

60. Ibid., 1931, 15.

61. *Chefoo, China, American Presbyterian Mission,* "Impressions and Experiences, 1927–1928" (pamphlet), 11.

62. *Chefoo Station Annual Reports,* 1924, 15; 1931, 15.

63. Ibid., 1937, 9.

64. For the history of PUMC see Mary Brown Bullock, *An American Transplant: The Rockefeller Foundation & Peking Union Medical College* (Berkeley: University of California Press, 1980).

65. Schools that formed the new union medical college: The Union Medical College of Shandong, The East China Medical School in Nanjing, The Hankou Medical College, and the Union Medical College of Peking which had sold its property to the Peking Union Medical College. In 1923 the North China Union Medical College for Women became a part of the Cheeloo union.

66. Crane, *PCUS Overseas Medical Missions,* 148–149.

67. Randolph Tucker Shields, "Medical Missions in China," *International Review of Missions,* 33 (1944): 290–291. See also *Training Christian Physicians for China: Shantung Christian University,* pamphlet (New York: Willard Price Co., circa 1924).

68. Crane, *PCUS Overseas Medical Missions,* 150, 152.

69. Shantung Christian University, *Bulletin of the School of Medicine,* 1930, University Bulletin No. 80.

70. Crane, *PCUS Overseas Medical Missions,* 157.

71. Shields, "Medical Missions in China," 291. Other Presbyterian physicians who served on the School of Medicine faculty were: Samuel Cochran, Arabella Gault, Theodore Greene, L. F. Heimburger, Lalla Iverson, Paul Laube, Philip B. Price, Thornton Stearns, Annie V. Scott, Susan Waddell, Martha Wylie, James Young, Rosa Bell (R.N.), Octavia Price (R.N.).

72. John C. Pollock, *A Foreign Devil in China: The Story of Dr. L. Nelson Bell, an American Surgeon in China* (Minneapolis: World Wide Publications, 1971), 43, 57.

73. Crane, *PCUS Overseas Medical Missions,* 102.

74. Ibid., 102; Bear, *History,* 5:253.

75. Bear, *History,* 4:252.

76. Pollock, *A Foreign Devil in China,* 72.

77. Ibid., 121–122; Bear, *History,* 4:291.

78. Pollock, *A Foreign Devil in China,* 123.

79. The primary research on kala azar was done at the Peking Union Medical College, which worked in close association with mission hospitals in north Jiangsu — primarily Xuzhou and Huaiyin (TKP) where field work and treatment was done. For the story behind the exciting research done to track down this elusive disease, see Mary Brown Bullock, *A Foreign Transplant,* 120–125.

80. Crane, *PCUS Overseas Medical Missions,* 106.

81. Pollock, *A Foreign Devil in China,* 117.

82. Theodore Chase Greene, *A Medical Mission in China: The Douw Hospital and its Work, 1926–1931,* mimeographed MSS, edited by Joan Swift Greene Smith, 1989.

83. Shields, "Medical Missions in China," 290.

84. Bullock, *An American Transplant,* 115.

85. Shields, "Medical Missions in China," 290.

Chapter 12: Teaching, Training, Schooling

1. I. L. Roots, ed., *The Chinese Church as Revealed in the National Christian Conference, Shanghai: 1922,* 112–113. William P. Fenn gives much higher figures: "By 1920 Protestants and Catholics could claim a combined total of more than a million students." *Christian Higher Education in Changing China, 1880–1950* (Grand Rapids, MI: Eerdmans, 1976), 41.

2. CC, 1925, Statistical Report; *AR,* 1927, 139.

3. Roots, *The Chinese Church as Revealed in the National Christian Conference,* 113; Fenn, *Christian Higher Education in Changing China,* 77.

4. Robert E. Speer and Hugh T. Kerr, *Report on Japan and China of the Deputation Sent by the BFM, PCUSA to Visit These Fields* (New York: Board of Foreign Missions, 1927), 343.

5. "One of the most unfortunate signs of the times is the practical shutting out of consistent Christian men from all government schools: the worship of Confucius therein being a compulsory law." *BMB* 1 (1905): 83.

6. Brown, *One Hundred Years,* 339.

7. By the 1930s, 90 percent of the cost of the primary schools, 74 percent of the middle schools and 33 percent of the college expense was provided by the Chinese constituency. Brown, *One Hundred Years,* 358.

8. *BMB* 3 (1908): 114.

9. The story is told by two graduates of the Yuanjiawa school: Peter Hu, "The Church in My Village," unpublished paper, 1985; Hu Shiu Ying, correspondence with F. A. Brown, 21 Apr. 1957.

10. North Jiangsu Mission, *Half our Burden,* 31.

11. *BMB* 3 (1908): 114.

12. CC, 1914, 10, 10.

13. *Central China Mission Station Reports,* 1916, 29; 1919, 19.

14. Ibid., 1921–1922, 34.

15. Ibid., 1922–1923, 42; 1923–1924, 11; 1927–1928, 14.

16. Fenn, *Christian Higher Education in Changing China,* 112.

17. Ibid., 84–100.

18. Bear, *History,* 4:36.

19. When the universities were nationalized by the PRC the name was changed to the United Board for Christian Higher Education in Asia. Fenn, *Christian Higher Education in Changing China,* 68.

20. Ibid., 158.

21. Northern Presbyterians supported the following schools: Hangzhou Christian College, Nanjing University, Ginling College for Women, Shandong Christian University and Yenching University. Lingnan University in Canton chose to remain under its own independent board in New York rather than join the United Board but retained strong relationships with the PCUSA board because of the Hackett Medical College, which became a part of Lingnan. The Southern Presbyterians supported Hangzhou Christian College and the Medical College of Shandong Christian University.

22. Fenn, *Christian Higher Education in Changing China,* 35.

23. Clarence B. Day, *Hangchow University: A Brief History* (New York: United Board for Christian Colleges in China, 1955).

24. "Hangchow Christian College," pamphlet (New York: Board of Trustees, 1924).

25. Department of Agricultural Economics, *The 1931 Flood in China* (Nanking: University of Nanjing, 1932), 41.

26. *University of Nanking, Report of the President,* 1919 (Shanghai: APMP, 1919), 82.

27. Ibid., 1919, 155.

28. Ibid., 1918, 3.

29. Fenn, *Christian Higher Education in Changing China,* 67, 70, 94.

30. Ibid., 46–50, 79–82.

31. Henry Winters Luce had been instrumental in raising funds for the move of the Dengzhou College to Weixian. Again he was one of the prime movers for the relocation of the college to Jinan. He resigned from the vice presidency of the Shandong College in 1917 because of policy differences with the president, J. Percy Bruce. See B. A. Garside, *One Increasing Purpose: The Life of Henry Winters Luce* (New York: Fleming H. Revell, 1948).

32. Yu-ming Shaw, *An American Missionary in China: John Leighton Stuart and Chinese-American Relations* (Cambridge, MA: Harvard University Press, 1992), 50.

33. Ibid., 55.

34. Ibid., 90–91. Nevertheless, the percentage of Christian students declined from 88 percent in 1924 to 32 percent in 1935. Bullock, *An American Transplant,* 116.

35. Dr. Wu, a prominent scholar and educator, resigned as chancellor after a few years because he felt he was only a figurehead. Stuart's biographer, Yu-ming Shaw, believes that Stuart was reluctant to give up authority. Shaw, *An American Missionary in China,* 60–64. But see also John Leighton Stuart, *Fifty Years in China* (New York: Random House, 1954), 49–81.

36. CC, 1912, 4; 1917, 6. Dr. Speer estimated that 31 percent of the Board's appropriations to China went for education. This probably did not include salaries. *Report on Japan and China,* 401.

37. CC, 1917, 11.

38. *A Monthly Cycle of Prayer for the China Missions,* 1926.

39. CC, 1918, 15.

40. CC, 1923, 104.

41. Xu Yi Hua, "Religion and Education: St. John's University as an Evangelizing Agency," Abstract, Ph.D. Dissertation, Princeton University, 1994. English was the mode of instruction at St. Johns. The criticism is not as applicable to the other colleges where Chinese was used.

42. Christian Literature Society, "Education for Service in the Christian Church in China, 1935," Survey report, PDH(Phil).

43. Brown, *One Hundred Years,* 358.

44. Fenn, *Christian Higher Education in Changing China,* 134.

45. United Board for Christian Higher Education in Asia, *New Horizons* (newsletter), 63 (Fall 1995/6): 5.

46. *The New York Times,* 29 Apr. 1987.

47. The questionnaire was mailed to twenty-six members of the Hangzhou Alumni Association in the U.S. Six were returned as being unknown or deceased. Eight carefully prepared responses were received.

Chapter 13: Crisis and Recovery

1. *AR,* 1928, 11.

2. Latourette, *History,* 821.

3. Sources used in this section: Spence, *The Search for Modern China,* 334–365; "Republican China, 1912–1949," in *The Cambridge History of China,* 12:527–720, 13: 116–167.

4. Chiang was baptized in a Methodist church in October 1930. How genuine was his conversion? Missionaries who knew him well believe his Christian faith was sincere. See Frank W. Price, *China: Twilight or Dawn* (New York: Friendship Press, 1948), 80–84.

5. Eliza Lancaster, ltr. to family, Shanghai, 28 Mar. 1927.

6. Lewis Lancaster, ltr. to friends, on board the S.S. *President Pierce,* 20 Apr. 1927.

7. Dr. John E. Williams, Vice-president of the University, had been shot by a soldier while crossing the street from the university to his home. The tribute to him by the University of Nanking Board reads as follows: The Board puts on record "its deep sense of the far-reaching value of Doctor Williams's services to the University — of his vital share in the conception of this union missionary undertaking, of his wise counsel, devoted sacrifices, and contagious optimism." Board Minutes 284, 1927, PDH(Phil).

8. Pearl S. Buck, ltr. to friends, Unzen, Japan, 13 Apr. 1927, PDH(Phil).

9. Professor Horace G. Robson, "Report of Investigation to the University of Nanjing Board," New York, 23 Apr. 1927, PDH(Phil).

10. Bear, *History,* 5:237.

11. Ibid., 5:270.

12. Ibid., 5:296.

13. Ruth Bracken, MCD, 3 May 1927; Bear, *History,* 5:316–317; Hamilton, *Glorious Living,* 88.

14. BFM Circular, 22 Sept. 1927; Reports from CC, 1927, and *AR,* 1928; Bear, *History, passim.*

15. Lloyd E. Eastman, "Nationalist China during the Nanking Decade 1927–1937," *Cambridge History of China,* 13:116.

16. Chesneaux, *China from the 1911 Revolution to Liberation,* 187.

17. R. G. Tiedemann, "The Persistence of Banditry: Incidents in Border Districts of the North China Plain," 419.

18. Frank A. Brown, "Memo. of Visit to Xuzhou," May 1927; F. A. Brown Papers, PDH(Mont).

19. Rev. Wang Heng Hsin, ltr. to Suchowfu Station, 14 Sept. 1928; F. A. Brown Papers PDH(Mont).

20. Bates, "The Protestant Endeavor in Chinese Society," III (1907–1922) 122–1089, 17.

21. *AR,* 1929, 71–72.

22. *New York Times,* 10 Nov. 1931. The source of the account was a Chinese girl who escaped and told her story to the missionaries. See also Edward Grant, "John W. Vinson — Another Name on the Roll Call of Faith," *Presbyterian Survey,* 22 (1932): 77.

23. E. H. Hamilton, *Afraid? Of What? A Book of Poems* (Hong Kong: Cathay Press, 1960), 5.

24. *AR(PCUS),* 1946, 86.

25. Brown, *One Hundred Years,* 1094.

26. William Ernest Hocking, ed., *Re-Thinking Missions: A Laymen's Inquiry after One Hundred Years* (New York: Harpers, 1932).

27. Lefferts A. Loetscher, *The Broadening Church: A Study of Theological Issues in the Presbyterian Church since 1869* (Philadelphia: University of Pennsylvania Press, 1954), 149.

28. In Loetscher, *The Broadening Church,* 150, 179; for the PCUS response see "Statement of the Executive Committee of Foreign Missions," *Christian Observer,* 28 Dec. 1932.

29. Pearl Sydenstricker grew up at the Southern Presbyterian Mission station at Zhenjiang. She returned to China as a missionary under the PCUS and taught in the Zhenjiang girls' school. In 1917 she married Lossing Buck, a PCUSA agricultural missionary in northern Anhui. She moved to her husband's station and became a member of the PCUSA mission. Her travels with her husband in the rural areas of northern China opened up a whole new world of discovery — the Chinese peasant. In 1920 the Bucks were transferred to Nanjing University with Lossing assigned to the Agricultural College and Pearl to the Department of English Literature. Their first child was retarded and Pearl began to write, feeling "it wise to

plunge into some form of mental effort" that would leave no time for her to think of herself. First came *East Wind: West Wind*. Then in 1931 the best seller *The Good Earth*. In 1934 she filed for divorce from Lossing Buck, married her publisher, Richard J. Walsh, and continued her meteoric career as a novelist. Although critical of the mission enterprise, the Board and her fellow missionaries, she never lost the conviction that there was something in Christianity worth taking to the nations. The great majority of her fellow missionaries rejected her unorthodox views on mission but undoubtedly read her novels. Her unique contribution to the China mission was that she changed the way Americans thought about the Chinese people. She humanized them. In *The Good Earth* the Chinese peasant had come alive. See Pearl S. Buck, *My Several Worlds: A Personal Record* (New York: The John Day Company, 1954); Dean K. Thompson, "Pearl Buck: Novels of Missionary Life" in *Go Therefore: 150 Years of Presbyterians in Global Mission* (Atlanta: General Assembly Mission Board, 1987); Charles Silver, "Pearl Buck, Evangelism and Works of Love" in *AP* 51 (Summer 1973); *The Several Worlds of Pearl S. Buck: Essays Presented at a "Centennial Symposium, Randolph-Macon Woman's College 26–28* Mar. 1992 (Westport, CT: Greenwood Press, 1994).

30. CC, 1933, 159.

31. John K. Fairbank, "The Chinese Revolution and American Missions," *China Notes* 11 (Autumn 1973): 41.

32. Leighton Stuart, "Open Letter in Regard to the Student Movement," circa 1919. PDH(Mont).

33. Chow Tse-tsung, *The May Fourth Movement: Intellectual Revolution in Modern China* (Stanford, CA: Stanford University Press, 1960), 323. See also Latourette, *History*, 696.

34. Fenn, *Christian Higher Education in Changing China*, 85.

35. James E. Bear, ltr. to friends, Shanghai, 12 May 1929, J. E. Bear Papers, Union Theological Seminary in Virginia Library.

36. *Shandong Mission Minutes*, 1925, 89.

37. CC, 1925, 86.

38. Mid-China Mission, *Report of Evaluation Committee*, circa 1930, F. A. Brown Papers, PDH(Mont).

39. R. E. Speer and H. T. Kerr, *Report on Japan and China of the Deputation Sent by the Board of Foreign Missions* (New York: Board of Foreign Missions, 1927), 405–406; Brown, *One Hundred Years*, 364.

40. Timothy Tingfang Lew, "Some of the Factors, Dangers and Problems in the Christian Missionary Enterprise in China Today through Chinese Eyes" (Address at the 34th Annual Session, Foreign Mission Conference of North America, Atlantic City, Jan. 1927).

41. Leung Siu Choh, "How May the Missions and Missionaries Best Serve the Chinese Church at the Present Time?" Paper presented at the Missionary Conference, Canton, Mar. 1925 PDH(Phil).

42. Ibid.

43. Janet E. Heininger, "Private Positions Versus Public Policy: Chinese Devolution and the American Experience in East Asia," *Diplomatic History* 6 (Summer 1982): 287.

44. *AR*, 1929, 25.

45. Speer and Kerr, *Report*, 215, 222.

46. Andrew Roy, *Never a Dull Moment: A Memoir of Family, China, and Hong Kong* (Beijing: Elissandra Roy, Home Publisher, n.d.), 28.

47. Speer and Kerr, *Report*, 287.

48. Ibid., 286–287.

49. Ibid., 288. Speer compares the figures for China with those of Japan, with 99 self-supporting churches, and Korea with 547. He cites the "old, much antagonized but apparently indestructible ideas of the Nevius Plan," which had been largely rejected in China but followed in Korea.

50. Bear, *History*, 5:444.

51. Mid China Mission, *Report of the Evaluation Committee*, 6.

52. Bear, *History*, 5:453.

53. "The Cooperative Plan — Suchowfu Hsieh Chu Hwei," 24 Oct. 1928, F. A. Brown Papers, PDH(Mont); Bear, *History*, 5:454.

54. Bear, *History*, 5:513.

55. Speer and Kerr, *Report*, 381; ltr. from Mrs. J. R. Lingle, Changsha Fuxiang Girls' School, 11 Mar. 1927, PDH(Phil).

56. Brown, *One Hundred Years*, 353–354.

57. The Central China Mission position: "We approve of the principle of government registration but we believe that registration should be deferred until the government becomes more established and until regulations are such as to make it possible to register the schools and at the same time maintain their truly Christian character." *Central China Mission Minutes*, 1927, 40.

58. In Shandong most schools applied for registration but the decision was left up to each station. *Shandong Mission Minutes*, 1932, 56; 1933, 46–50.

59. This policy was followed by a number of schools including Hangzhou Union Girls' School, Ningbo Middle Boys' School, Nanjing Ming Deh Girls' School, Xuzhou Boys' and Girls' Schools.

60. John D. Wells Boys' School in Xiangtan and the John Miller School in Changde were closed after protracted negotiations and strikes. The North Jiangsu Mission closed most of its schools.

61. Statistical tables, PCUSA and PCUS Minutes, 1927 and 1931.

62. Quoted by Bates, "The Protestant Endeavor in Chinese Society," III (1922–1937) 122–1088.

63. James C. Thomson, *While China Faced West: American Reformers in Nationalist China: 1928–1937* (Cambridge: Harvard University Press, 1969), 160.

64. *Hunan Mission Minutes*, 1930, 25.

65. *Kiangan Mission Minutes*, 1930, 29.

66. *North China Mission Minutes*, 1931, 22.

67. *Kiangan Mission Minutes*, 1937, 36.

68. Price, *History of Nanjing Theological Seminary*, 19.

69. Mid China Mission, *Report of Evaluation Committee*, 2; Statistical Tables, *AR (PCUS)*, 1937.

70. Statistical Tables, PCUS *Annual Report*, 1937.

71. Thomson, *While China Faced West*, 7.

72. CC, 1920, 3; 1923, 112.

73. Ernestine Van Buren, ed., *The Marguerite Mizell Story* (Dallas: First Presbyterian Church, 1987); Wang Weifan, conversation with author, October 1995.

74. Frank Wilson Price, *The Rural Church in China: A Survey* (New York: Agricultural Missions, 1948), 60, 61.

75. Price, *History of the Nanking Theological Seminary*, 22–23.

76. Price, *The Rural Church in China*, 1–35.

77. Ibid., 221.

78. Ibid., 18.

79. "Wenzhou Revisited," *Bridge*, 40 (Mar.–Apr. 1990): 4–14.

80. Bays, "Missions and Christianity in Modern China," 13.

81. In the year 1926 there were 116 PCUSA ordained ministers serving in China and 100 ordained ministers associated with the work of the various missions. In the year 1938 the number of ordained missionaries had dropped to 79 and the number of Chinese ministers had risen to 163. PCUS statistics are similar.

82. Elizabeth Minter, "A Tale of Two Texans in China" (Paper presented to the Presbyterian Historical Society of the Southwest, 1992), 4.

83. Statistical tables in the *AR* for these years.

Chapter 14: Under Fire

1. Sources used: Spence, *The Search for Modern China*, 410–483; Akira Iriye, "Japanese Aggression and China's International Position"; and Lloyd E. Eastman, "Nationalist China during the Sino-Japanese War," *Cambridge History of China*, 13:492–608.

2. The decision to open the dikes was bitterly criticized by subsequent historians. "The flood wrought even more devastation upon the Chinese populace than upon the Japanese." *Cambridge History of China*, 13:555.

3. Ibid., 13:556.

4. L. Nelson Bell, ltr. dated 1 Nov. 1937 (*China News Bulletin* No. 13, ECFM, 26 Nov. 1937).

5. *North China Mission Minutes*, 1938, 42.

6. Bill and Jessie Junkin, *Bits of China from the Life of Nettie DuBose Junkin* (Tazewell, VA, privately printed, 1986), 33.

7. Lawrence D. Kessler, "Surviving the Japanese Invasion of China: A Christian Community in Exile" (Paper presented at the Mid-Atlantic Region, Association for Asian Studies, 1 Nov. 1992).

8. Francis S. Sullivan, ed., "Memoirs of Mason and Lois Young in China," 14. (Typescript, 1990); *AR(PCUS)*, 1939, 31.

9. *Cambridge History of China*, 13:552.

10. Quoted in Romig, *To Bend and Rise as the Bamboo*, 79. See "The Rape of Nanking: A Nazi Who Saved Lives," *New York Times*, 12 Dec. 1996. The *Times* article identifies the German civilian who was chairman of the Safety Zone as John Rabe and gives new information about the Nanjing rape from a diary Mr. Rabe wrote.

11. *Kiangan Mission Minutes*, 1938, 20.

12. Quoted in Romig, *To Bend and Rise as the Bamboo*, 87.

13. *Kiangan Mission Minutes*, 1938, 20–21; *AR*, 1938, 41.

14. F. A. Brown, MCD, 19 June 1938.

15. *AR*, 1939, 44–45.

16. Lodwick, *Educating the Women of Hainan*, 186–188.

17. *AR(PCUS)*, 1940, 29.

18. Junkin, *Bits of China*, 45.

19. Craig Houston Patterson, *My China That Was*, 153.

20. CC, 1939, 34, 72.

21. *Kiangan Mission Minutes*, 1940, 37.

22. *AR(PCUS)*, 1940, 37.

23. *AR(PCUS)*, 1938, 25.

24. *East China Mission Minutes*, 1941, 62; *AR*, 1940, 37, 40. In 1939 the Central China Mission was renamed the East China Mission.

25. *Shandong Mission Minutes*, 1941, 21.

26. John Leighton Stuart, *Fifty Years in China*, 335.

27. Minter, "A Tale of Two Texans in China," 2.

28. *AR*, 1940, 38.

29. *AR(PCUS)*, 1938, 27.

30. Ibid., 1940, 34.

31. *AR*, 1941, 44.

32. *AR(PCUS)*, 1941, 43.

33. Ibid., 1939, 33.

34. *AR*, 1941, 41.

35. Frank A. Brown, MCD, 30 Oct. 1938.

36. F. A. Brown, ltr., "Faithful unto Death," 26 Sept. 1941.

37. Frank W. Price, *China: Twilight or Dawn?* (New York: Friendship Press, 1948), 150.

38. Sullivan, "Memoirs of Mason and Lois Young in China," 16–18.

39. Price, *China: Twilight or Dawn?*, 38.

40. Frank W. Price, *We Went to West China* (Nashville: Executive Committee of Foreign Missions, 1943), 6.

41. Ibid., 8.

42. *AR*, 1944, 24.

43. Price, *We Went to West China*, 21.

44. Roy, *Never a Dull Moment*, 41–88.

45. Ibid., 60–61.

46. Ibid., 72.

47. Bates, "The Protestant Endeavor in Chinese Society," Series III (1937–1945) 125–1122, 7.

48. Price, *Twilight or Dawn?*, 112.

49. *AR(PCUS)*, 1940, 29.

50. Asher Raymond Kepler was one of the great missionaries of the Presbyterian Church. From the beginning of his missionary career he became deeply committed to the cause of church union. During the revolution of 1911 Kepler was engaged in Red Cross relief among the wounded soldiers in Wuhan and was shot through the head by a stray machine gun bullet. He almost died before receiving medical attention. The wound partially paralyzed the muscles in his face. Extensive surgery at the Johns Hopkins University Hospital was necessary to repair the damage. The tribute paid to Dr. Kepler at his death by the BFM read in part: "From the beginning of his service, Dr. Kepler had a peculiar singleness of purpose — the upbuilding and strengthening of the church." Merwin, *Adventure in Unity*, 53–54.

51. Ibid., 118.

52. *AR(PCUS)*, 1938, 26.

53. Merwin, *Adventure in Unity*, 136.

54. Ibid., 139.

55. Ibid., 144.

56. Ibid., 144–148.

57. Lodwick, *Educating the Women of Hainan*, 198–201.

58. Conversation with my father, Rev. Frank A. Brown.

59. Ibid., 204–205. The misinformation about the massacre had originated with a Nationalist China communique from Chongqing and headlined in U.S. daily papers.

60. One middle school had moved to Free China, two to Portuguese Macau, while fourteen carried on in occupied China. Of the twenty hospitals, eleven continued in operation under Japanese control. *AR*, 1944, 27–29.

61. Passenger list of the M.S. *Gripsolm*. This list includes missionaries from Korea and Japan. Most China Inland Mission personnel, who were British citizens, are not included.

62. Langdon Gilkey, *Shantung Compound* (New York: Harper and Row, 1966).

63. Ibid., 23.

64. *The Cambridge History of China*, 13:533–534.

65. *AR*, 1944, 23.

66. In Carolyn Atkins and Betty Isbister, *Where the Cranes Fly: The Adventures of Edith F. Millican, M.D. in China* (Albuquerque, NM: Albuquerque Printing Co., 1987), 38.

67. *AR*, 1945, 41.

68. Gilkey, *Shantung Compound*, 206–208.

69. *Interned at the Weixian Camp:* Margaret Barnes, Samuel Dean, Arabella Gault, Orpha Gould, Eugene C. Huebener, Mrs. Richard Jenness, Rev. and Mrs. E. L. Johnson, Mrs. Watson Hayes. *Interned at the Pootung Camp in Shanghai:* Alexander MacLeod, Frank Millican. *Interned at the British Embassy Compound in Peking:* Rev. and Mrs. James P. Leynse. *Interned in the Philippines:* Rev. and Mrs. Henry Bucher, Miss Katherine Hand, Rev. and Mrs. William Mather, Dr. and Mrs. Brewster Mather, Rev. and Mrs. M. Harmer Patton, Dr. and Mrs. Theodore Stevenson, Dr. and Mrs. Marshall Welles, Rev. and Mrs. Gardner Winn, Mr. and Mrs. Donald Zimmerman. Miss Hilma Madelaire resided in Qingdao throughout the war.

70. Rev. and Mrs. William Junkin, Rev. and Mrs. John Walker Vinson and Dr. and Mrs. Thomas Chalmers Vinson.

71. Stuart, *Fifty Years in China,* 135–159.

72. Jessie Junkin, "Out of the Lion's Den," typescript, 1945; Jessie Junkin, "Wanted: Garbage and God," Notes for missionary talk, 1946; see also *Presbyterian Outlook,* 18 June 1945.

73. Paul R. Lindholm, *Shadows from the Rising Sun* (Quezon City, Philippines: New Day Publishers, 1978).

74. Price, *China: Twilight or Dawn?,* 29, 107.

75. W. C. McLauchlin, "A Survey of the Present Situation in Haichow, Suchien, TKP and Hwain Stations of the North Jiangsu Mission," circa Mar. 1946.

76. *AR,* 1947, 37.

77. Ibid., 1948, 50.

78. CC, 1947, 89.

79. Ibid., 96–97.

80. Ibid., 59–60.

81. *AR,* 1948, 52.

82. C. Darby Fulton, "The Narrative Report of the Executive Secretary to the Executive Committee of Foreign Missions on his visit to the Far East" (Nashville: Executive Committee, May 1947).

83. Charles West, Questionnaire, 28 June 1988.

84. Leighton Stuart was one of the most able missionaries of the Presbyterian Church. Although his diplomatic mission ended in failure, there is no doubt that it was worth the effort. If peace between the two factions could have been achieved, the Chinese people could have been spared an enormous amount of bloodshed. There is no doubt that Stuart gave the effort everything he had. His biographer writes that he was right in his long-term assessments: There would be an eventual Sino-Soviet split and communism in China would develop along a "Sinicized" form. See Shaw, *An American Missionary in China;* John Leighton Stuart, *Fifty Years in China,* xix, Chapters 9–11; Robert F. Smylie, "John Leighton Stuart: A Missionary Diplomat in the Sino-Japanese Conflict, 1937–1941," *AP* 53:3 (Fall 1975).

85. Frank A. Brown, *The Last Hundred Days* (Shanghai: pamphlet privately printed, 1949), 8–10.

86. For discussion as to the reasons for the fall of the KMT see the following: Thomson, *While China Faced West,* 5–18, 112–116, 150–160; *Cambridge History of China,* 13:770–782; Price, *China: Twilight or Dawn?,* 28–33, 60; Spence, *The Search for Modern China,* 498–504; Stuart, *Fifty Years in China,* 183–195.

87. *AR,* 1950, 37–43.

88. Wallace C. Merwin and Francis P. Jones, eds., *Documents of the Three-Self Movement* (New York: Far Eastern Office, Division of Foreign Missions, NCC, 1963), 15–16.

89. Ibid., 17–18.

90. Board of World Missions, PCUS, "A statement on policy in relation to governments, particularly in China today," early 1950.

91. Missionary ltr. from Xuzhou, 25 Oct. 1948.

92. Stanton Lautenschlager, "We Cannot Quit in China," *Presbyterian Life,* 3 Sept. 1949, 11.

93. Samuel H. Moffett, "Behind the Curtain: Report from Peking," *Presbyterian Life,* 22 Jan. 1949, 8.

94. Merwin and Jones, eds., *Documents of the Three-Self Movement,* 22.

95. Ibid., 24–25.

96. For the rise of the Three-Self Movement, see the author's *Christianity in the People's Republic of China,* rev. ed. (Atlanta: John Knox Press, 1986), 81–86, and Philip L. Wickeri, *Seeking the Common Ground* (Maryknoll, NY: Orbis, 1988).

97. For the text of the "Manifesto" see *Documents of the Three-Self Movement,* 19–20.

98. Minter, "A Tale of Two Texans," 9.
99. Samuel H. Moffett, Questionnaire, 28 June 1988.
100. Brown, *The Last Hundred Days,* 16–17.
101. Crane, "PCUS Overseas Medical Missions," 91.
102. Ibid., 160–162. The medical school had one year in Fuzhou, after which they were required to move back to Jinan.
103. Henry S. Nelson, *Doctor with Big Shoes: Missionary Experiences in China and Africa* (Franklin, TN: Providence House Publishers, 1995), 57–65.
104. Agnes and Pete Richardson, MCD, 18 Feb. 1951.
105. Roy, *Never a Dull Moment,* 99.
106. Ibid., 107.
107. Ibid., 111–118.
108. Richard C. Bush, Jr., *Religion in Communist China* (Nashville: Abingdon Press, 1970), 45.
109. *AR,* 1954, 22.
110. Ibid., 1956, 20.

Chapter 15: Epilogue

1. K. H. Ting, "An Update on the Church in China," address given at the Presbyterian China Missionary Reunion, Columbia Theological Seminary, Decatur, GA, 14 Oct. 1995.
2. "Message to Chinese Christians in Response to Bishop K. H. Ting's Opening Address," China Missionary Reunion, 16 Oct. 1994. The message was composed by a writing committee of Charles West, Arthur Romig and Elizabeth Manget Minter.
3. See the author's *Christianity in the People's Republic of China,* rev. ed. (Atlanta: John Knox Press, 1986).
4. The China Christian Council was organized in October 1980 by Christian leaders in the "post denominational era." It is not to be confused with two other organizations with similar names: (1) the PCUSA China Council, which was established in 1910 to coordinate the work of the eight Presbyterian missions and was composed entirely of missionaries. (2) The National Christian Council of China (NCCC), which was the ecumenical organization established in 1923 and included most Protestant denominations and missions. Both the PCUS China Council and the NCCC went out of existence at the time the missionaries were forced out of China (1949–1951).
5. *Bridge: Church Life in China Today,* edited by Deng Zhaoming, Christian Study Centre on Chinese Religion and Culture, Hong Kong.
6. A Roman Catholic and a Protestant church were opened in Beijing during the Cultural Revolution, but these were more "showpieces" attended mostly by foreign diplomats. Christians in Shanghai claim that the Mo En Church was the first to be opened to the Chinese public, but Mo En did not open until Sept. 1979.
7. For a description of the renewal of church life in Ningbo see "The Church in Ningbo: Recovery and Reconciliation," *Bridge* 7 (Sept. 1984): 13–14 and "Spiritual Education in Ningbo," *Bridge* 16 (May 1986): 5.
8. All estimates of church membership are from "How Many Christians Are There in China?" *Amity News Service,* Sept. 1996.
9. "Images and Impression from Zhejiang Province," *Bridge* 47 (May–June 1991): 16–17.
10. "Wenzhou Revisited," *Bridge* 40 (Mar.–Apr. 1990): 4.
11. *Amity News Service,* 1.4 (July 1992).
12. Janice and Philip Wickeri, "Peter, W. H. Tsai: A Tribute," *Amity News Service* 3 (1994), 10.
13. "Church Unity in Shanghai," *Bridge* 48 (July–Aug. 1991): 3.
14. "Rural Christianity in Anhui Province," *Bridge* 25 (Sept.–Oct. 1987): 13–15.

15. H. H. Whitlock, ltr. to author, 19 Apr. 1989.

16. Christina Yates Parr, ltr. to author, 19 Apr. 1991.

17. Don and Jessie Junkin McCall, report written at the request of the author entitled "Visiting Former PCUS Mission Churches in Jiangsu and Chekiang (Zhejiang) Provinces, Oct. 1994."

18. *Amity News Service,* 2.5 (Oct. 1993).

19. "Rev. Philip Wickeri — First Foreigner Ordained by Chinese Church in Forty Years," *Bridge* 48 (July–Aug. 1991): 16.

20. "Chinese Church Leader Calls for End to Bible Smuggling," *Amity News Service* 3.6 (Dec. 1994).

21. Presbyterian Church (USA), *1996 Mission Yearbook for Prayer and Study,* 297. An excellent channel through which contributions can be sent to the Amity Foundation is *China Connection,* 458 S. Pasadena Ave., Pasadena, CA 91105.

22. "The Church in Sunam," *Bridge* 14 (Nov.–Dec. 1985): 6.

23. Pat Johnson, ltr. to author, 28 Nov. 1993.

24. Henry S. Nelson, *Doctor with Big Shoes: Missionary Experiences in China and Africa* (Franklin, TN: Providence House Publishers, 1995), 84–95.

25. The author's visit to Taizhou, May 1993.

26. Conversation with Rev. Peter Han, May 1993. "Meeting point" refers to a place of regular worship that has not been fully organized or officially recognized by the RAB.

27. Ruth Bell Graham, "A Visit Home," *Decision,* Dec. 1980, 6.

28. McCall, Report of visit, Oct. 1994.

29. *Amity News Service,* 4.3 (June 1995).

30. McCall, Report of visit, Oct. 1994.

31. Ibid.

32. Author, interview with RAB officials, May 1993.

33. McCall, Report of Visit, Oct. 1994.

34. Wen Man Hsu, ltr. to Jean Vinson Urquhart, 15 Apr. 1989.

35. Author, interview with the Rev. Gu Yadong, May 1993.

36. *Amity News Service,* 2.5 (Oct. 1993).

37. "Irregularities in the Churches in Southern Shandong," *Bridge* 66 (July–Aug. 1994): 14.

38. "Shandong Leads the Way in Return of Church Property," *Amity News Service,* 4.1 (Feb. 1995).

39. "A Trip to Jinan and Qingdao," *Bridge* 19 (Sept.–Oct. 1986):7.

40. Ibid., 9.

41. Author, interview with staff of the Beijing Academy of Social Science and with Rev. Ying Gao, 8 June 1993. In 1994 members of the Gangwashi church alleged that the Religious Affairs Bureau had interfered in the appointment of their senior pastor.

42. *China News Update,* Sept. 1995, 10.

43. "Present Church Situation in Hunan," *Bridge* 45 (Jan.–Feb. 1991): 3–9.

44. *China News Update,* Sept. 1995, 9.

45. *Amity News Service,* 4.4 (Aug. 1995); "The Minority Ethnic Groups in Yunnan," *Bridge* 43 (Sept.–Oct. 1990): 3.

46. "The Dai Christians," *Bridge* 43 (Sept.–Oct. 1990): 10.

47. "A Visit to the Church in Hainan," *Religion in the People's Republic of China: Documentation* (Journal published in Kent, England, by the China Study Project), 18 (Dec. 1985): 18–19.

48. "The Miao People of Nanmao Encounter Christianity," *Bridge* 27 (Jan.–Feb. 1988): 9–10.

49. Marie Melrose, ltr. to author, 14 Mar. 1995; Robert Thomas, ltr. to author, May 1995.

50. "Churches in Northern Guangdong," *Bridge* 33 (Jan.–Feb. 1989): 11.

51. Ibid., 12.

52. See Price, *Our China Investment,* 176–179, for names of forty children of Southern Presbyterian missionaries who died in China between the years 1874 and 1926.

53. Harold Matthews, chairman and compiler, "Survey of Returning China Missionaries prepared at the request of the NCC China Committee," New York: 1951. Responses were received from 152 missionaries representing 22 Protestant mission boards. This significant evaluation is abbreviated as NCC 1951 Survey.

54. Responses were received from fifty-four missionaries (thirty-eight Northern, sixteen Southern Presbyterians). All had served in China sometime between the years 1921 and 1952.

55. Enid Douglas, Coordinator, "China Missionaries Oral History Project: An Overview," Oral History Program, Claremont Graduate School, Claremont, CA, 1973. Fifty-Four missionaries from fifteen different missions were interviewed. Five were Northern Presbyterians. The majority were from the Methodist and Congregational mission boards.

56. For a list of those interviewed see the bibliography in the Appendix.

57. One work in English should be noted: Luo Zhufeng, ed., *Religion under Socialism in China,* translated by Donald E. MacInnis and Zheng Xi'an, Research studies done by scholars at the Shanghai Academy of Social Studies (Armonk, NY: M. E. Sharpe, 1991).

58. Charles C. West, 1988 Questionnaire.

59. NCC, 1951 "Survey," 15.

60. West, 1988 Questionnaire.

61. C. Houston Patterson, 1988 Questionnaire.

62. NCC, 1951 "Survey," 15.

63. Arthur Romig, 1988 Questionnaire.

64. Paul Winn, 1988 Questionnaire.

65. Theodore Yates, 1988 Questionnaire.

66. NCC, 1951 "Survey," 15.

67. Patterson, 1988 Questionnaire.

68. Andrew Roy, 1988 Questionnaire.

69. NCC, 1951 "Survey," 2.

70. Cai Wenhao (Peter Tsai), "The Church in China — Yesterday, Today and Tomorrow," *Chinese Theological Review: 1985,* Janice Wickeri, ed. (Holland, MI: Foundation for Theological Education in Southeast Asia, 1985), 35.

71. Zhang Guangzheng, "Living as Christians Today: Sociological Insights," *Chinese Theological Review: 1988,* 56.

72. Latourette, *History,* 830.

73. Romig, 1988 Questionnaire.

74. Paul Lindholm, 1988 Questionnaire.

75. Mary Muriel Boone, 1988 Questionnaire.

76. Chen Zemin, "Living as Christians Today: Biblical Insights," *Chinese Theological Review: 1988,* 47.

77. E. J. Bingle and K. G. Grubb, eds., *World Christian Handbook,* 1952 ed. (London: World Dominion Press, 1952), 141–142.

78. Quoted in Bob Whyte, *Unfinished Encounter* (Harrisburg, PA: Morehouse Publishing, 1988), 133.

79. Thomson, *While China Faced West,* 227.

80. See Chapter 11, p. 234.

81. *World Christian Handbook,* 1952 ed., 141–142.

82. Alan Hunter, "Continuities in Chinese Protestantism, 1920–1990," *China Study Journal,* 6 (1991): 8.

83. Philip L. Wickeri, *Seeking the Common Ground* (Maryknoll, NY: Orbis, 1988), 125; Claremont China Oral History Project, 32.

84. Daniel H. Bays, "Missions and Christians in Modern China, 1850–1950" (Address

at the Symposium of the Northwest Regional China Council, Linfield College, Oregon, 14 July 1994), 7.

85. Claremont China Oral History Project, 37.

86. NCC, 1951 "Survey," 15.

87. J. Kenneth Foreman, 1988 Questionnaire; NCC, 1951 "Survey," 15.

88. G. Thompson Brown, "Why Has Christianity Grown Faster in Korea Than in China?" *Missiology* 22 (Jan. 1994): 77–88.

89. Kenneth Kepler, 1988 Questionnaire.

90. Statistics from *Shandong Mission Minutes,* 1938.

91. Philip Wickeri, interview, 26 May 1993.

92. Note should be made of Ralph R. Covell's recent book, which deals with this issue: *The Liberating Gospel in China: The Christian Faith among China's Minority Peoples* (Grand Rapids, MI: Baker Book House, 1995).

93. In 1935 North China Theological College had 133 students while the theological departments of Yenching and Cheeloo had a total of 62.

94. Muriel Boone, 1988 Questionnaire.

95. Donald MacInnis, "The North American Churches and China, 1949–1981," *IBMR* 5 (Apr. 1981): 50.

96. Frank W. Price, "End of an Era," *Presbyterian Outlook,* 8 Dec. 1952, 5.

97. The role of the missionary in shaping American policy and public opinion has been well documented by China historians: John King Fairbank, *Christianity in China: Early Protestant Missionary Writings,* 2; Michael H. Hunt, *The Making of a Special Relationship: The United States and China to 1914,* 154–183; Jonathan D. Spence, *The Search for Modern China,* 383–387. See also Patricia Neils, "Missionary Influence on US China Policy in the 1930s and '40s," unpublished paper, 1994. Ms. Neils writes that "50 percent of the foreign-culture experts in Washington, D.C. were missionary offspring" (p. 20).

98. Claremont China Oral History Project, 42, 46.

99. Ibid., 43.

100. Samuel H. Moffett, 1988 Questionnaire.

101. H. McKennie Goodpasture, quotation of John Holt Rice in "150 Years in Global Mission," *Mission Yearbook for Prayer and Study, 1987,* 6.

102. NCC, 1951 "Survey," 21.

103. Claremont China Oral History Project, 10. Three out of forty-four interviewed reported they "were led to abandon missionary work."

104. Helen Romig, 1988 Questionnaire.

105. K. H. Ting, Address in Lambeth Palace Chapel, 1 Oct. 1982, Whyte, *Unfinished Encounter,* 297–298.

Select Bibliography

Denominational Records and Official Publications

Presbyterian Church in the United States of America (PCUSA)
    Annual Reports of the Board of Foreign Missions
    Minutes and Annual Reports of the China Missions
    Minutes of the China Council
    The Foreign Missionary (1842–1886)
    The Presbyterian Monthly Record (1866–1886)
    The Church at Home and Abroad (1887–1894)
    Assembly Herald (1894–1918)
    The Presbyterian Magazine (1921–1933)
    Presbyterian Life (1948–1972)
    Woman's Work for Woman (1888–1924)
    A Monthly Cycle of Prayer for the China Missions (1926–1948)
    Hainan News Letter, American Presbyterian Mission (1927–1946)
    Archives, Staff Correspondence, Dept. of History, Philadelphia

Presbyterian Church in the United States (PCUS)
    Annual Reports of the Executive Committee of Foreign Missions
    Minutes of the China Missions
    The Missionary (1868–1811)
    The Missionary Survey (1912–1924)
    The Presbyterian Survey (1924–1995)
    Bi-Monthly Bulletin, SPM China Missions (1905–1909)
    Missionary Correspondence Dept. (1918–1951)
    Archives, Department of History, Montreat, NC

Other Periodicals

American Presbyterians: Journal of Presbyterian History. Published quarterly by the Presbyterian Historical Society (Department of History of the Presbyterian Church [U.S.A.]), Philadelphia.

Amity News Service. Published by The Amity Foundation Overseas Coordination Office, Hong Kong.

Bridge: Church Life in China Today. Published by the Christian Study Centre on Chinese Religion and Culture, Hong Kong.

China News Update. Occasional Newsletter published by the China Office, PC(USA).

China Notes. Published by the East Asia Office, National Council of Churches USA, New York.

China Study Journal. Published by the Department for China Relations, Council of Churches for Britain and Ireland, London 1986–. This journal continues the earlier publication *Religion in the People's Republic of China: Documentation.*

The Chinese Recorder. First published at Fuzhou, 1867. Published in Shanghai from 1911 to 1941.

International Bulletin of Missionary Research. Published quarterly by the Overseas Ministries Study Center, New Haven, CT.

Missiology. Published quarterly by the American Society of Missiology, Scottdale, PA.

Books, Articles and Unpublished Papers

Armstrong, O. V. "Marshall Feng Yu Hsiang a Guest in our home." Unpublished paper, 1932.

Atkins, Carolyn, and Betty Isbister. *Where the Cranes Fly: The Adventures of Edith F. Millican, M.D. in China, 1943–48.* Albuquerque, NM: Albuquerque Printing Company, 1987.

Barnett, Suzanne Wilson, and John King Fairbank, eds. *Christianity in China: Early Protestant Missionary Writings.* Cambridge: Harvard University Press, 1985.

Bates, Miner Searle. "The Protestant Endeavor in Chinese Society, 1890–1950." Manuscript collection in the Day Missions Library, Yale University, New Haven.

Bays, Daniel H. "Missions and Christianity in Modern China, 1850–1950." Address, Northwest Regional China Council symposium, *American Missionaries and Social Change,* Linfield College, July 1994.

Bear, James Edwin, Jr. *The Mission Work of the Presbyterian Church of the United States in China: 1867–1952.* 5 vols. Unpublished manuscript. Union Theological Seminary, Richmond, VA.

Beaver, R. Pierce, ed. *American Missions in Bicentennial Perspective.* Pasadena, CA: William Carey Library, 1977.

Berger, Paul. "Minutes of the Synod of North China, May 19–23, 1898." Unpublished paper, PDH(Phil).

Bingle, E. J., and Kenneth G. Grubb, eds. *World Christian Handbook.* 1952 ed. London: World Dominion Press, 1952.

Bland, J. O. P., and E. Backhouse. *China under the Empress Dowager: Being the History of the Life and Times of Tsu Hsi.* London: William Heinemann, 1910.

Board of Foreign Missions, PCUSA. *A Manual for the Use of Missionary Candidates and Missionaries.* 4th ed. New York: Mission House, 1882.

Board of World Mission, PCUS. *"I Have Fought a Good Fight."* Memorials of missionaries, 1948–1964. Nashville.

Boardman, Eugene Powers, *Christian Influence upon the Ideology of the Taiping Rebellion, 1851–1864.* Madison, WI: University of Wisconsin Press, 1952.

Bohr, Paul Richard. *Famine in China and the Missionary: Timothy Richards as Relief Administrator and Advocate of National Reform, 1876–1884.* Cambridge: Harvard University Press, 1972.

Broomhall, A. J. *Hudson Taylor and China's Open Century: Barbarians at the Gates.* Kent, England: Hodder and Stoughton, 1981.

Brown, Arthur Judson. *The Lien-Chou Martyrdom.* Pamphlet. New York: Board of Foreign Missions, PCUSA, circa 1905.

———. *New Forces in Old China.* New York: Revell, 1904.

———. *One Hundred Years: A History of the Foreign Missionary Work of the Presbyterian Church in the USA.* New York: Revell, 1936.

———. *Report of a Visitation of the China Missions, May 22–Sept. 19, 1901.* 3rd. ed. New York: Board of Foreign Missions, 1902.

Brown, Mrs. Charlotte Thompson. "Madame Chiang Kai-shek at the Front." *Presbyterian Survey* 28 (1938).

Brown, Frank A. *Charlotte Brown, A Mother in China: The Story of the Work of Charlotte Thompson Brown in China from 1909–1949.* Privately printed, 1953.

———. *The Last Hundred Days: A Diary.* Pamphlet. Nashville: Board of World Missions, 1950.

———. Manuscript collection in Presbyterian Department of History, Montreat.

Brown, G. Thompson. *Christianity in the People's Republic of China.* Rev. ed. Atlanta: John Knox Press, 1986.

———. "Why Has Christianity Grown Faster in Korea than in China?" *Missiology* 22 (1994).

Buck, Pearl S. *Is There a Case for Foreign Missions?* New York: John Day, 1933.

———. "The Laymen's Mission Report." *Christian Century* 49 (1932).

———. *My Several Worlds: A Personal Record.* New York: John Day Co., 1954.

Bullock, Mary Brown. *An American Transplant: The Rockefeller Foundation and Peking Union Medical College.* Berkeley: University of California Press, 1980.

Bush, Richard C., Jr. *Religion in Communist China.* Nashville: Abingdon Press, 1970.

Cai, Wenhao (Peter Tsai). "The Church in China — Yesterday, Today and Tomorrow." In *Chinese Theological Review: 1985,* Janice Wickeri, ed. Holland, MI: Foundation for Theological Education in Southeast Asia, 1985.

Caldwell, C. N. "The Opening of Taichow." *BMB* 1 (1906).

Canton School for the Blind. *Ming Sum: The School of the Understanding Heart.* 50th Anniversary Report. Hong Kong: The Standard Press, 1939.

Charles, Robert. "Olyphant and Opium: A Canton Merchant Who Just Said 'No.' " *IBMR* 16 (1992).

Chen, Zemin. "Living as Christians Today: Biblical Insights." In *Chinese Theological Review: 1988,* Janice Wickeri, ed. Holland, MI: Foundation for Theological Education in Southeast Asia, 1988.

Chesneaux, Jean, et al. *China from the 1911 Revolution to Liberation.* New York: Pantheon Books, 1977.

———. *China from the Opium Wars to the 1911 Revolution.* New York: Pantheon Books, 1976.

Chester, Samuel Hall. *Behind the Scenes.* Austin, TX: Press of Von Boeckman-Jones, 1928.

———. *Lights and Shadows of Mission Work in the Far East: Being the Record of Observations made during a visit to the Southern Presbyterian Mission in Japan, China, and Korea in the year 1897.* Richmond, VA: Presby. Committee of Publication, 1899.

———. *Memories of Four-Score Years.* Richmond, VA: Presby. Committee of Publication, 1934.

Choh, Leung Siu. "How May the Missions and Missionaries Best Serve the Chinese Church at the Present Time?" Paper presented at the Missionary Conference, Canton, March 1925.

Chow, Tse-tsung. *The May Fourth Movement: Intellectual Revolution in Modern China.* Stanford, CA: Stanford University Press, 1960.

Clark, Charles Allen. *The Nevius Plan of Mission work in Korea.* Seoul, Korea: Christian Literature Society, 1937.

Cohen, Paul A. *China and Christianity: The Missionary Movement and the Growth of Chinese Antiforeignism, 1860–1870.* Cambridge: Harvard University Press, 1963.

Corbett, Hunter, ed. *The American Presbyterian Mission in Shantung during Fifty Years: 1861–1911.* Shanghai: APMP, n.d.

Covell, Ralph. *The Liberating Gospel in China: The Christian Faith among China's Minority Peoples.* Grand Rapids, MI: Baker Books, 1995.

———. *W. A. P. Martin: Pioneer of Progress in China.* Washington, DC: Christian University Press, 1978.

Crane, Sophie Montgomery. "PCUS Overseas Medical Missions." Manuscript prepared for the PCUSA Global Mission Unit, 1992.

Day, Clarence B. *Hangchow University: A Brief History.* New York: United Board for Christian Colleges in China, 1955.

De Jong, Gerald F. *The Reformed Church in China, 1842–1951.* Grand Rapids, MI: Eerdmans, 1992.

Dodd, Samuel. "Statistics of Religion in the Synod of China for the year 1873." Unpublished paper, PDH(Phil).

Douglas, Enid, ed., "China Missionaries Oral History Project: Overview." Claremont, CA: Claremont Graduate School, 1973.

DuBose, Hampden C. *Memoirs of Rev. John Leighton Wilson, D.D. Missionary to Africa and Secretary of Foreign Missions.* Richmond, VA: Presby. Committee of Publications, 1895.

Entrican, Sara. *The Story of the Chifu [Chefoo] School [for the Deaf].* Pamphlet. Trenton, NJ: The Silent Worker, n.d.

Esherick, Joseph. *The Origins of the Boxer Uprising.* Berkeley: University of California Press, 1987.

Espey, John. *Minor Heresies.* New York: Alfred Knopf, 1945.

Fairbank, John King. *China: A New History.* Cambridge: The Belknap Press, 1992.

———. "The Chinese Revolution and American Missions." *China Notes* 11 (1973).

———. *The Great Chinese Revolution: 1800–1985.* New York: Harper and Row, 1986.

———, ed. *The Missionary Enterprise in China and America.* Cambridge: Harvard University Press, 1974.

———. *The United States and China.* 4th ed. Cambridge: Harvard University Press, 1978.

Fairbank, John K., and Edwin O. Reischauer. *China: Tradition and Transformation.* Boston: Houghton Mifflin Co., 1978.

Farnham, J. M. W. "Historical Sketch of Shanghai Station." In *Jubilee Papers of the Central China Presbyterian Mission,* J. C. Garritt, ed. Shanghai: APMP, 1895.

Fenn, William P. *Christian Higher Education in Changing China, 1880–1950.* Grand Rapids, MI: Eerdmans, 1976.

Fisher, Daniel W. *Calvin Wilson Mateer: Forty-five Years a Missionary in Shantung.* Philadelphia: Westminster Press, 1911.

Fitch, G. F. "Historical Sketch of Soochow Station." In *Jubilee Papers of the Central China Presbyterian Mission, 1844–1894,* J. C. Garritt, ed. Shanghai: APMP, 1895.

Fulton, C. Darby. *Narrative Report of the Executive Secretary to the Executive Committee of Foreign Missions on his visit to the Far East.* Nashville: ECFM, 1947.

Garritt, J. C., ed. *Jubilee Papers of the Central China Presbyterian Mission, 1844–1894.* Shanghai: APMP, 1895.

Garside, B. A. *One Increasing Purpose: The Life of Henry Winters Luce.* New York: Revell, 1948.

Gilkey, Langdon. *Shantung Compound.* New York: Harper and Row, 1966.

Goodpasture, H. McKennie. "China in an American, Frank Wilson Price: A Bibliographical Essay." *AP* 49 (1971).

Graham, Ruth Bell, "A Visit Home." *Decision,* December 1980.

Grant, Edward. "John W. Vinson — Another Name on the Roll Call of Faith." *Presbyterian Survey* 22 (1932).

Green, Ashbel. *Presbyterian Missions.* New York: Anson D. F. Randolph & Co., 1893.

Greene, Theodore Chase. *A Medical Mission in China: The Douw Hospital and Its Work, 1926–1931.* Edited and printed by Joan Swift Greene Smith, 1989.

Guinness, M. Geraldine. *The Story of the China Inland Mission.* 2 vols. 5th Ed. London: Morgan and Scott, 1900.

Hainan Presbyterian Mission. *Fifty Years in Hainan: American Presbyterian Mission 1881–1931.* Prepared by a committee of the mission on the occasion of its 50th anniversary.

Hamilton, E. H. *Afraid? Of What? A Book of Poems.* Hong Kong: Cathay Press, 1960.

———. "Nettie Donaldson Grier, M.D.: A Mender of Broken China." In *Glorious Living,* Hallie Paxson Winsborough, ed. Atlanta: Committee on Woman's Work, 1937.

Hartwell, Mrs. Charles K. "Mobile to China: A Valiant Woman's Mission." *The Alabama Review* 31 (1978).

Heininger, Janet E. "Private Positions Versus Public Policy: Chinese Devolution and the American Experience in East Asia." *Diplomatic History* 6 (1982).

Heng You. "Alice Carpenter and the Chinese Ming Sum School for the Blind." *AP* 68 (1990).

Henry, B. C. "The Projection of the Christian College in China located at Canton: Historical Resume." Paper presented to the Board of Foreign Missions, January 1885.

Hevia, James. "Leaving a Brand on China: Missionary Discourse in the Wake of the Boxer Movement." *Modern China* 18 (1992).

Hocking, William Ernest, ed. *Re-Thinking Missions: A Laymen's Inquiry after One Hundred Years.* New York: Harper and Bros., 1932.

Hood, George A. *Mission Accomplished? The English Presbyterian Mission in Lingtung, South China.* Frankfurt, Germany: Verlag Peter Lang, 1986.

Hunan Mission, PCUSA. *Brief Historical Sketch of the Work of the Presbyterian Church of America in Hunan Province.* Hankow: Religious Tract Society, circa 1936.

Hunt, Everett N., Jr. "The Legacy of John Livingston Nevius." *International Bulletin of Missionary Research* 15 (1991).

Hunt, Michael H. *The Making of a Special Relationship: The United States and China to 1914.* New York: Columbia University Press, 1983.

Hunter, Alan. "Continuities in Chinese Protestantism, 1920–1990." *China Study Journal,* 6 (1991).

Hyatt, Irwin T., Jr. *Our Ordered Lives Confess: Three Nineteenth-Century American Missionaries in East Shantung.* Cambridge: Harvard University Press, 1976.

Inslee, Eugenia. "Missionary Life in China Thirty Years Ago." *The Missionary,* 31 (1898).

Junkin, Bill and Jessie. *Bits of China from the life of Nettie DuBose Junkin.* Tazewell, VA: Privately printed. 1986.

Junkin, Jessie. "Out of the Lion's Den" and "Wanted: Garbage and God." Unpublished articles on prison camp experiences, 1945.

Junkin, Nettie DuBose, ed. *For the Glory of God: Memoirs of Dr. and Mrs. H. C. DuBose.* Lewisburg, WV: Published by the children of Dr. and Mrs. DuBose., n.d.

Kessler, Lawrence D. "A Helping Hand — Southern Presbyterians in Republican China." *American Asian Review,* Summer 1991.

———. *The Jiangyin Mission Station: An American Missionary Community in China, 1895–1951.* Chapel Hill, NC: University of North Carolina Press, 1996.

———. "Surviving the Japanese Invasion of China: A Christian Community in Exile." Paper presented at the Mid-Atlantic Region, Association for Asian Studies, Nov. 1992.

Latourette, Kenneth Scott. *The Chinese, Their History and Culture.* 3rd. ed., New York: Macmillan, 1946.

———. *A History of Christianity in China.* New York: Macmillan, 1929.

Lautz, Terrill E. *"Shantung Girl," Elisabeth Luce Moore: A Spoken History.* Hastings-on-Hudson, NY: Privately printed, 1989.

Lew, Timothy Tingfang. "Some of the Factors, Dangers and Problems in the Christian Missionary Enterprise in China Today through Chinese Eyes." Address at the 34th Annual Session, Foreign Mission Conference of North America, Atlantic City, Jan. 1927.

Lindholm, Paul R. *Shadows from the Rising Sun.* Quezon City, Philippines: New Day Publishers, 1978.

Ling, Pan. *In Search of Old Shanghai.* Hong Kong: Joint Publishing Co., 1983.

Little, Lacy L. *"Rivershade": A Historical Sketch of Kiangyin Station, China.* Pamphlet prepared by the station, n.d.

Liu, Kwang-Ching, ed. "Science and Salvation in China: The Life of W. A. P. Martin (1827–1916)." In *American Missionaries in China: Papers from Harvard Seminars.* Cambridge: Harvard University East Asian Research Center, 1970.

Lodwick, Kathleen L. *Educating the Women of Hainan: The Career of Margaret Moninger in China, 1915–1942.* Lexington, KY: University Press of Kentucky, 1995.

———. "Women at the Hainan Presbyterian Mission: Ministry and Diversion." *AP* 65 (1987).

Loetscher, Lefferts A. *The Broadening Church: A Study of Theological Issues in the Presbyterian Church since 1869.* Philadelphia: University of Pennsylvania Press, 1954.

Loomis, A. W. *Scenes in Chusan: or Missionary Labors by the Way.* Philadelphia: Presbyterian Board of Publications, 1859.

Lowrie, J. Walter. "The Story of Paotingfu." *The Assembly Herald* 4–5 (1901).

Lowrie, Walter, ed. *Memoirs of the Rev. Walter M. Lowrie, Missionary to China.* Edited by his father. New York: Robert Carter & Brothers, 1849.

Luo, Zhufeng, ed. *Religion under Socialism in China.* Research done by the Shanghai Academy of Social Studies. Translated by Donald E. MacInnis and Zheng Xi'an. Armonk, NY: M. E. Sharpe, 1991.

Lutz, Jessie G., *China and the Christian Colleges, 1850–1950.* Ithaca, NY: Cornell University Press, 1971.

———. "Protestant Christian Education in China, 1850–1950." *China Notes* 21 (1985).

Lyon, D. N., and J. H. Judson. "Historical Sketch of the Hangchow Station." In *Jubilee Papers of the Central China Presbyterian Mission,* J. C. Garritt, ed. Shanghai: APMP, 1895.

MacGillivray, D., ed. *A Century of Protestant Missions in China 1807–1907.* Being The Centenary Conference Historical Volume. Shanghai: APMP, 1907.

MacInnis, Donald. "The North American Churches and China 1949–1981." *International Bulletin of Missionary Research* 5 (1981).

———. *Religions in China Today: Policy and Practice.* Maryknoll, NY: Orbis, 1989.

Martin, Ralph G. *Henry and Clare: An Intimate Portrait of the Luces.* New York: G. P. Putnam and Sons, 1991.

Martin, W. A. P. *A Cycle of Cathay: or China South and North with Personal Reminiscences.* 3rd. ed. New York: Revell, 1900.

Mateer, Mrs. A. H. *Siege Days.* New York: Revell, 1903.

Mateer, Calvin. *A Review of "Methods of Mission Work."* Shanghai: Presbyterian Mission Press, 1900.

Mateer, Robert M. *Character Building in China: The Life Story of Julia Brown Mateer.* New York: Revell. 1912.

Matthews, Harold, ed. "Survey of Returning China Missionaries for the NCC China Committee." New York: NCC Division of Foreign Missions, 1951.

McCall, Donald, and Jessie Junkin. "Visiting Former PCUS Mission Churches in Jiangsu and Chekiang Provinces, October, 1994." Unpublished paper prepared at request of the author.

McIntosh, Gilbert. "Historical Sketch of the Presbyterian Mission Press." In *Jubilee Papers of the Central China Presbyterian Mission,* J. C. Garritt, ed. Shanghai: APMP, 1895.

McLauchlin, W. C. "A Survey of the Present Situation in Haichow, Sutchien, TKP [Huaiyin] and Huain Stations of the North Jiangsu Mission." Unpublished paper, March 1946.

Merwin, Wallace. *Adventure in Unity: The Church of Christ in China.* Grand Rapids, MI: Eerdmans, 1974.

Merwin, Wallace C., and Francis P. Jones, eds. *Documents of the Three-Self Movement.* New York: NCC Division of Foreign Missions, 1963.

Minter, Elizabeth. "A Tale of Two Texans in China." Paper presented to the Presbyterian Historical Society of the Southwest, 1992.

Moffett, Samuel Hugh. "Behind the Curtain: Report from Peking." *Presbyterian Life,* 22 Jan. 1949.

———. *A History of Christianity in Asia.* Vol. 1. New York: HarperCollins, 1992.

Moninger, Mary Margaret, ed. *The Isle of Palms: Sketches of Hainan.* Shanghai: Commercial Press, 1919. (Reprinted by Garland Press, New York, 1980.)

Montgomery, Annie L. "Beginning of Mission Work in Hwaianfu." Pamphlet. Nashville: ECFM, n.d.

Morrison, Eliza A. *Memoirs of the Life and Labours of Robert Morrison, D.D.* Compiled by his widow. 2 vols. London: Longman, Orne, Brown, and Green, 1839.

Morrison, J. H. *William Carey: Cobbler and Pioneer.* London: Hodder and Stoughton, 1924.

Murray, John. "Tsinanfu Station in the Earlier Years." In *The American Presbyterian Mission in Shantung,* Hunter Corbett, ed. Shanghai: APMP, 1914.

Neill, Stephen. *Colonialism and Christian Missions.* New York: McGraw-Hill Book Company, 1966.

Nelson, Henry S. *Doctor with Big Shoes: Missionary Experiences in China and Africa.* Franklin, TN: Providence House Publishers, 1995.

Nevius, Helen S. Coan. *Life of John Livingston Nevius.* New York: Revell, 1895.

Nevius, John Livingston. *Planting and Development of Missionary Churches,* 4th ed. Grand Rapids, MI: Baker Book House, 1958.

North Jiangsu Mission, PCUS. *Half Our Burden: A Statement and An Appeal through the ECFM to the Southern Presbyterian Church.* Shanghai: Commercial Press, 1915.

Noyes, Henry V. "The Presbytery of Canton, China." Handwritten manuscript, circa 1895. PDH(Phil).

Paton, David M. *Christian Missions and the Judgement of God.* London: SCM Press, 1953.

Patterson, B. C. "Autobiographical Notes." Manuscript PDH(Mont), 1952.

Patterson, Craig Houston. *From the Boxer Rebellion to Pearl Harbor: My China That Was.* Harrisonburg, Va.: privately printed, 1990.

Pin, Liao, ed. *The Grand Canal: An Odyssey.* Beijing: Foreign Language Press, 1987.

Pollock, John C. *A Foreign Devil in China: The Story of Dr. L. Nelson Bell, an American Surgeon in China.* Minneapolis: World Wide Publications, 1971.

Presbyterian Department of History. "Board Secretary Staff File." Incoming and Outgoing Correspondence with missionaries, 1852–1908. Philadelphia.

Price, Frank Wilson, *China: Twilight or Dawn.* New York: Friendship Press, 1948.

———. *History of Nanking Theological Seminary, 1911–1961.* New York: Board of Founders of Nanking Theological Seminary, 1961.

———. *The Rural Church in China, A Survey.* New York: Agricultural Missions, 19438

———. *We Went to West China.* Nashville: ECFM, 1943.

Price, P. Frank. *Our China Investment.* Nashville: ECFM, 1927.

Randolph-Macon Woman's College. *The Several Worlds of Pearl S. Buck: Essays Presented at a Centennial Symposium, March 1992.* Westport, CT: Greenwood Press, 1994.

Rankin, William. *Memorials of Foreign Missionaries.* Philadelphia: Presby. Board of Publication, 1895.

Rawlinson, Albert B. *Historical Sketch of the Mission in China.* Pamphlet. Philadelphia: Presby. Historical Society, n.d.

Records of the General Conference of the Protestant Missionaries of China held at Shanghai, May 7–20, 1890. Shanghai: APMP, 1890.

Reid, Gilbert. "The Shantung Mission — Its Progress and Promise." *The Church at Home and Abroad* 15 (1894).

Richardson, Agnes Rowland. *The Claimed Blessing: The Story of the Lives of the Richardsons in China, 1923–1951.* Cincinnati: C. J. Krehbiel Co., 1970.

Rockefeller Foundation, China Medical Commission, *Medicine in China.* New York: Rockefeller Foundation, 1914.

Romig, Arthur and Helen. *To Bend and Rise as the Bamboo: Letters from China 1931–1942.* Albuquerque, NM: Franklin's Press Masters, 1993.

Roots, I. L. ed. *The Chinese Church as Revealed in the National Christian Conference Held in Shanghai, May, 1922.* Report of Commission I. Shanghai: Oriental Press, 1922.

Roy, Andrew T. "Historical Overview of the Overseas Mission Policies of the United Presbyterian Church in the United States of America." General Assembly Mission Council, 1977.

———. *Never a Dull Moment: A Memoir of Family, China, and Hong Kong*. Beijing: Elissandra Roy, Home Publisher, n.d.

Scott, Charles E. "Tsingtao Station: Its Life and Work." In *The American Presbyterian Mission in Shantung during Fifty Years 1861–1911*, Hunter Corbett, ed. Shanghai: APMP, 1914.

Shaw, Yu-ming. *An American Missionary in China: John Leighton Stuart and Chinese-American Relations*. Cambridge: Harvard University Press, 1992.

Shields, Randolph. "Medical Education in China." *Presbyterian Survey* 26 (1936).

Silver, Charles. "Pearl Buck, Evangelism and Works of Love." *Journal of Presbyterian History* 51 (1973).

Smylie, Robert F. "John Leighton Stuart: A Missionary Diplomat in the Sino-Japanese Conflict, 1937–1941." *Journal of Presbyterian History* 53 (1975).

Soothill, W. E. *The Three Religions of China*. London: Oxford University Press, 1929.

Speer, Robert E., ed. *A Missionary Pioneer in the Far East: A Memorial of Divie Bethune McCartee*. New York: Revell, 1922.

———. *Presbyterian Foreign Missions*. Philadelphia: Presbyterian Board of Publications, 1901.

———. *Report on the China Missions of the Presbyterian Board of Foreign Missions*. 2nd ed. New York: BFM, 1897.

Speer, Robert E., and H. T. Kerr. *Report on Japan and China of the Deputation sent by the Board of Foreign Missions*. New York: BFM, 1927.

Speer, William. "First Stones in the Foundation of the Synod of China." *Chinese Recorder* 30 (1899).

Spence, Jonathan D. *God's Chinese Son: The Taiping Heavenly Kingdom of Hong Xiuquan*. New York: W. W. Norton, 1996.

———. *The Search for Modern China*. New York: W. W. Norton, 1990.

———. *To Change China: Western Advisers in China 1620–1960*. Boston: Little Brown and Company, 1969.

Stevens, Mary Thompson. "Letters from Mary Thompson Stevens to Her Mother from China, 1910–1919." Private collection.

Stuart, John Leighton. *Fifty Years in China: The Memoirs of John Leighton Stuart, Missionary and Ambassador*. New York: Random House, 1954.

Stuart, Warren H. "Mother Stuart." *The Missionary Survey* 2 (1913).

Sullivan, Francis S., ed. "Memoirs of Mason and Lois Young in China." Private collection.

Tang, Edmund, and Jean-Paul Wiest, eds. *The Catholic Church in Modern China: Perspectives*. Maryknoll, NY: Orbis, 1993.

Terrill, Ross. *Mao: A Biography*. New York: Harper and Row, 1981.

Thompson, Dean K. "John Leighton Stuart: Missionary and Ambassador to China." In *Go Therefore: 150 Years of Presbyterians in Global Mission*. Atlanta: General Assembly Mission Board, 1987.

———. "Pearl Buck: Novels of Missionary Life." In *Go Therefore: 150 Years of Presbyterians in Global Mission*. Atlanta: General Assembly Mission Board, 1987.

Thompson, Ernest Trice. *Presbyterians in the South*. 3 vols. Richmond: John Knox Press, 1973.

Thomson, James C. *While China Faced West: American Reformers in Nationalist China: 1928–1937*. Cambridge: Harvard University Press, 1969.

Tiedemann, R. G. "The Persistence of Banditry: Incidents in Border Districts of the North China Plain." *Modern China* 8 (1982).

Ting, K. H. "Facing the Future or Restoring the Past?" Address delivered in Toronto, November 1979.

————. "An Update on the Church in China." Address at the Presbyterian China Missionary Reunion, Columbia Theological Seminary, Decatur, GA, October 1995.

Twitchett, Denis, and John K. Fairbank, eds. *The Cambridge History of China.* Vol. 11 Late Ch'ing Dynasty, Vols. 12 and 13 Republican China. Cambridge: Cambridge University Press, 1978.

United States Consular Files for Chefoo (microfilm) 1866–1901. Washington, DC: National Archives.

Van Buren, Ernestine, ed. *The Marguerite Mizell Story.* Dallas, TX: First Presbyterian Church, 1987.

Van Evera, Pauline. "A Historical Sketch of the American Presbyterian Mission, Hangchow, China." PDH(Phil), 1936.

Wang, Weifan. "The Word Was Here Made Flesh." Lecture at the conference *China and Culture: A Sino-American Dialogue,* Columbia Theological Seminary, October 1992.

Webster, John C. B. "American Presbyterian Global Mission Policy: An Overview of 150 Years." *AP* 65 (1987).

Whyte, Bob. *Unfinished Encounter: China and Christianity.* Harrisburg, PA: Morehouse Publishing Co., 1988.

Wickeri, Janice and Philip. "Peter, W. H. Tsai: A Tribute." *Amity News Service* 3 (1994).

Wickeri, Philip L. *Seeking the Common Ground.* Maryknoll, NY: Orbis, 1988.

Wiest, Jean-Paul. *Maryknoll in China: A History, 1918–1955.* Armonk, NY: M. E. Sharpe, 1988.

Williams, Frederick Wells. *The Life and Letters of Samuel Wells Williams: Missionary, Diplomat, Sinologue.* New York: G. P. Putnam and Sons, 1889.

Woodbridge, Samuel Isett. *Fifty Years in China.* Richmond, VA: Presby. Committee on Publication, 1919.

————. *A Short History of Chinkiang.* Chinkiang: Chinkiang Literary Association, 1898.

Wylie, Alexander. *Memorials of Protestant Missionaries to the Chinese: Giving a list of their publications, and obituary notices of the Deceased.* Shanghai: Presbyterian Mission Press, 1867. Reprinted in Taipei by the Chengwen Publishing Co., 1967.

Xu, Yi Hua. "Religion and Education: St John's University as an Evangelizing Agency." Ph.D. diss., Princeton University, 1994.

Yang, Yongyi. "U.S. 'Missionary Mind Set' Impact on the 1911 Revolution. *Beijing Review* 27 (1988).

Yunnan Mission, PCUSA. "The Beginnings of the Yunnan Mission." Unsigned, undated manuscript, PDH(Phil).

Zhang, Guangzheng. "Living as Christians Today: Sociological Insights." In *Chinese Theological Review: 1988,* Janice Wickeri, ed. Holland, MI: Foundation for Theological Education in Southeast Asia, 1988.

Questionnaires and Interviews

Questionnaire mailed to all Presbyterian (PCUSA and PCUS) missionaries who had served in China, June 1988.

Questionnaire mailed to all members of Hangzhou Christian College alumni association who reside in the United States, Aug. 1994.

Interviews with the following former UPCUSA/PCUS missionaries:

Henry Bucher, Duarte, CA, June 1992

Clifford and Mary Chaffee, Duarte, CA, June 1992

E. H. and Estelle Hamilton, Decatur, GA, June 1988

Kenneth Kepler, Columbia, SC, 1994

Paul and Clara Lindholm, Duarte, CA, June 1992

Frank and Elizabeth Newman, Duarte, CA, June 1992

Arthur and Helen Romig, China Tour, 1993

Jessie Junkin McCall, Montreat, 1995
Henry and Katie Nelson, Zhenjiang, 1995
Francis and Helen Scott, Duarte, CA, June 1992
Theodore and Beatrice Scott, Duarte, CA, June 1992
Gardiner and Viola Winn, Duarte, CA, June 1992
Interviews with Chinese Church Leaders in China, May 1993:
K. H. Ting, President of the China Christian Council
Han Wenzao, Director of the Amity Foundation
Peter Wang, Director of Jiangsu Province Christian Council
Xu Rulei, Faculty member, Nanjing Seminary
Wang Weifan, Faculty member, Nanjing Seminary
Wen-hao (Peter) and Eleanor Tsai, Zhejiang Christian Council
Wang Be Da, elderly pastor in Hangzhou
Cao Sheng Jie, Vice President China Christian Council, Shanghai
Shen De Rong, member of the China People's Consultative Congress
George Wu, Methodist leader, former member of Three-Self Com.
Su Xu Yihua, Ph.D. candidate, Princeton University.
Gu Yadong, Pastor Christian Church, Xuzhou
Ying Gao, woman pastor at Beijing Chongwenmen Church
Deng Zhaoming, editor of *Bridge,* Hong Kong
Phil Wickeri, Overseas Coordinator, Amity Foundation, Hong Kong
Staff at the Academy of Social Science in Shanghai and Beijing

Person Index

415

Subject-Place Index